Also of Interest ...

Each of the following titles may be **packaged with Romney/Steinbart at a special price,** or sold separately!

Microsoft Excel for Accounting: Auditing and Accounting Information Systems

Katherine T. Smith, D.B.A.
L. Murphy Smith, D.B.A., CPA, Texas A&M University
Lawrence C. Smith, Jr., Ph.D., Louisiana Tech University
© 2003, ISBN 0-13-008552-9

Introduce your AIS and auditing students to the fundamental tools and techniques available in Microsoft Excel spreadsheet software!

Using this book, your students will learn how to complete their assignments in Excel—enabling them to work more efficiently while enhancing their understanding of accounting concepts. In addition, students will become more computer savvy with one of the most widely available and often used software products, Microsoft Excel. This knowledge will be beneficial both in college courses and future careers.

ACCOUNTING INFORMATION SYSTEMS CASES

Merle Martin
Monica Lam, both of California State University at Sacramento
© 2003, ISBN 0-13-035289-6

This collection of cases focuses on the 16 different learning objectives found in most accounting information systems textbooks (e.g., documentation techniques or application of internal controls). Many of the cases focus on relatively new AIS subject matter such as e-commerce, enterprise resource planning (ERP) models, and valuation of IT resources. For a complete table of contents, please go to www.prenhall.com/accounting and select this title under "Accounting Information Systems."

CAST: An Integrated Auditing and AIS Simulation

Frank A. Buckless
Laura R. Ingraham
Greg Jenkins, all of North Carolina State University
© 2003, ISBN 0-13-045186-X

The Comprehensive Assurance and Systems Tool (CAST) is a unique practice set intended to expose students to the many issues faced in the fields of assurance and information systems. Based on a real-world company and composed of multiple modules, CAST is designed to be flexible in its implementation across various courses during the junior and senior years of an undergraduate accounting curriculum. The major components include assurance services, manual accounting information systems, spreadsheet applications, general ledger software, and database design and development. Each component can be implemented in a stand-alone fashion or may be implemented in an integrated fashion across multiple courses (suggested approach). CAST will be delivered using traditional text materials, a CD-ROM, and an accompanying Web site. Instructors will receive all student materials and an instructor resource guide and solutions manual.

Prentice Hall's Companion Web Site

WWW.PRENHALL.COM/ROMNEY

Students learn better with Romney/Steinbart!

NINTH EDITION

ACCOUNTING INFORMATION SYSTEMS

NINTH EDITION

ACCOUNTING INFORMATION SYSTEMS

Marshall B. Romney

Brigham Young University

Paul John Steinbart

Arizona State University

Prentice
Hall

Upper Saddle River, New Jersey 07458

Library of Congress Cataloging-in-Publication Data

Romney, Marshall B.
    Accounting information systems / Marshall B. Romney, Paul John Steinbart.–9th ed.
      p. cm.
    Includes bibliographical references and index.
    ISBN 0-13-090903-3
      1. Accounting–Data processing. 2. Information storage and retrieval
systems–Accounting. I. Steinbart, Paul John. II. Title.

HF5679 .A34 2002
657'.0285–dc21   2002016932

Executive Editor: Deborah Hoffman
Editor-in-Chief: P.J. Boardman
Supplements Editor: Amy Whitaker
Senior Editorial Assistant: Jane Avery
Development Editor: Rebecca Johnson
Senior Project Manager, Media: Nancy Welcher
Executive Marketing Manager: Beth Toland
Managing Editor (Production): John Roberts
Production Editor: Kelly Warsak
Permissions Supervisor: Suzanne Grappi
Associate Director, Manufacturing: Vincent Scelta
Production Manager: Arnold Vila
Manufacturing Buyer: Michelle Klein
Art Director: Janet Slowik
Cover Design: Joan O'Connor
Cover Illustration: Comstock Images
Composition: Carlisle Communications
Full-Service Project Management: Carlisle Communications
Printer/Binder: Courier/Westford
Cover Printer: Phoenix Color Corp.

Pearson Education LTD.
Pearson Education Australia PTY, Limited
Pearson Education Singapore, Pte. Ltd
Pearson Education North Asia Ltd
Pearson Education, Canada, Ltd
Pearson Educación de Mexico, S.A. de C.V.
Pearson Education–Japan
Pearson Education Malaysia, Pte. Ltd

10 9 8 7 6 5 4 3 2
ISBN 0-13-090903-3

Brief Contents

Management Misinformation Systems by Russell L. Ackoff to Accompany Case 1-2
  www.prenhall.com/romney

Hardware Supplement   *www.prenhall.com/romney*

Overview of Manual Accounting Systems: Journals and Ledgers   *www.prenhall.com/romney*

References   *www.prenhall.com/romney*

Contents

PART II   CONTROL AND AUDIT OF ACCOUNTING INFORMATION SYSTEMS   189

PART IV   THE SYSTEMS DEVELOPMENT PROCESS   569

Preface

Today, professional accountants work in an exciting and complex environment that is constantly changing. Progress in information technology (IT) is occurring at an ever-increasing rate. Business organizations are changing their methods of operation and their management structures to meet the demands of an increasingly competitive environment. The economic and legal environment in which accountants work is also changing in unpredictable ways. These changes require today's accounting students to be better prepared than ever to enter the challenging world of the accounting profession.

The ninth edition of *Accounting Information Systems* provides students with the knowledge and skills they need to pursue successful careers in accounting. The text reflects how IT is altering the nature of accounting. Specifically, we discuss how such developments as the Internet, electronic commerce, EDI, and databases are fundamentally transforming the way organizations conduct their business activities. We also explain how these IT developments are changing the way businesses account for the results of those activities.

In addition to technology-driven changes, companies are responding to the increasingly competitive business environment by reexamining every internal activity in an effort to reap the most value at the least cost. As a result, accountants are being asked to do more than simply report the results of past activities. They must take a more proactive role in both providing and interpreting financial and nonfinancial information about the organization's activities. Therefore, throughout this text we discuss how accountants can improve the design and functioning of the accounting information system (AIS) so that it truly adds value to the organization. For example, each cycle chapter uses data modeling to illustrate how AISs can effectively integrate internally generated financial and nonfinancial data about organizational activities with other externally generated data (e.g., customer credit ratings and satisfaction).

As with the first eight editions, this book is written to help students acquire the understanding and knowledge of AISs that they must have to succeed in their chosen field. Today's accounting students will become tomorrow's users, auditors, and managers of computer-based information systems. As primary users of information systems in organizations, accountants must participate in their design and understand their operation. Accounting managers must measure and evaluate the performance of information systems. Internal and external auditors must assess the quality of information processing and evaluate the accuracy of information input and output. The major share of the accounting consultant's work is in the design, implementation, and evaluation of information systems.

To be successful in pursuing an accounting career, students must possess a basic knowledge of computer-based information systems and their role in performing the accounting function in contemporary business organizations.

Graduating students must understand the following key concepts:

➤ The business activities performed in the major business cycles and the flow of accounting data and information in those systems

➤ The collection and processing of data about those business activities

➤ The use of the latest IT developments to improve the efficiency and effectiveness of business activities

➤ The fundamentals of e-business and how they affect modern accounting information systems

➤ How to design an accounting information system (AIS) to provide the information needed to make key decisions in each business cycle

➤ The development, implementation, and maintenance of an AIS

➤ Internal control objectives and the effects of IT on these objectives, as well as the specific controls used to achieve those objectives

➤ Fundamental concepts of database technology and data modeling and their effect on AIS

➤ The tools of AIS work, such as REA diagrams, data flow diagrams, and flowcharting

This book is intended for use in a one-semester course in accounting information systems at the undergraduate or graduate level. Introductory financial and managerial accounting courses are suggested prerequisites, and an introductory course in data processing that covers a computer language or software package is helpful. The book can also be used as the main text in graduate or advanced undergraduate courses in management information systems.

MAJOR CHANGES IN THE NINTH EDITION

A significant effort has been made to shorten the ninth edition of the book and make it even easier for students to use and understand. This has been accomplished in the following ways:

1. A chapter and an appendix have been dropped from the book. Chapter 4 of the eighth edition, "Introduction to Data Processing," has been eliminated. Some of the chapter material, principally the data processing cycle, has been moved to Chapter 2, which now provides an overview of AIS processes. Information about files and databases has been integrated into the database chapter. As a result, in the ninth edition *all* of the material on files and databases is now discussed in Chapter 4. The remainder of the material that had been in the former Chapter 4, along with the appendix to that chapter, has been moved to our Web site.

2. Elementary concepts of data processing are introduced in Chapter 2 in connection with the steps of the accounting cycle.

3. References for each chapter, found at the end of the eighth edition, have been moved to our Web site *www.prenhall.com/romney.*

4. Some of the longer problems and cases at the end of some chapters have been moved to our Web site *www.prenhall.com/romney.*

In addition, the whole text was reexamined with a view to tightening the exposition and presenting every concept in as clear and straightforward a manner as possible.

The e-business chapter has been rewritten to bring more e-business concepts and principles into the book. The new chapter has a greater focus on the business viewpoint of e-business, describes how each step in the value chain is affected by e-business, and discusses the risks and controls that should be considered in e-business applications. Moreover, to give e-business a greater focus and importance, the chapter on e-business was moved from Chapter 7 in the eighth edition to Chapter 3 in the ninth edition. In addition, where appropriate, e-business concepts have been integrated into other chapters of the book.

Chapter 8 has been extensively revised to parallel the structure and format of the AICPA's new service, SysTrust, which provides assurance that an information system is, in fact, reliable. SysTrust uses four principles to determine if a system is reliable: availability, security, maintainability, and integrity.

We have improved and expanded our discussion of the REA data model in Chapter 5, as well as the cycle chapters (Chapters 11 through 15). In these chapters, the coverage of each business process cycle was also updated and improved by including such topics as e-business and enterprise resource planning (ERP) software.

IMPORTANT FEATURES

New On-line Support. Any student or instructor using AIS 9e has FREE access to Prentice Hall's content-rich, text-supported Web site at *www.prenhall.com/romney*. The AIS 9/e "Companion Web site" is designed to help students study the course material. Each text chapter is supplemented with an on-line study guide with immediate feedback, current news articles supported with exercises and activities, Internet exercises, PowerPoint slides, and more. Students can also access Prentice Hall's on-line tutor for additional help. Instructor supplements are passcode protected for security purposes and can be found on the instructor portion of this Web site.

Free on-line course support is available on Blackboard and Course Compass platforms. CourseCompass is Prentice Hall's nationally hosted solution.

Coverage of business strategies. The concept of the value chain classifies IT as a support activity. Thus, investments in IT are not an end in themselves, but must be linked to an organization's strategy and strategic position. Chapter 1 discusses basic strategies and the strategic positions that firms can pursue. This material is placed in the first chapter so that students immediately begin to think about how IT can be used to help organizations achieve their goals.

Coverage of e-business. As mentioned, e-business concepts and principles are thoroughly covered in the text.

Coverage of databases and data modeling. Accountants are increasingly becoming involved in database design. The discussion of relational databases in Chapter 4 has been improved. Chapter 5 has been revised to more clearly explain the REA approach to data modeling and it provides more examples. We also created additional homework problems designed to help students progressively hone their data modeling skills.

Focus on transaction cycles from a business process perspective. Chapters 11 through 14 cover the revenue, expenditure, production, and human resource business processes. In-depth coverage of how these processes are executed is combined with a thorough discussion of control issues. REA diagrams illustrate how data about these processes can be stored in integrated databases. Chapter 15 discusses both traditional general ledger and also ERP systems. Chapter 15 also covers additional measurement topics that are part of the "new finance," such as the balanced scorecard and the likely effects of XBRL on accounting and financial reporting.

Coverage of controls. Chapter 7 discusses control concepts using the COSO format. As discussed, specific controls in Chapter 8 follow the control format used by SysTrust.

Updated coverage of computer fraud and security. Chapter 9, on computer fraud, includes techniques that perpetrators are using to defraud companies. Many of these involve the Internet and other electronic commerce applications. Examples of recent frauds are included to illustrate fraud techniques.

The systems development process. Chapter 16 provides an overview of the development process and discusses systems analysis concepts, concluding with a definition of user needs. Chapter 17 discusses the various development strategies used to obtain a new AIS. Chapter 18 concludes with a discussion of how to design, implement, operate, and maintain a system to meet user needs.

Integrated cases. Each chapter begins with an **integrative** case, based on one of four fictional companies, that introduces the chapter's key concepts and topics. This case is integrated throughout the chapter, and a description of how the issues are resolved is provided in the summary and case conclusion.

Focus boxes and real-world examples. We include one to four focus boxes in each chapter. The focus boxes are summaries of articles describing how specific companies are using the latest IT developments to improve their AIS. Numerous real-world examples, featuring both large and small companies in a variety of industries, have also been added to each chapter to highlight and reinforce key concepts.

Chapter quizzes. At the end of each chapter is a short multiple-choice quiz, with answers provided at the end of the problem and case material. Students can use the quiz to test their understanding of the main topics in the chapter.

End-of-chapter discussion cases and problems. The end-of-chapter material is designed to help students develop and test their knowledge. It includes discussion questions and problems that integrate material from various parts of the chapter. Many problems were developed from reports in current periodicals. Other problems were selected from the various professional examinations, including the CPA, CMA, CIA, and SMAC exams.

End-of-chapter cases. Most chapters have two end-of-chapter cases. One is a stand-alone case; the other is the AnyCompany case, which provides students with the opportunity to apply their knowledge to the specific problems and challenges faced by a business in their local area. The AnyCompany case also gives students the chance to practice their written and oral communication skills in a realistic setting. The requirements for each AnyCompany case are tailored to the topics offered in the respective chapter. These suggested requirements are too extensive to permit assignment of all AnyCompany cases in one semester. Instead, we encourage instructors to select the case(s) with requirements that most closely match their course objectives. Alternatively, instructors can choose selected requirements from several chapters to create a customized term project that reflects the topics stressed in the course.

Graphics. The text contains hundreds of figures, diagrams, flowcharts, and tables that illustrate the concepts taught in the chapters.

References. On the Web site is an extensive bibliography, organized by chapter. This list contains references to the real-world examples used in each chapter and provides students with a starting point for further research on topics of interest.

Glossary. A comprehensive glossary located at the back of the book allows students to master the many terms used in the text.

AN OVERVIEW OF THE NINTH EDITION

Part I: Conceptual Foundations of Accounting Information Systems

Part I consists of the following six chapters which present the underlying concepts fundamental to an understanding of AIS:

Chapter 1 introduces basic terminology and discusses how an AIS can add value to an organization. It also discusses basic strategies and the strategic positions that firms can pursue, so that students can understand how IT can be used to help organizations achieve their goals.

Chapter 2 provides an overview of AIS topics, focusing on understanding basic business processes. It introduces the basic data processing steps used in an AIS. A simplified version of an REA diagram is also introduced to help students see the wide range of data that must be collected by the AIS. This information helps students to understand what an AIS does; as they read the remainder of the book, they see how advances in IT affect the manner in which those functions are performed. This coverage is especially useful if the curriculum has been changed so that the AIS course is now the first class accounting majors take after the course on principles.

Chapter 3 discusses the role of electronic commerce in today's business organizations. The chapter also discusses telecommunications concepts and applications as well as the Internet and the World Wide Web.

Chapter 4 introduces students to databases, with a particular emphasis on the relational data model and query languages. It also discusses transaction processing in automated systems, presenting basic information processing and data storage concepts.

Chapter 5 discusses data modeling and the design of a database AIS. It illustrates how the database technology covered in Chapter 4 can be used to design an AIS that more fully meets the information needs of managers. Chapter 5 also demonstrates how traditional financial statements and managerial reports can be derived from a database AIS.

Chapter 6 covers the most important tools and techniques used to understand, evaluate, design, and document information systems: data flow diagrams, and flowcharts.

Part II : Control and Audit of Accounting Information Systems

Part II consists of four chapters.

Chapter 7 discusses the threats to an AIS and why they are growing, as well as basic concepts of control. The chapter then discusses the major components of the COSO control model: the control environment; control policies, procedures, and activities; risk assessment; information and communication; and monitoring systems.

Chapter 8 discusses the many specific computer controls used in business organizations. The chapter material was organized so that these controls are explained in the context used by SysTrust: availability, integrity, security, and maintainability.

Chapter 9 focuses on computer fraud and security. The chapter defines fraud, explains how and why it occurs, discusses approaches and techniques used to perpetrate computer fraud, and provides methods for preventing and detecting it.

Chapter 10 reviews principles and techniques for the audit and evaluation of internal control in a computer-based AIS and introduces the topic of computer-assisted auditing. In auditing an information system, an auditor should make sure that audit objectives are met in six critical areas: overall security, program development, program modifications, processing of transactions, source data capture and input, and data storage.

Part III: Accounting Information Systems Applications

Part III consists of five chapters, each of which focuses on one of the business cycles. Each chapter highlights the differences between stand-alone legacy systems and integrated ERP systems.

Chapter 11 covers the revenue cycle, including sales, billing, accounts receivable, and cash receipts.

Chapter 12 covers the expenditure cycle, including purchasing, receiving, accounts payable, and cash disbursements.

Chapter 13 covers the production cycle, with a special focus on the implications of recent cost accounting developments, such as activity-based costing, for the design of the production cycle information system.

Chapter 14 discusses the human resources management/payroll cycle and explores the ways in which these two systems can be integrated.

Chapter 15 focuses on the general ledger and reporting activities in an organization, with particular emphasis on ERP systems. XBRL, the balanced scorecard, and data warehousing are also covered.

These five chapters have been written to reflect the three basic functions performed by the AIS: efficient transaction processing, provision of adequate internal controls to safeguard assets (including data), and preparation of information useful for effective decision making. A data model for each cycle is described, as are the effects of databases on the design and functioning of an AIS. The role of IT in providing a competitive advantage is stressed and numerous real-world examples are incorporated throughout this part.

Part IV: The Systems Development Process

Part IV consists of three chapters.

Chapter 16 introduces the systems development life cycle and discusses the introductory steps of this process (systems analysis, feasibility, and planning). Particular emphasis is placed on the behavioral ramifications of change.

Chapter 17 discusses an organization's many options for acquiring or developing an AIS (e.g., purchasing software, writing software, end-user–developed software, and outsourcing) and for speeding up or improving the development process (business process reengineering, prototyping, and computer-assisted software engineering).

Chapter 18 covers the remaining stages of the systems development life cycle (conceptual design, physical design, implementation, and operation and maintenance) and emphasizes the interrelationships among the phases.

Many real-world examples are included in these last chapters to enable students to understand the accountant's role in the systems development process.

Instructional Supplements

Our objective in preparing this textbook has been to simplify the teaching of AIS by enabling instructors to concentrate on classroom presentation and discussion, rather than on locating, assembling, and distributing teaching materials. As further support, the following supplementary materials are available on an Instructor's Resource CD, which is free of charge to adopters of the text.

Solutions Manual prepared by the authors
Instructors Manual/Test Item File (TIF) by Bill Cummings, Northern Illinois University
TestGen testing software computerized test item file by Timothy F. Carse
PowerPoint Presentation by Somnath Bhattacharya, Florida Atlantic University

Free text Web site support at *www.prenhall.com/romney* provides additional student resources, including an *On-line Study Guide* by Terri Brunsdon, University of Akron, which provides immediate feedback.

Instructors can access supplements on the instructor portion of the Web site which is passcode protected. Please see more detailed information under "Important Features."

Free On-line Course Support available on Blackboard and CourseCompass (Prentice Hall's nationally hosted solution) platforms.

"Also available" titles:

Getting Started with Peachtree, Errol Osteraa, Heald College

Getting Started with QuickBooks, Janet Horne, Los Angeles Pierce College

Getting Started with Simply Accounting, Jean Insinga, Middlesex Community-Technical College

Microsoft Excel for Accounting: Auditing and AIS, Katherine T. Smith, L. Murphy Smith, Texas A&M University; and Lawrence C. Smith, Jr., Louisiana Tech University

Accounting Information Systems Cases, Merle P. Martin and Monica Lam, California State University at Sacramento.

CAST: Integrated Auditing and AIS Simulation, Frank A. Buckless, Laura R. Ingraham, and J. Gregory Jenkins, all at North Carolina State University

CAST: Accounting Information Systems Simulation, Frank A. Buckless, Laura R. Ingraham, and J. Gregory Jenkins, all at North Carolina State University

CAST: Auditing Simulation, Frank A. Buckless, Laura R. Ingraham, and J. Gregory Jenkins, all at North Carolina State University

ACKNOWLEDGMENTS

We wish to express our appreciation to all supplements authors for preparing the various supplements that accompany this edition. We also thank Martha M. Eining of the University of Utah and Carol F. Venable of San Diego State University for preparing the comprehensive cases included on our Web site. We are grateful to Iris Vessey for her contributions to the problem material.

We appreciate the help of Wendy Carr of Brigham Young University in typing and preparing the various drafts of the Solutions Manual. We also appreciate the work of Angie Jensen of Brigham Young University for helping write some of the new Focus boxes in this edition.

Perhaps most importantly, we are indebted to the numerous faculty members throughout the world who have adopted the earlier editions of this book and who have been generous with their suggestions for improvement. We are especially grateful to those who participated in reviewing the ninth edition throughout various stages of the revision process.

Darrell Brown, Portland State University

Cheryl L. Dunn, Florida State University

George P. Geran, Florida Metropolitan University

Monojit Ghozal, Valdosta State University

Alfred R. Michenzi, Loyola College in Maryland

Susan M. Moncada, Indiana State University

Kanalis A. Ockree, Washburn University

John A. Pendley, University of Alabama in Huntsville

Arline Savage, Oakland University

Christine M. Schalow, California State University, San Bernardino

Charles W. Stanley, Baylor University

Louis J. Stewart, New York University

Bobby E. Waldrup, University of North Florida

We are grateful for permission received from four professional accounting organizations to use problems and unofficial solutions from their past professional examinations in this book. Thanks are extended to the American Institute of Certified Public Accountants for use of the CPA Examination materials, to the Institute of Certified Management Accountants for use of CMA Examination materials, to the Institute of Internal Auditors for use of CIA Examination materials, and to the Society of Management Accountants of Canada for use of SMAC Examination materials.

Of course, any errors in this book remain our responsibility. We welcome your comments and suggestions for further improvement.

Finally, we want to thank our wives and families for their love, support, and encouragement. We also want to thank God for giving us the ability to start and complete this book.

Marshall B. Romney
Provo, Utah
Paul John Steinbart
Tempe, Arizona

NINTH EDITION

ACCOUNTING INFORMATION SYSTEMS

C h a p t e r   1

Accounting Information Systems: An Overview

Learning Objectives

After studying this chapter, you should be able to:

- Explain what an accounting information system (AIS) is and describe the basic functions it performs.
- Discuss why studying the design and management of an AIS is important.
- Explain the role played by the AIS in a company's value chain and discuss ways that the AIS can add value to a business.
- Describe and contrast the basic strategies and strategic positions that a business can adopt.

Integrative Case: S&S, Inc.

After working for several years as a regional manager for a national retailing organization, Scott Parry decided to open his own business. Susan Gonzalez, one of his district managers, had also wanted to go into business for herself. Together they formed S&S, Inc., to sell consumer electronics devices. Scott and Susan decided to pursue a "clicks and bricks" strategy. They began by renting a large and attractive building in a busy part of the town, but planned to add an electronic storefront as well.

Scott and Susan each contributed enough money to see them through the first 6 months of business. They estimated that they needed to hire 10 to 15 employees–3 or 4 to stock the shelves, 3 or 4 customer sales representatives, and 4 to 6 checkout clerks. They plan to begin hiring these employees within the next 2 weeks.

Scott and Susan plan to hold the grand opening of S&S in 5 weeks. As they review what remains to be done to meet that deadline, they realize that they have not yet made the following important decisions:

1. How should they organize their accounting records so that the financial statements their banker requires can be easily produced?

2. How can they design a set of procedures to ensure that they meet all of their government obligations, such as remitting sales, income, and payroll taxes?
3. How should they price their products to be competitive yet earn a profit?
4. Should they extend credit, and if so, on what terms? How can they accurately track what customers owe and have paid?
5. How should they hire, train, and supervise their employees? What compensation and benefits packages should they offer, and how should they process payroll?
6. How can they track cash inflows and outflows so that S&S is not caught in a cash squeeze?
7. What is the appropriate product mix and quantities to carry, given S&S's limited showroom space?
8. What functionality should be provided on S&S's Web site?

Although Scott and Susan could make many of these decisions on the basis of an educated guess or "gut feel," they will probably make better decisions if they obtain additional information. A well-designed **accounting information system (AIS)** can solve some of these issues. Moreover, if properly designed, the AIS can provide some of the information needed to make the remaining decisions.

INTRODUCTION

We begin this chapter by defining what an AIS is. Next we discuss why the AIS is an important topic to study. Then we describe how an AIS adds value to an organization. We conclude by describing the basic strategies and strategic positions that organizations can pursue.

WHAT IS AN AIS?

A **system** is a set of two or more interrelated components that interact to achieve a goal. Systems are almost always composed of smaller subsystems, each performing a specific function important to and supportive of the larger system of which it is a part. For example, the college of business is a system composed of various departments, each of which is a subsystem. Yet the college itself is a subsystem of the university.

An AIS consists of five components:

1. The *people* who operate the system and perform various functions
2. The *procedures*, both manual and automated, involved in collecting, processing, and storing data about the organization's activities
3. The *data* about the organization's business processes
4. The *software* used to process the organization's data
5. The *information technology infrastructure*, including computers, peripheral devices, and network communications devices

Together, these five components enable an AIS to fulfill three important functions in any organization:

1. Collecting and storing data about the activities performed by the organization, the resources affected by those events, and the agents who participate in the various activities so that management, employees, and interested outsiders can review what has happened

2. Transforming data into information that is useful for making decisions that enable management to plan, execute, and control activities
3. Providing adequate controls to safeguard the organization's assets, including its data, to ensure that the data are available when needed and are accurate and reliable

WHY STUDY THE AIS?

An effective AIS is essential to any organization's long-run success. Without a means of monitoring the events that occur, there would be no way to determine how well the organization is performing. Every organization also needs to track the effects of various events on the resources that are under its control. Information about the agents who participate in those events is necessary to assign responsibility for actions taken. Therefore, many universities require both accounting and information systems majors to study AIS. This section explains how the AIS course fits into both the accounting and information systems curricula.

Study of the AIS Is Fundamental to Accounting

In *Statement of Financial Accounting Concepts No. 2*, the Financial Accounting Standards Board defined accounting as being an information system. It also stated that the primary objective of accounting is to provide information useful to decision makers. Therefore, it is not surprising that the Accounting Education Change Commission recommended that the accounting curriculum should emphasize that accounting is an information identification, development, measurement, and communication process. The commission suggested that the accounting curriculum should be designed to provide students with a solid understanding of three essential concepts:

1. The use of information in decision making
2. The nature, design, use, and implementation of an AIS
3. Financial information reporting

The other accounting courses that you take (financial accounting, managerial accounting, tax accounting, and auditing) focus on your role as a provider of information. In contrast, the AIS course focuses on understanding how the accounting system works: how to collect data about an organization's activities and transactions; how to transform that data into information that management can use to run the organization; and how to ensure the availability, reliability, and accuracy of that information. Thus, the AIS course complements the other accounting courses you will take.

You may intend to pursue a career in the public accounting profession. If so, you may become an auditor. Auditors need to understand the systems that are used to produce a company's financial statements. This course provides you with that knowledge; indeed, that is why many universities make the AIS course a prerequisite to the auditing course. Alternatively, you may want to specialize in tax. If so, you need to understand enough about your clients' AISs to be confident that the information used for their tax planning and compliance work is complete and accurate. A third option is management consulting. One of the fastest growing types of consulting services entails the design, selection, and implementation of new AISs. Indeed, the AICPA has recently created a new credential, the Certified Information Technology Professional

Focus 1-1

CITP – A New Specialty Designation for CPAs

The AICPA offers several specialty designations that can be earned by CPAs. One of these is the Certified Information Technology Professional (CITP). The CITP designation identifies CPAs who possess a broad range of technological knowledge and who understand how information technology can be used by organizations to achieve their business objectives. The new CITP designation reflects the AICPA's recognition of the importance of information technology and its interrelationship with accounting.

To be awarded the CITP designation, a CPA must earn a total of 100 points in the areas of business experience, lifelong learning, and an optional exam. Candidates must earn a minimum of 15 points, and a maximum of 75 points, in the area of business experience. The number of points awarded depends on the number of hours spent working in the following areas during the 3-year period preceding application for the CITP designation:

- Information Technology Strategic Planning
- Information Systems Management

- Systems Architecture
- Business Applications and E-Business
- Security, Privacy, and Contingency Planning
- Systems Development, Acquisition, and Project Management
- Systems Auditing and Internal Control
- Databases and Database Management

A candidate for the CITP designation must also earn a minimum of 30 points, up to a maximum of 70 points, in the category of lifelong learning. Lifelong learning includes continuing education, additional degrees, and obtaining or maintaining other technology-related certifications during the 3-year period preceding application for the CITP designation.

An optional exam is also available for candidates who have earned at least 60 points in the areas of business experience and lifelong learning. Candidates can earn 40 points by passing an exam that covers the eight topical areas listed in the preceding discussion of work experience.

Source: AICPA Web site (www.aicpa.org/accrspec/specdesg.htm).

(CITP), to provide CPAs a means of documenting their systems expertise (see Focus 1-1). The AIS course provides an introduction to that body of knowledge.

Not all accounting majors pursue careers in public accounting, however. Many of you will eventually find yourselves working in private industry or for not-for-profit organizations. Recently, the Institute of Management Accountants (IMA) conducted an intensive analysis of the job duties of corporate accountants. Table 1-1 presents the responses to a question asking respondents to indicate the five most critical work activities performed by accountants. Notice that respondents clearly indicated that work relating to accounting systems was the single most important activity performed by corporate accountants.

The AIS Course Complements Other Systems Courses

There are many other systems courses that cover the design and implementation of information systems, and which help you develop specialized skills in such areas as

Table 1-1   Ten Most Important Work Activities
Performed by Accountants

1. Accounting systems and financial reporting
2. Long-term strategic planning
3. Managing the accounting and finance function
4. Internal consulting
5. Short-term budgeting
6. Financial and economic analyses
7. Process improvement
8. Computer systems and operations
9. Performance evaluation (of the organization)
10. Customer and product profitability analyses

Source: Gary Siegel Organization, "The Practice Analysis of Management Accounting," An IMA Research Project (March 1996): 9.

databases, expert systems, and telecommunications. The AIS course differs from these other information systems courses in its focus on accountability and control. These issues are important because in most large businesses the managers are not the owners. Instead, the owners have entrusted management with assets and hold them accountable for their proper use.

Data and information are some of an organization's most valuable assets. To see why, consider what would happen if an organization lost all information about customers' balances, or if a competitor obtained a list of its most profitable customers. Clearly, the AIS must include controls to ensure the safety and availability of the organization's data. Controls are also needed to ensure that the information produced from that data is both reliable and accurate. These topics usually receive little attention in other systems courses. Thus, the AIS course complements other systems courses you may take and is an important part of the information systems curriculum.

The Focus of the AIS Course

Figure 1-1 shows that three factors influence the design of an AIS: developments in information technology (IT), the organization's strategy, and the organizational culture. The business press frequently reports the many ways in which IT is profoundly changing the way that accounting and many other business activities are performed. Because this impact is likely to continue, throughout this book we will focus on understanding how IT can be used to improve the performance of an AIS.

The AIS course, however, is more than a "computer course." To be sure, your professor will likely assign out-of-class projects designed to help you refine and improve your computer skills. Nevertheless, you also need to know how to evaluate the costs and benefits of new IT developments. This requires developing a basic understanding of business strategies and how IT can be used to implement those strategies as well as how new developments in IT create an opportunity to modify those strategies (note the arrow from IT to strategy in Figure 1-1). These topics are introduced in this chapter and will continue to be discussed throughout the text.

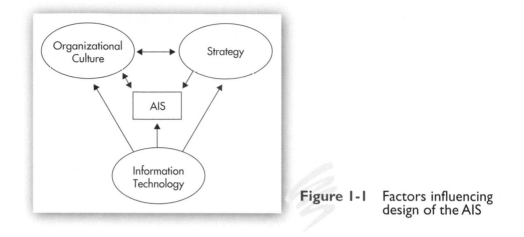

Figure 1-1 Factors influencing design of the AIS

Moreover, because an AIS functions within an organization, it should be designed to reflect the values of that organizational culture. Thus, Figure 1-1 also shows that the organizational culture influences the design of the AIS. Note, however, that the arrow between organizational culture and the AIS is bidirectional. Although the organization's culture should influence the design of its AIS, it is important to recognize that the design of the AIS can also influence the organization's culture by controlling the flow of information within the organization. For example, an AIS that makes information easily accessible and widely available is likely to increase pressures for more decentralization and autonomy. Throughout this text, therefore, we discuss the potential behavioral ramifications of making changes to a company's AIS.

THE ROLE OF THE AIS IN THE VALUE CHAIN

The objective of most organizations is to provide value to their customers.[1] This requires performing a number of different activities. Figure 1-2 shows that those activities can be conceptualized as forming a **value chain**.

An organization's value chain consists of five **primary activities** that directly provide value to its customers:

1. *Inbound logistics* consists of receiving, storing, and distributing the materials that are inputs used by the organization to create the services and products that it sells. For example, the activities of receiving, handling, and storing the steel, glass, and rubber comprise the inbound logistics activities for an automobile manufacturer.
2. *Operations* activities transform inputs into final products or services. For example, the assembly line activities in an automobile company convert raw materials into a finished car.
3. *Outbound logistics* are the activities involved in distributing finished products or services to customers. For example, shipping automobiles to car dealers is an outbound logistics activity.
4. *Marketing and sales* refers to the activities involved in helping customers to buy the organization's products or services. Advertising is an example of a marketing and sales activity.

---

[1]This section is based on Michael E. Porter and Victor E. Millar, "How Information Gives You Competitive Advantage," (July-August 1985), pp. 149–160.

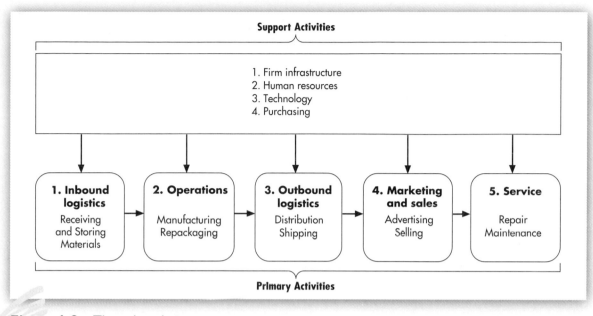

Figure 1-2 The value chain

5. *Service* activities provide post-sale support to customers. Examples include repair and maintenance services.

Organizations also perform a number of other **support activities** that enable the five primary activities to be performed efficiently and effectively. Those support activities can be grouped into four categories:

1. *Firm infrastructure* refers to the accounting, finance, legal support, and general administration activities that are necessary for any organization to function. The AIS is part of the firm infrastructure.
2. *Human resources* activities include recruiting, hiring, training, and providing employee benefits and compensation.
3. *Technology* activities improve a product or service. Examples include research and development, investments in new information technology, Web site development, and product design.
4. *Purchasing* includes all the activities involved in procuring raw materials, supplies, machinery, and the buildings used to carry out the primary activities.

Recall that systems are often composed of sets of subsystems. Thus, each step in an organization's value chain is itself a system consisting of a set of activities. For example, the sales and marketing step includes such activities as market research, calling on customers, order processing, and credit approval. In addition, an organization's value chain is itself a part of a larger system. Organizations interact with suppliers, distributors, and customers. As shown in Figure 1-3, this extended system forms a **supply chain**.

By paying attention to the interorganizational linkages in its supply chain, a company can help itself by helping the other organizations in the supply chain to improve

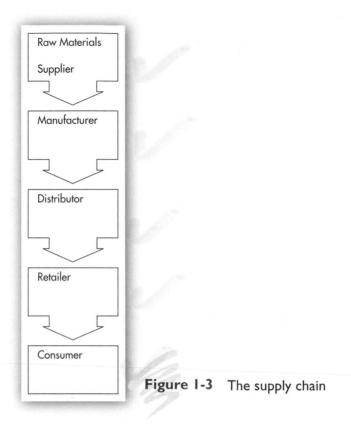

Figure 1-3   The supply chain

their performance. In our opening case, for example, S&S can improve its purchasing and inbound logistics activity by implementing a just-in-time inventory management system. S&S's costs are reduced because its purchasing and inbound logistics activities are performed more efficiently and because less of its capital is tied up in inventory. S&S can reap additional benefits if it links its new systems with its suppliers to help them perform some of their primary value chain activities more efficiently and effectively. For example, by providing more detailed and timely information about its inventory needs, S&S can help its suppliers more efficiently plan their production schedules to meet S&S's needs. This reduces their costs, and part of that reduction is likely to be passed on to S&S in the form of lower product costs.

How an AIS Can Add Value to an Organization

The value chain model shows that the AIS is a support activity. Thus, the AIS can add value to an organization by providing accurate and timely information so that the five primary value chain activities can be performed more effectively and efficiently. A well-designed AIS can do this by:

1. *Improving the quality and reducing the costs of products or services.* For example, an AIS can monitor machinery so that operators are notified immediately when the process falls outside acceptable quality limits. This not only helps maintain product quality but also reduces the amount of wasted materials and the costs of having to rework anything.

2. *Improving efficiency.* A well-designed AIS can help improve the efficiency of operations by providing more timely information. For example, a just-in-time manufacturing approach requires constant, accurate, up-to-date information about raw materials inventories and their locations.

3. *Improved decision making.* An AIS can improve decision making by providing accurate information in a timely manner. For example, Wal-Mart has created an enormous database that contains detailed information about sales transactions at each of its stores. It uses this information to optimize the amount of each product carried at each store. It also analyzes the data to discover patterns of items that seem to be purchased together, and uses such information to improve the layout of merchandise so as to encourage additional sales of related items. Similarly, Amazon.com uses its database of sales activity to suggest additional books that customers may want to purchase.

4. *Sharing of knowledge.* A well-designed AIS can make it easier to share knowledge and expertise, perhaps thereby improving operations and even providing a competitive advantage. For example, the largest public accounting firms all use their information systems to share best practices and to support communication between people located at different offices. Employees can search the corporate database to identify the relevant experts to provide assistance for a particular client; thus, all of a public accounting firm's accumulated international expertise can be made available to service any local client.

A well-designed AIS can also help an organization profit by improving the efficiency and effectiveness of its supply chain. For example, allowing customers to directly access the company's inventory and sales order entry systems can reduce the costs of sales and marketing activities. Moreover, if such access reduces customers' costs and time of ordering, both sales and customer retention rates may increase. Of course, creating such interorganizational information systems raises new control concerns that must be addressed. It also requires increased reliability and accuracy of the data in the AIS.

Data and Information

It is time to define some terms that we have been using. **Data** refers to any and all of the facts that are collected, stored, and processed by an information system. Figure 1-4 shows that three kinds of data need to be collected for any activity: facts about the event itself, the resources affected by that event, and the agents who participated in that event.

Consider, for example, the primary value chain activity of selling. Data need to be collected about the sale event itself (e.g., the date of the sale, total amount). Data also need to be collected about the resource being sold (e.g., the identity of the goods or services, the quantity sold, unit price). Finally, data need to be collected about the agents who participated in the sale event (e.g., the identity of the customer and the salesperson).

Once data have been collected, it is the job of the AIS to transform the facts so they can be used to make decisions. Thus, **information** is data that have been organized and processed to provide meaning. Table 1-2 presents six characteristics that make information useful and meaningful for decision making.

Decision Making

Researchers have developed many models of the decision-making and problem-solving process. All those models depict decision making as a complex, multistep activity. First, the problem has to be identified. Then the decision maker must select a method for solving the problem. Next, the decision maker must collect the data needed to

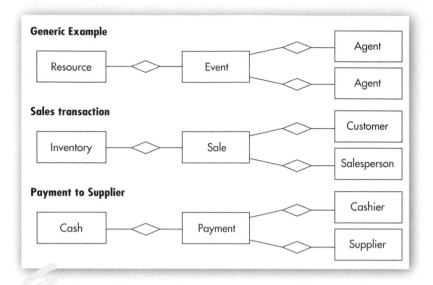

Figure 1-4   Data needs for each activity

Table 1-2   Characteristics of Useful Information

Relevant	Information is relevant if it reduces uncertainty, improves decision makers' ability to make predictions, or confirms or corrects their prior expectations.
Reliable	Information is reliable if it is free from error or bias and accurately represents the events or activities of the organization.
Complete	Information is complete if it does not omit important aspects of the underlying events or activities that it measures.
Timely	Information is timely if it is provided in time to enable decision makers to use it to make decisions.
Understandable	Information is understandable if it is presented in a useful and intelligible format.
Verifiable	Information is verifiable if two knowledgeable people acting independently would each produce the same information.

execute the decision model, and then interpret the outputs of the model and evaluate the merits of each alternative. Finally, the decision maker chooses and executes the preferred solution.

The AIS can provide assistance in all phases of decision making. Reports can help to identify potential problems. Different decision models and analytical tools can be provided to users. Query languages can facilitate the gathering of relevant data upon which to make the decision. Various tools, such as graphical interfaces, can help the decision maker interpret the results of a decision model and evaluate and choose among alternative courses of action. Finally, the AIS can provide feedback on the results of actions.

The degree to which an AIS can support decision making depends, however, on the type of decision being made. Decisions can be categorized either in terms of the degree of structure that exists or by their scope.

Decision structure

Decisions vary in terms of the degree to which they are structured. **Structured decisions** are repetitive, routine, and understood well enough that they can be delegated to lower-level employees in the organization. For example, the decision about extending credit to established customers requires only knowledge about the customer's credit limit and current balance. Structured decisions can often be automated.

Semistructured decisions are characterized by incomplete rules for making the decision and the need for subjective assessments and judgments to supplement formal data analysis. Setting a marketing budget for a new product is an example of a semistructured decision. Although such decisions usually cannot be fully automated, they are often supported by computer-based decision aids.

Unstructured decisions are nonrecurring and nonroutine. Examples include choosing the cover for a magazine, hiring senior management, and selecting basic research projects to undertake. No framework or model exists to solve such problems. Instead, they require considerable judgment and intuition. Nevertheless, unstructured decisions can be supported by computer-based decision aids that facilitate gathering information from diverse sources.

Decision scope

Decisions vary in terms of the scope of their effect. **Operational control** concerns the effective and efficient performance of specific tasks. Decisions relating to inventory management and extending credit are examples of operational control activities. **Management control** concerns the effective and efficient use of resources for accomplishing organizational objectives. Budgeting, developing human resource practices, and deciding on research projects and product improvements are examples of management control activities. **Strategic planning** concerns the establishing of organizational objectives and policies for accomplishing those objectives. Setting financial and accounting policies, developing new product lines, and acquiring new businesses are examples of strategic planning decisions.

A correspondence exists between a manager's level in an organization and his or her decision-making responsibilities. Top management faces unstructured and semistructured decisions involving strategic planning issues. Middle managers deal with semistructured decisions involving management control. Lower-level supervisors and employees face semistructured or structured decisions involving operational control.

Value of information for decision making

The information produced by a well-designed AIS can improve decision making in several ways. First, it identifies situations requiring management action. For example, a cost report with a large variance might stimulate management to investigate and, if necessary, take corrective action. Second, by reducing uncertainty, accounting information provides a basis for choosing among alternative actions. For example, accounting information is often used to set prices and determine credit policies. Third, information about the results of previous decisions provides valuable feedback that can be used to improve future decisions.

Nevertheless, although more information is often better, this is only true to a point. There are limits to the amount of information that the human mind can effectively absorb and process. **Information overload** occurs when those limits are passed. Information overload is costly, because decision-making quality declines while the costs of providing that information increase. Thus, information overload reduces the value of information. Consequently, information systems designers must consider how advances in IT can help decision makers more effectively filter and condense information, thereby avoiding information overload.

Moreover, it is important to recognize that there are costs associated with producing information. Those costs include the time and resources spent in collecting, processing, and storing data, as well as the time and resources used to distribute the resulting information to decision makers. There are also many opportunities to invest in additional IT to improve the overall performance of the AIS. Most organizations, however, do not have unlimited resources to invest in improving their information systems. Therefore, another important decision involves identifying which potential AIS improvements are likely to yield the greatest return. Making this decision wisely requires that accountants and information systems professionals understand their organization's overall business strategy.

THE AIS AND CORPORATE STRATEGY

Strategies and Strategic Positions

Michael Porter, world-renowned professor of business at Harvard, argues that there are two basic business strategies that companies can follow:[2]

1. A *product differentiation* strategy entails adding some features or services to your product that are not provided by competitors. Doing so allows a company to charge a premium price to its customers.
2. A *low-cost* strategy entails striving to be the most efficient producer of a product or service.

Sometimes a company can succeed in both producing a better product than its competitors and in doing so at costs below its industry average. Usually, however, companies must choose between the two basic strategies. If they concentrate on being the lowest cost producer, they will have to forego some value-added features that might differentiate their product. If they focus on product differentiation, they most likely will not have the lowest costs in their industry. Thus, a business strategy involves making choices.

Porter argues that the fundamental choice companies must make involves selecting a specific strategic position they wish to adopt. He describes three basic strategic positions:

1. A *variety-based* strategic position involves producing or providing a subset of the industry's products or services. Jiffy Lube International is an example of a company that has adopted a variety-based strategic position: It does not provide a wide range of automotive repair services, but focuses on oil changes and lubrication services.
2. A *needs-based* strategic position involves trying to serve most or all of the needs of a particular group of customers. This entails first identifying a target market. For example, AARP focuses on retirees.

[2]The material in this section is based on Michael E. Porter, " What Is Strategy?" *Harvard Business Review* (November-December 1996), pp. 61–78.

3. An access-based strategic position involves serving a subset of customers who differ from other customers in terms of factors such as geographic location or size, which creates different requirements for serving those customers. Edward Jones is an example of a company that has adopted an access-based strategic position: Its stock brokerage offices are located primarily in smaller towns and cities not served by the larger brokerage houses.

Porter explains that these three basic strategic positions are not mutually exclusive and, indeed, often overlap. For example, Southwest Airlines appears to have adopted elements of all three strategic positions. It can be classified as having a variety-based strategic position because it only offers a subset of the products provided by the airline industry (no first-class seating, no meals, no international flights). Southwest can also be classified as having a needs-based strategic position in that it has identified a specific target market (price-sensitive leisure travellers) for which it designs its services. Finally, Southwest also appears to have an access-based strategic position because it does not service all markets.

Choosing a strategic position is important because it enables a company to focus its efforts; otherwise it risks trying to be everything to everybody. Porter argues, however, that the specific strategic position an organization selects is not important. What is important is to design all of the organization's activities so that they mutually reinforce one another in filling that strategic position and in implementing the business strategy. When this occurs, a company reaps the benefits of *synergy*, wherein the entire system of activities performed by the organization is greater than the sum of each individual part. This makes it difficult for competitors to successfully imitate, because they must do more than just mimic specific procedures. Indeed, companies that have achieved a high degree of "fit" among their activities often do not worry about keeping their processes secret from competitors, because they know that they cannot be adopted piecemeal.

Information Technology and Business Strategy

As shown in Figure 1-1, developments in IT can affect strategy. The growth of the Internet provides a classic illustration. It has profoundly affected the way that many steps in the value chain are performed. For example, for products that can be digitized, the Internet enables organizations to significantly streamline their inbound and outbound logistics activities.

In addition to directly affecting the ways that organizations carry out their value chain activities, the Internet can also significantly affect both strategy and strategic positioning. For example, the Internet dramatically cuts costs, thereby helping companies to implement a low-cost strategy. If every company in a given industry, however, uses the Internet to adopt a low-cost strategy, then the effects may be problematic. Indeed, one possible outcome may be intense price competition among firms, with the likely result that most of the cost savings provided by the Internet get passed on to the industry's customers, rather than being retained in the form of higher profits. Moreover, because every company can use the Internet to streamline its value chain activities, it is unlikely that any particular company will be able to use the Internet to gain a sustainable long-term competitive advantage vis-à-vis its competitors. Therefore, once the majority of companies in an industry begin to fully integrate the Internet into their value chains, the effect may be to encourage companies to shift from following primarily a low-cost strategy toward adopting some form of product differentiation strategy.

The Internet may also affect the relative desirability of following the three strategic positions described earlier. For example, by drastically reducing or eliminating geographic barriers, the Internet makes a company's products available almost anywhere. Consequently, it may be more difficult to establish and maintain an access-based strategic position. This is just one example of how the Internet can affect an organization's strategy and choice of strategic position. Indeed, as Focus 1-2 explains, the Internet alters many fundamental characteristics of industry structure, thereby requiring companies to carefully reconsider their overall strategy.

Role of the AIS

An organization's AIS plays an important role in helping it adopt and maintain a strategic position. Achieving a close fit among activities requires that data be collected about each activity. It is also important that the information system collect and integrate both financial and nonfinancial data about the organization's activities.

Focus 1-2

The Internet Makes Strategy More Important Than Ever

The Internet has changed the way that many business processes are performed. It has also dramatically affected the five characteristics that determine the profitability of an entire industry: the bargaining power of buyers, the bargaining power of suppliers, barriers to entry, the threat of substitute products or services, and the level of rivalry among existing competitors.

Unfortunately for companies in most industries, the development of the Internet has tended to increase the relative power of one or more of these five factors, thereby decreasing the overall profitability of the average firm in a given industry. The Internet has reduced barriers to entry in many industries by reducing or eliminating the need to invest in and develop specific assets, such as a dedicated sales force. It increases the power of buyers by reducing switching costs and simplifying detailed comparisons across products and services. The Internet creates new methods of performing basic business processes, thereby creating new substitute products and services. It enables suppliers to bypass intermediaries and sell directly to end consumers. Finally, because the Internet decreases the level of variable costs relative to fixed costs, it increases pressures to compete more on price.

As a result of these factors, many companies find that although the Internet has made them more efficient and effective, they are unable to retain much of those benefits in the form of increased profits. In fact, if a company is not careful, it can find itself drawn into a vicious level of price competition that benefits only consumers. The only way companies can avoid that trap is to define a strategy and stake out a strategic position that effectively differentiates themselves from their competitors. Thus, the most important effect of the development of the Internet is the increased importance of strategy.

Source: Michael E. Porter, "Strategy and the Internet," *Harvard Business Review* (March 2001): 63–78.

Traditionally, the AIS has been referred to as a transaction processing system because its only concern was financial data and accounting transactions. For example, when a sale took place, the AIS would record a journal entry showing only the date of the sale, a debit to either cash or accounts receivable, and a credit to sales. Other potentially useful nonfinancial information about the sale, such as the time of day that it occurred, would traditionally be collected and processed outside of the AIS. Consequently, many organizations developed additional information systems to collect, process, store, and report information not contained in the AIS. Unfortunately, the existence of multiple systems creates numerous problems and inefficiencies. Often the same data must be captured and stored by more than one system, which not only results in redundancy across systems, but also can lead to discrepancies if data are changed in one system but not in others. In addition, it is difficult to effectively integrate data from the various systems.

Enterprise resource planning (ERP) systems are designed to overcome these problems as they integrate all aspects of a company's operations with its traditional AIS. Thus, when the sales force enters an order, the effect of the transaction automatically flows to all affected parts of the company. Inventory is updated, production schedules are adjusted, and purchase orders are initiated to acquire any needed raw materials and supplies. Moreover, important nonfinancial data, such as the time the activity occurred, is collected and stored in the same system.

A key feature of ERP systems is the integration of financial with other nonfinancial operating data. The value of such integration suggests that there may be strategic benefits to more closely linking the traditionally separate functions of information systems and accounting, and many organizations are beginning to combine these two functions. The importance of this trend is reflected in the fact that some universities have even merged their accounting and information systems departments.

The authors of this text believe that the disciplines of accounting and information systems have much in common and should be closely integrated. Therefore, we do not try to distinguish between an AIS and other types of information systems. Instead, we adopt the viewpoint that the AIS can and should be the primary information system of an organization and that it will provide users with the information they need to perform their jobs.

SUMMARY AND CASE CONCLUSION

Scott and Susan require a well-designed AIS to provide the information they need to effectively plan, manage, and control their business. S&S's AIS must be able to process data about sales and cash receipts, the purchase of and payment for merchandise and services, payroll and tax-related transactions, and the acquisition of and payment for fixed assets. The company's AIS must also provide the information needed to prepare financial statements.

Fortunately, there are many computer-based accounting packages available for the retail industry. As they begin looking at various popular software packages, however, Scott and Susan quickly learn that considerable accounting knowledge is required to choose the one that will best fit their business. Because neither has an accounting background, Scott and Susan decide that their next task will be to hire an accountant.

KEY TERMS

- accounting information system (AIS)
- system
- value chain
- primary activities
- support activities

- supply chain
- data
- information
- structured decision
- semistructured decision
- unstructured decision

- operational control
- management control
- strategic planning
- information overload
- enterprise resource planning (ERP) system

CHAPTER QUIZ

1. Data differ from information in which way?
   a. Data are output and information is input.
   b. Information is output and data are input.
   c. Data are meaningful bits of information.
   d. There is no difference.

2. Which of the following is not a characteristic that makes information useful?
   a. It is reliable.
   b. It is timely.
   c. It is inexpensive.
   d. It is relevant.

3. Which of the following is a primary activity in the value chain?
   a. purchasing
   b. accounting
   c. post-sales service
   d. human resource management

4. Top management continually emphasizes and supports investments designed to improve efficiency of the manufacturing process. Such a focus most likely reflects the pursuit of which type of strategy?
   a. product differentiation
   b. low cost
   c. needs-based
   d. variety-based

5. Which of the following is not a means by which information improves decision making?
   a. increasing information overload
   b. reducing uncertainty
   c. providing feedback about the effectiveness of prior decisions
   d. identifying situations requiring management action

6. In the value chain concept, upgrading IT is considered what kind of activity?
   a. primary activity
   b. support activity
   c. service activity
   d. structured activity

7. Lower-level management employees are most likely to make which of the following decisions?
   a. structured decisions involving strategic planning
   b. unstructured decisions involving managerial control
   c. structured decisions involving operational control
   d. unstructured decisions involving strategic planning

8. Which of the following is a function of an AIS?
   a. reducing the need to identify a strategy and strategic position
   b. transforming data into useful information
   c. allocating organizational resources
   d. automating decision making
9. A firm, its suppliers, and its customers collectively form which of the following?
   a. supply chain
   b. value chain
   c. ERP system
   d. AIS
10. A company that focuses its marketing efforts on a specific subset of the population (e.g., college students) is probably pursuing which type of strategic position?
    a. variety based
    b. needs based
    c. access based
    d. low cost

DISCUSSION QUESTIONS

1.1 Apply the value chain concept to S&S, Inc. Explain how it performs the various primary and supporting activities.
1.2 The value of information equals the difference between the decision benefits realized from using that information and the costs of producing it. Would you, or any organization, ever produce information if its expected costs exceeded its benefits? Provide some examples.
1.3 One function of the AIS is to provide adequate controls to ensure the safety of organizational assets, including data. Many people, however, often view control procedures as "red tape." Discuss how controls can improve overall efficiency and effectiveness.
1.4 One interesting property of digital assets is that they can be reproduced and distributed via the Internet at very little cost. What are some of the implications of having a product with a marginal cost close to zero?
1.5 Figure 1-1 shows that organizational culture and the design of an AIS influence one another. What does this imply about the degree to which an innovative system developed by one company can be transferred to another company?
1.6 Figure 1-1 shows that developments in IT affect both an organization's strategy and the design of its AIS. How can a company determine whether it is spending too much, too little, or just enough on IT?
1.7 To what extent can all the characteristics of useful information listed in Table 1-2 be simultaneously met?
1.8 Information technology enables organizations to easily collect large amounts of information about employees. Discuss the following issues:
    a. To what extent should management monitor employees' e-mail?
    b. To what extent should management monitor which Web sites are visited by employees?
    c. To what extent should management monitor employee performance by, for example, using software to track keystrokes per hour or other unit of time? If such information is collected, how should it be used?
    d. Should companies use software to electronically "shred" all traces of e-mail?
    e. Under what circumstances and to whom is it appropriate for a company to distribute information it collects about the people who visit its Web site?

Problems

1.1 Write a two-page report explaining the two basic strategies that S&S, Inc. can pursue and the three different strategic positions that it can adopt. Include in your report a discussion and examples of how IT can be used to support the different strategies and strategic positions.

1.2 Write a two-page report giving an example of each type of decision (operational control, management control, and strategic planning) that is made at S&S, Inc. Describe the degree of structure inherent in each of your examples. Discuss what kinds of information can be provided by S&S's AIS.

1.3 Information technology is continually changing the nature of accounting and the role of accountants. Write a two-page report describing what you think the nature of the accounting function in a large company will be like in the year 2010.

1.4 The annual report is considered by some to be the single most important printed document that companies produce. In recent years, annual reports have become large documents. They now include such sections as letters to the stockholders, descriptions of the business, operating highlights, financial review, management discussion and analysis, segment reporting, and inflation data as well as the basic financial statements. The expansion has been due in part to a general increase in the degree of sophistication and complexity in accounting standards and disclosure requirements for financial reporting.

   The expansion also is reflective of the change in the composition and level of sophistication of users. Current users include not only stockholders, but also financial and securities analysts, potential investors, lending institutions, stockbrokers, customers, employees, and, whether the reporting company likes it or not, competitors. Thus a report that was originally designed as a device for communicating basic financial information now attempts to meet the diverse needs of an ever-expanding audience.

   Users hold conflicting views on the value of annual reports. Some argue that they fail to provide enough information, whereas others believe that disclosures in annual reports have expanded to the point where they create information overload. Others argue that the future of most companies depends on acceptance by the investing public and by its customers; therefore, companies should take this opportunity to communicate well-defined corporate strategies.

Required

1. Identify and discuss the basic factors of communication that must be considered in the presentation of this information.

2. Discuss the communication problems a corporation faces in preparing the annual report that result from the diversity of the users being addressed.

3. Select two types of information found in an annual report, other than the financial statements and accompanying footnotes, and describe how they are helpful to the users of annual reports.

4. Discuss at least two advantages and two disadvantages of stating well-defined corporate strategies in the annual report.

5. Evaluate the effectiveness of annual reports in fulfilling the information needs of the following current and potential users:
   a. Shareholders
   b. Creditors

    c. Employees

    d. Customers

    e. Financial analysts

  6. Annual reports are public and accessible to anyone, including competitors. Discuss how this affects decisions about what information should be provided in annual reports. (CMA Examination, adapted)

1.5 Research the programming language XBRL and write a two-page report about its effect on financial reporting via the Internet.

Case 1-1   AnyCompany, Inc.: An Ongoing Comprehensive Case

The first case at the end of each chapter is an assignment that allows you to apply key concepts to a local company. This case, then, may become an ongoing case study on which you work throughout the term.

Visit a small to midsize business in your community and explain that you have been assigned to study a local company. Ask for permission to study the company and explain that you will need to meet with company employees several times during the term to get pertinent information. However, you will not need a great deal of their time or disrupt their business. Offer to share your findings and to make suggestions as a way of motivating the firm to allow you to study them.

REQUIRED

Once you have lined up a company, answer the following questions:

1. What types of information systems does the company have? What subsystems does it have? Describe each information system and explain its purpose.

2. Who are the major external users of company information? The major internal users? What information is produced for each set of users?

3. For two system outputs, identify the decisions that are made with that information, the data collected to produce the information, how the data are stored and processed to produce the information, and how instructions and procedures are given to the system and its users. Use the characteristics of information (reliable, timely, etc.) to evaluate the usefulness of the information provided.

4. What strategy is the company pursuing? How does its AIS help to achieve that strategy?

5. What strategic position is the company pursuing? How does its AIS help to achieve that position?

Case 1-2   Ackoff's Management Misinformation Systems

The Web site for this book contains Russell L. Ackoff's classic article "Management Misinformation Systems" from *Management Science*. In the article, Ackoff identified five common assumptions about information systems and then explained why he disagreed with them.

REQUIRED

Read the five assumptions, contentions, and Ackoff's explanations. For each of the five assumptions, decide if you agree or disagree with Ackoff's contentions. Prepare a report in which you defend your stand and explain your defense.

ANSWERS TO CHAPTER QUIZ

1. b	**3.** c	**5.** a	**7.** c	**9.** a
2. c	**4.** b	**6.** b	**8.** b	**10.** b

Overview
of Business
Processes

Learning Objectives

After studying this chapter, you should be able to:

- Explain the three basic functions an accounting information system (AIS) performs.
- Describe the documents and procedures used in an AIS to collect and process transaction data.
- Discuss the types of information that an AIS can provide.
- Describe the basic internal control objectives of an AIS and explain how they are accomplished.

Integrative Case: S&S, Inc.

The grand opening of S&S, Inc. is two weeks away. Scott Parry and Susan Gonzalez are working long hours to make the final arrangements for the store opening. Most of the employees have already been hired; training is scheduled for next week.

Susan has ordered what she thinks will be an adequate amount of inventory for the first month. The store is being remodeled and will have a bright, cheery decor. All seems to be in order—all, that is, except the accounting records.

Like many entrepreneurs, Scott and Susan have not given as much thought to their accounting records as they have to other parts of their business. They recognize that they need qualified accounting help and have hired a full-time accountant, Ashton Fleming. Scott and Susan think Ashton is perfect for the job because of his two years of experience with a national CPA firm. Ashton is looking forward to working for S&S because he has always wanted to be involved in building a company from the ground up.

During Ashton's first day on the job, Susan shows him where the invoices for the inventory that she purchased are located. Scott explains that the sales staff is paid a fixed salary plus commissions and that all other employees are paid hourly rates. Employees are paid every two weeks, with their first paychecks due next week. Susan then pulls out several folders and hands them to Ashton. One contains the documentation on their bank loan, with the first payment due several days after the grand opening. The other folders contain information on rental payments, utilities, and other expenses. Susan tells Ashton that she and Scott know little about accounting and are relying on him to help them decide how to run the accounting end of S&S. She adds that the only thing they have done so far is to open a checking account for S&S and that they have kept the check register updated to monitor their cash flow.

Ashton asks Scott what accounting software the company is using. Scott replies that with all the challenges they have had in opening up S&S, he and Susan have not had time to tackle that aspect yet. Scott adds that he and Susan did begin to look at some of the popular packages, but quickly realized that they did not know enough about accounting to make an intelligent choice. Scott then tells Ashton that his first task should be to purchase whatever accounting software he thinks will be best for S&S.

After Scott leaves, Ashton feels both excited and a little nervous about his responsibility for creating an accounting information system (AIS) for S&S. Although Ashton has audited many companies, he has never organized a company's books and is unsure how to go about it. A million questions run through his head. Here are just a few of them:

1. How am I going to organize things? Where do I start? What information do Scott and Susan need to run S&S effectively? How can that information be provided?
2. How am I going to collect and process data about all the types of transactions in which S&S will engage?
3. How do I organize all the data that will be collected?
4. How should I design the AIS so that the information provided is reliable and accurate?

INTRODUCTION

Chapter 1 noted that an AIS performs three basic functions:

1. Collecting and processing data about the organization's business activities efficiently and effectively.
2. Providing information useful for decision making.
3. Establishing adequate controls to ensure that data about business activities are recorded and processed accurately and to safeguard both that data and other organizational assets.

This chapter provides an overview of how an AIS performs these three functions. We begin by discussing the basic types of business activities in which an organization engages, the key decisions that must be considered when managing those activities, and the information needed to make those decisions. In doing so, we show that the nature and objectives of an organization affect the design of its AIS. Then we describe how data about business activities can be collected, processed, and transformed into useful information for management. We conclude the chapter with an introduction to internal controls.

BUSINESS ACTIVITIES AND INFORMATION NEEDS

Ashton decides that before he begins shopping for an accounting package for S&S, he must first understand how the company functions. This insight will enable him to identify the kinds of information Scott and Susan will need to manage S&S effectively. Then Ashton can determine the types of data and procedures that will be needed to collect that information.

Ashton creates a three-column table to summarize the results of his analysis. In the left column he lists basic business activities in which S&S will engage. Next, in the middle column, he lists key decisions that will need to be made for each of these activities. Finally, in the right column, he lists helpful information that Scott and Susan will need to make these decisions. Table 2-1 shows the results of this effort.

Ashton realizes that his list is not exhaustive, but he is satisfied that it provides a good overview of S&S. He also recognizes that not all the information needs listed in the right-hand column will be produced internally by S&S's AIS. Information about payment terms for merchandise purchases, for example, will be provided by vendors. Thus the AIS must be able to effectively integrate such external data with internally generated data so that Scott and Susan can use both types of information to run S&S.

Next, Ashton decides to reorganize the business activities listed in Table 2-1 into groups of related transactions. From his audit experience, Ashton knows that many of the business activities any organization performs can be described as pairs of events that involve a give-get exchange.[1] For example, S&S sells merchandise to customers in exchange for which it receives cash. Similarly, it buys inventory from suppliers and in exchange disburses cash to those suppliers.

Ashton notes that these basic exchanges correspond to what historically have been called **transaction cycles:**

➤ The **revenue cycle** includes the sales and cash receipts events.

➤ The **expenditure cycle** includes the purchases and cash disbursements events.

➤ The **human resources (payroll) cycle** includes the events of hiring and paying employees.

➤ The **production cycle** includes the events of transforming raw materials and labor into finished products.

➤ The **financing cycle** includes the events of obtaining funds from investors and creditors and repaying them.

Figure 2-1 shows how these various transaction cycles relate to one another and interface with the **general ledger and reporting system,** which is used to generate information for both management and external parties.

In many accounting software packages, the various transaction cycles are implemented as separate modules. Every organization does not need to implement every module. Retail stores like S&S, for example, do not have a production cycle and therefore do not need to implement that module. Moreover, some types of organizations have unique requirements. Financial institutions, for example, have demand-deposit

---

[1]The idea of modeling an AIS as a set of "Give and Take" exchanges was developed in Cheryl L. Dunn and William E. McCarthy, "Conceptual Models of Economic Exchange Phenomena: History's Third Wave of Accounting Systems," *Collected Papers of the Sixth World Congress of Accounting Historians,* Volume 1, Kyoto, Japan, pp 133–164; and in Guido Geerts and William E. McCarthy, "Modeling Business Enterprises as Value-Added Process Heirarchies with Resource-Event-Agent Object Templates," *Business Object Design and Implementation: OOPSLA 1995 Workshop Preceedings,* (October 16, 1995), Austin, TX: Springer.

Table 2-1   Overview of S&S's Business Activities, Key Decisions, and Information Needs

Business Activities	Key Decisions	Information Needs
Acquire capital	How much? Invest or borrow? If borrow, best terms?	Cash flow projections Pro-forma financial statements Loan amortization schedule
Acquire building and equipment	Size of building? Amount of equipment? Rent or buy? Location? How to depreciate?	Capacity needs Prices Market study Tax tables and regulations
Hire and train employees	Experience requirements? How to assess integrity and competence of applicants? How to train?	Job description Applicant job history and skills
Acquire inventory	What models to carry? How much to purchase? Which vendors? How to manage inventory (store, control, etc.)	Market analyses Inventory status reports Vendor performance and pay- ment terms
Engage in advertising and marketing	Which media? Content?	Cost analyses Market coverage
Sell merchandise	Markup percentage? Offer in-house credit? Which credit cards to accept?	Pro-forma income statement Credit card costs Customer credit status
Collect payments from customers	If offer credit, what terms? How to handle cash receipts?	Customer account status Accounts receivable aging report
Pay employees	Amount to pay? Deductions and withholdings? Process payroll in-house or use outside service?	Sales (for commissions) Time worked (for hourly employees) W4 forms Costs of external payroll service
Pay taxes	Payroll tax requirements Sales tax requirements	Government regulations Total wage expense Total sales
Pay vendors	Whom to pay? When to pay? How much to pay?	Vendor invoices Accounts payable

and installment-loan cycles that relate to transactions involving customer accounts and loans, respectively. In addition, the nature of a given transaction cycle differs across types of organizations. For example, the expenditure cycle of a service company, such as a public accounting or a law firm, does not involve processing transactions related to the purchase, receipt, and payment for merchandise that will be resold to customers.

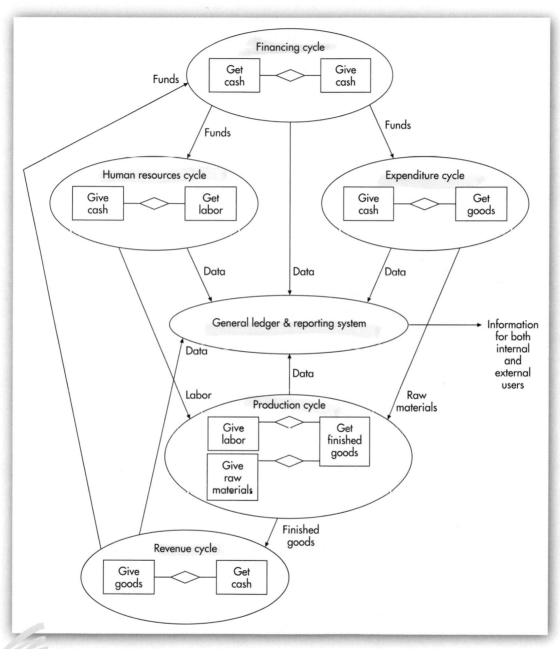

Figure 2-1 The AIS and its subsystems

Source: Adapted from classroom materials originally developed by Julie Smith David at Arizona State University and based on ideas developed in the sources listed in footnote 1.

After preparing Table 2-1 and Figure 2-1, Ashton believed that he understood S&S well enough to begin shopping for an accounting package that would serve as the core of its AIS. He recalled, however, several audits in which clients had multiple separate information systems, because their basic accounting software was not designed to accommodate the information needs of all managers. Ashton also vividly recalled attending one client's board meeting where he witnessed the negative effects of having multiple systems. The head of marketing had one report on year-to-date sales by product, the production manager had a different report that contained different sales figures, and the controller's report, which was produced by the general ledger system, had yet a third version of year-to-date sales. Over an hour had been wasted trying to reconcile those different reports! Ashton vowed that he would make sure that S&S did not ever find itself in such a mess. He would make sure that any accounting software package he selected would have the capability to integrate both financial and nonfinancial data about S&S's various business activities so that everyone could pull information from the same system.

TRANSACTION PROCESSING: DOCUMENTS AND PROCEDURES

The **data processing cycle** consists of four steps: data input, data storage, data processing, and information output. The trigger for data input is usually the performance of some business activity. As shown in Figure 2-2, data must be collected about three facets of each business activity:

1. Each event of interest
2. The resource(s) affected by each event
3. The agents who participate in each event

For example, S&S may find it useful to collect the following data about a sales transaction:

➤ Date of the sale
➤ Time of day the sale occurred
➤ Employee who made the sale
➤ Checkout clerk who processed the sale
➤ Checkout register at which the sale occurred, total amount of the sale, and item(s) sold
➤ Quantity of each item sold

Figure 2-2 Facets of business activites about which data must be collected

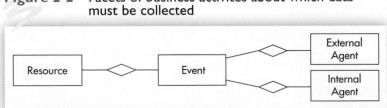

➤ Actual price of each item sold
➤ List price of item sold

For credit sales, additional information is also needed: special delivery instructions, the customer bill-to and ship-to addresses, and the customer name.

Each transaction cycle typically processes a large number of individual events or transactions. Most of these, however, can be categorized into a relatively small number of distinct types. For example, in retail stores like S&S, the majority of the individual transactions processed in the revenue cycle relate either to the sale of goods or services to customers or to the collection of cash from customers in payment for those sales. Table 2-2 lists the most common types of activities performed in each transaction cycle and the name of the document or form used to capture data about that event.

Data Input

Historically, most businesses used paper **source documents** to initially collect data about their business activities and then transferred that data into the computer. Today, however, most data about business activities are recorded directly through computer data entry screens. (Usually the data entry screen retains the same name as the paper source document it replaced.)

Well-designed source documents and data entry screens improve both control and accuracy of capturing data about business activities. Control is improved either by purchasing prenumbered source documents or by having the system automatically

Table 2-2   Common Business Activities and Source Documents

Business Activity	Source Document
Revenue Cycle	
Take customer order	Sales order
Deliver or ship order	Delivery ticket or bill of lading
Receive cash	Remittance advice or remittance list
Deposit cash receipts	Deposit slip
Adjust customer account	Credit memo
Expenditure Cycle	
Request items	Purchase requisition
Order items	Purchase order
Receive items	Receiving report
Pay for items	Check
Human Resources Cycle	
Collect employee withholding data	W4 form
Record time worked by employees	Time cards
Record time spent on specific jobs	Job time tickets or time sheet

assign a sequential number to each new transaction. Prenumbering simplifies verifying that all transactions have been recorded and that none of the documents has been misplaced. (Imagine trying to balance a checkbook if the checks were not prenumbered.) Well-designed paper forms and data entry screens improve accuracy by providing instructions or prompts about what data to collect, grouping logically related pieces of information close together, using check-off boxes or pull-down menus to present the available options, and using appropriate shading and borders to clearly separate data items.

If paper documents must still be exchanged with customers or suppliers, data input accuracy and efficiency can be further improved by using **turnaround documents,** which are records of company data sent to an external party and then returned to the system as input. Turnaround documents are prepared in machine-readable form to facilitate their subsequent processing as input records. An example is a utility bill that is read by a special scanning device when it is returned with its payment.

Source data automation is yet another means to improve the accuracy and efficiency of data input. Source data automation devices capture transaction data in machine-readable form at the time and place of their origin. Examples include ATMs used by banks, point-of-sale (POS) scanners used in retail stores, and bar code scanners used in warehouses.

Data Processing

Once data about a business activity has been collected, the next step usually involves updating previously stored information about the resources affected by that event and the agents who participated in that activity. For example, data about a sales transaction result in updating the information about inventory to reduce the quantity on hand of the items sold, as well as updating the customer's account balance. This updating can either be done periodically, such as once a day or week, or immediately as each transaction occurs.

Periodic updating of the data stored about resources and agents is referred to as **batch processing;** immediate updating as each transaction occurs is referred to as **on-line, real-time processing.** Batch processing is a legacy method that continues to be used for some applications, such as payroll, that naturally occur at fixed time periods. The obvious disadvantage of batch processing is that stored data are only current and accurate immediately after the periodic batch updating process. Consequently, most companies are switching to on-line, real-time processing for most applications. On-line data entry is more accurate than periodic batch input because the system can refuse incomplete or erroneous entries and, because the data are being entered at the time the transaction occurs, any errors can be easily corrected. Real-time processing ensures that stored information is always current, thereby increasing its usefulness for making decisions.

Indeed, many companies are using on-line, real-time processing because of the competitive advantages it offers. For example, a few years ago Federal Express updated its mission statement to include the phrase "Positive control of each package will be maintained by utilizing real-time electronic tracking and tracing systems." The company's on-line real-time system tells the exact location of each package and estimates its arrival time. Federal Express also provides customers with software that allows them to track their own parcels.

Data Storage

Imagine how difficult a textbook would be to read if it were not organized into chapters, sections, paragraphs, and sentences. Now imagine how hard it would be for S&S to find a particular invoice if all of its key documents were randomly dumped into file cabinets. Fortunately, most textbooks and company files are organized for easy retrieval. Likewise, information in an AIS can be organized for easy and efficient access. This section explains basic data storage concepts and definitions, using accounts receivable information as an example.

An **entity** is something about which information is stored. Examples of entities include employees, inventory items, and customers. Each entity has **attributes,** or characteristics of interest, which need to be stored. An employee pay rate and a customer address are examples of attributes. Generally, each type of entity possesses the same set of attributes. For example, all employees possess an employee number, pay rate, and home address. The specific data values for those attributes, however, will differ among entities. For example, one employee's pay rate might be $8.00, whereas another's might be $8.25.

Figure 2-3 shows that computers store data by organizing smaller units of data into larger, more meaningful ones. Data values are stored in a physical space called a **field.**

Figure 2-3   Data storage elements

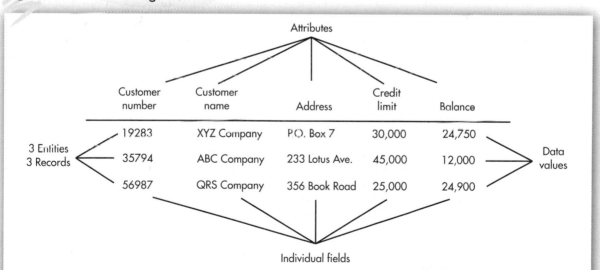

This accounts receivable file stores information about three separate entities: XYZ Company, ABC Company, and QRS Company. As a result, there are three records in the file. Five separate attributes are used to describe each customer: customer number, customer name, address, credit limit, and balance. There are therefore five separate fields in each record. Each field contains a data value that describes an attribute of a particular entity (customer). For example, the data value 19283 is the customer number for the XYZ Company.

The set of fields that contain data about various attributes of the same entity forms a **record.** In Figure 2-3, each row represents a different record and each column represents an attribute, or field. Thus, each intersecting row and column in Figure 2-3 is a field within a record, the contents of which are called a **data value.**

Related records are grouped to form a **file.** For example, all customer receivable records are stored in an accounts receivable file. A set of interrelated, centrally coordinated files is referred to as a **database.** For example, the accounts receivable file might be combined with customer, sales analysis, and related files to form a customer database.

In an AIS, the files used to store cumulative information about resources and agents are called ledgers. (In a manual system, ledgers are actually books; hence the phrase "keeping the books" refers to the process of maintaining and updating the ledgers.) Ashton decided that S&S, like most companies, should have both a general ledger and a set of subsidiary ledgers. The **general ledger** contains summary-level data for every asset, liability, equity, revenue, and expense account of the organization. A **subsidiary ledger** records all the detailed data for any general ledger account that has many individual subaccounts. For example, the general ledger contains one account that summarizes the total amount owed to the company by all customers. The subsidiary accounts receivable ledger has a separate record for each individual customer, each of which contains detailed information (name, address, account balance, credit limit, etc.) about a particular customer. Subsidiary ledgers are commonly used for accounts receivable, inventory, fixed assets, and accounts payable.

The general ledger account corresponding to a subsidiary ledger is called a control account. The relationship between the general ledger control account and the individual account balances in the subsidiary ledger plays an important role in maintaining the accuracy of the data stored in the AIS. Specifically, the sum of all entries in the subsidiary ledger should equal the amount in the corresponding general ledger control account. For example, the inventory subsidiary ledger would contain dollar balances for each inventory item carried by S&S. The sum of all the dollar balances in the inventory subsidiary ledger should equal the total dollar balance in the inventory control account in the general ledger. Any discrepancy between the total of the subsidiary ledger and the balance in the corresponding general ledger control account indicates that an error in the recording process has occurred.

Each general ledger account is assigned a specific number. The **chart of accounts** is a list of all general ledger accounts an organization uses. The structure of the chart of accounts is one of the most important aspects of an AIS, because it affects the preparation of financial statements and reports. Data stored in individual accounts can easily be summed for presentation in reports, but data stored in summary accounts cannot be easily broken down and reported in more detail. Consequently, it is important that the chart of accounts contain sufficient detail to meet an organization's information needs.

To illustrate, consider the consequences if S&S were to use only one general ledger account for all sales transactions. It would be easy to produce reports showing the total amount of sales for a given time period, but it would be very difficult to prepare reports separating cash and credit sales. Indeed, the only way to produce these latter reports would be to go back to the source documents to identify the nature of

Table 2-3   Sample Chart of Accounts for S&S

Account Code	Account Name	Account Code	Account Name
100–199	Current Assets	400–499	Equity Accounts
101	Checking Account	400	Common Stock
102	Savings Account	410	Retained Earnings
103	Petty Cash		
120	Accounts Receivable	500–599	Revenues
125	Allowance for Doubtful Accounts	501	Cash Sales
130	Notes Receivable	502	Credit Sales
150	Inventory	510	Sales Returns & Allowances
160	Supplies	511	Sales Discounts
170	Prepaid Rent	520	Interest Revenue
180	Prepaid Insurance	530	Miscellaneous Revenue
200–299	Noncurrent Assets	600–799	Expenses
200	Land	600	Cost of Goods Sold
210	Buildings	611	Wages Expense
215	Accumulated Depreciation —Buildings	612	Commissions Expense
		613	Payroll Tax Expense
230	Equipment	620	Rent Expense
235	Accumulated Depreciation —Equipment	630	Insurance Expense
		640	Supplies Expense
240	Furniture and Fixtures	650	Bad Debt Expense
245	Accumulated Depreciation —Furniture & Fixtures	701	Depreciation Expense— Buildings
250	Other Assets	702	Depreciation Expense— Equipment
300–399	Liabilities	703	Depreciation Expense— Furniture & Fixtures
300	Accounts Payable		
310	Wages Payable		
321	Employee Income Tax Payable	710	Income Tax Expense
322	FICA Tax Payable		
323	Federal Unemployment Tax Payable	900–999	Summary Accounts
324	State Unemployment Tax Payable	910	Income Summary
330	Accrued Interest Payable		
360	Other Liabilities		

each sales transaction. Clearly, this approach would not be practical. If, however, S&S used separate general ledger accounts for cash and credit sales, then reports showing both types of sales could be easily produced. Total sales could also be easily reported by summing each type of sale.

Table 2-3 shows the initial chart of accounts Ashton developed for S&S. Let us examine its structure. Each account number is three digits long, with each digit serving a specific purpose. The first digit represents the major account categories as they appear on S&S's financial statements: current assets, noncurrent assets, liabilities, equity accounts, revenues, expenses, and summary accounts. Notice that each major category is assigned a separate block of numbers, which corresponds with the sequence in which that category appears in the financial statements. Thus all current assets are numbered in the 100s, noncurrent assets are numbered in the 200s, and so on.

The second digit in each account code represents the primary financial subaccounts within each category. Again, the accounts are assigned numbers to match the order of their appearance in financial statements (in order of decreasing liquidity). Thus account 120 represents accounts receivable and account 150 represents inventory.

Finally, the third digit identifies the specific account to which the transaction data will be posted. For example, account 501 represents cash sales, and account 502 represents credit sales. Similarly, accounts 101 through 103 represent the various cash accounts used by S&S.

It is important to realize that the chart of accounts will differ, depending on the nature and purpose of the organization it represents. For example, the sample chart of accounts for S&S reflects the fact that the company is a corporation. In contrast, the chart of accounts for a partnership would include separate capital and drawing accounts for each partner, instead of common stock and retained earnings. Likewise, because S&S is a retail organization, it has only one type of general ledger inventory account. A manufacturing company, in contrast, would have separate general ledger accounts for raw materials, work in process, and finished goods inventories.

A chart of accounts should also provide room for growth. Notice that Ashton left a number of gaps in S&S's chart of accounts to allow for later insertion of additional accounts. For example, S&S does not currently have enough excess cash to invest in marketable securities. Later, when it can do so, a new general ledger account for marketable securities can be created and assigned the number 110. Ashton also knows that Scott and Susan hope to open additional stores in the future. When this occurs, he plans to add two more digits to the chart of accounts to represent each store in the chain, so that S&S can track sales, expenses, inventory, and other items in each individual store.

Accounts in the subsidiary ledgers often have longer account codes than those used in the general ledger. For example, Ashton plans that each individual account receivable will have a seven-digit code. The first three digits are 120, the code for accounts receivable in the general ledger. The additional four digits provide a means for identifying up to 10,000 individual customers. The accounts payable and inventory subsidiary ledgers will be organized in a similar manner.

This concludes our description of the documents and procedures commonly used to record and process data about transactions. In a small company like S&S, it will be Ashton's responsibility not only to design and manage the AIS but also to perform most of the procedures we have just described. These tasks are only part of Ashton's responsibilities, however. As Focus 2-1 explains, controllers in small businesses must play a number of roles. Similarly, we pointed out earlier that transaction processing is only one of three key functions of the AIS.

Focus 2-1

What Does a Small-Business Controller Do?

Controllers in small businesses play at least four distinct roles. The first role can be characterized as a technician. In this role, the controller is responsible for collecting and processing the data needed to prepare financial statements and a wide variety of managerial reports. Just turning out those reports, however, is not enough. The controller must understand the business issues behind the numbers well enough to help management interpret those numbers correctly. The controller must also work with various managers to learn exactly what information they need to do their jobs effectively, and then devise the means for providing that information.

The controller's second role is to act as "company cop." This entails ensuring that the company is in compliance with all applicable regulations and that assets, including data, are adequately safeguarded. It also involves establishing procedures to ensure that business activities are performed correctly and efficiently and that data about them are recorded accurately.

The third role the controller plays in a small business is that of booster and trainer. This entails helping managers and staff to understand how their individual duties fit into the company's overall goals and objectives. It also involves over-seeing sufficient cross-training of staff so that in the event of an employee's absence, due to vacations or illness, the business can continue to function smoothly. It may even include providing advice to young employees about career development, such as encouraging them to go back to school for further training. Moreover, in a small business, the controller may get involved in the kinds of employee counseling that in larger companies would be the province of a separate human resource management department.

A fourth role played by the small-business controller is that of technology and accounting expert. The controller must keep abreast of technology and accounting developments and how they affect both business operations and employee responsibilities. Developing and maintaining a good personal network are essential to meeting this role, because no one individual can keep abreast of all the accounting and technological changes that occur each year. One way to develop such a network is to get involved in the local Institute of Management Accountants (IMA) chapter.

In summary, the small-business controller is responsible for more than just keeping the books.

Source: Bonnie D. Labrack, "Small Business Controller," *Management Accounting* (November 1994): 38–41.

PROVIDING INFORMATION FOR DECISION MAKING

A second function of the AIS is to provide management with information useful for decision making. Whether presented in the form of paper reports or displayed on a computer screen, the information an AIS provides falls into two main categories: financial statements and managerial reports. Financial statements are primarily designed for external parties to use in making decisions about extending credit to or investing in the organization. Your other accounting and finance courses focus on financial statements in great detail. Therefore, this section provides an overview of some types of managerial reports that an AIS should be designed to provide.

Managerial Reports

An organization's AIS must be able to provide managers with detailed operational information about the organization's performance.[2] For example, Scott and Susan need reports about inventory status, relative profitability of products, relative performance of each salesperson, cash collections and pending obligations, and S&S's performance in meeting its delivery commitments.

Often, both traditional financial measures and operational data are required for proper and complete evaluation of performance. To illustrate, consider the evaluation of sales staff. Dividing sales revenue by the number of sales staff provides one measure of productivity. Dividing the *number* of sales transactions by the same denominator provides another way to look at productivity. Dividing sales revenue by the number of hours worked by sales staff provides yet another measure of productivity. Additional perspective is gained by calculating the average sale amount and the cost of sales staff salaries as percentages of sales revenue. All these measures are valid, and all five together provide a better overall evaluation of performance than any one does alone.

Most source documents capture both financial and operational data about business transactions. The key is to design the AIS so that both kinds of data are stored in a manner that facilitates their integration in reports. Traditionally, most AISs have failed in this regard because they were designed primarily to support the preparation of financial statements, rather than the decision needs of internal management.

Corporate accountants also must know how to reorganize existing internally generated data and present them in a manner that sheds new light on operational results. For example, innovation is one vital requirement for continued long-term growth. One way that companies can measure innovation success is to track and report the percentage of sales revenues that new products generate.

Some important data must be collected from external sources, however. Data about customer satisfaction is one good example. It is not sufficient simply to measure and track how long it takes to fill and deliver customer orders. That merely provides information about how well a company is meeting *its own* goals for customer service. Information about whether the company is meeting *its customers'* requirements and expectations is also needed. The only way to find this out is to ask customers directly. Consequently, certain companies, such as Apple Computer, regularly survey their customers. Other firms, such as the Big 3 U.S. automobile manufacturers, hire market research firms such as J.D. Powers to collect that data. Once again, it is important to design the AIS so that such externally generated data are integrated with internally generated measures in a manner that facilitates the preparation of reports based on both kinds of data.

Budgets and Performance Reports

Two important types of managerial reports are budgets and performance reports. A **budget** is the formal expression of goals in financial terms. One of the most common and important types of budgets is the cash budget. A **cash budget** shows projected cash inflows and outflows. This information is especially important to a small business,

---

[2]The material in this section is drawn largely from two articles by Robert S. Kaplan and David P. Norton: "The Balanced Scorecard – Measures that Drive Performance," *Harvard Business Review* (January–February 1992): 71–79; and "Putting the Balanced Scorecard to Work," *Harvard Business Review* (September–October 1993): 134–147.

because cash flow problems are a principal cause of small-business failures. A cash budget can provide advance warning of cash flow problems in time to permit corrective action to be taken.

Budgets are financial *planning* tools. Performance reports, in contrast, are used for financial *control*. A performance report lists the budgeted and actual amounts of revenues and expenses and also shows the variances, or differences, between these two amounts. Budgeted amounts, however, are estimates; consequently, there are almost certain to be variances for each item in the performance report. Therefore, the principle of management by exception should be used to interpret those variances. If the performance report shows actual performance to be at or near budgeted figures, a manager can assume that the item is under control and that no action needs to be taken. On the other hand, significant deviations from budgeted amounts, in either direction, signal the need to investigate the cause of the discrepancy and take whatever action is appropriate to correct the problem.

Behavioral Implications of Managerial Reports

According to an old saying, measurement affects behavior. As applied to business, this means that employees tend to focus their efforts primarily on those tasks that are measured and evaluated. This can be either good or bad, depending on the nature of the relationship between the behavior being measured and the organization's overall goals. To illustrate, consider the task of customer complaint resolution. The organization wants to satisfy its customers to the greatest extent possible at the lowest possible cost. If customer service representatives are evaluated solely in terms of the number of complaints resolved per unit of time, however, two types of problems may arise. The customer service representatives may be so focused on quickly resolving each complaint in the store's favor that they alienate some customers in the process. Or customer service representatives may "give away the store" just to appease and please every customer with a complaint.

Budgets can often result in dysfunctional behavior. For example, if a budget does not include all the funds required to purchase the equipment needed to meet performance goals, then managers may be tempted to rent the equipment. This solution might allow them to meet their performance targets and remain within budget, but may end up costing the company more than it would have spent to purchase the equipment outright.

Indeed, the budgeting process itself can be dysfunctional. Management may expend a great deal of effort in "number crunching," trying to get the budget numbers to turn out as desired, rather than focusing on how to accomplish the organization's mission and goals. Focus 2-2 discusses how to avoid this potential problem and turn the budgeting process into a value-added activity.

We have presented several examples of how reports produced by the AIS can unintentionally result in dysfunctional behavior. The key point to remember is that the AIS does not "neutrally" report on employee performance. Rather, it directly affects behavior. In the next section, we look at how the AIS can be designed to encourage employees to behave in ways congruent with the organizational goals of providing accurate, reliable information and safeguarding assets.

Focus 2-2

Avoiding Dysfunctional Budgeting Behavior

In most instances, to fly an airplane safely, you need to concentrate on where you are going, not on the instrument panel. Similarly, the key to running a business effectively is to focus on attaining the organization's goals, not on the budget process. This does not mean that budgeting has no value. Just as the instrument panel in a plane alerts the pilot about potential problems, budgets provide warning signs about organizational performance. The key to success in flying a plane or running a business, however, is not to spend too much time examining the instrument panel or budget. Accountants can use the following five-step process to help managers develop the proper perspective toward budgeting.

First, explain that the budget's purpose is to identify and allocate the resources needed to accomplish the organization's goals. Moreover, stress that the objective is not only to accomplish those goals, but also to do it as efficiently as possible.

Second, begin the budget process by identifying measurable goals. Each department manager needs to specify the unit's goals and how they relate to those of the entire organization.

Third, ask each department manager to develop several alternative strategies for accom-plishing these goals. No cost data should be involved at this time, however. Instead, the focus should be solely on identifying alternative methods for accomplishing objectives.

Fourth, the accounting department, rather than the department managers, should assign costs to each alternative strategy. This keeps each department manager focused on how that unit's goals and strategies relate to those of the entire organization, not on playing games to get the budget numbers "right."

Fifth, department managers should review the budget figures prepared by the accounting department. Each manager should be encouraged to develop alternative strategies that may more efficiently achieve each unit's goals. Any such changes should then be returned to the accounting department for assignment of costs. Steps four and five are repeated until managers are satisfied with the final budget.

The key to this process is a division of responsibilities between the accounting department and unit managers. Managers focus on setting goals and developing strategies to meet those goals; accountants do the number crunching to translate those goals and strategies into a budget. The result is that managers focus on running the organization, not on budgeting.

Source: Stephen M. Rehnberg, "Keep Your Head Out of the Cockpit," *Management Accounting* (July 1995): 34–37.

INTERNAL CONTROL CONSIDERATIONS

The third function of an AIS is to provide adequate internal controls to accomplish three basic objectives:

1. Ensure that the information produced by the system is reliable.
2. Ensure that business activities are performed efficiently and in accordance with management's objectives while also conforming to any applicable regulatory policies.
3. Safeguard organizational assets, including its data.

In this chapter we introduce two important methods for accomplishing these objectives: providing adequate documentation of all business activities and ensuring effective segregation of duties. Additional aspects of internal control are covered in Part 2 of this book.

Adequate Documentation

Adequate documentation of all business transactions is the key to accountability. Documentation allows management to verify that assigned responsibilities were completed correctly. Ashton recalls an example he encountered while working as an auditor that gave him a firsthand glimpse of the types of problems that can arise from inadequate documentation. One of his audit clients sold and serviced computers, providing free repairs during the warranty period. Service personnel were instructed to treat repairs as being under warranty unless explicitly informed otherwise. The client had no procedures, however, for tracking warranty periods. Consequently, the company was completing a great deal of free repair work that should have been charged to customers. Indeed, the results of the audit estimated that the client had failed to bill almost $1 million worth of repair work!

Well-designed documents and records can help organizations quickly identify potential problems. For example, gaps in the sequence of completed source documents might indicate that some documents have been misplaced, in which case some transactions may not have been recorded. Such a gap may also, however, be a sign of a more serious problem. For example, a missing check may have been written for fraudulent purposes.

Adequate documents and records can also ensure that an organization does not make commitments it cannot keep. For example, Ashton wants S&S to avoid promises to sell and deliver merchandise that it does not currently have in stock. Consequently, he wants S&S to use a perpetual inventory system. To maintain the accuracy of those records, he will periodically reconcile recorded amounts with physical counts of inventory on hand.

Adequately written descriptions of task procedures are also important. Ashton recalls another audit problem he encountered that related to a weakness in this area. The clerk responsible for processing customer payments had not been instructed how to handle checks for which no match could be found in the accounts receivable records. Consequently, the clerk had decided that the proper thing to do was to return such checks to customers along with a note requesting additional information about why the check had been sent. This added more than a week to the time it took to turn accounts receivable into cash. After this situation was uncovered, the clerk was instructed to endorse restrictively and deposit all such checks and then to initiate correspondence with the customer for resolution of the matter. To avoid similar problems in the future, the company also added this policy to the printed procedures manual.

Segregation of Duties

Segregation of duties refers to dividing responsibility for different portions of a transaction among several people. The objective is to prevent one person from having total

Focus 2-3

Stealing the Entire Company

The case of Thomas Brimberry and Stix & Co. illustrates how severe the problem of employee fraud can become. Brimberry began working at Stix & Co. as a clerk earning $20,000 a year. He had greater ambitions, however, and with other family members he borrowed heavily to buy into a nightclub. It failed, saddling him with $3,000 monthly debt payments. To make ends meet, he started to steal from his employer.

He began by opening a margin account in his wife's maiden name. He increased the account's borrowing power by inflating stockholdings or erasing debt. The documents authorizing these transactions were added to batches of similar transactions, all of which were processed by an unsuspecting clerk who did not always carefully examine each transaction.

At first, Brimberry succeeded in his illegal stock trades and was able to cover his debt payments. A run of bad trades, however, eventually left him $1 million in debt to Stix & Co. To cover this shortage, he began to counterfeit stock certificates. He carefully selected firms that did not pay dividends, so that no one at Stix would notice the failure to receive a dividend check. Stix's policy requiring two people to be present whenever stock certificates were put into or removed from the bank vault was not a problem. Brimberry says he simply chose clerks to accompany him who were "too busy or too dumb" to ask any questions about what he was doing.

Eventually, the illusion of rapid growth created by Brimberry's fake accounts made Stix & Co. a takeover target. Brimberry then contacted James Massa, a lawyer, and introduced him to the Stix & Co. board of directors as a big investor. Massa eventually bought a controlling interest in the firm, using $1 million that he and Brimberry had embezzled from Stix & Co. They then proceeded to steal at will, using their position as owners to fool the external auditors.

The scheme finally fell apart several years later when Brimberry and Massa began to argue about their relative share of the profits. Both were eventually convicted of embezzlement and sentenced to prison.

Source: John Curley, "How a Clerk Built Up a Brokerage Business by Hook or by Crook," *The Wall Street Journal* (February 7, 1985): A1, A22.

control over all aspects of a business transaction. Specifically, the functions of authorizing transactions, recording transactions, and maintaining custody of assets should be performed by different people. Segregation of these three duties helps to safeguard assets and improve accuracy because each person can look at and thereby limit the others' actions. Effective segregation of duties should make it difficult for an individual employee to steal cash or other assets successfully.

Segregation of duties is especially important in business activities that involve the receipt or disbursement of cash, because cash can be stolen so easily. For example, in processing cash receipts from customers, one person should be responsible for handling and depositing those receipts (the custody function) and another person should be responsible for updating the accounts receivable records (the recording function). Otherwise, a person who performed both functions could divert customer payments for personal use and conceal the theft by falsifying the accounts. Similarly, in the realm of cash disbursements, one person should be responsible for preparing and approving checks for payment (the authorization function), and another person should be responsible for signing and subsequently mailing those checks (the custody function). Indeed, Ashton recalls a fraud that occurred at one of his former audit clients because these cash disbursement functions were not adequately segregated. In that case, the treasurer signed all checks prepared by accounts payable, but instead of mailing them out himself, he returned the checks to accounts payable. After receiving the signed checks, however, the accounts payable manager would change the payee name and then cash the checks himself! After the fraud was detected, the treasurer was instructed to mail all checks after signing them. As this example shows, inadequate segregation of duties can create opportunities for the theft of organizational assets. Focus 2-3 provides an example of how bad this situation can get.

Small organizations like S&S, however, do not always have enough staff to segregate duties effectively. In such cases, effective control can still be achieved through close supervision and owner performance of some key business activities. For example, Ashton intends to recommend that Scott and Susan be the only ones authorized to write checks on the company's account. In addition, only Scott and Susan should have the authority to approve the granting of credit to new customers or the extension of additional credit to existing ones.

SUMMARY AND CASE CONCLUSION

An AIS plays three key roles in any organization: (1) collecting and storing data about the organization's business activities, (2) processing that data to provide information useful for managerial decisions, and (3) including adequate internal control procedures to ensure the reliability of information produced and to safeguard the organization's assets. Choosing the appropriate accounting package is essential to fulfilling the first two functions.

Ashton reflected on the steps he had followed to guide his selection of accounting software. He had begun by obtaining an understanding of S&S's basic business activities and of the key decisions that Scott and Susan would need to make to operate the business effectively. Since S&S is a retail merchandising company, its operations could be described in terms of four basic transaction cycles:

1. The *revenue cycle* encompasses all transactions involving sales to customers and the collection of cash receipts in payment for those sales.
2. The *expenditure cycle* encompasses all transactions involving the purchase of and payment for the merchandise sold by S&S, as well as other services it consumes, such as rent and utilities.
3. The *human resources cycle* encompasses all the transactions involving the hiring, training, and payment of employees.
4. The *financing cycle* encompasses all transactions involving the investment of capital in the company, borrowing money, payment of interest, and loan repayments.

These four cycles interface with the *general ledger and reporting subsystem,* which consists of all activities related to the preparation of financial statements and other managerial reports.

Ashton knew that Scott and Susan planned to open additional stores in the near future and also wanted to develop a Web site to conduct business over the Internet. Based on this information,

Ashton selected an accounting package that he believed would satisfy S&S's current and anticipated future needs. He realized his next step would be to install the software and produce some documentation of how the system worked.

KEY TERMS

- transaction cycles
- revenue cycle
- expenditure cycle
- human resources (payroll) cycle
- production cycle
- general ledger and reporting system
- data processing cycle
- source documents
- turnaround documents
- source data automation
- batch processing
- on-line, real-time processing
- entity
- attributes
- field
- record
- data value
- file
- database
- general ledger
- subsidiary ledger
- chart of accounts
- financing cycle
- budget
- cash budget
- segregation of duties

CHAPTER QUIZ

1. Which cycle includes the set of transactions involving interactions between an organization and its suppliers?
   a. revenue cycle
   b. expenditure cycle
   c. human resources cycle
   d. general ledger and reporting cycle
2. All of the information (name, gpa, major, etc.) about a particular student is stored in which of the following?
   a. file
   b. record
   c. attribute
   d. field
3. Which of the following would contain the total value of all inventory owned by an organization?
   a. source document
   b. general ledger
   c. cash budget
   d. subsidiary ledger
4. Which of the following is most likely to be a general ledger control account?
   a. accounts receivable
   b. petty cash
   c. prepaid rent
   d. retained earnings
5. Which of the following is useful for projecting the need for short-term borrowing?
   a. income statement
   b. performance report
   c. cash budget
   d. balance sheet

6. What report expresses goals in financial terms?
   a. performance report
   b. financial statement
   c. budget
   d. chart of accounts
7. How does the chart of accounts list general ledger accounts?
   a. alphabetical order
   b. chronological order
   c. order by size
   d. the order in which they appear in financial statements
8. Which of the following is the best way to compensate for inadequate segregation of duties?
   a. Prenumbering all source documents
   b. Preparing budgets and performance reports
   c. Directly involving ownership in key functions
   d. Maintaining sound hiring practices
9. Which of the following is one of the three key functions of the AIS?
   a. Processing transactions efficiently
   b. Providing adequate segregation of duties
   c. Designing easily read reports
   d. Developing a chart of accounts
10. Recording information about the resources affected, the agents participating in, and the facts about each event at the time that the event takes place is referred to as which of the following?
    a. batch processing
    b. on-line, real-time processing
    c. general ledger and reporting system
    d. chart of accounts

DISCUSSION QUESTIONS

2.1 Examine Table 2-1 and discuss how the various information items would be collected and reported by a company's AIS.

2.2 Many restaurants use customer checks with prenumbered sequence codes. Each food server is given a packet of these checks on which to write up customer orders. Food servers are told not to destroy any customer checks; if a mistake is made, they are to void that check and write a new one. All voided checks are to be turned in to the manager daily. How does this policy help the restaurant control cash receipts?

2.3 How does an organization's line of business affect the design of its AIS? Give several examples of how differences among organizations are reflected in their AISs.

2.4 At most movie theaters, one employee is usually responsible for issuing tickets and collecting cash while another person collects those tickets when patrons enter the theater. What is the reason for this practice?

2.5 Some individuals argue that accountants should focus on producing financial statements and leave the design and production of managerial reports to information systems specialists. What are the advantages and disadvantages of following this advice? To what extent should accountants be involved in producing reports that include more than just financial measures of performance? Why?

PROBLEMS

2.1 The chart of accounts must be tailored to an organization's specific needs. Discuss how the chart of accounts for each of the following organizations would differ from the one presented for S&S in Table 2-3.
   a. university
   b. bank
   c. government unit (city or state)
   d. manufacturing company
   e. expansion of S&S to a chain of 23 stores

2.2 Ollie Mace has recently been appointed controller of S. Dilley & Company, a family-owned manufacturing firm founded 28 years ago. The firm manufactures automotive parts. Its four major operating divisions are heat treating, extruding, small parts stamping, and machining. Last year's sales from each division ranged from $150,000 to over $3,000,000. Each division is physically and managerially independent, except for the constant surveillance of S. Dilley, the firm's founder.

   The accounting system for each division has evolved according to its needs and the abilities of its accounting staff. Mace is the first controller in the firm's history to have responsibility for overall financial management. Dilley expects to retire in a few years and wants Mace to improve the AIS before he retires so that it will be easier to monitor performance in each division.

   Mace decides that the financial reporting system should be redesigned to include the following features:

   • It should give managers uniform, timely, and accurate reports of business activity. Monthly reports should be uniform across divisions and be completed by the fifth of the following month to provide enough time to take corrective actions to affect the next month's performance. Company-wide financial reports should be available at the same time.

   • Reports should provide a basis for measuring the return on investment for each division. Thus, in addition to revenue and expense accounts, reports should show assets assigned to each division.

   • The system should generate meaningful budget data for planning and decision-making purposes. Budgets should reflect managerial responsibility and show costs for major product groups.

   Mace believes that a new chart of accounts is required to accomplish these goals. He wants to divide asset accounts into six major categories, such as current assets and plant and equipment. He does not foresee a need for more than 10 control accounts within each of these categories. From his observations to date, 100 subsidiary accounts are more than adequate for each control account.

   No division now has more than five major product groups. Mace foresees a maximum of six cost centers within any product group, including both the operating and nonoperating groups. He views general divisional costs as a non-revenue-producing product group. Altogether, Mace estimates that approximately 44 natural expense accounts plus 12 specific variance accounts would be adequate.

   Required
   Design a chart of accounts for S. Dilley & Company. Explain how you structured the chart of accounts to meet the company's needs and operating characteristics. Keep total account code length to a minimum, while still satisfying all of Mace's desires.
   (CMA Examination, adapted)

2.3 Washington County Hospital is located in a well-known summer resort area. The county population doubles during the summer months, and hospital activity increases correspondingly. A new administrator has decided to implement a responsibility accounting system. This program was announced when the quarterly cost reports were presented to department heads. Previously, cost data were infrequently supplied to department heads. Excerpts from the announcement of the new program follow:

> *The hospital has adopted a responsibility accounting system. From now on you will receive quarterly reports comparing actual with budgeted costs for your department. The reports will highlight the variances so that you can zero in on departures from budget (this is called management by exception). Responsibility accounting means that you are accountable for keeping your department's costs within budget. Variations from budget will help you identify which costs are out of line, and the size of the variance will indicate the relative importance of the deviations. Your first report accompanies this announcement. (See Table 2-4.)*

The new administrator constructed the annual budget for 1997 and set quarterly budgets at one-fourth the annual budget. The administrator compiled the budget by analyzing costs for the past three years. The analysis showed that all costs increased each year, with a dramatic increase this past year. The administrator considered setting the budget at the average amount for the past three years, hoping that the new system would help to control cost increases. He finally decided, however, to set the budget at 3 percent below last year's actual costs. The activity level measured by patient days and pounds of laundry was set at last year's level, too, because these numbers had remained basically constant over the past three years.

Table 2-4   Washington County Hospital: Performance Report, Laundry Department, July–September 2003

	Budget	Actual	(Over) Under Budget	Percent (Over) Under Budget
Patient Days	9,500	11,900	(2,400)	(25)
Pounds Processed—laundry	125,000	156,000	(31,000)	(25)
Costs:				
Laundry labor	$9,000	$12,500	$(3,500)	(39)
Supplies	1,100	1,875	(775)	(70)
Water, heating & softening	1,700	2,500	(800)	(47)
Maintenance	1,400	2,200	(800)	(57)
Supervisor's salary	3,150	3,750	(600)	(19)
Allocated administrative costs	4,000	5,000	(1,000)	(25)
Equipment depreciation	1,200	1,250	(50)	(4)
Totals	$21,550	$29,075	$(7,525)	(35)

Administrator's Comments: Costs are significantly above budget for the quarter. Particular attention needs to be paid to labor, supplies, and maintenance.

Required

a. Comment on the method used to set the budget.

b. What do budget variances mean? Is the administrator interpreting this information correctly? Explain.

c. Does the report presented in Table 2-4 accurately represent the department's performance efficiency? Why or why not?

(CMA Examination, adapted)

2.4 Denny Daniels is production manager for the jazz division of QRS, Inc., which manufactures audio CDs. Daniels is dissatisfied with the reports provided by the accounting department because they are virtually useless for helping him manage the production process. He also feels that the reports do not accurately reflect how hard or how effectively he works as a production manager. Daniels tried to discuss these perceptions and concerns with June Smith, the controller for the jazz division. He told her, "I think the cost report is misleading. I know I've had better production over a number of periods, but the cost report still says I have excessive costs. Look, I'm not an accountant, I'm a production manager. I know how to get a good-quality product out. Over a number of years, I've even cut the amount of raw materials used to do it. But the cost report doesn't show any of this. Basically, it's always negative, no matter what I do. There's no way you can win with accounting or the people at corporate who use these reports."

Smith gave Daniels little consolation. She stated that the accounting system and cost reports are designed by headquarters and cannot be changed. She added, "Although these accounting reports are pretty much the basis for evaluating the efficiency of your division and the means that corporate uses to determine whether you have done a good job, you shouldn't worry too much. You haven't been fired yet! Besides, these reports have been used for the last 25 years."

After talking with the production manager at the country division of QRS, Daniels concluded that most of what June Smith said was probably true. However, the country division was able to get corporate to agree to some minor cost reporting changes. Daniels also knew from the trade grapevine that turnover of production managers at QRS was considered high, even though relatively few were ever fired. Most seemed to end up quitting, usually in disgust, because they believed they were being evaluated unfairly. The following comment sums up the general feeling of production managers who had left QRS:

> *Corporate headquarters doesn't really listen to us. All they consider are those misleading cost reports. They don't want them changed, and they don't want any supplemental information. The accountants may be quick with numbers, but they don't know anything about production. As it was, I either had to ignore the cost reports entirely or pretend they were important, even though they didn't reflect how well I had done my job. No matter what they say about not firing people, negative reports mean negative evaluations. I'm better off working for another company.*

Table 2-5 is an example of the cost report that has Daniels in such an agitated state.

Required

a. Comment on how Denny's perceptions of the following elements are likely to affect his behavior and performance: June Smith, the controller; corporate headquarters; the cost report; himself; and the AIS.

b. Identify and explain three changes that should be made in the cost report to make the information more meaningful and useful to production managers like Daniels.

(CMA Examination, adapted)

Table 2-5 Sample Cost Report for Problem 2-4

QRS, Inc. Jazz Division Cost Report April 2003 (000 omitted)			
	Master Budget	**Actual Cost**	**Excess Cost**
Materials	$ 400	$ 437	$37
Labor	560	540	(20)
Overhead	100	134	34
Total	$1060	$1111	$51

2.5 An audit trail is a set of references that enables a person to trace a source document to its ultimate effect on the financial statements or work back from amounts in the financial statements to source documents. Describe in detail the audit trail for the following:
   a. Purchases of inventory
   b. Sale of inventory
   c. Employee payroll

2.6 Check a recent newspaper or magazine for an article about employee fraud. Write a two-page report summarizing how the fraud occurred and what control procedures could have prevented it.

2.7 Search popular business magazines (*Business Week, Fortune, Forbes*) for an article that describes a dysfunctional behavior resulting from a poorly designed managerial reporting and performance evaluation system. Write a two-page report summarizing the problem and explaining how the managerial report led to the unplanned (and undesired) behavior.

2.8 Shauna Washington started a business to sell art supplies and related curricula to home school families. The business grew quickly, with sales doubling three times during a five-year period. At that point, she sold the business because it had grown too large to manage from her home. Under the new owners, sales doubled again during the next two years. Profits, however, did not keep pace with sales. In addition, the firm had borrowed heavily to open a warehouse. Inventory costs and operating expenses at the warehouse were higher than anticipated and the monthly payments on the loan were proving to be burdensome. Recently, the number and amount of past due accounts have risen dramatically. Together, these problems have created a severe cash flow problem. If the cash flow situation does not improve quickly, the firm may have to declare bankruptcy, even though sales are continuing to increase.
   Required
   Describe some of the information that a good AIS could have provided for this firm and that, if provided in a timely manner, could have helped it avoid some of its problems.

Case 2-1   AnyCompany, Inc.: An Ongoing Comprehensive Case

Identify a local company (you may use the same company that you identified to complete Case 1-1) and answer the following questions:

1. How many transaction cycles does the company have? Does it have any additional ones that were not discussed in this chapter? If so, identify and describe them.
2. Select any two transaction cycles and list the major transactions that occur in each. Trace how those transactions are processed by explaining what happens at each step in the cycle. Evaluate the adequacy of the audit trail related to those transactions.
3. What source documents does the company use to capture the relevant data for the transactions you identified in step 2?
4. What reports are produced in the two business cycles that you identified in step 2? What decisions are influenced by these reports? Comment on the adequacy of the reports for their intended purpose.
5. Examine the company's chart of accounts. How is it structured? How well does that structure meet the information needs of decision makers? How flexible is it in terms of providing for future growth?

Case 2-2   S&S, Inc.

You have been hired to assist Ashton Fleming in designing an accounting system for S&S. Ashton has developed a list of the journals, ledgers, reports, and documents that he thinks S&S needs (see Table 2-6). He asks you to complete the following tasks:

1. Specify what data you think should be collected on each of the following documents:
   a. sales invoice
   b. purchase order
   c. receiving report
   d. employee time card
2. Design a report to manage inventory.
3. Design a report to assist in managing credit sales and cash collections.
4. Visit a local office supply store and identify what types of journals, ledgers, and blank forms for various documents (sales invoices, purchase orders, etc.) are available. Describe how easily they could be adapted to meet S&S's needs.

Table 2-6 Documents, Journals, and Ledgers for S&S

Title	Purpose
Documents	
Sales Invoice	Record cash and credit sales of merchandise
Service Invoice	Record sales of repair services
Delivery Ticket	Record delivery of merchandise to customers
Monthly Statement	Inform customers of outstanding account balances
Credit Memo	Support adjustments to customer accounts for sales returns & allowances and sales discounts; also support write-off of uncollectible accounts
Purchase Order	Order merchandise from vendors
Receiving Report	Record receipt of merchandise from vendors, indicating both quantity and condition of Items received
Time Card	Record time worked by employees
Specialized Journals	
Sales	Record all credit sales
Cash Receipts	Record cash sales, payments from customers, and other cash receipts
Purchases	Record all purchases from vendors
Cash Disbursements	Record all cash disbursements
General Journal	Record infrequent, nonroutine transactions; also record adjusting and closing entries.
Subsidiary Ledgers	
Accounts Receivable	Maintain details about each individual customer
Accounts Payable	Maintain details about each individual vendor
Inventory	Maintain details about each inventory item
Fixed Assets	Maintain details about each piece of equipment and other fixed assets
General Ledger	Maintain details about all major asset, liability, equity, revenue, and expense accounts

ANSWERS TO CHAPTER QUIZ

1. b	**3.** b	**5.** c	**7.** d	**9.** a
2. d	**4.** a	**6.** c	**8.** c	**10.** b

Introduction to
E-business

Learning Objectives

After studying this chapter, you should be able to:

- Explain what e-business is and how it affects organizations.
- Discuss methods for increasing the likelihood of success and for minimizing the potential risks associated with e-business.
- Describe the networking and communications technologies that enable e-business.

Integrative Case: S&S, Inc.

Ashton was reviewing S&S's performance with Scott and Susan. He finished his presentation with a great deal of excitement, noting that S&S was in the enviable position of being profitable during its first year of operation. Scott and Susan were pleased. "But we cannot rest on our laurels. Our competitors have established an e-business presence. I think that we need to expand our operations in that direction," Susan said. "Although I agree that we probably should establish an e-business presence," added Scott, "I am concerned about security. I don't want S&S to be victimized by hackers. I'm also worried about getting paid for any sales that we make—I have heard reports about small businesses losing money because of credit card fraud by on-line customers."

"Scott, those are, indeed, valid concerns," said Ashton, "but they can be addressed. Let me prepare a report for you outlining how S&S can safely, and effectively, get into e-business. While I am doing that, though, it is important that you and Susan decide exactly what kind of e-business activities you want S&S to perform. Although security-related issues are important, carefully designing S&S's e-business activities so that they effectively and accurately implement the company's overall business strategy is the real key to success."

INTRODUCTION

We use the term **e-business** to refer to all uses of advances in information technology (IT), particularly networking and communications technology, to *improve* the ways in which an organization performs all of its business processes. Thus, e-business encompasses not only an organization's external interactions with its suppliers, customers, investors, creditors, the government, and the media, but also includes the use of IT to redesign its internal processes. In contrast, **e-commerce** is a narrower concept that refers only to the electronic execution of business transactions such as buying and selling.

A myriad of new terms beginning with "e-" describe various technology-enabled business activities. More recently, additional terms beginning with "m-" have been coined to refer to business activities that are performed using wireless communications technology (the "m-" stands for *mobile*). We will not attempt to exhaustively list and define all these new terms because we believe that whether a business process uses wired or wireless communications devices is only a difference in medium that does not warrant introducing yet another set of terminology. However, the qualitative differences in terms of efficiency and effectiveness between technology-enabled and manual, paper-based business processes are sufficiently important to justify distinguishing e-business from traditional business activities.

Prior to the time when Internet access was common and easy, organizations had the option of choosing if and how to engage in e-business. At that time, e-business was a potential source of competitive advantage, but that is no longer true. Now, for organizations in many industries, engaging in e-business is no longer an option, but a necessity. Engaging in e-business alone does not provide a competitive advantage, but can when an organization uses it to more effectively implement its basic strategy and enhance the effectiveness and efficiency of its value chain activities.

This chapter provides accountants and systems professionals with a basic understanding of the opportunities and risks associated with e-business. It also discusses the IT that enables organizations to engage in e-business. By mastering the material in this chapter, accountants and systems professionals will be prepared to actively participate in planning, designing, and managing an organization's e-business initiatives.

E-BUSINESS MODELS

The term *e-business* can refer to technology-enabled interactions between individuals and organizations. This business-to-consumer (B2C) model has received much attention in the press. You may have participated in B2C e-commerce by purchasing books, music, or airline tickets on the Internet.

E-business is not limited to the B2C model, however. As shown in Table 3-1, businesses, governments, and educational institutions also engage in e-business with one another. In fact, the total dollar value of such interorganizational e-commerce is many times larger than that of B2C e-commerce. For convenience, we will use the general term B2B to refer to all of these types of interorganizational e-business.

Although many similarities exist between B2C and B2B e-business, there are also several important differences. B2C e-business often involves two parties that may not have engaged in a previous transaction with each other. Consequently, the issue of

Table 3-1   Categories of E-business

Type of E-business	Characteristics
B2C (Business to consumer)	• Organization-individual • Smaller dollar value • One-time or infrequent transactions • Relatively simple
B2B (Business to business) B2G (Business to government) B2E (Business to education)	• Inter-organizational • Larger dollar value • Established, ongoing relationships • Extension of credit by seller to customer • More complex

trust is important in B2C e-business. Consumers want to know that a company's Web site represents the electronic "storefront" of a legitimate business. They want reassurance that their orders will be filled correctly and that the company has established procedures to safeguard the privacy of any personal information they provide. In response to such concerns, several organizations offer services designed to provide assurances about the company behind a Web site. Focus 3-1 describes one such service, WebTrust, developed by the AICPA.

In contrast, with the exception of miscellaneous purchases, most B2B transactions take place between organizations that have established ongoing relationships with one another. For example, automobile manufacturers have preferred suppliers for such items as car seats, brakes, and tires. Similarly, most governmental units typically conduct repeated transactions with the same set of suppliers. Therefore, because most B2B transactions take place between parties that know each other, there is less need for third-party assurance services like WebTrust.

B2B e-business also differs from B2C in terms of complexity. B2C transactions are relatively simple. Typically, a consumer visits a company's Web site, looks at its offerings, places an order, and pays for the purchase at the time the sale occurs, usually with a credit card. The company then ships the goods and the transaction is completed. In contrast, in B2B transactions the selling organization oftentimes extends direct credit to customers and also allows them to make partial payments on their accounts. This adds complexity to accounting for and controlling sales and customer payments.

E-BUSINESS EFFECTS ON BUSINESS PROCESSES

E-business involves the use of communications and networking technology, rather than paper documents, to exchange information. **Electronic data interchange (EDI) is** a standard protocol for electronically transferring information between organizations

Focus 3-1

WebTrust: Providing Assurance for Electronic Commerce

Consumers interested in shopping on-line have a number of concerns. Is the company legitimate? Will it protect the confidentiality of any personal information submitted? What kinds of post-sales service and support are provided? How are complaints resolved?

To address such concerns, the AICPA has developed an assurance service called WebTrust. This program identifies best practices concerning the following aspects of e-business:

- Compliance with regulations concerning privacy and confidentiality of information collected by the organization
- Practices designed to ensure availability of the organization's Web site for conducting e-business
- Procedures designed to ensure the accuracy of processing e-business transactions and the organization's level of compliance with its stated business practices
- Level of security associated with the Web site
- Policies and procedures instituted to ensure enforceability of e-business transactions

Companies can hire a CPA firm to address any or all of these issues. Companies have the option of purchasing only a written report, documenting their level of compliance with WebTrust's best practices in one or more of the areas listed above. Alternatively, companies have the option of also purchasing the right to display a seal on their Web site indicating that a CPA firm has performed a WebTrust examination of their e-business practices.

The WebTrust program also identifies best practices for certificate authorities to ensure the integrity of key generation, distribution, and maintenance. Several major companies, including Verisign, Entrust, and Digital Signature Trust, have adopted the WebTrust standards for certificate authorities.

The WebTrust program differs from other types of certificates and seals in two important ways. First, a WebTrust report or seal is issued only after a thorough examination of a company's electronic commerce practices by an independent third party. Second, a WebTrust seal is valid only for 6 months. Thus, the WebTrust program requires regular reexamination of the company's e-business practices to ensure that it continues to follow best practices.

More details about the WebTrust criteria and the methods used to test compliance with them can be found by visiting the AICPA's main Web site at www.aicpa.org.

Source: Various AICPA press releases in 2000–2001, Technology Alerts issued by the AICPA Information Technology Membership section; and information available on the AICPA Web site (www.aicpa.org).

and across business processes. EDI permits information output by one system to be electronically transmitted and input into another system. By eliminating the need to manually reenter data, EDI improves accuracy and cuts costs by reducing the time and expense associated with mailing, processing, and storing paper documents.

Although EDI has been available since the 1970s, until recently its use was primarily restricted to large companies. For example, by 1997, nearly 90 percent of Fortune 500 companies used EDI, compared with less than 10 percent of smaller

Focus 3-2

What's the Big Deal about eBXML?

E-business involves the electronic exchange of information between organizations. Although it sounds simple, it can be quite complex. Many organizations have unique designs and formats for common business documents, such as purchase orders and sales invoices. If this information is to be exchanged electronically, there needs to be some standard format that all computer systems can read, regardless of what particular application program is being run. EDI contains such standards, but because it is a proprietary system, it has not been widely adopted by small and midsize businesses. What is needed is a set of open standards for transmitting business transaction data using the Internet.

What about HTML? HTML provides standard codes, but it focuses only on how information is displayed (e.g., bold, italicized); it does not define the content of the data. XML, on the other hand, uses tags that look similar to HTML tags but defines what each data item represents. A specialized variant of XML, called eBXML, uses tags specifically designed to define the contents of common business transactions. Using eBXML, an organization can exchange business transaction data with any other organization, regardless of its internal application. Moreover, because the United Nations supports eBXML, it will become the international standard for e-business.

Source: Various reports located on the eBXML Web site: www.ebxml.org.

businesses.[1] Cost was the primary barrier in that it could cost a company as much as $50,000 to join an existing EDI network.[2] Two recent developments, the Internet and XML, are removing that barrier. The Internet eliminates the need to use a special proprietary third-party network to transmit EDI messages. XML, which stands for eXtensible Markup Language, is a set of standards for defining the content of data on Web pages. A further refinement of XML, referred to as ebXML, defines standards for coding common business documents such as invoices, remittances, and purchase orders. An important feature of ebXML is that it eliminates the need for proprietary software to translate documents created by different companies, thereby providing an easier and less expensive alternative to EDI as a means of engaging in e-business. Focus 3-2 provides additional information about ebXML.[3]

Reaping the full benefits of EDI, however, requires that EDI be integrated with the company's AIS. Figure 3-1 illustrates the difference between integrated and stand-alone EDI systems. Notice that a stand-alone EDI system is merely another alternative to toll-free telephone numbers or fax systems. In all three cases, incoming orders must still be separately entered into the AIS, just as outgoing documents must be separately

---

[1]David Baum, "Transcending EDI," *Infoworld* (March 24, 1997): 67–68.
[2]Andy Reinhardt, "Log On, Link Up, Save Big," *Business Week* (June 22, 1998): 132–138.
[3]Chapter 15 discusses another varient of XML, called XBRL, which is designed to simplify the financial reporting process.

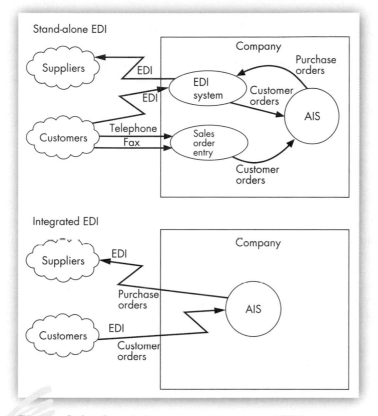

Figure 3-1   Stand-alone versus integrated EDI systems

entered into the EDI system. Stand-alone EDI systems not only fail to realize the full potential cost savings and accuracy improvements, but also fail to maximize customer service. Because they are not integrated with the AIS, stand-alone EDI systems do not allow customers to know, at the moment they are placing an order, if the requested items are in stock or will need to be back ordered.

EDI, the Internet, and advances in wireless communications reduce the costs and increase the speed and accuracy with which business processes are executed. As shown in Table 3-2, these technologies can transform and improve the primary and support activities in an organization's value chain.

Purchasing and Inbound Logistics

The Internet can improve the purchasing activity by making it easier for a business to identify potential suppliers and to compare prices. Data about purchases made by different organizational subunits can be centralized, thereby enabling an organization to determine total worldwide purchases of different products. Such information can then be used to negotiate better prices with key suppliers. The number of different suppliers used also can be reduced, thereby simplifying the purchasing activity and further cutting

Table 3-2   E-business Effects on Value Chain Activities

Value Chain—Primary Activities	E-business Opportunity
Inbound logistics	Acquisition of digitizable products
	Reduced inventory "buffers"
Operations	Faster, more accurate production
Outbound logistics	Distribution of digitizable products
	Continuous status tracking
Sales and Marketing	Improved customer support
	Reduced advertising costs
	More effective advertising
Post-Sale Support and Service	Reduced costs
	24/7 service availability

Value Chain—Support Activities	E-business Opportunity
• Purchasing	• Source identification and reverse auctions
• Human resources	• Employee self-service
• Infrastructure	• EFT, FEDI, other electronic payments

costs. Reverse auctions, in which suppliers bid against each other to provide goods or services, provide an opportunity to realize additional cost savings for some types of products.

Once the source of goods or services has been identified, IT provides several opportunities to improve the primary value chain activity of inbound logistics. More accurate and timely access to information about the status of shipments enables organizations to reduce the amount of inventory buffers they must carry. For products and services that can be digitized, such as books, CDs, software, and information, the entire inbound logistics function can be performed electronically. This yields tremendous cost savings, because the buying organization is relieved of the time and cost associated with receiving the product or service at the warehouse and routing it to the person who ordered it.

Internal Operations, Human Resources, and Infrastructure

Advanced communications technology can significantly improve the efficiency of internal operations. For example, auto parts supplier Grupo Antolin uses both wireless technology and EDI to manufacture 500,000 head liners (the interior of the roof), in more than 80 variations, for the Ford Explorer. Ford uses EDI to send Grupo Antolin information about the quantity and sequence of head liners needed. That information is then sent by radio frequency to portable terminals on the manufacturing plant floor so that assemblers know what to build. Wireless technology is also used to send assembly instructions to assembly-line robots, rather than requiring workers to key it in, thereby eliminating a potential source of human error. As a result, the operation can produce one assembly per minute.[4]

---

[4]John Teresko, "A Wireless Revolution," IndustryWeek.com, retrieved July 26, 2001 (*www.industryweek.com/CurrentArticles/Aap/articles.asp?ArticleId=1085*).

Improved access to information can also significantly improve planning. For example, Dell Computers credits its sophisticated Web-based sales order entry system with helping it to reduce inventory levels. In addition, Dell's build-to-order e-business model significantly improves Dell's cash flow, because it collects payment from its customers before paying suppliers for the components used to build the systems it sells.

Advances in communications and networking technology also can improve the efficiency and effectiveness of the human resources support activity in the value chain. A large proportion of the transactions processed by the human resources function are initiated by employees, such as new withholdings, changes in retirement allocations, and name changes. Enabling employees to directly make these changes will allow them more control of these aspects of their employment and likely increase morale. It can also generate significant cost savings by reducing the number of HR staff needed to process those changes. Moreover, the effectiveness of the HR function may improve because staff can now focus on value-added activities, such as negotiating terms with benefits providers, instead of on clerical tasks.

Advances in networking and communications technology can also improve the efficiency of an important part of organizational infrastructure: processing and properly accounting for customer payments.[5] Figure 3-2 shows that the use of EDI to

Figure 3-2 Information flows in electronic commerce

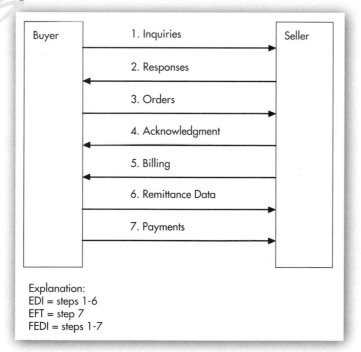

Explanation:
EDI = steps 1-6
EFT = step 7
FEDI = steps 1-7

---

[5]The material on electronic payment procedures and FEDI in this section is based on Philip P. Grannan, "Electronic Commerce Today; Financial EDI Solutions for Tomorrow," *Management Accounting* (November 1997): 38-41; and Understanding Financial EDI," by Ann B. Pushkin and Bonnie W. Morris, *Management Accounting* (November 1997): 42–46.

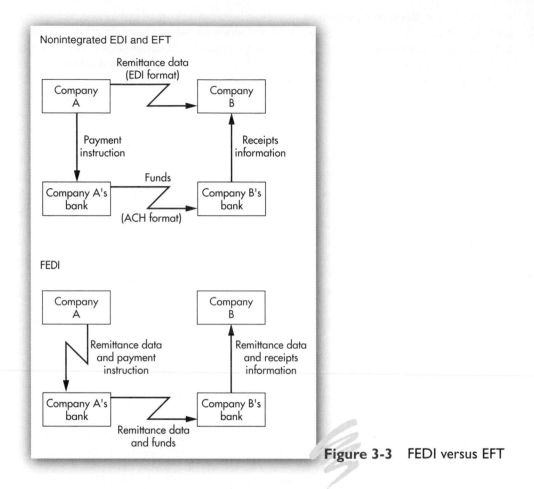

Figure 3-3   FEDI versus EFT

exchange information is only part of the buyer–seller relationship in business-to-business electronic commerce. The complete transaction also must include the exchange of funds to pay for the goods or services that were purchased.

The term **electronic funds transfer (EFT)** refers to making cash payments electronically, rather than by check. EFT is usually accomplished through the banking system's Automated Clearing House (ACH) network. Although almost all banks can send and receive funds through the ACH network, not every bank possesses the EDI capabilities to process the accompanying remittance data. Consequently, many companies have had to use one network for EFT and a separate network for EDI (see top panel in Figure 3-3). This complicates the seller's task of properly crediting customer accounts for payments, because information about the total amount of funds received arrives separately from information about which invoices that payment should be applied against. Similarly, the buyer's system must send information about payments to two different parties.

Financial electronic data interchange (FEDI) solves this problem by integrating the exchange of funds (EFT) with the exchange of other transaction-related information (EDI). As shown in the lower panel of Figure 3-3, with FEDI the buyer's AIS sends both remittance data and funds transfer instructions in one package. Similarly, the seller's AIS receives both the remittance data and funds simultaneously.

The full benefits of FEDI are realized when both the buyer's and seller's banks are EDI capable. In this case, the buyer's AIS sends one message, containing both the remittance data and EFT instructions, to its bank. The buyer's bank forwards that message to the seller's bank, which credits the seller's account and then sends both the remittance data and the notification of the funds transfer to the seller.

Even if the seller's bank is not EDI capable, however, the buyer still has two ways to implement FEDI. If the buyer's bank is EDI capable, then the buyer can still send the remittance data and funds transfer instructions in one message to its bank. Alternatively, the buyer can contract with a **financial value-added network (FVAN)** to implement FEDI. An FVAN is an independent organization that offers specialized hardware and software to enable the linking of various EDI networks with the ACH network the banking system uses for EFT. In this case, the buyer's AIS sends the remittance data and funds transfer instructions together to the FVAN. The FVAN translates the payment instructions from EDI format into ACH format and sends that information to the buyer's bank. The buyer's bank then makes a traditional EFT payment to the seller's bank. At the same time, the FVAN sends the remittance data to the seller in EDI format. Note that the seller receives the EFT and EDI portions separately; thus, both must contain a common reference number to facilitate proper matching. Consequently, although the buyer realizes the full advantage of FEDI under this arrangement, the seller does not.

Because of the accountability they provide, EFT and FEDI will likely continue to be widely used in B2B e-commerce. In B2C e-commerce, credit cards have been and probably will continue to be the principal medium used to pay for large retail sales. Not everyone has a credit card, however. Moreover, the transaction costs to sellers for accepting credit cards are higher than the costs of accepting checks from customers. Therefore, two other electronic payment media are likely to grow in use, especially for B2C e-commerce. The first is electronic bill payment, which is designed to replace paper checks to pay for services, like utility bills, and for installment purchases, like mortgages and autos. These electronic checks function similarly to paper checks, but can be processed at an even lower cost. The second alternative electronic payment method is some form of electronic cash that can be used to pay for purchases involving amounts too small to warrant the use and attendant fees of credit cards and electronic checks. This electronic cash may be stored as tokens in an electronic wallet on a computer or on some form of a smart card. Regardless of the media, it will be designed to function as cash, providing a convenient and anonymous means of paying for on-line purchases.

The emergence of application service providers is another e-business IT development that may significantly affect accounting and other infrastructure support activities. An **application service provider (ASP)** is a company that provides access to and use of application programs via the Internet. The ASP owns and hosts the software; the contracting organization accesses and uses the software remotely, via the Internet.

Traditionally, organizations have either purchased or written the business software they used. The ASP model presents the alternative option of ""renting" the necessary software. The primary advantage of the ASP model is potential cost savings. The ASP spreads its costs across multiple customers, so the cost to any individual customer of using the software is only a fraction of the cost of purchasing it. Organizations also avoid the costs associated with purchasing any necessary additional hardware to run the newest software. Moreover, the ASP model ensures that organizations will always be using the most current version of a particular software program.

The major disadvantages of the ASP model are the risks associated with relying on a third party to provide essential business services. Indeed, because the ASP model is relatively new, there is the risk that a particular supplier may go out of business, leaving its customers to scramble for alternatives. Security and privacy of data stored at the ASP are also concerns. On the one hand, ASPs may potentially provide greater security and privacy protection because, due to economies of scale, they can afford to employ better and more elaborate controls than could most individual organizations. On the other hand, because ASPs host data for many different organizations, including, quite possibly, direct competitors, there is the risk that sensitive data may be compromised. Consequently, accountants should analyze the business case for using an ASP and should also participate in the selection process by evaluating the financial viability of the various candidates. Table 3-3 lists important factors to consider when deciding whether to use an ASP.

The economics of the ASP model require a large potential customer base across which the costs can be spread, making it unlikely that ASPs will provide specialized applications that necessitate considerable customization for each customer. Thus, it is unlikely that most organizations will ever depend entirely on ASPs to satisfy their needs for computing services. Nevertheless, the ASP model is likely to grow in popularity as many organizations decide to manage their basic computing needs the same

Table 3-3   Factors to Consider When Evaluating ASPs

Potential Benefits	**Concerns**
• Lower costs	• Viability of ASP
• Automatic upgrading to current version of software	• Security and privacy of data
• Need fewer in-house IT staff	• Availability and reliability of service
• Reduced hardware needs	• Inadequate support or poor responsiveness to problems
• Flexibility	• Standard software that may not meet all customized needs
• Knowledgeable support	
• Security and privacy of data	

Example of Factors to Include in Service Level Agreement:
• Detailed specification of expected ASP performance (uptime, frequency of backup, use of encryption, data access controls, etc.)
• Remedies, including financial penalties, for failure of ASP to meet contracted service levels
• Ownership of data stored at ASP (the organization should maintain ownership to facilitate access in event that ASP goes out of business)

way that they manage their need for such basic utilities as power and water—by purchasing those services as needed from a third-party provider.

Outbound Logistics

Just as e-business can improve buyers' inbound logistics activities, it can also improve the efficiency and effectiveness of sellers' outbound logistics activities. Timely and accurate access to detailed information about shipments enables sellers to reduce transportation costs by combining shipments to customers located near to one another. More timely information about sales can help manufacturers optimize the amount of inventory they carry. For goods or services that can be digitized, the entire outbound logistics function can be performed electronically, which not only eliminates transportation costs, but also avoids the time and costs associated with selecting the goods and packing them for shipment.

Sales and Marketing

Perhaps the most obvious effect of e-business is on an organization's sales and marketing activities. Companies can create electronic catalogs on their Web sites to automate sales order entry. This capability not only makes it possible for customers to place orders when they want, but it can also significantly reduce staffing by eliminating the need to manually enter sales orders that were previously received by telephone, mail, or fax. For example, the Cisco Systems Web site enables a relatively small staff of salespeople to process billions of dollars in sales each year.

Nevertheless, even for companies that only sell on-line, effective Web sites do not eliminate all costs associated with the sales and marketing function. Customers will still have questions and need help in selecting products. Consequently, the most effective and successful Web sites provide some sort of live chat option or a link to a 24–hour toll-free telephone.

E-business may also improve the effectiveness of advertising and reduce its costs. Tailoring sales messages to individual customers improves their effectiveness. For example, once an Amazon.com customer selects one book, the site suggests related books that other customers have purchased in combination with the one the customer has already selected. Similarly, companies like Amazon can and do store and analyze data about customer purchases and then use that information to produce customized electronic coupons to solicit additional purchases. Such targeted advertising is more effective and less expensive than advertising in the traditional print media, radio, or television. Companies can stimulate more sales by using their Web sites to provide suggestions and advice about additional ways to use their products.

Post-sales Support and Service

E-business can significantly improve the quality of post-sales customer support. For example, setting up a Web page ensures that all customers receive consistent information. Quite often, numerous customers ask similar questions. These can be listed on a frequently asked questions (FAQ) feature, thereby reducing the number of customer inquiries that a customer service representative must handle. Of course, there will always be problems and issues that were not anticipated when designing the FAQ list that must be handled by customer service representatives. Using IT to resolve the routine issues, however, can both improve the overall quality of service and reduce costs. For example, some companies (e.g., AT&T and Nike) use a sequence of menu-driven forms at their Web sites to electronically "interview" their customers; only the most complex problems need to be routed to a customer service representative.[6] Such practices can significantly reduce the costs of customer support. Wells Fargo, for example, found that customers with on–line access to their accounts made 40 percent fewer calls to the bank than did customers without such access.[7]

E-BUSINESS SUCCESS FACTORS

The previous section described several ways that e-business can improve the efficiency and effectiveness of an organization's business processes. Two factors are critical in determining the success of such e-business initiatives. The first factor is the degree to which those e-business activities fit and support the organization's overall business strategy. The second factor is the ability to guarantee that e-business processes satisfy the three key characteristics required in any business transaction—validity, integrity, and privacy.

E-business and Organizational Strategy

It is important to remember that implementing e-business processes is not a basic strategy. Implementing e-business simply means using networking and communications IT to more efficiently and effectively perform business processes. The strategic value of doing so depends on the degree to which those processes help the organization implement and achieve its overall strategy.

Recall from Chapter 1 the two basic strategies any organization could pursue: being a low-cost producer or providing a differentiated product. E-business can be used to pursue either strategy. It is important that an organization understand which strategy it is pursuing, however, so that it does not inadvertently design its e-business processes in a manner that conflict with its chosen strategy.

For example, the optimal design of a Web site for a company pursuing a product differentiation strategy based on the quality of its customer service would likely be different from that of a company that sees itself as a low-cost provider of a commodity. In the latter case, the Web site might be designed to replace, as much as possible, the need to provide live customer service. Instead, the FAQ feature would be extensively developed. For additional support, customers might be requested to submit their questions via e-mail. If a toll-free telephone number were provided, it would probably be staffed at a minimal level. For quicker response, customers might be required to make a toll call. In contrast, the Web site of a company pursuing a strategy of differentiation through superior customer service might include not only an FAQ list, but also a chat feature so that customers could get real-time answers to their questions. Telephone support would likely be provided only through a toll-free number and would be staffed at a level that minimized wait time.

As another example of the need to link strategy with e-business practice, consider the use of reverse auctions to drive down acquisition costs. Reverse auctions can indeed result in lower costs, but they are also likely to inhibit the development of

---

[6]Peter Burrows. "Instant Info Is Not Enough," *Business Week* (June 22, 1998): 144.
[7]Ibid.

trusted relationships with key suppliers. Consequently, reverse auctions are more appropriate for a company that is seeking to be a low-cost provider of commodity type products than for a company that needs to nurture and maintain long-term relationships with suppliers of custom parts.

Three Key Properties of Business Transactions

The second factor critical to e-business success is ensuring that e-business processes have three fundamental characteristics that must be present in any business transaction—validity, integrity, and privacy (VIP).

1. Validity. Both parties to a transaction must be able to authenticate the identity of the other party to ensure that the transaction is valid and enforceable. A buyer must not be able to place an order, thereby causing the seller to invest time and resources in filling that order, and then repudiate the order. Conversely, a seller cannot be allowed to solicit orders and then renege on delivery.

2. Integrity. Both parties to a transaction must have confidence that the information exchanged is accurate and has not been altered during the transmission process.

3. Privacy. The privacy or confidentiality of business transactions and any information exchanged in those transactions must be maintained, if so desired by either party.

These characteristics are not unique to e-business; they have always been required for business transactions. E-business involves the same business processes, such as purchasing, receiving, and paying for goods or services, that have always been executed. The only difference is the information about those activities is now exchanged and processed electronically, rather than manually with paper documents. This difference in communications methods, however, affects the techniques used to achieve VIP.

In traditional business processes, authorizations and approvals—evidenced principally by means of signatures, notarizations, and signature guarantees—play an important role in ensuring validity. Manual and automated error detection and correction techniques can ensure accuracy. Procedures such as signatures across sealed envelopes and certified or hand delivery can ensure that the contents of a message have not been altered. Privacy is achieved by using techniques such as sealed envelopes and courier delivery. All of these concerns and objectives still apply to e-business transactions, but the methods used to satisfy them differ. In fact, those techniques, when properly implemented, may actually provide greater assurance about the VIP characteristics than is possible in traditional business processes.

In e-business transactions, the combination of message digests, digital signatures, and digital certificates achieves these VIP characteristics. Encryption plays an important enabling role for all three VIP characteristics. Not only does encryption directly provide privacy, but it is the underlying mechanism that creates the digital signatures and digital certificates which ensure the validity and integrity of the data being exchanged. Therefore, we discuss encryption techniques first, and then explain how encryption, digital signatures, digital certificates, and message digests together jointly provide VIP for e-business transactions.

Encryption techniques

Encryption entails converting a message from plain text to a secret code. This technique involves using a formula, called a key, to transform the original information.

There are two principal types of encryption systems. They differ in the number of such keys used and how those keys are distributed.

One type of encryption is called a single key system. The data encryption standard (DES) algorithm is a widely used commercial single key system.[8] **Single key encryption systems** are so named because they use the same key to encrypt and decrypt a message. The principal advantage of single key systems is that they are simple, fast, and efficient. A major problem, however, is the need for the sender to provide the recipient with the secret key. The effectiveness of the system depends on controlling who knows the secret key.

The second main approach to encryption, called **public key infrastructure (PKI),** uses two keys. One key, called the public key, is publicly available. The other key, called the private key, is kept secret, known only by the owner of that pair of keys. Either key (the public or the private) can be used to encode a message, but only the other key in that public–private pair can be used to decode that message.

The PKI approach has two principal advantages over single key systems. First, the public key is made publicly available, thereby eliminating problems attendant with distributing a single key. Second, the PKI approach is more secure than single key systems, because two different keys are used to encode and decode a message. Anyone can use the organization's public key to encrypt a message, but only that organization possesses the private key needed to decode that message.

The PKI approach to encryption is much slower than single key systems, however. Therefore, both types of encryption systems (DES and PKI) are typically used to conduct e-business. We will use an example of a B2B transaction involving S&S to illustrate the role encryption plays in facilitating e-business. First, however, we need to define four terms: digital signatures, digests, digital certificates, and certificate authorities.

A **digital signature** is an electronic message that uniquely identifies the sender of that message, just as a handwritten signature uniquely identifies the person signing a paper document. In a PKI system, encrypting a message with the sender's private key creates a digital signature. Such a message can only be decoded using the corresponding public key. Using any other public key to decode the message will produce gibberish.

The message that is used to create a digital signature is usually a digital summary, called a **digest,** of a plaintext business document. The digest is created by using a common utility program that calculates the digital values of every character in the plaintext document. If any individual character in the original document changes, the value of the digest also changes. This property provides a means for ensuring that the contents of a business document have not been altered or garbled during transmission. To illustrate, S&S could create a digital signature by using its private key to encypt a digest of a purchase order. Then, after receiving and decoding S&S's purchase order, the supplier can recalculate the digest of that purchase order by using the same utility program as S&S used. If this recalculated digest matches S&S's digital signature, then the supplier is assured that the purchase order is accurate and has not been altered.

A valid digital signature, however, proves only that the message was sent by the owner of the private key corresponding to the public key used to decode the message. It does not verify the identity of the private key's owner. A **digital certificate** identifies the

---

[8]Encryption standards are constantly evolving to maintain security. The DES algorithm is currently in the process of being signifiantly updated and replaced with the advanced encryption standard (AES) algorithm.

owner of a particular private key and the corresponding public key, and the time during which the certificate is valid. Thus, a digital certificate functions like a driver's license or passport. Digital certificates are issued by a reliable third party, called a **certificate authority.** Verisign, Entrust, and Digital Signature Trust are three widely known certificate authorities. The certificate authority's digital signature is also included on the digital certificate so that the validity of the certificate can be verified, just as a hologram, watermark, or other device is used to verify the validity of a driver's license or passport.

Example: Using Encryption to Conduct E-business

Figure 3-4 uses the context of S&S submitting a competitive bid to fill a contract with a local government to illustrate how both single key (e.g., DES) and PKI encryption techniques are used in a B2B e-business transaction. We assume that both S&S and the government entity have registered with a PKI certificate authority and possess valid digital certificates.

Step 1   Using the Internet to connect to the government agency's Web site, Scott or Susan clicks on the button to submit a bid. *The browser screen shows a lock symbol and may also display a message, indicating that a subsequent interaction will take place in a secure environment using encryption. The encryption software on both S&S's computer and the government agency's Web site exchanges digital certificates. The software on both computers looks up the certificate authority's public key and uses it to verify the validity of the certificate authority's digital signature on the digital certificate, thereby validating the information on the digital certificate. S&S's computer now possesses the government agency's public key, which was included in the agency's digital certificate. Similarly, the government agency now has S&S's public key.*

Step 2   Scott or Susan clicks a button to send a completed bid to the government agency. *Behind the scenes, the encryption software on S&S's computer performs the following:*
    a. *Uses a publicly available utility program to create a digital summary (or digest) of the plaintext bid.*
    b. *Encrypts the digest of the bid using S&S's private key. The encrypted digest is S&S's digital signature.*
    c. *Encrypts the entire bid using the DES single key algorithm. This provides a measure of privacy and security in the event that a competitor intercepts the bid.*
    d. *Uses the government agency's public key, obtained from the agency's digital certificate in step 1, to encrypt the DES key that was used to encrypt the bid in step 2c. This ensures that only the intended recipient of the bid (the government agency) will have the DES key needed to decode the bid.*

Step 3   Package including S&S's digital signature (created in step 2b), the encrypted bid (created in step 2c), and the encrypted DES key (created in step 2d) is sent to the government agency's Web site.

Step 4   The government agency's computer receives the package of encrypted material from S&S. Automatically, the encryption software on the government agency's computer does the following:
    a. *Uses S&S's public key, obtained from the digital certificates exchanged in step 1, to decode the digital signature sent by S&S. This produces the digest that S&S's computer created in step 2a.*
    b. *Uses its private key to decode the DES key that S&S used in step 2c to encrypt its bid.*

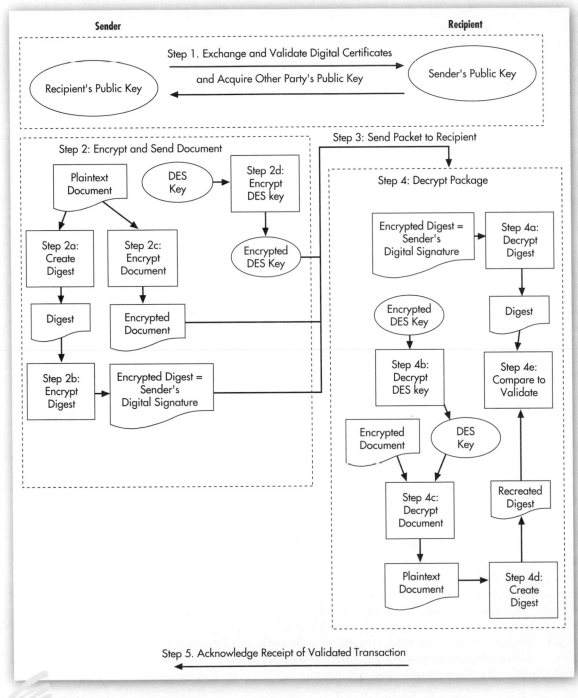

Figure 3-4 Use of encryption

c. *Uses that DES key to decode S&S's bid.*

d. *Uses the same publicly available utility program that S&S used in step 2a to create a digital summary of S&S's bid.*

e. *Compares the decoded digest produced in step 4a to the recreated digital summary created in step 4d. If the two match, the government agency is assured that (1) the bid was created and sent by S&S and (2) it was not altered or garbled during transmission.*

Step 5   The government agency sends S&S an electronic acknowledgment that its bid has been received.

Using both single key encryption systems, such as DES, and the dual key PKI approach maximizes effectiveness and efficiency. In the preceding example, the single key DES algorithm was used in step 2c to encrypt the basic business information being shared, because using the PKI approach to encrypt the same information would have taken much longer. The PKI approach was used in step 2d to provide a secure means of sharing the DES key. The same approach was also used in step 2b to create a digital signature and thereby ensure the validity of the transaction.

Accountants are responsible for ensuring the existence of adequate controls in their organization's information systems. This section explained how encryption could be used to provide the controls needed to execute e-business transactions. Chapters 7 through 10 provide in-depth coverage of many other issues concerning the design and testing of controls in an AIS.

INFRASTRUCTURE FOR E-BUSINESS

Advances in networking and communications technologies, especially the Internet, provide the necessary infrastructure for e-business. This section provides an introductory overview into networking concepts and discusses several strategic issues concerning alternative methods that organizations can use to implement e-business.

Types of Networks

The telecommunications networks many companies use to conduct e-commerce and manage internal operations consist of several components, and typically include some or all of the following: local area networks, wide area networks, value-added networks, and the Internet. A **local area network (LAN),** as its name implies, is a network of computers and other devices, such as printers, that are located in close proximity to each other (usually in the same building). In contrast, a **wide area network (WAN)** covers a wide geographic area and is often global. Companies typically own all the equipment that comprise their LANs, but usually do not own the long-distance data communications connections of their WANs. Instead, they contract to either use a value-added network or the Internet. A **value-added network (VAN)** is a long-distance communications system designed and maintained by an independent company. It offers specialized hardware and software to facilitate the exchange of data between various private networks. The **Internet** is an international network of computers (and smaller networks) that are interlinked. The connections that link those computers are called the Internet's *backbone*. **Internet service providers (ISPs)** such as AOL, AT&T, GTE, MCI, and Sprint provide access to the Internet. Although no one entity "owns" the Internet, portions of the backbone are owned and maintained by the major ISPs.

One big attraction of the Internet is its ease of use. Software called *browsers* enables users to easily navigate through vast amounts of information. Consequently, many companies have adapted their LANs to support these same basic Internet applications, including browsers. The term **intranet** refers to such internal networks that can be navigated with the same simple browser software used on the Internet, but which are inaccessible to the public. Intranets provide significant cost savings in disseminating and sharing information, thereby often increasing the effectiveness of operations. Many companies have realized the significant benefits to giving some of their suppliers and customers access to their intranets. This has led to the creation of **extranets,** which link the intranets of two or more companies. The basic difference between intranets, extranets, and the Internet relates to access. Intranets are private; access is restricted to only employees of the organization, and often to only a subset of employees. Access to extranets is also controlled, being limited to trusted trading partners. In contrast, access to the Internet is open to everyone.

The Internet makes e-business more cost effective by eliminating the need to use VANs, dial-up, or leased lines to exchange information between organizations. Because it is public and widely accessible, however, the Internet is not very secure. One solution is to encrypt all information sent over the Internet. The result of doing so creates what are referred to as **virtual private networks (VPNs),** so named because they provide the functionality of a privately owned network, while using the Internet. VPNs not only provide a secure environment for using the Internet, but are also a cost-effective method of providing remote access to the organization's intranets and extranets. The major cost savings associated with VPNs result from using the Internet to replace the combination of leased lines and toll-free telephone numbers traditionally used to provide employees and trading partners with remote access to the organizational network. Typically, this cost savings is greater than the cost of the VPN software and the need to upgrade to higher-capacity lines linking the organizational network to the Internet. Table 3-4 compares the costs of using VPNs with direct dial-up connections for providing remote access to organizational computing resources.

Table 3-4   Costs Associated with VPNs and Traditional Remote Access

VPN Cost Factors	**Traditional Remote Access Cost Factors**
• VPN set-up fees	• Servers and modem banks
• Higher capacity (T1 or T3) link between organizational network and the Internet	• Leased lines for direct, secure connections to trading partners
• VPN site license fees	• Toll-free telephone numbers
• National Internet access for users	• Long-distance charges (per minute of use)

Communications Software

Communications software manages the flow of data across a network. It performs the following functions:

➤ *Access control:* Linking and disconnecting the different devices; automatically dialing and answering telephones; restricting access to authorized users; and establishing parameters such as speed, mode, and direction of transmission.

➤ *Network management:* Polling to check if devices on the network are ready to send or receive data; queuing input and output; determining system priorities; routing messages; and logging network activity, use, and errors.

➤ *Data and file transmission:* Controlling the transfer of data, files, and messages among the various devices.

➤ *Error detection and control:* Ensuring that the data sent were indeed the data received.

➤ *Data security:* Protecting data during transmission from unauthorized access.

Communications software is written to work with a wide variety of protocols, which are rules and procedures for exchanging data. For example, the protocol used on the Internet is called **Transmission Control Protocol/Internet Protocol (TCP/IP).** This protocol creates what is called a packet-switching network. Figure 3-5 shows how TCP/IP enables communications over the Internet. When a message (either a file, document, or e-mail) is ready to be sent over the Internet, the TCP protocol breaks it up into small packets. Each packet is then given a header, which contains the destination address. The packets are then sent individually over the Internet. The IP protocol uses the information in the packet header to guide the packets so that they arrive at the proper destination. Once there, the TCP protocol reassembles the packets into the original message.

A communications channel is the medium that connects the sending and receiving devices in a data communications network. Common communications channels include telephone lines, fiber optic cables, terrestrial microwaves, satellite, and cellular radio frequencies. As shown in Figure 3-6 on page 69, a communications network often uses several different media to minimize the total data transmission costs.

Because the capacity of wireless is rapidly increasing, organizations are beginning to use radio frequencies to provide wireless communications links for their LANs. Cost and flexibility are other reasons for the growing popularity of wireless LANs. Focus 3-3 describes the potential benefits of wireless LANs.

The different communications channels each possess characteristics that affect the network's reliability, cost, and security. One important channel characteristic is its **bandwidth,** which refers to a channel's information carrying capacity. All else being equal, a communications channel with greater bandwidth will be more useful because it can transmit more information in less time. Higher bandwidth is essential for applications such as real-time video. Accountants can play an important role in evaluating the business case for investments designed to upgrade bandwidth by analyzing both the costs and the benefits of the proposed alternatives.

Network Configuration Options

LAN Configurations

Figure 3-7 on page 71 shows that LANs can be configured in one of three basic ways: as a star, a ring, or a bus.

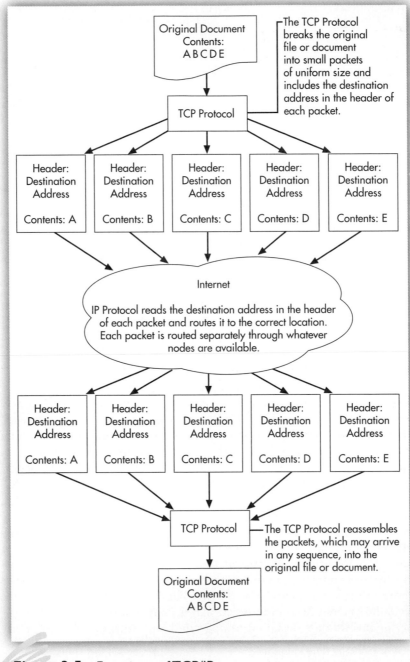

Figure 3-5 Functions of TCP/IP

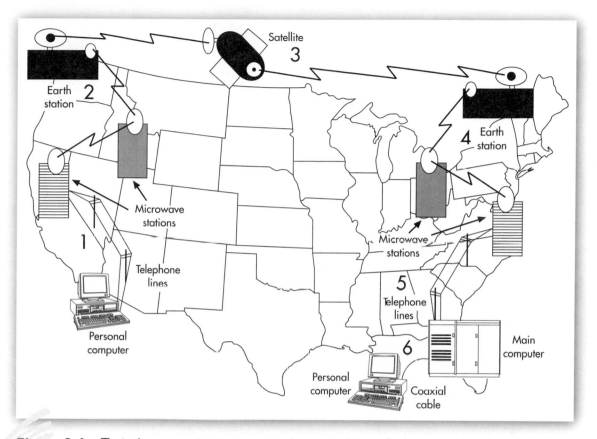

Figure 3-6   Typical communications network using cables, telephone wires, microwaves, and satellites

1. In a *star configuration*, each device is directly connected to the central server. All communications between devices are controlled by and routed through the central server. Typically, the server *polls* each device to see if it wants to send a message. If it does, the packet of data is sent to the server, which reads the destination address and routes it to the appropriate node. The star configuration is the most expensive way to set up a LAN because it requires the greatest amount of wiring. Its principal advantage, however, is that if one node goes down, the performance of the rest of the network is not affected.

2. In a *ring configuration*, each node is directly linked to two other nodes. As messages pass around the ring, each node checks the packet header to determine whether the data are intended for it. To control the flow of data and to prevent collisions, a LAN configured as a ring uses a software code called a token (hence, many LANs configured as rings are called token ring networks). The token continually passes around the ring. If a node wants to send a message, it grabs the token and attaches it to the message. The other nodes must then wait until the message reaches its destination and the token is once again free before they can send data. If one connection in the ring is broken, the network can continue to function, albeit more slowly, by routing all messages in the opposite direction.

Focus 3-3

Wireless LANs

Organizations have long realized the advantages of sharing data, applications, and hardware via a LAN. Recent advances in wireless communications can increase the flexibility of LANs. Wireless LANs (WLANs) can potentially increase productivity because users can connect from anywhere in the office complex, instead of being tethered to specific locations.

Creating a WLAN requires that every laptop and desktop computer have a wireless network interface card (NIC). (The desktop units serve as file and print servers for the WLAN.) A number of access points, which serve to transmit the signals, are also needed. Wireless LAN signals currently can be transmitted up to 1,500 feet and can accommodate 15 to 60 users, depending on the specific equipment and the nature of the building. A consultant can help determine the required number of access points for a given WLAN.

WLANs offer three important advantages over traditional wired LANs. First, employees become more mobile: As long as each laptop is equipped with a wireless NIC, it can access the LAN from anywhere in the building. Second, reconfiguring the network is easy and inexpensive because there is no need to rewire the building. Third,

because WLANs make it possible to easily display the same information on each meeting participant's laptop, they can eliminate the need for expensive multimedia projection equipment.

The major disadvantages of WLANs pertain to cost and security. At present, the hardware required to run a WLAN costs more than the same hardware required to set up a wired LAN. As noted earlier, however, this is offset to some degree by the ability to avoid the costs associated with installing new wiring in a building. WLANs create higher security risks because wireless signals can be easily intercepted. This is offset in part by the limited range of wireless transmissions. Nevertheless, sensitive data should probably be encrypted when sent over a WLAN.

As with all technologies, the capabilities (speed, transmission range, and capacity) of wireless communications continue to improve while the costs of the required components fall. Moreover, the flexibility of a WLAN increases productivity because employees can stay continuously connected to the network anywhere in the office complex. Consequently, it is likely that more and more organizations will replace their existing wired LANs with WLANs.

Source: Clyde T. Stambaugh and Don Chamberlain, "Ready to Pull the Plug?" *Journal of Accountancy* (August 2001): 53–55.

3. In a *bus configuration,* each device is connected to the main channel, or bus. Communication control is decentralized on bus networks. A software algorithm known as *carrier sense multiple access with collision detection* (CSMA/CD) controls communications between devices. When a node wants to send a message, it checks if the bus is free. If it is, then it sends the packets of data. The other nodes on the bus each check the header of the packet to determine whether the message is intended for them. If two nodes try to send a message at the same time, the messages are likely to collide. In that case, one node is arbitrarily given priority to resend its message. Bus configurations are easy to expand and are cheaper to set up than stars. Performance decreases, however, as the number of nodes connected to the bus increases.

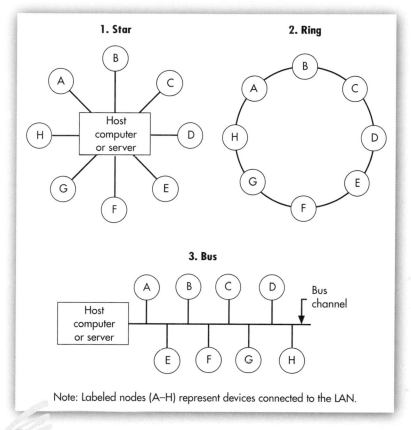

Note: Labeled nodes (A–H) represent devices connected to the LAN.

Figure 3-7   LAN configurations

There is no simple answer to the question of which LAN configuration is best. Performance is directly affected by the bandwidth of the communications channel (e.g., fiber optics, wireless, or copper wire) used to connect the nodes. Performance is inversely related to the number of nodes in the LAN. In addition, the size and power of the server significantly affect performance, especially in LANs configured as stars. To provide additional power, many companies such as Boeing, Wells Fargo Bank, J.C. Penney, and Lehman Brothers, are using their old mainframes as servers.

WAN configurations

Figure 3-8 shows three basic ways to configure a WAN: centralized, decentralized, or distributed.

1. In a *centralized WAN system,* all terminals and other devices are connected to a central corporate computer, which is usually a large mainframe. Centralized systems provide the advantages of better control, more experienced IT staff, and some economies of scale. The disadvantages of centralized systems are greater complexity, higher communications costs (because all messages must be sent through the central computer), and less flexibility in meeting the needs of individual departments and users.

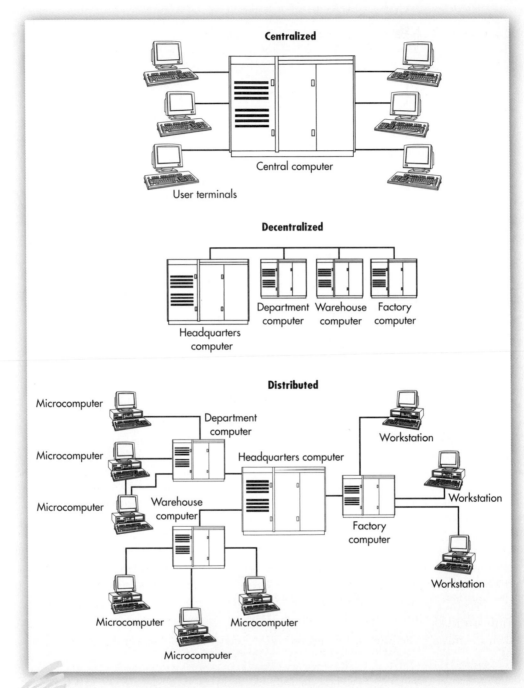

Figure 3-8 Comparison of centralized, decentralized, and distributed data processing

2. In a *decentralized WAN system,* each departmental unit has its own computer and LAN. Decentralized systems usually are better able to meet individual department and user needs than are centralized systems. In addition, communication costs are often lower, as much of the data needed are stored locally. The major disadvantages of decentralized systems are the complexity of coordinating data stored at many locations, increased hardware costs, and greater difficulty in implementing effective controls.

3. A *distributed data processing (DDP) system* is essentially a hybrid of the centralized and decentralized approaches. Each location has its own computers to handle local processing, thus providing the advantages of decentralized systems. Each local system is also linked to the corporate mainframe, however, thus providing many of the benefits associated with centralized systems.

     One advantage of DDP systems is that the various departmental computers back up one another, and there is less risk of catastrophic loss, as resources are in multiple locations. Another advantage is that each local system is treated as a module that can easily be added, upgraded, or deleted from the system. A disadvantage of DDP systems is that the multiple locations and varying needs complicate the tasks of coordinating the system and maintaining hardware, software, and data consistency. Standardizing documentation and control is also difficult, because authority and responsibility are distributed. Multiple locations and communications channels hinder adequate security controls and separation of duties. Another disadvantage of DDP is data duplication at multiple locations, which increases total storage costs and creates the opportunity for inconsistencies to arise.

Client/server configurations

Many WANs and most LANs are set up as client/server systems. Each desktop computer is referred to as a client. Each client sends requests for data to the servers. The server performs preprocessing on the database and sends only the relevant subset of data to the client for local processing.

Figure 3-9 shows that client/server systems can be configured as either a two-tier or a three-tier architecture. In a two-tiered system, the central database is stored on the server. Each client has its own copies of various application software and, therefore, must have both a powerful CPU that can handle considerable local processing and a large amount of disk storage space. The major advantages of two-tier systems are flexibility in meeting individual user needs and simplicity in overall design and control. The primary disadvantage is cost: Users require powerful clients to perform tasks at the local level and multiple copies of applications software must be purchased and maintained.

Three-tiered client/server systems attempt to reduce overall costs of corporate computing by utilizing two levels of servers. The top-tier server stores the central database. The second-tier servers host the applications programs. Most processing takes place at this middle tier. The clients primarily are used as interfaces and for formatting the results in the desired manner. This three-tier arrangement can reduce costs in several ways. First, because little processing is done at the client level, inexpensive "thin clients" or network PCs, which have smaller CPUs and limited RAM and secondary storage, can be used. Second, fewer copies of applications software need to be purchased and maintained. Third, data transmission costs are reduced, because the large chunks of data are sent primarily between the two server levels, and not to each individual client. Setting up a three-tier client/server architecture is expensive, however. In addition, applications development is more complex. Thus, as with other configuration choices, there is no one best solution. Instead, the optimal configuration depends on the needs of the specific organization.

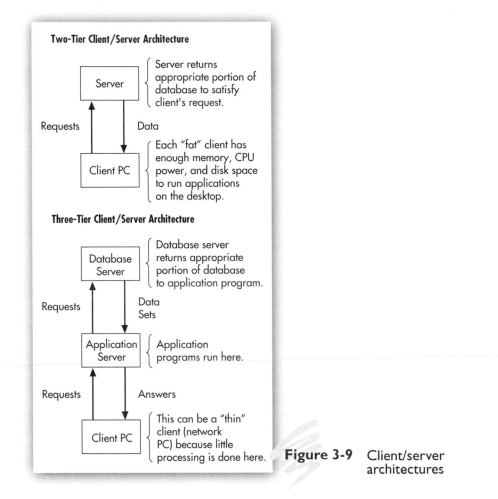

Figure 3-9   Client/server architectures

SUMMARY AND CASE CONCLUSION

Ashton prepared a report outlining how S&S could establish an e-business presence to enhance the effectiveness of its value chain activities. S&S could use the Internet to streamline the purchasing process by submitting most, if not all, of its orders via EDI instead of by mail. Several major suppliers used common carriers, such as Federal Express and United Parcel Service, to ship goods. Therefore, S&S could log into those carriers' Web sites to access real-time information about the status of incoming shipments. Internally, a corporate intranet would be developed to facilitate communication between stores, providing easy access to information about inventory levels at different locations. S&S would also create an extranet to allow major customers real-time access to information about the status of their orders. A consulting firm with extensive experience in designing Web sites would be hired to help S&S develop a Web site that would be more than just an electronic catalog, but would also include post-sale customer support service. Finally, S&S would hire a major accounting firm to address concerns about credit card fraud, compliance with federal and state privacy regulations, and other security issues.

KEY TERMS

- e-business
- certificate authority
- e-commerce
- local area network (LAN)
- electronic data interchange (EDI)
- wide area network (WAN)
- electronic funds transfer (EFT)
- value-added network (VAN)
- financial EDI (FEDI)

- Internet
- financial value-added network (FVAN)
- Internet service provider (ISP)
- application service provider (ASP)
- intranet
- single key encryption systems
- extranet
- public key infrastructure (PKI)

- virtual private network (VPN)
- digital signature
- Transmission Control Protocol/Internet Protocol (TCP/IP)
- digest
- bandwidth
- digital certificate

CHAPTER QUIZ

1. Which of the following acronyms stands for a company that rents software for remote access and use over the Internet?
   a. ISP
   b. FVAN
   c. VPN
   d. ERP
   e. ASP

2. Sending remittance data and payments together electronically is referred to as:
   a. EDI
   b. EFT
   c. FVAN
   d. FEDI

3. Which of the following is an example of an e-commerce transaction?
   a. allowing employees direct access to their benefits data on the company's intranet
   b. using an intranet to design a new product
   c. ordering merchandise from a supplier's Web site
   d. providing automated help in troubleshooting spreadsheet design issues

4. Which of the following is not one of the three basic characteristics that should exist in any business transaction?
   a. validity
   b. permanency
   c. integrity
   d. privacy

5. Which encryption approach is theoretically more secure, but also slower?
   a. secret key
   b. DES
   c. PKI
   d FEDI

6. Which of the following types of networks is used to provide trading partners with limited and controlled access to internal operating data?
   a. intranet
   b. extranet
   c. DDP
   d. WAN

7. In which one of the following LAN configurations are all of the devices linked directly to a host computer?
   a. Ring
   b. Star
   c. Bus
   d. DDP
8. Which of the following involves the use of encryption and the Internet to establish a secure link between two trading partners?
   a. EDI
   b. LAN
   c. WAN
   d. VPN
9. Which of the following can be used to prove that a party did in fact participate in an electronic transaction, thereby facilitating enforcement of a contract?
   a. Web site seal
   b. certificate authority
   c. digital signature
   d. digital certificate
10. Which of the following protocols promises to provide the benefits of EDI to small—and midsized—businesses?
    a. TCP
    b. BXML
    c. IP
    d. HTML

DISCUSSION QUESTIONS

3.1. Communication is vital to any organization, especially to a multidivisional company spread over a wide geographic area. Corporate structure is often aligned along these communication lines. Discuss the relationship between organizational structure and different types (e.g., centralized, decentralized, or DDP) network configurations. What types of mismatches, if any, between organizational structure and network configuration are possible? What are the likely results of such mismatches?

3.2. What are some potential advantages and disadvantages of establishing a corporate policy requiring that all business e-mail be encrypted?

3.3 E-business provides opportunities to improve the efficiency of all value chain activities. What circumstances will determine if the selling or the buying organization reaps the majority of the cost savings associated with e-business?

3.4. Traditionally, in B2B transactions, vendors required payment within 30 days, but offered discounts for earlier payment. How will the use of EDI and FEDI likely affect such practices?

3.5. Firms that successfully digitize their assets can reap significant cost advantages. Consider, for example, the business of selling reproductions of famous photographs and paintings. How is digitalization likely to affect the structure of this market? Will it increase or decrease the number of competitors? Why?

3.6. Would the presence or absence of a third-party–provided seal, such as WebTrust, influence your willingness to engage in electronic commerce with that company? Why or why not? Would your answer differ if you were a small-business owner, rather than an individual consumer?

3.7. Privacy advocates argue that individuals "own" all the information about themselves and therefore have the right to control the distribution of that information to third parties. An opposing argument is that you cannot outlaw "gossip" and the creation of a "reputation." Indeed, such gathering and sharing of information about people is an essential part of commerce. What is your opinion? Do we need a coherent set of laws regarding the sharing and dissemination of information communicated by e-mail? Why or why not?

3.8. A number of companies are developing proprietary types of electronic money. In effect, these companies are acting as independent treasuries. Do you think that such private currencies should be allowed? Or should governments regulate the coinage of electronic money, just as they regulate physical money?

PROBLEMS

3.1 Your friend owns a company with offices in several locations and asks you if she should implement a centralized, decentralized, or distributed data processing system. Prepare a two-page report that explains the advantages and disadvantages of each approach.

3.2 Research the current status of ASPs and write a report that addresses the following issues.
 a. Trends in the level of competition among ASPs and its effect on pricing
 b. Quality of data security and privacy provided by ASPs
 c. Trends in the use of ASPs across firms and industries. Specifically, is ASP usage associated with firm size? Does the level of ASP usage vary across industries (e.g., manufacturing, retail, financial services.)?
 d. How do ASPs demonstrate their levels of service reliability to potential customers?

3.3 Assume that a local company hires you to research the costs of VPNs versus toll-free long-distance dial-up access to its employees. Assume that the company must provide its employees with long-distance remote access to its internal network . Write a report that compares the relative costs of providing access using VPNs versus toll-free telephone numbers, while varying the following factors.
 a. The number of users who need long-distance remote access is 100, 1,000, or 5,000.
 b. The average times each user needs remote long-distance access to the network is only 1 time a week versus 1 time a day versus 10 times each day.
 c. The length of time each user connects to the network is 5 minutes versus 25 minutes.

3.4 Visit several Web pages for companies that are in the same industry. Select one that, in your opinion, is well designed and one that is poorly designed. Write a brief memo to your instructor comparing and contrasting the two Web pages. Include their universal resource locators (URLs) in your report.

3.5 Design a Web page for S&S. Write a brief report explaining and justifying your design choices. Describe how the Web page can be used to support one of the strategies discussed in Chapter 1. Include in your report the URL for your Web page.

3.6 Financial institutions face specific threats related to FEDI. Write a brief report describing the types of controls they use over both incoming and outgoing funds flows. Explain the purpose of each control activity.

3.7 A regional bank with offices in a four-state area wants to redesign its WAN. One decision involves the choice of a communications channel for long-distance links. Write a brief memo identifying the control threats that may arise if the bank uses each of the following as its primary long-distance communications channel:
   a. satellites
   b. microwave
   c. Internet
   d. FVAN
   e. leased telephone lines

3.8 Visit the Web site of a certificate authority and research the different types of certificates that it offers. Write a two-page report describing the level of assurance each different type of certificate provides and explain how that assurance is achieved. Identify the costs associated with each type of certificate and include an analysis of the situations in which each type of certificate is most useful.

3.9 Write a two-page report on taxation issues associated with e-business.

Case 3-1   AnyCompany, Inc.: An Ongoing Comprehensive Case

Visit a local company and obtain permission to study its e-business activities. Once you have lined up a company, write a report that summarizes the following information:

a. What is the general structure of the company's data communications network? Are processing and control centralized, decentralized, or distributed? Why?

b. Identify the data communications hardware and software the company employs.

c. Identify the data communications channels the company uses by determining the principal characteristics of each channel and the channel configurations used.

d. Does the company use EDI or FEDI? Why or why not?

e. What type of digital certificate, if any, does the company have? Why did the company choose that level of security? What requirements concerning digital signatures and digital certificates, if any, does the company expect its trading partners to meet? Why?

f. Does the company have a Web page? If so, how is it used? Critique the company's Web page and offer suggestions for improvements.

g. Does the company have any policies concerning the use of encryption?

h. How do the company's e-business activities support its strategy and strategic position?

i. Is the company using, or has it considered using, an ASP? Why or why not?

Case 3-2   Electronic Payments

Research the various methods of making payments electronically, such as smart cards, cyber-cash, credit cards, and EFT. Write a brief (maximum four pages, double-spaced) report that discusses the advantages and disadvantages of each approach.

ANSWERS TO CHAPTER QUIZ

1. e	**3.** c	**5.** c	**7.** b	**9.** c
2. d	**4.** b	**6.** b	**8.** d	**10.** b

Relational Databases

Learning Objectives

After completing this chapter, you should be able to:

- Explain the difference between database and file-based legacy systems.
- Describe what a relational database is and how it organizes data.
- Explain the difference between logical and physical views of a database.
- Create a set of well-structured tables to properly store data in a relational database.

Integrative Case: S&S, Inc.

S&S, Inc. has been very successful and now operates five stores and a popular Web site. Ashton Fleming believes that it is time to upgrade S&S's AIS so that Susan Gonzalez and Scott Parry can have easy access to the information they need to run their business. Most new AISs are based on a relational database. Ashton knows, however, that Scott and Susan are likely to have questions about the new system and whether a relational database is really appropriate for S&S, Inc. Therefore, he decides to prepare a brief report that explains why S&S's new AIS should be a relational database system. He organizes his report by addressing the following questions:

1. What is a database system and how does it differ from file-oriented systems?
2. What is a *relational* database system?
3. How do you design a well-structured set of tables in a relational database?

INTRODUCTION

Relational databases underlie most modern integrated AISs. This chapter and Chapter 5 explain how to participate in the design and implementation of a database AIS. This chapter defines the concept of a database. The emphasis is on understanding the structure of a relational database system, which is the most popular type of database used for transaction processing. Chapter 5 introduces two specific tools accountants use to facilitate database design: REA data modeling and Entity-Relationship diagramming.

Files Versus Databases

To fully appreciate the power of databases, it is important to understand some basic principles about how data are stored in computer systems. Figure 4-1 shows the basic elements of what is commonly called the data hierarchy. Information about the attributes of an entity, such as a customer's name and address, are stored in fields. All the fields containing data about one entity (e.g., one customer) form a record. A set of related records, such as all customer records, forms a file (e.g., the customer file). A set of interrelated, centrally coordinated files forms a database.

Figure 4-1 Accounts receivable file

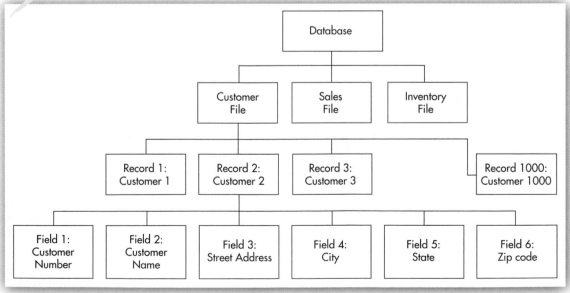

TYPES OF FILES

Two basic types of files exist. A **master file** is conceptually similar to a ledger in a manual AIS. Master files store cumulative information about an organization's resources and the agents with whom it interacts. For example, the inventory and equipment master files store information about important organizational resources. Similarly, the customer, supplier, and employee master files store information about important agents with whom the organization interacts.

Master files are permanent; they exist across fiscal periods. Individual records within a master file, however, are frequently changed. The most common type of change made to records in master files involves updating the data to reflect the effect of specific transactions. For example, the account balances of individual customer accounts in the customer master file are updated to reflect new sales transactions and payments received. Periodically, new records may also be added to a master file and sometimes, individual records may even be deleted.

The second basic type of file is called a **transaction file,** which is conceptually similar to a journal in a manual AIS. Transaction files contain records for the individual business transactions (events) that occur during a specific fiscal period. For example, S&S, Inc. would have a transaction file containing records of sales events and another transaction file containing records of customer payments. Both of these files would be used to update individual customer account balances in the customer master file. Transaction files are not permanent, but are usually only maintained on-line for one fiscal period.

For many years companies created new files and programs each time an information need arose. The result was a significant increase in the number of master files that organizations stored. For example, Bank of America at one time had 36 million customer accounts in 23 separate systems. One governmental agency had data stored in 22 separate systems.

This proliferation of master files created problems. Often the same data were stored in two or more separate master files (see Figure 4-2). This made it difficult to effectively integrate data stored in different files and to obtain an organization-wide view of the data. It also created problems because the specific data values stored in the different files may not have been consistent. For example, a customer's address may have been correctly updated in the master file used to ship merchandise, but the old address may still have been stored in the master file used for billing.

Databases

Database systems were developed to address the problems associated with the proliferation of master files. A **database** is a set of interrelated, centrally coordinated files. Figure 4-2 illustrates the differences between file-oriented and database systems. The database approach treats data as an organizational resource that should be used by and managed for the entire organization, not just the originating department or function. The focus is data integration and data sharing with all authorized users. Integration is achieved by combining master files into larger "pools" of data that many application programs can access. Figure 4-2 shows that this is accomplished by using a program called a **database management system (DBMS),** which acts as an interface between the database and the various application programs. The combination of the

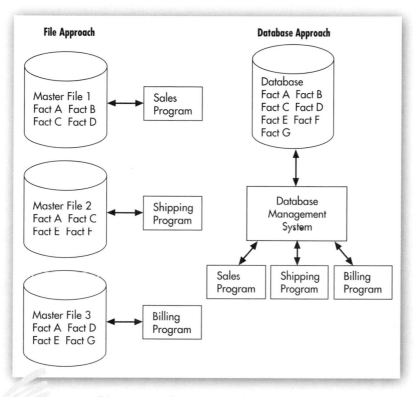

Figure 4-2   File-oriented versus database systems

database, the DBMS, and the application programs that access the database through the DBMS is referred to as the **database system.**

DATABASE SYSTEMS

Logical and Physical Views of Data

Database systems separate the logical and physical views of data. The **logical view** is how the user or programmer conceptually organizes and understands the data. For example, a sales manager may conceptualize all information about customers as being stored in the form of a table. The **physical view** refers to how and where the data are physically arranged and stored on disk, tape, CD-ROM, or other media. For example, Figure 4-3 shows a **record layout** of an accounts receivable file.

Separating the logical and physical views of data facilitates developing new applications because programmers can concentrate on coding the application logic (what the program will do) and do not need to focus on how and where the various data items are stored or accessed. Referring again to Figure 4-3, suppose a programmer wants a credit report showing the customer number, credit limit, and current balance.

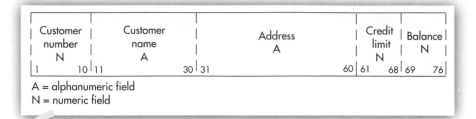

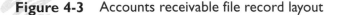

Figure 4-3   Accounts receivable file record layout

To write the program to produce such a report, she must understand the location and length of the fields needed (record positions 1 through 10 for customer number, for example) and the format of each field (alphanumeric or numeric). Clearly, the process becomes more complex if data are needed from several files.

In contrast, Figure 4-4 shows that the database management system software deals with the link between the way data are physically stored and each user's logical view of that data. Thus, the DBMS controls the database so that users can access, query, or update it without reference to how or where the data are physically stored.

Separating the logical and physical views of data also means that users can change their conceptualization about relationships among data items (their logical view of the task) without making changes in the way those data are physically stored. Likewise, the database administrator can change the physical storage of the data to improve system performance, without affecting users or application programs.

Schemas

A **schema** describes the logical structure of a database. There are three levels of schemas: the conceptual, the external, and the internal. Figure 4-5 on page 86 shows the relationships between these three levels.

The **conceptual-level schema** is the organization-wide view of the *entire* database. It lists all data elements and the relationships between them. The **external-level schema** consists of a set of individual user views of portions of the database, each of which is also referred to as a **subschema.** The **internal-level schema** provides a low-level view of the database. It describes how the data are actually stored and accessed, including information about pointers, indexes, record lengths, and so forth.

Figure 4-5 connects each of these levels with bidirectional arrows, which represent the mappings between the schemas. The DBMS uses these mappings to translate a user's or an application program's request for data (expressed in terms of logical names and relationships) into the corresponding pointers, indexes, and addresses needed to physically access the data.

Accountants are frequently involved in developing the conceptual- and external-level schemas, so it is important to understand the difference between the two. Consider the revenue cycle for S&S. The conceptual schema for the revenue cycle database would contain information about customers, sales, cash receipts, sales staff, cash, and inventory.

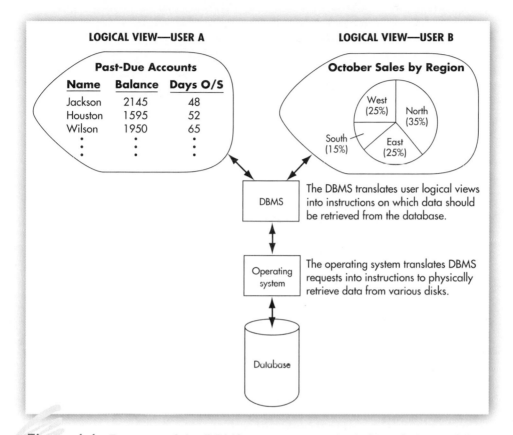

Figure 4-4   Function of the DBMS: to support multiple logical views of data

At the external level, a number of subschemas could be derived from this schema, each tailored to the needs of different users or application programs. Each subschema would also be designed to prevent access to those portions of the database that are not relevant to a particular user's job. For example, the external-level subschema for the sales order entry staff would include information about customer credit limits and current balances, inventory quantities and prices, but would probably not include information about the costs of inventory or current company bank account balances. The external-level subschema for the delivery staff would include information about the customer's address, but would probably not include information about each customer's credit limit or employee pay rates. Additional subschemas would define the relevant portions of the database that other employees must access to perform their jobs.

The Data Dictionary

A key component of a DBMS is the **data dictionary,** which contains information about the structure of the database. For each data element stored in the database, such as

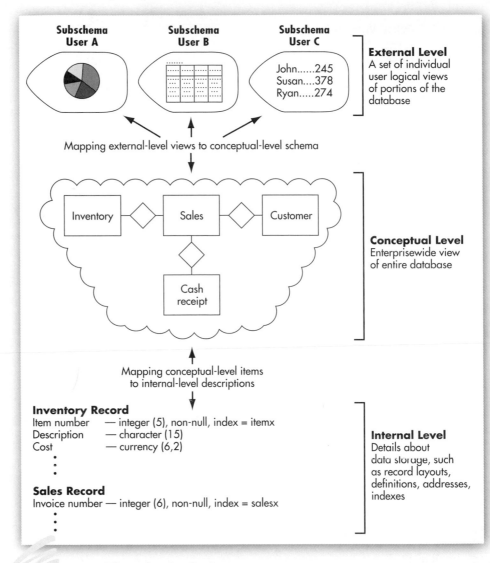

Figure 4-5   Three levels of schemas

the customer number, there is a corresponding record in the data dictionary describing it. Table 4-1 shows examples of the kind of information the data dictionary contains about each data element.

Accountants have a very good understanding of the data elements that exist in a business organization, where they originate, and where they are used. Consequently, accountants should participate in the development of the data dictionary.

The DBMS usually maintains the data dictionary. In fact, this is often one of the first applications of a newly implemented database system. Inputs to the data dictionary

Table 4-1 Example of a Data Dictionary

Data Element Name	Description	Records in Which Contained	Source	Field Length	Field Type	Programs in Which Used	Outputs in Which Contained	Authorized Users	Other Data Names
Customer number	Unique identifier of each customer	A/R record, customer record, sales analysis record	Customer number listing	10	Numeric	A/R update, customer file update, sales analysis update, credit analysis	A/R aging report, customer status report, sales analysis report, credit report	No restrictions	None
Customer name	Complete name of customer	Customer record	Initial customer order	20	Alphanumeric	Customer file update, statement processing	Customer status report, monthly statement	No restrictions	None
Address	Street, city, state, and zip code	Customer record	Credit application	30	Alphanumeric	Customer file update, statement processing	Customer status report, monthly statement	No restrictions	None
Credit limit	Maximum credit that can be extended to customer	Customer record, A/R record	Credit application	8	Numeric	Customer file update, A/R update, credit analysis	Customer status report, A/R aging report, credit report	R. Drummond W. Francom H. Heaton	CR_limit
Balance	Balance due from customer on credit purchases	A/R record, sales analysis record	Various sales and payment transactions	8	Numeric	A/R update, sales analysis update, statement processing, credit analysis	A/R aging report, sales analysis report, monthly statement, credit report	O. Cherrington J. Hansen K. Stocks	Cust_bal

include records of any new or deleted data elements, as well as changes in names, descriptions, or uses of existing data elements. Outputs include a variety of reports useful to programmers, database designers, and users of the information system. Sample reports include (1) a list of all programs in which a data item is used, (2) a list of all synonyms for the data elements in a particular file, (3) a list of all data elements used by a particular user, and (4) a list of all output reports in which a data element is used. These reports are useful in the design and implementation of a database system, provide documentation of the system, and can become part of the audit trail.

DBMS Languages

Every DBMS must provide a means of performing the three basic functions of creating, changing, and querying the database. The set of commands used to perform these functions are referred to as the data definition, data manipulation, and data query languages, respectively.

The **data definition language (DDL)** is used to (1) build the data dictionary, (2) initialize or create the database, (3) describe the logical views for each individual user or programmer, and (4) specify any limitations or constraints on security imposed on database records or fields. Table 4-2 shows an example of a DDL command used to create a table to store information about vendors.

Table 4-2   Example of Data Definition Language (DDL) Command

The following command creates a table to store information about suppliers:

```
CREATE TABLE          Supplier
    (Supplier#            INTEGER (5) NOT NULL,
    Name                 CHARACTER(15),
    Street_Address       CHARACTER(20),
    City                 CHARACTER(12),
    State                CHARACTER(2),
    Zipcode              CHARACTER(10),
    Balance              FLOATING(10)   )
```

This command creates a supplier table with seven columns. The supplier number and balance columns must contain only numeric values; supplier# will take integer values, whereas balance can be any numeric value, including decimal format. The remaining columns may contain either numbers or letters. The number in parentheses indicates the maximum number of characters that can be stored in that column. Finally, the constraint NOT NULL indicates that supplier# cannot be left blank.

Result of the command:

Supplier

⊞ Supplier : Table						_ □ ×
Supplier #	**Name**	**Address**	**City**	**State**	**Zipcode**	**Balance**
▶ 0	0	0	0	0	0	0
Record: I◄ ◄ 1 ► ►I ►* of 1						

Note: This command creates an empty table. Filling the table requires the use of DML commands.

The **data manipulation language (DML)** is used for data maintenance, which includes such operations as updating, inserting, and deleting portions of the database. The DML simplifies the writing of programs to accomplish these tasks by requiring references only to the names of data items, rather than to their physical storage locations. Table 4-3 shows examples of the three basic types of DML commands.

The **data query language (DQL)** is used to interrogate the database. Whereas the DML is used to change the contents of the database, the DQL merely retrieves, sorts, orders, and presents subsets of the database in response to user queries. Most DQLs contain a fairly powerful, but easy to use, set of commands that enables users to satisfy many of their own information needs, without a programmer's assistance. Table 4-4 presents a sample query command written in a popular query language called SQL (Structured Query Language). Appendix A presents more information about SQL and graphical query languages.

Many DBMSs also include a **report writer,** which is a language that simplifies report creation. Typically, users need only specify which data elements they want printed and how the report should be formatted. The report writer then searches the database, extracts the specified data items, and prints them out according to the user-specified format.

All users generally have access to both the DQL and the report writer. Access to the DDL and DML, however, should be restricted to those employees with administrative and programming responsibilities. This helps to limit the number of people who have the capability to make changes to the database.

Table 4-3   Example of Data Manipulation Language (DML) Operations

This command inserts a new row, containing information about St. Louis Electronics, into the supplier table:

```
INSERT
INTO    Supplier (Supplier#, name, street_address, city, state, zipcode, balance)
VALUES  (10004, 'St. Louis Electronics', '2455 Chippewa', 'St. Louis', 'MO',
         '63109-2643', 0)
```

This command updates the address of St. Louis Electronics:

```
UPDATE   Supplier
SET      Street_address = '3542 Chippewa',
         Zipcode = '63110-2214'
WHERE    Supplier# = 10004
```

This command deletes from the supplier table the row containing information about St. Louis Electronics:

```
DELETE
FROM    Supplier
WHERE   Supplier# = 10004
```

Table 4-4   Example of Data Query Language (DQL) Command

Query:

SELECT	Name, Balance
FROM	Vendor
ORDER BY	Balance, Descending

Result:

Name	Balance
South Side Electronics	3987.00
St. Louis Electronics Supply	3250.67
St. Louis Computer Warehouse	2311.85
Oakville Electronics	954.95

Record: 5 of 5

This query specifies that the name and balance columns (the SELECT command) in the vendor table (the FROM command) be displayed. The result is arranged in descending order (the ORDER BY and the DESCENDING commands) by the amount owed.

RELATIONAL DATABASES

A DBMS is characterized by the type of logical data model on which it is based. A **data model** is an abstract representation of the contents of a database. The overwhelming majority of new DBMSs are called relational databases because they use the relational data model developed by Dr. E. F. Codd in 1970. Therefore, this chapter focuses primarily on relational databases.

The **relational data model** represents everything in the database as being stored in the form of tables (see Figure 4-6). Technically, these tables are called **relations** (hence the name relational data model), but we will use the two words interchangeably. Moreover, keep in mind that the relational data model only describes how the data appear in the conceptual- and external-level schemas. The data are not actually stored in tables, but rather in the manner described in the internal-level schema.

Each row in a relation, called a **tuple** (which rhymes with *couple*), contains data about a specific occurrence of the type of entity represented by that table. For example, each row in the inventory table in Figure 4-6 contains all the pertinent data about a particular inventory item that S&S carries. Similarly, each row in the customer table contains all the information about a specific customer. Each column in a table contains information about one specific attribute of that entity. Thus, the columns in the sales table in Figure 4-6 represent specific characteristics about each sales transaction.

Inventory Table

Item Number	Description	Quantity on Hand	List Price
10573	19" Monitor	13	$495.00
10574	21" Monitor	8	$949.00
10622	Laser Printer	22	$395.00
10623	Color Laser Printer	5	$699.00
10624	Multi-functional Printer	12	$799.00

Record: 6 of 6

Inventory Table (Item number is primary key)

also foreign key

Customer Table

Customer #	Name	Street	City	State	Zip code	Credit Limit	Account Balance
11255	G. Hwang	2993 Main	Mesa	AZ	85281	$4,000.00	$875.00
12971	J. Jackson	466 W. Oak	Tempe	AZ	85286	$5,000.00	$2,588.00
13629	P. Szabo	246 E. Palm	Mesa	AZ	85281	$6,000.00	$3,955.00
15637	S. Martinez	2866 Spring	Tempe	AZ	85287	$5,000.00	$250.00
18229	B. Adams	1744 Apache	Tempe	AZ	85287	$3,000.00	$1,675.00

Record: 5 of 6

Customer Table (Customer number is primary key)

Sales Table

Invoice #	Date	Salesperson #	Customer #	Amount
10001	08-Sep-03	25	15637	$399.00
10002	10-Sep-03	22	12971	$1,748.00
10003	25-Sep-03	24	13629	$1,185.00
10004	02-Oct-03	25	11255	$399.00
10005	11-Oct-03	22	15637	$1,098.00
10006	25-Oct-03	25	18229	$990.00

Record: 7 of 7

Sales Table (Invoice Number is primary key)

Sales - Inventory Line Items Table

Invoice #	Item Number	Quantity	Actual Unit Price
10001	10573	1	$399.00
10002	10624	1	$799.00
10002	10574	1	$949.00
10003	10622	3	$395.00
10004	10573	1	$399.00
10005	10573	1	$399.00
10005	10623	1	$699.00
10006	10573	2	$495.00

Record: 9 of 9

Sales-Inventory Line Items Table (Combination of Invoice Number and Item Number forms primary key)

Figure 4-6 Sample relational tables for S&S, Inc.

Types of Attributes

Tables in a relational database have three types of attributes. A **primary key** is the attribute, or combination of attributes, that uniquely identifies a specific row in a table. For example, the primary key for the inventory table in Figure 4-6 is item number. Each different merchandise item that S&S sells can be uniquely identified by its item number. Often, the primary key is a single attribute. In some tables, however, two or more attributes jointly form the primary key. For example, the primary key of the sales-inventory line items table in Figure 4-6 is the combination of invoice number and item number.

A **foreign key** is an attribute appearing in one table that is a primary key in another table. Foreign keys are used to link tables. For example, the attributes customer number and salesperson number are foreign keys in the sales table in Figure 4-6; both are used to link the data about a particular sales transaction with information about the salesperson and customer who participated in that event.

Other non-key attributes in each table store important information about that entity. For example, the inventory table in Figure 4-6 also contains information about the description, quantity on hand, and list price of each item that S&S carries.

Basic Requirements of the Relational Data Model

The relational data model imposes several requirements on the structure of tables. The set of tables depicted in Figure 4-6 follows these constraints, representing a well-structured (normalized) database:

1. *Every column in a row must be single valued.* Notice that in each table in Figure 4-6 there is one, and only one, value in any given cell. Thus, each table is a "flat" file. This requirement is the reason why there is a table called sales-inventory line item. At S&S, each sales transaction can involve more than one different kind of inventory item table. For example, on sale number 10002, the customer bought both a monitor and a printer. Therefore, if item number was included as an attribute in the sales table, it would have to take on more than one value. Moreover, notice that a given item, for example a 19-inch monitor (item number 10573), can be sold to many different customers. Therefore, invoice number cannot be included as an attribute in the inventory table, because that table would no longer be a flat file.

Figure 4-7   Example of storing all data in one table

Invoice #	Date	Salesperson #	Other Salesperson data	Customer #
10001	08-Sep-03	25	name, date hired, etc.	15637
10002	10-Sep-03	22	name, date hired, etc.	12971
10002	10-Sep-03	22	name, date hired, etc.	12971
10003	25-Sep-03	24	name, date hired, etc.	13629
10004	02-Oct-03	25	name, date hired, etc.	11255
10005	11-Oct-03	22	name, date hired, etc.	15637
10005	11-Oct-03	22	name, date hired, etc.	15637
10006	25-Oct-03	25	name, date hired, etc.	18229

Table1 : Table

Record: 14 4   10 ▶ ▶I ▶* of 10   4

2. *Primary keys cannot be null.* The primary key is the attribute, or combination of attributes, that uniquely identifies a specific row in a table. For this to be true, the primary key of any row in a relation cannot be null (blank), for then there would never be a way to uniquely identify that row and retrieve the data stored there. A non-null value for the primary key indicates that a specific object exists and can be identified by reference to its primary key value. This constraint is referred to as the **entity integrity rule,** because it ensures that every row in every relation must represent data about some specific object in the real world.

3. *Foreign keys, if not null, must have values that correspond to the value of a primary key in another relation.* Foreign keys are used to link rows in one table to rows in another table. For example, the customer number and salesperson number attributes are foreign keys in the sales table in Figure 4-6, serving to link each sales transaction with the customer and salesperson who participated in that event. This is only possible, however, if the values of the customer number and salesperson number in the sales table correspond to actual customer and salesperson numbers that exist in some row in those tables. This constraint is referred to as the **referential integrity rule** because it ensures the consistency of the database. Foreign keys can contain null values, however. For example, some customers pay cash and for privacy reasons do not want to give S&S any way to identify and track them. Therefore, for such cash sales, the customer number field in the sales table would be blank.

4. *All non-key attributes in a table should describe a characteristic about the object identified by the primary key.* Most tables contain other attributes in addition to the primary and foreign keys. Consider the sales table shown in Figure 4-6. Invoice number is the primary key, and both customer number and salesperson number are foreign keys. The remaining attributes, (date and sale amount) are other important facts about the sales event. Details about the customer or salesperson who participated in that transaction, or about the items purchased, however, are stored in those tables, not in the sales table.

These four constraints produce a well-structured (normalized) database in which data are consistent and redundancy is minimized and controlled. The next section illustrates these benefits, by showing examples of the kinds of problems that can arise if these four constraints are violated.

Importance of a Well-Structured Relational Database

Figure 4-6 shows a set of well-designed tables to store information about S&S's sales transactions. We will compare this set of tables to the alternative of storing all the data in one large table to show the problems that can arise from improper table design (see Figure 4-7).

Other Customer data	Item Number	Description	Other Inventory data
name, address, etc.	10573	19" Monitor	Quantity on hand, etc.
name, address, etc.	10574	21" Monitor	Quantity on hand, etc.
name, address, etc.	10624	Multi-function Printer	Quantity on hand, etc.
name, address, etc.	10622	Laser Printer	Quantity on hand, etc.
name, address, etc.	10573	19" Monitor	Quantity on hand, etc.
name, address, etc.	10573	19" Monitor	Quantity on hand, etc.
name, address, etc.	10623	Color Laser Printer	Quantity on hand, etc.
name, address, etc.	10573	19" Monitor	Quantity on hand, etc.

Problems associated with storing all data in one table

One problem with trying to store all the data in one table is that it creates a great deal of redundancy. For example, examine sales invoice number 10002 in Figure 4-7. Because there are two separate inventory items sold, many data items—such as the date of the sale, customer name and other data, and salesperson data—are recorded multiple times. Likewise, because many sales include the 19-inch monitor, information about that particular item, such as its description and list price, is repeated every time someone buys that size monitor.

Because sales volume can be fairly high in a retail store (Figure 4-7 contains only five invoices), such redundancy can make file maintenance unnecessarily time consuming and error prone. Three specific types of problems can occur. The first is called an *update anomaly,* because changes (updates) to data values are not correctly recorded. For example, changing a customer's address requires searching the entire table and changing every occurrence of that customer's address. Overlooking even one row would create inconsistency in the database, because multiple rows, each with a different address, would then exist for the same customer. This could result in unnecessary duplicate mailings. It could also create errors in analyses such as counting the number of different customers who purchased something during a specific time period.

The other two types of problems associated with the approach depicted in Figure 4-7 are caused by the fact that customer, salesperson, and inventory data are not maintained independently of sales invoice data. One problem this creates is referred to as an *insert anomaly,* because there is no way to store information about prospective customers until they actually make a purchase. Until a customer makes a purchase, the sales invoice number column would be blank. The invoice number is part of the primary key for Figure 4-7, however, so it cannot be left blank.

The second problem associated with the way that the table in Figure 4-7 is designed is called a *delete anomaly,* because it involves unintended results that arise when deleting a row in that table. If a customer has made only one purchase, consisting of a single item, deleting that row from the table in Figure 4-7 would result in the loss of all information about that customer. For example, deleting the row for sales invoice 10006 because it is the end of a fiscal period also would delete all information about customer 18229 (B. Adams).

The solution: A set of tables

The problems associated with trying to store all the data in one table like that shown in Figure 4-7 can be avoided by creating the set of tables shown in Figure 4-6, which has a table for each separate entity of interest. First, notice that redundancy is greatly reduced. For example, all non-key attributes, such as customer addresses and inventory item unit prices, are stored just once. This avoids the potential of update anomaly problems. Note that redundancy is not entirely eliminated, however. Certain items, such as sales invoice number and item number, appear in more than one table. These attributes appear more than once only when they function as foreign keys, however. Consequently, the referential integrity rule ensures that there will be no update anomaly problems with the foreign keys.

An important feature of the schema depicted in Figure 4-6 is that data about various things of interest (customers, inventory, and sales transactions) are stored in separate tables. This makes it easier to add new data to the system. For example, information about prospective customers can be stored simply by adding another row in the customer table. Thus, the set of tables depicted in Figure 4-6 avoids the problem of an insert anomaly.

The schema shown in Figure 4-6 also simplifies the deletion of information. For example, deleting sales invoice 10006, representing the only sale to customer 18229 (B. Adams), would not result in the loss of all information about that customer, because information about each customer is stored in the customer table. Thus, the set of tables depicted in Figure 4-6 is free from delete anomalies.

Two Approaches to Database Design

There are two basic ways to design well-structured relational databases like the one depicted in Figure 4-6. One approach, called *normalization,* starts with the assumption that everything is initially stored in one large table. A set of rules is then followed to decompose that initial table into a set of normalized tables. The objective is to produce a set of tables in what is called third normal form (3NF), because such tables are free of the types of update, insert, and delete anomaly problems described earlier. The details of the normalization process are beyond the scope of this book, but can be found in any database textbook.

An alternative way to design well-structured relational databases involves semantic data modeling. Under this approach, the database designer uses knowledge about how business processes typically work and about the information needs associated with transaction processing to first draw a graphical picture of what should be included in the database. The resulting figure can then be directly used to create a set of relational tables that are in 3NF.

Semantic data modeling has two significant advantages over simply following the rules of normalization. First, because it makes use of the system designer's domain knowledge about business processes and practices, it facilitates the efficient design of transaction processing databases. Second, because the resulting graphical model explicitly represents information about the organization's business processes and policies, it facilitates communicating with the intended users of the system. Such communication is extremely important in ensuring that the resulting system meets the actual needs of users. Chapter 5 introduces two semantic data modeling tools that accountants and business systems professionals can use to design transaction processing databases, namely E-R (entity-relationship) diagramming and the REA data model.

DATABASE SYSTEMS AND THE FUTURE OF ACCOUNTING

Database systems may profoundly affect the fundamental nature of accounting. For instance, database systems may lead to the abandonment of the double-entry accounting model. The basic rationale for the double-entry model is that the redundancy of recording the amount of a transaction twice provides a check on the accuracy of data processing. Every transaction generates equal debit and credit entries, and the equality of debits and credits is checked and rechecked at numerous points in the accounting process. Data redundancy, however, is the antithesis of the database concept. If the amounts associated with a transaction are entered into a database system correctly, then it is necessary to store them only once, not twice. Computer data processing is sufficiently accurate to make unnecessary the elaborate system of checks and double checks, which characterizes the double-entry accounting model.

Database systems also have the potential to significantly alter the nature of external reporting. Considerable time and effort are currently invested in defining how companies should summarize and report accounting information to external users. Why not simply make a copy of the company's financial database and make it available to external users in lieu of the traditional financial statements? Users would then be free to manipulate and analyze the raw data in whatever manner they see fit. Focus 4-1 discusses this possibility in more detail.

Perhaps the most significant effect of database systems will be in the way that accounting information is used in decision making. The difficulty of formulating ad

---

Focus 4-1

Databases or Financial Statements?

Although information technology has dramatically changed the way that business is conducted, it has had relatively little effect on external reporting. Companies still produce periodic (quarterly and annual) financial reports of past activities based on historical costs. Moreover, they present that information at a highly aggregated level. It is estimated that the average financial database of a typical large company is on the order of 100 gigabytes. Yet annual reports contain, on average, only about 100 kilobytes of data. Consequently, users of annual reports see only a small portion of the data about the organization. In addition, the information is presented in a predefined format (the financial statements).

Why not replace the annual report with a copy of the company's financial database? Many companies already give their suppliers and customers limited access to their internal databases. Suppliers, for example, may be given access to inventory data so that they can plan production and deliveries to replenish shortages. They are not, however, given access to human resource or payroll data. Companies could similarly define a view of their database that excluded data too sensitive to be allowed to fall into the hands of competitors. This view of the database could be placed on CD-ROMs or made available over the Internet to investors, creditors, and other external users.

The technical capability for providing such database access exists. The computing power of current PCs makes processing such a database feasible for a wide range of users. External users would get a fuller picture of the organization's performance, and the information would also be more timely.

In such a system, the company's primary financial reporting function would involve the definition of data elements and database structure. Users would then be free to aggregate and classify that information using whatever decision model they believed to be appropriate.

Source: Robert K. Elliot, "Confronting the Future: Choices for the Attest Function," *Accounting Horizons* (September 1994):106–124.

hoc queries in accounting systems based on traditional files or nonrelational DBMS meant that accountants acted, in effect, as information gatekeepers. Financial information was readily available only in predefined formats and at specified times. Relational databases, however, provide query languages that are powerful and easy to use. Thus, managers need not get bogged down in procedural details about how to retrieve information. Instead, they can concentrate solely on specifying what information they want. As a result, financial reports can be easily prepared to cover whatever time periods managers want to examine, not just the time frames accountants traditionally use.

Relational DBMSs can also accommodate multiple views of the same underlying phenomenon. For example, tables storing information about assets can include columns not only for historical cost, but also for current replacement costs and market values. Thus, managers will no longer be forced to look at data in ways predefined by accountants.

Finally, relational DBMSs provide the capability of integrating financial and operational data. For example, data about customer satisfaction, collected by surveys or interviews, could be stored in the same table used to store information about current account balances and credit limits. Managers would thus have access to a richer set of data for making tactical and strategic decisions.

In all these ways, relational DBMSs have the potential to increase the use and value of accounting information for making the tactical and strategic decisions involved in running an organization. Accountants, however, must become knowledgeable about database systems so that they can participate in designing the accounting information systems of the future. Such participation is important for ensuring that adequate controls are included in those systems to safeguard the data and ensure the reliability of the information produced.

SUMMARY AND CASE CONCLUSION

Ashton prepared a report for Scott and Susan summarizing what he knew about database systems in general, and the relational data model in particular. His report explained that a database management system (DBMS) is the software that makes a database system work. A DBMS is based on a logical data model, which determines how users perceive the data as being stored.

Many DBMSs are based on the relational data model. This model represents data as being stored in the form of tables, which are called relations. Every row in a relational table has only one data value in each column. Neither row nor column position is significant. These properties support the use of simple, yet powerful query languages for interacting with a relational database. Users need specify only what data they want, and need not be concerned with how the data are retrieved. The DBMS functions as an intermediary between the user and the database, thereby hiding the complex addressing schemes actually used to retrieve and update the information stored in the database.

After reading Ashton's report, Scott and Susan agreed that it was time to upgrade S&S's AIS. They agreed with Ashton's suggestion that S&S hire a consulting firm to help guide the selection and installation of the new system. They also asked him to be involved in the design process to ensure that the new system meets their needs.

KEY TERMS

- Master file
- Data dictionary
- Transaction file
- Data definition language (DDL)
- Database
- Data manipulation language (DML)
- Database management system (DBMS)
- Data query language (DQL)

- Database system
- Report writer
- Logical view
- Data model
- Physical view
- Relational data model
- Record layout
- Relations
- Tuple
- Schema

- Primary key
- Conceptual-level schema
- Foreign key
- External-level schema
- Entity integrity rule
- Subschema
- Referential integrity rule
- Internal-level schema
- Normalization

CHAPTER QUIZ

1. The relational data model portrays data as being stored in:
   a. hierarchies
   b. tables
   c. objects
   d. files
2. Which of the following would be a master file?
   a. sales invoices
   b. all suppliers
   c. purchase orders
   d. cash disbursements
3. What is each row in a relational database table called?
   a. relation
   b. attribute
   c. record
   d. tuple
4. Which of the following is an individual user's view of the database?
   a. conceptual-level schema
   b. external-level schema
   c. internal-level schema
   d. logical-level schema
5. Which of the following would managers most likely use to retrieve information about sales during the month of October?
   a. DML
   b. DSL
   c. DDL
   d. DQL
6. Which of the following attributes would most likely be a primary key?
   a. supplier name
   b. supplier number
   c. supplier zip code
   d. supplier account balance

7. Which of the following is a software program that runs a database system?
   a. DQL
   b. DBMS
   c. DML
   d. DDL
8. The constraint that all primary keys must have non-null data values is referred to as which of the following?
   a. referential integrity rule
   b. entity integrity rule
   c. normalization rule
   d. relational data model rule
9. The constraint that all foreign keys must have either null values or the value of a primary key in another table is referred to as which of the following?
   a. referential integrity rule
   b. integrity entity rule
   c. normalization rule
   d. relational data model rule
10. Which of the following attributes in the cash receipts table (representing payments received from customers) would be a foreign key?
    a. cash receipt number
    b. customer check number
    c. customer number
    d. cash receipt date

DISCUSSION QUESTIONS

4.1 A database allows two distinct views of data: a logical view and a physical view. Contrast the two views, and discuss why separate views are necessary in database applications. Describe which perspective is most useful for each of the following employees: a programmer, a manager, and an internal auditor. How will understanding logical data structures assist accountants in designing and using database systems?

4.2 The relational data model represents data as being stored in tables. Spreadsheets are another tool that accountants use to employ a tabular representation of data. What are some similarities and differences in the way that both of these tools use tables? How might an accountant's familiarity with the tabular representation of spreadsheets facilitate or hinder learning how to use a relational DBMS?

4.3 The text explained how database technology may eliminate the need for double-entry accounting. This creates three possibilities: (1) the double-entry model will be abandoned, (2) the double-entry model will not be used directly, but an external-level schema based on the double-entry model will be defined for accountants' use, or (3) the double-entry model will be retained in database systems. Which alternative do you think is most likely to occur? Why?

4.4 Relational DBMS query languages provide easy access to information about the organization's activities. Does this mean that on-line, real-time processing should be used for all transactions? Does an organization need real-time financial reports? Why or why not?

PROBLEMS

4.1 The following data elements comprise the conceptual level schema for a database:

item number	customer number
cost	customer name
description	shipping address
quantity on hand	billing address
invoice number	credit limit
date	account balance
quantity sold	price
terms	

Required

a. Identify three potential users and design a subschema for each. Justify your design by explaining why each user needs access to that data element.

b. Using any relational database product, such as Microsoft Access, create the set of tables to implement your schema. Specify the primary key(s) and foreign key(s) for each table. Learn the command to enforce referential integrity and test your model by entering sample data in each table.

4.2 Most DBMS packages contain a data definition language, a data manipulation language, and a data query language. For each of the following examples, indicate which language would be used and why.

a. A database administrator defines the logical structure of the database.

b. The controller requests a cost accounting report containing a list of all employees being paid for more than 10 hours overtime in a given week.

c. A programmer develops a program to update the fixed assets records stored in the database.

d. The human resources manager requests a report noting all employees who are retiring within five years.

e. The inventory serial number field is extended in the inventory records to allow for recognition of additional inventory items with serial numbers containing more than 10 digits.

f. A user develops a program to print out all purchases made during the past two weeks.

g. An additional field is added to the fixed asset records to record the estimated salvage value of each asset.

4.3 Ashton wants to store the following data about S&S's purchases of inventory:

item number	vendor name	purchase order number
date of purchase	unit cost	description
vendor number	quantity purchased	quantity on hand
vendor address	purchasing agent	total amount of purchase
extended amount		

Required

a. Design a set of relational tables to store this data.

b. Identify the primary key for each table.

c. Implement your tables using any relational database product to which you have access.

d. Define which attributes are primary and foreign keys and implement referential integrity.

e. Test your specification by entering sample data in each table.

4.4 Create the set of relational tables in Table 4-A1 in any relational DBMS product to which you have access. Write queries to answer the following questions:
   a. How many different kinds of inventory items does S&S sell?
   b. How many sales were made during October?
   c. What was the total amount of sales in October?
   d. What was the average amount of a sales transaction?
   e. Which salesperson made the largest sale?
   f. How many units of each product were sold?
   g. Which product was sold most frequently?

4.5 Implement the set of relational tables shown in Figure 4-8 in a relational DBMS package to which you have access. Write queries to answer the following questions:
   a. Which customers (show their names) made purchases from Martinez?
   b. Who has the largest credit limit?
   c. How many sales were made in October?
   d. What were the item numbers, price, and quantity of each item sold on invoice number 103?
   e. How much did each salesperson sell?
   f. How many customers live in Arizona?
   g. How much credit does each customer still have available?
   h. How much of each item was sold? (Include the description of each item in your answer.)
   i. Which customers still have more than $1,000 in available credit?
   j. For which items are there at least 100 units on hand?

4.6 The BusyB Company wants to store data about its employees' skills. Each employee may possess one or more specific skills. In addition, several employees may have the same skill. The following facts need to be included in the database:

   employee name   supervisor   date hired
   skill number   skill name   date of birth
   pay rate   employee number   date skill acquired

   Required
   a. Design a set of relational tables to store these data.
   b. Identify the primary key for each table.
   c. Implement your schema using any relational DBMS to which you have access. Specify primary and foreign keys and learn the command to enforce referential integrity. Demonstrate the soundness of your design by entering sample data in each table.

4.7 Ashton wants to extend the schema depicted in Figure 4-6 to include information about payments from customers. He tells you that customers can make installment payments on each invoice. They may also write one check to pay for several different invoices. Ashton specifically wants to store the following information:

   customer name   total amount received
   invoice payment applies to   date of receipt
   customer number   amount applied to a specific invoice
   cash receipt number   employee processing payment

   Required
   a. Modify the set of relational tables in Figure 4-6 to store this additional data.
   b. Identify the primary key for each new table you created in step a.
   c. Implement your schema using any relational DBMS package available to you. Indicate which attributes are primary and foreign keys. Learn the command to enforce referential integrity and enter sample data in each table you created.

Inventory : Table

Item_Number	Description	Unit Cost	Unit Price	QOH
1010	Blender	14	29.95	200
1015	Toaster	12	19.95	300
1020	Mixer	23	33.95	250
1025	Television	499	699.95	74
1030	Freezer	799	999.95	32
1035	Refrigerator	699	849.95	25
1040	Radio	45	79.95	100
1045	Clock	79	99.95	300

Record: 9 of 9

Customer : Table

Customer_Number	Name	City	State	Credit_Limit
1000	Smith	Phoenix	AZ	2500
1001	Jones	St. Louis	MO	1500
1002	Jeffries	Atlanta	GA	4000
1003	Gilkey	Phoenix	AZ	5000
1004	Lankford	Phoenix	AZ	2000
1005	Zeile	Chicago	IL	2000
1006	Pagnozzi	Salt Lake	UT	3000
1007	Arocha	Chicago	IL	1000

Record: 9 of 9

Sales : Table

Invoice_Number	Date	Salesperson	Customer_Number	Amount
101	10/3/03	Wilson	1000	1549.90
102	10/5/03	Mahomet	1003	299.85
103	10/5/03	Jackson	1002	1449.80
104	10/15/03	Drezen	1000	799.90
105	10/15/03	Martinez	1005	849.95
106	10/16/03	Martinez	1007	99.95
107	10/29/03	Mahomet	1002	2209.70
108	11/3/03	Martinez	1000	779.90

Record: 9 of 9

Sales-Inventory : Table

Invoice_Number	Item_Number	Quantity	Extension
101	1025	1	699.95
101	1035	1	849.95
102	1045	3	299.85
103	1010	1	29.95
103	1015	1	19.95
103	1025	2	1399.90
104	1025	1	699.95
104	1045	1	99.95
105	1035	1	849.95
106	1045	1	99.95
107	1030	1	999.95
107	1035	1	849.95
107	1040	2	159.90
107	1045	2	199.90
108	1025	1	699.95
108	1045	1	99.95

Record: 17 of 17

Figure 4-8 Sample relational tables for Problem 4-5

Case 4-1   AnyCompany, Inc.: An Ongoing Comprehensive Case

Identify a local company (perhaps the same company that you identified to complete Case 1-1) that uses a database system and write a report that includes the following information:

1. The type of logical data model used by the DBMS.
2. The reasons why that particular product was chosen.
3. How the company transferred its data from its prior system to the database system.

4. Advantages the company has reaped from using the DBMS.
5. Any problems encountered in implementing the database system, and how those problems were handled.
6. The company's accountants' level of involvement in converting to the database system.

Case 4-2   Research Projects

As in all areas of information technology, DBMSs are constantly changing and improving. Research how businesses are using DBMS and write a report of your findings. Address the following issues:

1. Which popular DBMS products are based on the relational data model?
2. Which DBMS products are based on a logical model other than the relational data model?

3. What are the relative strengths and weaknesses of the different types (relational versus other logical models) of DBMSs?

ANSWERS TO CHAPTER QUIZ

1. b	**3.** d	**5.** d	**7.** b	**9.** a
2. b	**4.** b	**6.** b	**8.** b	**10.** c

Query Languages

QUERYING A RELATIONAL DATABASE

The relational data model allows three fundamental types of operations to be performed on tables:

1. *PROJECT* creates a new table (or relation) by selecting specified columns from the original table.
2. *RESTRICT* creates a new table by selecting from the original table those rows that meet specified conditions.
3. *JOIN* creates a new table by selecting the designated columns from two or more tables and then choosing the rows that meet specified conditions. The JOIN operation is used frequently, since a single relation often does not contain all the data necessary to satisfy a user inquiry.

The key property of the relational data model is that each of these three basic operations always results in the creation of a new table. This means that the result of a query using these operations can itself be the object of additional queries. It is this possibility for nesting queries that makes relational data query languages so powerful.

Relational query languages can be classified into two broad categories: text-based query languages and graphical query languages. Let us examine how each type works.

Structured Query Language: A Text-Based Query Language

The standard text-based query language provided by most, but not all, relational DBMSs is called **structured query language (SQL).** Many popular microcomputer accounting packages also provide SQL access to the general ledger. SQL is powerful, yet simple to use. Its power and simplicity enable easy generation of special-purpose reports so corporate accountants can meet management's information requests. Similarly, SQL permits auditors to easily retrieve information from client databases. Consequently, it is important to gain a basic understanding of how SQL works. In the remainder of this appendix, we introduce the principal SQL commands; additional information about SQL can be found in the reference manuals that accompany relational DBMS products.

SQL Syntax

Five basic keywords are used to construct most SQL queries:

1. *SELECT.* Used to list the columns that should be displayed in answering the query. This keyword implements the PROJECT operation.
2. *FROM.* Used to list the names of the tables that arc referenced in answering the query. If two or more table names are listed, the JOIN operation is applied to them.
3. *WHERE.* Used to specify which rows to retrieve when answering the query. This keyword implements the RESTRICT operation.
4. *ORDER BY.* Used to specify how to format the answer. The column that serves as the basis for ordering is listed, along with the desired sequence (ascending or descending).
5. *GROUP BY.* Used to specify which rows in a table should be subject to basic mathematical operations (such as SUM, MINIMUM, and MAXIMUM).

Sample SQL Queries

Let us now see how these five keywords can be used to retrieve information from the database shown in Table 4A-1.

Query 1: Show the dates and invoice totals for all sales in October, arranged in descending order by amount of the sale.
This query would be written in SQL as follows:

SELECT	Date, Invoice Total
FROM	Invoice
WHERE	Date BETWEEN 10/01/03 and 10/31/03
ORDER BY	Invoice Total, DESCENDING

Table 4A-2 shows the original invoice table and the response to this query.

Query 2: What are the invoice numbers of all sales made to D. Ainge, and who completed these sales?
This query would be written in SQL as follows:

SELECT	Sales Invoice #, Salesperson, Customer Name
FROM	Invoice, Customer
WHERE	Invoice.Customer # = Customer. Customer # AND Customer Name = 'D. Ainge'

Table 4A-3 shows the original tables and the result of the query.

Query 3: How many televisions were sold in October?
This query would be written in SQL as follows:

SELECT	Sum (quantity)
FROM	Line Item, Invoice, Inventory
WHERE	Line Item.Item # = Inventory.Item # AND Description = 'Television' AND Line Item.Sales Invoice # = Invoice.Sales Invoice # AND Date BETWEEN 10/01/03 and 10/31/03

This query shows that basic mathematical operators can be included in the SQL SELECT clause. In this case, the query is asking for the sum of the quantity sold column in the line item table. Table 4A-4 shows the result of this query.

Query 4: Display the names and addresses of all customers buying televisions in October.
This query would be written in SQL as follows:

SELECT	Customer Name, Street, City, State
FROM	Customer, Invoice, Line Item, Inventory
WHERE	Date BETWEEN 10/01/03 and 10/31/03 AND Description = 'Television' AND Invoice.Customer # = Customer.Customer # AND Invoice.Sales Invoice # = Line Item.Sales Invoice # AND Line Item.Item # = Inventory.Item #

The answer to this query is shown in Table 4A-5. Although only two lines long, the relational DBMS had to use all four tables to answer the query.

Query 5: How much did each salesperson sell so far this year?
This query would be written in SQL as follows:

SELECT	Sum (invoice total), Salesperson
FROM	INVOICE
GROUP BY	Salesperson

This query uses the GROUP BY keyword to instruct the DBMS to sum the invoice totals separately for each distinct value in the salesperson column. Table 4A-6 shows the result of this query.

Table 4A-1 Set of Relational Tables for Storing S&S Sales Data

Sales : Table

Sales Invoice #	Date	Salesperson	Customer #	Invoice Total
101	10/15/03	J. Buck	151	1447
102	10/15/03	S. Knight	152	4394
103	10/28/03	S. Knight	151	898
104	10/31/03	J. Buck	152	789
105	11/14/03	J. Buck	153	3994

Record: 6 of 6

Line Item : Table

Sales Invoice #	Item #	Quantity	Extended Amount
101	10	2	998
101	50	1	449
102	10	1	499
102	20	3	2097
102	30	2	1798
103	50	2	898
104	40	1	789
105	10	3	1497
105	20	1	699
105	30	2	1798

Record: 11 of 11

Customer : Table

Customer #	Customer Nam	Street	City	State
151	D. Ainge	123 Lotus Lane	Phoenix	AZ
152	G. Kite	40 Quatro Road	Mesa	AZ
153	F. Roberts	401 Excel Way	Chandler	AZ

Record: 4 of 4

Inventory : Table

Item #	Unit Price	Description
10	499	Television
20	699	Freezer
30	899	Refrigerator
40	789	Range
50	449	Microwave

Record: 6 of 6

106

Table 4A-2   Query 1

Show the dates and invoice totals for all sales in October, arranged in descending order by amount of the sale

Sales Invoice #	Date	Salesperson	Customer #	Invoice Total
101	10/15/03	J. Buck	151	1447
102	10/15/03	S. Knight	152	4394
103	10/28/03	S. Knight	151	898
104	10/31/03	J. Buck	152	709
105	11/14/03	J. Buck	153	3994

Sales : Table — Record: 6 of 6

The SELECT clause in the query invokes the relational PROJECT operation to display only the date and invoice total columns. The FROM clause specifies that these columns are to be found in the sales table. The WHERE clause then invokes the relational RESTRICT operation to display only those rows representing sales made during October. The ORDER BY clause specifies that the answer should be displayed in descending order by the amount in the invoice total column.

Date	Invoice Total
10/15/03	4394.00
10/15/03	1447.00
10/28/03	898.00
10/31/03	789.00

Query Response : Table — Record: 4

Analysis of SQL

As seen from these five examples, SQL is simple to use yet quite powerful. SQL's simplicity allows users to specify the desired result without having to specify how the data are to be retrieved. All five example queries specified only the conditions to be met in providing the answer; no looping or procedural commands were required to tell the system how to search for the desired records.

The simplicity of SQL reflects the properties of the relational data model, especially the nonimportance of row and column order. In contrast, the location of a data item in a nonrelational DBMS does provide important information. Consequently, users and application programmers working with nonrelational DBMSs must know how to navigate through the database to find the answers to their queries. For example, a DBMS based on the hierarchical (or tree) data model (e.g., IBM's IMS) represents data as being stored in hierarchies. Users of a hierarchical DBMS must navigate up and down the hierarchy to retrieve the desired data.

What are the invoice numbers of all sales made to D. Ainge, and who completed these sales?

Sales Invoice #	Date	Salesperson	Customer #	Invoice Total
101	10/15/03	J. Buck	151	1447
102	10/15/03	S. Knight	152	4394
103	10/28/03	S. Knight	151	898
104	10/31/03	J. Buck	152	789
105	11/14/03	J. Buck	153	3994

Sales : Table — Record: 6 of 6

The SELECT clause in the query invokes the relational PROJECT operation to select the shaded columns in the sales and customer tables. The FROM clause instructs the DBMS to apply the JOIN operator to the sales and customer tables. The first WHERE clause specifies that customer #, the common column in both tables, is used to join them.

Customer : Table

Customer #	Customer Name	Street	City	State
151	D. Ainge	123 Lotus Lane	Phoenix	AZ
152	G. Kite	40 Quatro Road	Mesa	AZ
153	F. Roberts	401 Excel Way	Chandler	AZ

Record: 4 of 4

Temp : Table

Sales Invoice #	Salesperson	Customer Name
101	J. Buck	D. Ainge
102	S. Knight	G. Kite
103	S. Knight	D. Ainge
104	J. Buck	G. Kite
105	J. Buck	F. Roberts

Record: 6 of 21

This temporary table is the result of executing the relational PROJECT and JOIN operations specified in the query. This temporary table would *not* appear on the screen; it is presented for illustrative purposes only. The second WHERE clause then invokes the relational RESTRICT operation to select only the shaded rows for display.

Query Response: Table

Sales Invoice #	Salesperson	Customer Name
101	J. Buck	D. Ainge
103	S. Knight	D. Ainge

Record: 3 of 21

The completed query looks like this. The customer name column can be deleted, if desired.

How many televisions were sold in October?

Sales : Table					
	Sales Invoice #	**Date**	**Salesperson**	**Customer #**	**Invoice Total**
	101	10/15/03	J. Buck	151	1447
	102	10/15/03	S. Knight	152	4394
	103	10/28/03	S. Knight	151	898
	104	10/31/03	J. Buck	152	789
	105	11/14/03	J. Buck	153	3994

Record: 6 of 6

This query needs information from the sales, line item, and inventory tables. The SELECT clause in the query invokes the relational PROJECT operation to select the shaded columns in all three tables. Those columns are joined to form a temporary table (not shown). The WHERE clause specifies the basis for linking the tables using columns common to each table (see arrows). It also invokes the relational RESTRICT operation to display only those rows that meet the query criteria.

Line Item : Table			
Sales Invoice #	**Item #**	**Quantity**	**Extended Amount**
101	10	2	998
101	50	1	449
102	10	1	499
102	20	3	2097
102	30	2	1798
103	50	2	898
104	40	1	789
105	10	3	1497
105	20	1	699
105	30	2	1798

Record: 11 of 11

Common fields in the files are used to link the tables, as shown by the arrows.

Inventory : Table		
Item #	**Unit Price**	**Description**
10	499	Television
20	699	Freezer
30	899	Refrigerator
40	789	Range
50	449	Microwave

Record: 6 of 6

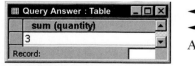

Query Answer : Table
sum (quantity)
3

Record:

Answer

109

Table 4A-5   Query 4

Display the names and addresses of all customers buying televisions in October

Inventory : Table

Item #	Unit Price	Description
10	499	Television
20	699	Freezer
30	899	Refrigerator
40	789	Range
50	449	Microwave

Record: |◄ ◄| 6 |► ►| ►*| of 6

The answer to this query only displays data taken from the customer table. However, data from all four tables are used to answer the query. The data used in each table are shaded. The description column in the inventory table is used to decide what item number relates to televisions (10).

Line Item : Table

Sales Invoice #	Item #	Quantity	Extended Amount
101	10	2	998
101	50	1	449
102	10	1	499
102	20	3	2097
102	30	2	1798
103	50	2	898
104	40	1	789
105	10	3	1497
105	20	1	699
105	30	2	1798

Record: |◄ ◄| 11 |► ►| ►*| of 11

The item number column in the line item table is used to identify on which invoice numbers televisions were sold (101, 102, and 105).

Sales : Table

Sales Invoice #	Date	Salesperson	Customer #	Invoice Total
101	10/15/03	J. Buck	151	1447
102	10/15/03	S. Knight	152	4394
103	10/28/03	S. Knight	151	898
104	10/31/03	J. Buck	152	789
105	11/14/03	J. Buck	153	3994

Record: |◄ ◄| 6 |► ►| ►*| of 6

The date column in the sales table is used to identify sales made in October (invoices 101,102).

Customer : Table

Customer #	Customer Name	Street	City	State
151	D. Ainge	123 Lotus Lane	Phoenix	AZ
152	G. Kite	40 Quatro Road	Mesa	AZ
153	F. Roberts	401 Excel Way	Chandler	AZ

Record: |◄ ◄| 4 |► ►| ►*| of 4

Sales invoices 101 and 102 correspond to customers 151 and 152. Those names and addresses are retrieved from the customer table and displayed as shown below.

Query Answer : Table

Customer Name	Street	City	State
D. Ainge	123 Lotus Lane	Phoenix	AZ
G. Kite	40 Quatro Road	Mesa	AZ

Record: |◄ ◄| 3 |► ►| ►*| of 21

Answer

Table 4A-6   Query 5

How much did each salesperson sell?

Sales Invoice #	Date	Salesperson	Customer #	Invoice Total
101	10/15/03	J. Buck	151	1447
102	10/15/03	S. Knight	152	4394
103	10/28/03	S. Knight	151	898
104	10/31/03	J. Buck	152	789
105	11/14/03	J. Buck	153	3994

Record: 6 of 6

The GROUP BY clause in the query directs that the invoice total column be summed for all rows in the sales table having the same value in the salesperson column (as indicated by the arrows).

Sum (Invoice Total)	Salesperson
6230.00	J. Buck
5292.00	S. Knight

Record: 2 of 21

Although providing such specific navigational instructions may, in some cases, result in faster retrieval times, it poses an extra burden on the end user to be aware of at least some aspects of the database structure. It also requires that special operators be included in the query language for using pointers or otherwise navigating from one record to another. This makes it harder for users to write ad hoc queries, which in turn increases the demands placed on application programmers to write those queries for users.

SQL is powerful because it is set based; every query inherently returns a subset of the tables referenced. In contrast, traditional programming languages such as COBOL, FOR-TRAN, and BASIC operate on just one record (row in a table) at a time. Consequently, using one of those languages to write these queries would have been much more complicated.

Graphical Query Languages

Most relational DBMSs also provide graphical query languages, which enable users to write queries by designing an example of what the desired answer should look like, instead of writing SQL code. Figure 4A-1 shows an example of a graphical language query and its SQL equivalent. Usually, the DBMS translates these "query-by-example" queries into the equivalent set of SQL commands in order to retrieve the desired data.

SQL Query: SELECT   Description, Sum (Qty Pur)
                 FROM   Inv-Pur, Inventory
                 WHERE   Inventory Item# = Inv-Pur Item#
                 GROUP BY   Description

The same query as written using the graphical language in ACCESS:

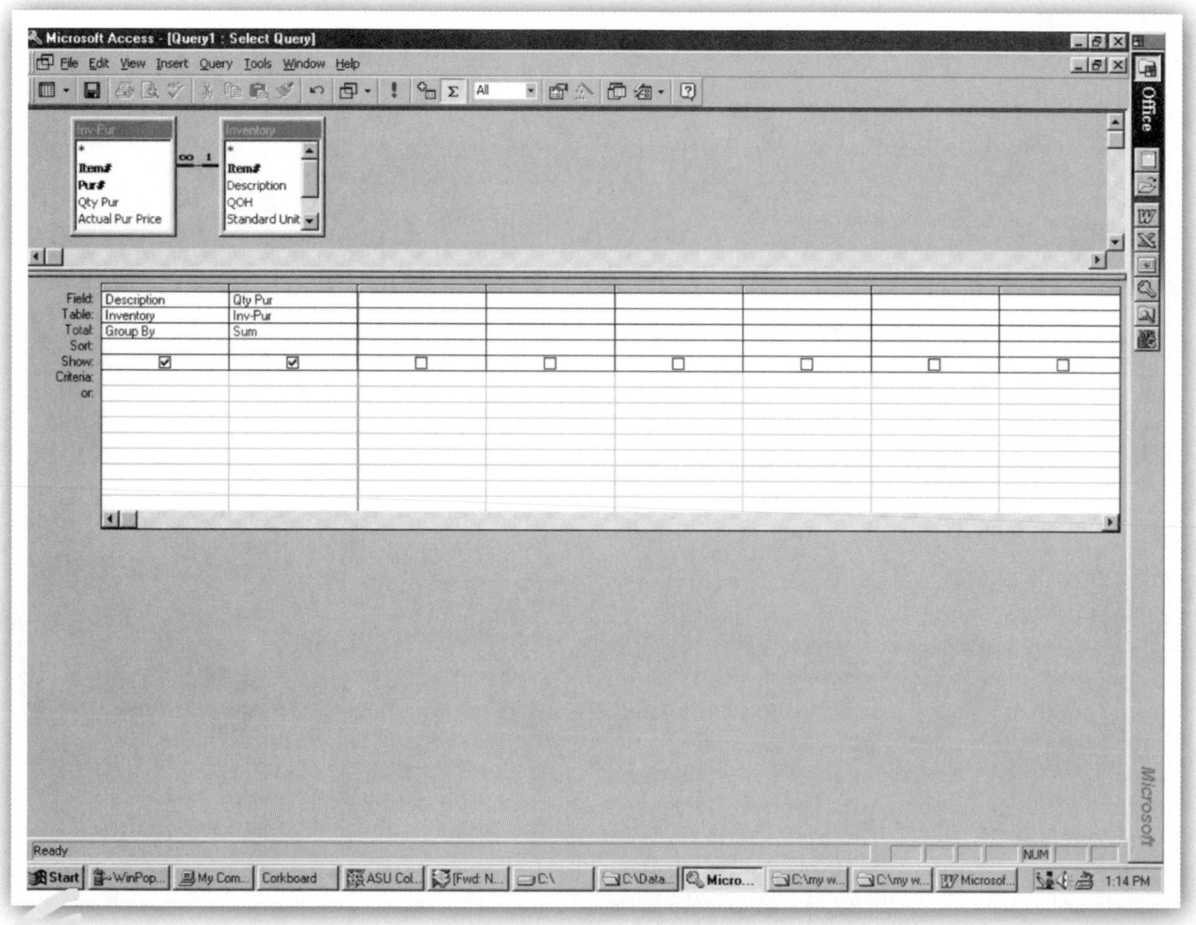

Figure 4A-1   Graphical language query and SQL equivalent

KEY TERM

• structured query language (SQL)

Data Modeling and Database Design

Learning Objectives

After studying this chapter, you should be able to:

- Discuss the steps for designing and implementing a database system.
- Use the REA data model to design an AIS database.
- Draw an entity-relationship (E-R) diagram of an AIS database.
- Build a set of tables to implement an REA model of an AIS in a relational database.
- Read an E-R diagram and explain what it reveals about the business activities and policies of the organization being modeled.

Integrative Case: S&S, Inc.

Ashton Fleming is frustrated. He is finding it difficult to communicate with the consultants about the desired structure of S&S's new database AIS. The consultants bring him lists of tables and attributes that will be included in the system, but Ashton is not confident that the proposed design will satisfy all of S&S's needs.

While mulling over his situation, Ashton began to sort through his stack of mail from the AICPA and his state CPA society. Suddenly, something caught his attention: a flyer announcing a two-day seminar on data modeling and database design to be held next week at a downtown hotel. The seminar's objective is to teach accountants how to design a relational database—and how to effectively communicate that design to others. Ashton immediately called and learned that registration was still open. He explained to Susan the benefits he thought the seminar could provide and Susan agreed to send him.

Ashton hopes to have answers for the following questions by the end of the seminar:

1. What are the basic steps to follow when designing a database?
2. When creating a relational database, how exactly do you decide which attributes belong in which tables?
3. How can you document an AIS that is implemented as a relational database?

INTRODUCTION

Like many companies, S&S is converting to the database approach for storing its accounting data. In this chapter, you will learn how to design and document a relational database for an accounting information system. You will see that there is much more to building a database than simply learning the syntax of how to use a particular DBMS. Building accurate databases requires a great deal of careful planning and design *before* you even sit down at the computer.

This chapter focuses on data modeling, one aspect of database design that accountants should understand. We introduce the REA accounting model and entity-relationship (E-R) diagrams and show how to use these tools to build a data model of an AIS. Then we describe how to implement the resulting data model in a relational database. Keep in mind, however, that although our discussion focuses on relational databases, the principles apply to building any type of database.

DATABASE DESIGN PROCESS

Figure 5-1 shows the six basic steps in database design. The first stage consists of initial planning to determine the need for and feasibility of developing a new system. This stage includes preliminary judgments about the proposal's technological and economic feasibility. The second stage includes identifying user information needs, defining the scope of the proposed new system, and using information about the expected number of users and transaction volumes to help you make preliminary decisions about hardware and software requirements. The third stage includes developing the different schemas for the new system, at the conceptual, external, and internal levels. The fourth stage consists of translating the internal-level schema into the actual database structures that will be implemented in the new system. This is also the stage when new applications are developed. The implementation stage includes all the activities associated with transferring data from existing systems to the new database AIS, testing the new system, and training employees how to use it. The final stage addresses using and maintaining the new system. This includes carefully monitoring system performance and user satisfaction to determine the need for making system enhancements and modifications. Eventually, changes in business strategies and practices or significant new developments in information technology initiate investigation into the feasibility of developing a new system and the entire process starts again (note the arrow returning to the planning stage).

Accountants can and should participate in all stages of the database design process, although the level of their participation in each stage is likely to vary. In the planning stage, accountants both provide some of the information used to evaluate the feasibility of the proposed project and participate in making that decision. In the requirements analysis and design stages, accountants participate in identifying user information needs, developing the logical schemas, designing the data dictionary, and specifying controls. Accountants with good AIS skills may participate in the coding stage. During the implementation stage, accountants can help test the accuracy of the new database and the application programs that will use that data. Finally, accountants use the database system to process transactions, and sometimes they even help manage it.

Accountants may provide the greatest value to their organizations by taking responsibility for data modeling. **Data modeling** is the process of defining a database

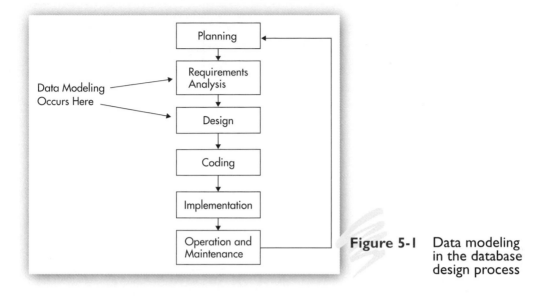

Figure 5-1   Data modeling in the database design process

so that it faithfully represents all aspects of the organization, including its interactions with the external environment. As shown in Figure 5-1, data modeling occurs during both the requirements analysis and design stages of database design. Two important tools that accountants can use to facilitate participation in data modeling are entity-relationship diagramming and the REA data model.

ENTITY-RELATIONSHIP DIAGRAMS

An **entity-relationship (E-R) diagram** is a graphical technique for portraying a database schema.[1] It is called an E-R diagram because it shows the various *entities* being modeled and the important *relationships* among them. An **entity** is anything about which the organization wants to collect and store information. In an E-R diagram, entities appear as rectangles, and relationships between entities are represented as diamonds. For example, the top E-R diagram in Figure 5-2 shows that most organizations collect and maintain information about their employees, supervisors, and departments. The middle E-R diagram shows that organizations also probably want to collect and maintain information about business transactions such as customer orders, sales, and cash receipts. The bottom diagram in the figure shows that E-R diagrams can be drawn for any purpose, such as modeling important components of sports.

An E-R diagram not only depicts the contents of a database, but also graphically models an organization. Thus, E-R diagrams can be used not only to design databases, but also to document and understand existing databases and to reengineer business processes. Business process reengineering is covered in Part IV; in this chapter we focus on using E-R diagrams for database design and for understanding the contents of existing databases.

---

[1]The material in this section is based on P. Chen, "The Entity Relationship Model—Toward a Unified View of Data," *Transactions on Database Systems* (March 1976, 1:1): 9–36.

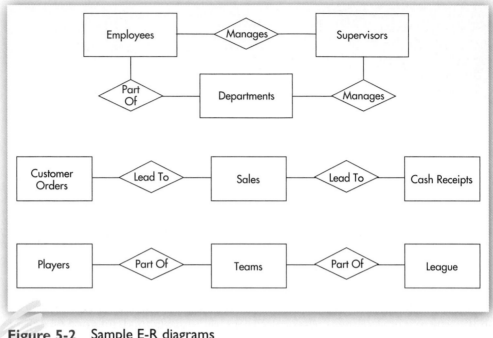

Figure 5-2   Sample E-R diagrams

As shown in Figure 5-2, E-R diagrams can include many different kinds of entities and relationships among those entities. An important step in database design, therefore, entails deciding which entities need to be modeled. The REA data model is useful for making that decision.

THE REA DATA MODEL

Specifically used for AIS database design, the **REA data model** is a conceptual modeling tool that focuses on the business semantics underlying an organization's value chain activities.[2] The REA data model provides guidance for database design by identifying what entities should be included in the AIS database and by prescribing how to structure relationships among the entities in that database.

Types of Entities

The REA data model classifies entities into three distinct categories: the *resources* the organization acquires and uses, the *events* (business activities) in which the organiza-

[2]The material in this section is adapted from William E. McCarthy, "An Entity-Relationship View of Accounting Models," *The Accounting Review* (October 1979): 667–686; William E. McCarthy, "The REA Accounting Model: A Generalized Framework for Accounting Systems in a Shared Data Environment," *The Accounting Review* (July 1982) : 554–578; and Guido L. Geerts and W.E. McCarthy, "An Ontological Analysis of the Primitives of the Extended-REA Enterprise Information Architecture," *Proceedings of the 7th Annual AIS Reasearch Symposium,* February 18-19, 2000 (Scottsdale, Arizona).

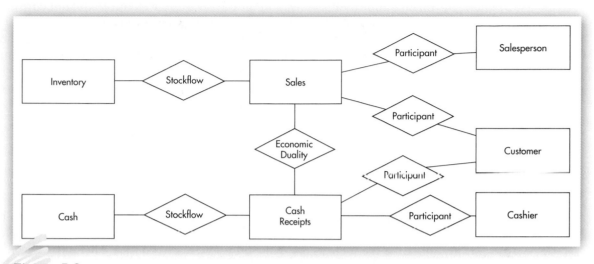

Figure 5-3   Sample REA diagram

tion engages, and the *a*gents participating in these events.[3] Figure 5-3 provides examples of these entities.

   Resources are those things that have economic value to the organization. In Figure 5-3, cash and inventory are resource entities. Machinery and equipment, supplies, warehouses, factories, and land are examples of other common organizational resources.

   Events are the various business activities about which management wants to collect information for planning or control purposes.[4] There are two event entities in Figure 5-3: sales and cash receipts.

   The REA data model helps people design databases that support the management of an organization's value chain activities. Therefore, most of the events in an REA data model fall into one of two categories: economic exchanges or commitments. **Economic exchanges** are the value chain activities that directly affect the quantity of resources. For example, the sales event decreases the quantity of inventory and the cash receipts event increases the amount of cash. **Commitments** represent promises to engage in future economic exchanges. For example, customer orders are commitments that lead to future sales. Often such commitments are necessary precursors to the subsequent economic exchange. Moreover, management

---

[3]Recently, some researchers have proposed a fourth type of entity, which they call locations. Stores and warehouses would be examples of this fourth type of entity. Nevertheless, such "location" entities are usually also resourses controlled by the organization. Therefore, the authors of this text see no compelling reason to create yet another type of entity and model locations as resources. If the locations at which events occur are not owned by the organization being modeled, location information should be stored as an attribute of the event.

[4]The discussion of events in this section is based on the work of Julie Smith David, "Three 'Events' That Define an REA Methodology for Systems Analysis, Design, and Implementation," working paper, Arizona State University, August 1997, and Guido L. Geerts and W.E. McCarthy, "An Ontological Analysis of the Primitives of the Extended-REA Enterprise Information Architecture," *Proceedings of the 7th Annual AIS Reasearch Symposium*, February: 18-19, 2000 (Scottsdale, Arizona).

needs to track commitments for planning purposes. For example, manufacturing firms often use information from customer orders to plan production.

Agents are the third type of entity in the REA model. **Agents** are the people and organizations that participate in events and about whom information is desired for planning, control, and evaluation purposes. Figure 5-3 includes two types of agent entities: employees (salesperson and cashier) and customers. Suppliers (or vendors) are another type of agent that would appear in an REA diagram of the expenditure cycle.

Basic REA Template

The REA data model prescribes a basic pattern for how the three types of entities (resources, events, and agents) should relate to one another. Figure 5-4 presents this basic pattern. Each event entity is linked to a resource entity. Events, such as the sale of merchandise, that change the quantity of a resource are linked to that resource in what is called a stockflow relationship. Other events, such as taking a customer order, that represent future commitments are linked to resources in what are called reserve relationships. Each event entity is also linked to two agent entities. The internal agent is the employee who is responsible for the resource affected by that event; the external agent is the outside party to the transaction.

Figure 5-4 also shows that each economic exchange event is linked in a give-to-get duality relationship with another economic exchange event. These economic duality relationships reflect the basic business principle that organizations typically engage

Figure 5-4   Basic REA template

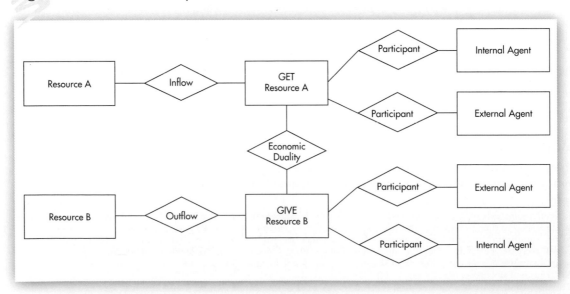

Source: Adapted from Figure 6 (p. 566) in William E. McCarthy, "The REA Accounting Model: A Generalized Framework for Accounting Systems in a Shared Data Environment," *The Accounting Review* (July 1982): 554–578; and Figure 1 (p. 35) in Cheryl L. Dunn and William E. McCarthy, "The REA Model: Intellectual Heritage and Prospects for Progress," *Journal of Information Systems* (Spring 1997): 31–51.

in activities that use up resources only in the hopes of acquiring some other resource in exchange. For example, the sales event, which requires giving up (decreasing) inventory, is related to the cash receipts event, which requires getting (increasing) the amount of cash. Indeed, Figure 5-5 shows that each accounting cycle can be described in terms of such give-to-get economic duality relationships.

Figures 5-3 through 5-5 show that the REA data model can be depicted using E-R diagrams. In the remainder of this chapter and throughout the book, we will refer to an E-R diagram developed according to the REA data model as an REA diagram. Let us now explain how to develop an REA diagram.

DEVELOPING AN REA DIAGRAM FOR ONE TRANSACTION CYCLE

Figure 5-6 shows the REA diagram Ashton developed for S&S's revenue cycle. This section explains how to develop such a diagram. Keep in mind that Figure 5-6 models only a subset of all S&S's business activities. To design an entire AIS for S&S, Ashton not only needs to further enhance this basic model, but must also develop similar models for S&S's other transaction cycles and then integrate those separate diagrams into an enterprise-wide model.

Developing an REA diagram for a specific transaction cycle consists of the following four steps:

1. Identify the pair of economic exchange events that represent the basic give-to-get economic duality relationship in that cycle.
2. Identify the resources affected by each economic exchange event and the agents who participate in those events.
3. Analyze each economic exchange event to determine whether it should be decomposed into a combination of one or more commitment events and an economic exchange event. If necessary, replace the original economic exchange event with the resulting set of commitment and economic exchange events.
4. Determine the cardinalities of each relationship.

Let us follow these four steps to see how Ashton developed Figure 5-6 to model S&S's revenue cycle.

Step 1: Identify Economic Exchange Events

Figure 5-4 shows that the basic REA template consists of a pair of events, one that increases some resource and one that decreases some resource. The basic economic exchange in the revenue cycle involves the sale of goods or services and the subsequent receipt of cash in payment for those sales. Thus, Ashton begins drawing the REA diagram for S&S's revenue cycle by creating the sales and cash receipts events entities as rectangles, and the economic duality relationship between them as a diamond.

In drawing an REA diagram for an *individual* transaction cycle, it is useful to divide the paper into three columns, one for each type of entity. Use the left column for resources, the center column for events, and the right column for agents. Readability is further enhanced if the event entities are drawn from top to bottom

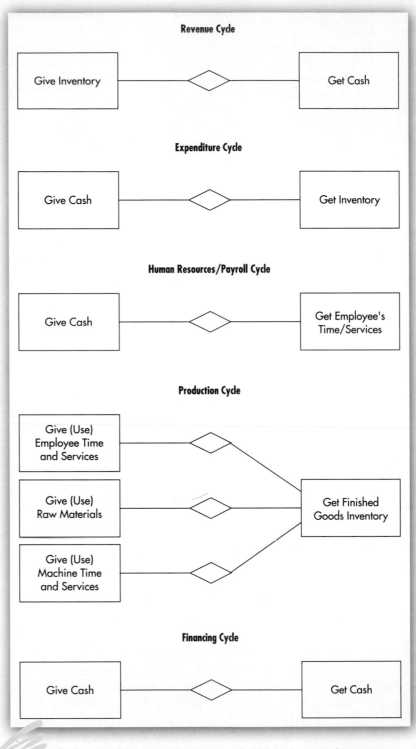

Figure 5-5 An AIS viewed as a set of give-to-get exchanges

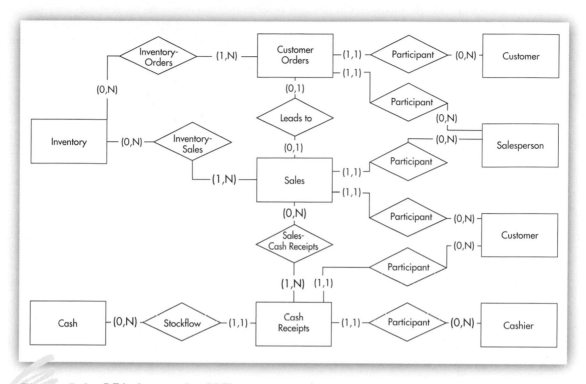

Figure 5-6   REA diagram for S&S's revenue cycle

corresponding to the sequence in which they occur. Thus, Ashton begins to draw Figure 5-6 by showing the sales event entity above the cash receipts event entity in the center column of the paper.[5]

Step 2: Identify Resources and Agents

Once the events of interest have been specified, the resources that are affected by those events need to be identified. To continue our example, Ashton observed that the sales event translates to giving inventory to customers and that the cash receipts event translates to receiving cash from customers. Therefore, he added the inventory and cash entities in the resources column and drew the stockflow relationships between those entities and the events that affected them.

What about accounts receivable? Accounts receivable is not modeled as a separate entity because it is not an independent object, but simply represents a timing difference between two events: sales and cash receipts. That is, accounts receivable simply represents sales for which customer payments have not yet been received. Consequently, if data about both sales and cash collections are already stored in the

---

[5]Placement conventions, such as the use of columns and sequential ordering of events, are not *required* to use the REA model to design a database. We suggest these rules only because following them often simplifies the process of drawing an REA diagram and produces REA diagrams that are easy to read.

database, all the information needed to calculate accounts receivable can be derived from the information stored about those two events. Later in this chapter we will explain how to extract information about accounts receivable from an AIS database built using the REA data model.

After specifying the resources affected by each event, it is necessary to identify the agents who participate in those events. There will always be at least one internal agent (employee) and, in most cases, an external agent (customer or vendor) who participate in each event. In the case of S&S's revenue cycle, customers and salespersons participate in the sales event. Customers and the cashier participate in the cash receipts event. Thus, Ashton included three agent entities in the REA diagram of S&S's revenue cycle: salespersons, customers, and cashiers. He then added relationships to indicate which agents participated in which events. To reduce clutter, he did not draw multiple copies of the customer entity.[6]

It is important to understand that the agents in an REA data model represent *functions,* not specific people. Thus, in Figure 5-6, Ashton modeled both the salesperson and cashier agents as separate entities. It is possible, however, that the same person may fill both roles. For example, in a cash sale, the salesperson also may act as the cashier and collect payment from the customer. The REA diagram would still include two agents to model this situation, however.

Finally, Ashton considered whether he needed to add any other relationships of interest between entities. The REA model requires that each event be linked to at least one resource and to at least two agents. This information needs to be supplemented by interviews with management to identify other possible relationships of interest. For example, if the organization assigns customers to specific salespeople to provide customized service, then a direct relationship between the two agent entities (salesperson and customer) would be added to the diagram. Ashton decided that he did not need to include any such relationship for S&S. At this point, his REA diagram for the revenue cycle looked like Figure 5-3.

Step 3: Include Commitment Events

The third step in drawing an REA diagram is analyzing each economic exchange event to determine whether it can be decomposed into a combination of one or more commitment and exchange events. Although Figure 5-3 accurately models S&S's sales to customers who come to the store, Ashton knows that S&S also receives orders from customers in three ways: over the Internet, by phone, and by mail. It is important that S&S has accurate up-to-date information about these orders so that Scott and Susan know when to reorder various inventory items. It is also important to know which orders have been shipped and when. Therefore, Ashton decides to replace the single economic exchange event labeled *sales* in Figure 5-3 with the combination of a commitment event, which he labels *customer orders,* and the economic exchange event, for which he keeps the label *sales.* Ashton decides that the sales event can be used to represent both shipments and in-store sales, because S&S collects almost identical information about both types of sales. The primary difference between the two events is that in-store sales will not have any shipping document number.

---

[6]As the number of entities in an REA diagram increases, a point may be reached where the diagram is easier to read if there are multiple copies of the same entity.

Ashton does not decompose the cash receipts economic exchange event, however. Whether the customer payment is received at the time the sale is made, as with most in-store purchases, or later by mail, the only thing S&S needs to track is the actual receipt of the payment.

But what about billing customers? Ashton did not model billing as an event because it is neither an economic exchange nor a commitment. Printing an invoice and mailing it to a customer does not increase or decrease the amount of any resource. Neither does it represent the organization's commitment to engage in a future economic exchange. The customer's obligation to pay the organization arises not from the billing activity, but from the delivery of the merchandise. The billing activity is simply an information-processing event that merely retrieves information from the database about previous customer orders and sales events. Organizations build databases to collect, process, and store information about their value chain activities. Printing documents and reports or querying the database, however, are just different ways of retrieving information about those activities for use in making decisions. Such information-processing activities do not change the contents of the database and, therefore, are not modeled as events in an REA diagram. Consequently, the activity of printing and mailing invoices does not need to appear in an REA diagram of an organization's revenue cycle.

Step 4: Determine Cardinalities of Relationships

The final step in drawing an REA diagram for one transaction cycle is to add information about the nature of the relationships between the various entities. In this text, we adopt the Batini[7] notation for representing cardinality information. Thus, the pairs of letters and numbers enclosed in parentheses next to each entity in Figure 5-6 represents the minimum and maximum cardinalities, respectively, with which that entity participates in that relationship. Unfortunately, no universal standard exists for representing information about cardinalities in REA diagrams. This chapter's appendix compares the notation used in this book with other commonly used conventions. Fortunately, once you understand what cardinalities mean, it is rather simple to translate from one notation to another.

What Are Cardinalities?   Entities represent a class or set of objects. For example, the customer entity represents all of the organization's customers and the sales entity represents all the individual sales transactions that occur during the current fiscal period. Each individual customer or sales transaction represents a specific instance of that entity.

Cardinalities indicate how many instances of one entity can be linked to one specific instance of another entity. For example, cardinalities indicate how many sales transactions can be linked to each individual customer and, conversely, how many customers can be linked to each individual sales transaction. In a relational database, each entity is a table and each instance is a row in that table. Therefore, in relational databases, cardinalities indicate how many rows in one table can be linked to each row in another table.

Figure 5-6 represents cardinalities as pairs of numbers next to each entity. The first number is the **minimum cardinality.** It indicates whether a row in this table *must* be linked to at least one row in the table on the opposite side of that relationship. A

---

[7]C. Batini, S. Ceri, and S. B. Navathe. 1992. *Conceptual Database Design. An Entity-Relationship Approach.* (Benjamin-Cummings: Redwood City, CA).

minimum cardinality of zero (0) means that a new row can be added to that table without being linked to any specific rows in the table on the other side of the relationship. For example, in Figure 5-6, the minimum cardinality of 0 next to the customer entity in the customer-sales relationship indicates that information about new (prospective) customers can be added to the customer table without having to be linked to any specific sales transactions. In contrast, a minimum cardinality of one (1) means that each row in that table must be linked to at least one row in the other table participating in that relationship. For example, in Figure 5-6, the minimum cardinality of 1 next to the sales entity in the customer-sales relationship indicates that information about a new sales transaction can be added only if it is linked to a row in the customer table.

The second number in each cardinality pair is the **maximum cardinality.** It indicates whether one row in that table *can* be linked to more than one row in the other table. A maximum cardinality of 1 means that each row in that table can be linked to, at most, only one row in the other table. Notice in the customer-sales relationship depicted in Figure 5-6 that the maximum cardinality next to the sales entity is 1. This means that each sales transaction can be linked to only one specific customer. In contrast, notice that the maximum cardinality next to the customer entity is N (which stands for *many*). This means that each row in the customer table can (but need not) be linked to more than one row in the sales table.

Three Types of Relationships   Three basic types of relationships between entities are possible, depending on the *maximum* cardinality associated with each entity.

1. A **one-to-one (1:1) relationship** exists when the maximum cardinality for each entity in that relationship is 1 (see Figure 5-7, Panel A).
2. A **one-to-many (1:N) relationship** exists when the maximum cardinality of one entity in the relationship is 1 and the maximum cardinality for the other entity in that relationship is N (see Figures 5-7, Panels B and C).
3. A **many-to-many (M:N) relationship** exists when the maximum cardinality for both entities in the relationship is N (Figure 5-7, Panel D).

Figure 5-7 shows that any of these possibilities might describe the nature of the relationship between the sales and cash receipts events. Figure 5-7, Panel A depicts a one-to-one (1:1) relationship between those two events. The maximum cardinality of 1 associated with the sales entity means that each sales event (row in the sales table) can be linked to *at most* one cash receipt event. This would reflect a policy that customers are not allowed to make installment payments. At the same time, the maximum cardinality of 1 associated with each cash receipt event means that each payment a customer submits is linked to *at most* one sales event. This indicates that customers must pay for each sales transaction separately.

Figures 5-7, Panel B and 5-7, Panel C depict two ways that one-to-many (1:N) relationships can occur. Figure 5-7, Panel B shows that each sales event may be linked to *many* cash receipt events. This indicates that customers may make installment payments, although they are not required. Figure 5-7, Panel B also shows, however, that each cash receipt event is linked to *at most* one sales event. This indicates that customers must pay for each sales transaction separately; they cannot build up an account balance over a period of time. In contrast, Figure 5-7, Panel C shows that each sales event can be linked to *at most* one cash receipt event. This indicates that customers cannot make installment payments. Figure 5-7, Panel C also shows that each cash receipt event *may* be linked to many different sales events. This indicates the existence of a policy allowing customers

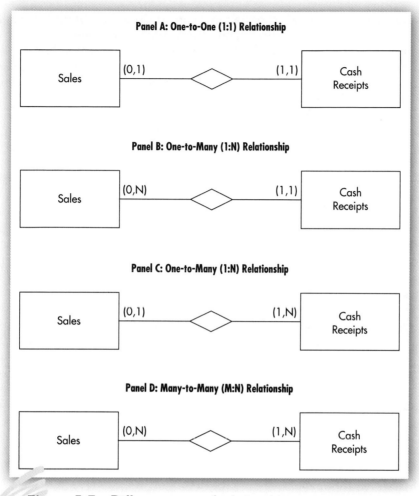

Figure 5-7   Different types of relationships

to make a number of purchases during a period of time (e.g., a month) and then pay off those purchases with one payment.

Figure 5-7, Panel D depicts a many-to-many (M:N) relationship between the sales and cash receipt events: Each sales event may be linked to *one or more* cash receipt events and each cash receipt event may be linked to *one or more* sales events. This reflects a situation in which the organization makes some cash sales, makes some sales that customers pay for in installments, and allows customers to pay for more than one sale with a single remittance.

Caution: Do not confuse the notation used for minimum and maximum cardinalities (a pair of numbers separated by a comma) with the notation used to describe the cardinality of a relationship between two entities (a pair of numbers separated by a colon).

Rules for Specifying Cardinalities   The database designer does not arbitrarily choose cardinalities. Instead, cardinalities reflect facts about the organization being modeled and its business practices. This information is obtained during the requirements definition stage of the database design process. Thus, Ashton had to clearly understand how the company conducts its business activities to ensure that Figure 5-6 was correct for S&S. Certain general principles, however, can provide a starting point for developing an REA data model for any organization.

Cardinality rules for agent-event relationships

Notice that in Figure 5-6 the minimum and maximum cardinalities associated with the event entity in every agent-event relationship are both one (1). This is almost always the case. The minimum cardinality associated with the event entity is 1 because there *must* be some agent who participates in that event. For example, a sales event must be linked to a customer. The maximum cardinality is usually also 1, because the organization wants to be able to hold some specific agent responsible for that event. To continue the previous example, a sale is made to some specific identifiable customer who is expected to pay for that sale. Similarly, to assign credit to the appropriate employee, the maximum cardinality of the event entity in relationships with internal agents (e.g., for the sales event, a salesperson) is also usually 1.

There is also a general principle concerning the cardinalities associated with the agent entity in agent-event relationships. Notice that in Figure 5-6 the cardinalities associated with each agent in the agent-event relationships all have zero minimums and N maximums. This combination is also quite typical. The maximum cardinality associated with internal agent entities in agent-event relationships is almost always N, because organizations expect that their employees will participate in numerous events. It is also usually N for external agents, because organizations often engage in repeat transactions with the same suppliers and customers. There are two reasons why the minimum cardinality associated with agent entities in agent-event relationships is usually zero (0). First, organizations want to be able to add information about potential customers and suppliers even though those agents may not have participated (yet) in any business transactions. Second, event entities are analogous to transaction files, whereas agent entities are analogous to master files. At the end of a fiscal year, the contents of event tables are typically archived and the new fiscal year begins with no rows in the various event tables. In contrast, information about agents is permanent in nature and is carried over from one fiscal period to the next. Therefore, at the beginning of a new fiscal year, customers may not be linked to any current sales events.

Thus, Ashton began by assuming that every agent-event relationship could be modeled according to this pattern: Event (1,1)-(0,N) Agent. Ashton then interviewed Scott and Susan to determine whether he needed to modify that assumption. Learning that there were no exceptions to this general practice, he left those cardinalities as shown in Figure 5-6.

Cardinality rules for resource-event relationships

Notice in Figure 5-6 that the minimum and maximum cardinalities associated with each resource in resource-event relationships are zero (0) and N, respectively. This is typical for most organizations for most resources, for the same reasons given earlier when explaining the typical minimum and maximum cardinalities associated with agents in agent-event relationships.

One exception to this general rule is that the maximum cardinality associated with the inventory resource is sometimes one (1). Figure 5-6 reflects the fact that S&S sells mass-produced merchandise. For each type of item carried, S&S must know the quantity on hand and quantity available for sale. The company also must know the quantity of each item bought or sold. S&S does not attempt to track which specific physical item was included in a given transaction, however. Consequently, each row in the inventory table in Figure 5-6 represents a kind of item. For S&S, the primary key is item number. Other organizations may call the primary key a part number or SKU number. The important thing to understand is that any row in S&S's inventory table can be linked to many different rows in the sales table.

Sometimes, however, organizations do track specific physical inventory items. Examples include original artwork, vehicles, or houses. For such merchandise, each row in the inventory table would represent a specific painting or house and would be identified by a primary key that is some type of serial ID number. In such cases, a given row in the inventory table could be associated with at most one sales transaction and, accordingly, would have a maximum cardinality of 1 instead of N.

Now consider the cardinalities associated with the event entity in resource-event relationships. Figure 5-6 reflects the general principle that the minimum cardinality associated with event entities in resource-event relationships is usually 1. For example, each sales event *must* include at least one row in the inventory table (for a sale to occur, S&S has to sell something). Similarly, each payment received from a customer must be deposited into some cash account. The only exception to this general rule arises if an event potentially can be linked to more than one resource entity. Consider an automobile repair business. Some services, such as tire rotations, may not include the sale of any parts; whereas other services, such as a brake repair, include both labor and parts. Thus, the sales event for such an auto repair business could be linked to an inventory entity, or to a repair services entity, or to both types of resources. Consequently, the minimum cardinality for the sales event would be 0 in both of those relationships. (Note: In rare situations, an event might be linked to one of several unique agent entities. In such cases, the minimum cardinality associated with the event entity again would be 0 instead of the normal 1.)

There are no general principles concerning the maximum cardinality associated with event entities in resource-event relationships, however. Instead, the maximum cardinality for an event depends on the nature of the resource affected by that event and by the organization's business policies. For example, Figure 5-6 shows that each cash receipt event can be linked to at most only one cash account. This indicates that S&S is following sound business practices and depositing all customer payments into its general checking account. (Scott and Susan may subsequently transfer excess monies to special investment accounts.) In contrast, Figure 5-6 shows that each customer order and sales event can be linked to many rows in the inventory table, because S&S allows, indeed encourages, its customers to order and buy as many different kinds of products as they desire. For example, a given sales transaction might include both a 21-inch monitor and a photo-quality printer. Consequently, in Figure 5-6, the maximum cardinality for both the customer orders and sales entities in their relationships with the inventory table is N.

Cardinality rules for event-event relationships

Figure 5-7 shows that almost any kind of cardinality pair is possible for each event entity in event-event relationships. The organization's business practices and policies must be understood to decide which possibility is correct. Ashton learned that S&S extends credit to its customers and mails them monthly statements listing all unpaid purchases. He also learned that many customers send S&S one check to cover all their purchases during a given time period. Thus, one cash receipt event could be linked to many different sales events. S&S also allows its customers to make installment payments on large purchases; thus, a given sales event could be connected to more than one cash receipt event. That is why Ashton modeled the relationship between the sales and cash receipt events as being many-to-many.

S&S ships each customer order individually, and waits until all items are in stock before filling an order. Therefore, Ashton modeled the relationship between the customer orders and sales events as being one-to-one.

The only general modeling principle that applies to event-event relationships is that for two temporally ordered events, the minimum cardinality for the first event is 0, because at the time it occurs, the other event has not yet happened. Often, but not always, the minimum cardinality for the event that happens second is 1, indicating that the first event had to have already occurred. For example, for companies that sell to customers either through catalogs or on the Web, customer orders (event 1) precede shipments to customers (event 2). Sometimes, however, both of the events need not occur. For example, S&S receives orders from its corporate customers before shipping them merchandise. In-store sales to walk-in customers, however, are not preceded with any order event. Consequently, in Figure 5-6, the minimum cardinality associated with the second event (sales) in the customer orders-sales relationship is also 0.

Figure 5-6 shows what Ashton's REA diagram for S&S's revenue cycle looked like after adding information about relationship cardinalities. The next step is to implement this model in a relational database.

IMPLEMENTING AN REA DIAGRAM IN A RELATIONAL DATABASE

Once an REA diagram has been developed, it can be used to design a well-structured relational database. In fact, creating a set of tables from an REA diagram automatically results in a well-structured relational database that is not subject to the update, insert, and delete anomaly problems discussed in Chapter 4.

Implementing an REA diagram in a relational database is a three-step process:

1. Create a table for each distinct entity and for each many-to-many relationship.
2. Assign attributes to appropriate tables.
3. Use foreign keys to implement one-to-one and one-to-many relationships.

Step 1: Create Tables for Each Entity and M:N Relationship

A properly designed relational database has a table for each distinct entity and for each many-to-many relationship in an REA diagram. In the case of S&S's revenue cycle shown in Figure 5-6, there are seven distinct entities: inventory, cash, customer orders, sales, cash receipts, employees, and customers. Although the REA diagram contains

Table 5-1   Facts to Be Stored in S&S's Revenue Cycle Database

Item #	Description	Cost
Price	Invoice #	Employee #
Customer #	Date	Total amount of sale
Time of sale	Employee name	Date hired
Date of birth	Pay rate	Customer name
Customer address	Customer account balance	Credit limit
Cash account #	Type of account	Cash account balance
Remittance #	Date of remittance	Amount of remittance
Amount applied to specific invoice	Call #	Date of call
Time of call	Product demonstrated	Customer called on
Salesperson making call	Customer order #	Date of order
Item ordered	Quantity ordered	Price
Customer making order	Salesperson taking order	Date of sale
Item sold	Quantity sold	Replacement or first-time purchase?

separate entities for the salesperson and the cashier, only one table, employees, is needed because S&S needs to know the identical information about its salespeople and its cashiers, such as name, date of birth, date hired, and pay rate.

Figure 5-6 also depicts three M:N relationships (customer orders-inventory, sales-inventory, and sales-cash receipts). Therefore, 10 tables are to be created to implement the REA diagram shown in Figure 5-6—one for each of the seven distinct entities and one for each of the three M:N relationships.

It is good practice to give each table the same name as the entity that it represents. Tables representing M:N relationships, however, are often titled by hyphenating the names of the two entities that are linked. Thus, in terms of Figure 5-6, we would create the tables customer orders-inventory, sales-inventory, and sales-cash receipts for those M:N relationships.

Step 2: Assign Attributes to Each Table

The next step is to determine which attributes should be included in each table.[8] During the data modeling process, users and management will have identified facts that they want to collect. Table 5-1 lists the facts that Ashton knows are essential to the database he is designing for S&S's revenue cycle.

---

[8]Some designers prefer to include attributes as part of the REA diagram. We choose not to do so in order to reduce the clutter on the diagram and to simplify our explanation of how to build the database. Regardless of when this step is preformed, identification of attributes and their proper assignment to specific entities or relationships is a critical part of database design.

Table Name	Primary Key	Foreign Keys	Other
		Attributes	
Inventory	Item #		Description, cost, price
Sales	Invoice #	Salesperson #, customer #	Date, time, amount
Employee	Employee #		Name, date hired, date of birth, pay rate
Customer	Customer #		Name, address, account balance, credit limit
Cash	Account #		Type, balance
Cash receipts	Remittance #	Customer #, cashier #	Date, amount
Customer orders	Order #	Customer #, salesperson #	Date
Orders-inventory	Order #, item #		Quantity ordered
Sales-inventory	Invoice #, item #		Quantity sold, price, replacement (Y/N)
Sales-cash receipts	Invoice #, remittance #		Amount applied

Figure 5-8   Tables created to implement REA diagram in Figure 5-6

Assign Primary Keys   Every table in a relational database must have a primary key, consisting of an attribute, or combination of attributes, that uniquely identifies each row in that table. Companies often create numeric identifiers for specific resources, events, and agents. These numeric identifiers are good candidates for primary keys. For example, S&S might use invoice number as the primary key of the sales table and customer number as the primary key of the customer table.

Usually the primary key of a table representing an entity is a single attribute. The primary key for M:N relationship tables, however, always consists of two attributes that represent the primary keys of each entity linked in that relationship. For example, the primary key of the sales-inventory table consists of both the invoice number (the primary key of the sales entity) and item number (the primary key of the inventory entity). Such multiple-attribute primary keys are called **concatenated keys.**

Assign Other Attributes to Appropriate Tables   Additional attributes besides the primary key are included in each table to satisfy transaction-processing requirements and management's information needs. Figure 5-8 shows the attributes that Ashton assigned to the various tables he created to implement S&S's revenue cycle REA diagram. Some of these attributes, such as the date and amount of each sale, are necessary for complete and accurate transaction processing and the production of financial statements and managerial reports. Other attributes are stored because they facilitate the effective management of an organization's resources, events, and agents. For example,

Scott and Susan can use data about the time when each sales transaction occurs to design staff work schedules.

Nonkey Attributes in M:N Relationship Tables   Let us examine the placement of the nonkey attributes in each of the M:N tables to see why they must be stored in those particular tables. Consider first the sales-cash receipts table. Recall that S&S allows its customers to make multiple purchases on credit and to make installment payments on their outstanding balances. Thus, one customer payment may need to be applied to several different invoices (sales transactions). Therefore, the attribute "amount applied" cannot be placed in the cash receipts table because it could take on more than one value, thereby violating the basic requirement of relational databases that every attribute in every row be single-valued (i.e., the requirement that every table be a flat file). Nor can the attribute "amount applied" be placed in the sales table, because the possibility of installment payments also creates a situation in which that attribute can have multiple values. The attribute "amount applied" is a fact about both a specific customer payment and sales transaction and, therefore, belongs in the M:N table linking those two events.

Now examine the sales-inventory table. Each row in this table contains information about a line item in an invoice. Although many of S&S's customers buy just one of each kind of product it sells, some sales to customers involve larger quantities. Consequently, S&S must record the quantity sold of each item. Each sales event, however, may include more than one inventory item. Thus, the attribute "quantity sold" may have several values on a single sales invoice, one for each item sold. Consequently, "quantity sold" cannot be an attribute in the sales table, because there can be more than one "quantity sold" associated with a given invoice number. In addition, S&S tracks inventory by kinds of items, not by specific identification. Therefore, a given item, such as Brand X's 21-inch monitor, may be sold in many different sales transactions. Consequently, "quantity sold" cannot be an attribute in the inventory table because it can take on multiple values. Therefore, because the attribute "quantity sold" applies to a specific item included in a specific sales transaction, it belongs in the M:N relationship table that links those two entities.

Price data

In Figure 5-8, notice that information about prices is stored as an attribute in both the inventory and sales-inventory tables. The inventory table stores the suggested list price for the item, which generally remains constant for a given fiscal period. The sales-inventory table stores the actual sales price, which varies during the course of the year as a result of sales promotions.

Cumulative data

Figure 5-8 also includes some attributes, such as "quantity on hand" in the inventory table and "account balance" in the customer table, that represent cumulative data. Theoretically, it is unnecessary to store these items separately in the database, because the system can readily compute them when necessary. For example, information about the quantity sold for each item is stored in the sales-inventory table. Information about quantities purchased would be stored in a similar table linking purchases and inventory. To determine quantity on hand, the AIS could simply calculate the difference between the quantity sold and the quantity purchased. In a similar manner, the cash receipts and cash disbursements tables contain information about cash inflows and outflows, respectively. The AIS can calculate the difference to display the current balance in the cash account.

Explicitly storing cumulative totals and balances, however, may improve response time to queries, which explains why Figure 5-8 shows several such summary attributes in appropriate tables. This should only be done, however, if the DBMS has the capability to automatically update these summary values as each new event occurs; otherwise, the summary values usually will be incorrect.

Step 3: Use Foreign Keys to Implement 1:1 and 1:N Relationships

M:N relationships must be implemented as separate tables to have a well-structured relational database. Although 1:1 and 1:N relationships also can be implemented as separate tables, it is usually more efficient to implement them by means of foreign keys. Recall from Chapter 4 that a foreign key is an attribute of one entity that is itself the primary key of another entity. For example, the attribute "customer number" might appear in both the customer and the sales tables. It would be the primary key of the customer table, but a foreign key in the sales table.

One-to-One Relationships   In a relational database, one-to-one relationships between entities can be implemented by including the primary key of one entity as a foreign key in the table representing the other entity. For purpose of designing a well-structured database, the choice of which table to place the foreign key in is arbitrary. Careful analysis of the minimum cardinalities of the relationship, however, may suggest which approach is likely to be more efficient.

Consider the 1:1 relationship between sales and customer payments depicted in Figure 5-7, Panel A. The minimum cardinality for the sales event is 0, indicating the existence of credit sales, and the minimum cardinality for the cash receipts event is 1, indicating that customer payments only occur after a sale has been made (e.g., there are no advance deposits). In this case, including invoice number (the primary key of the sales event) as a foreign key in the cash receipts event may be more efficient because then only that one table would have to be accessed and updated to process data about each customer payment. Moreover, for 1:1 relationships between two sequential events, including the primary key of the event that occurs first as a foreign key in the event that occurs second may improve internal control. We will talk more about internal controls in Parts II and III.

One-to-Many Relationships   As with 1:1 relationships, 1:N relationships also can be implemented in relational databases with foreign keys. To do this, place the primary key of the entity with the maximum cardinality of N as a foreign key in the entity that has a maximum cardinality of 1. For example, in Figure 5-8, the primary keys of the salesperson and customer tables are included as foreign keys in the sales table. Similarly, the primary keys of the cash, customer, and cashier tables are included as foreign keys in the cash receipts table. If we were to create tables for Figure 5-7, Panel B, the attribute "invoice number" would appear as a foreign key in the cash receipts table. If we created tables for Figure 5-7, Panel C, however, the attribute "remittance number" would appear as a foreign key in the sales table.

A potential exception to this general rule for implementing 1:N relationships may occur if the relationship includes two sequential event entities, and the event that normally occurs first is also the one that can participate many times in that relationship. In that case, implementing the relationship as a separate table might improve internal control.

Completeness Check

To implement the REA data model of S&S's revenue cycle depicted in Figure 5-6, Ashton has created the set of tables shown in Figure 5-8. In reviewing the list of facts (Table 5-1) stored in the database, however, Ashton notes that he has yet to assign to any database tables several facts relating to sales calls. He recalls that Scott and Susan want to begin collecting additional information about the performance of their outside sales staff, whose job is to call on corporate customers. Specifically, they want to know how many customers each salesperson talks to each day, what products the salesperson demonstrates, and the results of those calls. Ashton realizes that he must modify his REA data model and probably create additional tables to accommodate these items.

Ashton creates another event entity, which he labels "call on customer." He links it to both the salesperson and customer entities to depict the relevant agent-event relationships. Each sales call includes one salesperson talking with one customer. During the course of the year, each salesperson will make many sales calls and each customer is likely to receive multiple visits. Therefore, Ashton models both agent-event relationships as being 1:N, with the same minimum and maximum cardinalities for each entity as used in the agent-event relationships involving the customer order event.

During a sales call, a salesperson typically talks about and demonstrates more than one product. Conversely, a given product may be demonstrated during many different sales calls. Therefore, Ashton models the call on customer-inventory relationship as being M:N, with the same minimum and maximum cardinalities as in the customer order-inventory relationship.

If a sales call is successful, the customer will place an order with S&S. Not every call will result in an order, however. Scott and Susan told Ashton that although some customers might not place an initial order until after receiving several sales calls, for performance evaluation purposes they wanted to treat new orders as resulting from only the most recent preceding sales call. Furthermore, Scott and Susan noted that some new corporate customers might order in response to a catalog they received or as a result of visiting S&S's Web site. Therefore, Ashton modeled the call on customer-customer order relationship as being 1:1, but with zero minimum cardinalities for each event. Figure 5-9 reflects these revisions to Ashton's REA diagram, and Figure 5-10 shows the contents of the two new tables he created. He also modified the customer order table in Figure 5-8 to include the attribute "call number" as a foreign key linking that event to the call on customer event.

Ashton's need to modify his REA diagram to accommodate additional facts is not unusual. Indeed, it is often useful to create tables even before completely finishing an REA diagram, and then modify the diagram to include additional entities and relationships revealed through the process of assigning attributes to tables.

At this point, Ashton has almost completed the design of S&S's revenue cycle database. He notes that Figures 5-8, 5-9, and 5-10 satisfy the following basic requirements for designing well-structured relational databases as discussed in Chapter 4:

1. Every table has a primary key.
2. Other nonkey attributes in each table are either a fact about the thing designated by the primary key, or are foreign keys used to link that table to another table.
3. Every attribute in every table is single-valued (i.e., each table is a flat file).

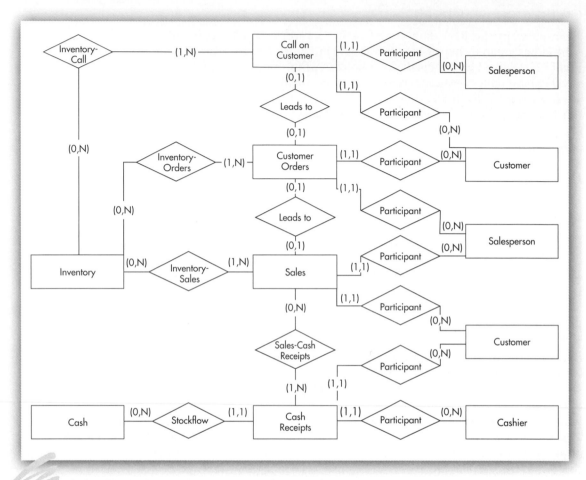

Figure 5-9 Expanded REA diagram for S&S revenue cycle
(including call on customer event)

Figure 5-10 Tables created to model call on customer event

Attributes			
Table Name	**Primary Key**	**Foreign Keys**	**Other**
Call on customer	Call #	Salesperson #, Customer #	Date, time, comments
Call - inventory	Call #, item #		

Note that the sets of tables listed in Figures 5-8 and 5-10 are the natural result of using the REA data model. Moreover, they not only satisfy the requirements for a properly designed database, but also reflect the underlying semantics about how S&S performs its revenue cycle business activities.

INTEGRATING REA DIAGRAMS ACROSS CYCLES

As mentioned, to design a functioning AIS for S&S, Ashton must develop REA diagrams for additional cycles and then integrate those diagrams. Figure 5-11 shows the first REA diagram he developed for S&S's expenditure cycle. It includes only the economic exchange events (compare with Figure 5-3).

Ashton then combined the diagrams for the revenue and expenditure cycles to provide Scott and Susan with one high-level overview of what would be included in their AIS. Figure 5-12 shows the resulting integrated REA diagram.

Ashton integrated the two individual REA diagrams by merging entities common to each. Thus, Figure 5-12 includes only one inventory entity and one cash entity.

Ashton then checked the completeness of Figure 5-12 by testing whether it satisfied these two rules:

1. Every resource entity should be linked to two stockflow events, one of which increments the resource and one that decrements it.
2. Every economic exchange event that increments a resource must be linked to an economic exchange event that decrements a resource, a principle referred to as economic duality.

Figure 5-11   Partial REA diagram for S&S expenditure cycle
(economic exchange events only)

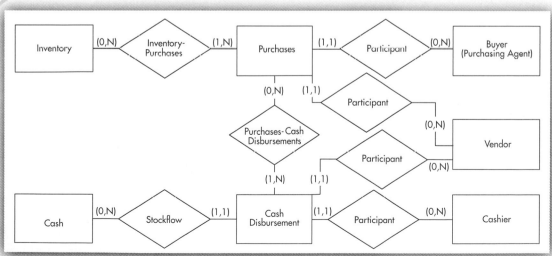

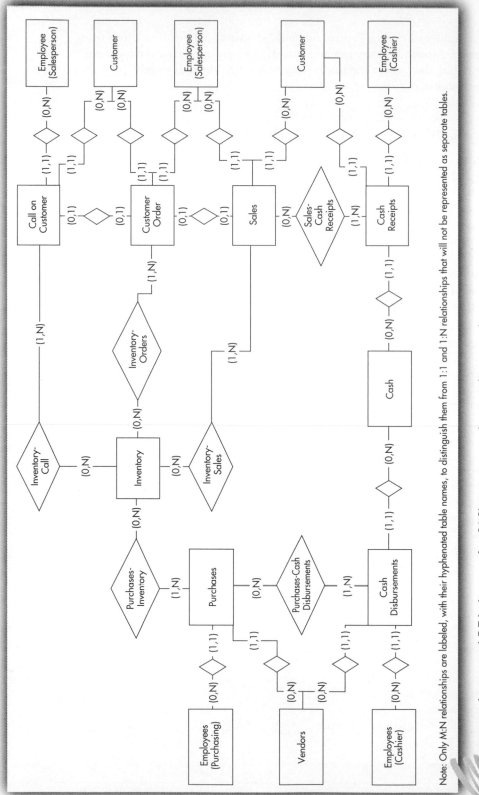

Figure 5-12 Integrated REA diagram for S&S's revenue and expenditure cycles

Note: Only M:N relationships are labeled, with their hyphenated table names, to distinguish them from 1:1 and 1:N relationships that will not be represented as separate tables.

Figure 5-12 satisfies both of these rules. The inventory resource is linked to the purchases event (which increments it) and to the sales event (which decrements it). Similarly, the cash resource is linked to both an increment event, cash receipts, and a decrement event, cash disbursements. In addition, purchases, an economic increment event, is linked to cash disbursements, an economic decrement event. Similarly, sales, an economic decrement event that reduces the inventory resource, is linked to cash receipts, an economic increment event that increases the cash resource.

USING REA DIAGRAMS

Thus far, we have shown how to use the REA data model to guide the design of an AIS. In that process, we developed an REA diagram for S&S. In this section, we discuss how REA diagrams also can be used to document business practices and to guide the retrieval of information from a database.

Documentation of Business Practices

REA diagrams are especially useful for documenting advanced AIS built using databases, because the cardinalities in REA diagrams provide information about the organization's business practices and the nature of its economic exchanges. For example, Figure 5-12 indicates that S&S extends credit to its customers and allows them to make installment payments on their purchases. It also indicates that S&S sells mass-produced goods (See pages 125–128 to review how this is depicted).

Correctly interpreting what the cardinalities in an REA diagram mean requires understanding exactly what an occurrence of each entity represents. This is usually easy for both agent and event entities. Each occurrence of an agent entity represents a specific person or organization. Similarly, each occurrence of an event entity represents a specific business activity or transaction. For example, each occurrence of the sales event represents a specific sales transaction.

Understanding what each occurrence of a resource entity represents, however, can sometimes be more difficult. Consider inventory, for example. An individual occurrence of this entity might represent either a specific physical object or a class of objects, depending on the nature of the inventory. In such cases, examining the attributes associated with that entity will indicate what it represents. For example, Figure 5-8 indicates that the inventory entity includes the attribute "quantity on hand," which means that each row in the inventory table represents a *kind* of inventory, not an individual object. Thus, one row in S&S's inventory table may store data about a specific 21-inch monitor brand, whereas another row may store data about a specific DVD drive model. S&S would want to know how many of each of these products it has on hand. Consequently, the attribute "quantity on hand" would be found in its inventory table.

In contrast, consider the situation when the inventory-sales relationship is modeled as being 1:N. This indicates that the organization must be selling unique products that it tracks by individual serial number. In this case, the inventory table would not include a "quantity on hand" attribute because there could only be one of each item.

The preceding discussion indicates that each organization will have its own unique REA diagram. At a minimum, because business practices differ across companies, so will relationship cardinalities. For example, if S&S frequently made partial shipments to fill customer orders, then the customer orders-sales relationship would probably be modeled as being 1:N. If S&S also frequently combined several orders from one customer into one large shipment, then the relationship would be modeled as being M:N. In fact, differences in business practices are likely to result in different entities being modeled. For example, if S&S only made sales to walk-in customers and did not take customer orders, then it would not need the customer order commitment event.

The cardinalities in an REA diagram also provide the reader with information about business controls. For example, each row in the cash entity represents a specific account. Thus, one row stores data about S&S's regular checking account, another about its payroll account, another about a money market investment account, and so on. Figure 5-12 models the cash-cash receipts relationship as being 1:N. This reflects a sound control practice of depositing all customer payments into the company's main checking account. Part II of this text discusses the concept of internal controls in more detail. In Part III, where we discuss each cycle in more detail, we present other examples of information about business controls that can be depicted in REA diagrams.

Although the development of the REA diagram for S&S's revenue cycle may seem to have been relatively straightforward and intuitive, data modeling can be a complex and repetitive process. One common challenge occurs when users employ different terminology. Focus 5-1 highlights the importance of involving the eventual users of the system in the data modeling process so that terminology is consistent.

Extracting Information from the AIS

A completed REA diagram also serves as a useful guide for querying an AIS database. Refer to Figures 5-8, 5-9, and 5-10, which depict Ashton's database AIS developed for S&S's revenue cycle using the REA data model. At first glance, it may appear that a number of elements found in traditional AIS, such as journals, ledgers, and information about such claims as accounts receivable, are missing. In reality, that information is present but stored in a different format.

Producing Journals and Ledgers   Queries can be used to generate journals and ledgers from a relational database built on the REA model. The information normally found in a journal is stored in the tables used to record data about events. For example, a sales journal can be produced by writing a query that displays the appropriate entries in the sales table for a given period. A query can be written to display every entry in the sales table, to produce a list of all sales events, both credit and cash sales. Traditionally, however, sales journals are used to record all *credit* sales. Therefore, the query to produce a credit sales journal would have to include both the sales and cash receipts tables. The logic of the query would include restricting the output to display only those sales that are not linked to a corresponding customer payment event that occurred on the same day as the sale. Similar processes can be followed to produce journals for events such as purchases or disbursements.

The information traditionally contained in ledgers is often stored in a relational database in a combination of resource and event tables. Consider one of the most common types of subsidiary ledgers: accounts receivable. Figures 5-8, 5-9, and 5-10 do not show any explicit accounts receivable table. As explained, the reason is that accounts receivable does not satisfy the REA model's definition of a resource. It is not an independent entity; rather, it represents an imbalance at any point in time between credit sales and cash receipts. Thus, accounts receivable does not need to be stored explicitly in the database. Instead, the total amount of accounts receivable can be

Focus 5-1

Why Should Users Participate in Data Modeling?

Data modeling is not an easy task, as Hewlett-Packard learned when it began designing a new database for its accounting and finance function. A major problem was that the same term meant different things to different people. For example, accounting used the term *orders* to refer to the total dollar amount of orders per time period, whereas the sales department used the term to refer to individual customer orders. Moreover, such confusions existed even within the accounting and finance function. For example, the reporting group used the term *product* to refer to any good currently sold to customers. Thus, the primary key for this entity was product number. In contrast, the forecasting group used the term *product* to refer to any good that was often still in the planning stage and had no product number assigned yet.

To solve these problems, Hewlett-Packard asked the different user groups to actively participate in the data modeling process. The first step was to convince all users of the need for and benefits of creating a data model for their function. Then it was necessary to carefully define the scope of the modeling effort. Hewlett-Packard found that the time invested in these early steps was worthwhile, because it facilitated the activities of clarifying definitions and developing attribute lists that took place later in the process. The latter activity was an iterative affair that included many revisions. Documentation was critical to this process. Each member of the modeling team and user groups had copies of the proposed lists, which made it easier to spot inconsistencies in definitions.

Hewlett-Packard credits the data modeling approach as contributing significantly to the project's overall success. Data modeling allowed the participants to concentrate first on understanding the essential business characteristics of the new system, instead of getting bogged down in specifying the contents of relational tables. This helped them to identify and resolve conflicting viewpoints early in the process, and paved the way for eventual acceptance of the resulting system. The key step, however, was in getting the different user groups to actively participate in the data modeling process. Otherwise, it is likely that the resulting data model would not have been accurate or widely accepted.

Source: Adapted from C. Randall Byers and Lysa Beltz, "Financial Data Modeling at Hewlett-Packard," *Journal of Systems Management* (January 1994): 28–33.

derived by calculating the total amount of sales for which customer payments have not yet been received. Table 5-2 describes some of the ways to do this, depending upon the nature of the relationship between the sales and cash receipts events.

The query logic presented in Table 5-2 derives the *total* amount of accounts receivable. To derive account balances for each customer, the query logic must be expanded to reference the customer table and to include the appropriate command (e.g., "group by" in SQL) to perform the calculations separately for each customer. The result of such a query would be a table with a row for each customer and a column showing the customer's outstanding balance. Another query could be written to sum the account balances in this table, thereby calculating total accounts receivable.

Table 5-2   Query Logic for Calculating Total Accounts Receivable Under Various Relationship Cardinality Scenarios

Situation 1:

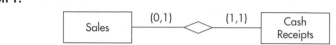

A 1:1 Relationship Between Sales and Cash Receipts
If the primary key of the cash receipts event, remittance advice number, is used as a foreign key in the sales table, then accounts receivable can be calculated by querying only the sales table. The query logic is simple: Sum the amount of all sales for which there is no remittance advice number. If the primary key of the sales table, invoice number, is used as a foreign key in the cash receipts table, then both tables must be referenced to compute accounts receivable. Because this is a 1:1 relationship, each customer payment applies to a specific sale in full. Therefore, accounts receivable equals the sum of all sales whose invoice numbers do not appear in the cash receipts table.

Situation 2:

A One-to-Many Relationship Between Sales and Cash Receipts
Invoice number is a foreign key in the cash receipts table. Note that in contrast to situation 1, a customer payment may not completely pay for a sale. Therefore, at least three queries are needed to calculate total accounts receivable: one to compute total sales, one to determine total cash collected for sales, and one to calculate the difference between those two values.

Situation 3:

A One-to-Many Relationship Between Cash Receipts and Sales
In this situation, remittance number is a foreign key in the sales table. Each sales transaction is paid in full by a cash receipt event, so the query logic is quite simple: Total accounts receivable is the sum of all sales for which there is no remittance number.

Situation 4:

A Many-to-Many Relationship Between Sales and Cash Receipts
In this case, a sale may be paid for by more than one cash receipt event and a cash receipt may pay for more than one sale. The amount applied to each sales transaction is stored as an attribute in the M:N relationship table that links sales and cash receipts, but the total amount remitted is an attribute of the cash receipts event. Thus, total accounts receivable can be derived by the same three queries used in situation 2: one query to compute total sales, another to compute total customer payments received, and a third to determine the difference between those two values.

Similar procedures can be used to derive other accounting concepts, such as accounts payable, that represent imbalances between two events.

Keep in mind, however, that the procedures for calculating accounts receivable described in the preceding paragraphs would not have to be followed every time this information was desired. Instead, the queries need only be written once and, after being tested for accuracy, can be stored for subsequent use. Moreover, because information about temporal interevent imbalances, such as accounts receivable and accounts payable, is needed so frequently, an implementation compromise is likely to be made so that account balance would be stored as a calculated attribute in the appropriate table. For example, the customer table depicted in Figure 5-8 has a column that stores that customer's account balance. This simplifies the query logic required to derive accounts receivable, because only the customer table would need to be accessed. To display the amount that a specific customer owes would mean writing a query that displayed a specific row in the customer table. Calculating the total amount of accounts receivable would mean summing the account balance column.

Providing Other Financial Statement Information   An REA diagram can guide the writing of queries to produce other information that would be included in financial statements. Querying a single table can derive many financial statement items. For example, summing the amount column in the sales table would yield sales for the current time period. Other information, however, such as accounts receivable, might require querying several tables. Correctly reading and understanding what the REA diagram says about how the data are stored is essential for knowing how to write such queries.

Preparing Managerial Reports   A major advantage of the REA data model is that it integrates nonfinancial and financial data in the AIS and makes both types of data easily accessible to management. For example, one attribute in the sales table in Figure 5-8 is the time that the sale occurred. Scott and Susan can use this data to track sales activity during different times of the day to better plan staffing needs. The sales-inventory table also includes a useful nonfinancial attribute: Is the purchase a replacement or the first-time acquisition of a product? Scott and Susan might be able to use this data to improve their marketing efforts. They could identify which new products seem to be popular replacements for older devices and then develop customized advertisements to be mailed to customers who had previously purchased the older type of device but who have not yet replaced it with the newer model.

In addition, the S&S revenue cycle database shown in Figures 5-8, 5-9, and 5-10 also can be expanded easily to integrate data from external sources. For example, to better evaluate customer credit status, Scott and Susan may decide to collect information from a credit rating agency, such as Dun & Bradstreet. This information could be added to the database by creating an additional column in the customer table to store the customer's credit rating. A similar process could be used to store information about suppliers that could be used in the vendor selection process.

In contrast to the REA data model, the general ledger in traditionally designed AISs uses the chart of accounts to store and organize data based on the structure of financial statements. In terms of the previous example, the traditional AIS contains only data about the financial aspects of a sales transaction, such as date and amount. Other data useful for evaluating operational performance, such as the time a sale occurred or if the customer was replacing an old device, would have to be stored in a separate database or information system. The existence of separate systems makes it more difficult for management to easily and quickly access the information it needs.

It is vitally important that an organization's AIS be capable of storing both traditional financial measures and other operational performance measures. As Robert Elliott explains:[9]

> Information technology (IT) is changing everything. It represents a new, post-industrial paradigm of wealth creation that is replacing the industrial paradigm and is profoundly changing the way business is done. Because of these changes in business, the decisions that management must make are very different from former decisions. *If the purpose of accounting information is to support business decision-making, and management's decision types are changing, then it is natural to expect accounting to change—both internal and external accounting* (emphasis added).

The REA data model can be used to build a database that allows the AIS to change in response to management's changing information requirements.

The REA data model shows that accounting need not be limited to the traditional double-entry model with its journals, ledgers, and chart of accounts. Instead, the REA data model supports the view that accounting is a process or system for collecting and disseminating information about an organization's business transactions. The means by which those objectives are accomplished, however, may change with new developments in information-processing technology. Indeed, Focus 5-2 suggests that some significant changes may be in store for how accounting is accomplished in many organizations. Nevertheless, although the mechanics of accounting may change, the need for the results (managerial reports and financial statements) of accounting remains.

SUMMARY AND CASE CONCLUSION

The database design process has six stages: planning, requirements analysis, design, coding, implementation, and operation. Because of their extensive knowledge of transaction processing requirements and general business functions, accountants should be active in every stage.

One way to perform the activities of requirements definition and conceptual design is to build a data model of the AIS. The REA accounting data model is developed specifically for building a database AIS. The REA model classifies data into three basic categories: resources, events, and agents. The REA model can be documented in the form of an E-R diagram, which shows the entities about which data are collected and highlights the important relationships among them. The cardinalities of the relationships depicted in REA diagrams also provide information about the basic business policies the company follows.

Developing an REA diagram requires four steps. First, identify the basic economic exchange of interest. Second, identify the resources affected by and the agents who participate in those exchange events. Third, determine if any of the economic exchange events can be decomposed into a set of commitment and exchange events. Fourth, use knowledge about the organization's business prac-

---

[9]Robert K. Elliot, "The Third Wave Breaks on the Shores of Accounting," *Accounting Horizons* (June 1992) : 61.

Focus 5-2

The Changing Nature of Accounting at IBM

In 1979, IBM used 315 separate worldwide accounting systems to support six accounting applications: general ledger, fixed assets, intracompany and intercompany transactions, accounts receivable, and accounts payable. During the 1980s, IBM worked to consolidate these systems, and by the end of 1991 had just 36 separate accounting systems. The remaining systems, however, still were not flexible enough to support the kind of company-wide decision making that IBM desired. Consequently, IBM set out to completely overhaul its accounting processes.

Instead of merely applying new technology to existing processes, IBM began by rethinking and redesigning the way business processes are performed from the ground up. A major component of this change included expanding the transaction-driven orientation of existing accounting systems to incorporate nonfinancial measures of business activities. The objective was to fully integrate financial and nonfinancial information so that both could be used in decision making. IBM also integrated information technology within the business processes so that data are recorded in real time, as the events unfolded. The final part of the solution included realigning ownership of the data so that the company will now be responsible for developing the corporate data model, specifying what data need to be recorded for each event, and providing users with the appropriate information retrieval tools. Relieved of these duties, functional managers will now be responsible for ensuring that appropriate data about each event are recorded and that adequate controls are in place. Individual users are then responsible for using the company-provided tools to retrieve the information they need.

IBM has used this procedure to merge four previously separate fund disbursement processes (payroll, travel expense, miscellaneous expense reimbursement, and time and attendance recording) into one integrated process. IBM estimates that the project will save more than $300 million over 10 years, while reducing the time required to process claims by 65 to 70 percent.

These changes dramatically affect the roles of the accounting staff and the controller. Most of the projected cost savings in the reimbursement project come from eliminating clerical jobs and redundant systems. Indeed, an internal study at IBM suggests that almost 60 percent of the work done by the accounting staff is clerical in nature and, therefore, can be eliminated. The controller becomes a key player in redesigning the AIS by identifying redundant processes and suggesting ways to use information technology to do things more efficiently, while maintaining adequate controls. At the same time, the controller's responsibility expands to include both nonfinancial and financial data. Consequently, the controller and the accounting staff participate more in the company's strategic decision-making process.

Source: Adapted from David P. Andros, J. Owen Cherrington, and Eric L. Denna, "Reengineering Your Accounting, The IBM Way," *Financial Executive* (July–August 1992): 28–31.

tices to add relationship cardinality information to the diagram. Finally, REA diagrams from different transaction cycles can be integrated into one larger diagram by linking across common entities, as in Figure 5-12.

A data model documented in an REA diagram can be implemented in a relational DBMS in three steps. First, tables are created for all entities and many-to-many relationships in the REA diagram. Second, primary keys and nonkey attributes are assigned to each table. Third, one-to-one and one-to-many relationships are implemented by means of foreign keys.

    Ashton Fleming followed these steps to implement a database AIS for S&S's revenue cycle. He drew Figure 5-3 to represent his understanding of the in-store sales and cash collections procedures S&S follows. After validating this REA diagram with Scott and Susan, Ashton expanded the revenue cycle REA model to include commitments and then integrated it with an REA model of the economic exchange events in the expenditure cycle, which resulted in Figure 5-12. He then demonstrated how to write queries to retrieve a variety of managerial reports and financial statements from the relational DBMS. Scott and Susan were quite impressed and eagerly anticipated Ashton extending the database to encompass all of S&S's business activities.

KEY TERMS

- data modeling
- entity-relationship
- (E-R) diagram
- entity
- REA data model
- resources

- events
- economic exchanges
- commitments
- agents
- cardinalities
- minimum cardinality

- maximum cardinality
- one-to-one relationship
- one-to-many relationship
- many-to-many relationship
- concatenated keys

CHAPTER QUIZ

1. Which of the following is not considered a resource in an REA data model?
   a. cash
   b. accounts receivable
   c. inventory
   d. equipment
2. Which of the following is not a type of entity in the REA data model?
   a. customers
   b. sales
   c. invoices
   d. delivery trucks
3. Which type of relationship cardinality *must* be implemented in a relational database as a separate table?
   a. one-to-one relationship
   b. one-to-many relationship
   c. many-to-many relationship
   d. all of the above
4. If a company pays for each purchase it makes with a separate check and does not make installment payments on any purchases, then the relationship between cash disbursements and purchases would be modeled as being which of the following?
   a. one-to-one relationship
   b. one-to-many relationship
   c. many-to-many relationship
   d. paid-in-full relationship

5. Which set of cardinality pairs most accurately models the sales of low-cost, mass-produced items by a retail store?
   a. inventory (0,N)–(0,N) sales
   b. inventory (0,N)–(1,N) sales
   c. inventory (1,N)–(1,N) sales
   d. inventory (1,N)–(0,N) sales
6. Data modeling occurs during which stages of database design?
   a. planning and requirements analysis
   b. requirements analysis and design
   c. design and coding
   d. coding and implementation
7. A company wants to store information about both currently used and alternate suppliers. Which set of cardinality pairs allows this?
   a. purchases (0,N)–(0,1) suppliers
   b. purchases (1,N)–(1,1) suppliers
   c. purchases (0,1)–(1,N) suppliers
   d. purchases (1,1)–(0,N) suppliers
8. The key of a many-to-many relationship between the sales and inventory events would be:
   a. invoice number
   b. item number
   c. both invoice number and item number
   d. either invoice number or item number
9. Which of the following statements about the REA data model is true?
   a. Every event must be linked to at least two agents.
   b. Every relationship must be implemented as a relational table.
   c. Every event must be linked to at least two resources.
   d. Every agent must be linked to at least two events.
10. Which of the following elements of the REA data model must be implemented as tables in a relational database?
    a. resources
    b. events
    c. agents
    d. all of the above

DISCUSSION QUESTIONS

5.1   It has been argued that advances in IT, especially the development of DBMS, have made the double-entry model of accounting obsolete. Specifically, the computer's ability to quickly and accurately sort and summarize transaction data has made the practice of maintaining ledgers to produce periodic reports unnecessary. Indeed, financial reports can now be produced at any time. What are the likely effects of these types of changes on the nature of accounting jobs in the future?

5.2   Traditional accounting systems are based on the chart of accounts, which establishes one predetermined basis for organizing and summarizing transaction data. How does the REA data model provide more flexibility in meeting the information needs of various decision makers? Provide specific examples.

5.3   A criticism of traditional accounting systems is that data are stored at too high a level of aggregation (summarization). That is, transaction data are recorded at the individual event level in journals, but once posted to ledgers, data are stored in summarized form. Thus, users find it easy to obtain information at only three levels of aggregation: (1) individual transactions (from the journals or transaction files), (2) totals for a particular account for a particular time period (by summarizing transaction activity), or (3) the cumulative balance in the ledger accounts. In contrast, one objective of the REA model and the events-based approach is to store accounting data at a less aggregated level. How important is this objective in meeting user needs? Are the three levels of aggregation provided by the traditional AIS sufficient to support all of an organization's information needs? Why or why not?

5.4   The traditional chart of accounts only stores financial information about transactions. An objective of the REA accounting model is to facilitate the integration of financial and nonfinancial information. Is it necessary to abandon the chart of accounts to accomplish this objective? Why or why not? (Hint: Think about how operational data, such as average time to fill and ship customer orders, can be stored in an AIS that uses the chart of accounts.)

5.5   The REA data model does not treat activities such as mailing invoices, recording vendor invoices, and preparing reports as being events. Why not?

PROBLEMS

5.1   Joe's is a small ice cream shop located near the local university's baseball field. Joe's serves walk-in customers only. The shop carries 26 flavors of ice cream. Customers can buy cones, sundaes, or shakes. When a customer pays for an individual purchase, a sales transaction usually includes just one item. When a customer pays for a family or group purchase, however, a single sale may include many different items. All sales must be paid for at the time the ice cream is served. Joe's maintains several banking accounts, but deposits all sales monies into its main checking account.
Required
Draw an REA diagram, complete with cardinalities, for Joe's revenue cycle.

5.2   Joe, the owner of the ice cream shop, purchases ice cream from two vendors. Over the years, he has developed good relationships with both vendors so that they allow Joe to pay them biweekly for all purchases made during the preceding two-week period. Joe calls in ice cream orders on Mondays and Thursdays. The orders are usually delivered the next day. Joe buys ice cream toppings from one of several local stores and pays for each such purchase at the time of sale with a check from the company's main checking account.
Required
Draw an REA diagram, complete with cardinalities, for Joe's expenditure cycle.

5.3   Draw an integrated REA diagram of Joe's revenue and expenditure cycles (see problems 5-1 and 5-2).

5.4   Sue's Gallery sells original paintings by local artists. All sales occur in the store. Sometimes customers purchase more than one painting. Individual customers must pay for purchases in full at the time of sale. Corporate customers, such as hotels, however, may pay in installments if they purchase more than 10 paintings. Although Sue's Gallery has several bank accounts, all sales monies are deposited intact into the main checking account.
Required
Draw an REA diagram for the gallery's revenue cycle. Be sure to include cardinalities.

5.5   Sue's Gallery only purchases finished paintings (it never commissions artists). It pays each artist 50 percent of the agreed price at the time of purchase and the remainder after the painting is sold. All purchases are paid by check from Sue's main checking account.

Required

Draw an REA diagram, complete with cardinalities, of the gallery's expenditure cycle.

5.6   Draw an integrated REA diagram of Sue's Gallery's revenue and expenditure cycles (see problems 5.4 and 5.5).

5.7   Develop a data model of S&S's expenditure cycle activities related to the acquisition of office equipment and other fixed assets. Assume that S&S makes installment payments for most fixed asset acquisitions, but occasionally pays for some equipment in full at the time of purchase.

Required

a. Draw an REA diagram of your data model.

b. Develop a set of relational tables that implements your data model. Specify each table's primary key and list several other nonkey attributes that should be included in each table.

5.8   S&S has incorporated and issued shares of common stock.

Required

a. Modify Figure 5-12 to reflect this change in structure. Include both the inflow of funds from the initial sale of S&S's stock and the outflow of funds in the form of dividends to those shareholders.

b. Develop a set of relational tables to implement these modifications. Specify the primary key for each table and list several other nonkey attributes that should be included. Use your own judgment in selecting which attributes of common stock transactions should be collected and stored.

5.9   Provide an example (in terms of companies with which you are familiar) for each of the business situations described by the following relationship cardinalities:

a. Sales (0,N) to Cash Collections (1,N)

b. Sales (1,1) to Inventory (0,1)

c. Purchases (0,N) to Cash Disbursements (1,N)

d. Purchases (0,1) to Cash Disbursements (1,N)

e. Purchases (1,N) to Cash Disbursements (1,1)

f. Employees (1,1) to Departments (1,N)

g. Purchases (0,1) to Inventory Receipts (1,N)

5.10 Model the cardinalities of the following business policies:

a. Sales-cash collection relationship for installment sales

b. Sales-cash collection relationship at most self-service gasoline stations

c. Customer order-sales relationship in a situation when occasionally several shipments are required to fill an order because some items were out of stock

d. Sales-inventory relationship for a custom homebuilder

5.11 The following tables and attributes exist in a relational database:

Table	Attributes
Vendor	Vendor#, name, street address, city, state
Purchases	P.O.#, date, amount, vendor#, purchasing agent
Inventory Receipts	Receiving report#, date, receiving clerk, remarks, P.O.#
Cash Disbursed	Check#, date, amount
Inventory Receipts–Cash Disbursed	Check#, receiving report#, amount applied to invoice

Required

Draw an REA diagram for this database. State any additional assumptions you need to make about cardinalities.

5.12 Sparky's Amusement Park is an entertainment park run by recent college graduates. It caters to young people and others who are young at heart. The owners are very interested in applying what they have learned in their information systems and marketing classes to operate a park better than any other in the area.

To accomplish these goals, guests of the park are given a personal "membership card" as they enter. This card will be used to identify each guest. Assume that a new card is issued each time a guest comes to the park. As a result, the system does not have to track one person over a period of time.

As at other parks, guests pay a flat fee for the day and then are able to ride all of the attractions (such as a double-looping roller coaster and the merry-go-round) for no extra charge. The owners, however, want to track the rides each guest takes and the attractions the guests use. They plan to have guests swipe their membership card through a computerized card reader, which automatically enters information into the computer system. This should allow the owners to gather data about the following:

- Number of people who use each piece of equipment (How many people rode the Ferris wheel today?)
- Number of times each piece of equipment is operated daily
- Times of day the attraction is busy or slow (When was the carousel the busiest?)
- Number of attractions each guest uses (How many different pieces of equipment did customer 1122 ride?)
- Number of rides each guest enjoys (How many different rides did customer 1122 enjoy? Did each guest go on any rides more than once?)

Required
a. Identify the entities (the people, places, things, and events in this business).
b. Identify the relationships between the entities.
c. Draw an REA diagram that models this situation using the following definitions:
   - Piece of equipment: the equipment that is operated in the park (e.g., Tilt-a-Whirl, roller coaster)
   - Ride: the specific time that the attraction is run
   - Guest: the people who enjoy the rides

(This problem is adapted from one developed for classroom use by Dr. Julie Smith David at Arizona State University.)

5.13 We-Fix-Computers, Inc. provides spare parts and service for a wide variety of computers. Customers may purchase parts to take home for do-it-yourself repairs, or they may bring their systems in for repair, in which they pay for both the parts and the labor associated with the type of service required. Some services do not include any new parts, just a labor charge for that service. Individual customers must pay for all parts purchases in full at the time of sale. Individual customers must pay 50 percent down when they bring their computers in for servicing and pay the balance at pickup. Corporate customers, however, are billed monthly for all sales (parts or service). Although We-Fix-Computers, Inc. has several different banking accounts, all sales are deposited intact into its main checking account.

Required
Draw an REA diagram of We-Fix-Computer's revenue cycle, complete with cardinalities.

5.14 We-Fix-Computers, Inc. purchases its inventory of parts from more than a dozen different vendors. Orders are usually delivered the next day; sometimes, however, suppliers ship only partial orders. We-Fix-Computers pays for some of its purchases COD, but usually pays by the 10th of the month for all purchases made the prior month. None of its suppliers allows it to make installment payments.

Required

Draw an REA diagram of We-Fix-Computer's expenditure cycle, complete with cardinalities.

5.15 Draw an integrated REA diagram of We-Fix-Computers, Inc.'s revenue and expenditure cycles (see problems 5.13 and 5.14).

5.16 The Mesa Veterinary Hospital is run by Dr. Brigitte Roosevelt. She has two employees in the office and has asked you to develop a database to help better track her data. Dr. Roosevelt currently uses her personal computer only for word processing, but she is interested in also using it to maintain pet histories and accounting information. She is excited about the transition and is counting on you to help her through the process. She describes her daily activities as follows:

When new customers come to Mesa Veterinary Hospital, the "parents" of the pets are required to complete an introductory form. This form includes the following:

- Parent name
- Address
- Day phone
- Night phone

They are also required to provide the following information about each pet, as some people own many pets:

- Pet name
- Breed
- Color
- Birth date

Dr. Roosevelt would like to enter this information once, and then have the system retrieve it for all subsequent visits.

When customers call to make appointments, one of the office clerks asks what kind of services they require (i.e., is it a routine exam, a surgery, etc.). Dr. Roosevelt sees only one pet during each appointment. If she is going to see one parent's two pets, then two separate appointments are necessary (but scheduled back-to-back). For each appointment, Dr. Roosevelt records the pet's weight, notes the reason for the appointment, and records her diagnosis. Depending on the diagnosis, the doctor will possibly prescribe any number of medications to cure the pet. Parents are charged $25 for each appointment, and must pay additionally for any medications prescribed for their pets. Dr. Roosevelt requires all pets to be brought back for another examination prior to refilling any prescriptions. Customers must pay for services and medication in full at the conclusion of their visits.

Dr. Roosevelt concludes the interview by requesting that in addition to the facts mentioned above, she wants the system to store the following attributes:

- Number of pets owned by each parent
- Total charge for the appointment
- Prescription price
- Drug name
- Length of appointment
- Diagnosis
- Date of appointment
- Service requested

Required

a. Given this brief overview, draw an REA diagram for the Mesa Veterinary Hospital and include cardinalities.

b. Assume you are going to implement your REA diagram using a relational database. Draw the tables necessary for this assignment. Include all attributes from the text and the additional ones listed. Create additional attributes only if necessary.

(This problem is adapted from one created for classroom use by Dr. Julie Smith David, Assistant Professor, Arizona State University.)

5.17 Your university hires you to implement a database system for the library network. You have interviewed several librarians, and the following summarizes these discussions:

- The library's main goal is to provide students and professors with access to books and other publications. The library, therefore, maintains an extensive collection of materials that are available to anyone with a valid university identification card.

- The standard procedure for loaning materials is that the student or faculty member comes to one of the three campus libraries and locates the book or journal on the shelves.

- Each book is assigned three unique numbers. First, the book is assigned a number by the publisher, called the International Standard Book Number (ISBN). This number allows the publishers to track each title and the number changes with each new addition. The second number is the Dewey decimal number, which is assigned to the title and written on the outside spine of the book. This number is used to organize the library shelves and is thus helpful to the students and faculty. It is therefore critical that this number be available to users on the on-line inquiry screens. The last number is a university book ID number. A different number is assigned to every book that is received so the library can track all copies of each book. This number is different from the other two numbers in that if the library has three copies of one book, each will have a unique university book ID number.

- When students or faculty check out books, the system must be able to track the specific copy that is being borrowed. Each book has a magnetic strip inserted in its spine, which is used as a security measure. If someone tries to take a book without checking it out, an alarm sounds.

- In general, students and faculty have equal clout in the library. Both are able to check out most books and to check out several books at one time. No one is allowed to remove periodicals from any library. The length of time that the book may be borrowed varies, however, depending on who checks it out. Students are allowed to check out a book for several weeks; faculty may borrow books for several months.

- When patrons check out books, they take their materials to the circulation desk. At that time, the librarian scans in each item's university book ID number and the borrower's ID number. The system then assigns a loan number to the transaction so that the system tracks each checkout uniquely (assume that each book is treated as a separate loan). At this time, each book's due date is calculated and marked on a slip located inside each book's front cover. Simultaneously, the magnetic strip is deactivated so the book may be removed from the library.

- After borrowers check out a book, they are expected to return it by its due date. In reality, everyone is allowed 30 days after the due date recorded on the checkout slip before the book is officially overdue. At that point, the book must be returned, and the borrower is assessed a $10 fine. If the book is permanently lost, then the borrower is fined $75 for the book's replacement. All fines must be paid in cash, in full. Students are not allowed to enroll for subsequent semesters until all library fines are paid; they also do not receive a diploma until all library fines are paid. Faculty must pay all outstanding fines by June 30 of each year.

- When a book is returned, the return must be entered into the system, and a unique return number is used to log the transaction. At that time, the loan record is updated to show that the book has been returned.

The following attributes have been identified as critical for the new system:

University book ID	Actual return date	Book return number#
Book publisher	Borrower ID	Dewey decimal number
Due date	Borrower name	Borrower address
Loan number	Book title	Book copyright date
Checkout date	Fine receipt number	Borrower e-mail address
Borrower phone number	Amount received	Library borrowed from
Cash account number	Library name	Librarian number
Librarian name	Amount of fine	Account balance
Book status (on the shelf or checked out)	Default library where book is shelved	Total number of books in a specific library
Type of borrower (faculty or student)	Borrower's fine balance owed	Loan status (still outstanding, or returned)
Librarian college degree	ISBN number	Author name

Required

a. Draw an E-R diagram for the library system, using the REA template as a starting point. Remember to include cardinalities.

b. Draw the tables that would be required to implement your E-R diagram. Only use the attributes listed above, unless others are absolutely necessary.

(This problem is adapted from one developed by Dr. Julie Smith David for classroom use at Arizona State University.)

Case 5-1   AnyCompany, Inc.: An Ongoing Comprehensive Case

Visit a local company (you may use the same company you selected in previous chapters) and study its revenue and expenditure cycles.

Required

a. Develop an REA model for both cycles, using an E-R diagram for documentation.

b. Develop a set of relational tables to implement your data model. Interview management and employees to determine what attributes should be included in your model.

Case 5-2   Practical Database Design

Hands-on practice in database design is important. Use a relational DBMS to implement either the basic data model for S&S's revenue cycle that was presented in this chapter, one of the enhanced data models from the homework problems, or some combination thereof. Then, perform the following tasks:

1. Create a user view of accounts receivable that is based on data stored in other tables.

2. Create a user view for sales order entry that includes information about quantity on hand of inventory items.

3. Write queries to develop an income statement and a balance sheet from your database (or at least those portions of each statement that are included in your data model).

ANSWERS TO CHAPTER QUIZ

1. b	**3.** c	**5.** b	**7.** d	**9.** a
2. c	**4.** a	**6.** b	**8.** c	**10.** d

Alternative Ways to Represent the Same Cardinality Information

Batini convention: Cardinality pair next to each entity states how many rows of the entity on the other side of the relationship can be linked to one row in the entity on this side of the relationship. Here, each sale must be linked to only one row in the customer table. Conversely, each customer can be linked to zero or many rows in the sales table.

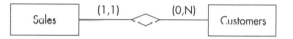

Elmasri convention (used in some MIS textbooks): Cardinality pair next to each entity states how many rows in that entity can be linked to one row in the entity on the other side of the relationship (i.e., a miror image of Batini convention). Each sale must be linked to only one customer, each customer can be linked to zero or many sales.

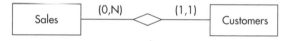

Maximums-only convention (used by Microsoft Access): Number next to an entity indicates how many rows in that entity can be linked to one row in the entity on the other side of the relationship. Here, each sale can be linked to at most one customer, each customer can be linked to at most many sales, and no information exists about minimums.

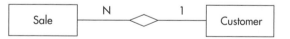

Graphical convention (similar to that used in Oracle Database products): Number of lines leading into an entity indicates how many rows in that entity can be linked to one row in the other entity. A 0 or 1 superimposed indicates minimum cardinalities. Here, each sale must be linked to only one customer, each customer may be linked to zero or many sales.

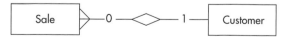

Systems Development and Documentation Techniques

Learning Objectives

After studying this chapter, you should be able to:

- Prepare and use data flow diagrams to understand, evaluate, and design information systems.
- Draw flowcharts to understand, evaluate, and design information systems.

Integrative Case: S&S, Inc.

What a hectic year it has been for Ashton Fleming! He has helped S&S get started, has overseen the installation of a simple AIS, and has helped S&S move into the world of e-business. As a result of its rapid growth, S&S has outgrown its initial AIS and Ashton has had to learn all about relational databases and data modeling. He has engaged Computer Applications (CA), a systems consulting firm, to help S&S select and install the new AIS.

During Ashton's first meeting with Kimberly Serra, CA's manager, she asked about S&S's system requirements and management's expectations. Ashton had yet to think through these issues, so he could not answer her specifically. When she asked how S&S's system worked, Ashton plunged into a discussion about the use of various company documents, but Kimberly seemed unable to fully absorb his detailed explanations. Ashton thought that part of his discussion was helpful, but overall it was irrelevant to the issue at hand.

Ashton came away impressed by CA and Kimberly. He also realized the need to understand S&S's information requirements more clearly. From his days as an auditor, Ashton knew the value of good system documentation in assisting unfamiliar users with both understanding and evaluating a system. Good system documentation would be a big help to him and Kimberly, as well as to Scott and Susan as they evaluate the current and proposed system.

After sharing his conclusions with Susan and Scott, Ashton's plan to document the current and proposed systems was well received. They supported his taking a leadership role in moving toward a new system and were especially interested in diagrams or charts that would help them understand how the system worked. Scott and Susan gave Ashton the following assignment:

1. What types of tools and techniques should S&S use to document its existing system so it is easy to understand and evaluate?
2. What development tools and techniques should S&S use to design its new computer-based information system?

INTRODUCTION

Documentation encompasses the narratives, flowcharts, diagrams, and other written material that explain how a system works. This information covers the who, what, when, where, why, and how of data entry, processing, storage, information output, and system controls. One popular means of documenting a system is to develop diagrams, flowcharts, tables, and other graphical representations of information. These are then supplemented by a **narrative description** of the system, a written step-by-step explanation of system components and interactions. In this chapter we explain data flow diagrams and flowcharts, the most common systems documentation tools. These tools save an organization both time and money.

Depending on your job function, documentation tools are important on one or more of the following levels:

1. At minimum, you must be able to *read* documentation to determine how the system works.
2. You may be required to *evaluate* internal control systems documentation to identify control strengths and weaknesses and recommend improvements. Alternatively, you may have to evaluate the documentation for a proposed system to determine if the system meets the company's needs.
3. The greatest amount of skill is needed to *prepare* documentation. If you are a member of a team that is developing a new system, then you must prepare documentation to show how both the existing and the proposed systems operate. Perhaps you will document your understanding of a company's system of internal controls for others to review.

An understanding of documentation tools is required regardless of the type of accounting career chosen. For example, Statement on Auditing Standards (SAS) 55, "Consideration of the Internal Control Structure in a Financial Statement Audit," requires that independent auditors understand a client's system of internal controls before conducting an audit. SAS 55 recommends that auditors use flowcharts to document large, complex systems. Auditors can spot internal control weaknesses and strengths more easily from such graphic portrayals.

This chapter discusses the following documentation tools:

1. *Data flow diagram,* a graphical description of the source and destination of data that shows data flow within an organization, the processes performed on the data, and how data are stored
2. *Document flowchart,* a graphical description of the flow of documents and information between departments or areas of responsibility within an organization

3. *System flowchart,* a graphical description of the relationship among the input, processing, and output in an information system

4. *Program flowchart,* a graphical description of the sequence of logical operations that a computer performs as it executes a program

These tools are used extensively in the systems development process. According to Microsoft, systems development is an extremely complex process, one that is far more complicated than building a Boeing 747. These tools are used to create order from chaos and complexity. In addition, the team members who develop information systems projects often change and these documentation tools help the new team members get up to speed quickly.

According to one study, data flow diagrams and flowcharts are the two most frequently used development and documentation tools. The study shows that 62.5 percent of information professionals use DFDs and that 97.6 percent use flowcharts. Over 92 percent of users were satisfied with the use of both DFDs and flowcharts and use both.

Both DFDs and flowcharts are easy to prepare and revise when one of the recently developed DFD or flowcharting software packages is used. These packages are easier to use, in fact, than most word processors. Once a few basic commands are mastered, users can quickly and easily prepare, store, revise, and print presentation-quality DFDs or flowcharts. To create a flowchart, the user selects the appropriate symbol, indicates where it should be placed, enters the appropriate text, and moves to the next symbol. Editing a flowchart is easy; users merely click on the appropriate symbol and add, delete, or move it.

The documentation tools explained in this chapter are used throughout the book. Data flow diagrams and systems flowcharts, for example, are used extensively to show how systems work and how data and information flow. They are also tested on professional examinations—as you can see by noting the number of questions in this book that are adapted from these exams. Learning about these tools will better prepare you for these examinations.

DATA FLOW DIAGRAMS

A **data flow diagram (DFD)** graphically describes the flow of data within an organization.[1] It is used to document existing systems and to plan and design new ones. There is no ideal way to develop a DFD, because different problems call for different methods. Some general guidelines for developing DFDs are shown in Focus 6-1.

Elements in a Data Flow Diagram

A DFD is composed of four basic elements: data sources and destinations, data flows, transformation processes, and data stores. Each is represented on a DFD by one of the symbols shown in Figure 6-1.

These four symbols are combined to show how data are processed. For example, the DFD in Figure 6-2 shows that the input to process C is data flow B, which comes from data source A. The outputs of process C are data flows D and E. Data flow E is

---

[1]Parts of this discussion are based on Tom DeMarco, *Structured Analysis and System Specification* (Upper Saddle River, New Jersey: Prentice-Hall, 1979). DeMarco has been at the forefront of structural analysis and design techniques and is a well-respected authority on the subject.

Focus 6-1

Guidelines for Drawing a DFD

1. *Understand the system.* To understand how the system works, observe the flow of information through an organization and interview the individuals who use and process the data.

2. *Ignore certain aspects of the system.* The purpose of a DFD is to diagram the origins, flow, transformation, storage, and destinations of data. Therefore, all control processes and control actions should be ignored. Only very important error paths should be included in the DFD. The details of unimportant error paths should be ignored. Determining how the system starts and stops is usually deferred to a later stage in the development process.

3. *Determine system boundaries.* Determine what to include in and exclude from the system. Include all relevant data elements in the DFD, because excluded items will not be considered during system development. When in doubt about an element's importance, include it until a definitive decision can be made to discard it.

4. *Develop a context diagram.* A context diagram is a good way of depicting system boundaries. In the diagram's center is a circle; inside of it is displayed the system of concern. The outside entities, with which the system interacts directly, are in boxes on either side, connected by data flows depicting the data passed between them. (See Figure 6-5 and its attendant discussion.) DFDs are prepared, in successively more detail, to depict data flows in the system.

5. *Identify data flows.* Identify all data flows entering or leaving the system's boundary, including where the data originate and the final destination. Any significant movement of information is usually a data flow. All data flows come from and go to either a transformation process, a data store (file), or a data source or destination. As each of these is

identified, it should be connected to the appropriate data flow. Data flows can move in two directions, shown as a line with arrows on both ends (see G in Figure 6-3).

6. *Group data flows.* A data flow can consist of one or more pieces of datum. Data elements that always flow together should be grouped together and shown as one data flow until they are separated. If the data elements do not always flow together, then they should be shown as two separate data flows.

7. *Identify transformation processes.* Place a circle wherever work is required to transform one data flow into another. All transformation processes should have one or more incoming and outgoing data flows.

8. *Group transformation processes.* Transformation processes that are logically related or occur at the same time and place should be grouped together. Never combine unrelated items into a single transformation process. If data are not processed together, or are sometimes processed differently, then separate them.

9. *Identify all files or data stores.* Data are stored temporarily or permanently in most systems. Each data repository, and each data flow into and out of it, should be identified.

10. *Identify all data sources and destinations.* All sources and destinations of data should be identified and included on the DFD.

11. *Name all DFD elements.* Except for data flows into or out of data stores (the data store name is often sufficient to identify the data-flow), data elements should be given unique and descriptive names representing what is known about them. This makes a DFD easier to read and understand as it provides the reader with key information. Naming data flows first forces the developer to concentrate on the all-important data flows, rather than on the processes or stores. Once data

(continued)

flows have been labeled, naming the processes and data stores is usually easy, because they typically take their names from the data inflows or outflows. Choose active and descriptive names, such as "daily inventory update" and "validate transaction," rather than "input data" or "update process." Process names should include action verbs such as update, edit, prepare, reconcile, and record.

12. *Subdivide the DFD.* A cluttered DFD is hard to read and understand. If you have more than five to seven processes on a single page, then use higher-level and lower-level DFDs. Decompose the context diagram into high-level processes, and then explode these high-level processes into successively lower-level processes. This process is explained in greater detail later in this chapter.

13. *Give each process a sequential number.* In a completed DFD, as shown in Figures 6-6 and 6-7 later in the chapter, each process is given a sequential number that helps readers move back and forth between the different DFD levels. Data flows should only go from lower-numbered to higher-numbered processes.

14. *Repeat the process.* DFD developers must work through organization data flows several times. Each subsequent pass helps refine the diagram and identify the fine points. As you refine the DFD, organize it to flow from top to bottom and from left to right.

15. *Prepare a final copy.* Draw a final copy of the DFD. Do not allow data flow lines to cross over each other; if necessary, repeat a data store or destination. Place the name of the DFD, the date prepared, and the preparer's name on each page.

Figure 6-1 Data flow diagram symbols

Symbol	Name	Explanation
□	Data sources and destinations	The people and organizations that send data to and receive data from the system are represented by square boxes. Data destinations are also refered to as data sinks.
 →	Data flows	The flow of the data into or out of a process is represented by curved or straight lines with arrows.
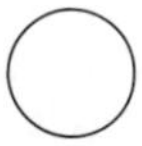 ○	Transformation processes	The processes that transform data from inputs to outputs are represented by circles. They are often refered to as bubbles.
—	Data stores	The storage of data is represented by two horizontal lines.

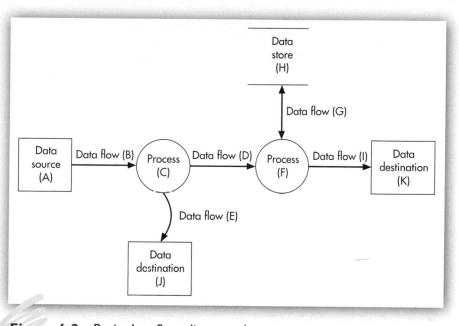

Figure 6-2   Basic data flow diagram elements

sent to data destination J. Process F uses data flows D and G as input and produces data flows I and G as output. Data flow G comes from and returns to data store H. Data flow I is sent to data destination K.

Figure 6-3 assigns specific titles to each of the processes depicted in Figure 6-2. Figures 6-2 and 6-3 will be used to examine the four basic elements of a DFD in more detail.

Data sources and destinations

A source or destination symbol on the DFD represents an organization or individual that sends or receives data that the system uses or produces. An entity can be both a source and a destination. **Data sources** and **data destinations** are represented by squares, as illustrated by items A (customer), J (bank), and K (credit manager) in Figure 6-3.

Data flows

A **data flow** represents the flow of data between processes, data stores, and data sources and destinations. Data that pass between data stores and either a data source or a destination must go through some form of data processing—that is, through a transformation process. Data flow arrows are labeled to indicate the type of data being passed. Thus, the reader knows exactly what information is flowing; no inferences are required. Data flows are represented in Figure 6-3 by items B (customer payment), D (remittance data), E (deposit), G (unlabeled; represents information entered into or retrieved from an accounts receivable data file), and I (receivables information).

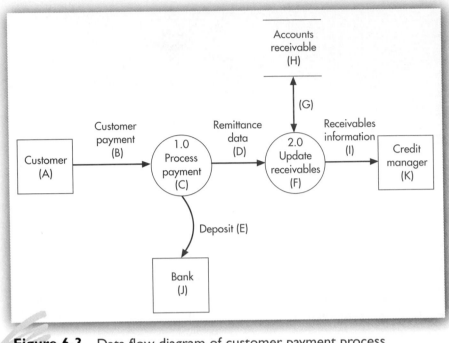

Figure 6-3   Data flow diagram of customer payment process

A data flow can consist of one or more pieces of datum. For example, data flow B (customer payment) consists of two parts: a payment and remittance data. Process 1.0 (process payment) splits these two data elements and sends them in different directions. The remittance data (D) flows to another process, where it is used to update accounts receivable records, and the payment (E) is sent to the bank with a deposit slip.

Because data flows may consist of more than one data element, the designer must determine the number of lines to show. The determining factor is if the data elements always flow together. For example, if customers sometimes send inquiries about the processing of their payments, the DFD could be revised as shown in Figure 6-4. The figure shows two lines because customer inquiries, although interacting with the same elements of the DFD, do not always accompany a payment. The two data ele-

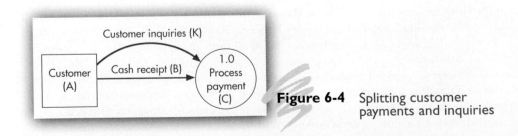

Figure 6-4   Splitting customer payments and inquiries

ments have different purposes, and customer inquiries occur less frequently. If represented by the same data flow, the separate elements would be obscured, and the DFD would be more difficult to interpret.

Processes

Processes represent the transformation of data. Figure 6-3 shows that process payment (C) takes the customer payment and splits it into the remittance data and the deposit (which includes the checks and deposit slip created within process payment). The updating receivables (F) process takes the remittance data (D) and the accounts receivables (H) data, producing an updated receivables record and sending receivables information to the credit manager.

Data stores

A **data store** is a temporary or permanent repository of data. DFDs do not show the physical storage medium (such as disks and paper) used to store the data. As with the other DFD elements, data store names should be descriptive. As shown in Figure 6-3, item H, data stores are represented by horizontal lines, with the respective name recorded inside.

Data dictionary

Data flows and stores are typically collections of data elements. For example, a data flow labeled "employee information" might contain elements such as name, address, job title, and birth date. A **data dictionary** contains a description of all data elements, stores, and flows in a system. Typically, a master copy of the data dictionary is maintained to ensure consistency and accuracy throughout the development process.

Subdividing the DFD

DFDs are subdivided into successively lower levels to provide ever-increasing amounts of detail, because few systems can be fully diagrammed on one sheet of paper. Users have differing needs, so a variety of levels can better satisfy these requirements.

The highest-level DFD is referred to as a **context diagram.** A context diagram provides the reader with a summary-level view of a system. It depicts a data processing system and the external entities that are the sources and destinations of the system's inputs and outputs.

Figure 6-5 is the context diagram that Ashton Fleming drew when he was analyzing the payroll processing procedures at S&S. It shows that the payroll processing system receives time card data from different departments and employee data from the human resources department. When these data are processed, the system produces (1) tax report and payments for governmental agencies, (2) employee payments, (3) a deposit in the payroll account at the bank, and (4) payroll data for management.

Ashton also wants to diagram the system's details, so he decides to decompose the context diagram into successively lower levels, each with an increasing amount of detail. In preparation, he wrote the narrative description of S&S's payroll processing procedures contained in Table 6-1. Take a few minutes to read this description and determine the following:

- How many major data processing activities are involved?
- What are the data inputs and outputs of each activity (ignoring all references to people, departments, and document destinations)?

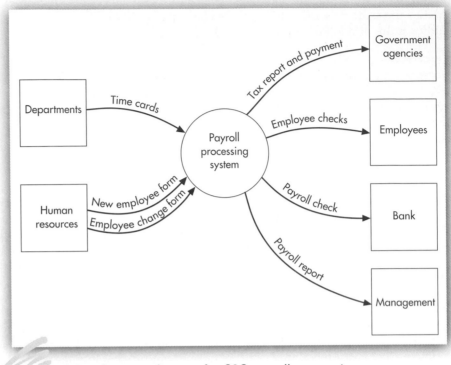

Figure 6-5   Context diagram for S&S payroll processing

Based on Ashton's description, you should have identified approximately five data processing activities. You may have noted more or fewer, depending on how you identified the activities. The first activity is updating the employee/payroll master file (first paragraph of the narrative). The second activity is handling employee compensation (second, fifth, and sixth paragraphs). Later in this chapter, you will see a breakdown of this activity into smaller parts in a lower-level DFD. A third activity is generating management reports (third paragraph). A fourth activity is paying taxes (fourth paragraph), and a fifth is posting entries to the general ledger (last paragraph). All data inflows and outflows, and the five activities, form the basis of the DFD as summarized in Table 6-2.

Using this information, Ashton exploded his context diagram and created the DFD shown in Figure 6-6. The data coming from the human resources department were grouped together and named "employee data." Notice that some data inputs and outputs have been excluded from this DFD. For example, in process 2.0, the data inflows and outflows that are not related to an external entity or to another process are not depicted (tax tables and payroll register in this case). These data flows are internal to the "pay employees" activity and are shown on the next DFD level.

Not fully satisfied with the level of detail he had captured, Ashton exploded process 2.0 (pay employees). Figure 6-7 provides more detail about the data processes

Table 6-1   Narrative Description of Payroll Processing at S&S

When employees are hired, they complete a new employee form. When a change to an employee's payroll status occurs, such as a raise or a change in the number of exemptions, human resources completes an employee change form. A copy of these forms is sent to payroll. These forms are used to create or update the records in the employee/payroll file and are then stored in the file. Employee records are stored alphabetically.

Some S&S employees are paid a salary, but most are hourly workers who record their time at work on time cards. At the end of each pay period, department managers send the time cards to the payroll department. The payroll clerk uses the time card data, data from the employee file (such as pay rate and annual salary), and the appropriate tax tables to prepare a two-part check for each employee. The clerk also prepares a two-part payroll register showing gross pay, deductions, and net pay for each employee. The clerk updates the employee file to reflect each employee's current earnings. The original copy of the employee paychecks is forwarded to Susan. The payroll register is forwarded to the accounts payable clerk. The time cards and the duplicate copies of the payroll register and paychecks are stored by date in the payroll file.

Every pay period the payroll clerk uses the data in the employee/payroll file to prepare a payroll summary report for Susan so that she can control and monitor labor expenses. This report is forwarded to Susan, with the original copies of the employee paychecks.

Every month the payroll clerk uses the data in the employee/payroll file to prepare a two-part tax report. The original is forwarded to the accounts payable clerk, and the duplicate is added to the tax records in the payroll file. The accounts payable clerk uses the tax report to prepare a two-part check for taxes and a two-part cash disbursements voucher. The tax report and the original copy of each document are forwarded to Susan. The duplicates are stored by date in the accounts payable file.

The accounts payable clerk uses the payroll register to prepare a two-part check for the total amount of the employee payroll and a two-part disbursements voucher. The original copy of each document is forwarded to Susan, and the payroll register and the duplicates are stored by date in the accounts payable file.

Susan reviews each packet of information she receives and approves and signs the checks. She forwards the cash disbursements vouchers to Ashton, the tax reports and payments to the appropriate governmental agency, the payroll check to the bank, and the employee checks to the employees. She files the payroll report chronologically.

Ashton uses the payroll tax and the payroll check cash disbursement vouchers to update the general ledger. He then cancels the journal voucher by marking it "posted" and files it numerically.

---

involved in paying employees, and it includes the tax tables and the payroll register data flow omitted from Figure 6-6. In a similar fashion, each of the processes shown in Figure 6-6 could be exploded to show a greater level of detail.

FLOWCHARTS

A **flowchart** is an analytical technique used to describe some aspect of an information system in a clear, concise, and logical manner. Flowcharts use a standard set of symbols to describe pictorially the transaction processing procedures a company uses and the flow of data through a system. General guidelines for preparing flowcharts

Table 6-2   Activities and Data Flows in Payroll Processing at S&S

Activities	Data Inputs	Data Outputs
Update employee/payroll file	New employee form Employee change form Employee/payroll file	Updated employee/payroll file
Pay employees	Time cards Employee/payroll file Tax rates table	Employee checks Payroll register Updated employee/payroll file Payroll check Payroll cash disbursements voucher
Prepare reports	Employee/payroll file	Payroll report
Pay taxes	Employee/payroll file	Tax report Tax payment Payroll tax cash disbursements voucher Updated employee/payroll file

Update general ledger	Payroll tax cash
	    disbursements voucher
	Payroll cash
	    disbursements voucher
		Updated general ledger

that are readable, clear, concise, consistent, and understandable are presented in Focus 6-2.

Flowchart Symbols

The symbols used to create flowcharts are shown in Figure 6-8. Each symbol has a special meaning that is easily conveyed by its shape. The shape indicates and describes the operations performed and the input, output, processing, and storage media employed. The symbols are drawn by a software program or with a **flowcharting template,** a piece of hard, flexible plastic on which the shapes of symbols have been diecut.

Flowcharting symbols can be divided into the following four categories, as shown in Figure 6-8:

1. *Input/output symbols* represent devices or media that provide input to or record output from processing operations.
2. *Processing symbols* either show what type of device is used to process data or indicate when processing is completed manually.
3. *Storage symbols* represent the devise used to store data that the system is not currently using.
4. *Flow and miscellaneous symbols* indicate the flow of data and goods. They also represent such operations as where flowcharts begin or end, where decisions are made, and when to add explanatory notes to flowcharts.

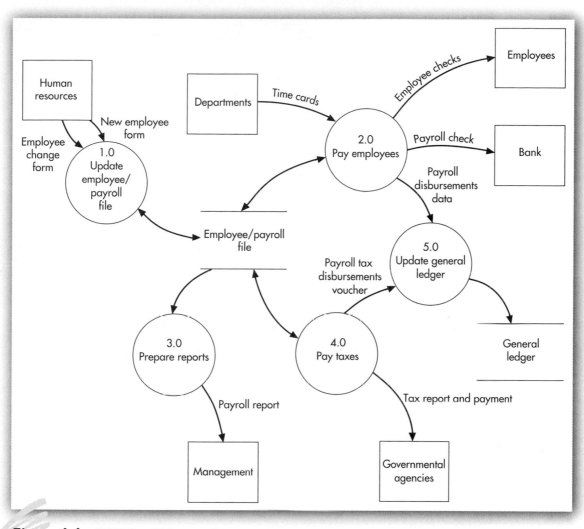

Figure 6-6   DFD for S&S payroll processing

Document Flowcharts

A **document flowchart** illustrates the flow of documents and information among areas of responsibility within an organization. Document flowcharts trace a document from its cradle to its grave. They show where each document originates, its distribution, the purposes for which it is used, its ultimate disposition, and everything that happens as it flows through the system.

A document flowchart is particularly useful in analyzing the adequacy of control procedures in a system, such as internal checks and segregation of functions. Flowcharts that describe and evaluate internal controls are often referred to as **internal control flowcharts.** The document flowchart can reveal weaknesses or inefficiencies

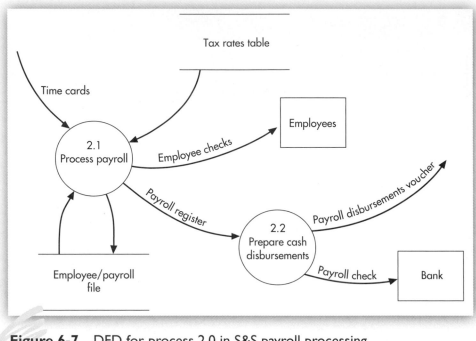

Figure 6-7   DFD for process 2.0 in S&S payroll processing

in a system, such as inadequate communication flows, unnecessary complexity in document flows, or procedures responsible for causing wasteful delays. Document flowcharts also can be prepared as part of the systems design process and should be included in the documentation of an information system.

The document flowchart that Ashton developed for the payroll process at S&S, as described in Table 6-2, is shown in Figure 6-9.

System Flowcharts

System flowcharts depict the relationship among the input, processing, and output of an AIS. A system flowchart begins by identifying both the inputs that enter the system and their origins. The input can be new data entering the system, data stored for future use, or both. The input is followed by the processing portion of the flowchart, that is, the steps performed on the data. The logic the computer uses to perform the processing task is shown on a program flowchart. The resulting new information is the output component, which can be stored for later use, displayed on a screen, or printed on paper. In many instances, the output from one process is an input to another.

The sales processing system flowchart in Figure 6-10 represents Ashton's proposal to capture sales data using state-of-the-art sales terminals. These terminals will edit the sales data and print a customer receipt. All sales data will be stored in a sales data file on a disk. At the end of each day, the data will be forwarded to S&S's computers, where it will be summarized and batch totals will be printed. A batch total is the

Focus 6-2

Guidelines for Preparing Flowcharts

1. Understand a system before flowcharting it. Interview users, developers, auditors, and management, or have them complete a questionnaire. Read through a narrative description of the system, or walk through system transactions.

2. Identify the entities to be flowcharted, such as departments, job functions, or external parties. Identify documents and information flows in the system as well as the activities or processes performed on the data. (For example, when reading a description of the system, the preparer could draw a box around the entities, a circle around the documents, and a line under the activities.)

3. When several entities, such as departments or functions, need to be shown on a flowchart, divide the flowchart into columns with a label for each. Flowchart the activities of each entity in its respective column.

4. Flowchart only the normal flow of operations, ensuring that all procedures and processes are in the proper order. Identify exception procedures by using the annotation symbol.

5. Design the flowchart so that flow proceeds from top to bottom and from left to right.

6. Give the flowchart a clear beginning and ending. Designate where each document originated, and show the final disposition of all documents so there are no loose ends that leave the reader dangling.

7. Use the standard flowcharting symbols, and draw them with a template or a computer.

8. Clearly label all symbols. Write a description of the input, process, or output inside the symbol. If the description will not fit, use the annotation symbol. Print neatly, rather than writing in cursive.

9. When using multiple copies of a document, place document numbers in the top right-hand corner of the symbol. The document number should accompany the symbol as it moves through the system.

10. Each manual processing symbol should have an input and an output. Do not directly connect two documents, except when moving from one column to another. When a document is moved to another column, it is usually best to show the document in both.

11. Use on-page connectors to avoid excess flow lines, which results in a neat-looking page. Use off-page connectors to move from one flowchart page to another. Clearly label all connectors to avoid confusion.

12. Use arrowheads on all flow lines. Do not assume that the reader will know the direction of the flow.

13. If a flowchart cannot fit on a single page, clearly label the pages 1 of 3, 2 of 3, and so on.

14. Show documents or reports first in the column in which they are created. They can then be shown moving to another column for further processing. A manual process is not needed to show documents being forwarded.

15. Show all data entered into or retrieved from a computer file as passing through a processing operation (a computer program) first.

16. Draw a line from the document to a file to indicate that it is being filed. A manual process is not needed to show a document entering a file.

17. Draw a rough sketch of the flowchart as a first effort. Be more concerned with capturing content than a perfect drawing. Few systems can be flowcharted in a single draft.

18. Redesign the flowchart to avoid clutter and a large number of crossed lines.

19. Verify the flowchart's accuracy by reviewing it with the people familiar with the system. Be sure all uses of flowcharting conventions are consistent.

20. Draw a final copy of the flowchart. Place the name of the flowchart, the date, and the preparer's name on each page.

Symbol	Name	Explanation
Input/Output Symbols		
	Document	A document or report: the document may be prepared by hand or printed by a computer
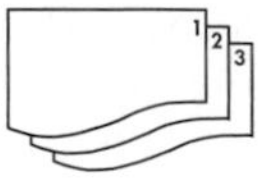	Multiple copies of one document	Illustrated by overlapping the document symbol and printing the document number on the face of the document in the upper right corner
	Input/output; Journal/ledger	Any function of input or output on a program flowchart. Also used to represent accounting journals and ledgers in a document flowchart
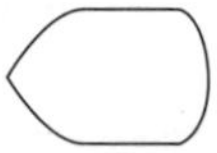	Display	Information displayed by an online output devise such as a terminal, monitor, or screen
	Online keying	Data entry by online devices such as a terminal or personal computer
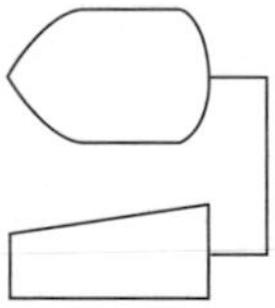	Terminal or personal computer	The display and online keying symbols are used together to represent terminals and personal computers
	Transmittal tape	Manually prepared control totals; used for control purposes to compare to computer-generated totals
Processing Symbols		
	Computer processing	A computer-performed processing function; usually results in a change in data or information
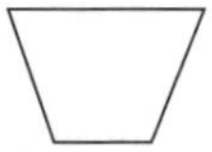	Manual operation	A processing operation performed manually
	Auxiliary operation	A processing function done by a device that is not a computer
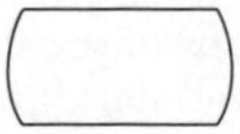	Off-line keying operation	An operation utilizing an off-line keying device (e.g., key to disk, cash register)

Figure 6-8 Common flowcharting symbols

Symbol	Name	Explanation
Storage Symbols		
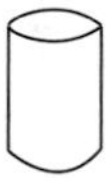	Magnetic disk	Data stored permanently on a magnetic disk; used for master files and databases
	Magnetic tape	Data stored on a magnetic tape
	Diskette	Data stored on a diskette
	On-line storage	Data stored in a temporary on-line file in a direct-access medium such as a disk
	File	File of documents manually stored and retrieved; inscribed letter indicates file-ordering sequence N=numerically, A=alphabetically, D=by date
Flow and Miscellaneous Symbols		
	Document or processing flow	Direction of processing or document flow; normal flow is down and to the right
	Data/information flow	Direction of data/information flow; often used to show data copied from one document to another
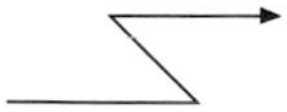	Communication link	Transmission of data from one location to another via communication lines
	On-page connector	Connects the processing flow on the same page; its usage avoids lines crisscrossing a page
	Off-page connector	An entry from, or an exit to, another page
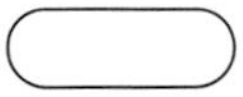	Terminal	A beginning, end, or point of interruption in a process or program; also used to indicate an external party
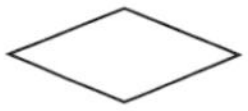	Decision	A decision-making step; used in a computer program flowchart to show branching to alternative paths
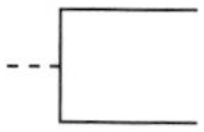	Annotation	Addition of descriptive comments or explanatory notes as clarification

Figure 6-8 Common flowcharting symbols (Continued)

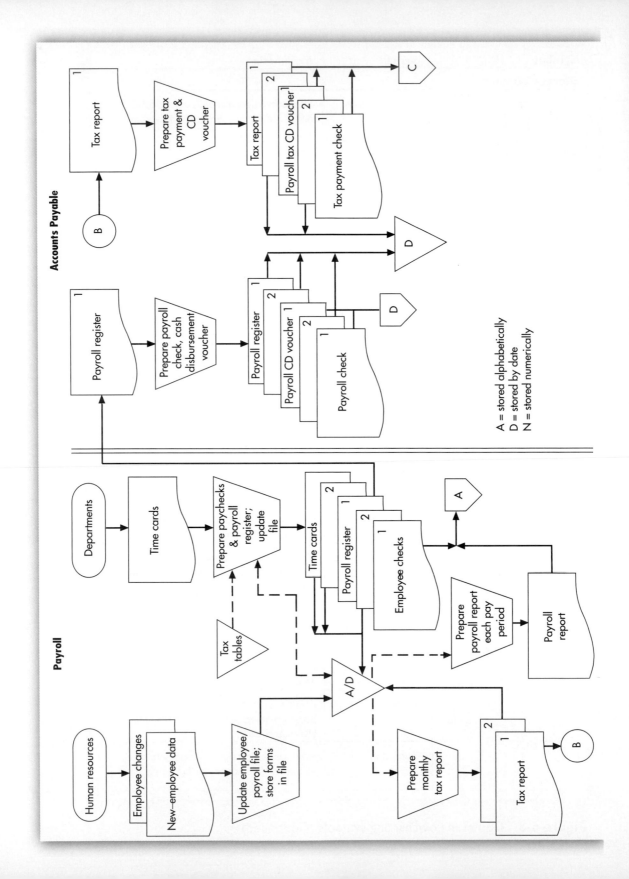

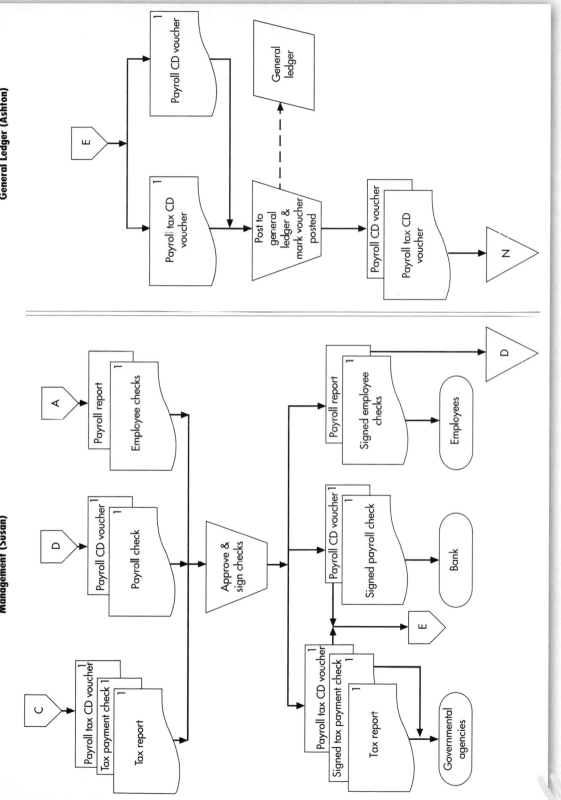

Figure 6-9 Document flowchart of payroll processing at S&S

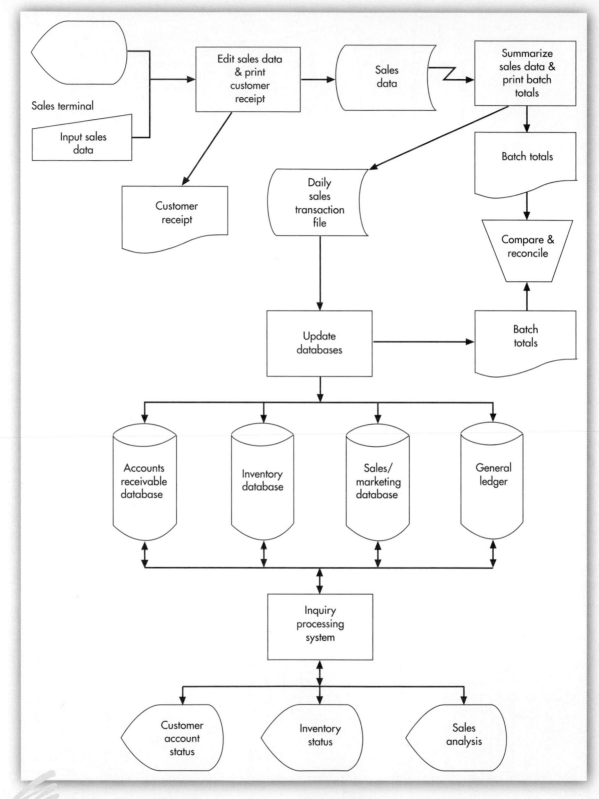

Figure 6-10   System flowchart of sales processing at S&S

sum of a numerical item contained in each transaction being processed. An example is total sales for all sales transactions. The summary data will then be processed, and batch totals will again be generated and printed. These amounts will be compared with the batch totals generated prior to processing, and all errors and exceptions will be reconciled. The accounts receivable, inventory, and sales marketing databases and the general ledger will be updated. Users can access the files at any time by using an inquiry processing system. This system will produce standard reports and allow users to access the data needed for special analyses.

System flowcharts are an important systems analysis, design, and evaluation tool. They are universally employed in systems work and provide an immediate form of communication among workers. The system flowchart is an excellent vehicle for describing information flows and procedures within an AIS.

Program Flowcharts

A **program flowchart** illustrates the sequence of logical operations performed by a computer in executing a program. The relationship between system and program flowcharts is shown in Figure 6-11.

Figure 6-11   Relationhip between system and program flowcharts. A program flowchart describes the specific logic to perform a process shown on a system flowchart.

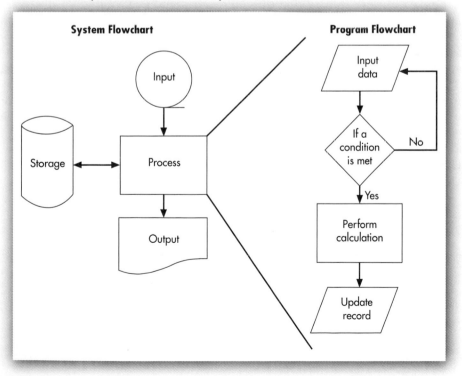

Program flowcharts employ a subset of the symbols shown in Figure 6-8. Once designed and approved, the program flowchart serves as the blueprint for coding the computer program.

SUMMARY AND CASE CONCLUSION

Ashton prepared the DFDs and flowcharts of S&S's payroll processing system (Figures 6-6, 6-7, 6-9, and 6-10) to document and explain the operation of the existing system. He was pleased to see that Scott and Susan were able to grasp the essence of the system from this documentation. The DFDs indicated the logical flow of data and the flowcharts illustrated the physical dimensions of the system: The origin and final disposition and the interworkings of the documents in each department were clear.

Susan and Scott agreed that Ashton should document the remainder of the system. The documentation would help all of them understand the current system. It would also help Ashton and the consultants design the new system. In fact, the payroll documentation had already helped them identify a few minor changes they wanted to make in their system. Using the information from Figure 6-9, Susan now understands why the payroll clerk sometimes had to borrow the only copy of the payroll report that was prepared. She thus recommended that a second copy be made and kept in the payroll department. Susan also questioned the practice of keeping all the payroll records in one employee/payroll file. To keep the file from becoming unwieldy, she recommended that it be divided into three files: personal employee data, pay period documentation, and payroll tax data. A discussion with the payroll clerk verified that this approach would make payroll processing easier and more efficient.

Over the next few weeks, Ashton documented the remaining accounting cycles. This process helped him identify inefficiencies and unneeded reports. He also found that some system documents were inadequately controlled. In addition, he got several ideas about how an automated system could help him reengineer the business processes at S&S. By substituting technology for manpower, outdated processes and procedures could be eliminated to make the system more effective.

When Ashton completed his analysis and documentation of the current system, Susan and Scott asked him to continue his work in designing a new system using a relational database. To do that, Ashton must thoroughly understand the information needs of the various employees in the company. Then he can design a new system using the tools, such as DFDs and flowcharts, that were examined in this chapter (systems development is discussed in Chapters 16 through 18).

KEY TERMS

- documentation
- narrative description
- data flow diagram (DFD)
- data sources
- data destinations
- data flow
- processes
- data store
- data dictionary
- context diagram
- flowchart
- flowcharting template
- document flowchart
- internal control flowchart
- system flowchart
- program flowchart

CHAPTER QUIZ

1. A DFD is a representation of which of the following?
   a. relationship among input, processing, and output of an AIS
   b. flow of data in an organization
   c. decision rules in a computer program
   d. computer hardware configuration

2. Documentation methods such as DFDs and flowcharts save both time and money, adding value to an organization.
   a. True
   b. False

3. Which of the following statements is false?
   a. Flowcharts make use of many symbols.
   b. A flowchart emphasizes the flow of documents or records containing data.
   c. DFDs help convey the timing of events.
   d. Both a and b are false.

4. A DFD consists of the following four basic elements: data sources and destinations, data flows, transformation processes, and data stores. Each is represented on a DFD by a different symbol.
   a. True
   b. False

5. Which of the following is not one of the guidelines that should be followed in naming DFD data elements?
   a. If a name cannot completely describe the data or process, then decompose the flow or process further.
   b. Make sure the names describe all the data or the entire process.
   c. Name only the most important DFD elements.
   d. Choose active and descriptive names.

6. The understanding of documentation skills that accountants require varies with their job function. However, they should at least be able to do which of the following?
   a. Read documentation to determine how the system works.
   b. Critique and correct documentation that others prepare.
   c. Prepare documentation for a newly developed information system.
   d. Teach others how to prepare documentation.

7. Which of the following statements is false?
   a. A flowchart is an analytical technique used to describe some aspect of an information system in a clear, concise, and logical manner.
   b. Flowcharts use a standard set of symbols to describe pictorially the flow of documents and data through a system.
   c. Flowcharts are easy to prepare and revise when the designer utilizes a flowcharting software package.
   d. A system flowchart is a narrative representation of an information system.
   e. A program flowchart shows the logic used in computer programs.

8. Which of the following flowcharts illustrates the flow of information among areas of responsibility in an organization?
   a. program flowchart
   b. computer configuration chart
   c. system flowchart
   d. document flowchart

9. Which of the following is not one of the recommended guidelines for making flowcharts more readable, clear, concise, consistent, and understandable?
   a. Divide the flowchart into columns with labels.
   b. Flowchart all information flows, especially exception procedures and error routines.
   c. Design the flowchart so that flow proceeds from top to bottom and from left to right.
   d. Show the final disposition of all documents to prevent loose ends that leave the reader dangling.
   e. Each manual processing symbol should have an input and an output.
10. Data sources and destinations are represented in a data flow diagram as:
   a. a square
   b. a curved arrow
   c. a circle
   d. two parallel lines
   e. none of the above

DISCUSSION QUESTIONS

6.1 Identify the DFD elements in the following narrative: A customer purchases a few items from a local grocery store. Jill, a salesclerk, enters the transaction in the cash register and takes the customer's money. At closing, Jill gives both the cash and the register tape to her manager.

6.2 Do you agree with the following statement: "Any one of the systems documentation procedures, such as a DFD, can adequately document a given system"? Explain.

6.3 Compare the guidelines for preparing flowcharts and DFDs. What general design principles and limitations are common to both documentation techniques?

6.4 Your classmate asks you to explain flowcharting conventions using real-world examples. Draw each of the major flowchart symbols from memory, placing them into one of six categories: input/output, processing, storage, data flow, and miscellaneous. For each symbol, suggest several uses.

PROBLEMS

6.1 Prepare systems flowcharting segments for each of the following operations:
   a. processing transactions stored on magnetic tape to update a master file stored on magnetic tape
   b. processing transactions stored on magnetic tape to update a database stored on a disk
   c. converting source documents off-line to magnetic tape using an optical character reader (OCR)
   d. processing OCR documents on-line to update a database on magnetic disk
   e. reading data from a disk file into the computer to be printed on a report
   f. keying data from source documents to a temporary file stored on a disk
   g. manually sorting and filing invoices
   h. processing source data on-line using a terminal from a remote location, which is connected to a central computer system for updating and recording source data in a database stored on magnetic disk

6.2 The Happy Valley Utility Company uses turnaround documents in its computerized customer accounting system. Meter readers are provided with preprinted computer forms, each containing the account number, name, address, and previous meter readings. Each form also contains a formatted area in which the customer's current meter reading can be marked in pencil. After making their rounds, meter readers turn in batches of these documents to the computer data preparation department, where they are processed by a mark-sense document reader that transfers their contents to magnetic tape.

This magnetic tape file is then sent to the computer center, where it is used as input for two computer runs. The first run sorts the transaction records on the tape into sequential order by customer account number. On the second run, the sorted transaction tape is processed against the customer master file, which is stored on a magnetic disk. Second-run outputs are (1) a printed report listing summary information and any erroneous transactions detected by the computer and (2) customer bills printed in a special OCR-readable font. Bills are mailed, and customers are requested to return the stub portion along with payment.

Customer payments are received in the mail room and checked for consistency against the returned stubs. Checks are then sent to the cashier's office. The mail room provides the computer data preparation department with three sets of records: (1) stubs with compatible amounts, (2) stubs with differing amounts, and (3) a list of amounts received from customers without stubs. For the latter two types of records, data preparation personnel use a special typewriter to prepare corrected stubs. An OCR document reader then processes all the stubs and transfers their contents onto magnetic tape.

The magnetic tape containing the payment records is then sent to the computer center, where it is sorted on the computer into sequential order by customer account number and processed against the customer master file to post the payment amounts. Two printed outputs from this second process are (1) reports listing erroneous transactions and summary information and (2) past-due customer balances.

Required
a. Draw a system flowchart of the billing operations, commencing with the computer preparation of the meter reading forms and ending with the mailing of customer bills.
b. Draw a system flowchart depicting customer payments processing, starting with the mail room operations and ending with the computer run that posts the payment amounts to the customer master file.

6.3 The Dewey Construction Company processes its payroll transactions to update both its payroll master file and its work-in-process master file in the same computer run. Both the payroll master file and the work-in-process master file are maintained on disk and accessed directly.

Data to be input to this system are keyed onto a tape using a key-to-tape encoder. The tape is then processed to update the files. This processing run also produces a payroll register on magnetic tape, employee paychecks and earnings statements, and a printed report listing error transactions and summary information.

Required
Prepare a system flowchart of the process described.

6.4 Prepare a document flowchart to reflect how ANGIC Insurance Company processes its casualty claims. The process begins when the claims department receives a notice of loss from a claimant. Claims prepares and sends the claimant four copies of a proof-of-loss form on which the claimant must detail the cause, amount, and other aspects of the loss. Claims also initiates a record of the claim, which is sent with the notice of loss to the data processing department, where it is filed by claim number.

The claimant must fill out the proof-of-loss forms with an adjuster's assistance. The adjuster must concur with the claimant on the estimated amount of loss. The claimant and adjuster each keep one copy of the proof-of-loss form. The claimant sends the two remaining copies to the claims department. Separately, the adjuster submits a report to the claims department, confirming the estimates on the claimant's proof-of-loss form.

The claims department authorizes a payment to the claimant, forwards a copy of the proof-of-loss form to data processing, and files the original proof-of-loss form and the adjuster's report alphabetically. The data processing department prepares payment checks and mails them to the customers, files the proof-of-loss form with the claim record, and prepares a list of disbursements, which it transmits to the accounting department.

6.5 Beccan Company is a discount tire dealer operating 25 retail stores in the metropolitan area. Beccan sells both private-brand and name-brand tires. The company operates a centralized purchasing and warehousing facility and employs a perpetual inventory system. All purchases of tires and related supplies are placed through the company's central purchasing department to optimize quantity discounts. The tires and supplies are received at the central warehouse and distributed to the retail stores as needed. The perpetual inventory system at the central facility maintains current inventory records, designated reorder points, and optimum order quantities for each type and size of tire and other related supplies. Beccan uses the following five documents in its inventory control system.

- *Retail stores requisition.* The retail stores submit this document to the central warehouse when they need tires or supplies. The shipping clerks in the warehouse department fill the orders from inventory and authorize delivery to the stores.
- *Purchase requisition.* The inventory control clerk in the inventory control department prepares this document when the quantity on hand for an item falls below the designated reorder point. It is then forwarded to the purchasing department.
- *Purchase order.* The purchasing department prepares this document when items need to be ordered. It is then submitted to an authorized vendor.
- *Receiving report.* The warehouse department prepares this document when ordered items are received from vendors. The receiving clerk completes the document by indicating the vendor's name and the date and quantity of the shipment received.
- *Invoice.* An invoice is received from vendors, specifying the amounts Beccan owes.

The following departments are involved in Beccan's inventory control system:

- *Inventory control department.* Responsible for the maintenance of all perpetual inventory records for all stock items. This inventory includes current quantity on hand, reorder point, optimum order quantity, and quantity on order for each item carried.
- *Warehouse department.* Maintains the physical inventory of all items carried in stock. All orders from vendors are received (receiving clerk) and all distributions to retail stores are filled (shipping clerks) in this department.
- *Purchasing department.* Places all orders for items needed by the company.
- *Accounts payable department.* Maintains all open accounts with vendors and other creditors, in addition to processing payments.

Required

Prepare a document flowchart that indicates the interaction and use of these documents among all departments at Beccan Company's central facility. It should provide adequate internal control over the receipt, issuance, replenishment, and payment of tires and supplies. You may assume that there is a sufficient number of document copies to ensure that the perpetual inventory system has the necessary basic internal controls.

(CMA Examination, adapted)

6.6   As the internal auditor for No-Wear Products of Hibbing, Minnesota, you have been asked by your supervisor to document the company's current payroll processing system. Based on your documentation, No-Wear hopes to develop a plan for revising the current information system to eliminate unnecessary delays in paycheck processing. Your best explanation of the system came from an interview with the head payroll clerk:

> *The payroll processing system at No-Wear Products is fairly simple. Time data are recorded in each department using time cards and clocks. It is annoying, however, when people forget to punch out at night and we have to record their time information by hand. At the end of the period, our payroll clerks enter the time card data into a payroll file for processing. Our clerks are pretty good—though I've had to make my share of corrections when they mess up the data entry.*
>
> *Before the payroll file is processed for the current period, human resources sends us data on personnel changes, such as increases in pay rates and new employees. Our clerks enter this information into the payroll file so it is available for processing. Usually, when mistakes get back to us, it's because human resources is recording the wrong pay rate or an employee has left and the department forgets to remove the record.*
>
> *The data are then processed and individual employee paychecks are generated. Several important reports are also generated for management—though I don't know exactly what they do with them. In addition, the government requires regular federal and state withholding reports for tax purposes. Currently, the system generates these reports automatically, which is nice.*

Required

a. Prepare a context diagram for the current payroll processing system at No-Wear Products.

b. Develop a DFD to document the payroll processing system at No-Wear Products.

6.7   Ashton Fleming has decided to analyze the accounts payable process at S&S. His intent is to document how the present system works so the transition to a computerized system will be easier. He also hopes to improve any weaknesses he discovers in the system. In the following narrative, Ashton explains what happens at S&S:

> *Before S&S pays a vendor invoice, the invoice must be matched against the purchase order used to request the goods and the receiving report that the receiving department prepares. Because all three of these documents enter the accounts payable department at different times, a separate alphabetical file is kept for each type of document. The purchase orders that are forwarded from purchasing are stored in a purchase order file. The receiving reports are stored in a receiving report file. When vendor invoices are received, the accounts payable clerk records the amount due in the accounts payable ledger and then files the invoices in the vendor invoice file.*
>
> *S&S's policy is to make sure all accounts are paid within 30 days to take advantage of the early-payment discounts that suppliers offer. When it comes time to pay a particular bill, the accounts payable clerk retrieves the vendor invoice and attaches the purchase order and the receiving report. These matched documents are forwarded to Ashton Fleming.*
>
> *Ashton reviews the documents to ensure they are complete and prepares a two-part check. The checks and the other three documents are forwarded to Susan for her approval and signature. Ashton records the check amount in the cash disbursements journal.*

Susan reviews the documents to ensure they are valid payables and then signs the checks. She forwards the check to the vendor and returns the documents and the second copy of the check to the accounts payable clerk. The clerk files the documents alphabetically in a paid invoice file.

At the end of every month, the accounts payable clerk uses information from the accounts payable ledger to prepare an accounts payable report. This report is forwarded to Susan for her review. After she is finished with the report, Susan files it chronologically.

Required
a. Prepare a DFD to document accounts payable processing at S&S.
b. Prepare a document flowchart to document accounts payable processing at S&S.

6.8 Since opening its doors in Hawaii two years ago, Oriental Trading has enjoyed tremendous success. As a wholesaler, Oriental Trading purchases textiles from Asian markets and resells them to local retail shops. To keep up with the strong demand for textiles in the Hawaiian Islands, Oriental Trading is expanding its local operations. At the heart of the expansion is the introduction of a new information system to handle the tremendous increase in purchases.

You have conducted several interviews with department supervisors who interact with the acquisition/payment system. The following is a summary of your discussions:

A purchase requisition is sent from the inventory system to Sky Ishibashi, a clerk in the purchasing department. Sky prepares a purchase order from information in the vendor and inventory files and mails it to the vendor. The vendor returns a vendor acknowledgment to Sky indicating receipt of the purchase order. Sky then sends a purchase order notification to Elei Mateaki, a clerk in the accounts payable department.

When the receiving department accepts vendor goods, the inventory system notifies Elei by sending him a receiving report. Elei also receives invoices from the various vendors. He matches the invoices with the purchase order notification and the receiving report and updates the accounts payable master file. Elei then sends a payment authorization to the accounting department. There, Andeloo Nonu prepares and mails a check to the vendor. When the check is issued, the system automatically updates the accounts payable master file and the general ledger.

Required
Develop a context diagram and a DFD of the acquisition/payment system at Oriental Trading.

6.9 Ashton Fleming has worked furiously for the past month trying to completely document the major business information flows at S&S. Upon completing his personal interviews with cash receipts clerks, Ashton asks you to develop a comprehensive DFD for the cash receipts system. Ashton's narrative of the system follows:

Customer payments include cash received at the time of purchase and account payments received in the mail. At day's end, the treasurer endorses all checks and prepares a deposit slip for the checks and the cash. A clerk then deposits the checks, cash, and deposit slip at the local bank each day.

When checks are received as payment for accounts due, a remittance slip is included with the payment. The remittance slips are used to update the accounts receivable file at the end of the day. The remittance slips are stored in a file drawer by date.

Every week, a cash receipts report and an aged trial balance are generated from the data in the accounts receivable ledger. The cash receipts report is sent to Scott and Susan. A copy of the aged trial balance by customer account is sent to the credit and collections department.

Required

Develop a context diagram and a DFD for the cash receipts system at S&S.

6.10 A mail order skin and body care company advertises in magazines. Magazine subscribers initiate most orders by completing and sending coupons directly to the company. The firm also takes orders by phone, answers inquiries about products, and handles payments and cancellations of orders. Products that have been ordered are sent either directly to the customer or to the company's regional offices that handle the required distribution. The mail order company has three basic data files, which contain customer mailing information, product inventory information, and billing information based on invoice number. During the next few years, the company expects to become a multimillion-dollar operation. Recognizing the need to computerize much of the mail order business, the company has begun the process by calling you.

Required

Draw a context diagram and at least two levels of DFDs for the preceding operations.

6.11 The local community college requires that each student complete a registration request form and mail or deliver it to the registrar's office. A clerk enters the request into the system. First, the system checks the accounts receivable subsystem to ensure that no fees are owed from the previous quarter. Next, for each course, the system checks the student transcript to ensure that he or she has completed the course prerequisites. Then the system checks class position availability and adds the student's Social Security number to the class list.

The report back to the student shows the result of registration processing: If the student owes fees, a bill is sent and the registration is rejected. If prerequisites for a course are not fulfilled, the student is notified and that course is not registered. If the class is full, the student request is annotated with "course closed." If a student is accepted into a class, then the day, time, and room are printed next to the course number. Student fees and total tuition are computed and printed on the form. Student fee information is interfaced to the accounts receivable subsystem. Course enrollment reports are prepared for the instructors.

Required

Prepare a context diagram and at least two levels of DFDs for this operation.

6.12 Charting, Inc., a new audit client of yours, processes its sales and cash receipts documents in the following manner:

1. *Payment on account.* Each morning a mail clerk in the sales department opens the mail. The mail clerk prepares a remittance advice (showing customer and amount paid) if one is not received. The checks and remittance advices are then forwarded to the sales department supervisor, who reviews each check and forwards the checks and remittance advices to the accounting department supervisor.

   The accounting department supervisor, who also functions as credit manager in approving new credit and all credit limits, reviews all checks for payments on past-due accounts and then forwards the checks and remittance advices to the accounts receivable clerk, who arranges the advices in alphabetical order. The remittance advices are posted directly to the accounts receivable ledger cards. The checks are endorsed by stamp and totaled. The total is posted to the cash receipts journal. The remittance advices are filed chronologically. After receiving the cash from the previous day's cash sales, the accounts receivable clerk prepares the daily deposit slip in triplicate. The third copy of the deposit slip is filed by date, and the second copy and the original accompany the bank deposit.

2. *Sales.* Sales clerks prepare sales invoices in triplicate. The original and second copy are presented to the cashier. The sales clerk retains the third copy in the sales book. When the sale is for cash, the customer pays the sales clerk, who presents the money to the cashier with the invoice copies.

The cashier approves a credit sale from an approved credit list after the sales clerk prepares the three-part invoice. After receiving the cash or approving the invoice, the cashier validates the original copy of the sales invoice and gives it to the customer. At the end of each day, the cashier recaps the sales and cash received and forwards the cash and the second copy of the sales invoices to the accounts receivable clerk.

The accounts receivable clerk balances the cash received with cash sales invoices and prepares a daily sales summary. The credit sales invoices are posted to the accounts receivable ledger, and then all invoices are sent to the inventory control clerk in the sales department for posting to the inventory control cards. After posting, the inventory control clerk files all invoices numerically. The accounts receivable clerk posts the daily sales summary to the cash receipts and sales journals and files the sales summaries by date.

The cash from cash sales is combined with the cash received on account to make up the daily bank deposit.

3. *Bank deposits.* The bank validates the deposit slip and returns the second copy to the accounting department, where the accounts receivable clerk files it by date.

Monthly bank statements are reconciled promptly by the accounting department supervisor and filed by date.

Required

You recognize that there are weaknesses in the existing system and believe a document flowchart would be beneficial in evaluating this client's internal control in preparing for your examination of the financial statements.

a. Complete the flowchart given in Figure 6-12, for sales and cash receipts of Charting, Inc., by labeling the appropriate symbols and indicating information flows. The chart is complete as to symbols and document flows.

b. Using the guidelines for preparing flowcharts in Focus 6-2 and the flowcharting symbols shown in Figure 6-8, critique the flowchart shown in Figure 6-12. List the ways the flowchart violates the guidelines or uses improper symbols.

(CPA Examination, adapted)

6.13 A partially completed charge sales system flowchart appears in Figure 6-13. The flowchart depicts the charge sales activities of the Bottom Manufacturing Corporation.

A customer's purchase order is received, and a six-part sales order is prepared therefrom. The six copies are initially distributed as follows:

Copy 1—Billing copy, to billing department

Copy 2—Shipping copy, to shipping department

Copy 3—Credit copy, to credit department

Copy 4—Stock request copy, to credit department

Copy 5—Customer copy, to customer

Copy 6—Sales order copy, file in sales order department

When each copy of the sales order reaches the appropriate department or destination, it calls for specific internal control procedures and related documents. Some procedures and related documents are indicated on the flowchart; others are labeled by the letters a to r.

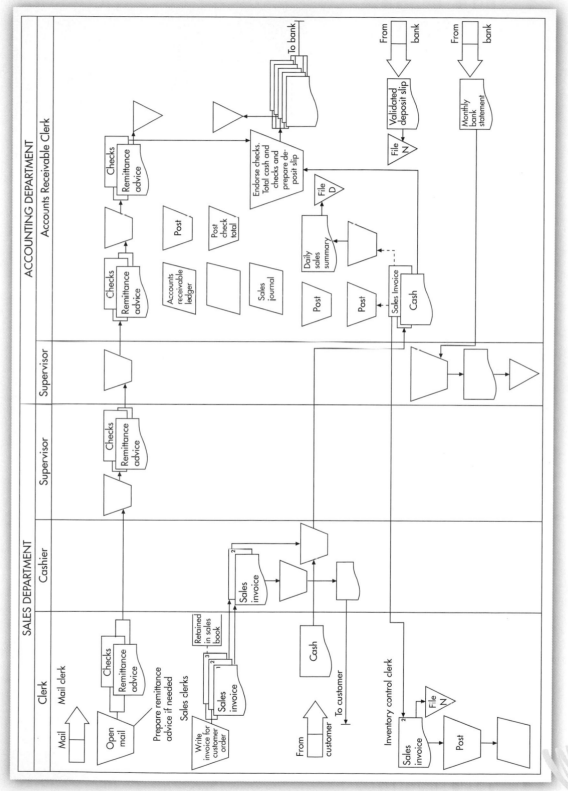

Figure 6-12 Charting, Inc. flowchart for sales and cash receipts

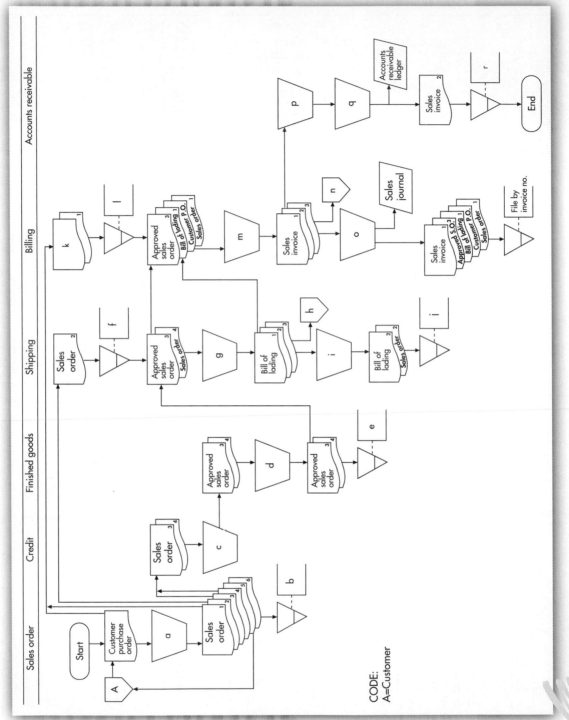

Figure 6-13 Bottom manufacturing corporation flowchart of credit sales activities

Required

a. List the procedures or the internal documents that are labeled letters c to r in the flowchart of Bottom Manufacturing Corporation's charge sales system. Organize your answer as follows. (note that the explanations of the letters a and b in the flowchart are entered as examples):

b. Using the guidelines for preparing flowcharts in Focus 6-2 and the flowcharting symbols shown in Figure 6-8, critique the flowchart shown in Figure 6-13. List the ways the flowchart violates the guidelines or uses improper symbols.

(CPA Examination, adapted)

Flowchart Symbol Letter	Procedures or Internal Document
a	Prepare six-part sales order.
b	File by order number.

Case 6-1   AnyCompany, Inc.: An Ongoing Comprehensive Case

Identify a local company (you may use the same company you identified in Case 1-1) and perform the following steps:

1. Select one of the company's business cycles for study. Examine all available documentation of the cycle's information system.

2. Prepare a report as follows:

   a. Describe who is involved in processing the data in the information system. Include in your report a partial organizational chart showing the relationships among employees.

   b. Describe the information flowing through the organization. Include in your report a context diagram and as many levels of DFDs as necessary to show the flow of information in the cycle.

   c. Describe what documents are used in the system. Include in your report a document flowchart showing the main documents used in processing transactions in the cycle, from origination to final destination. Also include a sample of the system documents.

   d. Identify the files and databases the company uses, and describe how and when they are updated. Include in your report a system flowchart that shows the following: (1) all inputs to the computerized system, (2) all processing performed, and (3) all system output.

   e. Describe other development tools used to create and document the system.

3. In assignment 2, you used techniques and tools with a system that already existed. As an alternative to those assignments, analyze a system that is currently being developed.

Case 6-2   Dub 5

You are the systems analyst for the Wee Willie Williams Widget Works (also known as Dub 5, which is a shortened version of 5 Ws). Dub 5 produces computer keyboard components. It has been producing keyboards for IBM, its biggest customer, for more than 20 years and has recently signed an exclusive 10-year contract to provide the keyboards for all IBM personal computers. As the systems analyst, you have been assigned the task of developing a DFD for Dub 5's order processing system. You have finished gathering all the information you need to develop the first-pass DFD and now want to complete the diagram.

Customer orders, which are all credit sales, arrive via mail and by phone. When an order is processed, a number of other documents are prepared. You have diagrammed the overall process and the documents produced, as shown in Figure 6-14.

The following documents are created:

- The order processing department creates a packing slip, which is then used by the warehouse department to fill the order. The packing slip accompanies the goods shipped from the warehouse.

- A customer invoice is prepared and mailed once the goods have been shipped.

- A monthly customer statement is mailed to the customer.

- When orders are not accepted, an order rejection is sent to the customer, explaining why the order cannot be filled.

Figure 6-14   Overall process for Dub 5

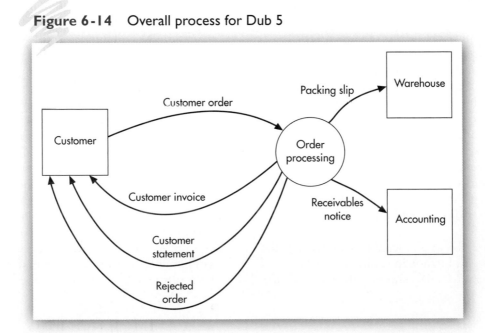

- A receivables notice, which is a copy of the customer invoice, is sent to the accounting department so that accounts receivable records can be updated.

After reviewing your notes, you write the following narrative summary:

> When an order comes in, the order processing clerk checks the customer's credit file to confirm credit approval and ensure that the amount falls within the credit limit. If either of these conditions is not met, the order is sent to the credit department. If an order meets both conditions, the order processing clerk enters it into the system on a standard order form. The information on the form is used to update the company's customer file (in which the name, address, and other information is stored), and the form is then placed in the company's order file.
>
> When the credit department receives a rejected order, the credit clerk first determines why the order has been rejected. If the credit limit has been exceeded, the customer is sent a personalized copy of a standard letter explaining that his or her credit limit has been exceeded and that the merchandise will be shipped as soon as Dub 5 receives payment. If the customer has not been approved for credit, a credit application is sent to the customer along with a letter stating that the order will be shipped as soon as credit approval is granted.
>
> Before preparing a packing slip, the order processing employee checks the inventory records to determine if the company has the products ordered on hand. If the items are in stock, a packing slip is prepared for every order form that is completed.
>
> Once notification of shipped goods has been received, a three-part customer invoice is prepared. One copy is kept by the order processing department, one is sent to the customer, and one is sent to the accounting department so that the receivables file can be updated. The receivables file contains all account information except name and address. A note in the customer file indicates that the invoice has been sent. Every month, Dub 5 mails customer statements.
>
> From the information presented, complete a DFD for Dub 5.

ANSWERS TO CHAPTER QUIZ

1. b	**3.** c	**5.** c	**7.** d	**9.** b
2. a	**4.** a	**6.** a	**8.** d	**10.** a

Part II
Control and
Audit of
Accounting
Information
Systems

C h a p t e r   7

Control and Accounting Information Systems

Learning Objectives

After studying this chapter, you should be able to:

- Describe the threats to an AIS and discuss why these threats are growing.
- Explain the basic concepts of control as applied to business organizations.
- Describe the major elements in the control environment of a business organization.
- Describe control policies and procedures commonly used in business organizations.
- Evaluate a system of internal accounting control, identify its deficiencies, and prescribe modifications to remedy those deficiencies.
- Conduct a cost-benefit analysis for particular threats, exposures, risks, and controls.

Integrative Case: Springer's Lumber & Supply

After completing his bachelor's degree in accounting at Idaho State, Jason Scott has been hired as an internal auditor for Northwest Industries, a diversified forest products company. He is assigned to audit Springer's Lumber & Supply, Northwest's building materials outlet in Bozeman, Montana. His supervisor, Maria Pilier, has asked him to trace a sample of purchase transactions from purchase requisition to cash disbursement to verify that proper control procedures were followed. By mid-afternoon Jason is frustrated with this task, and for good reasons:

- The purchasing system is poorly documented.
- He keeps finding transactions that have not been processed as Ed Yates, the accounts payable manager, said they should be.
- Purchase requisitions are missing for several items that had been personally authorized by Bill Springer, the purchasing vice president.
- Some vendor invoices have been paid without supporting documents, such as purchase orders and receiving reports.

- Prices charged for some items seem unusually high, and there are a few discrepancies in item prices between the vendor invoice and the corresponding purchase order. Yates seemed to have a logical answer for every question Jason raised. Yates ended the discussion by advising Jason that the real world is not always as tidy as the world portrayed in college textbooks. When Jason discussed his findings with Maria, he learned that she also has some concerns.
- Springer's is the largest supplier in the area and has a near monopoly.
- Management authority is held by the company president, Joe Springer, and his two sons, Bill (the purchasing vice president) and Ted (the controller). Several relatives and friends are on the payroll. Together the Springers own 10 percent of the company.
- Lines of authority and responsibility within the company are loosely defined and confusing.
- Maria believes that Ted Springer may have engaged in "creative accounting" to make Springer's one of Northwest's best-performing retail outlets.

After talking to Maria, Jason ponders the following issues:

1. Because Ed Yates had a logical explanation for every unusual transaction, should Jason describe these transactions in his report?
2. Is a violation of proper control procedures acceptable if it has been authorized by management?
3. Maria's concerns about Springer's loosely defined lines of authority and possible use of creative accounting are matters of management policy. With respect to Jason's control procedures assignment, does he have a professional or an ethical responsibility to get involved?

INTRODUCTION

Our society has become increasingly dependent on accounting information systems, which have grown increasingly more complex to meet our escalating needs for information. As system complexity and our dependence on them increase, companies face the growing risk of their systems being compromised. The four types of threats a company faces, as summarized in Table 7-1, are discussed in the first part of this chapter.

AIS THREATS

One threat companies face is natural and political disasters such as fires, excessive heat, floods, earthquakes, high winds, and war. An unpredictable disaster can completely destroy an information system and cause a company to fail. When a disaster strikes, many companies can be affected at the same time. For example, a flood in Chicago destroyed or damaged 400 data processing centers. Examples of these types of disasters include the following:

➤ The two terrorist attacks on the World Trade Center in New York City and the attack on the Federal Building in Oklahoma City destroyed or disrupted the systems in those buildings.

➤ In 1993, unrelenting rains caused the Mississippi and Missouri Rivers to overflow and flood parts of eight states. Many organizations lost their computer systems, including the city of Des Moines, Iowa, whose computers were buried under 8 feet of water.

Table 7-1   Threats to Accounting Information Systems

Threats	Examples
Natural and political disasters	Fire or excessive heat
	Floods
	Earthquakes
	High winds
	War
Software errors and equipment malfunctions	Hardware failures
	Software errors or bugs
	Operating system crashes
	Power outages and fluctuations
	Undetected data transmission errors
Unintentional acts	Accidents caused by human carelessness, failure to follow established procedures, and poorly trained or supervised personnel
	Innocent errors or omissions
	Lost or misplaced data
	Logic errors
	Systems that do not meet company needs or are incapable of handling their intended tasks
Intentional acts (computer crimes)	Sabotage
	Computer fraud
	Embezzlement

➤ An earthquake in Los Angeles destroyed numerous systems; caused others to be damaged by falling debris, water from ruptured sprinkler systems, and dust; and severed communication lines. Companies in San Francisco suffered a similar fate a few years earlier.

➤ The Defense Science Board has predicted that by 2005 attacks on information systems by foreign countries, espionage agents, and terrorists will be widespread.

A second threat to companies is software errors and equipment malfunctions such as hardware failures, software errors or bugs, operating system crashes, power outages and fluctuations, and undetected data transmission errors. Examples include the following:

➤ Bugs in a new tax accounting system were to blame for California's failure to collect $635 million in business taxes.

➤ At the Bank of New York, a field used to count the number of transactions was too small to handle the volume on a busy day. The error shut the system down and left the bank $23 million short when it tried to close its books. It had to borrow money overnight at a significant cost.

A third threat to companies is unintentional acts such as accidents or innocent errors and omissions. These are usually caused by human carelessness, failure to follow established procedures, and poorly trained or supervised personnel. Users often lose or misplace data and accidentally erase or alter files, data, and programs. Computer operators and users can enter the wrong input or erroneous input, use the wrong version of a program, use the wrong data files, or misplace the files. Systems analysts and programmers make logic errors, develop systems that do not meet the company's needs, or develop systems incapable of handling their intended tasks. Examples include the following:

➤ A data entry clerk at Giant Food, Inc. mistakenly keyed in a quarterly dividend of $2.50 instead of $0.25. As a result, the company paid over $10 million in excess dividends.

➤ A bank programmer mistakenly calculated interest for each month using 31 days. During the 5 months before the mistake was discovered, over $100,000 in excess interest was paid out on the savings accounts.

A fourth threat that companies face is intentional acts, typically referred to as computer crimes. This threat can take the form of **sabotage,** in which the intent is to destroy a system or some of its components. Computer fraud is another crime, where the intent is to steal something of value such as money, data, or computer time or services. It can also involve **embezzlement,** which is the theft or misappropriation of assets by employees, accompanied by the falsification of records to conceal the theft. Examples include the following:

➤ A technology enthusiast, John Draper, discovered that the whistle offered as a prize in Cap'n Crunch cereal exactly duplicated the frequency of a WATS line. He used his discovery to defraud the phone companies by making a large number of free telephone calls.

➤ An AIS manager at a Florida newspaper went to work for a competitor after he was fired. Before long, the first employer realized that its reporters were constantly being scooped. The newspaper finally discovered that the AIS manager still had an active account and password and regularly browsed its computer files for information on exclusive stories.

The greatest risks to information systems and the greatest dollar losses result from innocent errors and omissions. Carl Jackson, past president of the Information Systems Security Association, estimates that 65 percent of security problems are caused by human errors, 20 percent by natural and political disasters, and 15 percent by fraud.

When companies do not protect their systems from these four threats, they may face an additional threat, a lawsuit. This legal threat is explained in Focus 7-1.

Why AIS Threats Are Increasing

As a result of these problems, controlling the security and integrity of computer systems has become an important issue. Most AIS managers indicate that control risks have increased in the last few years. For example, studies have shown that more than 60 percent of organizations have experienced a major control failure in recent years. Among the many reasons for the increase in security problems are the following:

➤ Increasing numbers of client/server systems mean that information is available to an unprecedented number of workers. Computers and servers are everywhere; there are PCs on most desktops, and laptop computers are commonplace. ChevronTexaco, for example, has over 35,000 PCs.

Focus 7-1

Information Security Threats Could Also Cost in Court

Many CIOs are bracing themselves for what may be a deluge of liability lawsuits for information security breaches. If this were to happen, not only would a company pay for whatever damages it suffers from a breach, but it could also be held responsible for damages suffered by its customers. For example, in August 2001, after fighting the Code Red Worm, Qwest encountered another fight with Washington's attorney general's office. After the virus had left some of Qwest's customers with interrupted DSL coverage for 10 days, 15 to 20 customers complained to the attorney general's office. Although Qwest insisted that it was not at fault for an attack made by somebody else, the attorney general's office asked that the company refund its customers.

Soon judges and juries will have to decide if companies are legally responsible for insufficient security. Even though no legal precedents have been set as yet, corporate officers could be personally liable for breaches of security. In an effort to protect America's IT infrastructure, the government is starting to create regulations that will hopefully reduce the danger of certain lawsuits. However, chances are that companies will still have to increase security and stay aware if they hope to avoid successful claims.

Sarah D. Scalet in an article in *CIO* offers the following tips for avoiding successful lawsuits:

- **"Establish and implement an in-house security policy."** Develop a definite policy for how the company safeguards data and make sure the policy is well documented.

- **"Have a security audit done."** Ensure that the company is adhering to its information security policy by contracting a third person to test it. Having a third and unbiased party review a company's information security can help prove that the company is actively seeking to stay abreast of potential security risks.

- **"Remember security in contracts."** When outsourcing, a company must be sure the other company has in place and is following adequate security procedures.

- **"Don't make promises you can't keep."** A company should never promise faultless security, but rather appropriate security measures. Making big promises can leave you at risk for breach of contract lawsuits.

- **"Pay attention to regulations affecting your industry."** Countries sometimes have laws on the protection of customer information. Make sure the company is aware of the laws in the countries where it is doing business.

- **"Consider purchasing e-commerce insurance."** Cyber insurance covers online risks not covered by basic business insurance. Cyber insurance covers such occurences as attacks involving denial of service, malicious code, and inappropriate web content.

- **"Pay attention to what similar companies are doing."** Keep track of what other companies are doing so that you can prove that you are doing as much as anybody else for security.

Source: Sarah D. Scalet, "See You in Court," *CIO* (November 1, 2001): 62–70.

➤ Because LANs and client/server systems distribute data to many users, they are harder to control than centralized mainframe systems. At ChevronTexaco, information is distributed among many systems and thousands of employees working locally and remotely as well as nationally and internationally.

➤ WANs are giving customers and suppliers access to each other's systems and data, making confidentiality a major concern. For example, Wal-Mart allows certain vendors to access particular information in its computers as a condition of their alliance. Imagine the potential confidentiality problems if these vendors also formed alliances with Wal-Mart competitors such as Kmart and Target.

Unfortunately, many organizations do not adequately protect their data due to one or more of the following reasons:

➤ Computer control problems are often underestimated and downplayed, and companies view the loss of crucial information as a distant, unlikely threat. For example, less that 25 percent of 1,250 participants in an Ernst & Young study thought computer security was an extremely important issue. That figure was down from about 35 percent in the prior year's survey.

➤ The control implications of moving from the centralized, host-based computer systems of the past to those of a networked system or an Internet-based system are not fully understood.

➤ Many companies do not realize that data security is crucial to their survival. Information is a strategic resource, and protecting it must be a strategic requirement. For example, one company lost millions of dollars over a period of several years because it did not protect its data transmissions. A competitor tapped into its phone lines and obtained faxes of new product designs sent to an offshore plant.

➤ Productivity and cost pressures motivate management to forgo time-consuming control measures.

Why Computer Control and Security Are Important

Fortunately, companies are now recognizing the problems and taking positive steps to increase computer control and security. For example, they are becoming proactive in their approach. They are devoting full-time staff to security and control concerns and educating their employees about control measures. Many are establishing and enforcing formal information security policies. They are making controls a part of the applications development process and are moving sensitive data off the unsecured client servers to a more secure environment, such as a mainframe.

As an accountant, you must understand how to protect systems from the threats they face. You must also have a good understanding of IT and its capabilities and risks. This knowledge can help you to use IT to achieve an organization's control objectives.

Achieving adequate security and control over the information resources of an organization should be a top management priority. Although internal control objectives remain the same regardless of the data processing method, a computer-based AIS requires different internal control policies and procedures. For example, although computer processing reduces the potential for clerical errors, it may increase the risks of unauthorized access to or modification of data files. In addition, segregating the authorization, recording, and asset custody functions within an AIS must be achieved differently, as computer programs may be responsible for one or more of these functions. Fortunately, computers also provide opportunities for an organization to enhance its internal controls.

Assisting management in the control of a business organization is a primary objective of an AIS. The accountant can help achieve this objective by designing effective control systems and by auditing (or reviewing) control systems already in place to ensure their effectiveness.

Any potential adverse occurrence or unwanted event that could be injurious to either the AIS or the organization, is referred to as a **threat.** The potential dollar loss should a particular threat became a reality is referred to as the **exposure** from the threat, and the likelihood that the threat will come to pass is the **risk** associated with the threat.

Management expects accountants to be control consultants. That is, accountants are to (1) take a proactive approach to eliminating system threats and (2) detect, correct, and recover from threats if and when they occur.

It is important to recognize that it is much easier to build controls into a system at the initial design stage than to add them after the fact. For that reason, accountants and other control experts should be important members of the team that develops or modifies an information system.

The four chapters in Part II focus on control concepts. This chapter explains general principles of control in business organizations and describes key control procedures most suitable for a typical AIS. Chapter 8 describes how control principles apply to a computer-based AIS and explains the control procedures most applicable to them. Chapter 9 provides an in-depth examination of the causes and remedies for fraud. Chapter 10 examines the processes and procedures used in auditing a computer-based AIS.

OVERVIEW OF CONTROL CONCEPTS

Internal control is the plan of organization and the methods a business uses to safeguard assets, provide accurate and reliable information, promote and improve operational efficiency, and encourage adherence to prescribed managerial policies. These internal control purposes are sometimes at odds with each other. For example, many people are pushing for radical business process reengineering so they can have better and faster information and improve operational efficiency. Others resist those changes because they impede the safeguarding of company assets and require significant changes in managerial policies.

The **internal control structure** consists of the policies and procedures established to provide a reasonable level of assurance that the organization's specific objectives will be achieved. The system provides only reasonable assurance, because one that provides complete assurance would be difficult to design and would be prohibitively expensive.

Internal controls perform three important functions. **Preventive controls** deter problems before they arise. Hiring highly qualified accounting personnel, appropriately segregating employee duties, and effectively controlling physical access to assets, facilities, and information are effective preventive controls. Because not all control problems can be prevented, **detective controls** are needed to discover problems as soon as they arise. Examples of detective controls are duplicate checking of calculations and preparing bank reconciliations and monthly trial balances. **Corrective controls** remedy problems discovered with detective controls. They include procedures taken to identify the cause of a problem, correct resulting errors or difficulties, and modify the system so that future problems are minimized or eliminated. Examples include maintaining backup copies of key transaction and master files and adhering to procedures for correcting data entry errors as well as those for resubmitting transactions for subsequent processing.

In 1977 shock waves reverberated through the accounting profession when Congress incorporated language from an AICPA pronouncement into the **Foreign Corrupt Practices Act.** The primary purpose of the act was to prevent the bribery of foreign officials in order to obtain business. A significant effect of the act, however, was to require corporations to maintain good systems of internal accounting control. Needless to say, this requirement has generated tremendous interest among management, accountants, and auditors in the design and evaluation of internal control systems.

Study by the Committee of Sponsoring Organizations

The **Committee of Sponsoring Organizations (COSO)** is a private sector group consisting of the American Accounting Association, the AICPA, the Institute of Internal Auditors, the Institute of Management Accountants, and the Financial Executives Institute. In 1992, COSO issued the results of a study to develop a definition of internal controls and to provide guidance for evaluating internal control systems. The report has been widely accepted as the authority on internal controls.

The study took 3 years and involved tens of thousands of hours of research, discussion, analysis, and due process. It involved hundreds of people, including members of the five COSO organizations, corporate chief executives and board members, legislators, regulators, lawyers, consultants, auditors, and academics. The report spells out employees' responsibilities for the proper functioning of controls and describes the external auditor's role in assessing controls.

The COSO study defines internal control as the process implemented by the board of directors, management, and those under their direction to provide reasonable assurance that control objectives are achieved with regard to the following:

1. Effectiveness and efficiency of operations
2. Reliability of financial reporting
3. Compliance with applicable laws and regulations

According to COSO, internal control is a process because it permeates an organization's operating activities and is an integral part of basic management activities. Internal control provides reasonable, rather than absolute, assurance, because the possibilities of human failure, collusion, and management override of controls make this process an imperfect one.

COSO represents a significant move away from an internal control definition that is confined to accounting controls to one that addresses a wide range of board of directors and management objectives. COSO's internal control model has five crucial components. These five components are summarized in Table 7-2 and are discussed in greater depth later in the chapter.

Study by the Information Systems Audit and Control Foundation

The Information Systems Audit and Control Foundation (ISACF) developed the Control Objectives for Information and related Technology (COBIT). COBIT is a

Table 7-2   Five Interrelated Components of COSO's Internal Control Model

Component	Description
Control environment	The core of any business is its people—their individual attributes, including integrity, ethical values, and competence—and the environment in which they operate. They are the engine that drives the organization and the foundation on which everything rests.
Control activities	Control policies and procedures must be established and executed to help ensure that the actions identified by management as necessary to address risks to achievement of the organization's objectives are effectively carried out.
Risk assessment	The organization must be aware of and deal with the risks it faces. It must set objectives, integrated with the sales, production, marketing, financial, and other activities so that the organization is operating in concert. It must also establish mechanisms to identify, analyze, and manage the related risks.
Information and communication	Surrounding the control activities are information and communication systems. They enable the organization's people to capture and exchange the information needed to conduct, manage, and control its operations.
Monitoring	The entire process must be monitored, and modifications made as necessary. In this way the system can react dynamically, changing as conditions warrant.

framework of generally applicable information systems security and control practices for IT control. The framework allows (1) management to benchmark the security and control practices of IT environments, (2) users of IT services to be assured that adequate security and control exist, and (3) auditors to substantiate their opinions on internal control and to advise on IT security and control matters.

The framework addresses the issue of control from three vantage points, or dimensions:

1. Business Objectives. To satisfy business objectives, information must conform to certain criteria that COBIT refers to as business requirements for information. The criteria are divided into seven distinct yet overlapping categories that map into the COSO objectives: effectiveness (relevant, pertinent, and timely), efficiency, confidentiality, integrity, availability, compliance with legal requirements, and reliability.
2. IT resources, which include people, application systems, technology, facilities, and data.
3. IT processes, which are broken into four domains: planning and organization, acquisition and implementation, delivery and support, and monitoring.

COBIT, which consolidates standards from 36 different sources into a single framework, is having a big impact on the information systems profession. It is helping managers learn how to balance risk and control investment in an information system environment. It provides users with greater assurance that the security and IT controls provided by internal and third parties are adequate. It guides auditors as they substantiate their opinions and as they provide advice to management on internal controls.

THE CONTROL ENVIRONMENT

A **control environment** consists of the following factors:

1. Commitment to integrity and ethical values
2. Management's philosophy and operating style
3. Organizational structure
4. The audit committee of the board of directors
5. Methods of assigning authority and responsibility
6. Human resources policies and practices
7. External influences

Commitment to Integrity and Ethical Values

It is important for management to create an organizational culture that stresses integrity and ethical values. Companies can endorse integrity as a basic operating principle by actively teaching and practicing it. For example, top management should make it clear that honest reports are more important than favorable ones. Management should not assume that everyone accepts honesty. They should consistently reward and encourage honesty and give verbal labels to honest and dishonest behavior. If companies simply punish or reward honesty without labeling it as such or explaining the principle, or if the standard of honesty is inconsistent, then employees will most likely be inconsistent in their moral behavior.

Management should develop clearly stated policies that explicitly describe honest and dishonest behaviors. These policies should especially cover issues that are uncertain or unclear, such as conflicts of interest and the acceptance of gifts. For example, most purchasing agents would agree that accepting a $5,000 bribe from a supplier is dishonest, but a weekend vacation at a hunting cabin is not as clear-cut. A major cause of dishonesty comes from rationalizing these situations; it is not uncommon for the criterion of expediency to replace the criterion of right versus wrong.

All dishonest acts should be thoroughly investigated and those found guilty should be dismissed. Dishonest employees should be prosecuted to let employees know that this type of behavior will not be allowed.

Management's Philosophy and Operating Style

The more responsible that management's philosophy and operating style are, the more likely it is that employees will behave responsibly in working to achieve the organization's objectives. If management shows little concern for internal controls, then employees are less diligent and effective in achieving specific control objectives. For example, Maria Pilier found that lines of authority and responsibility at Springer's were loosely defined, and she suspected that management may have engaged in creative accounting to show its performance in the best light. Meanwhile, Jason Scott found evidence of poor internal control practices in the purchasing and accounts payable function. It is quite possible that these two conditions are related—that is, that management's loose attitude contributed to purchasing's inattentiveness to good internal control practices.

Management's philosophy and operating style can be assessed by answering questions such as the following:

➤ Does management take undue business risks to achieve its objectives, or does it assess potential risks and rewards prior to acting?

➤ Does management attempt to manipulate such performance measures as net income so that its performance can be seen in a more favorable light?

➤ Does management pressure employees to achieve results regardless of the methods, or does it demand ethical behavior? In other words, does management believe the ends justify the means?

Organizational Structure

A company's organizational structure defines its lines of authority and responsibility and provides the overall framework for planning, directing, and controlling its operations. Important aspects of organizational structure include the centralization or decentralization of authority, the assignment of responsibility for specific tasks, the way responsibility allocation affects management's information requirements, and the organization of the accounting and information system functions. An overly complex or unclear organizational structure may indicate more serious problems. ESM, a brokerage company dealing in government securities, used a multilayered organizational structure to hide a $300 million fraud. Company officers funneled cash to themselves and hid it by reporting a fictitious receivable from a related company in their financial statements.

In today's business world, drastic changes are occurring in management practices and in the organization of companies. Hierarchical organizational structures, with many layers of management who supervise and control the work of those under them, are disappearing. They are being replaced with flat organizations that have self-directed work teams of employees formerly assigned to separate and segregated departments. Team members are empowered to make decisions without seeking multiple layers of approval to complete their work. The emphasis is on continuous improvement rather than on the periodic reviews and appraisals characteristic of earlier evaluations. These changes have an enormous impact on a company's organizational structure and on the nature and type of controls used there.

The Audit Committee of the Board of Directors

All corporations listed on the New York Stock Exchange must have an **audit committee** composed entirely of outside (nonemployee) directors. The audit committee is responsible for overseeing the corporation's internal control structure, its financial reporting process, and its compliance with related laws, regulations, and standards. The committee works closely with the corporation's external and internal auditors. One of the committee's responsibilities is to provide an independent review of the actions of corporate managers on behalf of company shareholders. This review serves as a check on management integrity and increases the confidence of the investing public in the propriety of financial reporting.

Methods of Assigning Authority and Responsibility

Management should assign responsibility for specific business objectives to specific departments and individuals and then hold them accountable for achieving those objectives. Authority and responsibility may be assigned through formal job descriptions, employee training, and operating plans, schedules, and budgets. Of particular importance is a formal company code of conduct addressing such matters as standards of ethical behavior, acceptable business practices, regulatory requirements, and conflicts of interest.

A written **policy and procedures manual** is an important tool for assigning authority and responsibility. The manual spells out management policy with respect to handling specific transactions. In addition, it documents the systems and procedures employed to process those transactions. It includes the organization's chart of accounts and sample copies of forms and documents. The manual is a helpful on-the-job reference for employees and a useful tool in training new employees.

Human Resources Policies and Practices

Policies and practices about hiring, training, evaluating, compensating, and promoting employees affect an organization's ability to minimize threats, risks, and exposures. Employees should be hired and promoted based on how well they meet written job requirements. Resumes, reference letters, and background checks are important means of evaluating the qualifications of job applicants. Training programs should familiarize new employees with their responsibilities as well as organization policies and procedures. Finally, policies with respect to working conditions, compensation, job incentives, and career advancement can be a powerful force in encouraging efficiency and loyal service.

The importance of thorough background checks is underscored by the case of Philip Crosby Associates (PCA), a consulting and training firm. PCA undertook an exhaustive search to select a financial director. The company finally hired John Nelson, an MBA and CPA with a glowing reference from his former employer. In reality, the CPA and reference were phony. Nelson was actually Robert W. Liszewski, who had recently served an 18-month jail sentence for embezzling $400,000 from an Indiana bank. By the time PCA discovered this fact, Liszewski had embezzled $960,000 using wire transfers to a dummy corporation supported by forged signatures on contracts and authorization documents.

Additional control policies are needed for employees with access to cash or other property. They should be required to take an annual vacation, and during this time their job functions should be performed by other staff members. Many employee frauds are discovered when the perpetrator is suddenly forced by illness or accident to take time off. Periodic rotation of duties among key employees can achieve the same results. Of course, the very existence of such policies deters fraud and enhances internal control. Finally, fidelity bond insurance coverage of key employees protects companies against losses arising from deliberate acts of fraud by bonded employees.

External Influences

External influences that affect an organization's control environment include requirements imposed by stock exchanges, by the Financial Accounting Standards Board (FASB), and by the Securities and Exchange Commission (SEC). They also include regulatory agency requirements, such as those for banks, utilities, and insurance companies. Examples include enforcement of the internal control provisions of the Foreign Corrupt Practices Act by the SEC, and audits of financial institutions by the Federal Deposit Insurance Corporation (FDIC).

CONTROL ACTIVITIES

The second component of COSO's internal control model (see Table 7-2) is control activities, which are policies and rules that provide reasonable assurance that management's control objectives are achieved. Generally, control procedures fall into one of the following five categories:

1. Proper authorization of transactions and activities
2. Segregation of duties
3. Design and use of adequate documents and records
4. Adequate safeguards of assets and records
5. Independent checks on performance

Focus 7-2 discusses how a violation of specific control activities, combined with control environment factors, resulted in fraud within a Midwestern school district.

Proper Authorization of Transactions and Activities

Employees perform tasks and make decisions that affect company assets. Because management lacks the time and resources to supervise each activity and decision, they establish policies for employees to follow and then empower them to perform accordingly. This empowerment, called **authorization,** is an important part of an organization's control procedures.

Authorizations are often documented by signing, initializing, or entering an authorization code on a transaction document or record. Computer systems are now capable of recording a **digital signature** (or fingerprint), a means of signing a document with a piece of data that cannot be forged.

Employees who process transactions should verify the presence of the appropriate authorization(s). Auditors review transactions to verify proper authorization, as their absence indicates a possible control problem. For example, when reviewing purchases, Jason Scott discovered that some did not have a purchase requisition. Instead, they had been "personally authorized" by Bill Springer, the purchasing vice president. In addition, Jason found that some vendor invoice payments had been authorized without proper supporting documents, such as purchase orders and receiving reports. These findings raise questions about the adequacy of Springer's internal control procedures.

Certain activities or transactions may be of such consequence that management grants **specific authorization** for them to occur. For example, management review and approval is often required for sales in excess of $20,000, capital expenditures in excess of $10,000, or uncollectible write-offs in excess of $5,000. In contrast, management can authorize employees to handle routine transactions without special approval, a procedure known as **general authorization.** Management should have written policies on both specific and general authorization for all types of transactions.

Focus 7-2

Control Problems in a School District

THE DIRECTOR of finance for a Midwestern school district with 42 separate schools hired a CPA firm to audit the school district's books. The audit was accompanied by a report showing that the district's system had some serious internal control deficiencies. The director, a former auditor, set out to improve the control system. The district (1) selected a new software package that all sites would use, (2) standardized accounting and bookkeeping procedures, (3) instituted consistent purchase order procedures, (4) implemented a separation of duties, and (5) created a control system for student vending machine cash and inventory.

As the changes were being made, the director noted that book collection fees for the middle school were low. He asked the district's internal auditor to investigate. The auditor contacted the middle school secretary, who was responsible for making daily deposits of all student fees and writing checks to the central office for book fees. The secretary said the low amount was due to the increase in the number of fees waived by the principal for students who qualified for free or reduced lunches.

The principal denied that he was waiving the fee. The principal, the auditor, and the director examined the fee cards for each child. Their investigation showed that the daily deposits into the activity checking account did not agree with the dates stamped paid on the student fee cards. A search of the premises revealed no uncashed checks. So where did the money go, and how did the secretary manage to take it when most of the fees were paid with checks made out to the school?

They finally discovered that the secretary was also in charge of the faculty welfare and vending machine receipts fund. The district was not responsible for the fund, and so it was never audited or examined. Nor was the fund subject to the newly implemented system of internal controls. Deposits to the welfare fund were checks from the faculty and cash from the vending machines.

An examination of the available records revealed how the $20,000 fraud took place. The secretary stole all cash received from the vending machines. She also wrote and recorded checks to vendors, and on some checks she erased the name of the payee and replaced it with her name. She deposited student fees into the faculty welfare fund to cover up the stolen money.

The secretary was immediately discharged for improper bookkeeping practices. Because the secretary was bonded, the district was able to recover all of its missing funds.

The school district made changes to strengthen its control. Internal auditors now examine all funds at the schools. The control of faculty welfare funds was transferred to a faculty member. The investigation also revealed that the secretary had a prior criminal record; therefore, a background check was implemented so that all future hires could be screened.

Segregation of Duties

Good internal control demands that no single employee be given too much responsibility. An employee should not be in a position to perpetrate *and* conceal fraud or unintentional errors. As shown in Figure 7-1, effective segregation of duties is achieved when the following functions are separated:

➤ *Authorization*—approving transactions and decisions

➤ *Recording*—preparing source documents; maintaining journals, ledgers, or other files; preparing reconciliations; and preparing performance reports

➤ *Custody*—handling cash, maintaining an inventory storeroom, receiving incoming customer checks, writing checks on the organization's bank account

If two of these three functions are the responsibility of a single person, then problems can arise. For example, the former city treasurer of Fairfax, Virginia, was convicted of embezzling $600,000 from the city treasury. When residents used cash to pay their taxes, she would keep the currency. She recorded tax collections on the property tax records, but did not report them to the city controller. Eventually she made an adjusting journal entry to bring her records into agreement with those of the controller. When the treasurer received cash to pay for business license fees or court fees, she recorded these transactions on a cash register and deposited this money daily. She stole some of this cash and made up discrepancies in the bank deposit by substituting miscellaneous checks received in the mail that would not be missed when they went unrecorded. Because the treasurer was responsible for both the *custody* of

Figure 7-1   Separation of duties

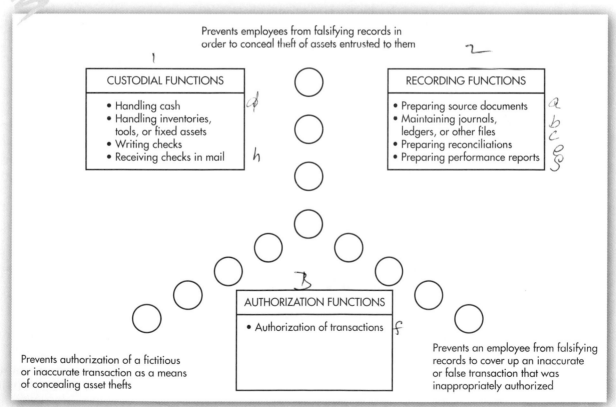

cash receipts and the *recording* of those receipts, she was able to steal cash receipts and falsify the accounts to conceal the theft.

The utilities director of Newport Beach, California, who was responsible for *authorizing* transactions and had *custody* of cash, was charged with embezzling $1.2 million. He forged invoices or easement documents (the right to pass through a person's land) authorizing payments to a real or fictitious property owner. Finance department officials gave him the checks to deliver to the property owners. He forged signatures, endorsed the checks to himself, and deposited them in his own account. Because he was given physical custody of checks relating to transactions that he had authorized, he was able to authorize fictitious transactions and steal the payments.

The payroll director of the Los Angeles Dodgers, who was responsible for both authorization and recording functions, pleaded guilty to embezzling $330,000 from the team. He credited employees for hours not worked and then received a kickback of 50 percent of their extra compensation. He also added fictitious names to the Dodgers payroll and cashed the paychecks. The fraud was discovered when the payroll director became ill and another employee took over his duties. Since the perpetrator was responsible for both *authorizing* the hiring of new employees and for *recording* employee hours worked, he did not need to prepare or handle the actual paychecks. The club treasurer would simply mail the checks to an address specified by the payroll director.

In modern information systems, the computer often can be programmed to perform one or more of the already mentioned functions—in essence, replacing employees. The principle of separating duties remains the same; the only difference is that the computer, not a human, performs the function. For example, many gas stations are now equipped with pumps that allow customers to insert a credit card to pay for their gas. In such cases, the custody of the "cash" and the recording function are both performed by the computer. In addition to improving internal controls, these machines actually improve the process of serving the customer by increasing convenience and eliminating lines to pay for the gas.

In a system that incorporates an effective separation of duties, it should be difficult for any single employee to commit embezzlement successfully. Detecting fraud where two or more people are in **collusion** to override the controls is more difficult. For example, two women employed by a credit card company colluded to steal funds. One woman was authorized to set up credit card accounts, the other to write off unpaid accounts of less than $1,000. The first woman created a new account for each of them using fictitious data. When the amounts outstanding neared the $1,000 limit, the woman in collections wrote them off. The first woman would then create two new cards, and the process would be repeated. The women were caught when the jilted boyfriend of one of them sought revenge; he called the credit card company and disclosed the fraudulent scheme.

Design and Use of Adequate Documents and Records

The proper design and use of documents and records helps ensure the accurate and complete recording of all relevant transaction data. Their form and content should be kept as simple as possible to promote efficient record keeping, minimize recording errors, and facilitate review and verification. Documents that initiate a transaction should contain a space for authorizations. Those used to transfer assets to someone else should have a space for the receiving party's signature. To reduce the likelihood of documents being used fraudulently, they should be sequentially prenumbered so each can be accounted for. A good audit trail facilitates tracing individual transactions through the system, the correction of errors, and the verification of system output.

Adequate Safeguards of Assets and Records

When people consider safeguarding assets, they most often think of cash and physical assets, such as inventory and equipment. In today's world, however, one of a company's most important assets is its information. Accordingly, steps must be taken to safeguard both information and physical assets. The following procedures safeguard assets from theft, unauthorized use, and vandalism:

➤ Effectively supervising and segregating duties

➤ Maintaining accurate records of assets, including information

➤ Restricting physical access to assets (Cash registers, safes, lockboxes, and safety deposit boxes limit access to cash, securities, and paper assets. Restricted storage areas are used to protect inventories. For example, over $1 million was embezzled from Perini Corp. because of poor controls. Blank checks were kept in an unlocked storeroom. Employees simply took a check, made it out to a fictitious vendor, ran it through the check signing machine which was also left unlocked, and cashed the check.)

➤ Protecting records and documents (Fireproof storage areas, locked filing cabinets, and off-site backup locations are effective means of protecting records and documents. Access to blank checks and documents should be limited to authorized personnel. In Inglewood, California, a janitor was charged with stealing 34 blank checks while cleaning the city finance office. He forged the names of city officials on the checks and cashed them in amounts ranging from $50,000 to $470,000.)

➤ Controlling the environment (Sensitive computer equipment should be located in a room with adequate cooling and special fire protection. The room should be elevated and reinforced to protect the equipment from flooding and falling objects.)

➤ Restricting access to computer rooms, computer files, and information (Access controls are discussed in Chapter 8.)

Independent Checks on Performance

Internal checks to ensure that transactions are processed accurately are another important control element. These checks should be independent, because they are generally more effective if performed by someone other than the person who is responsible for the original operation. Various types of independent checks are discussed in the following subsections.

Reconciliation of two independently maintained sets of records

One way to check the accuracy and completeness of records is to reconcile them with other records that should have the same balance. For example, a bank reconciliation verifies that company checking accounts agree with bank statements. Another example is comparing the accounts receivable subsidiary ledger total with the accounts receivable total in the general ledger.

Comparison of actual quantities with recorded amounts

The cash in a cash register drawer at the end of each clerk's shift should be the same as the amount recorded on the cash register tape. All inventories should be counted at least annually and the results compared with inventory records. High dollar value items, such as jewelry or furs, should be counted more frequently.

Double-entry accounting

The maxim that debits must equal credits provides numerous opportunities for internal checks. For example, debits in a payroll entry may be allocated to numerous inventory and/or expense accounts by the cost accounting department. Credits are allocated to several liability accounts for wages and salaries payable, taxes withheld, employee insurance, union dues, and so on, by the payroll department. At the conclusion of these two complex operations, the comparison of total debits with total credits provides a powerful check on the accuracy of both processes. Any discrepancy indicates the presence of one or more errors.

Batch totals

In a batch processing application, source documents are assembled in groups and **batch totals** (also called **control totals**) are manually computed before source data are entered into the system. As the data are processed, the control totals should be generated during each processing step. An employee who was not involved in preparing the original batch totals should compare the two sets of totals. Otherwise, a person who generated the original control totals and reconciled the two sets of totals could easily hide errors or fraudulent transactions.

Discrepancies between the two totals indicate an error in the previous processing step. Examples include lost records, unauthorized records added to the batch, or data transcription or data processing errors. The cause of discrepancies should be identified and the errors corrected before the transactions are processed further. Limiting batch sizes (such as to 50 records) reduces the time required to find the cause of any individual discrepancy.

Five batch totals are used in computer systems, as follows:

1. A **financial total** is the sum of a dollar field, such as total sales or total cash receipts.
2. A **hash total** is the sum of a field that would usually not be added, such as the sum of customer account numbers or employee identification numbers.
3. A **record count** is the number of documents processed.
4. A **line count** is the number of lines of data entered. For example, the line count would be five if a sales order shows that five different products were sold to a customer.
5. A **cross-footing balance test.** Many worksheets have row totals and column totals. This test compares the grand total of all the row totals with the grand total of all the column totals to check that they are equal.

The home-based business Sarah Robinson runs in Springville, Utah, is used to illustrate the use of batch totals to prevent accounting and recording errors.

1. When Sarah receives checks in the mail, she prepares a receipts list showing customer names and amounts received, computes a batch total (the total dollar amount of all checks) and writes it on the receipts list, and prepares a deposit slip.
2. After she deposits the checks, she compares the bank-validated copy of the deposit slip with her original batch total on the receipts list.
3. Using a copy of Sarah's receipts list, her CPA posts credits to the appropriate customer accounts and updates each customer's balance. He computes the new total balance of the accounts receivable file, determines the difference between the old and new file totals,

and verifies that this difference agrees with Sarah's batch total. This comparison serves as an independent check on the accuracy of posting receipts to the customer accounts.

4. Her CPA prepares a summary journal entry and posts it to the general ledger, again verifying that the entry amount is equal to Sarah's batch total.

Batch totals provide an independent check on the accuracy of each processing step. If a discrepancy is discovered, the difference between the batch totals often provides a clue about where the error occurred. For example, if the difference equals a transaction amount, that transaction may have been omitted. If the difference is exactly double a transaction amount, it may have been incorrectly debited instead of credited (added instead of subtracted). If the discrepancy involves a nonzero digit, there may be a **transcription error,** in which a digit is entered incorrectly during processing (e.g., 94 for 54, causing an error of 50). If it is evenly divisible by 9, the likely cause is a **transposition error,** in which two adjacent digits were inadvertently exchanged (e.g., 46 for 64).

Simple errors can have large financial consequences. For example, a single transposition error almost cost the U.S. Treasury $14 million. A clerk at the Federal Reserve Bank of Philadelphia transposed two digits while calculating the interest on newly issued 5-year Treasury notes. The operator erroneously entered the interest rate as 8.67 precent rather than 6.87 percent. Fortunately, an investor detected the error when he received a notification of the amount to be paid. The bank was able to correct the error before the checks were issued and mailed. The bank quickly implemented new control procedures to ensure that the problem did not reoccur.

Independent review

After one person processes a transaction, a second person sometimes reviews the work of the first. The second person checks for proper authorization signatures, reviews supporting documents, and checks the accuracy of crucial data items such as prices, quantities, and extensions.

RISK ASSESSMENT

The third component of COSO's internal control model (see Table 7-2) is risk assessment. Accountants play an important role in helping management control a business by designing effective control systems and evaluating existing ones to ensure that they are operating effectively. Accountants can evaluate an internal control system using the risk assessment strategy shown in Figure 7-2. We will now walk you through the major steps in this strategy.

Identify Threats

Companies face the following types of threats:

- ➤ *Strategic* (e.g., doing the wrong things)
- ➤ *Operating* (e.g., doing the right things, but in the wrong way)
- ➤ *Financial* (e.g., having financial resources lost, wasted, or stolen or incurring inappropriate liabilities)
- ➤ *Information* (e.g., receiving faulty or irrelevant information, unreliable systems, and incorrect or misleading reports)

For example, many organizations implement electronic data interchange (EDI) systems that provide instantaneous communications and eliminate paper documents.

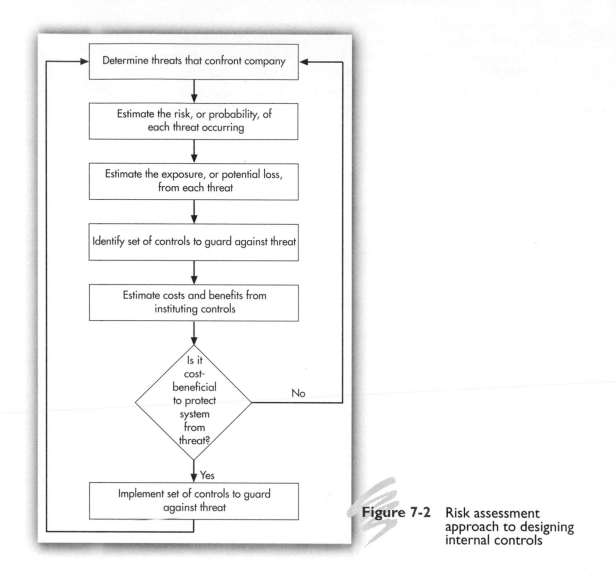

Figure 7-2   Risk assessment approach to designing internal controls

An EDI system allows them to create electronic documents, transmit them over private networks or the Internet to their customers' and suppliers' computers, and receive in return electronic responses.

Companies that implement an EDI system must identify the following threats the system will face:

1. *Choosing an inappropriate technology.* The companies might move to EDI before their customers and suppliers are ready. They may also choose to use EDI when there is a more effective means of communicating with their customers and suppliers electronically.

2. *Unauthorized system access.* Hackers can break into the system and steal data or sabotage the system.

3. *Tapping into data transmissions.* Hackers can eavesdrop on a data transmission and copy the transmission, distort it, or prevent it from arriving at its destination.

4. *Loss of data integrity.* Errors may be introduced into the data due to employee or software errors, erroneous input, faulty transmissions, and so forth.

5. *Incomplete transactions.* The receiving computer may not receive the complete data package from the sending computer.

6. *System failures.* Hardware or software problems, power outages, sabotage, employee mistakes, or other factors may cause the EDI system to fail or be inaccessible for a time.

7. *Incompatible systems.* Some companies have difficulty interacting with other systems because of incompatible computer systems.

Estimate Risk

Some threats pose a greater risk because the probability of their occurrence is more likely. For example, a company is more likely to be the victim of a computer fraud than of a terrorist attack, and employees are more likely to make unintentional errors than they are to commit intentional acts of fraud.

Estimate Exposure

The risk of an earthquake may be small, but the exposure can be enormous; it could completely destroy a company and force it into bankruptcy. The exposure from a fraud is usually not as great, as most frauds do not threaten a company's existence. The exposure from unintentional errors has a broad range of effects, depending on the nature of the error and how long it persists. Risk and exposure must be considered together. As either increases, both the materiality of the threat and the need to protect against it rise.

Identify Controls

Management must identify one or more controls that will protect the company from each threat. In evaluating the benefits of specific internal control procedures, management should consider their effectiveness and timing. All other factors being equal, a preventive control is superior to a detective one. However, if preventive controls fail, detective controls are essential for discovering the problem and corrective controls help recover from the problem. Thus, preventive, detective, and corrective controls complement each other, and a good internal control system should employ all three.

Estimate Costs and Benefits

No internal control system can provide foolproof protection against all internal control threats. The cost of a foolproof system would be prohibitive. In addition, because many controls negatively affect operational efficiency, too many controls slow the system and make it inefficient. Therefore, the objective in designing an internal control system is to provide reasonable assurance that control problems do not take place.

The benefit of an internal control procedure must exceed its cost. Costs are easier to measure than benefits, however. The primary cost element is personnel, including the time to perform control procedures, the costs of hiring additional employees to achieve effective segregation of duties, and the costs of programming controls into a computer system. Internal control benefits stem from reduced losses. One way to calculate benefits involves **expected loss,** the mathematical product of risk and exposure.

$$\text{Expected loss} = \text{risk} \times \text{exposure}$$

Table 7-3   Cost-Benefit Analysis of Payroll Validation Procedure

	Without Validation Procedure	With Validation Procedure	Net Expected Difference
Cost to reprocess entire payroll	$10,000	$10,000	
Risk of payroll data errors	15%	1%	
Expected reprocessing cost ($10,000 × risk)	$1,500	$100	$1400
Cost of validation procedure	$0	$600	$(600)
Net expected benefit of validation procedure			$800

The benefit of a control procedure is the difference between the expected loss with the control procedure(s) and the expected loss without it.

Determine Cost-Benefit Effectiveness

After estimating benefits and costs, management determines if the control is cost beneficial. For example, at Atlantic Richfield, data errors occasionally required an entire payroll to be reprocessed, at a cost of $10,000. Management determined that a data validation step would reduce error risk from 15 percent to 1 percent, at a cost of $600 per pay period. The cost-benefit analysis that management used to determine if the validation step should be employed is shown in Table 7-3.

If the proposed payroll validation procedure is not utilized, then the expected loss to the company is $1,500. Because the expected loss with the validation step is $100, the control provides an expected benefit of $1,400. After deducting the control costs of $600, the validation step provides a net benefit of $800 and clearly should be implemented.

In evaluating the costs and benefits of internal control, management must consider factors other than those in the expected benefit calculation. For example, if an exposure threatens an organization's existence, it may be worthwhile to spend more than indicated by the cost-benefit analysis to minimize the possibility that the organization will perish. This extra cost can be viewed as a catastrophic loss insurance premium.

Focus 7-3 discusses how Dow Chemical assesses risk and designs control systems.

INFORMATION AND COMMUNICATION

The fourth component of COSO's internal control model (see Table 7-2) is information and communication. The primary purpose of an AIS is to record, process,

Focus 7-3

Risk Analysis at Dow Chemical

RISK ANALYSIS is often perceived as an expensive and lengthy process that outside consultants perform with a minimum of employee contact. Consequently, few end users actually understand or even desire the recommended controls and are reluctant to implement or enforce them. Dow Chemical is out to change this attitude; it has recently developed a simple and quick way to help users evaluate risk.

The key component of the Dow security program is the risk analysis matrix (RAM). The RAM is a grid-based question-and-answer chart that helps users identify potential threats and the associated data and assets that require protection. The first step in using the RAM is to classify undesirable events in terms of their effects. In the grid that follows, the vertical axis has three columns related to security objectives: data integrity (unauthorized data modification or destruction), data sensitivity (unauthorized data disclosure), and data availability (unavailability of data or system services). The horizontal axis pinpoints the accidental acts (such as an error or omission) and the deliberate acts (such as a hacker or employee fraud) from which data must be protected. After undesirable events are identified, employees affected by the system are then assembled. For example, if a regional sales office

is to have a LAN installed, a salesperson, a LAN technician, and a clerk from the sales office are invited to a special meeting.

The manager of security prepares the matrix as a visual aid and asks the participants to consider the risks associated with each of its squares. For example, they might discuss what could happen if data were accidentally modified by an employee. Each square is considered in turn (reducing data integrity due to deliberate acts, unauthorized data disclosure due to an accident, etc.) until the chart is complete.

The next step is to determine which controls will address each security concern. For example, sensitive documents should be shredded to guard against their falling into the wrong hands. Another example is using a tape backup system to guard against the main server being accidentally destroyed. That is followed by management determining the economic feasibility of the controls. The last step is to assign implementation responsibilities to team members.

Many security managers find security to be a daunting proposition and do not know where to start. Dow Chemical claims that companies can now empower themselves and develop their own system of controls. No longer do they have to rely on someone else to do it for them.

Risk Analysis Matrix			
	Data Integrity	**Data Sensitivity**	**Data Availability**
Accidental Acts Errors and Omissions	Major or minor concern	Confidential or nonconfidential	Essential or nonessential
Deliberate Acts Fraud and Misuse	Major or minor concern	Confidential or nonconfidential	Essential or nonessential
	Data Destruction or **Modification**	**Data Disclosure**	**Data Inaccessibility**

store, summarize, and communicate information about an organization. This means that accountants must understand how (1) transactions are initiated, (2) data are captured in machine-readable form or converted from source documents to machine-readable form, (3) computer files are accessed and updated, (4) data are processed to prepare information, and (5) information is reported to internal users and external parties. Accountants must also understand the accounting records and procedures, supporting documents, and specific financial statement accounts involved in processing and reporting transactions.

These items make it possible for the system to have an audit trail. An **audit trail** exists when individual company transactions can be traced through the system from where they originate to where they end up on the financial statements. Likewise, the numbers on the financial statements can be traced back through the system to the individual transactions making up the balance.

According to the AICPA, an AIS has five primary objectives:

1. Identify and record all valid transactions. For example, if a company intentionally records a fictitious sale, it can overstate revenues and income. If a company forgets to record some expenses at the year's end, expenses are understated and net income is overstated.

2. Properly classify transactions. For example, improperly classifying an expense as an asset overstates assets and net income.

3. Record transactions at their proper monetary value. For example, an account receivable that becomes uncollectible should be written off.

4. Record transactions in the proper accounting period. Recording 2000 sales in 1999 overstates sales and net income for 1999 and has the opposite effect for 2000.

5. Properly present transactions and related disclosures in the financial statements. Failing to disclose a lawsuit or a contingent liability could mislead the reader of a financial statement.

Accounting systems generally consist of several accounting subsystems, each designed to process transactions of a particular type. Although they differ with respect to the type of transactions processed, all accounting subsystems follow the same sequence of procedures. These procedures are referred to as accounting cycles. The five major accounting cycles and their related control objectives and procedures are detailed in Chapters 11 through 15.

MONITORING PERFORMANCE

The fifth component of COSO's internal control model (see Table 7-2) is monitoring. Key methods of monitoring performance include effective supervision, responsibility reporting, and internal auditing.

Effective Supervision

Effective supervision involves training and assisting employees, monitoring their performance, correcting errors, and safeguarding assets by overseeing employees who have access to them. Supervision is especially important in organizations that cannot afford elaborate responsibility reporting or are too small to have an adequate segregation of duties.

Responsibility Accounting

Responsibility accounting systems include budgets, quotas, schedules, standard costs, and quality standards; performance reports that compare actual with planned performance and highlight significant variances; and procedures for investigating significant variances and taking timely action to correct the conditions leading to such variances.

Internal Auditing

Internal auditing involves reviewing the reliability and integrity of financial and operating information and providing an appraisal of internal control effectiveness. It also involves assessing employee compliance with management policies and procedures and applicable laws and regulations, and evaluating the efficiency and effectiveness of management. Unlike external auditors, internal auditors place great emphasis on a company's management controls; thus, they can detect excess overtime, underused assets, obsolete inventory, padded travel expense reimbursements, excessively loose budgets and quotas, poorly justified capital expenditures, and production bottlenecks. Objectivity and effectiveness require that the internal audit function be organizationally independent of accounting and operating functions. For example, the head of internal auditing should report to the audit committee of the board of directors rather than to the controller or chief financial officer.

One alert internal auditor noted that a department supervisor took the entire office staff out to lunch in a limousine on her birthday. During the remainder of the audit, he noted other evidences of an extravagant lifestyle. Questioning if her salary could support her lifestyle, he began a more in-depth investigation. He found that she had set up several fictitious vendors, sent the company invoices from these vendors, and then cashed the checks when they were mailed to her. Over a period of several years, she had embezzled over $12 million.

SUMMARY AND CASE CONCLUSION

After 3 days in Bozeman, Jason and Maria returned to Northwest's main office and filed their audit report. One week later, they were summoned to the office of Roger Sawyer, Northwest's director of internal auditing, to explain their findings. Shortly thereafter, a high-level internal audit team was dispatched to Bozeman to take a closer look at the situation.

When the audit team returned, Jason and Maria inquired about their findings and were told the situation was still under investigation. Six months later, a company newsletter included an announcement that the Springer family had sold their remaining 10 percent interest in the Bozeman business to Northwest and had resigned from their management positions. Two Northwest executives were transferred in to replace them. Still, there was no word on the audit findings.

Two years later, Jason and Maria were assigned to a job supervised by Frank Ratliff, a member of the high-level internal audit team. After hours, Frank told them the story. Based on Jason and Maria's reports, the investigation team had examined a large sample of purchasing transactions and all employee timekeeping and payroll records for a 12-month period. The team had also taken a detailed physical inventory. The investigators discovered that the problems identified by Jason—including missing purchase requisitions, purchase orders, and receiving reports, as well as excessive prices—were widespread. They found that these problems occurred almost exclusively in transactions with three large vendors from whom Springer's had purchased several million dollars' worth of inventories and supplies. The team discussed the unusually high item prices with the vendors, but did not receive a satisfactory explanation. However, a check of the county business licensing bureau revealed that Bill Springer held a significant ownership interest in each of these three companies. By authorizing excessive prices to companies he partially owned, Springer had earned a share of several hundred thousand dollars of excessive profits, all at the expense of Northwest Industries.

The investigation team also found evidence that several of Springer's employees were paid for more hours than documented by timekeeping records. Finally, the team had determined Springer's inventory account was materially overstated. The physical inventory revealed that a significant portion of recorded inventory did not exist, and that other portions were obsolete. The adjusting journal entry reflecting Springer's real inventory wiped out much of the outlet's profits over the past 3 years.

When confronted, the Springers vehemently denied any laws had been broken. Northwest considered going to the authorities for a formal fraud investigation, but were concerned their case was not strong enough to prove in court. They were also worried that adverse publicity might damage the company's position in Bozeman. After months of negotiation, the Springers agreed to the settlement reported in the newsletter. Part of the settlement was that no public statement would be made about any alleged fraud or embezzlement involving the Springers. According to Frank, this policy was not unusual. In many cases of fraud, settlements are reached quietly, with no legal action taken, so the company can avoid adverse publicity.

KEY TERMS

- sabotage
- embezzlement
- threat
- exposure
- risk
- internal control
- internal control structure
- preventive controls
- detective controls
- corrective controls
- Foreign Corrupt Practices Act

- Committee of Sponsoring Organizations (COSO)
- control environment
- audit committee
- policy and procedures manual
- authorization
- digital signature
- specific authorization
- general authorization
- collusion

- batch totals (control totals)
- financial total
- hash total
- record count
- line count
- cross-footing balance test
- transcription error
- transposition error
- expected loss
- audit trail

CHAPTER QUIZ

1. COSO identified five interrelated components of internal controls. Which of the following is not one of those five?
   a. risk assessment
   b. internal control policies
   c. monitoring
   d. information and communication

2. Sarah Robinson computed a batch total by adding the total amount of all checks. What is this type of batch total called?
   a. cross-footing balance test
   b. line count
   c. record count
   d. hash total
   e. none of the above

3. Which of the following statements is true?
   a. The COSO report is narrow in scope and is limited to financial controls.
   b. The COSO report states that internal control is a process that should provide reasonable assurance that control objectives are achieved.
   c. The Foreign Corrupt Practices Act had no impact on internal accounting control systems.
   d. It is easier to add controls to an already designed system than to include them during the initial design stage.

4. All other things being equal, which of the following is true?
   a. Detective controls are superior to preventive controls.
   b. Corrective controls are superior to preventive controls.
   c. Preventive controls are equivalent to detective controls.
   d. Preventive controls are superior to detective controls.

5. Which of the following statements about the control environment is false?
   a. Management's attitudes toward internal control and ethical behavior have little impact on employee beliefs or actions.
   b. An overly complex or unclear organizational structure may be indicative of more serious problems.
   c. A written policy and procedures manual is an important tool for assigning authority and responsibility in many organizations.
   d. Supervision is especially important in organizations that cannot afford elaborate responsibility reporting or are too small to have an adequate separation of duties.

6. To achieve effective segregation of duties, certain functions must be separated. Which of the following is the correct listing of the accounting-related functions that must be segregated?
   a. control, recording, and monitoring
   b. authorization, recording, and custody
   c. control, custody, and authorization
   d. monitoring, recording, and planning

7. Which of the following is not an independent check?
   a. bank reconciliation
   b. periodic comparison of subsidiary ledger totals to control accounts
   c. trial balance
   d. re-adding the total of a batch of invoices and comparing it with your first total

8. Which of the following is a control procedure relating to both the design and use of documents and records?
   a. locking blank checks in a drawer
   b. reconciling the bank account
   c. sequentially prenumbering sales invoices
   d. comparing actual physical quantities with recorded amounts

9. Which of the following is the correct order of the risk assessment steps discussed in the chapter?
   a. Identify threats, estimate risk and exposure, identify controls, and estimate costs and benefits.
   b. Identify controls, estimate risk and exposure, identify threats, and estimate costs and benefits.
   c. Estimate risk and exposure, identify controls, identify threats, and estimate costs and benefits.
   d. Estimate costs and benefits, identify threats, identify controls, and estimate risk and exposure.

10. Your current system is deemed to be 90 percent reliable. A major threat has been identified with an exposure of $3,000,000. Two control procedures exist to deal with the threat. Implementation of control A would cost $100,000 and reduce the risk to 6 percent. Implementation of control B would cost $140,000 and reduce the risk to 4 percent. Implementation of both controls would cost $220,000 and reduce the risk to 2 percent. Given the data, and based solely on an economic analysis of costs and benefits, what should you do?
   a. Implement control A only.
   b. Implement control B only.
   c. Implement both controls A and B.
   d. Implement neither control.

DISCUSSION QUESTIONS

7.1 Answer the following questions about the audit of Springer's Northwest Lumber & Supply.
   a. What deficiencies existed in the control environment at Springer's?
   b. Do you agree with the decision to settle with the Springers rather than prosecute them for fraud and embezzlement? Why or why not?
   c. Should the company have told Jason and Maria the results of the high-level audit? Why or why not?

7.2 Effective segregation of duties is sometimes not economically feasible in a small business. What internal control elements do you think can help compensate for this threat?

7.3 Craig Robinson has just purchased a PC and intends to computerize his sister Sarah's manual system. What effect will this have on the use of batch totals in cash receipts processing?

7.4 Some people believe that, instead of producing tangible benefits, business controls create resentment and loss of company morale. Discuss this position.

7.5 In recent years, Supersmurf's external auditors have given clean opinions on its financial statements and favorable evaluations of its internal control systems. Discuss whether it is necessary for this corporation to take any further action to comply with the Foreign Corrupt Practices Act.

7.6 When you go to a movie theater, you buy a prenumbered ticket from the window or counter cashier. This ticket is then handed to another person at the entrance to the movie. What kinds of irregularities is the theater trying to prevent? What controls is it using to prevent these irregularities? What remaining risks or exposures can you identify?

PROBLEMS

7.1 You are an audit supervisor who has recently been assigned to a new client, Go-Go Corporation, which is listed on the New York Stock Exchange. You recently visited Go-Go's corporate headquarters to become acquainted with key personnel and to conduct a preliminary review of the company's accounting policies and systems. During this visit, the following events occurred.
   a. You met with Go-Go's audit committee, which consists of the corporate controller, treasurer, financial vice president, and budget director.
   b. You recognized the treasurer as a former aide to John Boatsky, who was convicted of fraud in an insider trading scandal 3 years ago.
   c. Management explained its plans to change accounting methods for depreciation from the accelerated to the straight-line method. Management implied that, if your firm does not concur with this change, Go-Go will employ other auditors.
   d. You learned that the financial vice president manages a staff of five internal auditors.
   e. You noted that all management authority seems to reside with three brothers, who serve as chief executive officer, president, and financial vice president.
   f. You were told that the performance of division and department managers is evaluated on a subjective basis, because Go-Go's management believes that formal performance evaluation procedures are counterproductive.
   g. You learned that the company has reported increases in earnings per share for each of the past 25 quarters; however, earnings during the current quarter have leveled off and may decline.
   h. You reviewed the company's policy and procedures manual, which listed policies for dealing with customers, vendors, and employees.
   i. Your preliminary assessment is that the accounting systems are well designed and employ effective internal control procedures.
   Required
   The information you have obtained suggests potential problems relating to one or more elements of Go-Go's internal control structure. Identify these problems and explain each in relation to internal control structure concepts.

7.2 The first column in Table 7-4 lists transaction amounts that have been summed to obtain a batch total. Assume the amounts and the batch total are correct. Columns a through d contain batch totals computed from the same amounts after these transaction amounts were processed in a subsequent processing step. One processing error occurred during each of the four cases.
   Required
   For each case, you are to do the following:
   a. Compute the difference between the batch total obtained after processing and the correct batch total shown on the left.
   b. Explain specifically how this difference is helpful in discovering the processing error.
   c. Identify the processing error.

7.3 Explain how the principle of separation of duties is violated in each of the following situations. Also suggest one or more procedures to reduce the risk and exposure highlighted in each example.
   a. A payroll clerk recorded a 40-hour work week for an employee who had quit the previous week. He then prepared a paycheck for this employee, forged her signature, and cashed the check.
   b. While opening the mail, a cashier set aside, and subsequently cashed, two checks payable to the company on account.

Table 7-4   Transaction Amounts from Source Documents and Batch Totals

Transaction amounts	a	b	c	d
$3,630.62	$3,630.62	$3,630.62	$3,630.62	$3,630.62
1,484.86	1,484.86	1,484.86	1,484.86	1,484.86
2,164.67	2,164.67	2,164.67	2,164.67	2,164.67
946.43	946.43	946.43	946.43	946.43
2,626.28	−2,626.28	2,626.28	2,626.28	2,626.28
969.97	969.97	969.97	969.97	969.97
2,772.42	2,772.42	2,772.42	3,772.42	2,772.42
934.25	934.25	934.25	934.25	934.25
1,620.94	1,620.94	1,620.94	1,620.94	1,620.94
4,566.86	4,566.86	4,656.86	4,566.86	4,566.86
1,249.32	1,249.32	1,249.32	1,249.32	1,249.32
1,070.27	1,070.27	1,070.27	1,070.27	1,070.27
2,668.51	2,668.51	2,668.51	2,668.51	2,668.51
1,762.62	1,762.62	1,762.62	1,762.62	873.26
873.26	873.26	873.26	873.26	$27,578.66
$29,341.28	$24,088.72	$29,431.28	$30,341.28	

c. A cashier prepared a fictitious invoice from a company using his brother-in-law's name. He wrote a check in payment of the invoice, which the brother-in-law later cashed.

d. An employee of the finishing department walked off with several parts from the storeroom and recorded the items in the inventory ledger as having been issued to the assembly department.

e. A cashier cashed a check from a customer in payment of an account receivable, pocketed the cash, and concealed the theft by properly posting the receipt to the customer's account in the accounts receivable ledger.

7.4 McClain's Lumberyard uses the following procedures to sell lumber to its customers:
   a. The customer tells an office clerk the sizes and quantities of lumber he wants to purchase.
   b. The clerk records the items on a sales document, calculates the total cost, and collects the customer's payment.
   c. A worker obtains the lumber from the yard and loads it into the customer's car or truck. If the purchase is large and the customer wishes, McClain's will deliver the order.

Required
Explain several aspects of the design and use of the sales document that will facilitate control of cash receipts and inventories by McClain's.

7.5 The Gardner Company, a client of your firm, has come to you with the following problem: It has three clerical employees who must perform the following functions.
   a. Maintain the general ledger.
   b. Maintain the accounts payable ledger.
   c. Maintain the accounts receivable ledger.
   d. Prepare checks for signature.
   e. Maintain the disbursements journal.
   f. Issue credits on returns and allowances.

g. Reconcile the bank account. ✓
h. Handle and deposit cash receipts. ✓

Assuming equal abilities among the three employees, the company asks you to assign the eight functions to them to maximize internal control. Assume that these employees will perform no accounting functions other than the ones listed.

Required

a. List four possible unsatisfactory pairings of the functions.
b. State how you would distribute the functions among the three employees. Assume that with the exception of the nominal jobs of the bank reconciliation and the issuance of credits on returns and allowances, all functions require an equal amount of time.

(*CPA Examination, adapted*)

7.6 The Future Corporation is a small manufacturing company located in Aggie, Texas. It operates one plant and employs 50 workers in its manufacturing facility. Employees are paid weekly. Each week, the department supervisors supply the payroll clerk with signed time sheets and a list of any employees hired or terminated by the supervisor. The payroll clerk compares the time sheets with the time cards and prepares and signs payroll checks. The paychecks are then given in sealed envelopes to the supervisors, who in turn give them to the respective employees.

Required

Identify several internal control weaknesses in Future Corporation's payroll system. For each weakness, describe how internal control could be improved.

7.7 You are auditing the Alaska branch of Far Distributing Company. This branch has substantial annual sales, which are billed and collected locally. As a part of your audit, you find that the procedures for handling cash receipts are as follows:

- Cash collections on over-the-counter and COD sales are received from the customer or delivery service by the cashier. Upon receipt of cash, the sales ticket is stamped "paid" and a copy is filed for future reference. The only record of COD sales is a copy of the sales ticket, which the cashier holds until receiving cash from the delivery service.
- Mail is opened by the secretary to the credit manager, and remittances are given to the credit manager for review. The credit manager then places the remittances in a tray on the cashier's desk. At the daily deposit cutoff time, the cashier delivers the checks and cash on hand to the assistant credit manager, who prepares remittance lists and makes up the bank deposit, which the assistant manager also takes to the bank. The assistant credit manager also posts remittances to the accounts receivable ledger cards and verifies the cash discount allowable.
- You also ascertain that the credit manager obtains approval from the executive office at Far Distributing Company, located in Chicago, to write off uncollectible accounts. In addition, the manager has retained in custody, as of the end of the fiscal year, some remittances received on various days during the last month.

Required

a. Describe irregularities that might occur under the current procedures for handling cash collections and remittances.
b. List the procedures that you would recommend to strengthen internal control over cash collections and remittances.

(*CPA Examination, adapted*)

7.8 Your junior accountant has prepared the following description of the accounting and internal control procedures relating to purchases by the Branden Company, a midsize manufacturer of special-order machinery:

After approval by manufacturing department supervisors, materials purchase requisitions are forwarded to the purchasing department supervisor, who distributes the requisitions to his employees. These employees prepare prenumbered purchase orders in triplicate, account for all numbers, and send the original purchase order to the vendor. One copy of the purchase order is sent to the receiving department, where it is used as a receiving report. The other copy is filed in the purchasing department.

When the materials are received, they are moved directly to the storeroom and issued to the supervisors on an informal request basis. The receiving department sends a receiving report (with its copy of the purchase order attached) to the purchasing department and forwards copies of the receiving report to the storeroom and to the accounting department.

Vendors' invoices for material purchases, received in duplicate in the mail room, are sent to the purchasing department and directed to the employee who placed the related order. This employee then compares (1) the invoice with the copy of the purchase order on file in the purchasing department for price and terms; and (2) the invoice quantity received as reported by the shipping and receiving department on its copy of the purchase order. The purchasing department employees also check discounts, footings, and extensions, after which they initial the invoice to indicate approval for payment. The invoice is then submitted to the voucher section of the accounting department, where it is coded for account distribution, assigned a voucher number, entered in the voucher register, and filed according to payment due date.

Required

Discuss the internal control weaknesses at Branden Company. Suggest supplementary or revised procedures for remedying each weakness with regard to (a) requisition of materials and (b) receipt and storage of materials.

(CPA Examination, adapted)

7.9 During a recent review, ABC Corporation discovered that it has a serious internal control problem. It is estimated that the exposure associated with this problem is $1 million and that the risk is presently 5 percent. Two internal control procedures have been proposed to deal with this problem. Procedure A would cost $25,000 and reduce risk to 2 percent. Procedure B would cost $30,000 and reduce risk to 1 percent. If both procedures were implemented, risk would be reduced to one-tenth of 1 percent.

Required

a. What is the estimated expected loss associated with ABC Corporation's internal control problem before any new internal control procedures are implemented?
b. Compute the revised estimate of expected loss if procedure A were implemented, if procedure B were implemented, and if both procedures were implemented.
c. Compare the estimated costs and benefits of procedure A, procedure B, and both procedures combined.
d. Considering only the estimates of cost and benefit, which procedure(s) should be implemented? What other factors might be relevant to the decision?

Case 7-1   AnyCompany, Inc.: An Ongoing Comprehensive Case

Visit a local company and obtain permission to study its system of internal controls. Once you have lined up a company, do the following:

1. Obtain copies of organizational charts, job descriptions, and related documentation on how authority and responsibility have been assigned within the organization. Do lines of authority and responsibility seem to be clearly defined?

2. Determine if the company has an internal audit function. If so, visit with an internal audit supervisor or manager and learn (a) to whom in the organization the head of internal auditing reports and (b) what kinds of jobs internal auditing generally performs.

3. If the company is a corporation whose equity securities are publicly traded, determine the following:
   a. Has the company taken steps to document its compliance with the internal control provisions of the Foreign Corrupt Practices Act of 1977? If possible, examine and evaluate this documentation.
   b. Is an audit committee part of the board of directors? If so, obtain a membership list and a copy of the committee's charter or bylaws.

4. Interview someone who hires employees for positions in accounting and data processing. Find out the following information.

   a. What sort of background checks are performed before these employees are hired?
   b. Is fidelity bond coverage normally obtained for them?
   c. Does the company require rotation of duties and enforced vacations for these employees?

5. Select any one of the five accounting data processing cycles described in Chapters 11 through 15 and examine the company's internal control procedures for that accounting cycle.
   a. Identify the persons responsible for the transaction authorization, record keeping, and asset custody functions.
   b. Learn how transaction documents and/or records are used to facilitate internal control.
   c. Follow the audit trail by tracing one accounting transaction from its original source document through its entry in journals, ledgers, files, and so on, and ultimately the general ledger accounts.
   d. Identify the policies and procedures used to safeguard assets and records.
   e. Identify several internal check procedures.

Case 7-2   The Greater Providence Deposit & Trust Embezzlement

On a Saturday afternoon in the spring of 1988, Nino Moscardi received an anonymous note in his mail. Moscardi, president of Greater Providence Deposit & Trust, was shocked to read that an employee of the bank was putting through bogus loans. On the following Monday, Moscardi directed the bank's internal auditors to investigate certain transactions detailed in the note. The investigation led to James Guisti, manager of a North Providence branch office and a trusted 14-year employee who had once worked as one of the bank's auditors. Guisti was later charged with embezzling $1.83 million from the bank through 67 phony loans taken out over a 3-year period.

Court documents revealed numerous details of Guisti's embezzlement scheme. For example, the first bogus loan was written in April 1985 for $10,000. The loans were 90-day notes requiring no collateral and ranging in amount from $10,000 to $63,500. Guisti originated the loans; when each one matured, he would take out a new loan, or rewrite the old one, to pay the principal and interest due. Some loans had been rewritten five or six times.

The 67 loans were taken out in various names, including his wife's maiden name, his father's name, and the names of two of his friends. These people denied they received any stolen funds or knew anything about the embezzlement. In addition, one loan was in the name of James Vanesse, who police said did not exist. The Social Security number on Vanesse's loan application was issued to a female, and the phone number belonged to a North Providence auto dealer.

Court records also disclosed the details of police interviews with bank employees to determine how the loan money was dispensed. According to Lucy Fraioli, a customer service representative who co-signed checks to the five names to which Guisti had originated loans, Guisti was her supervisor and she thought nothing was wrong with the checks, though she did not know any of the five people. Marcia Perfetto, head teller at the branch, told police that she had cashed checks for Guisti made out to four of the five persons. Asked if she gave the money to Guisti when he gave her the checks to cash, she answered, "Not all of the time," though she could not recall ever having given the money directly to any of the four, whom she said she did not know.

According to news reports, Guisti was authorized to make consumer loans up to a certain dollar limit without loan committee approvals, which is a standard industry practice. Guisti's lending limit was $10,000 until January 1987, when it was increased to $15,000. In February 1988 it was increased again to $25,000. Some of the loans, however, including the one for $63,500, far exceeded his lending limit. In addition, all loan applications should have been accompanied by a report on the applicant's credit history, purchased from an independent credit rating firm. The loan taken out in a fictitious name would not have had a credit report and should have been flagged by a loan review clerk at the bank's headquarters.

News reports raised several questions about why the fraud had not been detected earlier. State regulators had examined the bank's books in September 1986. The bank's own internal auditors also failed to detect the fraud. In checking for bad loans, however, bank auditors do not examine all loans and generally focus on loans much larger than the ones in question. In addition, Greater Providence had recently dropped its computer services arrangement with a local bank in favor of an out-of-state bank, and this changeover may have reduced the effectiveness of the bank's control procedures. Finally, the bank's loan review clerks were frequently rotated, making follow-up on questionable loans more difficult.

Court records indicate that Guisti was a frequent gambler and used the proceeds of the embezzlement to pay gambling debts. The bank's losses totaled $624,000. Its bonding company, Hartford Accident and Indemnity Company, covered the loss, which was less than the $1.83 million in bogus loans, because Guisti used a portion of the borrowed money to repay some loans as they came due.

According to financial reports made available by Greater Providence officials, the bank had assets of $220 million and outstanding loans of $184 million as of the end of 1987, and it earned a record $1.6 million for 1987. It had eight branches in the Providence area.

The bank had experienced other adverse publicity during that period. In 1985, the bank was fined $50,000 after pleading guilty to failure to report a series of cash transactions exceeding $10,000, which is a felony. In 1986, the bank was taken private by its current owners, but only after a lengthy public battle with State Attorney General Arlene Violet. The state charged that the bank had inflated its assets and overestimated its capital surplus to make its balance sheet look stronger. The bank denied this charge.

1. Discuss how Greater Providence Deposit & Trust might improve its control procedures over the disbursement of loan funds to minimize the risk of this type of fraud. In what way does this case indicate a lack of proper segregation of duties?
2. Discuss how Greater Providence might improve its loan review procedures at bank headquarters to minimize its fraud risk. Was it a good idea to rotate the assignments of loan review clerks? Why or why not?
3. Discuss whether Greater Providence's auditors should have been able to detect this fraud.
4. Are their any indications that the control environment at Greater Providence may have been deficient? If so, how could they have contributed to this embezzlement?

Source: John Kostrezewa, "Charge: Embezzlement," *Providence Journal-Bulletin* (July 31, 1988): F-1.

ANSWERS TO CHAPTER QUIZ

1. b	3. b	5. a	7. d	9. a
2. e	4. d	6. b	8. c	10. b

Computer-Based Information Systems Control

Learning Objectives

After studying this chapter, you should be able to:

- Identify and explain the four principles of systems reliability and the three criteria used to evaluate if the principles have been achieved.
- Identify and explain the controls that apply to more than one principle of reliability.
- Identify and explain the controls that help ensure that a system is available to users when needed.
- Identify and explain the security controls that prevent unauthorized access to information, software, and other system resources.
- Identify and explain the controls that help ensure that a system can be properly maintained, while still providing for system availability, security, and integrity.
- Identify and explain the integrity controls that help ensure that system processing is complete, accurate, timely, and authorized.

Integrative Case: Seattle Paper Products

During his fifth month at Northwest Industries, Jason Scott is assigned to audit Seattle Paper Products (SPP), a Northwest subsidiary. Jason's first task is to review 50 randomly selected payables transactions, track down all supporting documents, and verify that all transactions have been properly authorized and correctly processed. Within a short time he locates vendor invoices and disbursement vouchers for all 50 transactions, and he finds purchase orders and receiving reports for 45 of the transactions. After reviewing these documents, Jason is satisfied that these 45 transactions are valid and accurate.

The other five transactions involve the purchase of services, which are processed on the basis of vendor invoices approved by management. One particular invoice, from Pacific Electric Services, lists $450 for maintenance and repair work but has no authorization signature. Jason locates five more invoices from Pacific Electric, all for maintenance and repair services in amounts ranging from $300 to $500. These five bear the initials "JLC," for Jack Carlton, the general supervisor of the plant. Much to Jason's surprise, Carlton denies initialing them and claims he has never heard of Pacific Electric. Jason finds no such firm in the phone book.

Jason cannot believe he has found another hidden problem. After brooding over his bad luck, he begins to think about the following questions:

1. Is Jack Carlton telling the truth? If so, where did the Pacific Electric Services invoices come from?
2. If Carlton is not telling the truth, what is he up to?
3. If Pacific Electric Services is a fictitious company, how could SPP's control systems allow its invoices to be processed and approved for payment?

INTRODUCTION

In today's world, more and more companies depend on IT to process business information electronically. Organizations use IT to operate their businesses, manufacture products, and perform services. Companies can no longer build a moat around their information systems and lock everyone else out. Instead, they must share information and use IT to link their information systems to those with whom they interact frequently: customers, vendors, employees, business partners, shareholders, and governmental entities. This increase in connectivity has made information systems more vulnerable.

Achieving adequate security and control over an organization's information resources should be a top management priority. Although internal control objectives remain the same regardless of how business is conducted or how extensively IT is used, the way information security and control are achieved has changed significantly in recent years. With the expected developments in e-commerce and IT, it is also highly likely that these changes will continue.

As information systems have evolved, so must internal control systems. When businesses moved from a paper-based system to a mainframe-based computer system, new controls had to be developed to mitigate or control the risks introduced by these new computer-based information systems. Likewise, when businesses moved from a centralized mainframe-based system to a distributed model, such as a client/server system, new controls had to be developed. Now, as we move into an Internet-based e-commerce environment, new controls will need to be developed to help control the new risks that arise. Fortunately, advances in information systems and in IT also provide opportunities for an organization to enhance its internal controls.

In today's interconnected global economy, an unreliable information system harms not only the company and employees who use it, but also the company's supply chain. Recognizing the need for information systems assurance, the AICPA and the Canadian Institute of Chartered Accountants (CICA) have introduced a new evaluation service, called **SysTrust,** that independently tests and verifies a system's reliability.

This service provides management, customers, vendors, and business partners with the assurance that an information system is indeed reliable.

What Constitutes a Reliable System?

SysTrust uses the following four principles to determine if a system is reliable:

1. *Availability*. The system is available for operation and use at times set forth in service-level statements or agreements. This means users must be able to enter, update, and retrieve data during the agreed-upon times.

2. *Security*. The system is protected against unauthorized physical and logical access. This helps prevent (a) the improper use, alteration, destruction, or disclosure of information and software, and (b) the theft of system resources.

3. *Maintainability*. The system can be modified as required without affecting system availability, security, and integrity. Only authorized, tested, and documented changes should be made to a system and related data. For all planned and completed changes, resources must be available to manage, schedule, document, and communicate the changes to management and authorized users.

4. *Integrity*. System processing is complete, accurate, timely, and authorized. A system has integrity if it accomplishes its intended function in an unimpaired manner, free from unauthorized or inadvertent system manipulation.

For each of the four principles of reliability, the following three criteria have been developed to evaluate if the principle has been achieved:

1. The entity has defined, documented, and communicated performance objectives, policies, and standards that achieve each of the four principles. SysTrust defines **performance objectives** as the overall goals that an entity wishes to achieve; **policies** as the rules that provide a formal direction for achieving the objectives and that enable performance; and **standards** as the required procedures that are implemented to meet the policies.

2. The entity uses procedures, people, software, data, and infrastructure to achieve each principle in accordance with established policies and standards.

3. The entity monitors the system and takes action to achieve compliance with the objectives, policies, and standards for each principle.

The controls that are used to achieve these reliability principles are discussed next. Those that apply to most or all of the four principles are discussed first, followed by the controls related more specifically to each principle.

CONTROLS RELATED TO MORE THAN ONE RELIABILITY PRINCIPLE

The following controls apply to more than one reliability principle: strategic planning and budgeting, developing a system reliability plan, and performing documentation. Table 8-1 summarizes the key controls discussed in this section.

Strategic Planning and Budgeting

As presented in Chapter 1, an organization's information system must be aligned with its business strategies. To accomplish this feat, organizations require a multiyear (often a 3- to 5-year) **strategic plan** that serves as a technological road map and lays out the

Table 8-1   Summary of Key General Reliability Controls

Control Category	Threats/Risks	Controls
Strategic Planning & Budgeting	IS does not support business strategies, poor resource use, information needs not met or can't be paid for	Multiyear strategic plan that is periodically evaluated, research and development group to assess emerging technologies impact on business operations, budgets to support plan.
Developing a system reliability plan	Inability to ensure system reliability	Assign plan responsibility to top-level manager; continuously review and update plan; identify, document, and test user reliability requirements and performance objectives, policies, and standards; identify and review all new or changed legal requirements; log user requests for change; document, analyze, and report system reliability problems; determine ownership, custody, access, and maintenance responsibility of information resources; develop security awareness program and communicate it to all existing employees; require new employees to sign security agreement; perform risk assessment for all changes to systems environment
Documentation	Ineffective design, operation, review, audit, and modification of systems	Administrative documentation (standards and procedures for data processing, analysis, design, programming, file handling and storage), systems documentation (application inputs, processing steps, outputs, errorhandling), operating documentation (equipment configurations, programs, files, setup and execution procedures, corrective actions)

projects the company must complete to achieve its long-range goals. To gather information for the plan, companies need a research and development group that is responsible for assessing how emerging technologies impact the business and its operations. The plan must address the company's hardware, software, personnel, and infrastructure requirements. Each year the board of directors and top management should prepare and approve the plan and its supporting budgets.

The plan should be evaluated several times a year to ensure that the organization can develop or acquire important new system components and maintain existing ones. As part of these evaluations, the manager of the information system should assesses the functionality, stability, complexity, cost, degree of business automation, and strengths and weaknesses of the existing system to determine if it adequately supports the company's business needs. In addition, users should be asked if their systems meet current and anticipated business needs and how new technologies could be used to improve their systems.

An organization cannot follow its strategic plan unless funds are budgeted for the anticipated changes. A budget should be established for emergencies or for unanticipated maintenance requirements. There should be a relationship between current and prior budget allocations. See Chapter 2 for a more in-depth discussion on budgets.

Developing a System Reliability Plan

In a recent study, 66 percent of those reporting problems with their systems said one of the reasons was inadequate monitoring of controls and security. Another 44 percent said insufficient understanding of control concepts and control design was a contributing factor. This highlights a significant problem in many companies—their lack of an effective plan to ensure the reliability of their information system. Developing and continuously updating a comprehensive reliability plan is one important control that a company can implement.

A top-level manager should be assigned formal responsibility and accountability to develop, supervise, and enforce the plan. The plan should be communicated, on a timely basis, to all authorized system users and personnel responsible for implementing and monitoring the plan. The most common means of doing so is in memos, meetings, policies and procedures manuals, and interaction with the organization's help desk. The plan should be continuously reviewed and updated.

According to SysTrust, a good way to begin developing a systems reliability plan is to identify and document (1) the availability, security, maintainability, and integrity requirements for authorized users, and (2) performance objectives, policies, and standards for the four principles of reliability. User requirements are usually documented in service-level agreements or other company documents. Companies should have a formal process to identify and review all new or changed laws, regulations, contracts, or other service-level agreements that can affect user requirements or system performance objectives, policies, or standards. Likewise, all user requests for change should be logged and reviewed.

Procedures should exist to ensure that actual system availability, security, maintainability, and integrity are tested regularly and the results are compared with performance objectives, policies, and standards. The results of these tests and comparisons, and all system reliability problems, should be documented and reported to management, and all problems resolved. The log of problems and variances should be analyzed periodically to identify trends that might impact system reliability and appropriate changes made.

Organizations must identify all significant information resources, such as hardware, programs, data, and transactions. They should then decide who owns the resource, who has custody of it, who can have physical and logical access to it, and who is responsible for establishing and maintaining its security and reliability.

As part of the reliability plan, a security awareness program can help employees understand the importance of systems security and reliability. This program should be communicated to all existing employees. Newly hired employees should be required to sign an agreement that they will abide by the security policy when they begin work.

All systems undergo change and a risk assessment should be performed and evaluated when a change occurs within or outside of the physical environment of the system. Any change in system components should be evaluated with respect to its impact on the systems performance objectives, policies, and standards.

Documentation

Another important control affecting the four reliability principles is the implementation of documentation procedures and standards to ensure clear and concise documentation. Quality documentation facilitates communication and regular progress reviews during systems development and can be used as a reference and training tool for newly hired systems employees. It also simplifies program maintenance, especially when updating applications written by someone else, and eases problems related to job turnover, such as a programmer quitting in the middle of a major project.

Documentation may be classified into three basic categories:

1. **Administrative documentation** describes the standards and procedures for data processing, including the justification and authorization of new systems and system changes; standards for systems analysis, design, and programming; and procedures for file handling and storage.
2. **Systems documentation** describes each application system and its key processing functions. It includes narrative material, flowcharts, and program listings. It shows application inputs, processing steps, outputs, and error handling procedures.
3. **Operating documentation** describes what is needed to run a program, including the equipment configuration, program and data files, procedures to set up and execute the job, conditions that may interrupt program execution, and corrective actions for program interruptions.

AVAILABILITY

Some of the reasons why systems may become unavailable to users are hardware and software failures, natural disasters, and deliberate acts of sabotage. One popular means of sabotage, which often significantly limits an organization's e-business activities, is called a denial-of-service attack. Denial-of-service attacks are discussed in greater depth in Chapter 9.

To ensure information system availability, organizations need to minimize system downtime and develop disaster recovery plans. These two controls are discussed in this section and are summarized in Table 8-2.

Minimizing System Downtime

Significant financial losses can be incurred if hardware or software malfunctions cause an information system to fail. Among the methods to minimize system downtime are policies and procedures, appropriate insurance, preventive maintenance, an uninterrupted power system, and fault tolerance.

Organizations should develop and implement policies and procedures for dealing with outages, errors (system, program, and data), loss or destruction of data, and

Table 8-2   Summary of Key Availability Controls

Control Category	Threats/Risks	Controls
Minimizing system downtime	System outages or failure that interrupts critical business operations, loss or destruction of data	Policies and procedures to handle outages, errors, loss or destruction of data, and other problems; disaster and business interruption insurance; regular preventive maintenance on key components; uninterrupted power system; fault tolerance
Disaster recovery plan	Prolonged interruption of data processing and business operations due to fire, natural disaster, sabotage, or vandalism	Coordinator's responsibility is to implement a plan, determine recovery priorities, assign responsibility for recovery activities, document and test plan, continuously review and revise plan; remote storage of backup data and program files (electronic vaulting, grandfather–father–son), procedures for recovering lost or destroyed files (checkpoint and rollback), insurance coverage, backup computer and telecommunications facilities (reciprocal agreements, hot and cold sites, duplicate hardware, software, and data storage devices)

other types of problems. Operating personnel should be familiar with these policies and procedures and be able to follow them in the event of problems. If a system does fail, adequate disaster and business interruption insurance can speed an organization's ability to restore system availability and to recover from any losses incurred.

Preventive maintenance includes regularly testing system components and replacing those in poor condition. An **uninterruptible power supply (UPS)** system is an auxiliary power supply that regulates the flow of power to the computer, preventing loss of data due to momentary power surges or dips. In the event of a complete power failure, a UPS provides a backup power supply to keep the computer system operating for a limited amount of time, until it can be safely shut down. **Fault tolerance** describes the system's ability to continue operating when system components (such as PCs, terminals, data transmission lines, and disk drives) fail. It is achieved using redundant components that take over in the event of failure.

In today's interconnected world of e-business, the security of an organization's system often depends on overall Internet security. Therefore, organizations should consider how an extended network or system outage would affect the organization and then make all possible and appropriate contingency plans. For example, an organization may require the assistance of many other organizational entities to adequately respond to a denial-of-service attack.

Disaster Recovery Plan

Every organization should have a **disaster recovery plan** so that data processing capacity can be restored as smoothly and quickly as possible in the event of a major disaster. Being without an information system can be quite costly; some companies report losses as high as $500,000 per hour of downtime. John Alden Life Insurance estimates that, without its disaster recovery plan, Hurricane Andrew would have put the company out of business in three days. Many of the 350 companies that had their systems destroyed in the World Trade Center bombing in 1993 were unprepared; 150 of them went out of business. Because the damages were so much greater in the September 11, 2001, attack on the World Trade Center, the number of companies to go out of business will probably be even greater. Certainly, no company without an excellent disaster recovery plan, including backup copies of its data, could possibly hope to survive the collapse of those buildings

A survey of 200 large U.S. businesses showed that only one-third have a disaster recovery plan with off-site data storage for their client/server applications. As Focus 8-1 and 8-2 illustrate, those that have them are well rewarded for their planning and foresight when disaster strikes.

The objectives of a recovery plan are to (1) minimize the extent of the disruption, damage, and loss; (2) temporarily establish an alternative means of processing information; (3) resume normal operations as soon as possible; and (4) train and familiarize personnel with emergency operations. Disaster recovery and other contingency plans should be tested on a regular basis and updated as circumstances change or as otherwise needed. A sound disaster recovery plan should contain the following elements.

Priorities for the recovery process

The disaster recovery plan should identify the applications necessary to keep the organization running, the hardware and software necessary to sustain the applications, and the sequence and timing of all recovery activities.

Insurance

The disaster recovery plan should include insurance coverage to defer costs of equipment replacement, recovery activities, and business interruption.

Backup data and program files

Procedures should exist for recovering lost or destroyed files. All program and data files should be backed up regularly and frequently and stored at a secure site some distance from the main computer. As a result of the bombing of the Federal Building in Oklahoma City, the Federal Employees Credit Union offices were destroyed and 18 of its 33 employees died. Even though all its records and computers were destroyed, duplicate copies of all crucial information had been stored off-site. Two days later, the company reopened its doors in a new location with new computer and phone systems.

Backup files may be transported to the remote site physically; or they can be sent electronically to the backup facility by way of **electronic vaulting.** Many electronic

Focus 8-1

A Model for Disaster Recovery Planning

The value of a disaster recovery plan is underscored by numerous case histories. Perhaps the best known is the story of the worst bank fire in history and how the bank recovered by following a plan that has since become a disaster recovery planning model.

On Thanksgiving Day, a huge fire swept through the offices of Northwest National Bank of Minneapolis, destroying bank transaction records and data processing facilities. It was described as one of the worst fires in the city's history. Yet the following Monday, bank employees were back on the job in new quarters—handling deposits, withdrawals, investments, loans, and other routine bank transactions. The fire could have threatened the bank's ability to remain in business, but it did not, thanks to a detailed disaster recovery plan. Because a record of nearly every bank transaction was stored elsewhere in computers or on microfilm, the bank lost few, if any, important records. The day after the fire, computers at a local service bureau were hard at work making new copies of the destroyed records. The recovery plan provided bank executives with a detailed blueprint for lining up new office space, replacing computer equipment and supplies, procuring new office equipment, and making other arrangements essential to the continuation of Northwest's banking operations.

In another example, an early morning fire struck the Bank of the Sierra in Porterville, California, destroying its corporate offices and melting its mainframe computer. Though the facility was seemingly well protected by a sprinkler system and a halon-gas fire-extinguishing system, this fire burned through the building's roof, which collapsed, crushing the sprinkler system and releasing the halon gas into the air. The bank's central databases and related records, including all personal and mortgage loan records, credit card records, and unprocessed checks, were lost.

Using a 150-page disaster recovery plan grounded in Northwest National Bank's experience, Bank of the Sierra officials quickly identified team members, crucial tasks, and required equipment, and began an overnight effort to restore bank services. By 10:00 A.M. the following morning, 9 hours after the fire started, backup files were on-line and tellers were conducting business at branch windows as if nothing had happened. For processing of the bank's 25,000 to 40,000 daily transactions, a data processing hot site in nearby San Ramon was used. Updated files were downloaded from the hot site to a mainframe computer, provided by a Denver company, from which printouts were flown back to Porterville daily. Within 6 days after the fire, the bank had cleaned up its transaction processing backlog and its customer accounts were current.

vaulting services have employees install their software on their computers so that they can use Internet connections to contact the computers and automatically back up data, usually in the middle of the night. If data are lost or need to be accessed, the Internet connection provides prompt on-line access to the backup data. To protect data privacy, all data are encrypted before being transmitted.

Batch processing files are backed up using the **grandfather–father–son concept.** In batch processing, when a master file on tape is updated with a set of transactions, a new master file is created on a new tape file. If a master file is destroyed, it can be

Focus 8-2

How Nasdaq Recovered from September 11

Recently, the value of a disaster recovery plan has been underscored by the latest increase in terrorist activity. The most notable example is the September 11, 2001, attack on the World Trade Center Towers. The damage caused by two airplanes managed to wipe some businesses out of existence. However, due to an effective disaster recovery plan, Nasdaq was up and running 6 days after the attack.

Nasdaq's headquarters was located on the 49th and 50th floors of One Liberty Plaza, just across the street from the World Trade Center. When the first plane hit, Nasdaq's security guards immediately evacuated personnel from the building. Most of the employees were out of the building by the time the second plane crashed into the other tower. Although employees were evacuated from the headquarters and the office in Times Square had temporarily lost telephone service, Nasdaq was able to relocate to a backup center at the Marriott Marquis. Once there, Nasdaq executives went through their list of priorities: first, their personnel; second, the state of their traders; third, the physical damage; and lastly, the trading industry situation.

Effective communication became essential in determining the condition of the above priorities. Nasdaq attributes much of its success in communicating and coordinating with the rest of the industry to its dress rehearsals for Y2K. While preparing for the changeover, Nasdaq had regular nationwide teleconferences with all the exchanges. This helped the company organize similar conferences after the attack. Nasdaq had already planned for one potential crisis, and this proved helpful in recovering from another unexpected crisis. By prioritizing and teleconferencing, the company was able to quickly identify the situation and the traders who would need extra help before Nasdaq could open the market again.

Nasdaq's extremely redundant and dispersed systems also helped the company quickly reopen the market. Each trader is linked to two Nasdaq connection centers, and there are 20 connection centers in the United States. The centers are connected to each server using two separate paths and sometimes two distinct vendors. Servers are kept in different buildings and have two network topologies. Even with the electricity out in Lower Manhattan, Nasdaq's systems were relatively unaffected.

When personnel could no longer occupy the Manhattan office and phone lines were out in the Times Square office, Nasdaq still had offices in Maryland and Connecticut, which allowed it to monitor the regulatory processes. This also lessened the risk of losing all Nasdaq's senior management. Even if large numbers of people had been lost in One Liberty Plaza, the company still would have had members of its senior management in other locations.

Nasdaq also took such precautions as having its executives carry more than one mobile phone in case one service provider goes down and investing in interruption insurance to help defer the costs of closing the market. Planning and foresight saved Nasdaq from losing what could have been tens of millions of dollars.

Source: Tom Field, "How Nasdaq Bounced Back," *CIO* (November 1, 2001): 54–58.

recreated using prior generations of the master file and the appropriate transaction file. For example, suppose that on Wednesday night the current master file is destroyed. It could be recreated using the Tuesday master file (father file) and the Tuesday transaction file. If Tuesday's file was also destroyed, it could be recreated using the Monday master file (grandfather file) and Monday's transaction file. The Wednesday master file, as previously mentioned, could then be reconstructed with the new Tuesday master file and the Tuesday transaction file.

A similar procedure is used to ensure that on-line databases and master files can be reconstructed. Periodically during processing, a checkpoint is created; the system makes a copy of the database or master file at that point in time and the information needed to restart the system. The checkpoint file is stored on a separate disk or tape file. If a problem occurs, the system can be restarted by determining the last checkpoint and then reprocessing all subsequent transactions.

In a procedure called **rollback,** a preupdated copy of each record is created prior to processing a transaction. If a hardware failure occurs, the records are rolled back to the preupdate value and the transaction is reprocessed from the beginning.

PC hard drives are often backed up on CDs, diskettes, and tape files; however, if the backup copies are stored next to the PC, they can also be destroyed by a disaster that wipes out the PC. That is exactly what happened when First Interstate Bancorp suffered a fire in its headquarters building in Los Angeles. First Interstate now repeatedly reminds employees to back up their files and take them home at the end of each day. Salomon, a large brokerage firm, has a system that creates weekly backup copies of all files on its 3,000 workstations worldwide. They also have a copy of all application programs on a duplicate computer system.

It is important to document the backup procedures and periodically practice restoring a system from the backup data. In this way, employees know how to quickly restart the system in the event of a failure.

Specific assignments

A disaster recovery plan requires a coordinator who is responsible for implementing all phases of the plan. This individual will then assign responsibility for recovery activities to specific individuals and teams. These activities should include arranging for new facilities, operating the computer, installing software, establishing data communications facilities, recovering vital records, and arranging for forms and supplies.

Backup computer and telecommunications facilities

Backup facilities can be arranged in several ways. One is to establish a reciprocal agreement with an organization that has compatible facilities so that each party can temporarily use the other's data processing facilities in the event of an emergency. For example, four banks whose computers and data were damaged or destroyed in the 1993 World Trade Center bombing were able to use the New York Clearing House Association backup facilities to complete $90 billion of transactions on the day of the bombing.

A second way is to contract with a vendor to provide contingent sites for emergency use. A **hot site** is a facility configured to meet the user's requirements. A **cold site** provides everything necessary to quickly install computer equipment (power, air conditioning, and support systems), but does not have the computers installed. A cold site user must contract with its vendor to ensure prompt delivery of equipment and software in the event of an emergency. For example, several organizations were able to reroute information system operations to disaster recovery facilities in other parts of the country after the September 11, 2001, World Trade Center disaster.

In a multilocation organization, users can distribute processing capacity so that other facilities can take over if one location is damaged or destroyed. In some cases, a system may be so important that a company invests in duplicate hardware, software, or data storage devices. For example, the system at Caesar's Palace in Las Vegas is so vital that an exact duplicate of the entire system, including an up-to-the-minute copy of the database, is maintained 500 feet from the main system.

Periodic testing and revision

The recovery plan is incomplete until it has been satisfactorily tested by simulating a disaster and having each disaster recovery team carry out its prescribed activities. The plan should be retested twice a year. Most plans fail their initial test, and even tested plans rarely anticipate and deal with all problems that surface when a disaster strikes. In addition, the recovery plan must be continuously reviewed and revised to ensure that it reflects current computer applications, equipment configurations, and personnel assignments.

Complete documentation

The disaster recovery plan should be fully documented, with copies stored securely at multiple locations.

SECURITY

Several classifications of controls that help ensure the security of a system are discussed in this section: segregation of duties within the system's function, physical and logical access controls, protection of personal computers and client/server networks, and Internet and e-commerce controls. Table 8-3 summarizes the key security controls discussed in this section.

Segregation of Duties Within the Systems Function

In a highly integrated information system, procedures once performed by separate individuals are now combined. Therefore, any person who has unrestricted access to the computer, its programs, and live data could have the opportunity to both perpetrate and conceal fraud. To combat this threat, organizations must implement compensating control procedures such as the effective segregation of duties within the information system function. Authority and responsibility must be clearly divided among the following functions:

1. *Systems administration.* Systems administrators are responsible for ensuring that the different parts of an information system operate smoothly and efficiently.
2. *Network management.* Network managers ensure that all applicable devices are linked to the organization's internal and external networks and that the networks operate continuously and properly.

Table 8-3 Summary of Key Security Controls

Control Category	Threats/Risks	Controls
Segregation of duties in systems function	Computer fraud	Clearly divide authority and responsibility among systems administration, network management, security management, change management, users, systems analysts, programmers, computer operators, information systems librarian, and the data control group.
Physical access controls	Damage to computers and files; unauthorized access to confidential data	Put computers in locked rooms; restrict access to authorized personnel; maintain a few securely locked and carefully monitored entrances; require proper employee ID; require visitors to sign a log as they enter and leave the site; use a security alarm system; restrict access to private, secured telephone lines, authorized terminals, and PCs; install locks on PCs and other computer devices; restrict access to off-line programs, data, and equipment; locate critical system components away from hazardous materials; install fire and smoke detectors and fire extinguishers.
Logical access controls	Unauthorized access to systems software, application programs, data files, and other system resources	Data security classifications (no restrictions, employees only, owners and top management only, etc.), determine access privileges of employees and outsiders, review activities of those who can read, add, delete, and change data. Recognize users by what they know (passwords, PIN, answers to personal questions), or possess (ID card, active badge), or by personal characteristics (fingerprints, voice patterns, retina prints, facial patterns, signature dynamics, and keyboarding patterns), compatibility checks, access control matrix.
Protection of personal computers and client/ server networks	Damage to computer files and equipment; unauthorized access to confidential data; users who are not security conscious	Inventory PCs and uses, tailor security to risk and exposure, train users in PC controls, lock disk drives, label with unremovable tags, limit data stored or downloaded, prohibit personal software or copying company software for personal uses, keep sensitive data in secure environment, automatically shut down idle network PCs, back up hard drives regularly, encrypt or password protect files, wipe disks clean with utility program, place protective walls around operating systems, boot PCs within a security system, use multilevel password control, employ specialists or security programs to detect holes in a network, audit and record security breaches.
Internet & e-commerce controls	Damage to data files and equipment; unauthorized access to confidential data	Passwords, encryption, routing verification, virus detection software, firewalls, tunneling, electronic envelopes, deny employees access to the Internet, and Internet servers not connected to other company computers.

3. *Security management.* Security management is charged with ensuring that all aspects of the system are secure and protected from all internal and external threats.

4. *Change management.* These individuals manage all changes to an organization's information system to ensure they are made smoothly and efficiently and to prevent errors and fraud.

5. *Users.* User departments record transactions, authorize data to be processed, and use system output.

6. *Systems analysis.* Systems analysts help users determine their information needs and then design an information system to meet those needs.

7. *Programming.* Programmers take the design provided by systems analysts and create an information system by writing the computer programs.

8. *Computer operations.* Computer operators run the software on the company's computers. They ensure that data are properly input to the computer, processed correctly, and needed output is produced.

9. *Information system library.* The information system librarian maintains custody of corporate databases, files, and programs in a separate storage area called the information system library.

10. *Data control.* The data control group ensures that source data have been properly approved, monitors the flow of work through the computer, reconciles input and output, maintains a record of input errors to ensure their correction and resubmission, and distributes systems output.

It is important that different people perform these functions. Allowing a person to do two or more jobs exposes the company to the possibility of fraud. For example, if a programmer for a credit union was allowed to use actual data to test her program, she could erase her car loan balance while conducting the test. Likewise, if a computer operator has access to programming logic and documentation, he might, while processing the company payroll program, be able to alter the program to increase his salary.

In addition to adequate segregation of duties, organizations should ensure that the people who design, develop, implement, and operate the company's information system are qualified and well trained, as explained in Chapter 7. The same holds true for those in charge of system security.

Physical Access Controls

Both the physical ability to use computer equipment, referred to as **physical access,** and the ability to gain access to company data, called **logical access,** should be restricted. Physical access security can be achieved using the following controls:

➤ Place computer equipment in locked rooms and restrict access to authorized personnel.

➤ Have only one or two entrances to the computer room. The entrances should be securely locked and monitored carefully by security guards and closed-circuit television systems.

➤ Require proper employee ID, such as a security badge, for passage through an access point. Modern security badges incorporate photos and magnetic, electric, or optical codes that can be read only by special badge readers. With advanced ID techniques, each employee's entry and exit may be automatically recorded in a log that is maintained on the computer and periodically reviewed by supervisory personnel.

➤ Require visitors to sign a log as they enter and leave the site. Brief them on company security policies, assign visitor's badges, and escort them to their destinations.

➤ Use a security alarm system to detect unauthorized access during off-hours.

➤ Restrict access to private, secured telephone lines or to authorized terminals or PCs.

➤ Install locks on PCs and other computer devices.

➤ Restrict access to off-line programs, data, and equipment.

➤ Locate hardware and other critical system components away from hazardous or combustible materials.

➤ Install fire and smoke detectors and fire extinguishers that do not damage computer equipment.

Logical Access Controls

Users should be allowed access only to the data they are authorized to use and then only to perform specific, authorized functions such as reading, copying, and adding to and deleting data. It is also important to protect data from those outside the organization. For example, a manufacturing company's competitor broke into its system and browsed its data until it discovered a bid on a billion-dollar project. The competitor narrowly underbid the company and won the contract. The intrusion was discovered by an auditing system, but not before the bid was lost.

To restrict logical access, a system must differentiate between authorized and unauthorized users, utilizing what the user knows or possesses, where the user is accessing the system, or some personal characteristic. Perhaps the most common approach is what a person knows. For example, the computer could ask users personal questions, such as their mother's maiden name. Users also could be asked to enter a personal identification number (PIN).

User IDs and passwords

The most frequent knowledge identifier is a **user identification (ID) and authentication system.** When signing on to a system, users identify themselves by entering a unique **user ID,** such as an employee number or account number. (Note that a user's name may not be a unique identifier.)

Users then enter a **password,** a series of characters that is known only to the user and the system. If the user-entered ID and password match those in the computer, then the system assumes it is an authorized user. The downside of passwords is that they can be guessed, lost, written down, or given away, creating the potential for unauthorized and, in some cases, dangerous persons to gain system access. For example, a convicted child rapist working in a Boston hospital used a former employee's password to gain access to confidential patient files. He proceeded to obtain telephone numbers of families that had children. Users should be held accountable for maintaining the confidentiality of their user IDs and passwords and for any actions performed by someone signing on using them.

Following the recommendations in Focus 8-3 can minimize the risks associated with passwords.

Physical possession identification

People also can be identified by **physical possession identification** (what they physically possess), such as an ID card that contains a person's name, ID number, picture, and other pertinent information. Computer and security devices such as door locks

Focus 8-3

Ensuring Password Integrity

1. Require users to keep their ID numbers and passwords confidential. The system should not display ID numbers or passwords on the screen as they are entered. Users should never reveal passwords. At Pacific Bell, teenage hackers posed as company employees and persuaded system users to give them the passwords they needed to access the system.

2. Randomly assign passwords to users, as user-selected passwords are often easily guessed.

3. Change passwords frequently to maintain confidentiality. Several months after she was fired, a woman in California logged on to her former company's computers to copy and damage files. The police raided her home and seized millions of dollars of company software. The company had invalidated her password, but because passwords were not changed regularly, one she stole just before she left allowed her access to the system.

4. Assign electronic ID numbers to each authorized device. Authorized devices should be the only ones allowed to interact with the system, and only to access certain data. For example, access to payroll records could be restricted to computers and terminals in the payroll department and appropriate top management.

5. Disconnect and deactivate the ID of anyone unable to provide a valid ID number or password within three attempts. This prevents hackers from programming a computer to try all combinations of user IDs and passwords. One company in Fort Worth had the ability to implement this control, but decided that it ate up too many system resources. After its internal auditors found evidence of repeated log-on attempts, they activated the software and found five employees who were trying to guess the passwords required to access confidential data. All five employees were terminated.

6. Immediately investigate devices from which repeated attempts to access the system with invalid ID numbers or passwords originate.

7. Require employees to log off their computers when not in use. It is especially important not to leave computers unattended during on-line interactions with confidential corporate databases.

8. Restrict user or terminal transactions to specified times, such as normal business hours.

9. Immediately restrict an employee's access to data when she is transferred to another department. For example, someone leaving the payroll department should no longer have access to payroll data.

10. Immediately deactivate the user ID and password of any employee who is terminated. In a security review conducted by Ernst & Young, 240 ex-employees still retained access to their company's dial-in system.

11. Use password scanning programs to detect weak, or easily guessed, passwords.

12. Require smart cards that generate a new and unique password every minute. The system uses the same algorithm and, because times are synchronized, generates the same password.

Focus 8-4

"Active Badges" Keep Silent Tabs on Employees' Whereabouts

George Orwell's Big Brother is watching more keenly than ever at the Olivetti Research Laboratory and the computer laboratory at Cambridge University in Cambridge, England. Employees there are sporting infrared tracking devices called active badges that allow a computer network to silently keep tabs on each person's whereabouts. In addition to enhancing physical security in corporate buildings, this automatic tracing system can be used to track objects in airports, ranging from luggage to lost children.

The small clip-on badges hanging from shirt pockets and dangling from belts are equipped with transceivers that emit uniquely coded signals every few seconds. The signals are picked up by infrared sensors located in each room and transferred to workstations and PCs that serve as nodes on a distributed computer network. When telephone calls come in to the facility, the receptionist can call up the system, locate the individual, and transfer the call to the nearest telephone.

The practical benefits of active badges, such as not missing phone calls, have turned some doubters into believers and willing badge users. One potential stumbling block is that the system responds to the badge, not the individual. Whoever wears that uniquely coded badge can assume the identity of the proper owner. Solving the authentication problem is the target of a related research project.

The introduction of this technology raises certain legal and ethical issues. Critics argue that the new technology sacrifices individual privacy in favor of convenience and efficiency. Some employees wearing active badges may feel like house-arrest victims whose bracelets trigger an alarm when they leave home. Some people feel that it is great technology in the right hands, but that a bad manager could make an employee's life miserable.

---

can read ID cards. Unfortunately, they can also be lost, stolen, or given away. Security can be increased significantly if a user is required to have both an ID card and a password before receiving access to the system. However, even these systems can be compromised. For example, a hacker broke into the Motorola system by calling the help desk and saying he was an employee working at home who had forgotten his ID card (the card generated random passwords that change every few seconds). The help desk believed him and let him into the corporate network. Fortunately, he did no permanent damage to the company's system.

Focus 8-4 describes another physical possession ID, an active badge that transmits a radio signal picked up by special receivers.

Biometric identification

Biometric identification devices identify unique physical characteristics such as fingerprints, voice patterns, retina prints, facial patterns and features, body odor, signature dynamics, and keyboarding patterns (the way a user types certain groups of characters). When a person desires access to the system, his or her biometric identifications are matched against those stored in the computer. For example, Oracle has a palm-size device that compares a user's fingerprints with sets stored in a central database. The device also tracks blood flow and pressure, which allows it to differentiate between a real fingerprint and one on a wax model or glove. Large banks are beginning to install retina scanners on their ATMs to prevent unauthorized access. The scanners capture and digitize the pattern of blood vessels produced when light is reflected off a retina, which contains about 10 times more information than a fingerprint.

The U.S. Bureau of Immigration and Naturalization has begun to use electronic hand readers to verify a person's identification. The handprint of a passport applicant is captured and stored on a wallet-size card. When a cardholder enters the country, his or her card and hand are placed in a special reading device that matches the two. In airports equipped with hand readers, passports do not have to be shown when a cardholder reenters the country. The eventual goal is to put coded handprint data on machine-readable passports.

The ideal biometric device can adapt to slight personal changes, but will reject unauthorized users. Unfortunately, problems still exist. For example, voice recognition devices may reject a person with a head cold or one whose voice is muffled over a phone line, while retina scanners may reject someone with bloodshot eyes. Another disadvantage is that, with the exception of voice scanners, users must have remote biometric identification devices or be physically present to use the system.

Compatibility tests

Companies should have a framework that allows management and the departments that own information and data to classify it based on how a loss of security or confidentiality would impact the business. Some data will require no restrictions, such as the data put on a Web site for general access. Some data may be restricted to employees. Other data are confidential and access should be limited to only the owners and top management. In most organizations, several security (or confidentiality) levels are defined and used. Once the data and programs have been classified, owners and top management can determine the access privileges of employees and outsiders. In making this determination, proper segregation of duties should be maintained. Data integrity and security are so important that no single person in the organization should have the authority to read, add, delete, and change data unless someone else is responsible for reviewing the activities.

When an individual tries to access data or programs or operate the system, a **compatibility test** should be performed to determine if the user is authorized to perform the desired action. For example, factory employees would not be authorized to make entries involving accounts payable, and purchasing agents would not be allowed to enter sales orders. This procedure is necessary to prevent both unintentional errors and deliberate attempts to manipulate the system.

Compatibility tests use an **access control matrix,** which is a list of authorized user ID numbers and passwords; a list of all files, data, and programs; and the access each user has to them. Figure 8-1 shows an access control matrix with codes for four types of access. User 12345-ABC is permitted only to read and display file C and is restricted from any kind of access to other files or programs. User 12389-RST, apparently a programmer, is authorized to make any type of change in program 2 and to read and display records in file B. User 12567-XYZ, probably a supervisor, is authorized to read and display the contents of all files and programs.

USER IDENTIFICATION		FILES			PROGRAMS			
Code Number	Password	A	B	C	1	2	3	4
12345	ABC	0	0	1	0	0	0	0
12346	DEF	0	2	0	0	0	0	0
12354	KLM	1	1	1	0	0	0	0
12359	NOP	3	0	0	0	0	0	0
12389	RST	0	1	0	0	3	0	0
12567	XYZ	1	1	1	1	1	1	1

Codes for type of access:
  0 = No access permitted
  1 = Read and display only
  2 = Read, display, and update
  3 = Read, display, update, create, and delete

Figure 8-1   Access control matrix

Protection of Personal Computers and Client/server Networks

In the rush to move from mainframe to client/server networks, many companies have failed to develop adequate systems of internal controls for their client/server networks. They are now forced to retrofit those applications with appropriate security features. Other companies have built mission-critical client/server applications that cannot be used because they lack adequate security features. PCs and networks of PCs are more vulnerable to security risks than are mainframes for several reasons:

1. PCs are everywhere, which means physical access is difficult to control. Each network PC becomes a device that must be controlled. The more legitimate users there are, the greater the risk of an attack on the network. For example, Chevron Texaco distributes information to tens of thousands of employees using more that 40,000 PCs.
2. PC users are generally less aware of the importance of security and control.
3. Many more people are familiar with the operation and use of PCs.
4. Adequate segregation of duties is difficult because PCs are located in user departments, and one person may be responsible for both development and operations.
5. Networks are accessed from remote locations using modems, the Internet, EDI, and other communications systems. The sheer number and variety of these access points significantly increase the risks networks face.

6. PCs are portable and the most elaborate security system in the world cannot protect the data a PC contains if it is lost, stolen, or misplaced.

Many of the policies and procedures for mainframe control are applicable to PCs and networks. The following controls are also important:

➤ Train users in PC-related control concepts and their importance. Security should be an essential part of the application development process. Users who develop their own application programs should be taught how to test and document them.

➤ Restrict access by using locks and keys on PCs and, where appropriate, on disk drives. Equipment should be clearly labeled with nonremovable tags.

➤ Establish policies and procedures to (1) control the data that can be stored or downloaded to PCs, (2) minimize the potential that PCs removed from company premises are stolen, (3) prohibit users from loading personal software onto company PCs, copying company software for personal uses, or making unauthorized use of the system. It was a lack of these controls (or the failure to enforce them) that allowed employees at a major stock brokerage in San Francisco to use the company's computer system to buy and sell cocaine.

➤ Portable PCs should not be stored in cars and should be carried onto airplanes rather than checked. Those that contain confidential data should be locked at night and otherwise secured when not in use. At the British Defense Ministry, a laptop was stolen that contained the entire war plan for Operation Desert Storm.

➤ Keep sensitive data in the most secure environment possible, such as storing it on a server or mainframe, as opposed to a PC. Alternatively, sensitive data can be placed on removable diskettes or disk drives and stored in a locked safe. Someone used a screwdriver at Levi Strauss's main headquarters to remove a hard drive from a PC. It contained personal data (name, social security number, birth dates, and bank account numbers) for 20,000 of its employees. This data could be used to apply for fraudulent credit cards and to withdraw cash from bank accounts.

➤ Install software that automatically shuts down a terminal or a computer attached to a network after it has been idle for a predetermined amount of time.

➤ Back up hard drives regularly.

➤ Encrypt or password protect files so that stolen data will not be useful.

➤ Use a super erase utility program that actually wipes the disk clean when confidential data are deleted. The delete command on most PCs merely erases the index to the data rather than the data itself. Many common utility programs can retrieve deleted (rather than erased) data.

➤ Build protective walls around operating systems to keep users from altering crucial system files.

➤ Because PCs are most vulnerable when turned on, they should be booted up within a security system. Users should not be able to use any part of the system until they have been properly authorized. Any attempt to remove security software from the system should render the keyboard inoperable.

➤ Where a physical segregation of duties is not possible, use multilevel password control to limit employee access to incompatible data and provide an effective segregation of duties.

➤ Use specialists or security programs to detect holes in a network. Security programs mimic an intruder and provide valuable information about how secure the network activity is and where improvements should be made. Care should be exercised to make sure these programs are not used improperly. For example, Satan (System

Administrator Tool for Analyzing Networks), a free security program offered on the Internet, actually helps open networks to outsiders in certain situations.

➤ Audit and record what users do and when they do it, so that security breaches can be traced and corrected.

➤ Educate users about the risks of computer viruses and how they can be minimized (see Chapter 9).

In most organizations, PCs are electronically linked using local and wide area networks. One advantage of PC networks is improved security and control procedures and enforcement through the central network controller. In particular, password controls can be required, PC use can be centrally monitored, virus protection procedures can be enforced, and backup procedures can be performed automatically.

Developing an internal control strategy for PCs begins by inventorying all PCs and identifying their uses. Then each PC should be classified according to the risks and exposures associated with its applications. For example, a PC used to maintain accounts payable records and prepare cash disbursements may be subject to more risk and exposure than one used for word processing. Next, a security program should be tailored to each PC according to the degree of risk and exposure and the nature of the system applications. Perhaps the most sensitive PC applications are accounting systems under one individual's control, which implies an inadequate segregation of duties. In such cases, sound human resource practices must be followed, such as background checks prior to hiring, fidelity bond coverage, enforced vacations, and periodic rotation of duties.

Internet and E-commerce Controls

Following are reasons why caution should be exercised when conducting business on the Internet:

➤ The Internet's sheer size and complexity are overwhelming, as is the large, global base of people that depend on the Web. The number of Internet users is growing dramatically.

➤ The Internet offers tremendous variability in quality, compatibility, completeness, and stability of network products and services.

➤ Before an Internet message arrives at its destination, it can easily pass through 6 to 10 computers. Anyone at one of these computers could read or make an electronic copy of the Internet message. Even other people can read messages sent on a company's secure **intranet** (an internal Internet), as a large company found out recently during a security audit. The audit disclosed that confidential e-mail messages sent between executives in the main office could be read by a network administrator working in another building 30 miles away.

➤ Many Web sites have security flaws. One study of 2,200 sites found that between 70 and 80 percent had serious security flaws. High-profile sites were more likely to have serious flaws than less popular sites.

➤ Hackers are attracted to the Internet. For example, six young people were arrested in Denmark for using the Internet to break into the National Weather Service computers. Fortunately, the hackers did not bring the system to its knees, which could have grounded all commercial airline flights that depend on the center's weather forecasts. The hackers were discovered when obsolete employee passwords began appearing in the system. In another case, a 16-year-old hacker used his home computer and the Internet to break into more than a hundred international networks. Although they have no proof, some investigators fear that the hacker was able to steal secret nuclear data.

Several effective controls can be used to secure Internet activity. Some of the most important have already been discussed, such as passwords, encryption technology (see Chapter 3), and routing verification procedures. Others, such as virus detection, are discussed in Chapter 9.

Organizations can use a **firewall** to control against unauthorized access, either by outsiders or by employees who attempt to access parts of the system to which they do not have access. As shown in Figure 8-2, a firewall is hardware and software that control communications between a company's internal network, sometimes referred to as the trusted network, and an external network, or untrusted network, such as the Internet or a value-added network. The firewall is a barrier between the networks that prevents unwanted information from flowing into and out of the trusted network. Complex networks are sometimes divided into subnets, each with its own firewall. Organizations often use firewalls to separate internal networks, thereby protecting sensitive data from unauthorized internal use. Firewalls must be capable of protecting themselves from attack, hostile traffic, and unauthorized modification. Firewalls often use redundant hardware, software, and other technology to reduce outages and failures.

Firewalls can and should be implemented at two levels. At the first level, routers should intercept all incoming and outgoing data packets, examine the source or destination information, and decide whether to let that packet proceed. Packets that pass this test should then be routed to the appropriate application gateway, which provides a second level of security. The application gateway can be programmed to examine the contents of incoming and outgoing packets and determine if they should be allowed to pass further.

Figure 8-2   The role of a firewall

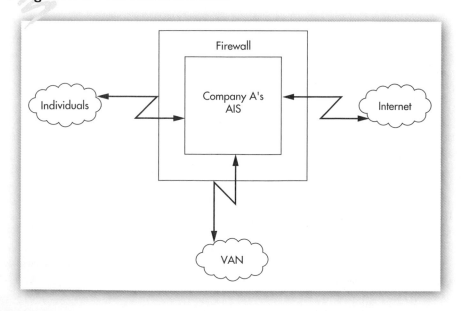

Firewalls, like any locks, can be penetrated. Consequently, companies also implement intrusion detection systems to provide real-time warning that unauthorized access is occurring. In addition, firewalls can be bypassed by wireless communications links between the IS and outside parties. Thus, computer security and internal audit professionals need to continuously monitor and review *all* links in their organizations' communications networks.

Control efforts now focus on constructing an impenetrable firewall to prevent unauthorized system access. It is much easier to have strong access controls at a single point of entry than to try controlling numerous points of entry. Digital Equipment Corp. installed a firewall, called Screening External Access Link (SEAL), between its internal corporate network and the Internet. SEAL has not allowed a single intruder in 11 years. However, other companies have not been so lucky. Over one Thanksgiving holiday, a hacker was able to bore through the firewall at General Electric and access proprietary information. GE had to shut down its Internet access for 72 hours to assess the damage and correct the problem.

Internet security can also be achieved using an approach called **tunneling.** In tunneling, networks are connected via the Internet—firewall to firewall—and data are divided into small segments called Internet Protocol (IP) packets, encrypted, mixed with millions of packets from thousands of other computers, and sent through the Internet. At the receiving end, the packets are decrypted and reassembled into the original message. This allows companies to use the Internet to create a virtual private network and avoid the cost of leasing private lines to connect the networks. Tunneling also can be used to safeguard individual networks within an organization.

An **electronic envelope** can protect e-mail messages. The envelope is created using the private or public key encryption techniques discussed in Chapter 3. If the secrecy of the keys is maintained, the authenticity and integrity of an encrypted e-mail can be guaranteed. The person receiving the e-mail opens the envelope by using the key to decrypt the message.

Some companies, such as Philip Morris, have been so wary of hackers, viruses, and other undesirable aspects of Internet usage that they have denied their employees access to the Internet and outside e-mail. Other companies have a one-way, outgoing Internet connection only, so that employees can get into the Internet to do research. There is no access into the system from the outside. However, this limits the Internet's effectiveness, as people cannot receive e-mail.

Other companies take the opposite approach. They set up an Internet server that is not connected to their other computer systems in any way. The only items stored on the server are data that the company wants to make available to Internet users and is not afraid to lose. If hackers manage to bring the system to its knees, the company simply restarts the system and reloads the data stored in the system.

Internet security has a way to go before it can be considered secure. As a company introduces a new security program, a hacker often finds a way to compromise it. For example, security locks on Netscape's Web browser were broken twice within a couple of months of the software's release. To motivate hackers to inform the company about future security problems, Netscape began offering prizes to anyone who found new loopholes in its software.

MAINTAINABILITY

The two categories of controls that help ensure the maintainability of a system are: (1) project development and acquisition controls and (2) change management controls. These controls are discussed below and summarized in Table 8-4.

Project Development and Acquisition Controls

It is important to have a formal, appropriate, and proven methodology to govern the development, acquisition, implementation, and maintenance of information systems and related technologies. The methodology should contain appropriate controls for management review and approval, user involvement, analysis, design, testing, implementation, and conversion. The methodology also should make it possible for management to trace information inputs from their source to their final disposition or from their final disposition back to the original source (the audit trail). The methodologies used to develop or acquire systems are discussed in more detail in Chapters 16 through 18.

Table 8-4   Summary of Key Maintainability Controls

Control Category	Threats/Risks	Controls
Project development and acquisition controls	Systems development projects consume excessive resources.	Long-range strategic master plan, data processing schedules, assignment of each project to a manager and team, project development plan, project milestones, performance evaluations, system performance measurements (throughput, utilization, response time), and post-implementation reviews.
Change management controls	Systems development projects consume excessive resources, unauthorized systems changes.	Change management control policies and procedures, periodic review of all systems for needed changes, standardized format for changes, log and review change requests, assess impact of changes on system reliability, categorize and rank all changes, procedures to handle urgent matters, communicate changes to management and users, management approval of changes, assign specific responsibilities while maintaining adequate segregation of duties, control system access rights, make sure changes go through all appropriate steps, test all changes, develop plan for backing out of mission-critical system changes, implement a quality assurance function, and update documentation and procedures.

Focus 8-5

Harnessing Runaway Systems

Westpac Banking Corporation of Sydney, Australia, instigated a 5-year systems development project to redefine the role of information technology. The project, designated Core System 90 (CS90), was budgeted at $85 million. Its objective was to decentralize Westpac's information systems by equipping branch managers with computer-aided software engineering (CASE) tools and expert systems, to generate new financial products. Decentralization would enable Westpac to respond more rapidly to customer needs while downsizing its internal AIS department.

Some 3 years after it began the project, Westpac took stock of CS90 and concluded that it was out of control. Despite an outlay of nearly $150 million on the project, no usable results had been attained. In addition, bank officials determined that the scheduled completion date could not be realized. Facing serious problems with its loan portfolio and asset management programs, Westpac decided that it could not afford to risk several more million dollars on CS90. So, the bank fired IBM, the systems integrator* and the primary software developer, and brought in Andersen Consulting (now called Accenture) to review the project and develop recommendations for salvaging it.

Westpac's CS90 boondoggle is merely one example of what has become an all-too-frequent story: a computer project that is over budget and behind schedule, often due to a systems integrator that is unable to deliver on lofty promises. Industry experts refer to such projects as runaways. Over a several year period, KPMG took over some 50 runaway computer projects, and it estimates that, in about two-thirds of these cases, the problems arose from mismanagement by a systems integrator.

Computer systems built by a third party are subject to the same cost overruns and missed deadlines as systems developed internally. Therefore, it makes sense to use the same basic rules of project management and control, including close monitoring of system progress during development. Unfortunately, many companies are not doing this.

Instead, they rely on the integrator's assurance that the project will be completed on time. Too often, the integrator falls behind schedule but does not tell the client, figuring that the project can still be completed on time if a big push is made at the last minute. In such cases, the CIO and other AIS executives are as much at fault as the systems integrator, according to experts in salvaging runaway systems.

These experts suggest that a systems integration project should be monitored by a sponsors committee, established by the CIO, and chaired by the project's internal champion. Department managers for all units that will use the system should be on this committee. The role of this committee should be to establish formal procedures for measuring and reporting the status of the project. The best approach is to divide the project into manageable tasks, assign responsibility for each task, and then meet on a regular basis (at least monthly) to review progress and assess quality.

Equally important are steps that should be taken at the outset of the project. Before third parties are called in to bid on a project, clear specifications must be developed, including exact descriptions and definitions of the system, explicit deadlines, and precise acceptance criteria for each stage of the project. Although specification development may seem expensive, it usually

---

*A systems integrator is a vendor who takes the responsibility for managing a cooperative systems development effort involving its own development personnel, those of the buyer, and possibly the systems development personnel of one or more other vendors, using common standards as much as possible.

saves money in the long run. For example, Suffolk County, New York, recently spent 12 months and $500,000 preparing detailed specifications for a new $16 million criminal justice information system before accepting bids. The county then hired Unisys Corporation and Grumman Data Systems to develop the system. County officials believe that their diligent upfront efforts helped ensure their new system's success and saved the county $3 million in hardware costs.

Some systems integrators may object to detailed specifications and rigorous project control methods. For example, after reviewing Suffolk County's specifications, only 6 of the 22 integrators that had originally expressed interest bid on the project. This should be viewed as a blessing, rather than a problem. Those integrators who disdain a company's attempts to rigorously control the cost and quality of its systems projects are likely the same ones responsible for most of the profusion of runaway systems.

Examples abound of poorly managed development or acquisition projects that have wasted large sums of money because certain basic principles of management control were ignored. Consider that the Oklahoma State Insurance Fund terminated a development contract with Policy Management Systems for a software system that would issue policies and processes and track claims and premiums. The contract was canceled when the project fell several months behind schedule and went $1 million over budget. As explained in Focus 8-5, Westpac Banking Corporation terminated a large-scale systems integration project after spending over $150 million.

To minimize failures, the basic principles of responsibility accounting should be applied to the development or acquisition of an information system. Adherence to these principles greatly reduces the potential for cost overruns and project failures while substantially improving the efficiency and effectiveness of the information system. Project development and acquisition control include the following key elements:

1. *Strategic master plan.* The need for a strategic master plan was discussed earlier in the chapter.

2. *Project controls.* A **project development plan** shows how a project will be completed, including the modules or tasks to be performed, who will perform them, the dates they should be completed, and the cost of each. The plan should specify **project milestones**—or significant points when progress is reviewed and actual and estimated completion times are compared. Each project should be assigned to a manager and team who should be held responsible for the success or failure of the project. A **performance evaluation** of the project team members should be done as each plan is completed.

3. *Data processing schedule.* To maximize the use of scarce computer resources, all data processing tasks should be organized according to a **data processing schedule.**

4. *System performance measurements.* For a system to be evaluated properly, it must be assessed using **system performance measurements.** Common measurements include **throughput**

(output per unit of time), **utilization** (percentage of time the system is being productively used), and **response time** (how long it takes the system to respond).

5. *Postimplementation review.* After a development project is completed, a **postimplementation review** should be performed to determine if the anticipated benefits were achieved. Reviews help to control project development activities and to encourage accurate and objective initial cost and benefit estimates.

Change Management Controls

To properly control information system changes, companies need formal change management control policies and procedures. These controls should include the following:

➤ Periodicially review all systems for needed changes.

➤ Require all requests to be submitted in a standardized format.

➤ Log and review requests from authorized users for changes and additions to systems.

➤ Assess the impact of requested changes on system reliability objectives, policies, and standards.

➤ Categorize and rank all changes using established priorities.

➤ Implement specific procedures to handle urgent matters, such as logging all emergency changes that require deviations from standard procedures and having management review and approve them after the fact. Make sure there is an audit trail for all urgent matters.

➤ Communicate all changes to management and keep change requestors informed of the status of their requested changes.

➤ Require IT management to review, monitor, and approve all changes to hardware, software, and personnel responsibilities.

➤ Assign specific responsibilities to those involved in the change and monitor their work. Make sure that the specific assignments result in an adequate segregation of duties.

➤ Control system access rights to avoid unauthorized systems and data access.

➤ Make sure all changes go through the appropriate steps (development, testing, and implementation).

➤ Test all changes to hardware, infrastructure, and software extensively in a separate, nonproduction environment before placing it into live production mode.

➤ Make sure there is a plan for backing out of any changes to mission-critical systems in the event that it does not work or does not operate properly.

➤ Implement a quality assurance function to ensure that all standards and procedures are followed and to assess if change activities achieve their stated objectives. These findings should be communicated to user departments, information systems management, and top management.

➤ Update all documentation and procedures when changes are implemented.

INTEGRITY

The primary objective of **application controls** is to prevent, detect, and correct errors in transactions as they flow through the various stages of a specific data processing program. In other words, they ensure the integrity of a specific application's inputs, stored data, programs, data transmissions, and outputs.

In the opening case, Jason Scott discovered several fictitious invoices at SPP that may have been processed by the accounts payable and cash disbursements system. If so, this represents a failure in the application's integrity controls. However, inadequate **general controls,** which ensure that the organization's overall computer-based control environment is stable and well managed, also may have contributed to this control breakdown. General controls and application controls are important and necessary, because application controls will be much more effective in the presence of strong general controls.

If application controls are weak, the information system output is likely to contain errors. Erroneous data can lead to poor management decision making and can negatively affect a company's relationships with customers, suppliers, and other external parties. For example, several states sued Experian (formerly TRW), a large credit reporting bureau, for reporting inaccurate credit information and violating consumer privacy. These lawsuits were reportedly triggered by thousands of consumer complaints about inaccurate and negative information surfacing on their credit reports.

This section will discuss six categories of integrity controls: source data controls, input validation routines, on-line data entry controls, data processing and data storage controls, output controls, and data transmission controls. Batch totals, another integrity control, were discussed in Chapter 7. These integrity controls are summarized in Table 8-5.

Source Data Controls

Companies must establish control procedures to ensure that all source documents are authorized, accurate, complete, properly accounted for, and entered into the system or sent to their intended destination in a timely manner. The following source data controls regulate the integrity of input:

➤ *Forms design.* Source documents and other forms should be designed to help ensure that errors and omissions are minimized. For better control, forms are often prenumbered. Forms design is discussed in more detail in Chapter 18.

➤ *Prenumbered forms sequence test.* When sequentially prenumbered forms are utilized, the system should be programmed to identify and report missing or duplicate form numbers.

➤ *Turnaround documents.* A turnaround document is a record of company data sent to an external party and then returned by the external party to the system as input. Turnaround documents are prepared in machine-readable form to facilitate their subsequent processing as input records. An example is a utility bill that a special scanning device reads when the bill is returned with a payment. Because turnaround documents are system outputs that come back as machine-readable input records, they are much more accurate than input records prepared by manual keying.

➤ *Cancelation and storage of documents.* Documents that have been entered into the system should be canceled so they can not be inadvertently or fraudulently reentered into the system. Paper documents can be defaced, such as stamping them paid. If a document is stored electronically, a flag can be placed in the database to show that the document has been canceled. Original source documents should be retained for as long as needed to satisfy legal requirements.

➤ *Authorization and segregation of duties.* Source documents should be prepared only by authorized personnel acting within their authority. Adequate segregation of

Table 8-5 Summary of Key Integrity Controls

Control Category	Threats/Risks	Controls
Source data controls	Invalid, incomplete, or inaccurate source data input	Forms design; sequentially prenumbered forms; turnaround documents; cancellation and storage of documents; review for appropriate authorization; segregation of duties; visual scanning; check-digit verification; and key verification.
Input validation routines	Invalid or inaccurate data in computer-processed transaction files	As transaction files are processed, edit programs check key data fields using these edit checks: sequence, field, sign, validity, limit, range, reasonableness, redundant data, and capacity checks. Enter exceptions in an error log; investigate, correct, and resubmit them on a timely basis; re-edit them; and prepare a summary error report.
On-line data entry controls	Invalid or inaccurate transaction input entered through on-line terminals	Field, limit, range, reasonableness, sign, validity, and redundant data checks; user IDs and passwords; compatibility tests; automatic system data entry; prompting operators during data entry; preformatting; completeness test; closed-loop verification; a transaction log maintained by the system; clear error messages; and data retention sufficient to satisfy legal requirements.
Data processing and storage controls	Inaccurate or incomplete data in computer-processed master files	Policies and procedures (governing the activities of data processing and storage personnel; data security and confidentiality, audit trails, and confidentiality agreements); monitoring and expediting data entry by data control personnel; reconciliation of system updates with control accounts or reports; reconciliation of database totals with externally maintained totals; exception reporting, data currency checks, default values, data matching; data security (data library and librarian, backup copies of data files stored at a secure off-site location, protection against conditions that could harm stored data); use of file labels and write protection mechanisms; database protection mechanisms (database administrators, data dictionaries, and concurrent update controls); and data conversion controls.
Output controls	Inaccurate or incomplete computer output	Procedures to ensure that system outputs conform to the organization's integrity objectives, policies, and standards; visual review of computer output; reconciliation of batch totals; proper distribution of output; confidential outputs being delivered are protected from unauthorized access, modification, and misrouting; sensitive or confidential output stored in a secure area; users review computer output for completeness and accuracy; shred confidential output no longer needed; error and exception reports.
Data transmission controls	Unauthorized access to data being transmitted or to the system itself; system failures; errors in data transmission	Monitor network to detect weak points, backup components, design network to handle peak processing, multiple communication paths between network components, preventive maintenance, data encryption, routing verification (header labels, mutual authentication schemes, callback systems), parity checking, and message acknowledgment procedures (echo checks, trailer labels, numbered batches).

duties should be maintained in determining who is authorized to complete source documents.

➤ *Visual scanning.* Source documents should be scanned for reasonableness and propriety before being entered into the system.

➤ *Check digit verification.* Authorized ID numbers (such as an employee number) can contain a **check digit** that is computed from the other digits. For example, the AIS could take a Social Security number, such as 123-45-6789, and calculate a tenth digit from the other nine and add it to the Social Security number to form a 10-digit ID number. Data entry devices can be programmed to perform **check digit verification** by using the first nine digits to calculate the tenth digit each time an ID number is entered. If an error is made in entering any of the 10 digits, the calculation made on the first 9 digits will not match the tenth, or check, digit.

➤ *Key verification.* **Key verification** is expensive and used only for crucial input such as customer numbers, amounts, and quantities ordered. It consists of an employee rekeying data into the computer, which compares the two sets of keystrokes and highlights discrepancies for correction.

Jason Scott discovered that prenumbered forms were not used at SPP. However, sequentially prenumbered vouchers could have been used, with a separate voucher attached to each vendor invoice and its supporting documents. In addition, supplier numbers were not controlled using check digits. In fact, there was no formal process of approving additions to the supplier (accounts payable) file. If a supplier's invoice was approved for payment, that supplier became an approved creditor. Jason noted in his report that the proper use of either sequentially prenumbered vouchers or check digit verification of supplier numbers could have helped prevent SPP from paying fictitious invoices.

Input Validation Routines

Input validation routines are programs that check the integrity of input data as the data are entered into the system. These programs are called **edit programs,** and the integrity checks they perform are called **edit checks.** In on-line processing, edit checks are performed during the source data entry process. As shown in Figure 8-3, a separate program performs input validation in batch processing prior to regular processing. In on-line processing, the system should not accept incorrect data until corrected. The following edit checks are used in input validation routines:

➤ A **sequence check** tests if a batch of input data is in the proper numerical or alphabetical sequence.

➤ A **field check** determines if the characters in a field are of the proper type. For example, a check on a numerical field would indicate an error if it contained blanks or alphabetic characters.

➤ A **sign check** determines if the data in a field have the appropriate arithmetic sign. For example, data in an inventory balance field should never possess a negative sign.

➤ A **validity check** compares ID numbers or transaction codes with those already authorized. For example, if a sale to customer 65432 is entered, the computer must locate customer 65432 in the customer database to confirm that the sale was indeed made to a valid customer.

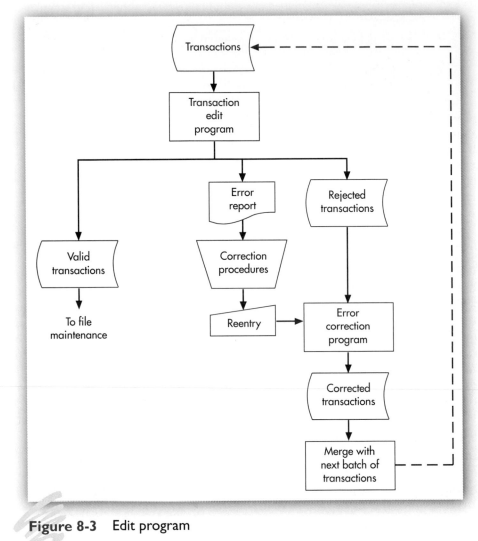

Figure 8-3   Edit program

➤ A **limit check** tests a numerical amount to ensure that it does not exceed a predetermined upper or lower limit. For example, the hours-worked field in weekly payroll input can be compared with a maximum amount, such as 60 hours.

➤ A **range check** is similar to a limit check except that it has both upper and lower limits. Range checks are used on transaction date fields, since a date should be within a few days of the current date.

➤ A **reasonableness test** determines the logical correctness of input and stored data. For example, a $1,000 monthly salary increase is reasonable for an executive with a current salary of $15,000 per month but not for a data entry clerk making $1,500 per month.

➤ A **redundant data check** uses two identifiers in each transaction record to confirm that the correct database record has been updated. For example, the customer account number and the first five letters of the customer's name can be used to retrieve the correct customer master record from the accounts receivable file.

➤ A **capacity check** ensures that the data will fit into the assigned field. For example, 458,976,253 will not fit in an eight-digit field.

Procedures should be established to detect, correct, and report all errors and to ensure that they are followed. Information about data input or data processing errors (date they occur, cause of the error, date corrected and resubmitted) should be entered in an **error log.** Errors should be investigated, corrected, and resubmitted on a timely basis (usually with the next batch of transactions) and reedited using the same input validation routine. Periodically, the error log should be reviewed to ensure that all errors have been corrected and then used to prepare an **error report** that summarizes errors by record type, error type, cause, and disposition.

On-line Data Entry Controls

The goal of on-line data entry control is to ensure the integrity of transaction data entered from on-line terminals and PCs by minimizing errors and omissions. On-line data entry controls include the following:

➤ Field, limit, range, reasonableness, sign, validity, and redundant data checks, as described in the previous section, are useful controls.

➤ User ID numbers and passwords limit data entry to authorized personnel.

➤ Compatibility tests ensure that employees entering or accessing data are actually authorized to make those particular entries or view the data.

➤ Where possible, the system should automatically enter transaction data, which saves keying time and reduces errors. For example, the system can determine the next available document number and enter it into the transaction record. The system also can generate new ID numbers that satisfy the check digit algorithm and do not duplicate existing numbers and then enter them into the input record.

➤ **Prompting,** in which the system requests each input data item and waits for an acceptable response.

➤ **Preformatting,** in which the system displays a document with highlighted blank spaces and waits for the data to be entered.

➤ A **completeness check** on each input record determines if all required data items have been entered.

➤ **Closed-loop verification** is used to check the accuracy of input data. For example, if a clerk enters an account number, the system could retrieve and display the account name so that the clerk could determine if the correct account number had been entered. Closed-loop verification can be used instead of a redundant data check to protect against entry of a valid but incorrect identification number.

➤ A **transaction log** that includes a detailed record of all transaction data, a unique transaction identifier; the date and time of entry; terminal, transmission line, and operator identification; and the sequence in which the transaction was entered. If an on-line file is damaged, the log can be used for reconstruction purposes. If a malfunction temporarily shuts down the system, the log can be used to ensure that transactions are not lost or entered twice.

➤ Clear **error messages** that indicate when an error has occurred, which item is in error, and what the operator should do to correct it.

➤ The data needed to reproduce on-line data entry documents should be retained as necessary to satisfy legal requirements.

Data Processing and Storage Controls

Information is generally what gives a company a competitive edge and makes it viable. Because it is such a valuable resource, information must be protected from unauthorized disclosure and destruction. For example, a technician working late to repair a printing press at Webco Press in Lapeer, Michigan, was trusted to complete his assignment without supervision. The technician gained access to Webco's mainframe computer and made a printout of the company's customer list, complete with prices. He attempted to sell the customer list to a Webco competitor for $5,000 but was apprehended. In another example, Mattel Corp. lost critical competitive information when the laptops of several of its executives were stolen.

Common controls that help preserve the integrity of data processing and stored data are as follows:

➤ *Policies and procedures.* These should be established for the following aspects of data processing and storage: computer operators, data storage personnel, job scheduling (to prevent unauthorized job runs), data security and confidentiality (to identify the types of data maintained and the level of protection required for each, and to maintain records of confidential documents, records, and files); and audit trails (to track those with access to confidential data). Employees should sign contracts that require them to maintain the confidentiality of company data.

➤ *Data control function.* Applications in which a large number of paper forms are entered into the system should have a data control function set up. Data control logs the data as they are received, checks for user authorizations, monitors processing, reconciles control totals after each processing step, notifies users of incorrect inputs, and reenters all error corrections.

➤ *Reconciliation procedures.* At the end of every day, or periodically if there is continuous processing, all transactions and other system updates should be reconciled to control reports, file status/update reports, or other control mechanisms. In addition, general ledger accounts should be reconciled to subsidiary account totals on a regular basis. For example, the inventory control account balance in the general ledger should equal the sum of the item balances in the inventory database. The same is true for the accounts receivable, capital assets, and accounts payable control accounts.

➤ *External data reconciliation.* Database totals should periodically be reconciled with data maintained outside the system. For example, the number of employee records in the payroll file can be compared with the total from human resources to detect attempts to add fictitious employees to the payroll database.

➤ *Exception reporting.* When files are scanned or processed, all unusual conditions should be listed. For example, the sign check might detect a negative inventory or customer account balance.

➤ *Data currency checks.* Stored data become out of date, as when suppliers or customers move or go out of business and employees retire or quit. To identify such conditions, a "date of last transaction" field can be scanned periodically to identify records that are more than a year old.

➤ *Default values.* In certain instances, fields are left blank if a standard **default value** is to be used. For example, if the hours worked field in the payroll input is left blank, an employee could be paid for 40 hours.

➤ *Data matching.* In certain cases, two or more items of data must be matched before an action can take place. For example, the system could verify that information on the vendor invoice matches that on both the purchase order and the receiving report before paying a vendor.

➤ *File labels.* These labels can protect data files from inadvertent misuse. An **external label,** a gummed paper label attached to a storage device (e.g., diskette), contains the file name, contents, and date processed. **Internal labels** are written in machine-readable form on the data recording media. There are three different internal labels. A **volume label** identifies the entire contents of each separate data recording medium, such as a hard disk, diskette, or tape reel. A **header label,** located at the beginning of each file, contains the file name, expiration date, and other identification data. A **trailer label,** located at the end of the file, contains file control totals, which are checked against those accumulated during processing.

➤ *Write protection mechanisms.* These protect against the accidental writing over or erasing of data files. A **tape file protection ring** is a plastic ring that, when removed, prevents a tape file from being written upon. Many diskettes have on/off switches that perform the same function. Unfortunately, these write protection mechanisms can easily be circumvented.

➤ *Database protection mechanisms.* Database systems use database administrators, data dictionaries, and concurrent update controls to provide data protection. The administrator establishes and enforces procedures for accessing and updating the database. The data dictionary ensures that data items are defined and used consistently. **Concurrent update controls** protect records from errors that occur when two or more users attempt to update the same record simultaneously. This is accomplished by locking out one user until the system has finished processing the update entered by the other.

➤ *Data conversion controls.* As data from old files and databases are entered into new data structures, conversion controls are needed to ensure that the new data storage mediums are free of errors. The old and new systems should be run in parallel at least once and the results compared to identify discrepancies. Data conversion should be carefully supervised and reviewed by internal auditors.

➤ *Data security.* A properly supervised data library is one essential means of preventing loss of data. A data library, a librarian that logs data files in and out, internal and external labels, write protection mechanisms, and backup copies of data files stored at a secure off-site location help ensure data integrity. The data file storage area also should be protected against fire, dust, excess heat or humidity, and other conditions that could harm stored data.

Output Controls

Companies should establish, document, and follow procedures designed to ensure that all system outputs conform to the organization's integrity objectives, policies, and standards. The procedures would ensure that the company does the following:

➤ Reviews all output for reasonableness and proper format.
➤ Reconciles corresponding output and input control totals on a daily basis.
➤ Distributes computer output to the appropriate user departments.

➤ Protects sensitive or confidential outputs that are being delivered to users from unauthorized access, modification, and misrouting.

➤ Stores sensitive or confidential output in a secure area.

➤ Requires users to carefully review the completeness and accuracy of all computer output that they receive.

➤ Shreds or otherwise destroys highly confidential data such as obsolete customer listings, research data, and payroll registers.

➤ Corrects any errors found on output reports.

Special care should be taken when introducing new systems or new methods of providing information. For example, Experian developed a highly secure Web site for customers to access their credit reports; the site had firewalls, encryption, and identity verifications to prevent a user from ordering someone else's credit report. Two days after the site was launched, the *Washington Post* ran a story about the Web site that resulted in more than 2,000 requests in a matter of hours. This load, which was much heavier than Experian had anticipated, turned up a bug that caused the reports to queue up in the wrong order. As a result, people were sent the wrong credit report. Fortunately, the output controls Experian put into the system spotted the problem after only 213 reports were delivered. What could have been a major disaster was only a minor one because of the system controls.

Data Transmission Controls

Organizations must take steps to properly protect confidential information when it is transmitted from one location to another. They must reduce the risk of data transmission failures such as unauthorized access, data modification, and data being sent to the wrong location. To do this, companies should monitor the network to detect weak points, maintain backup components, and design networks so that capacity is sufficient to handle peak processing periods. They also should establish multiple communication paths between crucial network components so the system can function if one of the paths fails. By way of preventive maintenance, companies can upgrade to conditioned telecommunications lines that are faster and more efficient, have fewer problems with static, and are less likely to fail.

Data transmission errors are minimized using data encryption, routing verification, parity checking, and message acknowledgment techniques.

Data encryption (cryptography)

Due to the phenomenal growth of the Internet and electronic commerce, **data encryption (cryptography)** has become an extremely important control. Cryptography is the science of secret codes and is used to ensure that data transmissions and electronic commerce transactions limit data access or use to authorized personnel, protect data from unauthorized tampering or electronic eavesdropping, and determine, with almost absolute certainty, who sent a message. Data encryption controls are discussed in greater depth in Chapter 3.

Routing verification procedures

Several **routing verification procedures** can ensure that messages are not routed to the wrong system address. Transmitted data can be given a header label that identifies its destination, which the system uses to verify that the destination is valid and authorized to receive it. **Mutual authentication schemes** require both computers to exchange their passwords before communication can take place. In a **callback system,** a user enters a password and is identified as an authorized user. Then the computer disconnects and calls the user back to verify the user's identity, password, telephone number, or location.

Parity checking

Computers use a combination of bits to represent a single character. For example, the digits 5 and 7 might be represented by 0101 and 0111, respectively. When data are transmitted, bits may be lost or received incorrectly. To detect these errors, a **parity bit** is added to every character. In even parity, each bit has an even number of ones. In this example, the parity bit for 5 is zero (0101 0), because 5 already has an even number of ones. The parity bit for 7 would be a one (0111 1) so there are an even number of ones. In odd parity, there are an odd number of ones. **Parity checking** is verifying that there are an even (or odd) number of ones and is performed by devices that receive data. Two-dimensional parity checking tests parity both vertically and horizontally. Dual checking is important in telecommunications, because noise bursts frequently cause two or more adjacent bits to be lost. A one-dimensional parity check will not detect all such errors.

Message acknowledgment techniques

A number of message acknowledgment techniques are used to let the sender of an electronic message know that a message was received.

> *Echo check.* When data are transmitted, the system calculates a summary statistic such as the number of bits in the message. The receiving unit performs the same calculation—a procedure known as an **echo check**—and sends the result to the sending unit. If the counts agree, the transmission is presumed to be accurate.

> *Trailer label.* The receiving unit can check for a trailer label to verify that the entire message was received.

> *Numbered batches.* If a large message is transmitted in segments, each can be numbered sequentially so that the receiving unit can properly assemble the segments.

When a data transmission error is detected, the receiving unit will signal the sending unit and the data are retransmitted. Generally, the system will do this automatically and the user is unaware that it has occurred. Occasionally, the system may not be able to accomplish automatic retransmissions and will request that the sender retransmit the data.

Data transmission controls for EDI and EFT

Data transmission controls take on added importance in organizations that use electronic data interchange (EDI) or electronic funds transfer (EFT) because of the risk of unauthorized access to proprietary data. EFT systems are also vulnerable to fraudulent fund transfers. In these types of environments, sound internal control is achieved using a number of control procedures. Physical access to network facilities should be strictly controlled. Electronic identification should be required for all authorized network terminals. Strict logical access control procedures are essential, with passwords and dial-in phone numbers changed on a regular basis. Encryption should be used to secure stored data as well as data being transmitted. Details of all transactions should be recorded in a log that is periodically reviewed for evidence of invalid transactions.

RELIABILITY CONTROLS: AN ON-LINE PROCESSING EXAMPLE

Many of the reliability controls described in the chapter can be illustrated using a credit sale as an example. The following transaction data are used: sales order number, customer account number, inventory item number, quantity sold, sale price, and delivery date. If the customer purchases more than one product, the inventory item number, quantity sold, and price fields will occur more than once in each sales transaction record. Processing these transactions includes the following steps: (1) entering and editing the transaction data; (2) updating the customer and inventory record (the amount of the credit purchase is added to the customer's balance; for each inventory item, the quantity sold is subtracted from the quantity on hand); and (3) preparing and distributing shipping and/or billing documents.

Data Entry

Data can be entered into the system through a keyboard or by capturing the data electronically using a source data automation device such as a scanner that reads Universal Product Codes (UPCs). For adequate control, all significant transaction data are checked at least once. Generally, tests performed by the computer, such as edit checks, are less costly and more effective than tests performed by people, such as key verification and visual inspection. The earlier in the process a data entry error is caught, the easier and less costly it is to correct. A significant advantage of on-line systems is the immediate correction of any detected errors.

As needed, the following controls can be used to check the accuracy of transaction data that are entered into the system:

➤ When a user accesses an on-line system, logical access controls confirm the identity of the data entry device (personal computer, terminal) and the validity of the user's ID number and password.

➤ A compatibility test is performed on all user interactions to ensure that only authorized tasks are performed.

➤ The system automatically assigns the transaction the next sequential sales order number and the current date as the date of the invoice.

➤ To assist authorized personnel in entering sales data, the system asks for all required input (completeness test). After each prompt, the system waits for a response.

➤ Each response is tested using one or more of the following controls: validity checks (valid customer and inventory numbers), field and sign checks (only positive, numeric characters in the quantity, date, and price fields), and limit or range checks (delivery date).

➤ When the customer number is entered, the system retrieves the corresponding customer name from the database and displays it on the screen (closed-loop verification). The operator visually examines the customer name. If it matches the name on the sales order document, the operator signals the system to proceed with the transaction. If not, the operator rechecks the customer number and enters the correct value.

➤ When the inventory item number is entered, the system and the operator go through the same procedures as they do with the customer number.

File Updating

Because the file update program accesses the customer and inventory database records, it performs additional input validation tests by comparing data in each transaction record with data in the corresponding database record. These tests often include the following:

➤ Validity checks on the customer and inventory item numbers

➤ Sign checks on inventory-on-hand balances (after subtracting quantities sold)

➤ Limit checks that compare each customer's total amount due with their credit limit

➤ Range checks on the sale price of each item sold relative to the permissible range of prices for that item

➤ Reasonableness tests on the quantity sold of each item relative to normal sales quantities for that customer and that item.

➤ At predetermined times, backup copies of all transactions processed and the database are created and conveyed to a secure off-site location for storage purposes

Preparing and Distributing Output

Outputs include billing and/or shipping documents and a control report. Output controls that can be utilized are as follows:

➤ Billing and shipping documents are forwarded electronically to the appropriate users.

➤ Users in the shipping and billing departments perform a limited review of the documents by visually inspecting them for incomplete data or other obvious deficiencies.

➤ The control report is sent automatically to its intended recipients, or they can query the system for the report. If they query the system, logical access controls confirm the identity of the device making the query and the validity of the user's ID number and password.

RELIABILITY CONTROLS: A BATCH PROCESSING EXAMPLE

Processing these transactions in a batch processing mode includes the following steps:

1. *Prepare batch totals.* These totals are recorded on batch control forms added to each group of sales documents.

2. *Deliver the transactions to the electronic data processing (EDP) department.* There each batch is checked for proper authorization and recorded in a control log.

3. *Enter the transaction data into the system.* Data entry errors generally fall into one of two types. Operator errors arise when an operator reads a source document incorrectly or accidentally strikes the wrong key. These errors are generally benign and can be corrected immediately. Incorrect source data, such as an unauthorized sales transaction or an invalid account number, is more problematic and should be corrected before the sales transaction data are processed any further.

4. *Sort and edit the transaction file.* Either before or after the sales transaction file is sorted into customer number sequence, a program performs several edit checks. Rejected transactions are listed on a control report with the computed batch totals. Data control reconciles the batch totals, investigates and corrects any errors, and submits the corrected transactions.

5. *Update the master files.* The sales transaction file is processed against customer (accounts receivable) and inventory databases or master files. If the databases or master files are stored off-line, care must be taken to ensure that the correct file copies are retrieved from the file library and loaded onto the system. The operator must check the file name and processing date on the external labels before loading the files. The file update program checks the internal header label before processing begins. Each file has a trailer label containing a record count and other file totals. These are checked and updated during the file updating run.

6. *Prepare and distribute output.* Outputs include billing and/or shipping documents and a control report. The control report contains batch totals accumulated during the file update run and a list of transactions rejected by the update program.

7. *User review.* Users in the shipping and billing departments perform a limited review of the documents for incomplete data or other obvious deficiencies.

Figure 8-4 illustrates these seven steps and identifies the application controls that should be utilized in each.

SUMMARY AND CASE CONCLUSION

Jason Scott and his supervisor were unable to identify the source of the fictitious invoices. They asked the police to identify the owner of the Pacific Electric Services bank account. The police discovered that Patricia Simpson, a data entry clerk at SPP, was the owner of the account. Under questioning by a certified fraud examiner, Patricia admitted to an embezzlement scheme in which she created fictitious invoices, inserted them into batches of invoices submitted to her for data entry, modified the batch control totals, and destroyed the original batch control sheet. According to Patricia, the scheme had been initiated only 3 months previously, and no one else at SPP was involved. She also claimed that all fictitious invoices were in the name of Pacific Electric Services.

Jason examined SPP's cash disbursement records to corroborate Patricia's story. He wrote a program that reads cash disbursements transaction files and identifies disbursements to Pacific Electric Services. Then he undertook the daunting task of retrieving several hundred files containing disbursement transactions over the past 2 years from SPP's archives. He identified 40 fraudulent transactions totaling over $20,000. Contrary to Patricia's account, the first of these transactions occurred 18 months earlier.

Since Patricia had not been truthful about the duration of her scheme, Jason wondered if she might also have used other fictitious company names. By this time, however, she was not supplying any further information, on the advice of her lawyer. So Jason wrote another computer program to scan the cash disbursement records and retrieve the supplier account number, name, address, and authorization code for every vendor invoice processed without a supporting purchase order or receiving report. This test eventually yielded a file containing 175 supplier records, for which payment authorizations had been granted by 23 different employees at SPP. Jason sorted this file by authorization code and prepared 23 printouts containing data about the suppliers with which each

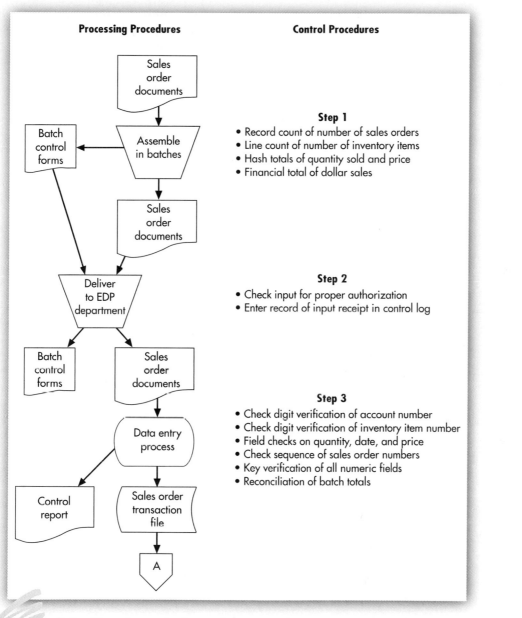

Figure 8-4 Flowchart of sales order processing and related control procedures (continues on next page)

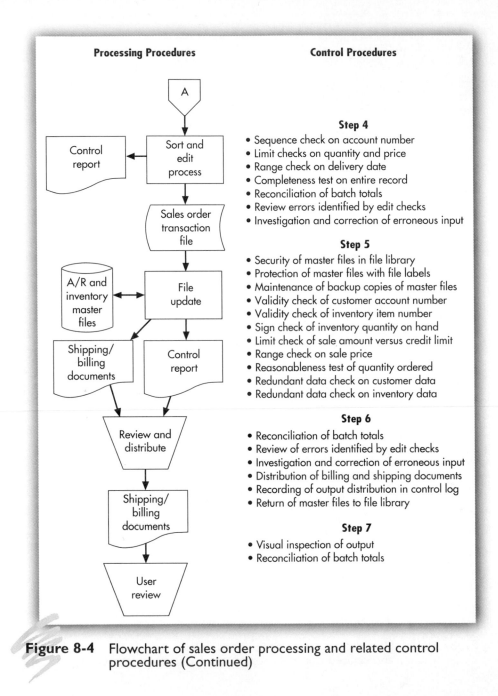

Processing Procedures

Control Procedures

Step 4
- Sequence check on account number
- Limit checks on quantity and price
- Range check on delivery date
- Completeness test on entire record
- Reconciliation of batch totals
- Review errors identified by edit checks
- Investigation and correction of erroneous input

Step 5
- Security of master files in file library
- Protection of master files with file labels
- Maintenance of backup copies of master files
- Validity check of customer account number
- Validity check of inventory item number
- Sign check of inventory quantity on hand
- Limit check of sale amount versus credit limit
- Range check on sale price
- Reasonableness test of quantity ordered
- Redundant data check on customer data
- Redundant data check on inventory data

Step 6
- Reconciliation of batch totals
- Review of errors identified by edit checks
- Investigation and correction of erroneous input
- Distribution of billing and shipping documents
- Recording of output distribution in control log
- Return of master files to file library

Step 7
- Visual inspection of output
- Reconciliation of batch totals

Figure 8-4   Flowchart of sales order processing and related control procedures (Continued)

of these employees contracted. Each printout was sent to the corresponding employee, with a request to confirm the authenticity of every supplier on his or her list. After having received all of these printouts, Jason concluded that the embezzlement scheme was indeed confined to Pacific Electric Services.

SPP implemented the following changes in its accounts payable and cash disbursements system in response to the auditor's recommendations:

1. There must be an approved purchase order for every disbursement, including those solely for service purposes.

2. Disbursements can be made only to approved suppliers, and every supplier must be approved by a purchasing agent who is not involved in the cash disbursements process. Approved suppliers are assigned an account number that contains a check digit. That account number must be included in every cash disbursement record. The purchasing department now maintains a count of the number of approved suppliers. This list is regularly compared with a computer-generated count of the number of supplier records in the accounts payable file.

3. When payment of vendor invoices is approved, a voucher record is prepared to document the approval. This voucher accompanies the invoice and any supporting documents through all subsequent processing steps. These vouchers are sequentially prenumbered, and all outstanding voucher numbers are accounted for on a regular basis.

4. An employee other than the person who approves the payments prepares batch totals for the daily batch of cash disbursement transactions. The accounts payable department retains a copy of the batch control sheet for comparison with the final batch control report generated by the cash disbursement system.

As he learned about the changes SPP made to improve its internal control system, Jason reflected on how management rejected similar changes suggested by Northwest's internal audit staff, including those made by his supervisor, just a year ago. Jason realized he has learned an important truth about internal control: There are many companies and managers who do not realize the importance of internal control until they have been burned.

KEY TERMS

- SysTrust
- performance objectives
- policies
- standards
- strategic plan
- administrative documentation
- systems documentation
- operating documentation
- preventive maintenance
- uninterruptible power supply (UPS)
- fault tolerance
- disaster recovery plan

- electronic vaulting
- grandfather–father–son concept
- rollback
- hot site
- cold site
- physical access
- logical access
- user identification (ID) and authentication system
- user ID
- password
- physical possession identification

- biometric identification
- compatibility tests
- access control matrix
- intranet
- firewall
- tunneling
- electronic envelope
- project development plan
- project milestones
- performance evaluation
- data processing schedule
- system performance measurements

- throughput
- utilization
- response time
- postimplementation review
- application controls
- general controls
- check digit
- check digit verification
- key verification
- input validation routines
- edit programs
- edit checks
- sequence check
- field check
- sign check

- validity check
- limit check
- range check
- reasonableness test
- redundant data check
- capacity check
- error log
- error report
- prompting
- preformatting
- completeness check
- closed-loop verification
- transaction log
- error messages
- default value

- external label
- internal labels
- volume label
- header label
- trailer label
- tape file protection ring
- concurrent update controls
- data encryption
  (cryptography)
- routing verification procedures
- mutual authentication schemes
- callback system
- parity bit
- parity checking
- echo check

CHAPTER QUIZ

1. What controls are designed to ensure that an organization's computer-based control environment is stable and well managed?
   a. general controls
   b. application controls
   c. detective controls
   d. preventive controls

2. All of the following are effective control procedures to ensure that operators do not make unauthorized changes to programs and files except:
   a. rotating duties
   b. having multiple operators in the computer room during processing
   c. requiring formal written authorization for and documentation of program changes
   d. maintaining and reviewing a log of all operator activity and interventions

3. Password effectiveness is enhanced by all of the following except:
   a. changing passwords frequently
   b. user selection of passwords
   c. not displaying the password on the screen
   d. automatic disconnection after several failed attempts

4. What is the best method to reduce the risk of electronic eavesdropping?
   a. using parity bits
   b. compatibility tests
   c. data encryption
   d. checkpoints and rollback procedures

5. Descriptions of each application program, including narratives, flowcharts, and code, are called:
   a. administrative documentation
   b. accounting documentation
   c. operating documentation
   d. systems documentation

6. Which term describes controls that are designed to prevent, detect, or correct errors in transactions as they flow through the various stages of a specific data processing program?
   a. general controls
   b. application controls
   c. administrative controls
   d. data processing controls

7. According to SysTrust, all of the following are principles a company can use to determine if a system is reliable except:
   a. availability
   b. controllability
   c. maintainability
   d. integrity

8. When the computer sums the first four digits of a customer number to calculate the value of the fifth digit and then compares that calculation to the number typed during data entry, it is an example of which of the following?
   a. field check
   b. parity check
   c. check digit verification
   d. batch total

9. What term describes the edit check that would detect the entry of a customer number that does not exist?
   a. check digit
   b. limit check
   c. sequence check
   d. validity check

10. In an on-line system, the user enters the customer number and the system responds by displaying the customer name and asking the user for verification. This is called a:
    a. closed-loop verification test
    b. redundant data check
    c. compatibility test
    d. completeness test

DISCUSSION QUESTIONS

8.1   A computer implementation project is often performed in a state of crisis, with the implementation group working feverishly to keep pace with the implementation schedule. In this atmosphere, corners are often cut with respect to documentation and application controls. What arguments would be effective to prevent these types of shortcuts?

8.2   Theoretically, a control procedure should be adopted if its benefit exceeds its cost. Explain how the benefits and costs of the following controls can be estimated.
   a. Segregation of duties
   b. Data protection procedures
   c. Logical access controls
   d. Input validation routines

8.3   Prudential-Bache Securities in New York contracted with Comdisco Computing Service Corporation in New Jersey to back up its data (more than 500,000 securities transactions per day) by transmitting it on a real-time basis to an electronic vaulting service. The service includes use of a high-speed data transmission line and an automated tape library. Comdisco also agreed to make a hot site available to Prudential-Bache in the event that a disaster shuts down its central data center. The hot site has a direct link to the vaulting system, ensuring that all but the last 15 minutes of trading data would be recovered.

Though terms of the contract were not disclosed, this arrangement is certainly a very expensive proposition for Prudential-Bache. Discuss how this contract could have been justified on a cost-benefit basis. In addition, name at least three steps that Prudential-Bache should take to prevent unauthorized access to its backup data.

8.4   For control purposes, the function of transaction authorization should be performed by employees outside the systems department. However, computers are increasingly being programmed to initiate transactions, such as issuing a purchase order when an inventory balance is low. Discuss whether such automatic transaction generation represents a violation of good internal control principles.

8.5   The Foster Corporation recently fired its AIS director after experiencing several years of budget overruns in systems development and computer operations. You have been appointed as interim director and are charged with investigating the problems the department has experienced. There is little written information about the activities of the department or the policies under which it was managed. The previous director communicated assignments, standards, and performance evaluations verbally. This management style was popular with some employees but unpopular with many others, some of whom have left the company.

The major systems project under development is an AIS. Objectives for the project are loosely defined, although a good deal of analysis, design, and programming has been completed. The project director estimates the project is half finished. The computer operations department runs jobs on an as-received basis. The operations supervisor suggests that a more reliable system is needed to satisfy demand during peak periods and cope with expected processing growth.

Identify and briefly describe several elements of control that appear to be lacking in this situation and that should be implemented in the information systems department.

PROBLEMS

8.1   Your company has purchased several personal computers. One has been installed in the stores department, which is responsible for disbursing stock items and maintaining stores records. In your audit, you find that one employee, trained in computer applications, receives the requisitions for stores, reviews them for completeness and approvals, disburses the stock, maintains the records, operates the computer, and authorizes adjustments to the total amounts of stock accumulated by the computer.

When you discuss the applicable controls with the department manager, you are told that the personal computer is assigned exclusively to that department. Therefore, it does not require the same types of controls that are applicable to large computer systems.

Required

Comment on the manager's contentions, discussing briefly five types of control that would apply to this personal computer application.

8.2 You are the general manager of a manufacturing company in Woodbridge, Virginia. During the past 6 months, your company has consistently lost bids to a competitor whose bids always seen to be slightly lower. On a hunch that this could not keep happening by chance, you hire a private detective. She reports that one of your employees with access to the computer is stealing your bid data and selling it to the competitor for $25,000 per bid.

Required

a. Identify the likely deficiencies in internal control over your company's computer systems that could have allowed this fraud to occur.

b. How else could bids have been stolen and sold?

c. How would you guard against each of these methods?

8.3 Consider the set of numeric computer input data in Table 8-6.

Required

a. From the data in Table 8-6, calculate and show one specific example of the following:
   Hash total
   Record count
   Financial total

b. For each of the following controls, give a specific example from the four records in Table 8-6 of an error or probable error that would be caught by the control (list the error—do not merely describe it).
   Field check
   Sequence check
   Limit check
   Reasonableness test
   Cross-footing balance test

Table 8-6 Computer Input Data, Problem 8.3

Employee Number Col. 1–3	Pay Rate Col. 4–6	Hours Worked Col. 7–8	Gross Pay Col. 9–13	Deductions Col. 14–18	Net Pay Col. 19–23
121	250	38	$ 9500	01050	08450
123	275	40	11000	01250	09750
125	200	90	16000	02000	12000
122	280	40	11200	11000	00200

8.4   You are the data security administrator for a small company. Its system uses two programs: a payroll system and an inventory processing system. It maintains three files: a payroll master file, an inventory master file, and a transaction log. The following users should have the indicated access to the system:

User	Access
Salesperson	Read and display records in the inventory file
Inventory control analyst	Read, display, update, create, and delete records in the inventory file
Payroll analyst	Read, display, and update records in the payroll file
Human resources manager	Read, display, update, create, and delete records in the payroll file
Payroll programmer	Perform all payroll system operations; read and display payroll file records and transaction log records
Inventory programmer	Perform all operations on the inventory system; read and display inventory file records and transaction log records
Data processing manager	Read and display all programs and files
Yourself	Perform all operations in all programs and files

Required

a. Create an access control matrix that allows the users to have the indicated levels of access. For each user, assign a six-character user code and select access authority codes. Use the following access authority coding system.
   0 = no access permitted
   1 = read and display only
   2 = read, display, and update
   3 = read, display, update, create, and delete

b. What changes would you make to the access privileges of the employees mentioned earlier?

8.5   What control(s) would you recommend to prevent the following situations from occurring?
   a. The "time worked" field for salaried employees should contain a 01 for one week. One employee's field contained the number 40, and a check for $9,872.51 was accidentally prepared and mailed.
   b. A programmer obtained the master payroll file, loaded it into the system, and changed his monthly salary from $4,400 to $6,000.
   c. The accounts receivable file on disk was inadvertently destroyed and could not be reconstructed after being substituted for the accounts payable file in a processing run.
   d. A company lost almost all its vital business data in a fire that destroyed the room in which it stored its magnetic disk and tapes.

e. A programmer quit the firm in the middle of an assignment. Because no other programmers could make sense of the work already completed, the project was started over from scratch.

f. A bank programmer obtained the disks containing the program that calculates interest on customer accounts. She loaded the program into the computer and modified it so the fractions of a cent from each interest calculation, which would otherwise be rounded off, were added to her account.

g. During keying of customer payment records, the digit 0 in a payment of $102.34 was mistakenly typed as the letter O. As a result, the transaction was not processed correctly, and the customer received an incorrect statement.

8.6 What control(s) would you recommend in an on-line computer system to prevent the following situations from occurring?

a. A teenager gained unauthorized access to the system by programming a PC to enter repeated user numbers until a correct one was found.

b. An employee gained unauthorized access to the system by observing her supervisor's user number and then correctly guessing the password after 12 attempts.

c. A salesperson for a PC manufacturer, keying in a customer order from a remote laptop computer, entered an incorrect stock number. As a result, an order for 50 monitors was placed for a customer who wanted to order 50 PCs.

d. A salesperson received a laptop computer to enter sales orders while calling on customers. She used it to increase her own monthly salary by $500.

e. A salesperson keying in a customer order from a remote computer inadvertently omitted the delivery address from the order.

f. A company's research and development center utilizes remote PCs tied into its computer center 100 miles away. Using a wiretap, the company's largest competitor stole secret plans for a major product innovation.

g. A server at a bank served terminals at eight drive-in windows. When the server failed, the bank was forced to shut down the windows for 2 hours during a busy Friday afternoon.

h. A 20-minute power failure that shut down a firm's computer system resulted in loss of data for several transactions that were being entered into the system from remote terminals.

8.7 The headquarters of Gleicken Corporation, a private company with $3.5 million in annual sales, is located in California. For its 150 clients, Gleicken provides an on-line legal software service that includes data storage and administrative activities for law offices. The company has grown rapidly since its inception 3 years ago, and its data processing department has mushroomed to accommodate this growth. Because Gleicken's president and sales staff spend a great deal of time out of the office soliciting new clients, planning the EDP facilities has been left to the data processing professionals.

Gleicken recently moved its headquarters into a remodeled warehouse on the outskirts of the city. While remodeling the warehouse, the architects retained much of the original structure, including the wooden-shingled exterior and exposed wooden beams throughout the interior. The company's hardware is situated in a large open area with high ceilings and skylights. This openness makes the data processing area accessible to the rest of the staff and encourages a team approach to problem solving. Before Gleicken began to occupy its new facility, city inspectors declared the building safe (adequate fire extinguishers, sufficient exits, etc.).

Gleicken wanted to provide further protection for its large database of client information. Therefore, it instituted a tape backup procedure that automatically backs up the database every Sunday evening to avoid interrupting daily operations and procedures. All the tapes are labeled and carefully stored on shelves in the data processing department reserved for this purpose. The departmental operator's manual has instructions on how to use these tapes to restore the database should the need arise. In the event of an emergency, there is a home phone list of the individuals in the data processing department. Gleicken has recently increased its liability insurance for data loss from $50,000 to $100,000.

This past Saturday the Gleicken headquarters building was completely destroyed by fire. The company must now inform its clients that all their information has been destroyed.

Required
a. Describe the computer security weaknesses present at Gleicken Corporation that made it possible for a disastrous data loss to occur.
b. List the components that should have been included in the disaster recovery plan at Gleicken Corporation in order to ensure computer recovery within 72 hours.
c. What factors, other than those included in the plan itself, should a company consider when formulating a disaster recovery plan?
d. What threats, other than the fire, should Gleicken have protected itself from?

8.8   The Moose Wings Cooperative Flight Club owns a number of airplanes and gliders. It serves fewer than 2,000 members, who are numbered sequentially from the founder, Tom Eagle (0001), to the newest member, Jacques Noveau (1368). Members rent the flying machines by the hour, and all must be returned on the same day. The club uses a computer on its premises and a dial-up line to send the billing data to a computer utility. The utility bills members monthly.

The following six records were among those entered for the flights taken on November 1, 2003.

Member #	Flight Date DDMMYY	Plane Used*	Takeoff Time	Landing Time
1234	311103	G	0625	0846
4111	011103	C	0849	1023
1210	011103	P	0342	0542
0023	011103	X	0159	1243
012A	011103	P	1229	1532
0999	011103	L	1551	1387

*G = glider; C = Cessna; P = Piper Club; L = Lear Jet

Required
a. For each of the five data fields, suggest one or more edit controls that could be included in the program for detecting possible errors.
b. Identify and describe any errors in the records.
c. Suggest other controls to prevent input errors if on-line entry were employed.

8.9   Taibert Corporation hired an independent computer programmer to develop a simplified payroll application for its newly purchased computer. The programmer developed an on-line data entry system that minimized the level of knowledge required by the operator. It was based on keying answers to input cues that appeared on the terminal's viewing screen. Examples of the cues follow:
a. Access routine:
  1. Operator access number to payroll file?
  2. Are there new employees?
b. New employees routine:
  1. Employee name?
  2. Employee number?

      3. Social security number?
      4. Rate per hour?
      5. Single or married?
      6. Number of dependents?
      7. Account distribution?
   c. Current payroll routine:
      1. Employee number?
      2. Regular hours worked?
      3. Overtime hours worked?
      4. Total employees this payroll period?

The independent auditor is attempting to verify that certain input validation (edit) checks exist. The checks should ensure that errors resulting from omissions, invalid entries, or other inaccuracies are detected as soon as the answers to the input cues are entered.

Required

Identify the various types of input validation (edit) checks an auditor would expect to find in the EDP system. Describe the assurances provided by each identified validation check. Do not discuss the review and evaluation of these controls.

8.10 Babbington-Bowles is an advertising agency that employs 625 salespersons, who travel and entertain extensively. Each month, salespersons are paid both salary and commissions. The nature of their job is such that expenses of several hundred dollars a day might be incurred. In the past these expenses were included in each monthly paycheck. Salespersons were required to submit their expense reports, with supporting receipts, by the 20th of each month. These reports would be reviewed and then sent to data entry in a batch. Suitable controls were incorporated on each batch during input, processing, and output. This system worked well from a company viewpoint, and the internal auditor was convinced that while minor padding of expense accounts might occur, no major losses have been encountered.

    However, the salespersons were unhappy. They pointed out that they were often forced to carry several thousand dollars for an entire month. If they were out of town around the 20th, they might not be reimbursed for their expenses for 2 months. They requested that Babbington-Bowles provided a service whereby a salesperson or his or her representative could submit receipts and expense reports to the accounting department and receive a check almost immediately.

    The data processing manager agreed to the following procedures. The salespeople could enter their expenses on-line on a company Web site. The salesperson's name would be entered on the Web-based form, with the required expense amounts broken down into the standard categories. A program would process these data to the proper accounts and, if everything checked out suitably, mail a check to the salesperson or send a direct deposit into their account.

Required

Identify five important controls, and explain why they might be incorporated in the system. These controls may be physical, they may relate to jobs and responsibilities, or they may be part of the program.

Case 8-1   AnyCompany, Inc.: An Ongoing Comprehensive Case

Visit a local company and obtain permission to study its system of internal controls. Once you have lined up a company, do the following:

1. Obtain copies of organizational charts, job descriptions, and related documentation on how authority and responsibility have been assigned within the information systems function. Evaluate if lines of authority and responsibility seem to be clearly defined and if incompatible duties have been appropriately segregated.
2. Determine how the company evaluates the progress of systems development projects during the design and implementation stages.
3. Observe how the company controls physical access to its mainframe computer site, as well as to its personal computers and online terminals. Evaluate if the company's access controls seem to be effective.
4. Determine the procedures used by the company to protect its stored program and data files from loss or destruction, including procedures for recovery of any program or data files that may be lost. Evaluate if these procedures appear to be sound.
5. Examine the company's policies and procedures relating to the use of passwords to control logical access to its system resources. Evaluate these policies and procedures.
6. Briefly examine copies of the company's administrative, systems, and operating documentation. Evaluate the quality and completeness of this material.
7. Determine the techniques used by the company to minimize the risk of system downtime.
8. Ask if the company has a written disaster recovery plan for its computer facilities. If so, examine a copy of the plan and assess its strengths and weaknesses.

Case 8-2   The State Department of Taxation

The department of taxation in your state is developing a new computer system for processing individual and corporate income tax returns. The new system features direct data input and inquiry capabilities. Identification of taxpayers is provided by using the social security number for individuals and federal tax identification number for corporations. The new system should be fully implemented in time for the next tax season.

The new system will serve three primary purposes:

1. Data will be input directly into the system from tax returns using computer terminals located at central headquarters.
2. The returns will be processed using the main computer facilities at central headquarters. Processing will include four steps:
   a. Verifying mathematical accuracy
   b. Auditing the reasonableness of deductions, tax due, etc., through the use of edit routines, which also include a comparison of current and prior years' data.

c. Identifying returns that should be considered for audit by department revenue agents

d. Issuing refund checks to taxpayers

3. Inquiry service will be provided to taxpayers upon request through the assistance of tax department personnel at five regional offices. A total of 50 terminals will be placed at each regional office. A taxpayer will be allowed to determine the status of his or her return or get information from the last three years' returns by calling or visiting one of the department's regional offices.

The state commissioner of taxation is concerned about data security during input and processing, over and above protection against natural hazards such as fire and flood. This includes protection against the loss or damage of data during data input and processing as well as the improper input or processing of data. In addition, the tax commissioner and the state attorney general have discussed the general problem of data confidentiality that may arise from the nature and operation of the new system. Both individuals want to have potential problems identified before the system is fully developed and implemented so that the proper controls can be incorporated into the new system.

REQUIRED

1. Describe the potential confidentiality problems that could arise in each of the following three areas of processing, and recommend the corrective action(s) to solve each problem identified:

a. Data input

b. Processing of returns

c. Data inquiry

2. The state tax commission wants to incorporate controls to provide data security against the loss, damage, improper input, or use of data during data input and processing. Identify the potential problems (outside of natural hazards such as fire or floods) for which the department of taxation should develop controls, and recommend the possible controls for each problem identified.

ANSWERS TO CHAPTER QUIZ

1. a	**3.** b	**5.** d	**7.** b	**9.** d
2. c	**4.** c	**6.** b	**8.** c	**10.** a

Computer Fraud and Security

Learning Objectives

After studying this chapter, you should be able to:

- Define fraud and describe the process one follows to perpetuate a fraud.
- Discuss why fraud occurs, including the pressures, opportunities, and rationalizations that are present in most frauds.
- Compare and contrast the approaches and techniques that are used to commit computer fraud.
- Describe how to deter and detect computer fraud.

Integrative Case: Northwest Industries

It was late on the last Sunday of March when Jason Scott finished his tax return. Before sealing the envelope, he reviewed his return for a final time. Jason quickly compared the documents used to prepare his return with the actual numbers. Everything was in order except his withholding amount. For some reason, the federal income tax withholdings on his final paycheck was $5 higher than on his W-2 form. He decided to use the W-2 amount and made a note to check with payroll to find out what happened to the other $5. The next day was a typical Monday at Northwest Industries and Jason was swamped. After reviewing his to-do list, he decided to dismiss the $5 difference because the amount was immaterial.

At lunch on April 16, several people were joking about their last-minute attempts to complete their tax returns. In the course of the conversation, one of Jason's coworkers grumbled about the company taking out $5 more from his check than he was given credit for on his W-2. No one followed up on the comment, and it was not until after lunch that the coincidence hit Jason: He was not the only one to have a $5 discrepancy between his withholdings and his W-2 statement. After obtaining the appropriate clearances, it was once again time to investigate. By the end of the following day, Jason was worried. Most of the 1,500 company employees had a $5 discrepancy between their reported withholdings and the actual amount withheld. Interestingly enough, the W-2 of Don Hawkins, a programmer in charge of the payroll system, showed that thousands of dollars more in withholdings had been reported to the IRS than had been withheld from his paycheck.

It certainly looked to Jason like Northwest had a serious problem. He knew that when he reported the situation, management was going to ask the following questions:

1. What constitutes a fraud, and is the withholding problem a fraud?
2. If this is indeed a fraud, how was it perpetrated? What motivated Don to commit it?
3. Why did the company not catch these mistakes earlier? Was there a breakdown in controls?
4. What can the company do to detect and prevent fraud?
5. Just how vulnerable are computer systems to fraud?

INTRODUCTION

Fraud is any and all means a person uses to gain an unfair advantage over another person. Fraudulent acts include lies, suppressions of the truth, tricks, and cunning, and they often involve a violation of a trust or confidence. Losses from fraud in the United States are estimated to be about $500 billion a year.

Either someone within an organization or an external party can commit fraud. Not surprisingly, former and current employees (sometimes called knowledgeable insiders) are much more likely to perpetrate fraud than are nonemployees. Because employees understand a company's system and its weaknesses, they are better able to commit a fraud, evade detection, and cover their tracks. The controls most organizations use to protect corporate assets make it more difficult for an outsider to steal from a company. Fraud perpetrators are often referred to as **white-collar criminals,** to distinguish them from criminals who commit violent crimes.

Internal fraud can be broken down into two categories: misappropriation of assets and fraudulent financial reporting. **Misappropriation of assets,** or **employee fraud,** is committed by a person or group of persons for personal financial gain. The fraud discovered by Jason Scott is a misappropriation of assets.

The National Commission on Fraudulent Financial Reporting (the Treadway Commission) defines **fraudulent financial reporting** as intentional or reckless conduct, whether by act or omission, that results in materially misleading financial statements. Fraudulent financial reporting is of special concern to independent auditors. The Treadway Commission studied 450 lawsuits against auditors and found undetected fraud to be a factor in half of them. Financial statements can be falsified to deceive investors and creditors, to cause a company's stock price to rise, to meet cash flow needs, or to hide company losses and problems. The perpetrators receive indirect benefits: They keep their jobs, their stock rises, and they receive pay raises and promotions they do not deserve. They can also gain more power and influence than they should.

The Treadway Commission recommended four actions to reduce the possibility of fraudulent financial reporting:

1. Establish an organizational environment that contributes to the integrity of the financial reporting process.
2. Identify and understand the factors that lead to fraudulent financial reporting.

3. Assess the risk of fraudulent financial reporting within the company.
4. Design and implement internal controls to provide reasonable assurance that fraudulent financial reporting is prevented.

This chapter discusses fraud in four main sections. The first section describes the fraud process and the second section explores the reasons why fraud occurs. The third section describes the approaches to computer fraud and the specific techniques used to commit it. The fourth section analyzes several ways companies can deter and detect computer fraud.

THE FRAUD PROCESS

Three characteristics are associated with most fraud:

1. The *theft* of something of value, such as cash, inventory, tools, supplies, equipment, or data. The theft of assets is the most common type of employee fraud. Most fraudulent financial reporting consists of the overstatement of assets or revenues. Few employees or companies are motivated to steal or overstate liabilities. Likewise, few frauds include the theft or direct overstatement of equity accounts.
2. The *conversion* of the stolen assets into cash. For example, stolen inventory and equipment must be sold or otherwise converted into cash.
3. The *concealment* of the crime to avoid detection. When assets are stolen or overstated, the only way to balance the basic accounting equation is to inflate other assets or to decrease liabilities or equity. Unless perpetrators find some way to keep the accounting equation in balance, their theft or misrepresentation can be discovered. Concealment often takes more effort and time and leaves behind more evidence than the actual theft. For example, taking cash requires only a few seconds, whereas altering records to hide the theft can be more challenging and time consuming.

A common and effective way to hide a theft is to charge the stolen item to an expense account. For example, one employee stole $10,000 and charged it to a miscellaneous expense account. Assets were reduced by $10,000 but so was equity, since expense accounts decrease net income as they are closed out, which in turn lowers the retained earnings amount. As another example, an enterprising payroll clerk added a fictitious name to his company's payroll records, intercepted the paycheck, and cashed it. Although the company was missing funds, its books were balanced because there was a debit to a wages expense and a credit to cash. In both cases, the perpetrator's exposure is limited to a year or less, because the expense accounts are zeroed out at the end of the year. On the other hand, perpetrators who hide a theft by affecting another balance sheet account must continue the concealment. Hence one of the most popular ways to cover up a fraud is to hide the theft in an income statement account.

Another way to hide a decrease in assets is by lapping. In a **lapping** scheme, the perpetrator steals cash received from customer A to pay its accounts receivable. Funds received at a later date from customer B are used to pay off customer A's balance. Funds from customer C are used to pay off B, and so forth. The cover-up must continue indefinitely unless the money is replaced, because the theft will be uncovered if the scheme is stopped.

In a **kiting** scheme, the perpetrator covers up a theft by creating cash through the transfer of money between banks. For example, suppose a fraud perpetrator opens checking accounts in three banks, called bank A, B, and C, and deposits $100 in each account. Then the perpetrator "creates" cash by depositing a $1,000 check from bank A into bank B and then withdraws the $1,000 from bank B. Since there are insufficient funds in bank A to cover the $1,000 check, the perpetrator deposits a $1,000 check from bank C to bank A before his check to bank B clears. Since bank C also has insufficient funds, $1,000 must be deposited to bank C before the check to bank A clears. The check to bank C is written from bank B, which also has insufficient funds. The scheme continues, with checks and deposits occurring as needed to keep the checks from bouncing.

WHY FRAUD OCCURS

Researchers have compared the psychological and demographic characteristics of three groups of people: white-collar criminals, violent criminals, and the general public. Although they found significant differences between violent and white-collar criminals, they found few differences between white-collar criminals and the general public. White-collar criminals tend to mirror the general public in education, age, religion, marriage, length of employment, and psychological makeup.

Fraud perpetrators share a number of common characteristics. Most spend their illegal income rather than invest or save it. Once they begin the fraud, it is very hard for them to stop. They usually begin to rely on the extra income. If the perpetrators are not caught shortly after they begin, they typically become brazen and their desire for more money can encourage them to increase the amount they take. As time passes, many perpetrators grow careless, overconfident, or greedy and usually make a mistake that leads to their apprehension.

Perpetrators of computer fraud tend to be younger and possess more computer knowledge, experience, and skills. Some computer fraud perpetrators are more motivated by curiosity and the challenge of "beating the system" than by the actual gain. They may view their actions as a game rather than as dishonest behavior. Others commit computer fraud to gain stature among others in the computer community. One study shows that computer crime is an equal opportunity employer: 32 percent of the perpetrators being women and 43 percent minorities.

Some fraud perpetrators are disgruntled and unhappy with their jobs and are seeking revenge against their employers. Others are regarded as ideal employees who are dedicated, hard working, and in a position of trust. Most have no previous criminal record. Prior to committing fraud, they were honest citizens who were valued and respected members of their communities. Why, then, would they risk everything by committing fraud? Research shows that three conditions are necessary for fraud to occur: a pressure or motive, an opportunity, and a rationalization.

Pressures

A **pressure** is a person's motivation for committing a fraud. Three types of motivation that often lead to fraud are summarized in Table 9-1. Pressures can be financial, such as living beyond one's means or having heavy debts or unusually high bills. Often, the perpetrator feels such pressures cannot be shared with others.

An illustration of someone who succumbed to financial pressures is Raymond Keller of Stockport, Iowa. Raymond was a local boy who worked his way up from driving a coal truck to owning a grain elevator. He made money by trading on commodities

Table 9-1   Pressures that Can Lead to Fraud

Financial	Work-Related	Other
Living beyond means	Low salary	Challenge
High personal debt	Nonrecognition of	Family/peer pressure
"Inadequate" income	performance	Emotional instability
Poor credit ratings	Job dissatisfaction	Need for power or control
Heavy financial losses	Fear of losing job	Excessive pride or ambition
Bad investments	Overaggressive bonus	
Health care expenditures	plans	
Large gambling debts		
Need to support a drug		
or alcohol addiction		
Greed		

and built a lavish house overlooking the Des Moines River. No one knows why his financial situation declined. Some say he lost a lot of money speculating on the commodities markets; others say it was a grain embargo that virtually halted the buying and selling of grain. Whatever the reason, Raymond had a severe cash shortage and went deeply into debt. He asked some farmers to wait for their money, and he gave others bad checks. Finally, the seven banks to which he owed over $3 million began to call in their loans. So Raymond began to sell grain, which he stored for local farmers, to cover his losses. When a state auditor showed up at his door unexpectedly, Raymond chose to take his life rather than face the consequences of his fraud.

Pressures can also be work related. Some employees steal data so they can take it to a new job or to a company they are starting. Some employees turn to fraud because they have strong feelings of resentment or believe they have been treated unfairly. They may feel that their pay is too low, that their contributions to the company are not appreciated sufficiently, or that the company is taking advantage of them. Some fear losing their job and commit a fraud hoping to preserve their position by making themselves or their company look better. In one case, an accountant in California, who was passed over for a raise, increased his salary by 10 percent, the amount of an average raise. When apprehended, he defended his actions by saying he was only taking what was rightfully his. When asked how he would have felt if he had increased his salary by 11 percent, he responded that he would have been stealing 1 percent.

Other motivations that lead to fraudulent actions include family or peer pressure, emotional instability, and the challenge of beating the system. Many computer hackers commit fraud for the challenge of subverting the controls and breaking into a system. In one case, a company boasted in its advertisements that its new information system was so secure that outsiders would not be able to break into it. Within 24 hours of the system's implementation, a team of individuals had broken into the system and left a message that the impenetrable system had just been compromised.

Opportunities

An **opportunity** is the condition or situation that allows a person to commit and conceal a dishonest act. The list of opportunities that make fraud easy to commit and conceal is almost endless. Table 9-2 notes some of the more frequently mentioned opportunities noted in fraud research studies.

Opportunities often stem from a lack of internal controls. For example, a company might lack proper procedures for authorizations, clear lines of authority, or independent checks on performance. Likewise, there may not be a separation of duties among the authorization, custodial, and record-keeping functions. However, the most prevalent opportunity for fraud results from a company's failure to *enforce* its system of internal controls.

One control feature that many companies lack is a background check on all potential employees. A background check would have saved one company from the "phantom controller." In that case, the company president stopped by the office one night, saw a light on in the controller's office, and went to see why he was working so late. He was surprised to find a complete stranger at work. An investigation showed the controller was not an accountant and had been fired from three of his previous five jobs in the last 8 years. Because he was unable to do the accounting work, he had hired someone to come in at night to do his work for him. Before his scam was discovered, the controller had defrauded the company of several million dollars.

Table 9-2   Perceived Opportunities

Internal Control Factors	Other Factors
Failure to enforce internal controls	Too much trust in key employees
Lack of proper procedures for authorizations	Close association with suppliers/customers
	Incompetent supervisory personnel
No separation of duties between authorization, custody, and record-keeping functions	Operating on a crisis basis
	Failure to discipline violators
	Confusion about ethics
No independent checks on performance	Lack of explicit conflict-of-interest statements
No separation of accounting duties	Inadequate physical security
Lack of clear lines of authority	Inadequate staffing and/or training
Lack of frequent reviews	Poor management philosophy
Inadequate documentation	Lack of employee loyalty
No background checks	Unclear company policies
Lack of frequent reviews	Apathy
	Inattention to details

Other situations that make it easy for someone to commit a fraud are excessive trust in key employees, incompetent supervisory personnel, inattention to details, inadequate staffing, lack of training, and unclear company policies.

Many frauds also arise when employees build mutually beneficial personal relationships with customers or suppliers. For example, a buyer could agree to purchase goods at an inflated price in exchange for a kickback from the vendor. Frauds can also occur when a crisis arises and the company disregards its normal control procedures. For instance, one Fortune 500 company was hit with three multi-million dollar frauds in the same year. All three took place when the company was trying to resolve a series of crises and failed to follow the standard internal control procedures.

Rationalizations

Most fraud perpetrators have an excuse or a **rationalization** that allows them to justify their illegal behavior. Perpetrators rationalize either that they are not actually being dishonest or that their reasons for committing fraud are more compelling than honesty and integrity. Perhaps the most common rationalization is that the perpetrator is just "borrowing" the stolen assets because he or she has every intention of repaying the company.

Some perpetrators rationalize that they are not hurting a real person. It is just a faceless and nameless computer system that will be affected or a large, impersonal company that will not miss the money. For example, one perpetrator took pains to steal no more than $20,000, which was the maximum that the insurance company would reimburse the company for losses.

The list of rationalizations people use is lengthy. Here are some of the most frequently used:

> ➤ You would understand if you knew how badly I needed it.
> ➤ What I did was not that serious.
> ➤ It was for a good cause. (This is the Robin Hood syndrome, robbing from the rich to give to the poor.)
> ➤ I occupy a very important position of trust. I am above the rules.
> ➤ Everyone else is doing it, so it cannot be that wrong.
> ➤ No one will ever know.
> ➤ The company owes it to me, and I am taking no more than is rightfully mine.

Fraud occurs when people have high pressures, abundant opportunities, and the ability to rationalize away their personal integrity. Fraud is not likely to occur when people have few pressures, little opportunity to commit and conceal fraud, and high personal integrity that makes them less likely to rationalize fraud. Unfortunately, in most cases there is a mixture of these three forces that makes it difficult to determine if a particular person is likely to commit a fraud.

COMPUTER FRAUD

The U.S. Department of Justice defines **computer fraud** as any illegal act for which knowledge of computer technology is essential for its perpetration, investigation, or prosecution. More specifically, computer fraud includes the following:

> ➤ Unauthorized theft, use, access, modification, copying, and destruction of software or data

➤ Theft of money by altering computer records or the theft of computer time

➤ Theft or destruction of computer hardware

➤ Use or the conspiracy to use computer resources to commit a felony

➤ Intent to illegally obtain information or tangible property through the use of computers

Using a computer, fraud perpetrators are able to steal more of something in much less time and with much less effort. For instance, they can steal millions of dollars in less than a second. Perpetrators can commit a fraud and leave little or no evidence. Therefore, computer fraud is often much more difficult to detect than other types of fraud.

The Rise in Computer Fraud

Organizations that track computer fraud estimate that 80 percent of U.S. businesses have been victimized by at least one incident of computer fraud, at a cost of up to $10 billion per year. However, for the following six reasons, no one knows exactly how much companies lose to computer fraud:

1. *Not everyone agrees on what constitutes computer fraud.* For example, some people restrict the definition to a crime that takes place inside a computer or is directed at one. For others, it is any crime in which the perpetrator uses the computer as a tool. Many people do not believe that making an unlicensed copy of software constitutes computer fraud. Software publishers think otherwise, however, and prosecute those who make illegal copies. Similarly, some people do not think it is a crime to browse through someone else's computer if they have no intentions of harming the organization or its data.

2. *Many computer frauds go undetected.* At one time, the FBI estimated that only 1 percent of all computer crime is detected; other estimates are between 5 and 20 percent.

3. *An estimated 80 to 90 percent of the frauds that are uncovered are not reported.* Only the banking industry is required by law to report all frauds. The most commonly cited reason for failure to report computer fraud is a company's fear that adverse publicity would result in copycat fraud and a loss of customer confidence, which could cost more than the fraud itself. As a result, fraud estimates are based on the limited numbers of frauds that are both detected and reported. What is known is that computer fraud is large and growing. During a one year period, the dollar losses from unauthorized employee abuses in the United States increased 15-fold, from $181,400 to $2.81 million per incident. A few years ago it was estimated that computers at the Defense Department were attacked more than half a million times and that the number of incidents increases 50 to 100 percent per year. Defense Department staffers and outside consultants made 38,000 "friendly hacks" on their networks to evaluate security. Almost 70 percent of them were successful. Unfortunately, systems management at the Defense Department was only able to detect 4 percent of the attacks; the others went unnoticed. At the Pentagon, which has the government's most advanced hacker-awareness program, only 1 in 500 break-ins was detected and reported. As early as 1979, *Time* labeled computer fraud a "growth industry." Some of the reasons attributed to the steady growth of fraud include the growing number of competent computer users, easier access to remote computers through both the Internet and other data networks, and the belief of many companies that "it won't happen to us."

4. Most networks have a low level of security. Dan Farmer, who wrote SATAN (a network security testing tool), tested 2,200 high-profile Web sites at government institutions, banks, and newspapers. Only 3 of the sites detected him and contacted him to find out his intentions. Farmer concluded that 2 of the 3 sites had serious vulnerabilities, and most firewalls and other protective measures at the sites were ineffective.

5. Many Internet pages give step-by-step instructions on how to perpetrate computer crimes and abuses. For instance, an Internet search found more than 17,000 matches for "denial of service," a rapidly growing form of computer abuse. There are also thousands of pages on how to break into routers and disable Web servers.

6. Law enforcement is unable to keep up with the growing number of computer frauds. The FBI is one of two federal agencies (the other is the U.S. Secret Service) charged with investigating computer crime. Due to the lack of funding and people with the necessary skills, however, the FBI is only able to investigate 1 in 15 computer crimes.

One type of computer fraud, economic espionage, is growing especially fast. **Economic espionage,** the theft of information and intellectual property, increased by 323 percent during one 5-year period. Almost 75 percent of the estimated annual losses of $100 billion were to an employee, former employee, contractor, or supplier. At any point in time, the FBI is investigating about 800 separate incidents of economic espionage. One noteworthy case of industrial espionage is the allegations against Reuters Analytics. Reuters was accused of breaking into the computers of its competitor, Bloomberg, and stealing lines of code. The lines were supposedly used in software that enables financial institutions to analyze historical data on the stock market.

Computer Fraud Classifications

Various researchers have examined fraud to determine the types of assets stolen and the approaches used. As shown in Figure 9-1, a way to categorize computer fraud is to use the data processing model: input, processor, computer instructions, stored data, and output.

Input

The simplest and most common way to commit a fraud is to alter computer input. It requires little if any computer skills. Instead, perpetrators need only to understand how the system operates so they can cover their tracks.

Paul Sjiem-Fat used desktop publishing technology to perpetrate one of the first cases of computer forgery. Sjiem-Fat created bogus cashier's checks and used them to buy computer equipment, which he subsequently sold in the Caribbean. He was

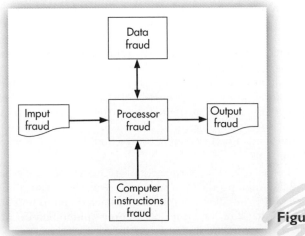

Figure 9-1   Computer fraud classifications

caught while trying to steal $20,000 from the Bank of Boston. The bank called in the Secret Service, who raided his apartment and found nine bogus checks totaling almost $150,000. Sjiem-Fat was prosecuted and sent to prison.

Another perpetrator opened an account at a New York bank, then had a printer prepare blank deposit slips. The slips were similar to those available in bank lobbies, except that his account number was encoded on them. Early one morning he replaced all the deposit slips in the bank lobby with his forged ones. For three days, all bank deposits using the forged slips went directly into the perpetrator's account. After those three days, the perpetrator withdrew the money, then disappeared. Because he used an alias, his identity was never uncovered nor was he ever found.

In disbursement frauds, the perpetrator causes a company either to pay too much for ordered goods or to pay for goods never ordered. One perpetrator used a desktop publishing package to prepare fraudulent bills for office supplies that were never ordered, then mailed those bills to companies across the country. The perpetrator kept the dollar amount low enough ($300) so that most companies did not bother to require purchase orders or approvals. An amazingly high percentage of the companies paid the bills without question.

To commit inventory fraud, a perpetrator can enter data into the system to show that stolen inventory has been scrapped. For example, several employees at an East Coast railroad entered data into the company's system to show that more than 200 railroad cars were scrapped or destroyed. They removed the cars from the railway system, then repainted and sold them.

To commit payroll frauds, perpetrators can enter data to increase their salary, create a fictitious employee, or retain a terminated employee on the records. Under the latter two approaches, the perpetrator proceeds to intercept and cash the illegal checks.

In a cash receipts fraud, the perpetrator hides the theft by falsifying system input. For example, an employee at the Arizona Veteran's Memorial Coliseum sold customers full-price tickets, entered the sales as half-price tickets, and pocketed the difference.

Processor

Computer fraud can be committed through unauthorized system use, including the theft of computer time and services. For example, some companies do not permit employees to use company computers to keep personal or outside business records. Violating this policy would constitute a fraud. While most people would not call it fraud, **employee goofing** (surfing the Internet for personal entertainment on company time) has become a serious problem at many companies. One study estimates that employees with Internet access, on average, lose 1 to 2 hours of productivity a week goofing.

Computer instructions

Computer fraud can be accomplished by tampering with the software that processes company data. This may include modifying the software, making illegal copies, or using it in an unauthorized manner. It also might include developing a software program or module to carry out an unauthorized activity. This approach to computer fraud used to be one of the least common, because it required a specialized knowledge about computer programming that was beyond the scope of most users. Today, however, such frauds are much more frequent because of the many Web pages that instruct users on how to create viruses and other computer-based schemes.

Data

Computer fraud can be perpetrated by altering or damaging a company's data files or by copying, using, or searching them without authorization. In numerous situations, disgruntled employees have scrambled, altered, or destroyed data files. For example, an employee removed the external labels from hundreds of tape files; another employee used a powerful magnet to scramble the data on magnetic files.

Company data also can be stolen. In one case, the office manager of a Wall Street law firm found information about prospective mergers and acquisitions in the firm's word processing files. He sold the information to friends and relatives, who made several million dollars by illegally trading securities. In another case in Europe, a disgruntled employee removed a company's data files from the computer room. He then drove to the off-site storage location and removed the company's backup files. He demanded $500,000 in return for the files, but was arrested while trying to exchange the tapes for the ransom. In another case, a software engineer stole secrets about the manufacture of Intel microprocessors. Because the manufacturing plans could be read but not copied or printed, he videotaped the plans screen by screen.

At Levi Strauss & Co., a thief removed a hard drive that contained the names, addresses, Social Security numbers, and bank account numbers of over 20,000 employees. Although the hard drive can be replaced for a couple of hundred dollars and the data restored to it from a backup copy of the data, the potential loss could run into the hundreds of millions of dollars if the sensitive data are used to apply for fraudulent credit cards or loans.

Data also can be destroyed, changed, or defaced—particularly if stored on a company Web site. For instance, vandals broke into the NCAA's Web site just before the pairings were announced for the basketball tournament and posted swastikas, racial slurs, and a white-power logo. The U.S. Air Force, CIA, and NASA have also been the victims of high-profile attacks on their Web sites. An analyst at the Computer Security Institute described the problem as "cyberspace vandals with digital spray cans."

One noted hacker stated that all companies that use the Web, especially those with important trade secrets or valuable IT assets, are under constant attack. The attackers include disaffected employees, industrial spies, foreign governments, hackers and crackers, terrorist groups, and competitors.

Output

Computer fraud can be carried out by stealing or misusing system output. System output is usually displayed on monitors or printed on paper. Unless properly safeguarded, monitor and printer output is subject to prying eyes and unauthorized copying. A study by a Dutch engineer shows that many computer monitors emit a televisionlike signal that can be picked up, restructured with the help of some inexpensive electronic gear, and displayed on a standard television screen. Under ideal conditions these signals can be picked up from terminals as far away as two miles. During one experiment, the engineer was able to set up his equipment in the basement of an apartment building and read the screen on a terminal located on the eighth floor.

Computer Fraud and Abuse Techniques

Over the years, perpetrators have devised many methods to commit computer fraud. This section discusses some of the more common techniques, as summarized in Table 9-3.

Table 9-3 Computer Fraud and Abuse Techniques

Technique	Description
Cracking	Unauthorized access to and use of computer systems, usually by means of a personal computer and a telecommunications network. Crackers are hackers with malicious intentions.
Data diddling	Changing data before, during, or after it is entered into the system to delete, alter, or add key system data.
Data leakage	Unauthorized copying of company data such as computer files.
Denial-of-service attack	Attacker sends e-mail bombs (hundreds of messages per second) from randomly generated false addresses; Internet service provider's e-mail server is overloaded and shuts down.
Eavesdropping	Listening to private voice or data transmissions, often using a wiretap.
E-mail forgery	Sending an e-mail message that looks as if it were sent by someone else.
E-mail threats	Sending a threatening message to try and get the recipient to do something that would make it possible to defraud them.
Hacking	Unauthorized access to and use of computer systems, usually by means of a personal computer and a telecommunications network. Hackers do not intend to cause any damage.
Internet misinformation	Using the Internet to spread false or misleading information about companies.
Internet terrorism	Using the Internet to disrupt electronic commerce and to destroy company and individual communications.
Logic time bomb	Program that lies idle until some specified circumstance or a particular time triggers it. Once triggered, the bomb sabotages the system by destroying programs, data, or both.
Masquerading or impersonation	Perpetrator gains access to the system by pretending to be an authorized user; enjoys same privileges as the legitimate user.
Password cracking	Intruder penetrates a system's defenses, steals the file containing valid passwords, decrypts them, and then uses them to gain access to system resources such as programs, files, and data.
Piggybacking	Tapping into a telecommunications line and latching on to a legitimate user before he or she logs into the system; legitimate user unknowingly carries perpetrator into the system.
Round-down	Computer rounds down all interest calculations to two decimal places. Remaining fraction of a cent is placed in an account controlled by the perpetrator.
Salami technique	Tiny slices of money are stolen over a period of time. (Expenses are increased by a fraction of a percent; increments are placed in a dummy account and later pocketed by the perpetrator.)
Scavenging	Gaining access to confidential information by searching corprate records. Scavenging methods range from searching trashcans for printouts or copies of confidential information to scanning the contents of computer memory.
Social engineering	Perpetrator tricks an employee into providing the information needed to get into a system.
Software piracy	Copying computer software without the publisher's permission.

(continued)

287

Spamming	E-mailing the same message to everyone on one or more Usenet news groups or LISTSERV lists.
Superzapping	Unauthorized use of special system programs to bypass regular system controls and perform illegal acts.
Trap door	Perpetrator enters the system using a back door that bypasses normal system controls and perpetrates fraud.
Trojan horse	Unauthorized computer instructions in an authorized and properly functioning program.
Virus	Segment of executable code that attaches itself to software, replicates itself, and spreads to other systems or files. Triggered by a predefined event, a virus damages system resources or displays a message on the monitor.
War dialing	Programming a computer to search for an idle modem by dialing thousands of phone lines. Perpetrator enters the system though the idle modem, captures the personal computer attached to the modem, and gains access to the network(s) to which the personal computer is attached.
Worm	Similar to a virus, except that it is a program rather than a code segment hidden in a host program. A worm also copies and actively transmits itself directly to other systems. It usually does not live very long, but is quite destructive while alive.

A **Trojan horse** is a set of unauthorized computer instructions in an authorized and otherwise properly functioning program. It performs some illegal act at a preappointed time or under a predetermined set of conditions. Trojan horses are often placed in software that is billed as helpful add-ons to popular software programs. For example, several thousand America Online subscribers were sent messages containing an offer of free software. Users who opened the attachments unknowingly unleashed a Trojan horse that secretly copied the subscriber's account name and password and forwarded it to the sender. Another type of Trojan horse monitors a user's keystrokes, captures credit card numbers, and sends them by e-mail to the software's creator.

In another case, visitors to adult sites were told to download a special program to see the pictures. This program had embedded code that turned off the volume on their modems, disconnected them from their Internet service providers, and connected them to a service in the former USSR. The program kept them connected to this site, at $2 a minute, until they turned off their computers. Over 800,000 minutes were billed, with some phone bills as high as $3,000, before the scam was detected.

The **round-down technique** is used most frequently in financial institutions that pay interest. In the typical scenario, the programmer instructs the computer to round down all interest calculations to two decimal places. The fraction of a cent that is rounded down on each calculation is put into the programmer's account or one that he or she controls. No one is the wiser, since all the books balance. Over time these fractions of a cent can add up to a significant amount, especially when interest is calculated daily.

With the **salami technique,** tiny slices of money are stolen over a period of time. For example, a disgruntled chief accountant for a produce-growing company in

California used this technique to get even with his employer. He used the company's computer system to falsify and systematically increase all the company's production costs by a fraction of a percent. These tiny increments were put into the accounts of dummy customers and then pocketed by the accountant. Every few months the fraudulent costs were raised another fraction of a percent. Because all expenses were rising together, no single account or expense would call attention to the fraud. The accountant was eventually caught when an alert teller failed to recognize the payee name on a check the perpetrator was trying to cash and brought it to her manager's attention.

A **trap door,** or back door, is a way into a system that bypasses normal system controls. Programmers use trap doors to modify programs during systems development and normally remove them before the system is put into operation. When a trap door is not removed before the program is implemented, anyone who discovers it can enter the program and commit a fraud. Programmers can also insert trap doors before they are terminated, allowing them access to the system after they leave.

Superzapping is the unauthorized use of special system programs to bypass regular system controls and perform illegal acts. The name of this technique is derived from a software utility, called Superzap, developed by IBM to handle emergencies, such as restoring a system that has crashed.

Software piracy is copying software without the publisher's permission. It is estimated that for every legal copy of software sold, between seven and eight illegal ones are made. Within days of being released, most new software is on a bulletin board and available free to those who want to download it illegally. An estimated 26 percent of software used in the United States is pirated. In some countries, this figure is over 90 percent. The software industry estimates the economic losses of piracy at between $15 billion and $18 billion a year.

Piracy is such a serious problem that the Software Publishers Association (SPA, which represents more than 500 software publishers) files lawsuits against companies and individuals. One lawsuit claimed the University of Oregon's Continuing Education Center violated copyright law by making illegal and unauthorized copies of programs and training manuals. The university settled the case by agreeing to (1) pay a $130,000 fine; (2) launch a campaign to educate its faculty, staff, and students on the lawful use of software; and (3) host a national conference on copyright law and software use. In another case, the Business Software Alliance found 1,400 copies of unlicensed software at an adult vocational school in the Los Angeles Unified School District and claimed $5 million in damages.

Individuals convicted of software piracy are subject to fines of up to $250,000 and jail terms of up to 5 years. However, the SPA often negotiates more creative punishments. For example, a Puget Sound student caught distributing copyrighted software over the Internet was required to write a 20-page paper on the evils of software piracy and copyright infringement and also had to perform 50 hours of community service wiring schools for Internet usage. Failure to comply with either item would have subjected him to a $10,000 fine and resulted in a lawsuit for copyright infringement.

Data diddling is changing data before, during, or after it is entered into the system. The change can be made to delete, alter, or add key system data. For example, a clerk for a Denver brokerage altered a transaction to record 1,700 shares of Loren Industries stock worth about $2,500 as shares in Long Island Lighting worth more than $25,000.

Data leakage refers to the unauthorized copying of company data. The *Encyclopedia Britannica* claimed losses in the millions of dollars when an employee made copies of its customer list and began selling them to other companies. Ten Social Security Administration employees sold 11,000 Social Security numbers (and other identifying information such as the mother's maiden name) to credit card fraudsters.

Piggybacking is tapping into a telecommunications line and latching on to a legitimate user before the user logs into a system. The legitimate user unknowingly carries the perpetrator into the system.

In **masquerading,** or **impersonation,** the perpetrator gains access to the system by pretending to be an authorized user. This approach requires a perpetrator to know the legitimate user's ID number and password. Once inside the system, the perpetrator enjoys the same privileges as the legitimate user being impersonated.

In **social engineering,** perpetrators trick employees into giving them the information they need to get into the system. They might call saying they are conducting a security survey and lull the person into disclosing confidential information. They may call help desks and claim to be an employee who has forgotten a password, or may call users and say they are from network engineering and are testing the system and need a password. They also pose as buyers or salespeople to get plant tours and obtain information that may help them break into the system.

A **logic time bomb** is a program that lies idle until some specified circumstance or a particular time triggers it. Once triggered, the bomb sabotages the system by destroying programs, data, or both. Most bombs are written by disgruntled programmers who want to get even with their company. Donald Burleson, a former security officer, set off a bomb that erased 168,000 sales commissions records. As a result, company paychecks were held up for a month. The program, which was attached to a legitimate one, was designed to go off periodically and erase more records. A fellow programmer who was testing a new employee bonus system discovered the bomb before it could go off again. The company's computers were shut down for two days while the bomb was diffused.

Hacking, or **cracking,** is the unauthorized access to and use of computer systems, usually by means of a personal computer and a telecommunications network. Hackers do not intend to cause any damage. They are usually motivated by the challenge of breaking into computer systems and are just browsing or looking for things to copy and keep. Crackers are hackers with malicious intentions. For example, during Operation Desert Storm, Dutch crackers broke into 34 different military computer sites and extracted confidential information. Among the information stolen were the troop movements and weapons used in the Iraq war. The group offered to sell the information to Iraq, but the government declined, probably because of the fear of being set up.

Hackers and crackers have broken into the computers of governmental agencies such as the U.S. Department of Defense, NASA, and the Los Alamos National Laboratory. One 17-year-old cracker, nicknamed Shadow Hawk, was convicted of electronically penetrating the Bell Laboratories national network, destroying files valued at $174,000, and copying 52 proprietary software programs worth $1.2 million. He published confidential information, such as telephone numbers, passwords, and instructions on how to breach AT&T's computer security system, on underground bulletin boards. He was sentenced to nine months in prison and given a $10,000 fine. Like Shadow Hawk, many hackers are fairly young, some as young as 12 and 13.

Scavenging, or **dumpster diving,** is gaining access to confidential information by searching corporate records. Scavenging methods range from searching trashcans for printouts or carbon copies of confidential information to scanning the contents of computer memory. In one case, Jerry Schneider, a high school student, noticed a trashcan full of papers on his way home from school. Rummaging through them, he discovered operating guides for Pacific Telephone computers. Over time his scavenging activities resulted in a technical library that later allowed him to steal $1 million worth of electronic equipment. In another case, in South America, a man attached a video camera to a car battery, hid it in some bushes, and pointed it at the company president's window. The president had an office on the first floor and his computer monitor faced the window. A significant business acquisition almost fell through as a result of the information on the videotape.

Eavesdropping enables perpetrators to observe private communications or transmissions of data. One way to intercept signals is by setting up a **wiretap.** The equipment needed to wiretap an unprotected communications line is readily available at local electronics stores. One alleged wiretapping fraud involved Mark Koenig, a 28-year-old consultant to GTE, and four associates. Federal agents say they pulled personal identification numbers and other crucial information about Bank of America customers from GTE telephone lines, and used the data to make 5,500 fake ATM cards. Koenig and his friends allegedly intended to use the cards over one long weekend to withdraw money from banks all over the country. Authorities were tipped off, however, and the criminals were apprehended before they could use the cards.

Fraud perpetrators are beginning to use unsolicited **e-mail threats** to defraud people. For example, Global Communications sent a message to many people threatening legal action if an unspecified overdue amount was not paid within 24 hours. The message also stated that court action could be avoided by calling Mike Murray at an 809 area code (which is for islands in the Caribbean). People who called got a clever recording that sounded like a live person and responded to the caller's voice. The responses were designed to keep callers on the phone as long as possible, because they were being billed at $25 per minute.

In another instance, a man posed as a woman on a chat line and lured men into erotic conversations. After a while "she" offered them revealing pictures of herself. The men who asked for the pictures got, instead, a very angry letter from her "husband" threatening physical violence unless they paid him money.

It is also possible to commit **e-mail forgery** in a couple of different ways. One way is to send an e-mail message through a re-mailer who removes the message headers, thereby making the message anonymous. Another way is to make the e-mail message look as if someone else sent it. For example, a former Oracle employee was charged with breaking into the company's computer network, falsifying evidence, and committing perjury for forging an e-mail message to support her charge that she was fired for breaking up a relationship with the company's chief executive. She faces up to six years in jail for her activities.

A **denial-of-service attack** occurs when an attacker sends **e-mail bombs:** The perpetrator sends so many messages (hundreds per second) from randomly generated false addresses that the Internet service provider's e-mail server is overloaded and shuts down. Other denial-of-service attacks include sending so much data to a network or Web server that it crashes. These attacks go by such creative names as Bonk, Boink, Syn-flood,

Ping of Death, WinNuke, and LandAttack. One Syn-flood attack shut down more than 3,000 Web sites for 40 hours on one of the busiest shopping weekends of the year.

Internet terrorism occurs when crackers use the Internet to disrupt electronic commerce and to destroy company and individual communications. For example, a cracker developed a program that erased messages and unleashed it at Usenet, an Internet bulletin board system. The program destroyed 25,000 messages before it could be removed from the system.

Internet misinformation is using the Internet to spread false or misleading information about companies. This can be done in a number of ways, including inflammatory messages in on-line chats, setting up Web sites, and spreading urban legends. For example, a representative from the Tommy Hilfiger Corp. was supposedly kicked off the Oprah Winfrey show for making racist remarks. This information, together with a call to boycott the company, quickly spread throughout the world on the Internet. This urban legend was totally false, and Hilfiger quickly went to the Net to deny the story. McDonald's spent seven years fighting a large number of false accusations that were spread using pamphlets and Web sites. McDonald's finally won the case after 313 days of testimony and an expenditure of $16 million. McDonald's was awarded $94,000. Immediately after the verdict, one anti-McDonald's Web site mocked the verdict and called its campaign against McDonald's "unstoppable."

Crackers who search for an idle modem by programming their computers to dial thousands of phone lines are **war dialing.** Crackers can enter through the idle modem, capture the PC attached to the modem, and then gain access to the network to which it is connected. This approach got its name from the movie *War Games.*

Password cracking occurs when an intruder penetrates a system's defenses, steals the file containing valid passwords, decrypts them, and then uses them to gain access to system resources such as programs, files, and data.

Spamming is e-mailing the same message to everyone on one or more Usenet newsgroups or LISTSERV lists. The spammer may consider this a fun prank or a perfect, inexpensive, and legal way to reach potential customers; however, many in the Internet community take a dim view of these pranks and types of business practices. In retaliation, some spammers have been spammed in return with thousands of messages, causing their e-mail service to fail. Such retaliation, however, affects many innocent users of the same system and can result in their e-mail accounts being closed. A better approach is to e-mail the person in charge of the spammer's site. (If the spammer's address is gorilla@zoo.com, his administrator is postmaster@zoo.com.) An example of a spam is one called "MAKE.MONEY.FAST," which was sent to thousands of groups. It was nothing more that the Usenet equivalent of a chain letter.

Computer Viruses

A **computer virus** is a segment of executable code that attaches itself to software. Most viruses have two phases. In the first phase, the virus replicates itself and spreads to other systems or files. The replication phase is usually triggered by some predefined event, such as the computer being turned on; using or exiting software; creating, opening, or closing a document; reaching a specific date; or the software containing the virus being used a specific number of times. In the attack phase, which also is triggered by some predefined event, the virus carries out its mission. Both phases can be triggered at the same time, or the virus can be secretly replicated and set to go off at a later time. Many viruses lie dormant for extended periods of time without causing any specific damage, except to propagate themselves.

Viruses can destroy or alter data or programs, take control of the computer, destroy the hard disk's file allocation table, delete or rename files or directories, reformat the hard disk, change the content of files, or keep users from booting the system or accessing data on a hard disk. A virus can intercept and change transmissions, print disruptive images or messages on the screen or change its color, or cause the screen image to disappear. As the virus spreads, it takes up space, clogs communications, and hinders system performance. A particularly bad virus attack shut down a bank with 200 servers and 10,000 desktop computers for four days. During the downtime, the bank was locked out of its system and customer accounts could not be accessed. A firm that specializes in fixing virus attacks was eventually able to restore the system.

There are several ways computers can become infected: (1) by opening an e-mail attachment that contains a virus, (2) by opening a file that contains a virus, (3) by booting, or starting, the computer with an infected diskette (called a boot sector virus), and (4) by running a program that has been infected (a program file virus). Symptoms of a computer virus include computers that will not boot, programs that will not execute, unexpected read or write operations, an inability to save files to the A: drive, bad sectors on diskettes, long program load times, abnormally large file sizes, slow systems operation, and unusual screen activity, error messages, or file names.

Viruses are contagious and are easily spread from one system to another. For example, the National Computer Security Association estimated that in just one year, the number of U.S. businesses infected by viruses tripled, even though the use of antivirus software increased. To spread rapidly, a virus must be introduced into a network with a large number of computers. In a relatively short time, the virus can spread to thousands of systems. When the virus is confined to a single machine or to a small LAN, it will soon run out of computers to infect. A virus also spreads when users send e-mail messages, share programs or files, or when they access and use programs from external sources such as bulletin boards and suppliers of free software. Research shows that e-mail containing hidden viruses is the fastest growing way to spread them. E-mail and macro viruses contained in common word processing and spreadsheet files are the most common viruses.

Many computer viruses have long lives because they can create copies of themselves faster than they can be destroyed. A number of viruses, such as Stone and Jerusalem-B, have spread so furiously that they have become epidemics. According to a survey conducted by Dataquest, 63 percent of the 600,000 personal computer users surveyed had experienced a virus and 38 percent of those affected had lost data. Virus creators are beginning to make viruses that mutate each time they infect a computer, making them much more difficult to detect and destroy.

A **worm** is like a virus, except that it is a program rather than a code segment hidden in a host program. Worms often reside in e-mail attachments, which, when opened or activated, can damage the user's system. Worms often reproduce by mailing themselves to the recipient's mailing list, resulting in an electronic chain letter. Some recent worms have completely shut down the e-mail systems at a number of firms. A worm usually does not live very long, but is quite destructive while alive. One of the more destructive worms, written by Robert T. Morris, affected 6,000 computers in a very short time. Focus 9-1 details the impact of this worm on systems across the country.

Focus 9-1

A Worm Run Amok

SCIENTISTS at Berkeley's Experimental Computing Facility noticed a rash of unknown users trying to log on to their system. The break-in attempts increased in frequency until they could no longer be monitored. Within minutes, the program invaded computer processing space and brought Berkeley's mammoth system to a halt. At this point the scientists realized a program was trying to access the system.

Within 30 minutes, it was clear that the program was not limited to the Berkeley system. It was invading the *entire* Internet. Within hours, computer experts discovered the existence of a powerful "worm" in the Internet. While scientists attempted to stop the worm, law enforcement officials and the press were beginning their own investigations of the unauthorized entry. Information on a possible suspect was scarce until an unidentified phone caller tipped a *New York Times* writer by inadvertently referring to the criminal programmer as "RTM".

Robert Tappan Morris loved computers and challenges. He acquired a passion for computer security issues while working with his father, a scientist at Bell Labs. At Harvard he received extensive recognition for problem-solving work using the school's main computer facility, which was linked to the Internet. Robert's most successful projects centered on improving Bell Systems Internet operations and its operating system, UNIX. At age 20, Robert's skills in UNIX security were so extensive that his father had him address a computer security conference at the National Security Agency. The next day he delivered the same address to the Naval Research Laboratory.

While Robert was attending graduate school at Cornell University, the first computer viruses were receiving national media attention. This sparked Robert's interest in developing an undetectable worm that would invade the Internet. His goal was to reach as many computers as possible. With Robert's background in UNIX security issues and his unlimited access to the Cornell computer system, developing a worm was easy. Robert had discovered three programming flaws in the UNIX operating system that allowed him unauthorized access to any computer on the Internet. Using a bug in the Sendmail subprogram, Robert developed a worm capable of entering a given system without authorization. The worm was designed to replicate and use Sendmail to enter related systems entirely undetected.

When the worm was finished, Robert illegally logged on to the artificial intelligence lab computer at MIT from his system at Cornell and released his creation. After dinner Robert attempted to log on, but the computer did not respond. He immediately knew something was wrong and after several attempts to remedy the problem, the significance of the danger was clear. Robert had made a fatal programming error that allowed the worm to replicate out of control throughout the Internet.

Cleaning out the Internet system and recreating the files that the worm destroyed took several months.

Robert was arrested and charged with a felony violation of the 1986 Counterfeit Access Device and Computer Fraud and Abuse Act, which prohibits unauthorized computer access. In 1990 he was convicted of computer crime and sentenced to three years probation, 400 hours of community service, and a $10,000 fine.

It takes little technical knowledge to create a worm or virus. In fact, several Web sites provide unsophisticated users with an application that enables them to create worms. One such application has been downloaded more than 15,000 times.

PREVENTING AND DETECTING COMPUTER FRAUD

Because fraud is a serious problem, organizations must take every precaution to protect their information systems. Taking certain measures can significantly decrease the potential for fraud and any resulting losses. For example, a company can create a climate that makes fraud less likely, increase the difficulty of committing a fraud, reduce the amount of loss if a fraud occurs, increase the likelihood of detecting fraud, prosecute fraud perpetrators, and increase the penalty for committing fraud. These measures are summarized in Table 9-4.

Make Fraud Less Likely to Occur

Some computer consultants claim that the most effective method of obtaining adequate system security is to rely on the integrity of company employees. At the same time, research shows that current and former employees commit the most fraud. Thus, employees are both the greatest control strength and weakness. Organizations can take steps to increase employee integrity and reduce the likelihood of employees committing a fraud, as described in the following sections.

Use proper hiring and firing practices

As discussed in Chapter 7, one important managerial responsibility is to hire and retain honest people. Similarly, a company should take care when firing employees. To prevent sabotage or copying confidential data before they leave, dismissed employees should be removed from sensitive jobs immediately and denied access to the computer system. One employee, after learning he had been terminated, lit a butane lighter under a smoke detector located just outside the computer room. It set off a sprinkler system that ruined most of the computer hardware in the room.

Because they are not subjected to normal hiring practices such as background checks, some people, intent on breaking into systems, pose as janitors or temporary employees to gain access to the company's site and often to its information system. Once they have legitimate access to the building or the system, they can use any number of techniques to commit fraud or sabotage the system. For this reason, all company personnel, including cleaning crews and temporary employees, should be subject to all hiring and firing policies.

Manage disgruntled employees

Many employees who commit fraud are seeking revenge or justice for some wrong they perceive has been done to them. Hence, companies should have procedures for identifying these individuals and either help them resolve their feelings or remove them from jobs with system access. One way to avoid disgruntled employees and to maintain high company morale is to provide grievance channels and employee counseling. Employees need someone outside the normal chain of command to talk with about their grievances and problems. Having someone who will listen to them and help them resolve their problems can significantly decrease the number of dissatisfied

Table 9-4 Summary of Ways to Prevent and Detect Computer Fraud

Make Fraud Less Likely to Occur
- Use proper hiring and firing practices.
- Manage disgruntled employees.
- Train employees in security and fraud prevention measures.
- Manage and track software licenses.
- Require signed confidentiality agreements.

Increase the Difficulty of Committing Fraud
- Develop a strong system of internal controls.
- Segregate duties.
- Require vacations and rotate duties.
- Restrict access to computer equipment and data files.
- Encrypt data and programs.
- Protect telephone lines.
- Protect the system from viruses.
- Control sensitive data.
- Control laptop computers.
- Monitor hacker information.

Improve Detection Methods
- Conduct frequent audits.
- Use a computer security officer.
- Set up a fraud hot line.
- Use computer consultants.
- Monitor system activities.
- Use forensic accountants.
- Use fraud detection software.

Reduce Fraud Losses
- Maintain adequate insurance.
- Store backup copies of program and data files in a secure off-site location.
- Develop a contingency plan for fraud occurrences.
- Use software to monitor system activity and recover from fraud.

Prosecute and Incarcerate Fraud Perpetrators

employees. This is often not easy to accomplish, because most employees fear that airing their feelings could have negative consequences for their careers.

Train employees in security and fraud prevention measures

Many top executives believe that employee training and education are the most important elements of any security program. Fraud is much less likely to occur in an environment where employees believe security is everyone's business. An ideal corporate culture for fraud deterrence exists when employees are proud of their company and are protective of its assets. They believe they have a responsibility to report fraud, because what harms the company harms them. This culture does not just happen. It has to be created, taught, and practiced. Therefore, a company should educate and train employees in the following areas:

➤ *Security measures.* Employees should be taught why security measures are important and should be motivated to take them very seriously. Security should be monitored and enforced as a way of reinforcing this training.

➤ *Telephone disclosures.* Employees should not give out confidential information over the telephone without knowing for sure who is calling. Employees can use tactics such as dialing the caller back and verifying a person's identity by asking penetrating and specific questions that only that person would be able to answer.

➤ *Fraud awareness.* Employees should be made aware of fraud's prevalence and its dangers. They should be taught why people commit fraud and how to deter and detect it.

➤ *Ethical considerations.* The company should promote its ethical standards in its practices and through company literature such as employee handouts. Acceptable and unacceptable behavior should be defined so that employees are aware of a company's ethical position should a problem arise. Many business practices fall into a gray area between right and wrong, especially in the computer industry. For example, many professionals see nothing wrong with using corporate computer resources for personal use or gaining unauthorized access to another company's databases and browsing through them. When arrested for unauthorized browsing, one programmer was shocked that he was prosecuted, because he believed his activities were a common industry practice.

➤ *Punishment for unethical behavior.* Employees should be informed of the consequences of unethical behavior (reprimands, dismissal, and prosecution). This information should be disseminated not as a threat but as the consequence of choosing to act unethically. For example, employees should be informed that using a computer to steal or commit fraud is a federal crime and anyone doing so faces immediate dismissal and/or prosecution. Likewise, the company should display notices of program and data ownership and inform employees of the penalties of misuse.

Educating employees in security issues, fraud awareness, ethical considerations, and the consequences of choosing to act unethically can make a tremendous difference. This education can be accomplished by conducting informal discussions and formal meetings, issuing periodic departmental memos, distributing written guidelines and codes of professional ethics, circulating reports of securities violations and their consequences, and promoting security and fraud training programs.

Manage and track software licenses

Software license management, a fast-growing area of IT management, helps companies to comply with their software licenses. Of key concern is making sure there are enough licenses to meet user demands and that there are not more users than licenses. This protects companies from software piracy lawsuits. It can also save a company money by ensuring that it does not pay for more licenses than it actually uses or needs.

Require signed confidentiality agreements

All employees, suppliers, and contractors should be required to sign and abide by a confidentiality agreement.

Increase the Difficulty of Committing Fraud

One way to deter fraud is to design a system with sufficient controls to make fraud difficult to perpetrate. These controls help ensure the accuracy, integrity, and safety of system resources. This section discusses how companies can develop a strong system of internal controls and details some of the more important fraud prevention techniques.

Develop a strong system of internal controls

It is management's responsibility to develop a secure and adequately controlled system. Managers typically delegate the design of adequate control systems to systems analysts, designers, and end users. The corporate information security officer and the operations staff are typically responsible for ensuring that control procedures are followed.

To develop efficient and cost-effective controls, designers should follow the risk assessment strategy shown in Figure 7-2. These controls are much more effective when placed in the system as it is built, rather than as an afterthought. Management must also establish a set of procedures to ensure control compliance and enforcement.

It is especially important to ensure that internal controls are in place during the end-of-the-year holiday season. Research shows that a disproportionate amount of computer fraud and security break-ins takes place during this time. Some reasons for this are (1) extended employee vacations when fewer people are around to "mind the store," (2) students are out of school and have more time on their hands, and (3) counterculture hackers get lonely this time of year and increase their attacks on systems.

Segregate duties

As discussed in Chapter 7, there must be an adequate segregation of duties to prevent individuals from stealing assets and covering their tracks.

Require vacations and rotate duties

Many fraud schemes, such as lapping and kiting, require the ongoing attention of the perpetrator. If mandatory vacations were coupled with a temporary rotation of duties, such ongoing fraud schemes would fall apart. For example, when federal investigators raided an illegal gambling establishment, they found that Roswell Steffen, who earned $11,000 a year, was betting up to $30,000 a day at the racetrack. Investigators at Union Dime Savings Bank discovered he had embezzled and gambled away $1.5 million of the bank's money over a three-year period. A compulsive gambler, Steffen began by borrowing $5,000 to place a bet on a sure thing that did not pan out. He embezzled ever increasing amounts in an effort to win back the original money he had "borrowed."

Steffen committed his fraud by transferring money from inactive accounts to his own account. If the owner of an inactive account complained, Steffen, the chief teller who had the power to resolve these types of problems, replaced the money by taking it from another inactive account. After being caught and asked how the fraud could have been prevented, he said the bank could have coupled a two-week vacation period with several weeks of rotation to another job function. That would have made his embezzlement, which required his physical presence at the bank and his constant attention, almost impossible to cover up.

Restrict access to computer equipment and data files

Computer fraud can be reduced significantly if access to computer equipment and data files is restricted. Physical access to computer equipment should be restricted, and legitimate users should be authenticated before they are allowed to use the system. Unfortunately, companies often fail to delete or change ID codes and passwords when employees leave or are transferred to another department. A favorite electronic espionage tactic is to gain access to a building and plug into an Ethernet jack in the wall and talk to the system. This can be prevented by configuring the system to only respond to hardware that it recognizes.

Encrypt data and programs

Another way to protect data is to translate them into a secret code, thereby making them meaningless to anyone without the means to decipher them. Data encryption is explained in Chapter 3.

Protect telephone lines

Computer hackers (called **phreakers** when they attack phone systems) use telephone lines to transmit viruses and to access, steal, and destroy data. They also steal telephone services. One company lost $4.5 million in three days when its system was compromised and details on how to use its phone lines were published on the Internet. Phreakers also break into voice mail systems, as the New York Police Department learned. Staff changed the voice mail greeting to say that officers were too busy drinking coffee and eating doughnuts to answer the phone and to call 119 (not 911) in case of an emergency.

One effective method to protect telephone lines is to attach an electronic lock and key to them. When one such device was tested, researchers concluded that it would take a hacker 188 days working nonstop to break the more than 1 trillion combinations. Few hackers would make the attempt, and if they did, they would most likely be detected before they were successful. When a new phone system is installed, never use the default passwords as they are all published on the Internet. On established systems, change the passwords frequently.

Some crackers gain access to systems through dial-up modem lines. For example, a company in Silicon Valley refused to let workers have Internet access at work because of the fear that crackers would compromise its systems. Engineers at the company thought they needed Internet access to get their work done and bought $50 modems for their analog telephone lines. Security took away their access by replacing their analog lines with digital lines. Not to be outdone, the engineers requested fax lines, which were analog. Security never found out about the fax lines until a disgruntled ex-employee had his computer dial all company numbers looking for the screech of a modem. The former employee entered through the modem line and caused considerable damage to the system. Another Silicon Valley company, Sun Microsystems, has made it a firing offense to use a modem on a desktop computer, and employees caught using them are sent packing that very day.

Protect the system from viruses

There are hundreds of thousands of virus attacks every year, and an estimated 90 percent of the PCs that suffer a virus attack are reinfected within 30 days by the same virus or some other virus. A system can be protected from viruses by following the guidelines listed in Focus 9-2.

Focus 9-2

Keeping Your Microcomputers Virus-Free

Here are some practical suggestions for protecting computers from viruses:

- Install reliable antivirus software that scans for, identifies, and destroys viruses. Some antivirus packages use neural networks to seek out software that behaves like a virus. The suspected code is sent to a software lab via the Internet and tested. If the code is a virus, the lab develops an antidote and sends it back to the user via the Internet.

- Scan all incoming e-mail for viruses at the server level rather than when it hits users' desktops.

- Do not put your diskettes or CD in strange machines; your diskette or CD may become infected. Do not let others put their diskettes in your drives; your machine may become infected. Scan all new diskettes and CDs and all new files with antiviral software before any data or programs are copied to your machine.

- Use write-protect tabs that prohibit writing to diskettes. A virus cannot spread to a write-protected diskette.

- Obtain software, diskettes and CDs only from known and trusted sources. Although the likelihood of contracting a virus in this manner is small, even this software may be infected.

- Be wary of software, diskettes or CDs from unknown sources. They may be virus bait, especially if their prices or functionality sound too good to be true.

- Deal with trusted software retailers. Some dealers rewrap and sell used software as if it were new.

- Some software suppliers use electronic techniques to make tampering evident. Ask if the software you are purchasing has such protection.

- Write-protect new software diskettes before installing them to prevent infection and to provide you with backup.

- Check new software on an isolated machine with virus detection software. Software direct from the publisher has been known to have viruses.

- When you restart, use the "power-off—power-on" to clear and reset the system. It is possible for a virus to survive a warm start-up using the Ctrl-Alt-Del or Reset keys.

- It is safer to start up or boot the machine from a write-protected diskette than from a hard disk. This type of start-up will resist viruses that obtain control via the hard disk's boot sector.

- Have two backups of all files. Data files should be backed up separately from programs to avoid contaminating backup data. Keep write-protected copies of original disks and restore from them.

- Restrict the use of public bulletin boards. All outside software should be certified as virus-free before loading it into the system.

Source: Deloitte and Touche, *Information Protection Review,* 2(1): 6.

Fortunately, some very good virus protection programs are available. Virus protection programs are designed to remain in computer memory and search for viruses trying to infiltrate the system. The intrusion is usually detected when an unauthorized user attempts to access an executable program. When an infection attempt is detected, the software freezes the system and flashes a message to the user. The user can then instruct the program to remove the virus. Virus detection programs, which spot an infection soon after it starts, are more reliable than virus protection programs.

Virus identification programs scan all executable programs to find and remove known viruses from the system. These programs work by scanning the system for specific characteristics of known virus strains.

Make sure that the latest versions of the antivirus programs are used. National City Bank in Cleveland, Ohio, installed some new laptops on its system. The manufacturer and the bank checked the laptops for viruses, but did not use the latest antivirus software. A virus spread from the hard drive of the laptops to 300 network servers and 12,000 workstations. It took the bank over two days to completely eradicate the virus from all bank systems.

Control sensitive data

To protect its sensitive data, a company should classify all of its data as to importance and confidentiality and then apply and enforce appropriate access restrictions. It should shred discarded paper documents. Controls can be placed over data files to prevent or discourage copying. Employees should be informed of the consequences of using illegal copies of software, and the company should institute controls to ensure that illegal copies are not in use. Sensitive and confidential information, backup tapes, and system documentation should be locked away when not in use. Servers and PCs should also be locked when unattended. Companies should never store all data in one place or give an employee access to everything. To avoid infection by a network computer, local area networks can use dedicated servers that allow data to be downloaded but never uploaded. Closed-circuit televisions can be used to monitor areas where sensitive data or easily stolen assets are handled.

Some organizations with particularly sensitive data are installing diskless PCs or workstations. All data are stored centrally in a network and users download the necessary data each day. At day's end, all data to be saved must be stored in the network, thereby controlling the problem of unguarded information created and stored in desktop computers. Users can delete or destroy only the data on their screens; thus, the company's data are secure and the system is virtually immune to disasters that a user might intentionally or unintentionally cause. In addition, without disks, users cannot introduce viruses into the system with contaminated diskettes; nor does the company lose valuable data, because employees cannot copy company data on diskettes and remove them from the premises.

Control laptop computers

Special care should be given to laptop computers, because thieves are increasingly breaking into cars and hotel rooms to steal them for the confidential information they contain. According to one insurance company, 1 of 14 laptops purchased is stolen. To improve laptop security, companies should do the following:

➤ Make staff aware of the significant threats laptops face.
➤ Establish laptop security policies that require employees who are traveling to back up data to a separate source, and to never leave a laptop unattended, or lock it to a large object when left unattended.
➤ Engrave the company name or logo and a phone number on the PC.
➤ Install software that makes it impossible for the computer to boot up without a password.

➤ Password protect and encrypt data on the hard disk so that if a laptop is stolen, the data cannot be used.

➤ Install motion detectors that can emit a loud shriek if the machine is moved.

➤ Install software that periodically disables the laptop's sound and dials a toll-free number to check in. Laptops reported stolen are told to call every five minutes so police can locate them.

➤ Instruct employees to store confidential data on a disk or CD, rather than the hard drive, and always keep the disks or CDs in their possession or locked in a safe place.

Monitor hacker information

Underground journals, books, and cracker Web sites contain a great deal of information on how to break into systems. For example, there are articles on how to breach a server, generate virus code, and hide your identity in cyberspace. Details on how to take advantage of newly discovered security holes are published almost daily. It is important to monitor these sites and find postings that pertain to systems that your company uses so they can be protected from hacker attacks.

Improve Detection Methods

Many companies are currently being defrauded without their knowledge. The following steps can be taken to detect fraud as soon as possible.

Conduct frequent audits

One way to increase the likelihood of detecting fraud and computer abuses is to conduct periodic external and internal audits as well as special network security audits. Auditors should regularly test system controls and periodically browse data files looking for suspicious activities. However, care must be exercised to make sure employees' privacy rights are not violated. Informing employees that auditors will conduct a **random surveillance** not only helps resolve the privacy issue but also significantly deters computer crime. One large financial institution that implemented this strategy uncovered several abuses, including some that resulted in the termination of one employee and the reprimand of another. Systems auditing is detailed in Chapter 10.

Use a computer security officer

Most frauds are not detected by internal or external auditors. In a study published in the *Sloan Management Review,* auditors uncovered only 4.5 percent of 259 cases of fraud. Normal system controls uncovered 45 percent, accidental discovery uncovered 32 percent, and computer security officers found 8 percent. The study shows that assigning responsibility for fraud deterrence and detection to a **computer security officer** has a significant deterrent effect. This person should be independent of the information system function. The security officer can monitor the system and disseminate information about improper system uses and their consequences. Charles Schwab has implemented this strategy and has a fraud unit of more than 20 IT people who constantly assess and monitor internal and external network traffic operations.

To prevent economic espionage, the computer security officer should head an information security committee that includes all departments that create, access, maintain, and use confidential information. The committee should develop procedures to identify, store, handle, transmit, and dispose of confidential information. It should also develop a comprehensive information security program, including components such as nondisclosure statements for employees, contractors, vendors, and visitors. It is especially important that the computer security officer work closely with the person in charge of building security, as that is often a company's weakest security leak.

Set up a fraud hot line

People witnessing fraudulent behavior are often torn between two conflicting feelings. They want to protect company assets and report fraud perpetrators, yet they are uncomfortable in the whistle-blower role and find it easier to remain silent. This reluctance is even stronger if they are aware of whistle-blowers who have been ostracized or persecuted by their coworkers or superiors, or have had their careers damaged.

An effective way to resolve this conflict is to provide employees with hot lines so they can anonymously report fraud. In one study, researchers found that anonymous tips uncovered 33 percent of the 212 frauds studied. The insurance industry set up a hot line in an attempt to control an estimated $17 billion a year in fraudulent claims. In the first month, more than 2,250 calls were received; 15 percent of these resulted in investigative action. The downside of hot lines is that many of the calls are not worthy of investigation. Some are made seeking revenge, others are vague reports of wrongdoing, and others have no merit.

A potential problem with a hot line is that those who operate it may report to people who are involved in top-management fraud. Using a fraud hot line set up by a trade organization or commercial company can overcome this threat. This company can pass reports of management fraud directly to the board of directors.

Use computer consultants

Many companies use outside computer consultants or in-house teams to test and evaluate their security procedures and computer systems. Each security weakness or means of breaching the system that is detected is closely evaluated, and corresponding protective measures are implemented. Some companies dislike this approach, because they do not want their weaknesses exposed or their employees to know that the system can be breached.

Several of the largest accounting firms have more than 1,000 computer risk management specialists, and more than half of their chargeable hours are spent on security matters. The Federal Reserve Bank of New York has three full-time people (Tiger Teamers) who test the system for weaknesses. These teams try everything possible to compromise a company's system. To get into offices to locate passwords or access computers, the teamers masquerade as janitors, temporary workers, or confused delivery personnel. They also use sexy decoys to distract guards, climb through roof hatches, and drop through ceiling panels. Some outside consultants claim that they can get into 90 percent or more of the companies they attack.

In one documented case, a consultant was hired to find out who was leaking corporate secrets to a competitor. The culprit was a young vice president who was not careful with his laptop or passwords. When the vice president would not believe him, the consultant had a beautiful member of his staff put on a slinky little dress and talk her way past security guards by telling them she wanted to surprise her husband with her pregnancy test results. A few minutes later she left the building with the vice president's laptop.

So-called white-hat organizations monitor hackers and their activities and then publish the findings on Web pages. These pages explain how to perpetrate all known hacking activities. The sites then explain how network administrators can protect themselves from each hacking approach, and they provide information system managers with a valuable way to learn about the latest security threats and how to protect themselves from those threats.

Monitor system activities

All system transactions and activities should be recorded in a log which indicates who accessed what data, when, and from which terminal. These logs should be reviewed frequently to monitor system activity and trace any problems to their source.

Several risk analysis and management software packages are available to review computer systems and networks. These systems evaluate established security measures and test for weaknesses and vulnerabilities. A series of reports is then generated that explains the weaknesses found and suggests improvements. Cost parameters can be entered so that a company can balance acceptable levels of vulnerability and cost-effectiveness. Intrusion-detection programs and software utilities also can detect illegal entry into systems.

Use forensic accountants

Forensic accountants specialize in fraud auditing and investigation, and of late this has been the fastest-growing area in accounting. Many forensic accountants have degrees in accounting and have received specialized training with the FBI, the IRS, or other law enforcement agencies. A professional designation has also been created to recognize this field. The Association of Certified Fraud Examiners in Austin, Texas, has developed a Certified Fraud Examiner (CFE) certification program. To become a CFE, candidates must pass a two-day exam. Today there are more than 15,000 CFEs worldwide.

Use fraud detection software

People who commit fraud tend to follow certain patterns and leave behind clues, such as things that do not make sense. Software has been developed to uncover these fraud symptoms. For example, a health insurance company could use fraud detection software to review how often procedures are performed, if a diagnosis and the procedures performed fit a patient's profile, how long a procedure takes, and how far patients live from the doctor's office. ReliaStar Financial used a fraud detection package from IBM to detect the following:

➤ Hundreds of thousands of dollars in fraudulent claims from a Los Angeles chiropractor. The software noticed that all of the chiropractor's patients lived more than 50 miles from the doctor's office and flagged the bills for investigation.

➤ A Long Island otolaryngologist who was submitting bills weekly for a rare and expensive procedure that is normally done only once or twice in a lifetime.

➤ A podiatrist who saw four patients and then billed ReliaStar for almost 500 separate procedures.

Other companies have **neural networks** (programs that mimic the brain and have learning capabilities) which are quite accurate in identifying suspected fraud. For example, the Visa and MasterCard operation at Mellon Bank uses neural network software to track 1.2 million accounts. Its neural network can spot the illegal use of a credit card and notify the owner shortly after it is stolen. The software can also spot trends before bank investigators do. For example, one investigator learned about a new scam from another bank. When he went to the system to have it check for the scam, he noticed that the neural network had already identified the scam and had printed out a list of transactions that fit its pattern. The software cost Mellon Bank less than $1 million and paid for itself in six months.

Reduce Fraud Losses

No matter how hard a company tries to prevent fraud, chances are that it will occur. Therefore, an important strategy is to seek to minimize potential fraud losses. Some of these methods include the following:

➤ Maintain adequate insurance.

➤ Keep a current backup copy of all program and data files in a secure off-site location.

➤ Develop a contingency plan for potential fraud occurrences and other disasters. Use special software designed to monitor system activity and help companies recover from frauds and malicious actions. One such software utility helped a company recover from a rampage caused by a disgruntled employee who had received a negative performance evaluation. The perpetrator ripped cards and cables out of PCs, changed the inventory control files, and edited the password file to stop people from logging on to the LAN. Shortly after the incident, the software identified the corrupted files and flashed an alert to company headquarters. The damage was undone by issuing simple commands to the utility software, which restored the corrupted file to its original status.

Prosecute and Incarcerate Fraud Perpetrators

Most fraud cases go unreported and unprosecuted for several reasons:

1. Many cases of computer fraud are as yet undetected.

2. Companies are reluctant to report computer crimes because a highly visible computer fraud is a public relations disaster. Fraud also reveals the vulnerability of a company's computer system, possibly attracting more acts of fraud. Unreported fraud creates a false sense of security; people think systems are more secure than they really are.

3. Law enforcement officials and the courts are so busy with violent crimes that they have little time for fraud cases in which no physical harm is present. All too often, prosecuting attorneys treat teen hacking and cracking as a childish prank and let them plea bargain down to a misdemeanor.

4. Fraud is difficult, costly, and time consuming to investigate and prosecute. Until 1986, law enforcement officials were without a law that dealt specifically with computer crimes. As a result, they had to prosecute using laws written for other purposes. This problem was partially resolved when the U.S. Congress passed the Computer Fraud and Abuse Act of 1986. The law covers computers used by the federal government, financial institutions, and certain medical organizations, as well as in interstate or foreign

commerce. The law makes it illegal to knowingly gain access to computers with intent to defraud. Trafficking in computer access passwords is also prohibited. The crime is a felony if more than $1,000 worth of software is damaged or if money, goods, or services are stolen. The penalties are severe: 1 to 5 years for the first offense, 10 years for the second, and 20 years for the third and subsequent offenses. Fines can be up to $250,000 or twice the value of the stolen data. Although the law has resulted in increased prosecutions, many say it is vague and is an easy target for defense attorneys. The laws are supplemented by computer fraud statutes in every U.S. state.

5. Many law enforcement officials, lawyers, and judges lack the computer skills needed to investigate, prosecute, and evaluate computer crimes. Increased training, which is time consuming and costly, is necessary for officials to understand and detect computer fraud.

6. When fraud cases are prosecuted and a conviction is obtained, the sentences received are often very light. For example, Judge John Lord, when sentencing convicted white-collar criminals, stated that the perpetrators were God-fearing, highly civic-minded men, who had spent their lifetimes in sincere and honest dedication and service to their families, churches, country, and communities. He said he could never send them to jail. One investigator noted that the average sentence for a fraud perpetrator was one year in jail for every $10 million stolen.

One of the most famous cases of a light sentence involved C. Arnoldt Smith, former owner of the San Diego Padres who was named Mr. San Diego of the Century. Smith was very involved in the community and made large political contributions. When investigations showed that he had stolen $200 million from his bank, he pleaded nolo contendere (no contest). He was given a sentence of four years' probation and a fine of $30,000. The fine was to be paid at the rate of $100 a month for the following 25 years, with no interest. Mr. Smith was 71 at the time. The embezzled money was never recovered.

SUMMARY AND CASE CONCLUSION

Jason Scott believed Don Hawkins had committed a fraud, but he needed more details to support that conclusion. In preparation for his meeting with management, he expanded the scope of his investigation. A week later, Jason presented his findings to the president of Northwest. To introduce the problem and to make it hit a little closer to home, Jason presented the president with a copy of his own withholding report filed with the IRS and pointed out the president's withholdings. Then he showed him a printout of withholdings from the payroll records and pointed out the $5 difference, as well as the difference of several thousand dollars in Don Hawkins's withholdings. This immediately got the president's attention, and Jason proceeded to tell him how he believed a fraud had been perpetrated.

During the latter part of the prior year, the payroll system had undergone some minor modifications. Don had been in charge of the project. Due to pressing problems with several other projects, the payroll project had been completed without the usual review by other systems personnel. Jason arranged for a member of the audit staff, who was a former programmer, to review the code changes. She found a few lines of unusual code in the program for generating the withholdings report for the IRS. The code subtracted $5 from most employees' withholdings and added it to Don's withholdings. Don got his hands on the money when the IRS sent him a huge refund check.

It appeared that Don intended to use the scheme every year, as he had not removed the incriminating code. He must have been fairly confident of his scheme, because he had not tried to modify the company's copy of the withholdings report. Somehow he knew there was no reconciliation of withholdings from the payroll records with the IRS report. It was a simple plan, and it could have gone undetected for years if Jason had not overheard someone in the cafeteria talk about a $5 difference.

Jason quietly investigated Don and found he had a reputation of being disgruntled. He had been passed over last year for a managerial position in the programming department and had been unhappy ever since. He made numerous comments to coworkers about favoritism and unfair treatment. He even mentioned getting even with the company somehow. Don had also recently purchased a fairly expensive sports car. No one knew where he got the money, but Don did mention to a coworker that he had made a sizable down payment when he bought the car in April.

When the president asked the inevitable question of how the company could prevent this type of fraud from happening again, Jason suggested the following guidelines:

1. A review of the company's internal controls should be conducted to analyze its effectiveness in preventing fraud. One control that already existed, reviewing program changes, could have prevented Don's scheme had it been followed. As a result, Jason suggested a stricter enforcement of the existing controls.
2. New controls should be put into place to detect fraud. For example, Jason suggested a reconciliation of the withholdings on the IRS report with those on the payroll records.
3. Employees should be trained in fraud awareness, security measures, and ethical issues.

Jason also urged the president to prosecute the case. The president was reluctant to do so because of the adverse publicity and the problems it would cause for Don's wife and children. Jason's supervisor tactfully suggested that if other employees found out that Don was not prosecuted, it would send the wrong message to the rest of the company. The president finally conceded to prosecute if the company could prove that Don was guilty. The president agreed to hire a forensic accountant to build a stronger case against Don and try to get him to confess.

KEY TERMS

- fraud
- white-collar criminals
- misappropriation of assets
- employee fraud
- fraudulent financial reporting
- lapping
- kiting
- pressure
- opportunity
- rationalization
- computer fraud
- economic espionage
- employee goofing
- Trojan horse
- round-down technique
- salami technique
- trap door
- superzapping
- software piracy
- data diddling
- data leakage
- piggybacking
- masquerading
- impersonation
- social engineering
- logic time bomb
- hacking
- cracking
- scavenging
- dumpster diving
- eavesdropping
- wiretap
- e-mail threats
- e-mail forgery
- denial-of-service attack
- e-mail bombs
- Internet terrorism
- Internet misinformation
- war dialing
- password cracking
- spamming
- computer virus
- worm
- phreakers
- random surveillance
- computer security officer
- forensic accountants
- neural networks

CHAPTER QUIZ

1. Which of the following is a fraud in which later payments on account are used to pay off earlier payments that were stolen?
   a. lapping
   b. kiting
   c. Ponzi scheme
   d. salami technique

2. Which type of fraud is associated with as many as 50 percent of all lawsuits against auditors?
   a. kiting
   b. fraudulent financial reporting
   c. Ponzi schemes
   d. lapping

3. Which of the following statements is false?
   a. The psychological profiles of white-collar criminals differ from those of violent criminals.
   b. The psychological profiles of white-collar criminals differ from those of the general public.
   c. Computer fraud perpetrators are different from other types of white-collar criminals.
   d. Computer fraud perpetrators often do not view themselves as criminals.

4. Which of the following conditions are usually necessary for a fraud to occur? (There is more than one right answer.)
   a. pressures
   b. opportunities
   c. explanations
   d. rationalizations

5. Which of the following is not an example of computer fraud?
   a. theft of money by altering computer records
   b. intent to obtain information illegally through use of a computer
   c. failure to perform preventive maintenance on a computer
   d. unauthorized modification of a software program

6. A set of instructions to increase a programmer's pay rate by 10 percent is hidden inside an authorized program. It changes and updates payroll files. What is this computer fraud technique called?
   a. virus
   b. worm
   c. trap door
   d. Trojan horse

7. What is the computer fraud technique called that involves a set of instructions hidden inside a calendar utility that copies itself until memory is filled and the system crashes?
   a. logic bomb
   b. worm
   c. virus
   d. Trojan horse

8. Which of the following control procedures is most likely to deter lapping?
   a. encryption
   b. continual update of the access control matrix
   c. background check on employees
   d. periodic rotation of duties

9. Which of the following is the most important, basic, and effective control to deter fraud?
   a. enforced vacations
   b. logical access control

c. segregation of duties

d. virus protection controls

10. Which of the following are methods of reducing fraud losses? (There may be more than one right answer.)

a. insurance

b. regular backup of data and programs

c. contingency plan

d. segregation of duties

Discussion Questions

9.1 Do you agree that the most effective method of obtaining adequate system security is to rely on the integrity of company employees? Why or why not? Does this seem ironic? What measures should a company take to ensure the integrity of its employees?

9.2 You are the president of a multinational company. One of your senior executives confessed to kiting $100,000. Explain what kiting is and what your company can do to prevent it. How would you respond to your employee's confession? What issues must you consider before pressing formal charges?

9.3 One December morning, the computers at U.S. Leasing Company began acting sluggish. Computer operators were relieved when a software troubleshooter from Digital Equipment called several hours later. They were more than happy to let him help correct the problem they were having with the Digital software. The troubleshooter asked for a phone number for the computers as well as a logon number and passwords—a common procedure employed by Digital in handling software problems.

The next morning, the computers were worse. A call to Digital confirmed U.S. Leasing's suspicion: Someone had impersonated a Digital repairman to gain unauthorized access to the system and destroy the entire computer database. U.S. Leasing was also concerned that the intruder had devised a program that would let him get back into the system even after all the passwords were changed.

What techniques might the impostor have employed to breach U.S. Leasing's internal security? What could U.S. Leasing do to avoid these types of incidents in the future?

9.4 To address the need for tighter data controls and lower support costs, Manufacturers Hanover has adopted a new diskless PC. It is little more than a mutilated personal computer described as a "gutless wonder." The concept behind the diskless PC is simple: A LAN server-based file system of high-powered diskless workstations is spread throughout an organization and connected with a central repository or mainframe. The network improves control by limiting user access to company data previously stored on desktop hard drives. The user can destroy or delete only the information currently on the screen, so a company's financial data are protected from user-instigated catastrophes. The diskless computer also saves money in user support costs by distributing applications and upgrades automatically, as well as by offering on-line help.

What threats does the diskless PC minimize? Do the security advantages of the new system outweigh potential limitations?

9.5 Biometric security systems are becoming a cost-effective solution to the troubling problem of computer security. These security devices measure our unique physical traits, such as speech patterns, eye and finger physiology, and written signature dynamics. The ideal system must be reliable and yet flexible enough to handle minor changes in physical characteristics such as a cut finger or a hoarse voice. The system also requires that the user be physically present to gain access. Hertz and Security Pacific Bank are two companies seeking to use the new technology.

For both companies, the security devices will aid in ensuring that only authorized individuals have access to computer systems and their related operations.

Why are biometric security devices increasing in popularity? What are the advantages and disadvantages of these systems in comparison with traditional security measures such as passwords and locked doors?

9.6 A few days after the inventory control system for Revlon, the cosmetics giant, went down, officials discovered that Logisticon, a software developer, caused the downtime. Seven months earlier, Revlon had signed an agreement to have Logisticon install a real-time invoice and inventory processing system. Prior to completion of phase I of the project, Revlon discovered a series of programming bugs. Revlon proceeded to withhold any additional payment on the contract to Logisticon, who contended that the software was fine but that the computer hardware was faulty. When Revlon refused payment, Logisticon sought repossession: It used a telephone dial-in feature in the software to make a disabling phone call and render the system unusable.

After a three-day standoff, Logisticon reactivated Revlon's inventory system. Revlon filed suit in California Superior Court charging Logisticon with trespassing, breach of contract, and misappropriation of trade secrets (use of Revlon passwords). Logisticon filed a countersuit for breach of contract. Revlon and Logisticon later settled out of court.

Would Logisticon's actions be classified as sabotage or repossession? Why? Would you find the company guilty of committing a computer crime? Be prepared to defend your position to the class.

9.7 Improved computer security measures create their own set of problems: user antagonism, sluggish response time, and hampered performance. Many professionals believe that the most effective way to promote computer security is to educate users about good moral conduct. According to Richard Stallman, president of the Free Software Foundation, MIT programmer, and computer activist, software licensing is antisocial because it prohibits the growth of the technology by keeping information away from the neighbors. He believes high school and college students should have unlimited access to computers without security measures in order to teach constructive and civilized behavior. He states that a protected system is a puzzle and, because it is human nature to solve puzzles, eliminating computer security so that there is no temptation to break in would reduce hacking.

Do you agree with Stallman's statements? Do you agree that software licensing is antisocial? Is ethical teaching the solution to computer security problems? Would the removal of computer security measures reduce the incidence of computer fraud? Why or why not?

9.8 Discuss the following statement by Roswell Steffen, a convicted embezzler: "For every foolproof system, there is a method for beating it." Do you believe a completely secure computer system is possible? Explain. If internal controls are less than 100 percent effective, why should they be employed at all?

9.9 What motives do people have for hacking? Why has hacking become so popular in recent years? Do you regard it as a crime? Explain your position.

PROBLEMS

9.1 An experienced senior auditor was assigned to investigate a possible fraudulent situation characterized by extremely high, unexplained merchandise shortages at one location of the company's department store chain. During the course of the investigation, the auditor determined the following:

1. The supervisor of the receiving department was the owner and operator of a small boutique carrying many of the same labels as the chain store. The chain store's general manager was unaware of the ownership interest.

2. The receiving supervisor signed receiving reports showing that the total quantity shipped by a supplier had been received. A total of 5 to 10 percent of each shipment was diverted to the boutique.

3. The chain's buyers were unaware of the short shipments, because the receiving supervisor would enter the correct quantity on the move ticket accompanying the merchandise to the sales areas.

4. The chain's accounts payable department paid vendors for the total quantity shown on the receiving report.

5. Based on the supervisor's instructions, quantities on the move tickets were not compared with those on the receiving report.

Required

Classify each of the five situations as a fraudulent act, an indicator of fraud, or an event unrelated to the investigation. Justify your answers.

(CIA Examination, adapted)

9.2 A small but growing firm has recently hired you to investigate a potential fraud. The company heard through its hot line that the purchases journal clerk periodically enters fictitious acquisitions. The nonexistent supplier's address is given as a post office box, which the clerk rents. He forwards notification of the fictitious purchases for recording in the accounts payable ledger. Payment is ultimately mailed to the post office box. He then deposits the check in an account established in the name of the nonexistent supplier.

Required

a. Define fraud, fraud deterrence, fraud detection, and fraud investigation.

b. List four red-flag indicators (personal as opposed to organizational) that might point to the existence of fraud in this example.

c. List two procedures you could follow to uncover the fraudulent behavior of the purchases journal clerk in this situation.

(CIA Examination, adapted)

9.3 Most experts maintain that the computer frauds that are publicly revealed represent only the tip of the iceberg. Although the major threat to computer security is perceived by many to be external, the more dangerous threats come from insiders. Management must recognize these problems and develop and enforce security programs to deal with the many types of computer fraud.

Required

Explain how each of the following six types of fraud is committed. Using the format provided, also identify a different method of protection for each and describe how it works.

Type of Fraud	*Explanation*	*Identification and Description of Protection Methods*
a. Input manipulation		
b. Program alteration		
c. File alteration		
d. Data theft		
e. Sabotage		
f. Theft of computer time		

(CMA Examination, adapted)

9.4 The Treadway Commission study shows that fraudulent financial reporting usually occurs as the result of environmental, institutional, or individual influences and opportune situations.

These influences and opportunities, present to some degree in all companies, motivate individuals and companies to engage in fraudulent financial reporting. The prevention and detection of fraudulent financial reporting require that these influences and opportunities be identified and evaluated in terms of the risks they pose to a company. These risk factors include internal ethical and control factors as well as external environmental conditions.

Required

a. Identify two company situational pressures that would increase the likelihood of fraud.

b. Identify three corporate opportunities that make fraud easier to commit and detection less likely.

c. For each of the following, identify the external environmental factors that should be considered in assessing the risk of fraudulent financial reporting.
   - The company's industry
   - The company's business environment
   - The company's legal and regulatory environment

d. According to the Treadway Commission, what can top management do to reduce the possibility of fraudulent financial reporting?

(CMA Examination, adapted)

9.5 The impact of employee and management fraud is staggering both in terms of dollar costs and the effect on the victims. For each of the following independent cases of employee fraud, describe the recommendations internal auditors should make to prevent similar problems from occurring in the future.

a. A retail store that was part of a national chain experienced an abnormal inventory shrinkage in its audiovisual department. The internal auditors, noting this shrinkage, included an in-depth evaluation of the department in the scope of their store audit. During their review the auditors learned from an employee that a particular customer bought a large number of small electronic components and that the customer always went to a certain cashier's checkout line. The auditors' work revealed that the cashier and the customer had colluded to steal a number of electronic components. The cashier did not record the sale of several items the customer took from the store.

b. During an unannounced visit to a large hospital, internal auditors discovered a payroll fraud when they observed the distribution of paychecks. The supervisors of each department distributed paychecks to employees and were supposed to return unclaimed checks to the payroll department. When the auditors took control of, and followed up on, an unclaimed paycheck for an employee in the food service department, they discovered that the employee had quit four months previously. The employee and the supervisor had had an argument, and the employee had simply left and never returned. The supervisor had continued to turn in a time card for the employee and had taken the unclaimed checks and cashed them.

c. While performing an audit of cash disbursements at a manufacturing firm, internal auditors discovered a fraud committed by an accounts payable clerk. She made copies of supporting documents and used them to support duplicate payments to a supplier of manufacturing materials. The clerk, who had opened a bank account in a name similar to that of the supplier, took the duplicate checks and deposited them in her bank account.

(CMA Examination, adapted)

9.6 Rent-A-Wreck's policy requires a "sealed bid" to sell motor vehicles that are no longer efficient. In reviewing the sale of some vehicles that had been declared obsolete, the auditor found that management had not always complied with the stated policy. Records indicated that several vehicles on which major repairs had recently been performed were sold at negotiated prices. Management assured the auditor that by performing limited repairs and negotiating with knowledgeable buyers, better prices had been obtained for the salvaged vehicles than had the required sealed-bid procedures been followed. The auditor suspected that there might be more involved than management indicated. Further investigation revealed that the vehicles had been sold to employees at negotiated prices well below market value. The auditor's work eventually resulted in three managers and five other employees pleading guilty to criminal charges and making restitution to the organization.

Required

a. Based on this scenario, outline the symptoms or indications of possible fraud that would have aroused the auditor's suspicion.

b. Suggest audit procedures that the auditor could have employed to establish the fact that fraud had in fact occurred.

(CIA Examination, adapted)

9.7 A few years ago, news began circulating about a computer virus named Michelangelo that was set to "ignite" on March 6, the birthday of the famous Italian artist. The virus itself was spread via diskettes used with PCs. When a software package containing the virus was introduced to the computer system, the virus would attach to the computer's operating system boot sector. On the magical date, the virus would release itself, freezing the system's boot function and destroying all of its data.

When March 6 arrived, the virus did minimal damage. Preventive techniques limited the damage to isolated personal and business computers. Though the excitement surrounding the virus was largely illusory, Michelangelo helped the computer-using public realize its own system's vulnerability to outside attack.

Required

a. What is a computer virus? Cite at least three reasons why no system is completely safe from a computer virus.

b. Why do viruses represent a serious threat to information systems? What damage can a virus do to a computer system?

c. Why is a virus often classified as a Trojan horse?

d. What steps can individuals and companies take to prevent the spread or propagation of a computer virus?

9.8 The auditor of a bank is called to a meeting with a senior operations manager because of a customer's report that an auto loan payment was not credited. According to the customer, the payment was made at a teller's window using a check drawn on an account in that bank. The payment was made on its due date, May 5. On May 10, the customer decided to sell the car and called the bank for a payoff on the loan. The payment had not been credited to the loan. The customer came to the bank on May 12 to inquire about the payment and meet with the manager. The manager found that the payment had been credited the night before the meeting (as of May 11); the customer was satisfied because no late charge would have been assessed until May 15. The manager asked if the auditor was comfortable with this situation.

The auditor located the customer's paid check in the deposit department and found that it had cleared as of May 5. The auditor traced the item back through the computer records and found that the teller had processed the check as being cashed. The auditor traced the payment through the entry records of May 11 and found that the payment had been made with cash instead of a check.

Required

What type of embezzlement scheme does this appear to be, and how does that scheme operate?

(CIA Examination, adapted)

9.9 It was a typical Wednesday on the UCLA campus when everything began going wrong in the student computer lab. The computer lab was filled to capacity as the end of the semester neared. Nearly 70 students were logged in to the UCLA computer network, run by Netware software, when the system came to a halt. Students tried running software without success, and many students could not even log in without getting a frustrating ABORT RETRY message from the Netware operating system.

System directors initially suspected a cable break or an operating system failure as the culprit, but diagnostics revealed nothing. After several frustrating hours, a staff member began running a virus detection program and uncovered a Jerusalem virus on the lab's main server. The virus was eventually traced to diskettes used by unsuspecting UCLA students. When staff workers used the infected computers to gain supervisor access to the operating system, the virus spread.

The virus cost UCLA about 25 person-hours and disrupted the lives of frantic students preparing for finals. Later that evening the system was brought back on-line after infected files were replaced with backup copies.

Required

a. What conditions made the UCLA system a potential breeding ground for the Jerusalem virus?

b. What symptoms indicated that a virus was present?

c. What advice would you give UCLA's director of computing to prevent the same incident from recurring?

Case 9-1   David L. Miller: Portrait of a White-collar Criminal

There is an old saying in crime-fighting circles: Crime doesn't pay. However, for David Miller crime has paid rich dividends. It paid for two Mercedes-Benz sedans, a $280,000 suburban house, a condominium at Myrtle Beach, South Carolina, $500 suits, and $75 tailored and monogrammed shirts. It also paid for diamond, sapphire, ruby, and emerald rings for his wife and a new car for his father-in-law. Though he has confessed to embezzling funds from six different employers over a 20-year period, he has never been prosecuted and has never been incarcerated. In large part, Miller's freedom is the result of the fear that companies have about turning in employees who defraud them.

Miller's first employer was also his first victim. In 1965, after 10 months of selling insurance in Wheeling, West Virginia, he was fired for stealing about $200. After holding an assortment of odd jobs, he moved to Ohio and worked as an accountant for a local baker. Miller was caught embezzling funds and paid back the $1,000 he had stolen. Again, he was not reported to the authorities and was quietly dismissed.

Miller returned to Wheeling and went to work for Wheeling Bronze, Inc., a bronze-castings maker. In December 1971, the president of Wheeling Bronze discovered that several returned checks were missing and that there was a $30,000 cash shortfall. After an extensive search, workers uncovered a number of canceled checks with forged signatures in an outdoor sandpile. Miller was questioned and confessed to the scheme. He was given the choice of paying back the stolen amount or going to jail. Miller's parents took out a mortgage on their home to pay back the stolen money. No charges were ever filed, and Miller was dismissed.

Several months later Miller found a job in Pennsylvania working for Robinson Pipe Cleaning. When Miller was caught embezzling funds, he again avoided prosecution by promising to repay the $20,000 he had stolen.

In 1974, Crest Industries hired Miller as an accountant. Miller proved to be the ideal employee and was quickly promoted to the position of office manager. He was very dedicated, worked long hours, and did outstanding work. Soon after his promotion he purchased a new home, a new car, and a new wardrobe.

In 1976, Miller's world unraveled again when Crest's auditors discovered that $31,000 was missing. Once again there was a tearful confession and a promise to repay all money stolen. Miller confessed that he had written several checks to himself and had then recorded payments to suppliers on the carbon copies of the checks. To cover his tracks, he intercepted and altered the company's monthly bank statements. He had used the money he had stolen to finance his lifestyle and to repay Wheeling Bronze and Robinson Pipe Cleaning.

Miller claimed in his confession that he had never before embezzled funds. He showed a great deal of remorse, so much so that Crest even hired a lawyer for him. He gave Crest a lien on his house, and he was quietly dismissed. Because the president of Crest did not want the publicity to harm Miller's wife and three children, Crest never pressed charges against him.

Miller next took a job as an accountant in Steubenville, Ohio, with Rustcraft Broadcasting Company, a chain of radio and television stations. Rustcraft was acquired in 1979 by Associated Communications, and Miller moved to Pittsburgh to become Associated's new controller.

Miller immediately began dipping into Associated's accounts. Over a 6-year period Miller embezzled approximately $1.36 million, $445,000 of that in 1984 when he was promoted to CFO. Miller used various methods to embezzle the money. One approach to circumvent the need for two signatures on every check was to ask another executive who was leaving on vacation to sign several checks "just in case" the company needed additional cash while he was gone. Miller used most of these checks to siphon off funds to his personal account. To cover the theft, Miller retrieved the canceled check from the bank reconciliation and destroyed it. The amount stolen was then charged to a unit's expense account to balance the company's books.

While working at Associated, Miller was able to lead a very comfortable lifestyle. He bought a new house and several expensive cars. He bought vacation property and an extravagant wardrobe, and he was generous with tips and gifts. His $130,000 salary could not have supported this lifestyle, yet no one at Associated ever questioned the source of his conspicuous consumption.

Miller's lifestyle came crashing down in December 1984 while he was on vacation. A bank officer called to inquire about a check written to Mr. Miller. An investigation ensued, and Miller confessed to embezzling funds. As part of the 1985 out-of-court settlement with Miller, Associated Communications received most of Miller's personal property.

Miller cannot explain why he was never prosecuted. He always insisted that he was going to pay the company back. Such statements would usually satisfy his employers and get him off the hook. He believes that these agreements actually contributed to his subsequent thefts. For example, one rationale for starting to steal from a new employer was to pay back the former one.

After leaving Associated, Miller was hired by a former colleague. Miller underwent therapy and believes he has resolved his problem with compulsive embezzlement.

When interviewed about his past activities, Miller thought his problem with theft was an illness, just like alcoholism or compulsive gambling.

The illness was driven by a subconscious need to be admired and liked by others. He thought that by spending money, others would like him. Ironically, he was universally well liked and admired at each job, and it had nothing to do with money. In fact, one coworker at Associated was so surprised at the news of the thefts that he said it was like finding out that your brother was an ax murderer. In the interview, Miller also claimed that he is not a bad person. He says he never intended to hurt anyone, but once he got started, he just could not stop.

1. How does Miller fit the profile of the average fraud perpetrator? How does he differ? How did these characteristics make him difficult to detect?
2. Discuss the threefold fraud process (theft, conversion, concealment) Miller followed in embezzling funds from Associated Communications. What specific concealment techniques did Miller use?
3. What pressures motivated Miller to embezzle? What opportunities allowed him to steal and cover up his theft? How did Miller rationalize his actions?
4. Miller had a framed T-shirt in his office that said, "He who dies with the most toys wins." What does this tell you about Miller? What lifestyle red flags could have tipped off the company to the possibility of fraud?
5. Identify several reasons why companies hesitate in prosecuting white-collar criminals. What are the problems with such rationalizations? What could law enforcement officials do to encourage more rigorous prosecution of white-collar criminals?
6. Identify the primary action each of the victimized companies could have taken to prevent Miller's embezzlement. What other controls could help in preventing future fraud?

Source: Bryan Burrough, "David L. Miller Stole from His Employer and Isn't in Prison," *Wall Street Journal* (September 19, 1986): 1.

Case 9-2   Lexsteel Corporation

Lexsteel Corporation is a leading manufacturer of steel furniture. The company has manufacturing plants and distribution facilities throughout the United States, but the purchasing, accounting, and treasury functions are centralized at corporate headquarters in Fresno, California.

While discussing a recent management letter with the external auditors, Ray Landsdown, controller of Lexsteel, became aware of potential problems with the accounts payable system. The auditors had to perform additional audit procedures to attest to the validity of accounts payable and cutoff procedures. The auditors have recommended a detailed systems study of the current procedures to assess the company's exposure to potential embezzlement and fraud and to identify ways to improve management controls.

Landsdown has assigned the study task to Dolores Smith, a relatively new accountant in the department. Because Smith could not find adequate documentation of the accounts payable procedures, she interviewed those employees involved and constructed a flowchart of the current system. This flowchart is shown in Figure 9-2, and descriptions of the current procedures follow.

COMPUTER RESOURCES

The host computer mainframe is located at corporate headquarters with interactive, remote job entry terminals at each branch location. In general, data entry occurs at the source and is transmitted to an integrated database maintained on the host computer. Data transmission occurs over leased telephone lines between the branch offices and the host computer. The software allows flexibility for managing user access and editing data input.

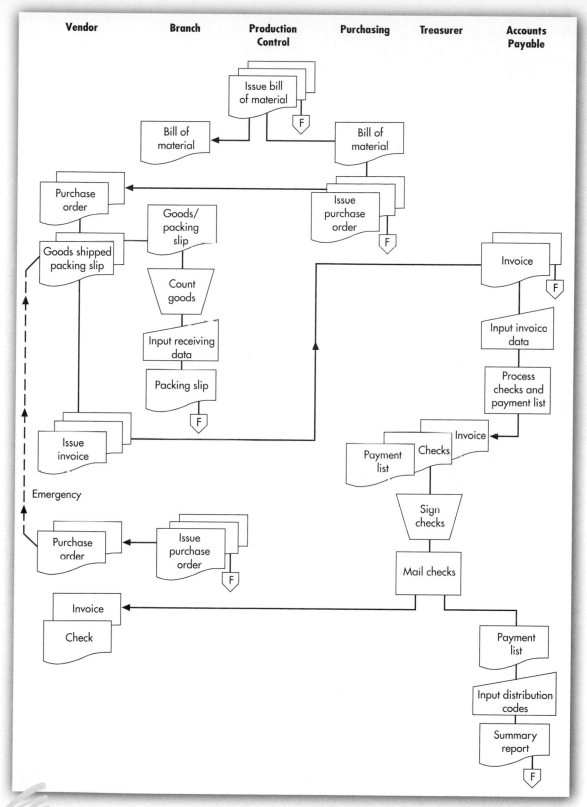

Figure 9-2 Accounts payable procedures at Lexsteel

317

PROCEDURES FOR PURCHASING RAW MATERIALS

The host computer at corporate headquarters generates production orders and appropriate bills of material. From these bills of material, purchase orders for raw materials are generated by the centralized purchasing function and mailed directly to the vendors. Each purchase order instructs the vendor to ship the materials directly to the appropriate manufacturing plant. Assuming that the necessary purchase orders have been issued, the manufacturing plants proceed with the production orders received from corporate headquarters.

Upon receipt of goods, the manufacturing plant examines and verifies the count against the packing slip and transmits the receiving data to accounts payable at corporate headquarters. In the event that raw material deliveries fall behind production, each branch manager is given the authority to order materials and issue emergency purchase orders directly to the vendors. Data about the emergency orders and verification of materials receipt are transmitted via computer to accounts payable at corporate headquarters. Since the company employs a cost-effective computerized perpetual inventory system, physical counts of raw materials are not performed.

ACCOUNTS PAYABLE PROCEDURES

Vendor invoices are mailed directly to corporate headquarters and entered by accounts payable personnel when received. This often occurs before the branch offices transmit the receiving data. The final day the invoice can be paid is entered as the payment due date. Using information listed on the invoice, the data entry person often must calculate this due date.

Once a week, invoices due the following week are printed in chronological entry order on a payment listing, and the corresponding checks are drawn. The checks and the payment listing are sent to the treasurer's office for signature and mailing to the payee. The check number is printed by the computer, displayed on the check and the payment listing, and validated as the checks are signed. After the checks are mailed, the payment listing is returned to accounts payable for filing. When there is insufficient cash to pay all the invoices, the treasurer retains certain checks and the payment listing until all checks can be paid. When the remaining checks are mailed, the listing is then returned to accounts payable. Often weekly check mailings include a few checks from the previous week, but rarely are there more than two weekly listings involved.

When accounts payable receives the payment listing back from the treasurer's office, the expenses are distributed, coded, and posted to the appropriate plant/cost center accounts. Accounts payable processes weekly summary performance reports for each cost center and branch location reflecting all data entry to that point.

1. Identify and discuss three areas where Lexsteel Corporation may be exposed to fraud or embezzlement due to weaknesses in the procedures described. Recommend improvements to correct these weaknesses.
2. Describe three areas where management information could be distorted due to weaknesses in Lexsteel's procedures. Recommend improvements to correct these weaknesses.
3. Identify three strengths in Lexsteel's procedures, and explain why they are strengths.

(CMA Examination, adapted)

ANSWERS TO CHAPTER QUIZ

1. a　　3. b　　5. c　　7. c　　9. c
2. b　　4. a, b, d　　6. d　　8. d　　10. a, b, c

Auditing of Computer-Based Information Systems

Learning Objectives

After studying this chapter, you should be able to:

- Describe the scope and objectives of audit work, and identify the major steps in the audit process.
- Identify the objectives of an information system audit, and describe the four-step approach necessary for meeting these objectives.
- Design a plan for the study and evaluation of internal control in an AIS.
- Describe computer audit software and explain how it is used in the audit of an AIS.
- Describe the nature and scope of an operational audit.

Integrative Case: Seattle Paper Products

Shortly after learning how to use a computer audit software package, Jason Scott was assigned to a project at Seattle Paper Products (SPP). The company is modifying its sales department payroll system to change the way it calculates sales commissions. Under the old system, commissions were a fixed percentage of dollar sales. The new system is considerably more complex, with commission rates varying according to the product sold and the total dollar volume of sales.

Jason's assignment is to use the audit software to write a parallel simulation test program to calculate sales commissions and compare them with those generated by the new system. Jason obtained the necessary payroll system documentation and the details on the new sales commission policy. After a few days his program was ready to run.

Jason obtained the file containing sales transaction data from the last payroll period and used it to run his program. To his surprise, his calculations were $5,000 less than those produced by SPP's new program; in fact, individual differences existed for about half of the company's salespeople. Jason double-checked his program code but could not locate any errors. He selected a salesperson for whom there was a discrepancy and recalculated the commission by hand. The result agreed with his program. He reviewed the new commission policy with the sales manager, line by line, and concluded that he understood the new policy completely. Jason is now convinced that his program is correct and that the error lies with the new program. Based on this conclusion, he ponders the following questions:

1. How could a programming error of this significance be overlooked by experienced programmers who thoroughly reviewed and tested the new system?
2. Is this an inadvertent error, or could it be another fraud?
3. What can be done to find the error in the program?

INTRODUCTION

This chapter focuses on the concepts and techniques used in auditing an AIS. Auditors are employed for a wide range of tasks and responsibilities. Many organizations employ internal auditors to evaluate company operations. The General Accounting Office and state governments employ auditors to evaluate management performance and compliance with legislative intent in government departments. The Department of Defense employs auditors to review the financial records of companies with defense contracts. Publicly held companies hire external auditors to provide an independent review of their financial statements.

This chapter is written primarily from the perspective of the internal auditor. Internal auditors are directly responsible for helping management improve organizational effectiveness and efficiency, including assisting in the design and implementation of an AIS that contributes to the organization's goals. In contrast, external auditors are primarily responsible to corporate shareholders and investors and are only indirectly concerned with the effectiveness of a corporate AIS. Despite this distinction, many of the internal audit concepts and techniques discussed in this chapter apply to external audits.

The first section of this chapter provides an overview of auditing, the scope and objectives of internal audit work, and the steps in the auditing process. The second section describes a methodology and set of techniques for evaluating internal controls in an AIS. The third section discusses techniques for evaluating the reliability and integrity of information in an AIS. Finally, operational audits of an AIS are reviewed.

THE NATURE OF AUDITING

The American Accounting Association has formulated the following general definition of **auditing.** Auditing is a systematic process of objectively obtaining and evaluating evidence regarding assertions about economic actions and events to ascertain the degree of correspondence between those assertions and established criteria and communicating the results to interested users.[1]

Auditing requires a step-by-step approach characterized by careful planning and judicious selection and execution of appropriate techniques. Auditing involves the collection, review, and documentation of audit evidence. In developing recommenda-

---

[1]Committee on Basic Auditing Concepts, *A Statement of Basic Auditing Concepts* (Sarasota, FL.: American Accounting Association, 1973), 2.

tions, the auditor uses established criteria, such as the principles of management and control described in earlier chapters, as a basis for evaluation.

Auditors used to audit around the computer and ignore the computer and its programs. They merely examined the system's printed records and output, thinking that if output was correctly obtained from system input, then processing must be reliable. A more current approach, auditing through the computer, uses the computer to check the adequacy of system controls, data, and output. Most audit techniques discussed in this chapter involve auditing through the computer.

Internal Auditing Standards

According to the Institute of Internal Auditors (IIA), the purpose of an internal audit is to evaluate the adequacy and effectiveness of a company's internal control system and determine the extent to which assigned responsibilities are actually carried out. The IIA's five audit scope standards outline the internal auditor's responsibilities:

1. Review the reliability and integrity of operating and financial information and how it is identified, measured, classified, and reported.
2. Determine if the systems designed to comply with operating and reporting policies, plans, procedures, laws, and regulations are actually being followed.
3. Review how assets are safeguarded, and verify the existence of assets as appropriate.
4. Examine company resources to determine how effectively and efficiently they are used.
5. Review company operations and programs to determine if they are being carried out as planned and if they are meeting their objectives.

Today's organizations use a computerized AIS to process, store, and control company information. To achieve the preceding five objectives, an internal auditor must be qualified to examine all elements of the computerized AIS and use the computer as a tool to accomplish these auditing objectives. In other words, computer expertise is essential to conducting an internal audit.

Types of Internal Auditing Work

Three different types of audits are commonly performed:

1. The **financial audit** examines the reliability and integrity of accounting records (both financial and operating information) and correlates with the first of the five scope standards.
2. The **information systems audit** reviews the controls of an AIS to assess its compliance with internal control policies and procedures and its effectiveness in safeguarding assets. Its scope roughly corresponds to the IIA's second and third standards.
3. The **operational,** or **management, audit** is concerned with the economical and efficient use of resources and the accomplishment of established goals and objectives. Its scope corresponds to the fourth and fifth standards.

An Overview of the Auditing Process

All audits follow a similar sequence of activities and may be divided into four stages: planning, collecting evidence, evaluating evidence, and communicating audit results. Figure 10-1 presents an overview of the auditing process, specifying many of the procedures typically performed within each of these stages. This section discusses the four auditing stages and activities in greater detail.

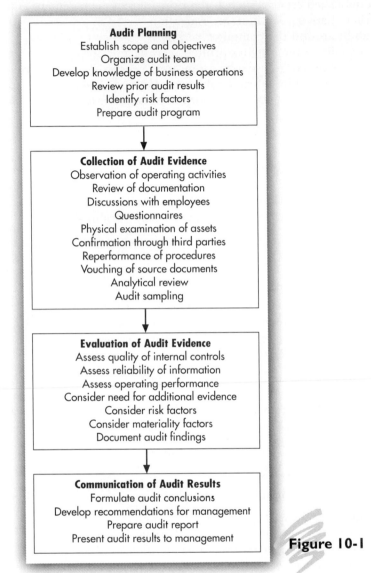

Audit Planning
Establish scope and objectives
Organize audit team
Develop knowledge of business operations
Review prior audit results
Identify risk factors
Prepare audit program

Collection of Audit Evidence
Observation of operating activities
Review of documentation
Discussions with employees
Questionnaires
Physical examination of assets
Confirmation through third parties
Reperformance of procedures
Vouching of source documents
Analytical review
Audit sampling

Evaluation of Audit Evidence
Assess quality of internal controls
Assess reliability of information
Assess operating performance
Consider need for additional evidence
Consider risk factors
Consider materiality factors
Document audit findings

Communication of Audit Results
Formulate audit conclusions
Develop recommendations for management
Prepare audit report
Present audit results to management

Figure 10-1 Overview of the auditing process

Audit planning

The purpose of audit planning is to determine why, how, when, and by whom the audit will be performed. The first step in audit planning is to establish the scope and objectives of the audit. For example, the audit scope of a publicly held corporation extends to its corporate stockholders with the purpose of evaluating the fairness of financial statement presentation. In contrast, an internal audit may examine an entire division, a specific department, or a computer application. It may focus on internal controls, financial information, operating performance, or some combination of the three.

An audit team with the necessary experience and expertise is formed. Team members become familiar with the auditee by conferring with supervisory and operating personnel, reviewing system documentation, and reviewing the findings of prior audits.

An audit should be planned so that the greatest amount of audit work focuses on the areas with the highest risk factors. There are three types of risk when conducting an audit:

1. **Inherent risk** is the susceptibility to material risk in the absence of controls. For example, a system that employs on-line processing, networks, database software, telecommunications, and other forms of advanced technology has more inherent risk than a traditional batch processing system.

2. **Control risk** is the risk that a material misstatement will get through the internal control structure and into the financial statements. A company with weak internal controls has a higher control risk than one with strong controls. Control risk can be determined by reviewing the control environment and considering control weaknesses identified in prior audits and evaluating how they have been rectified.

3. **Detection risk** is the risk that auditors and their audit procedures will not detect a material error or misstatement.

To conclude the planning stage, a preliminary audit program is prepared to show the nature, extent, and timing of the procedures necessary for achieving audit objectives and minimizing audit risks. A time budget is prepared, and staff members are assigned to perform specific audit steps.

Collection of audit evidence

Most audit effort is spent collecting evidence. The following are among the most commonly used methods of collecting audit evidence:

➤ *Observation* of the activities being audited (e.g., watching how employees enter the computer site or how data control personnel handle data processing work as it is received).

➤ *Review of documentation* to understand how a particular AIS or internal control system is supposed to function.

➤ *Discussions* with employees about their jobs and how they carry out certain procedures.

➤ *Questionnaires* that gather data about the system.

➤ *Physical examination* of the quantity and/or condition of tangible assets such as equipment, inventory, or cash.

➤ *Confirmation* of the accuracy of certain information, such as customer account balances, through communication with independent third parties.

➤ *Reperformance* of selected calculations to verify quantitative information on records and reports (e.g., the auditor could recompute a batch total or recalculate the annual depreciation charge).

➤ *Vouching* for the validity of a transaction by examining all supporting documents, such as the purchase order, receiving report, and vendor invoice supporting an accounts payable transaction.

➤ *Analytical review* of relationships and trends among information to detect items that should be further investigated (For example, an auditor for a chain of dress shops discovered that at one shop the ratio of accounts receivable to sales was far too high. An investigation revealed that the manager had diverted funds from collections to her personal use).

Because many audit tests and procedures cannot feasibly be performed on the entire set of activities, records, assets, or documents under review, they are often performed on a sample basis. A typical audit will usually be a mix of audit procedures. For example, an audit designed to evaluate AIS internal controls would make greater use of observation, review of documentation, discussions with employees, and reperformance of control procedures. An audit of financial information would focus on physical examination, confirmation, vouching, analytical review, and reperformance of account balance calculations.

Evaluation of audit evidence

The auditor evaluates the evidence gathered in light of the specific audit objective and decides if it supports a favorable or unfavorable conclusion. If inconclusive, the auditor plans and executes additional procedures until sufficient evidence is obtained to reach a definitive conclusion.

Materiality and reasonable assurance are important when deciding how much audit work is necessary and when evaluating evidence. Because errors are bound to exist in any system, auditors focus on detecting and reporting those that have a significant impact on management's interpretation of the audit findings. Determining **materiality,** what is and is not important in a given set of circumstances, is primarily a matter of judgment. Materiality is generally more important to external audits, when the overall emphasis is on the fairness of financial statement presentation, than to internal audits, when the focus is on determining adherence to management's policies.

The auditor seeks **reasonable assurance** that no material error exists in the information or process audited. Because it is prohibitively expensive to seek complete assurance, the auditor must be willing to accept some risk that the audit conclusion is incorrect. It is important to realize that when inherent or control risk is high, the auditor must obtain greater assurance to offset the greater uncertainty and risks.

At all stages of the audit, findings and conclusions are carefully documented in audit working papers. Documentation is especially important at the evaluation stage, when final conclusions must be reached and supported.

Communication of audit results

The auditor prepares a written (and sometimes oral) report summarizing the audit findings and recommendations, with references to supporting evidence in the working papers. This report is presented to management, the audit committee, the board of directors, and other appropriate parties. After the audit results are communicated, auditors often perform a follow-up study to ascertain if recommendations have been implemented.

The Risk-Based Audit Approach

The following four-step approach to internal control evaluation, referred to as the risk-based audit approach, provides a logical framework for carrying out an audit:

1. Determine the threats (errors and irregularities) facing the AIS.
2. Identify the control procedures implemented to minimize each threat by preventing or detecting the errors and irregularities.
3. Evaluate the control procedures. Reviewing system documentation and interviewing appropriate personnel to determine if the necessary procedures are in place is called a

systems review. Then **tests of controls** are conducted to determine if these procedures are satisfactorily followed. These tests include activities such as observing system operations; inspecting documents, records, and reports; checking samples of system inputs and outputs; and tracing transactions through the system.

4. Evaluate weaknesses (errors and irregularities not covered by control procedures) to determine their effect on the nature, timing, or extent of auditing procedures and client suggestions. This step focuses on the control risks and if the control system as a whole adequately addresses them. If a control deficiency is identified, the auditor asks about **compensating controls,** or procedures that compensate for the deficiency. Control weaknesses in one area may be acceptable if they are compensated for by control strengths in other areas.

The risk-based approach to auditing provides auditors with a clear understanding of the errors and irregularities that can occur and the related risks and exposures. This understanding provides a sound basis for developing recommendations to management on how the AIS control system should be improved.

INFORMATION SYSTEMS AUDITS

The purpose of an information systems audit is to review and evaluate the internal controls that protect the system. When performing an information system audit, auditors should ascertain that the following objectives are met:

1. Security provisions protect computer equipment, programs, communications, and data from unauthorized access, modification, or destruction.
2. Program development and acquisition are performed in accordance with management's general and specific authorization.
3. Program modifications have management's authorization and approval.
4. Processing of transactions, files, reports, and other computer records is accurate and complete.
5. Source data that are inaccurate or improperly authorized are identified and handled according to prescribed managerial policies.
6. Computer data files are accurate, complete, and confidential.

Figure 10-2 depicts the relationship among these six objectives and information system components. Each of these objectives is discussed in detail in the following sections. Each description includes an audit plan to accomplish each objective, as well as the techniques and procedures necessary for carrying out the plan.

Objective 1: Overall Security

Table 10-1 contains a framework for auditing computer security. It shows the following:

1. *Types of security errors and fraud faced by companies.* These include accidental or intentional damage to system assets; unauthorized access, disclosure, or modification of data and programs; theft; and interruption of crucial business activities.
2. *Control procedures to minimize security errors and fraud.* These include developing an information security/protection plan, restricting physical and logical access, encrypting data, protecting against viruses, implementing firewalls, instituting data transmission controls, and preventing and recovering from system failures or disasters.

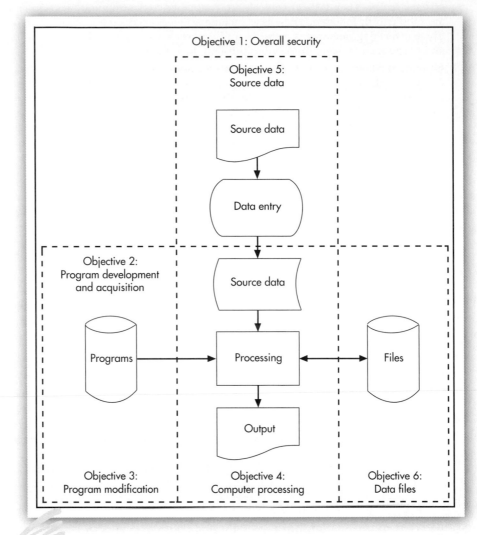

Figure 10-2   Information systems components and related audit objectives

3. *Systems review audit procedures.* These include inspecting computer sites; interviewing personnel; reviewing policies and procedures; and examining access logs, insurance policies, and the disaster recovery plan.

4. *Tests of controls audit procedures.* Auditors test security controls by observing procedures, verifying that controls are in place and work as intended, investigating errors or problems to ensure they were handled correctly, and examining any tests previously performed. For example, one way to test logical access controls is to try to break into a system. During a U.S. government agency security audit, auditors used agency terminals to gain unauthorized access to its computer system, disable its security-checking proce-

Table 10-1   Framework for Audit of Computer Security

Types of Errors and Fraud
- Theft of or accidental or intentional damage to hardware and files
- Loss or theft of or unauthorized access to programs, data files, and other system resources
- Loss or theft of or unauthorized disclosure of confidential data
- Unauthorized modification or use of programs and data files
- Interruption of crucial business activities

Control Procedures
- Information security/protection plan
- Restrictions on physical access to computer equipment
- Logical access controls based on password protection and other authentication procedures
- Data storage and transmission controls such as encryption
- Virus protection procedures
- File backup and recovery procedures
- Fault-tolerant systems design
- Disaster recovery plan
- Preventive maintenance
- Firewalls
- Information systems insurance

Audit Procedures: System Review
- Inspect computer sites
- Review the Information Security/Protection Plan
- Interview information system personnel about security procedures
- Review written documentation about physical access policies and procedures
- Review logical access policies and procedures

- Review file backup and recovery policies and procedures
- Review data storage and transmission policies and procedures
- Review procedures employed to minimize system downtime
- Review vendor maintenance contracts
- Examine system access logs
- Examine disaster recovery plan
- Examine information system casualty insurance policies

Audit Procedures: Tests of Controls
- Observe computer site access procedures
- Observe the preparation and off-site storage of backup files
- Review records of password assignment and modification
- Investigate how unauthorized access attempts were dealt with
- Verify the extent and effectiveness of data encryption use
- Verify the effective use of data transmission controls
- Verify the effective use of firewalls
- Verify the effective use of virus protection procedures
- Verify the use of preventive maintenance and uninterruptible power
- Verify amounts and limitations on insurance coverage
- Examine the results of test simulations of disaster recovery plan

Compensating Controls
- Sound personnel policies
- Effective user controls
- Segregation of incompatible duties

dures, and control the system from the terminal. The security breakdown was possible because of poor administrative controls and inadequate security software.

5. *Compensating controls.* If security controls are seriously deficient, the organization faces substantial risks. Sound personnel policies and effective segregation of incompatible duties can partially compensate for poor computer security. Good user controls will also help, if user personnel can recognize unusual system output. Because it is unlikely these controls can compensate indefinitely for poor computer security, auditors should strongly recommend that security weaknesses be corrected.

Objective 2: Program Development and Acquisition

Table 10-2 provides a framework for reviewing and evaluating the program development process. Two things can go wrong in program development: (1) inadvertent errors due to misunderstanding of system specifications or careless programming, and (2) unauthorized instructions deliberately inserted into the programs. These problems can be controlled by requiring both management and user authorization and approval, thorough testing, and proper documentation.

The auditor's role in systems development should be limited to an independent review of systems development activities. To maintain the objectivity necessary for performing an independent evaluation function, auditors should not be involved in developing the system. During the systems review, auditors should gain an understanding of development procedures by discussing them with management, system users, and information system personnel. They should also review the policies, procedures, standards, and documentation listed in Table 10-2.

To test systems development controls, auditors should interview managers and system users, examine development approvals, and review the minutes of development team meetings. The auditor should review thoroughly all documentation relating to the testing process and ascertain that all program changes were tested. The auditor should examine the test specifications, review the test data, and evaluate the test results. If unexpected test results were obtained, the auditor should ascertain

Table 10-2   Framework for Audit of Program Development

Types of Errors and Fraud
- Inadvertent programming errors
- Unauthorized program code

Control Procedures
- Review software license agreements
- Management authorization for program development and approval of programming specifications
- Management authorization of software acquisition
- User approval of programming specifications
- Thorough testing of new programs
- User acceptance testing
- Complete systems documentation, including approvals

Audit Procedures: System Review
- Independent and concurrent review of the systems development process
- Review systems development/acquisition policies and procedures
- Review systems authorization and approval procedures
- Review programming evaluation standards
- Review program documentation standards
- Review program testing and test approval procedures
- Review procedures for ensuring all acquired software has a proper copyright license agreement
- Discuss systems development procedures with management, system users, and information system personnel
- Review final application system documentation

Audit Procedures: Tests of Controls
- Interview users about their involvement in systems acquisition/development and implementation
- Review minutes of development team meetings for evidence of involvement
- Verify management and user sign-off at milestone points in the development process
- Review test specifications, test data, and results of systems tests
- Review software license agreements

Compensating Controls
- Strong processing controls
- Independent processing of test data by auditor

how the problem was resolved. Strong processing controls (see objective 4) sometimes can compensate for inadequate development controls. If auditors rely on compensatory processing controls, they should obtain persuasive evidence of compliance, using techniques such as independent processing of test data. If this type of evidence cannot be obtained, they may have to conclude that a material weakness in internal control exists and that the risk of significant errors or fraud in application programs is unacceptably high.

Objective 3: Program Modification

Table 10-3 presents a framework for auditing application program and system software changes. The same errors and fraud that can occur during program development can happen during program modification. For example, one programmer assigned to

Table 10-3   Framework for Audit of Program Modifications

Types of Errors and Fraud
- Inadvertent programming errors
- Unauthorized program code

Control Procedures
- Listing of program components that are to be modified
- Management authorization and approval of program modifications
- User approval of program change specifications
- Thorough testing of program changes, including user acceptance test
- Complete program change documentation, including approvals
- Separate development, test, and production versions of program
- Changes implemented by personnel independent of users and programmers
- Logical access controls

Audit Procedures: System Review
- Review program modification policies, standards, and procedures
- Review documentation standards for program modification
- Review program modification testing and test approval procedures
- Discuss program modification policies and procedures with management, system users, and information systems personnel

- Review final documentation for some typical program modifications
- Review test specifications, test data, and results of systems tests
- Review logical access control policies and procedures

Audit Procedures: Tests of Controls
- Verify user and information system management approval for program changes
- Verify that program components to be modified are identified and listed
- Verify that program change test procedures comply with standards
- Verify that program change documentation complies with standards
- Verify that logical access controls are in effect for program changes
- Observe program change implementation and verify that (1) separate development, test, and production versions are maintained, and (2) changes are not implemented by either user or programming personnel
- To test for unauthorized or erroneous program changes, use (1) source code comparison program, (2) reprocessing, and (3) parallel simulation

Compensating Controls
- Independent audit tests for unauthorized or erroneous program changes
- Strong processing controls

modify his company's payroll system inserted a command to erase all company files if a termination notice was ever entered into his own payroll record. When the programmer was fired, his termination notice caused the system to crash and erase key files.

When a program change is submitted for approval, a list of all required updates should be compiled and then approved by management and program users. All program changes should be thoroughly tested and documented. During the change process, the developmental version of the program must be kept separate from the production version. After the amended program has received final approval, the change is implemented by replacing the production version with the developmental version.

During systems review, auditors should gain an understanding of the change process by discussing it with management and user personnel. The policies, procedures, and standards for approving, modifying, testing, and documenting the changes should be examined. A complete set of final documentation materials for recent program changes, including test procedures and results, should be reviewed. Finally, the auditor should review the procedures used to restrict logical access to the developmental version of the program.

An important part of an auditor's tests of controls is to verify that program changes were identified, listed, approved, tested, and documented. This step requires that the auditor observe how changes are implemented to verify that separate development and production programs are maintained and that changes are implemented by someone independent of the user and programming functions. The auditor should review the development program's access control table to verify that only those users assigned to carry out the modification had access to the system.

To test for unauthorized program changes, auditors can use a source code comparison program. After auditors thoroughly test a newly developed program (objective 2), they keep a copy of its source code. At any subsequent time, the auditor may use the comparison program to compare the current version of the program with the original source code. If no changes have been authorized, these two versions should be identical. Therefore, any unauthorized differences should result in an investigation. If the difference represents an authorized change, the auditor can refer to the program change specifications to ensure that the changes were authorized and correctly incorporated.

Two additional techniques detect unauthorized program changes. The **reprocessing** technique also uses a verified copy of the source code. On a surprise basis, the auditor uses the program to reprocess data and compare that output with the company's data. Discrepancies in the two sets of output are investigated to ascertain their cause. **Parallel simulation** is similar to reprocessing except that the auditor writes a program instead of saving a verified copy of the source code. The auditor's results are compared with the company's results, and any differences are investigated. Parallel simulation can be used to test a program during the implementation process. For example, Jason used this technique to test a portion of SPP's new sales department payroll system.

Auditors should observe the testing and implementation, review related authorizations and documents, and, if necessary, perform independent tests for each major program change. If this step is skipped and program change controls are subsequently determined to be inadequate, it may not be possible to rely on program outputs. In addition, auditors should always test programs on a surprise basis as a precaution against unauthorized program changes being inserted after the examination is completed and then removed just prior to the next scheduled audit.

If internal controls over program changes are deficient, a compensating control is source code comparison, reprocessing, or parallel simulation performed by the auditor. In addition, the presence of sound processing controls, independently tested by the auditor, can partially compensate for such deficiencies. However, if the deficiencies are caused by inadequate restrictions on program file access, the auditor should strongly recommend actions to strengthen the organization's logical access controls.

Objective 4: Computer Processing

Table 10-4 provides a framework for auditing computer processing controls. The focus of the fourth objective is the processing of transactions, files, and related computer records to update files and databases and to generate reports.

During computer processing, the system may fail to detect erroneous input, improperly correct input errors, process erroneous input, or improperly distribute or disclose output. Table 10-4 shows the control procedures to detect and prevent these errors and the systems review and tests of control procedures the auditor employs. The purpose of these audit procedures is to gain an understanding of the controls, evaluate their adequacy, and observe operations for evidence that the controls are in use.

Auditors must periodically reevaluate processing controls to ensure their continued reliability. If processing controls are unsatisfactory, user and source data controls may be strong enough to compensate. If not, a material weakness exists and steps should be taken to eliminate the control deficiencies.

Several specialized techniques allow the auditor to use the computer to test processing controls. They include processing test data, using concurrent audit techniques, and analyzing program logic. Each of the techniques has its own advantages and disadvantages, which means that they are more appropriate in some situations and less appropriate in others. No one technique is good for all circumstances. Auditors should not disclose which technique they use, as that may lessen the effectiveness of the audit test. Each of these procedures is now explained.

Processing test data

One way to test a program is to process a hypothetical series of valid and invalid transactions. The program should process all of the valid transactions correctly and identify and reject all of the invalid ones. All logic paths should be checked for proper functioning by one or more of the test transactions. Examples of invalid data include records with missing data, fields containing unreasonably large amounts, invalid account numbers or processing codes, nonnumeric data in numeric fields, and records out of sequence.

The following resources are helpful when preparing test data:

➤ A listing of actual transactions
➤ The test transactions the programmer used to test the program
➤ A **test data generator program,** which automatically prepares test data based on program specifications

In a batch processing system, the company's program and a copy of relevant files are used to process the test data. The results are compared with the predetermined

Table 10-4   Framework for Audit of Computer Processing Controls

Types of Errors and Fraud
- Failure to detect incorrect, incomplete, or unauthorized input data
- Failure to properly correct errors flagged by data editing procedures
- Introduction of errors into files or databases during updating
- Improper distribution or disclosure of computer output
- Intentional or unintentional report inaccuracies

Control Procedures
- Computer data editing routines
- Proper use of internal and external file labels
- Reconciliation of batch totals
- Effective error correction procedures
- Understandable operating documentation and run manuals
- Competent supervision of computer operations
- Effective handling of data input and output by data control personnel
- File change listings and summaries prepared for user department review
- Maintenance of proper environmental conditions in computer facility

Audit Procedures: Systems Review
- Review administrative documentation for processing control standards
- Review systems documentation for data editing and other processing controls
- Review operating documentation for completeness and clarity
- Review copies of error listings, batch total reports, and file change lists

- Observe computer operations and data control functions
- Discuss processing and output controls with operators and information system supervisory personnel

Audit Procedures: Tests of Controls
- Evaluate adequacy of processing control standards and procedures
- Evaluate adequacy and completeness of data editing controls
- Verify adherence to processing control procedures by observing computer operations and the data control function
- Verify that selected application system output is properly distributed
- Reconcile a sample of batch totals, and follow up on discrepancies
- Trace disposition of a sample of errors flagged by data edit routines to ensure proper handling
- Verify processing accuracy for a sample of sensitive transactions
- Verify processing accuracy for selected computer-generated transactions
- Search for erroneous or unauthorized code via analysis of program logic
- Check accuracy and completeness of processing controls using test data
- Monitor on-line processing systems using concurrent audit techniques
- Recreate selected reports to test for accuracy and completeness

Compensating Controls
- Strong user controls
- Effective source data controls

correct output; discrepancies indicate processing errors or control deficiencies that should be thoroughly investigated.

In an on-line system, auditors enter test data using a data entry device, such as a personal computer or a terminal, and observe and log the system's response. If the system accepts erroneous or invalid test transactions, the auditor reverses the effects of the transactions, investigates the problem, and corrects the deficiency.

Although processing of test transactions is usually effective, it does have the following disadvantages:

1. The auditor must spend considerable time developing an understanding of the system and preparing an adequate set of test transactions.

2. Care must be taken to ensure that test data do not affect the company's files and databases. The auditor can reverse the effects of the test transactions or process the transactions in a separate run using a copy of the file or database. However, a separate run removes some of the authenticity obtained from processing test data with regular transactions. Also, since the reversal procedures may reveal the existence and nature of the auditor's test to key personnel, it can be less effective than a concealed test.

Concurrent audit techniques

Millions of dollars of transactions can be processed in an on-line system without leaving a satisfactory audit trail. In such cases, evidence gathered after data processing is insufficient for audit purposes. In addition, because many on-line systems process transactions continuously, it is difficult or impossible to stop the system to perform audit tests. Thus, the auditor uses **concurrent audit techniques** to continually monitor the system and collect audit evidence while live data are processed during regular operating hours. Concurrent audit techniques use **embedded audit modules,** which are segments of program code that performs audit functions. They also report test results to the auditor and store the evidence collected for the auditor's review. Concurrent audit techniques are time-consuming and difficult to use, but are less so if incorporated when programs are developed.

Auditors commonly use five concurrent audit techniques. An **integrated test facility (ITF)** technique places a small set of fictitious records in the master files. The records may represent a fictitious division, department, or branch office or a customer or supplier. Processing test transactions to update these dummy records will not affect the actual records. Because fictitious and actual records are processed together, company employees usually remain unaware that this testing is taking place. The system must distinguish ITF records from actual records, collect information on the effects of the test transactions, and report the results. The auditor compares processing with expected results to verify that the system and its controls are operating correctly.

In a batch processing system, the ITF technique eliminates the need to reverse test transactions and is easily concealed from operating employees. ITF is well suited to testing on-line processing systems, because test transactions can be submitted on a frequent basis, processed with actual transactions, and traced throughout every processing stage. All this can be accomplished without disrupting regular processing operations; however, care must be taken not to combine dummy and actual records during the reporting process.

The **snapshot technique** examines the way transactions are processed. Selected transactions are marked with a special code that triggers the snapshot process. Audit modules in the program record these transactions and their master file records before and after processing. Snapshot data are recorded in a special file and reviewed by the auditor to verify that all processing steps have been properly executed.

System control audit review file (SCARF) uses embedded audit modules to continuously monitor transaction activity and collect data on transactions with special audit significance. The data are recorded in a SCARF file or **audit log.** Transactions recorded in a SCARF file include those exceeding a specified dollar limit, involving inactive accounts, deviating from company policy, or containing write-downs of asset values. Periodically the auditor receives a printout of the SCARF file, examines the information to identify any questionable transactions, and performs any necessary follow-up investigation.

Audit hooks are audit routines that flag suspicious transactions. For example, internal auditors at State Farm Life Insurance determined that their policyholder system was vulnerable to fraud every time a policyholder changed his or her name or address and then subsequently withdrew funds from the policy. Staff devised a system of audit hooks to tag records with a name or address change. The internal audit department is now notified when a tagged record is associated with a withdrawal and can appropriately investigate the transaction for fraud. When audit hooks are used, auditors can be informed of questionable transactions as they occur. This approach, known as **real-time notification,** displays a message on the auditor's terminal. Additional information about State Farm's use of audit hooks, including how a major fraud was detected, is contained in Focus 10-1.

Continuous and intermittent simulation (CIS) embeds an audit module in a database management system. The CIS module examines all transactions that update the DBMS using criteria similar to those of SCARF. If a transaction has special audit significance, the module independently processes the data (in a manner similar to parallel simulation), records the results, and compares them with those obtained by the DBMS. If any discrepancies exist, the details are written on an audit log for subsequent investigation. If serious discrepancies are discovered, the CIS may prevent the DBMS from executing the update process.

Analysis of program logic

If an auditor suspects that a particular application program contains unauthorized code or serious errors, then a detailed analysis of the program logic may be necessary. This process is time-consuming and requires programming language proficiency, so it should be used only as a last resort. To perform the analysis, auditors refer to systems and program flowcharts, program documentation, and a listing of the program source codes. The following software packages serve as aids in this analysis:

- ➤ **Automated flowcharting programs,** which interpret program source code and generate a corresponding program flowchart.
- ➤ **Automated decision table programs,** which generate a decision table representing the program logic.
- ➤ **Scanning routines,** which search a program for occurrences of a specified variable name or other character combinations.
- ➤ **Mapping programs,** which identify unexecuted program code. This software could have uncovered the program code that the unscrupulous programmer inserted to erase all computer files when he was terminated, as detailed in an earlier example.
- ➤ **Program tracing,** which sequentially prints all application program steps (line numbers or paragraph names) executed during a program run. This list is intermingled with regular output so auditors can observe the precise sequence of events that unfold during program execution. Program tracing helps auditors detect unauthorized program instructions, incorrect logic paths, and unexecuted program code.

Focus 10-1

Using Audit Hooks at State Farm Life

THE STATE FARM LIFE INSURANCE COMPANY computer system has a host computer in Bloomington, Illinois, and 26 smaller computers in regional offices. In the regional offices, more than 1,500 terminals and personal computers are used to update almost 4 million individual policyholder records in the host computer. The system processes more than 30 million transactions per year. The system keeps track of policyholder funds valued at more than $6.7 billion.

This on-line, real-time system updates files and databases as transactions occur. Paper audit trails have virtually vanished, and documents supporting changes to policyholder records have been virtually eliminated or are only held a short time before disposition.

Anyone with access and a working knowledge of the system could potentially commit fraud. The internal audit staff had the challenge of identifying the life insurance transactions in which fraud was possible. To accomplish this task, the internal auditors brainstormed ways to defraud the system and interviewed various sys-

tem users who provided extremely valuable insights.

Auditors currently have 33 embedded audit hooks monitoring 42 different types of transactions. One audit hook monitors unusual transactions in transfer accounts, which are clearing accounts for temporarily holding funds that are to be credited to multiple accounts.

The audit hooks have been very successful. One employee fraudulently obtained cash by processing a loan on her brother's life insurance policy. She then forged her brother's endorsement and cashed the check. To cover up the fraud, she had to repay the loan before the annual status report was sent to her brother. To do so, she used a series of fictitious transactions involving a transfer account. The fraud was uncovered almost immediately when the transfer account audit hook recognized the first of these fictitious transactions and notified the auditor.

Within a month of the notification, the case had been investigated and the employee was terminated.

Source: Linda Marie Leinicke, W. Max Rexroad, and John D. Ward, "Computer Fraud Auditing: It Works," *Internal Auditor* (August 1990).

Objective 5: Source Data

Table 10-5 shows the internal controls that prevent, detect, and correct inaccurate or unauthorized source data. It also shows the systems review and tests of control procedures that auditors use for evaluation. In an on-line system, the source data entry and processing functions are one operation. Therefore, source data controls, such as proper authorization and editing data input, are integrated with processing controls.

Auditors use an **input controls matrix,** such as the one depicted in Figure 10-3, to document the review of source data controls. The matrix shows the control procedures applied to each field of an input record.

Auditors should make sure that the data control function is independent of other functions, maintains a data control log, handles errors, and ensures the overall

Table 10-5   Framework for Audit of Source Data Controls

Types of Errors and Fraud
- Inaccurate source data
- Unauthorized source data

Control Procedures
- Effective handling of source data input by data control personnel
- User authorization of source data input
- Preparation and reconciliation of batch control totals
- Logging of the receipt, movement, and disposition of source data input
- Check digit verification
- Key verification
- Use of turnaround documents
- Computer data editing routines
- File change listings and summaries prepared for user department review
- Effective procedures for correcting and resubmitting erroneous data

Audit Procedures: System Review
- Review documentation about responsibilities of data control function
- Review administrative documentation for source data control standards
- Review methods of authorization and examine authorization signatures

- Review accounting systems documentation to identify source data content and processing steps and specific source data controls used
- Document accounting source data controls using an input control matrix
- Discuss source data control procedures with data control personnel as well as the users and managers of the system

Audit Procedures: Tests of Controls
- Observe and evaluate data control department operations and specific data control procedures
- Verify proper maintenance and use of data control log
- Evaluate how items recorded in the error log are dealt with
- Examine samples of accounting source data for proper authorization
- Reconcile a sample of batch totals and follow up on discrepancies
- Trace disposition of a sample of errors flagged by data edit routines

Compensating Controls
- Strong user controls
- Strong processing controls

efficiency of operations. It is usually not economically feasible for small businesses and PC installations to have an independent data control function. To compensate, user department controls must be stronger over data preparation, batch control totals, edit programs, restrictions on physical and logical access to the system, and error handling procedures. These procedures should be the focus of the auditor's systems review and tests of controls when there is no independent data control function.

Although source data controls may not change often, the strictness with which they are applied may. Therefore auditors should test them on a regular basis. The auditor tests the system by evaluating samples of source data for proper authorization. A sample of batch controls should be reconciled. A sample of data edit errors should be evaluated to check that they were resolved and resubmitted into the system.

If source data controls are inadequate, user department and computer processing controls may compensate. If not, the auditor should strongly recommend steps to correct the source data control deficiencies.

Record Name: Employee Weekly Time Report Input Controls	Field Names:	Employee number	Last name	Department number	Transaction code	Week ending (date)	Regular hours	Overtime hours	Comments
Financial totals						✓	✓		
Hash totals		✓							
Record counts									Yes
Cross-footing balance									No
Key verification		✓				✓	✓		
Visual inspection									All fields
Check digit verification		✓							
Prenumbered forms									No
Turnaround document									No
Edit program									Yes
Sequence check		✓							
Field check		✓		✓		✓	✓		
Sign check									
Validity check		✓		✓	✓	✓			
Limit check						✓	✓		
Reasonableness test						✓	✓		
Redundant data check		✓	✓	✓					
Completeness test					✓	✓	✓	✓	
Overflow procedure									
Other:									

Figure 10-3   Input controls matrix

Objective 6: Data Files

The sixth objective concerns the accuracy, integrity, and security of data stored in machine-readable files. Data storage risks include the unauthorized modification, destruction, or disclosure of data. Many of the controls discussed in Chapter 8 are used to protect the system against these risks. If file controls are seriously deficient, especially with respect to physical or logical access or to backup and recovery procedures, then the auditor should strongly recommend they be rectified. Table 10-6 summarizes the errors, controls, and audit procedures for this objective.

Table 10-6 Framework for Audit of Data File Controls

Types of Errors and Fraud
- Destruction of stored data due to inadvertent errors, hardware or software malfunctions, and intentional acts of sabotage or vandalism
- Unauthorized modification or disclosure of stored data

Control Procedures
- Secure file library and restrictions on physical access to data files
- Logical access controls using passwords and access control matrix
- Proper use of file labels and write-protection mechanisms
- Concurrent update controls
- Use of data encryption for highly confidential data
- Use of virus protection software
- Maintenance of backup copies of all data files in an off-site location
- Use of checkpoint and rollback to facilitate system recovery

Audit Procedures: System Review
- Review documentation for functions of file library operation
- Review logical access policies and procedures
- Review operating documentation to determine prescribed standards for
  —use of file labels and write-protection mechanisms
  —use of virus protection software
  —use of backup data storage
  —system recovery, including checkpoint and rollback procedures

- Review systems documentation to examine prescribed procedures for
  —use of concurrent update controls and data encryption
  —control of file conversions
  —reconciling master file totals with independent control totals
- examine disaster recovery plan
- discuss data file control procedures with systems managers and operators

Audit Procedures: Tests of Controls
- Observe and evaluate file library operations
- Review records of password assignment and modification
- Observe and evaluate file-handling procedures by operations personnel
- Observe the preparation and off-site storage of backup files
- Verify the effective use of virus protection procedures
- Verify the use of concurrent update controls and data encryption
- Verify completeness, currency, and testing of disaster recovery plan
- Reconcile master file totals with separately maintained control totals
- Observe the procedures used to control file conversion

Compensating Controls
- Strong user controls
- Effective computer security controls
- Strong processing controls

The auditing-by-objectives approach is a comprehensive, systematic, and effective means of evaluating internal controls in an AIS. It can be implemented using an audit procedures checklist for each objective. The checklist should help the auditor reach a separate conclusion for each objective and suggest compensating controls when an objective is not fully achieved. A separate version of the checklist should be completed for each significant application.

Auditors should review system designs while there is still time to adopt their suggestions for control and audit features. Techniques such as ITF, snapshot, SCARF, audit hooks, and real-time notification should be incorporated into a system during the design process, rather than as an afterthought. Similarly, most application control techniques are easier to design into the system than to add after the system is developed.

COMPUTER SOFTWARE

A number of computer programs, called **computer audit software (CAS)** or **generalized audit software (GAS),** have been written especially for auditors. They are available from software vendors and the larger public accounting firms. In essence, CAS is a computer program that, based on the auditor's specifications, generates programs that perform the audit functions. CAS is ideally suited for examination of large data files to identify records needing further audit scrutiny. For example, Focus 10-2 describes how the U.S. government uses CAS to battle the federal budget deficit. Table 10-7 contains a list of CAS functions and one or more audit examples for each function.

Figure 10-4 shows how CAS is used. The auditor's first step is to decide on audit objectives, learn about the files and databases to be audited, design the audit reports, and determine how to produce them. This information is recorded on specification sheets and entered into the system via a data entry program. This program creates specification records that the CAS uses to produce one or more auditing programs. The auditing programs process the source files and perform the

---

Focus 10-2

Battling Federal Budget Deficits with Audit Software

THE U.S. GOVERNMENT is finding that computer audit software is a valuable tool in its attempts to reduce massive federal budget deficits. For example, the software is being used to identify fraudulent Medicare claims and pinpoint excessive charges by defense contractors.

A computer audit by the General Accounting Office (GAO) cross-checked figures with the IRS and discovered that thousands of veterans lied about their income to qualify for pension benefits. The audit revealed that 116,000 veterans receiving pensions on the basis of need failed to disclose $338 million in income from savings accounts, stock dividends, or rents. More than

13,600 veterans underreported their income, and one did not report income of over $300,000.

Before the computer check was instituted, the Veterans Administration (VA) relied on the vets for accurate income reports. Once the VA notified beneficiaries that their income would be verified with the IRS and the Social Security Administration, the pension rolls dropped by more than 13,000, at a savings of $9 million a month, the GAO reported.

The VA plans to use the same system for checking income levels of those applying for medical care. If their income is found to be above a certain level, patients will be required to make co-payments.

Table 10-7   General Functions of Computer Audit Software

Function	Explanation	Examples
Reformatting	Read data in different formats and data structures, and convert to a common format and structure	Read inventory records from purchasing database and convert to an inventory file usable by the GAS program
File manipulation	Sort records into sequential order; merge files sequenced on the same sort key	Sort inventory records by location; merge customer transaction files with receivables master file
Calculation	Perform the four basic arithmetic operations: add, subtract, multiply, and divide	Foot client accounts receivable file; recalculate client inventory valuation; recalculate client depreciation; sum employee payroll by department
Data selection	Review data files to retrieve records meeting specified criteria	Identify customer accounts having a balance exceeding the credit limit; select all purchase transactions in excess of a specified dollar amount
Data analysis	Examine records for errors or missing values; compare fields in related records for inconsistencies	Perform data editing of client files; compare personnel and payroll files to verify consistency
File processing	Provide programming capability for file creation, updating, and downloading to a personal computer	Use parallel simulation to verify that client gross pay calculations are correct; download sample of client inventory records to personal computer for further analysis to support inventory test counts
Statistics	Stratify file records by item valuation; select statistical samples; analyze statistical sampling results	Stratify customer accounts by size of account balance and select a stratified sample of accounts for audit confirmation
Report generation	Format and print reports and documents	Prepare analysis of financial statement ratios and trends; prepare accounts receivable aging schedule; prepare audit confirmations

auditing operations needed to produce the specified audit reports. Frequently, an initial CAS computer run is performed to extract key auditing information and place it in an audit work file. Additional audit reports and analyses are generated by subsequent computer runs that use the audit work file as input.

The following case illustrates the value of audit software. In a small New England town, a new tax collector was elected, defeating the incumbent. The new tax collector requested an audit of the city's tax collection records. Using CAS, the auditor accessed the tax collection records for the past 4 years, sorted them by collection date, summed the amount of taxes collected monthly, and prepared a 4-year summary report of monthly tax collections. The analysis revealed that tax collections during January and July, the two busiest months, had declined by 58 percent and 72

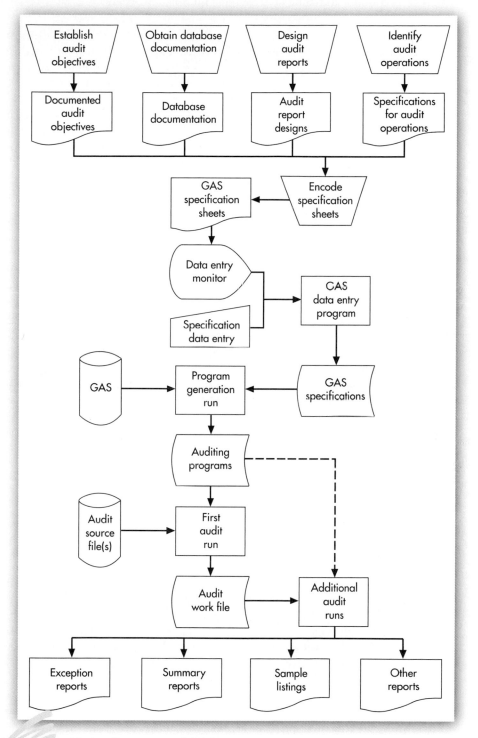

Figure 10-4 Overview of GAS processing

percent, respectively. Auditors used the CAS to compare the tax collection records, one by one, with the city's property records. The ensuing report identified several discrepancies, including one case where the former tax collector used another taxpayer's payment to cover her own delinquent tax bills. The former tax collector was arrested and charged with embezzlement.

The primary purpose of CAS is to assist the auditor in reviewing and retrieving information in computer files. When the auditor receives the CAS reports, most of the audit work still remains to be done. Items on exception reports must be investigated, file totals must be verified against other sources of information such as the general ledger, and audit samples must be examined and evaluated. Although the advantages of using CAS are numerous and compelling, CAS cannot replace the auditor's judgment or free her from other phases of the audit.

OPERATIONAL AUDITS OF AN AIS

The techniques and procedures used in operational audits are similar to those of information systems and financial audits. The basic difference is that the information systems audit scope is confined to internal controls, whereas the financial audit scope is limited to systems output. In contrast, the operational audit scope is much broader, encompassing all aspects of information systems management. In addition, operational audit objectives include evaluating such factors as effectiveness, efficiency, and goal achievement.

The first step in an operational audit is audit planning, during which the scope and objectives of the audit are established, a preliminary review of the system is performed, and a tentative audit program is prepared.

Evidence collection includes the following activities:

➤ Reviewing operating policies and documentation
➤ Confirming procedures with management and operating personnel
➤ Observing operating functions and activities
➤ Examining financial and operating plans and reports
➤ Testing the accuracy of operating information
➤ Testing controls

At the evidence evaluation stage, the auditor measures the actual system against an ideal one, a system that follows the best principles of systems management. One important consideration is that the results of management policies and practices are more significant than the policies and practices themselves. That is, if good results are achieved through policies and practices that are theoretically deficient, then the auditor must carefully consider whether recommended improvements would substantially improve results. In any event, the auditor should thoroughly document the findings and conclusions and communicate the audit results to management.

Being a good operational auditor requires some degree of management experience. Those with strong auditing backgrounds but weak or no management experience often lack the perspective necessary to understand the management process. Thus, the ideal operational auditor is a person with audit training and experience and a few years' experience in a managerial position.

SUMMARY AND CASE CONCLUSION

Jason is trying to determine how his parallel simulation program generated sales commission figures that differed from those of SPP's program. When he studied the figures, he noticed that in all the differences, the sales commission was higher than average. This meant there might have been a systematic error in one of the programs. After verifying that his program was correct, he asked to review a copy of SPP's program.

The program was very lengthy, so Jason used the scanning technique to search the code for a specified set of characters. Under the new policy, the commission rate changes when sales for the period exceed $40,000. Jason searched the code for occurrences of "40000," which directed him to the place where the commission rate structure resides. To his astonishment, he discovered a commission rate of 0.085 for sales in excess of $40,000, while the policy called for only 0.075. Some quick calculations confirmed this was the source of the differences between the two programs.

Jason reported the findings to his supervisor, who called the audit manager. They arranged a meeting between the audit manager and the head of the systems development team. The meeting was quite embarrassing for the team head and her staff, but the coding error was acknowledged and corrected.

The audit manager called Jason to congratulate him and informed him that if the programming error had gone undetected, SPP would have paid over $100,000 per year in excess sales commissions. Jason was grateful to receive the manager's praise, but he also took the opportunity to point out deficiencies in the programming practices employed by the development team. First, the commission rate table had been embedded in the program code; good programming practice would require that it be stored in a separate table to be used by the program when needed. Second, he suggested that the incident called into question the quality of SPP's program development and testing practices. Jason asked if a more extensive operational audit of those practices might be appropriate. The audit manager agreed that this might be worth examining, and he promised to raise the issue at his next meeting with Northwest's director of internal auditing.

KEY TERMS

- auditing
- financial audit
- information systems audit
- operational audit
- management audit
- inherent risk
- control risk
- detection risk
- materiality
- reasonable assurance
- systems review
- tests of control
- compensating controls
- reprocessing

- parallel simulation
- test data generator program
- concurrent audit techniques
- embedded audit modules
- integrated test facility (ITF)
- snapshot technique
- system control audit review file (SCARF)
- audit log
- audit hooks
- real-time notification
- continuous and intermittent simulation (CIS)

- automated flowcharting programs
- automated decision table programs
- scanning routines
- mapping programs
- program tracing
- input controls matrix
- computer audit software (CAS)
- generalized audit software (GAS)

CHAPTER QUIZ

1. Which of the following is a characteristic of auditing?
   a. Auditing is a systematic, step-by-step process.
   b. Auditing involves the collection and review of evidence.
   c. Auditing involves the use of established criteria to evaluate evidence.
   d. All of the above are characteristic of auditing.

2. Which of the following is not one reason that an internal auditor should participate in internal control reviews during the design of new systems?
   a. It is more economical to design controls during the design stage than to do so later.
   b. It eliminates the need for testing controls during regular audits.
   c. It minimizes the need for expensive postimplementation modifications.
   d. It permits the design of audit trails while they are economical.

3. Which type of audit involves a review of general and application controls, with a focus on determining if there is compliance with policies and adequate safeguarding of assets?
   a. information systems audit
   b. financial audit
   c. operational audit
   d. compliance audit

4. At what step in the audit process do the concepts of reasonable assurance and materiality enter into the auditor's decision process?
   a. planning
   b. evidence collection
   c. evidence evaluation
   d. Materiality is important in all three steps.

5. What is the process of examining if the necessary controls have been designed into the system called?
   a. risk analysis
   b. systems review
   c. tests of controls
   d. risk-based approach to auditing

6. Which of the following procedures is not used to detect unauthorized program changes?
   a. source code comparison
   b. parallel simulation
   c. reprocessing
   d. reprogramming code

7. Which of the following is a concurrent audit technique that monitors all transactions and collects data on those that meet certain characteristics specified by the auditor?
   a. integrated test facility
   b. snapshot techniques
   c. SCARF
   d. audit hooks

8. Which of the following is a computer technique that assists an auditor in understanding program logic by identifying all occurrences of specific variables?
   a. mapping program
   b. program tracing
   c. automated flowcharting
   d. scanning routine

9. Which of the following is a computer program written especially for audit use?
   a. GAS
   b. SCARF
   c. ITF
   d. CIS
10. The focus of an operational audit is on which of the following?
    a. reliability and integrity of the financial information
    b. efficient use of resources
    c. internal controls
    d. safeguarding assets

DISCUSSION QUESTIONS

10.1   Auditing an AIS effectively requires that an auditor have some knowledge of computers and their accounting applications. However, it may not be feasible for every auditor to be a computer expert. Discuss the extent to which auditors should possess computer expertise to be effective auditors.

10.2   Should internal auditors be members of systems development teams that design and implement an AIS? Why or why not?

10.3   Berwick Industries is a fast-growing corporation that manufactures industrial containers. The company has a sophisticated AIS that uses advanced technology. Berwick's executives have decided to pursue listing the company's securities on a national stock exchange, but they have been advised that their listing application would be stronger if they were to create an internal audit department.

At present, no Berwick employees have auditing experience. To staff its new internal audit function, Berwick could (a) train some of its computer specialists in auditing, (b) hire experienced auditors and train them to understand Berwick's information system, (c) use a combination of the first two approaches, or (d) try a different approach. Which approach would you support, and why?

10.4   The assistant finance director for the city of Tustin, California, was fired after city officials discovered that she had used her access to city computers to cancel her daughter's $300 water bill. An investigation revealed that she had embezzled a large sum of money from Tustin in this manner over a long period. She was able to conceal the embezzlement for so long because the amount embezzled always fell within a 2 percent error factor used by the city's internal auditors. Should Tustin's internal auditors have discovered this fraud earlier? Discuss.

PROBLEMS

10.1   You are the director of internal auditing at a university. Recently, you met with Issa Arnita, the manager of administrative data processing, and expressed the desire to establish a more effective interface between the two departments. Issa wants your help with a new computerized accounts payable system currently in development. He recommends that your department assume line responsibility for auditing suppliers' invoices prior to payment. He also wants internal auditing to make suggestions during system development, assist in its installation, and approve the completed system after making a final review.

Required

Would you accept or reject each of the following, and why?

a. The recommendation that your department be responsible for the preaudit of suppliers' invoices
b. The request that you make suggestions during development of the system
c. The request that you assist in the installation of the system and approve the system after making a final review

(CIA Examination, adapted)

10.2   As an internal auditor for the Quick Manufacturing Company, you are participating in the audit of the company's AIS. You have been reviewing the internal controls of the computer system that processes most of its accounting applications. You have studied the company's extensive documentation of its systems and have interviewed the MIS manager, operations supervisor, and other employees to complete your standardized computer internal control questionnaire.

You report to your supervisor that the company has designed a successful set of comprehensive internal controls into its computer systems. He thanks you for your efforts and asks for a summary report of your findings for inclusion in a final overall report on accounting internal controls.

Required

Have you forgotten an important audit step? Explain. List five examples of specific audit procedures that you might recommend before reaching a final conclusion.

10.3   As an internal auditor, you have been assigned to evaluate the controls and operation of a computer payroll system. To test the computer systems and programs, you are to submit independently created test transactions with regular data in a normal production run.

Required

a. List four advantages of this technique.
b. List two disadvantages of this technique.

(CIA Examination, adapted)

10.4   You are involved in the internal audit of accounts receivable, which represent a significant portion of the assets of a large retail corporation. Your audit plan requires the use of the computer, but you encounter the following reactions.

a. The computer operations manager says that all time on the computer is booked for the foreseeable future and that it will not be available to help the auditor with his work.
b. The computer scheduling manager suggests that your computer program be cataloged into the computer program library (on disk storage) so that it can be run when computer time becomes available.
c. You are refused admission to the computer room.
d. The systems manager tells you that it will take too much time to adapt the computer audit program to the computer's operating system and that company programmers will write the programs needed for the audit.

Required

For each of the four situations described, state the action the auditor should take to proceed with the accounts receivable audit.

(CIA Examination, adapted)

10.5   You are a manager for the regional CPA firm of Dewey, Cheatem, and Howe (DC&H). You are reviewing your staff's working papers of an audit of the state welfare agency. You find that the test data concept was used to test the agency's computer program that maintains accounting records. Specifically, your staff obtained a duplicate copy of the program and of the welfare accounting data file from the manager of computer operations and borrowed the test transaction data file used by the welfare agency's programmers when the program was written. These were processed on DC&H's home office computer. A copy of the edit summary report that listed no errors was included in the working papers, with a notation by the audit senior that the test indicates good application controls.

You note that the quality of the audit conclusions obtained from this test is flawed in several respects, and you decide to ask your subordinates to repeat the test.

Required

Identify three existing or potential problems with the way this test was performed. For each problem, suggest one or more procedures that might be performed during the revised test to avoid flaws in the audit conclusions.

10.6   You are auditing the financial statements of Aardvark Wholesalers, Inc. (AW), a wholesaler with operations in 12 western states and total revenues of about $125 million. AW uses a computer system in several of its major accounting applications. Accordingly, you are carrying out an information system audit to evaluate internal controls in their computer system.

From an AW manual, you have obtained the following job descriptions for key personnel:

Director of information systems: Reports to administrative vice president. Responsible for defining the mission of the information systems division and for planning, staffing, and managing a department that optimally executes this mission.

Manager of systems and programming: Reports to director of information systems. Responsible for managing a staff of systems analysts and programmers whose mission is to design, program, test, implement, and maintain cost-effective data processing systems. Also responsible for establishing and monitoring documentation standards.

Manager of operations: Reports to director of information systems. Responsible for cost-effective management of computer center operations, for enforcement of processing standards, and for systems programming, including implementation of operating system vendor upgrades.

Data entry shift supervisor: Reports to manager of operations. Responsible for supervision of data entry operators and monitoring of data preparation standards.

Operations shift supervisor: Reports to manager of operations. Responsible for supervision of computer operations staff and monitoring of processing standards.

Data control clerk: Reports to manager of operations. Responsible for logging and distributing computer input and output, monitoring source data control procedures, and custody of program and data files.

Required

a. Prepare an organizational chart for AW's information systems division.
b. Name two positive and two negative aspects (from an internal control standpoint) of this organizational structure.
c. What additional information, if any, would you require before making a final judgment on the adequacy of AW's separation of functions in the information systems division?

10.7   Robinson's Plastic Pipe Corporation uses a computerized inventory data processing system. The basic input record to this system has the format shown in Table 10-8. You are performing an audit of source data controls for this system, and you have decided to use an input controls matrix for this purpose.

Table 10-8   Parts Inventory Transaction File

Field Name	Field Type	Positions
Item number	Numeric	1–6
Transaction date	Date	7–12
Transaction type	Alphanumeric	13
Document number	Alphanumeric	14–21
Quantity	Numeric	22–26
Unit cost	Monetary	27–33

Required

Prepare an input controls matrix using the same format and listing the same input controls as shown in Figure 10-3; however, replace the field names shown in Figure 10-3 with those of the inventory transaction file shown in Table 10-8. Place checks in the cells of the matrix that represent input controls you might expect to find for each field.

10.8   As an internal auditor for the state auditor's office, you have been assigned to review the implementation of a new computer system in the state welfare agency. The agency is installing an on-line computer system to maintain the state's database of welfare recipients. Under the old system, state residents applying for welfare assistance completed a form giving their name, address, and other personal data, plus details about their income, assets, dependents, and other data needed to establish their eligibility. The data on these forms are checked by welfare examiners to verify their authenticity. The welfare examiners then certify the applicant's eligibility for assistance and determine the form and amount of aid.

Under the new system, welfare applicants will provide their case data to clerks, who will simultaneously enter the data into the system using on-line terminals. Each applicant record will be assigned a "pending" status until a welfare examiner can verify the authenticity of the crucial data used in determining eligibility for assistance. When this verification process has been completed, the welfare examiner will enter a change in the status code from "pending" to "approved," and then the system will execute a program to calculate the appropriate amount of aid.

Periodically, the circumstances (income, assets, dependents, etc.) of welfare recipients change and the database must be updated accordingly. Welfare examiners will enter these change transactions into the system as soon as their accuracy has been verified. The system will then immediately recalculate the recipient's welfare benefit. At the end of each month, checks are generated and mailed to all eligible welfare recipients.

Welfare assistance in your state amounts to several hundred million dollars annually. You are concerned about the possibilities of fraud and abuse.

Required

a. Describe how you could employ concurrent audit techniques within this system to reduce the risks of fraud and abuse.

b. Describe how computer audit software could be used to review the work of welfare examiners in verifying applicant eligibility data. For this purpose you may assume that the state auditor's office has access to computerized databases maintained by other state and local government agencies.

11.9   You are an internal auditor for the Military Industrial Company. You are presently preparing test transactions for the company's weekly payroll processing program. Each input record to this program contains the following data items.

Spaces	Data Item
1–9	Social Security number
10	Pay code (1 = hourly; 2 = salaried)
11–16	Wage rate or salary
17–19	Hours worked, in tenths
20–21	Number of exemptions claimed
22–29	Year-to-date gross pay, including cents
30–80	Employee name and address

The program performs the following edit checks on each input record:

- Field checks to identify any records that do not have numeric characters in the fields for wage rate/salary, hours, exemptions, and year-to-date gross pay
- A validity check of the pay code
- A limit check to identify any hourly employee records with a wage rate higher than $20
- A limit check to identify any hourly employee records with hours worked greater than 70 hours
- A limit check to identify any salaried employee records with a weekly salary greater than $2,000 or less than $100

Records that do not pass these edit checks are listed on an error report. For those that pass the edit checks, the program performs a series of calculations. First, the employee's gross pay is determined. Gross pay for a salaried employee is equal to the salary amount contained within spaces 11 to 16 of the input record. Gross pay for an hourly employee is equal to the wage rate times the number of hours up to 40, plus 1.5 times the wage rate times the number of hours in excess of 40 hours.

The program computes federal withholding tax for each employee by multiplying gross pay times a tax rate determined from Table 10-9. The program next computes state withholding tax for each employee by multiplying gross pay times a tax rate determined from Table 10-10.

Table 10-9   Computation of Federal Withholding Tax

Number of Exemptions	Gross Pay Range			
	$0–$99.99	$100–$249.99	$250–$499.99	Over $500
0–1	0.06	0.12	0.18	0.24
2–3	0.04	0.10	0.16	0.22
4–5	0.02	0.08	0.14	0.20
Over 5	0.00	0.06	0.12	0.18

Table 10-10 Computation of State Withholding Tax

Number of Exemptions	Gross Pay Range	
	$0–$499.99	Over $500
0–3	0.03	0.05
Over 3	0.01	0.03

The program next computes the employee's pension contribution, which is 3 percent of gross pay for hourly employees and 4 percent of gross pay for salaried employees. Finally, the program computes the employee's net pay, which is gross pay minus tax withholdings and pension contribution. Once these calculations have been completed for one employee record, the program prints that employee's paycheck and summary earnings statement and then proceeds to the next employee input record to perform edit checks and payroll calculations, continuing this cycle until all input records have been processed.

Your short-term goal is to prepare a set of test transactions containing one of each possible type of error and another set of test transactions that will test each of the computational alternatives one at a time. Transactions to test for multiple errors in one record, or to test for multiple combinations of logic paths, are to be developed later.

The test transactions you prepare need not include a Social Security number or an employee name and address (your assistant will add those after reviewing a file printout). Accordingly, each of your test transactions will consist of a series of 20 characters representing data in spaces 10 to 29 of an input record. For example, for an hourly employee who has a wage rate of $9.50, worked 40.5 hours, claims two exemptions, and has a year-to-date gross pay of exactly $12,000, the test transaction would be 10009504050201200000.

Required

a. Prepare a set of test transactions; each transaction should contain one of the errors tested for by the edit checks. Determine the expected results of processing for each of these test transactions.

b. Prepare a set of test transactions that test every possible way gross pay may be calculated. Determine the expected gross pay for each of these transactions.

c. Prepare a set of test transactions that test every possible way federal withholding tax may be computed. Determine the expected value of the federal withholding tax for each of these test transactions.

d. Prepare a set of test transactions that test every possible way state withholding tax may be computed. Determine the expected value of the state withholding tax for each of these test transactions.

e. Prepare a set of test transactions that test every possible way the pension contribution may be computed. Determine the expected value of the pension contribution for each of these test transactions.

10.10 The internal audit department of Sachem Manufacturing Company is considering the purchase of computer software that will aid the auditing process. Sachem's financial and manufacturing control systems are completely automated on a large mainframe computer. Melinda Robinson, the director of internal auditing, believes that Sachem should acquire computer audit software to assist in the financial and procedural audits that her department conducts. Robinson is considering the following types of software packages:

- A generalized audit software package that assists in basic audit work such as the retrieval of live data from large computer files. The department would review this information using conventional audit investigation techniques. More specifically, the department could perform criteria selection, sampling, basic computations for quantitative analysis, record handling, graphical analysis, and the printing of output (i.e., confirmations).
- An ITF package that uses, monitors, and controls dummy test data as they are processed by existing programs. It also checks the programs and the existence and adequacy of program data entry and processing controls.
- A flowcharting package that graphically presents the flow of information through a system and pinpoints control strengths and weaknesses.
- A parallel simulation and modeling package that uses actual data to conduct the same tests using another program, a computer logic program developed by the auditor. The package can also be used to seek answers to difficult audit problems (involving many comparisons) within statistically acceptable confidence limits.

Required

a. Without regard to any specific computer audit software, identify the general advantages of using computer audit software to assist with audits.
b. Describe the audit purpose facilitated and the procedural steps to be followed by the internal auditor in using the following:
   - Generalized audit software package
   - Integrated test facility package
   - Control flowcharting package
   - Program (parallel) simulation and modeling package

(CMA Examination, adapted)

10.11 The Thermo-Bond Manufacturing Company maintains its fixed asset records on its computer. The fixed asset master file includes the data items listed in Table 10-11.

Table 10-11 Fixed Asset Master File

Item Number	Location	Description
1	1–6	Asset number
2	7–30	Description
3	31	Type code
4	32–34	Location code
5	35–40	Date of acquisition
6	41–50	Original cost
7	51–56	Date of retirement*
8	57	Depreciation method code
9	58–61	Depreciation rate
10	62–63	Useful life (years)
11	64–73	Accumulated depreciation at beginning of year
12	74–83	Year-to-date depreciation

*For assets still in service, the retirement date is assigned the value 99/99/99.

Required

Refer to Table 10-7, which describes the general functions of computer audit software. Then explain several ways such software could be used by an auditor in performing a financial audit of Thermo-Bond's fixed asset account.

10.12 An auditor is conducting an examination of the financial statements of a wholesale cosmetics distributor with an inventory consisting of thousands of individual items. The distributor keeps its inventory in its own distribution center and in two public warehouses. It maintains an inventory computer file on a computer disk, and at the end of each business day it updates the file. Each record of the inventory file contains the following data:

Item number	Cost per item
Description of item	Date of last purchase
Quantity on hand	Date of last sale
Location of item	Quantity sold during year

The auditor will have a CAS and a disk containing inventory data as of the date of the distributor's physical inventory count. The auditor will perform the following audit procedures:

1. Observe the distributor's physical count of inventories as of a given date, and test a sample for accuracy.
2. Compare the auditor's test counts with the inventory records.
3. Compare physical count data with the inventory records.
4. Test the mathematical accuracy of the distributor's final inventory valuation.
5. Test inventory pricing by obtaining item costs from buyers, vendors, or other sources.
6. Examine inventory purchase and sale transactions on or near the year-end date to verify that all such transactions were recorded in the proper accounting period.
7. Ascertain the propriety of inventory items located in public warehouses.
8. Analyze inventory for evidence of possible obsolescence.
9. Analyze inventory for evidence of possible overstocking or slow-moving items.
10. Test the accuracy of individual data items listed in the distributor's inventory master file.

Required

Describe how the use of the general-purpose software package and the copy of the inventory file data might be helpful to the auditor in performing each of these auditing procedures.

(CPA Examination, adapted)

Case 10-1 AnyCompany, Inc.: An Ongoing Comprehensive Case

Select a local company with an internal auditing department, and obtain permission to study its internal auditing policies and procedures. Then complete the following steps and prepare a report describing your findings and conclusions:

1. Determine to whom internal auditing reports. Does this reporting arrangement provide the internal audit function with sufficient independence?
2. Does the internal audit function perform information system, financial, and operational audits? Does it perform other kinds of audits? About what percentage of its total audit work falls into each of these categories?
3. Determine how the internal auditors perform information system audits. If possible, obtain copies of audit programs, checklists, and/or questionnaires used in performing these audits. Comment on the company's approach to information system auditing.
4. In performing information system audits, do the internal auditors use methods of auditing through the computer, such as reprocessing, parallel simulation, program tracing, test data processing, and concurrent audit techniques? Describe how the internal auditors use these methods.
5. In carrying out financial audits, does the internal audit function employ computer audit software? If so, obtain a copy of the documentation and describe the functions it can perform. If possible, observe how the audit software is used to carry out a financial audit, and examine copies of the output.
6. Ask the internal auditors to explain specific audit jobs during which they discovered something unusual and/or were able to recommend improvements in controls or operating procedures that saved the company substantial amounts of time or money.

Case 10-2 Preston Manufacturing Company

You are performing a financial audit of the general ledger accounts of the Preston Manufacturing Company. At the beginning of the current fiscal year, the company converted its general ledger accounting from a manual to a computer-based system. The new system uses two computer files, the contents of which are specified as follows:

Each day as detailed transactions are processed by Preston's other computerized accounting systems, summary journal entries are accumulated; at the end of the day, they are added to the general ledger file. At the end of each week and each month, the general journal file is processed against the general ledger control file to compute a new current balance for each account and to print a trial balance.

The following resources are available as you complete the audit:

- Your firm's generalized computer audit software package, which can perform the general functions listed in Table 10-7

General Journal		
Field Name	**Field Type**	**Size**
Account number	Numeric	6
Amount	Monetary	9.2
Debit/credit code	Alphanumeric	1
Date (MM/DD/YY)	Date	6
Reference document type	Alphanumeric	4
Reference document number	Numeric	6

General Ledger Control		
Field Name	**Field Type**	**Size**
Account number	Numeric	6
Account name	Alphanumeric	20
Beginning balance/year	Monetary	9.2
Beg-bal-debit/credit code	Alphanumeric	1
Current balance	Monetary	9.2
Cur-bal-debit/credit code	Alphanumeric	1

- A complete copy of the general journal file for the entire year
- A copy of the general ledger file as of the fiscal year-end (current balance = year-end balance)
- A printout of Preston's year-end trial balance listing the account number, account name, and balance of each account on the general ledger control file.

Design a series of procedures utilizing the CAS to analyze the data in these files and prepare the reports needed to carry out your financial audit. Your application design should include the following:

1. A description of the data content of each output report, preferably in the form of a tabular layout chart of the report format
2. A description of the auditing objectives of each report and how the report would be used in subsequent auditing procedures to achieve those objectives

ANSWERS TO CHAPTER QUIZ

1. d	3. a	5. b	7. c	9. a
2. b	4. d	6. d	8. d	10. b

Part III

Accounting Information Systems Applications

The five chapters in Part III describe in detail how a company's AIS supports its business processes. In response to the Y2K issue, many large organizations replaced their disparate stand-alone legacy systems with integrated information systems, such as **enterprise resource planning (ERP) systems.** As shown in Figure III-1, ERP systems integrate an organization's business activities by storing data about those activities in a centralized database.

Figure III-1 shows that at the heart of an ERP system is a database that is shared by and accessible to all the various functions in the organization. This central database enables information relating to one set of business activities to be shared by other business processes in order to efficiently and effectively coordinate activities. Consequently, a business activity in one cycle often triggers a complex sequence of activities that may involve all of the remaining cycles depicted in Figure III-1. For example, in a manufacturing company, new customer orders may result in scheduling additional production. In turn, this may also trigger the purchase of additional raw materials and hiring additional temporary help to meet excess demands. Moreover, the General Ledger and Reporting system can provide up-to-date reports to management to facilitate planning, controlling, and evaluating the performance of the organization's business activities.

The five chapters in Part III describe how this integration occurs by separately examining each of the components depicted in Figure III-1. Each chapter describes the basic business activities that are performed, the threats to effective and efficient performance of those processes and the applicable control procedures for dealing with those threats, and the key decisions that need to be made and the information needed to support those decisions. We begin with the Revenue Cycle, which consists of all of the activities associated with the basic economic exchange of selling goods or services and collecting cash from customers for those goods or services. Next we describe the Expenditure Cycle, which involves the activities associated with acquiring and paying for goods and services. Then we discuss the Production Cycle, which consists of the activities

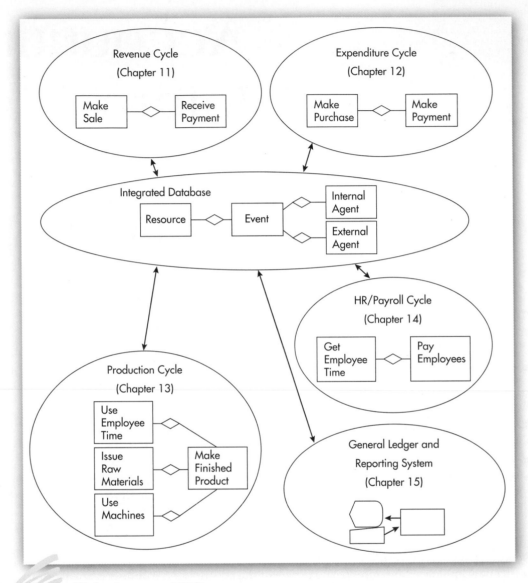

Figure III-1   Integrated ERP system
(Adapted from classroom materials created by Julie Smith David at Arizona State University)

associated with using labor and equipment to transform raw materials into finished goods. The fourth chapter focuses on the Human Resources/Payroll Cycle, addressing issues associated with the effective development and management of an organization's most valuable resource: its employees. In the final chapter we look at the General Ledger and Reporting System, examining issues associated with providing management with timely and accurate financial and nonfinancial information about the effectiveness and efficiency with which the organization executes its various business activities.

The Revenue Cycle: Sales and Cash Collections

Learning Objectives

After studying this chapter, you should be able to:

- Describe the basic business activities and related data processing operations performed in the revenue cycle.
- Discuss the key decisions that need to be made in the revenue cycle and identify the information needed to make those decisions.
- Document your understanding of the revenue cycle.
- Identify major threats in the revenue cycle and evaluate the adequacy of various control procedures for dealing with those threats.
- Read and understand a data model (REA diagram) of the revenue cycle.

Integrative Case: Alpha Omega Electronics

Alpha Omega Electronics (AOE) manufactures a variety of inexpensive consumer electronic products, including calculators, digital clocks, radios, pagers, toys, games, and small kitchen appliances. AOE's primary customers are retail stores, but the company has recently begun selling in bulk to mail-order firms that advertise in catalogs and magazines. Figure 11-1 shows a partial organization chart for AOE.

Linda Spurgeon, president of AOE, called an executive meeting to discuss two pressing issues. First, AOE has been steadily losing market share for the past 3 years. Second, cash-flow problems have necessitated increased short-term borrowing. At the executive meeting, Trevor Whitman, vice president of marketing, explained that one reason for AOE's declining market share is that competitors are apparently providing better customer service. When Linda asked for specifics, however, Trevor admitted that his opinion was based on recent conversations with two major customers. Moreover, he also admitted that he could not readily identify AOE's 10 most profitable customers. Linda then asked Elizabeth Venko, the controller, about AOE's cash flow problems. The most recent accounts receivable aging schedule indicated a significant increase in the number of past-due customer accounts. Consequently, AOE has had to increase its short-term borrowing because of delays in collecting customer payments. In addition, the Best Value Company, a retail chain that has been one of AOE's major customers, recently went bankrupt. Elizabeth admitted that she is unsure if AOE will be able to collect the large balance due from Best Value.

Linda was frustrated with the lack of detailed information regarding both issues. She ended the meeting by asking Elizabeth and Trevor to work with Ann Brandt, vice president of information systems, to develop improved reporting systems so that AOE could more closely monitor and take steps to improve both customer service and cash-flow management. Specifically, Linda asked Elizabeth, Trevor, and Ann to address the following issues:

1. How could AOE improve customer service? What information does marketing need to perform its tasks better?
2. How could AOE identify its most profitable customers and markets?
3. How can AOE improve its monitoring of credit accounts? How would any changes in credit policy affect both sales and uncollectible accounts?
4. How could AOE improve its cash collection procedures?

As the AOE case indicates, deficiencies in the information system used to support revenue cycle activities can create significant problems for an organization. As you read this chapter, think about how AOE's information system can be redesigned to provide more efficient and effective support of its revenue cycle activities.

Figure 11-1 Partial organization chart for AOE

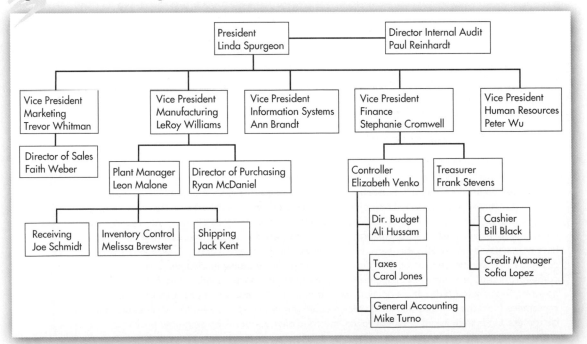

INTRODUCTION

The revenue cycle is a recurring set of business activities and related information processing operations associated with providing goods and services to customers and collecting cash in payment for those sales (see Figure 11-2). The primary external exchange of information is with customers. Information about revenue cycle activities also flows to the other accounting cycles (via the centralized database, which is not shown in Figure 11-2, to reduce clutter). For example, the expenditure and production cycles use information about sales transactions to initiate the purchase or production of additional inventory to meet demand. The human resource management/payroll cycle uses information about sales to calculate sales commissions and bonuses. The general ledger and reporting function uses information produced by the revenue cycle to prepare financial statements and performance reports.

The revenue cycle's primary objective is to provide the right product in the right place at the right time for the right price. To accomplish that objective, management must make the following key decisions:

➤ To what extent can and should products be customized to individual customers' needs and desires?

➤ How much inventory should be carried, and where should that inventory be located?

Figure 11-2   The context diagram of the revenue cycle

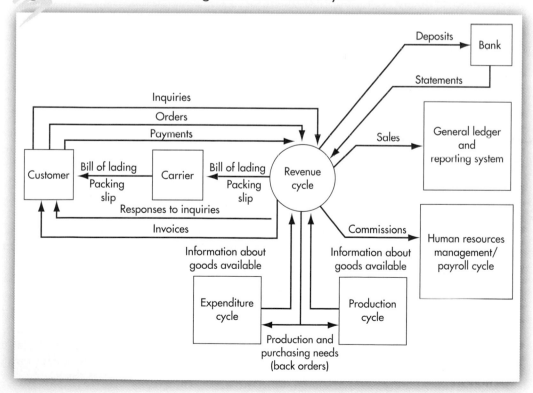

➤ How should merchandise be delivered to customers? Should the company perform the shipping function itself or outsource it to a third party that specializes in logistics?

➤ What are the optimal prices for each product or service?

➤ Should credit be extended to customers?

➤ How much credit should be given to individual customers?

➤ What credit terms should be offered?

➤ How can customer payments be processed to maximize cash flow?

In addition, management must monitor and evaluate the efficiency and effectiveness of revenue cycle processes. This requires easy access to detailed data about the resources employed in the revenue cycle, the events that affect those resources, and the agents who participate in those events. Moreover, to be useful and relevant for decision making, that data must be accurate, reliable, and timely.

This chapter examines the three basic functions of the AIS in the revenue cycle: capturing and processing data about business activities, storing and organizing that data to support decision making, and providing controls to ensure the reliability of data and the safeguarding of organizational resources. We begin by describing the basic business activities performed in the revenue cycle. Then we examine the methods used to collect, store, and process data about revenue cycle activities. Next, we examine the major control objectives in the revenue cycle and discuss how to design the AIS to mitigate the threats associated with revenue cycle activities. We conclude the chapter by presenting an integrated data model that stores and organizes information about revenue cycle activities in a manner that enables management to make key decisions and effectively monitor performance.

REVENUE CYCLE BUSINESS ACTIVITIES

Figure 11-3 shows the four basic business activities performed in the revenue cycle.

Sales Order Entry

The revenue cycle begins with the receipt of orders from customers. The sales order department, which reports to the vice president of marketing (refer back to Figure 11-1), performs the sales order entry process. Figure 11-4 shows that the sales order entry process entails three steps: taking the customer's order, checking and approving customer credit, and checking inventory availability. Figure 11-4 also includes an important related event that may be handled either by the sales order department or by a separate customer service department (which typically also reports to the vice president of marketing), that of responding to customer inquiries.

Taking customer orders

Customer orders can be received in many different ways: in store, by mail, by phone, over a Web site, or by a salesperson in the field. In recent years, organizations have discovered a number of ways to use IT to improve the efficiency and effectiveness of the sales order entry process. One way to improve sales order entry

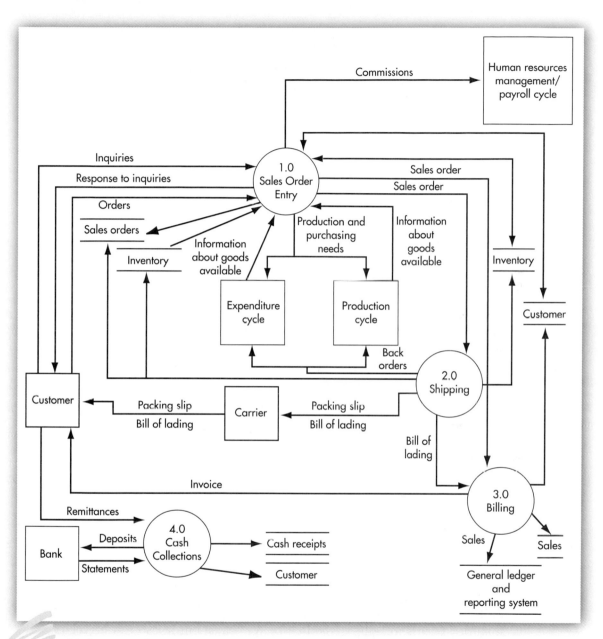

Figure 11-3 Level 0 data flow diagram of the revenue cycle

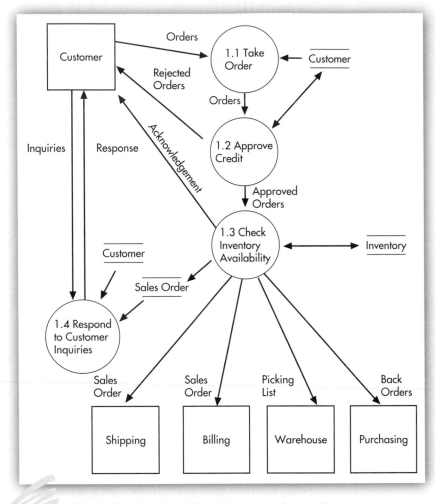

Figure 11-4   Level 1 data flow diagram: sales order entry

efficiency is by allowing customers to enter sales order data themselves. This automatically occurs for sales generated by Web sites, but it also can be accomplished for both in-store and mail-order sales. For example, retail stores such as Service Merchandise, as well as many mail-order firms, have customers mark item numbers and quantities on preprinted order forms that an optical character recognition (OCR) device can read.

Web sites provide another way to automate sales order entry. Their use not only reduces the costs associated with taking customer orders, but also provides an opportunity to increase sales by allowing customers to design their own products. Such interactive sales order entry systems are referred to as choiceboards. For example, visitors to Dell Computer's Web site can try numerous combinations of components and features until they find a configuration that meets their needs at a price they can afford. This not only increases sales, but also enables Dell to build products in response to orders, thereby eliminating the need to carry a large inventory of finished goods. Moreover, because Dell receives payment at the time of order, its cash flow is dramatically improved.

Yet another way to improve the sales order entry process involves using electronic data interchange (EDI) to link directly with customers. With EDI, retail stores would send their orders directly to AOE's sales order system in a format that would eliminate the need for data entry. Some manufacturers and distributors even use EDI to assume responsibility for managing a retail customer's inventory, an arrangement referred to as vendor-managed inventory (VMI). With VMI, the customer provides the supplier with access to data from the customer's point-of-sale (POS) system. The supplier uses that data to monitor inventory levels and automatically initiates replenishment when inventory falls to specified levels. VMI arrangements benefit both parties. Retailers save money by outsourcing the costs associated with inventory management and by reducing the likelihood of stockouts (lost sales). Manufacturers and distributors benefit because more accurate sales forecasts enable them to optimize production and delivery schedules, and the reduced likelihood of retailer stockouts increases total sales.

Information technology also provides many opportunities to improve sales force efficiency and effectiveness, a process referred to as sales force automation. For example, e-mail is an economical way to inform sales staff of pricing changes and sales promotions and remind them about a particular customer's special needs and interests. It also provides for management's real-time approval for special deals. E-mail also reduces the need for salespeople to return to the home office, thereby increasing the proportion of time they can spend with customers. Technology also enhances the quality of sales presentations. Laptop computers enable salespeople to make multimedia presentations, which improves their ability to demonstrate and explain the capabilities and features of complex technical products. Focus 11-1 describes several ways that one company uses sales force automation tools to increase sales.

Regardless of how customer orders are initially received, it is important that all data required to process the order be collected and accurately recorded. Therefore, the following edit checks must be performed to ensure complete accuracy:

➤ *Validity checks* of the customer account and inventory item numbers, by matching them to information in the customer and inventory master files, respectively

➤ A *completeness* test to ensure that all necessary information, including both the ship-to and bill-to addresses for the customer, is present

➤ *Reasonableness tests* that compare the quantity being ordered to past history for that item and customer

As these edit checks are performed, data are recorded on a sales order document. The document is usually an electronic form displayed on a computer monitor screen. As shown in Figure 11-5, the **sales order** contains information item numbers, quantities, prices, and other terms of the sale.

Focus 11-1

Sales Force Automation

The sales staff of McKesson General Medical, a division of McKesson Corp., uses an 8-by-10-by-1-inch pen-based electronic tablet to support its sales efforts. Each night detailed information about the purchasing histories of the doctors whom the salesperson will call on the next day are downloaded into the device. The software then suggests appropriate products to show and can recommend alternatives for any items currently out of stock. Salespeople like the device because they can use it easily while walking around the office or hospital with doctors.

Initial trials of the system resulted in a 30 percent increase in sales. A major reason is the device improves salespeople's ability to explain and demonstrate new products. Software that uses if-then logic enables a salesperson to make the same kind of detailed presentation of a new product that the manufacturer's product manager would make.

Salespeople report that the new sales force automation tool not only increases sales per call, but also significantly reduces the time required to make those sales. Their enthusiasm is reflected in their willingness to spend up to $6,000 of their own money to purchase the device.

Source: Tim Stevens, "Medical Miracle: Technology-Assisted Selling Is Just What the Doctor Ordered," *IndustryWeek* (March 1, 1999); available at http://www.industryweek.com/CurrentArticles/asp/articles.asp?ArticleId=496.

Credit approval

Most business-to-business sales are made on credit. Credit sales should be approved before they are processed. For existing customers with well-established payment histories, a formal credit check for each sale is usually unnecessary. Instead, order takers have general authorization to approve orders from customers in good standing, meaning those without past-due balances. This usually is accomplished by establishing a **credit limit** (maximum allowable account balance) for each customer based on the customer's past credit history and ability to pay. In such cases, approving customer credit involves checking the customer master file to verify the account exists, identifying the customer's credit limit, and verifying that the amount of the order plus any current account balance does not exceed this limit. This process can be automated by using another edit check during the order entry process, the limit check.

➤ A limit check could compare the amount of the order and any existing customer account balance to that customer's credit limit (If the new order does not cause the customer's account balance to exceed the credit limit, then the order is accepted. If the proposed order would cause the customer's account balance to exceed the credit limit, then an e-mail message can be sent to the credit manager to decide whether to approve or reject the order.)

Specific authorization for approving credit is used for new customers, when an order exceeds the customer's credit limit, or when the customer has outstanding past-due balances. This type of authorization should be made by the credit manager.

12345

SALES ORDER
Alpha Omega Electronics
2431 Bradford Lane
St. Louis, MO 63105–2311

Sold To: Hardware City
35 Appliance Way
Phoenix, AZ 85201

Ship To: Hardware City
6742 Mesa Dr.
Mesa, AZ 85284

Date: March 17, 2003	Customer Purchase Order No. 7291	Salesperson JKL	Shipping Instructions: Rush

Quantity Ordered	Quantity Shipped	Quantity Back Ordered	Item Number	Description	Unit Price	Amount
100	100		2741	Calculator	17.95	1795.00
50	50		3315	Pager	49.95	2497.50

Thank You!

Figure 11-5   Sample AOE sales order

Checking inventory availability

The next step is to determine if there is sufficient inventory available to fill the order, so that customers can be informed of the expected delivery date. The accuracy of this process is important, because if inventory records are not accurate and up-to-date, customers may become justifiably upset when unexpected delays occur in filling their orders.

If sufficient inventory is available to fill the order, the sales order is completed and the quantity-available field in the inventory file for each item ordered is reduced by the amount ordered. The shipping, inventory control, and billing departments are then notified of the sale, and an acknowledgment may be sent to the customer. If there is not sufficient inventory on hand to fill the order, a **back order** for those items must be created. In manufacturing companies, creating a back order involves notifying the production department to initiate the production of the requested items. In retail companies, the purchasing department would be notified about the need to order the required items.

Once inventory availability has been determined, the system then creates a **picking ticket** that lists the items, and quantities of each item, that the customer ordered. The picking ticket authorizes the inventory-control function to release merchandise to the shipping department. Although traditionally a paper document, picking tickets today are often electronic forms that may be displayed on portable handheld devices or on monitors built into forklifts. To further improve efficiency, the picking ticket often lists the items by the sequence in which they are stored in the warehouse, rather than in the order listed on the sales order.

Responding to customer inquiries

Besides processing customer orders, Figure 11-4 shows that the sales order entry process also includes responding to customer inquiries. Sometimes these inquiries precede an order, and often they occur after orders have been placed. In either case, responding to customer inquiries is extremely important. Indeed, the quality of customer service provided is often key to a company's success.

Customer service is so important that many companies use special software packages, called customer relationship management (CRM) systems, to support this vital process. CRM systems help organize detailed data about customers so the data can be used to facilitate more efficient and more personalized service. For example, information about customer preferences and transaction history can be used to suggest other products the customer may want to consider. Detailed data about customer requirements and business practices can also be used to proactively contact customers about the need to reorder.

The goal of customer relationship management is to retain customers. A general marketing rule of thumb is that it costs at least five times as much to attract and make a sale to a new customer as it does to make a repeat sale to an existing customer. Retention requires more than merely satisfying customers. It requires creating loyalty. Research indicates that if customer satisfaction is rated on a 1-to-5 scale, with 5 representing completely satisfied and 1 representing completely dissatisfied, customers who rated their satisfaction level at 5 were many times more likely to make repeat purchases than were customers who only rated their satisfaction level at 4. Moreover, that same research indicates that the key to generating total satisfaction, and thereby retaining customers, is the quality and nature of the post-sale customer contacts. Therefore, CRM systems should not be viewed as a way to keep customers at arm's-length and reduce, or totally automate, all interaction with them. Instead, CRM systems should be seen as tools to improve the level of customer service provided. The goal is to turn satisfied customers into loyal customers by enriching the relationship.

Many customer inquiries are routine, however. Consequently, companies can and should use IT to automate the response to common requests, such as questions about account balances and order status, so that sales order and customer service representatives can concentrate their time and effort on handling the more complex, nonroutine inquiries. For example, Web sites provide a cost-effective alternative to traditional toll-free telephone customer support, automating that process with a list of frequently asked questions (FAQs). Discussion boards can also be provided, so that customers can share information and useful tips with one another. Web sites also enable customers to use PINs to directly access their account information and to check on the status of orders.

It is impossible, however, to anticipate every question customers may ask. Therefore, Web sites designed to provide customer service should probably include an instant messaging or chat feature to enable customers to obtain real-time expert assistance and advice for dealing with special issues the FAQ list does not satisfactorily address.

The effectiveness of a Web site depends largely on its design. Companies should regularly review records of customer interaction on their Web sites to quickly identify potential problems. A hard-to-use Web site may actually hurt sales by frustrating customers and creating ill will. Conversely, a well-designed Web site can provide insights that may lead to increased sales. For example, National Semiconductor analyzes which products receive the most attention from visitors to its Web site. When sales managers noticed the increased interest in new heat sensors, they were able to revise their sales forecasts and ramp up production early enough to satisfy a marked increase in orders for that product. Without the advance warning provided by analyzing Web site traffic, National Semiconductor would not have been prepared for the upsurge in customer demand and probably would have lost some of those new orders to competitors.

Shipping

The second basic activity in the revenue cycle (circle 2.0 in Figure 11-3) is filling customer orders and shipping the desired merchandise. As shown in Figure 11-6, this

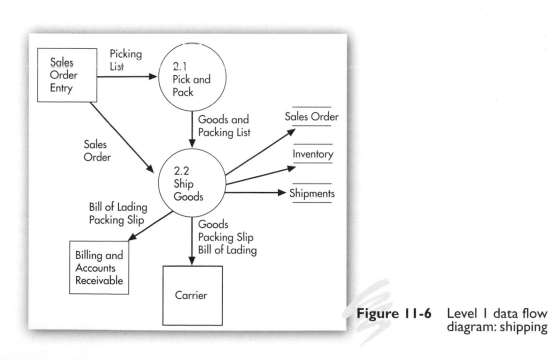

Figure 11-6   Level 1 data flow diagram: shipping

process consists of two steps: (1) picking and packing the order, and (2) shipping the order. The warehouse and shipping departments perform these activities, respectively. Both functions include custody of inventory and, as shown in Figure 11-1, report ultimately to the vice president of manufacturing.

Pick and pack the order

The picking ticket printed by sales order entry triggers the pick and pack process. Warehouse workers use the picking ticket to identify which products, and the quantity of each product, to remove from inventory. Warehouse workers record the quantities of each item actually picked, either on the picking ticket itself if a paper document is used, or by entering the data into the system if electronic forms are used. The inventory is then transferred to the shipping department.

AOE, like many companies, has made significant investments in automated warehouse systems consisting of computers, bar code scanners, conveyer belts, and forklifts to reduce the time and cost of moving inventory into and out of the warehouse. For example, J.C. Penney equips its forklifts with radio frequency data communication (RFDC) terminals to provide drivers with information about which items to pick next and where they are located. Drivers no longer need to return to a central printer to receive instructions. Once picked, items are run through a bar code scanner, which provides real-time and accurate recording of all inventory movements into and out of the warehouse. This is essential for perpetual inventory systems.

Automated warehouse systems not only cut costs and improve efficiency in handling inventory, but can also enable more customer-responsive shipments. For example, Levi Strauss & Company's advanced warehouse system uses bar code scanners on conveyor belts to route jeans and shirts so that they can be packed and shipped to customers in matched sets. Customers are also sent an electronic packing slip indicating the size, style, and colors of clothing in a pending shipment. The cartons are then bar-coded so retailers can quickly check in the merchandise and move it to the selling floor. These services not only save retailers time and money but also help improve turnover of Levi Strauss products, thereby increasing the manufacturer's sales.

Ship the order

The shipping department compares the physical count of inventory with the quantities indicated on the picking ticket and with the quantities indicated on the copy of the sales order that was sent directly to shipping from sales order entry. Discrepancies can arise either because the items were not stored in the location indicated on the picking ticket or the perpetual inventory records were inaccurate. In such cases, the shipping department needs to initiate the back ordering of the missing items and enter the correct quantities shipped on the packing slip.

After the shipping clerk counts the goods delivered from the warehouse, the sales order number, item number(s), and quantities are entered using on-line terminals. This process updates the quantity-on-hand field in the inventory master file. It also produces a packing slip and multiple copies of the bill of lading. The **packing slip** lists the quantity and description of each item included in the shipment (it may be a copy of the picking list). The **bill of lading** is a legal contract that defines responsibility for the goods in transit. It identifies the carrier, source, destination, and any special shipping instructions, and it indicates who (customer or vendor) must pay the carrier (see Figure 11-7).

STRAIGHT BILL OF LADING—SHORT FORM **Not Negotiable.**

Shipper's No. _____

Carrier _____ **Carrier's No.** _____

RECEIVED, subject to the classifications and tariffs in effect on the date of the issue of this Bill of Lading.

at _____ **20_____ from** _____

the property described below, in apparent good order, except as noted (contents and condition of contents of packages unknown), marked, consigned, and destined as indicated below, which said carrier (the word carrier being understood throughout this contract as meaning any person or corporation in possession of the property under the contract) agrees to carry to its usual place of delivery at said destination, if on its route, otherwise to deliver to another carrier on the route to said destination. It is mutually agreed, as to each carrier of all or any of said property over all or any portion of said route to destination, and as to each party at any time interested in any or all of said property, that every service to be performed hereunder shall be subject to all terms and conditions of the Uniform Domestic Straight Bill of Lading set forth (1) in Uniform Freight Classification in effect on the date hereof, if this is a rail or a rail-water shipment, or (2) in the applicable motor carrier classification or tariff if this is a motor carrier shipment.

    Shipper hereby certifies that he is familiar with all the terms and conditions of the said bill of lading, including those on the back thereof, set forth in the classification or tariff which governs the transportation of this shipment, and the said terms and conditions are hereby agreed to by the shipper and accepted for himself and his assigns.

Consigned to _____

(Mail or street address of consignee—For purposes of notification only.)

Destination _____ State _____ Zip Code _____ County _____

Delivery Address ★ _____

    (★ To be filled in only when shipper desires and governing tariffs provide for delivery thereat.)

Route _____

Delivering Carrier _____ Car or Vehicle Initials _____ No. _____

No. Packages	Kind of Package, Description of Articles, Special Marks, and Exceptions	*Weight (Sub. to Cor.)	Class or Rate	Check Column	Subject to Section 7 of Conditions of applicable bill of lading, if this shipment is to be delivered to the consignee without recourse on the consignor, the consignor shall sign the following statement.
					The carrier shall not make delivery of this shipment without payment of freight and all other lawful charges.
					(Signature of Consignor.)
					If charges are to be prepaid, write or stamp here, "To Be Prepaid."

*If the shipment moves between two ports by a carrier by water, the law requires that the bill of lading shall state whether it is "carrier's or shipper's weight."

NOTE—Where the rate is dependent on value, shippers are required to state specifically in writing the agreed or declared value of the property.

The agreed or declared value of the property is hereby specifically stated by the shipper to be not exceeding

                    per

†"The fibre boxes used for this shipment conform to the specifications set forth in the box maker's certificate thereon, and all other requirements of Uniform Freight Classification."

†Shipper's imprint in lieu of stamp; not a part of bill of lading approved by the Interstate Commerce Commission.

Received $ _____ to apply in pre-payment of the charges on the property described hereon.

          Agent or Cashier

Per _____
(This signature here acknowledges only the amount prepaid.)

Charges advanced:
$

_____ **Shipper, per** _____ **Agent, Per** _____

Permanent post office address of shipper, _____ _____ _____

Figure 11-7 Sample bill of lading

A copy of the bill of lading and the packing slip accompany the shipment. If the customer is to pay the shipping charges, this copy of the bill of lading may serve as a freight bill, to indicate the amount the customer should pay to the carrier. In other cases, the freight bill is a separate document.

The shipping department keeps a second copy of the bill of lading to track and confirm the transfer of goods to the carrier. Another copy of the bill of lading and the packing slip are sent to the billing department to indicate that the goods have been shipped and that an invoice should be prepared and mailed. The carrier also retains a copy of the bill of lading for its records.

One major decision that needs to be made when filling and shipping customer orders concerns the choice of delivery method. Traditionally, many companies have maintained their own truck fleets for deliveries. Large companies such as GM have even assigned entire departments to this function. Increasingly, however, manufacturers are outsourcing this function to commercial carriers such as Ryder System, Inc., Roadway Services, Inc., and Schneider National Company. Outsourcing deliveries reduces costs and allows manufacturers to concentrate on their core business activity (the production of goods). Selecting the proper carrier, however, requires collecting and maintaining information about carrier performance (e.g., percentage of on-time deliveries, damage claims) and integrating that information in the AIS.

Another important decision concerns the location of distribution centers. Increasingly, many customers are asking suppliers and manufacturers to deliver products only when needed. Consequently, suppliers and manufacturers must use logistics software tools to identify the optimal locations to store inventory in order to minimize the total amount of inventory carried and to meet each customer's delivery requirements.

Globalization adds complexity to outbound logistics. The efficiency and effectiveness of different distribution methods, such as trucking or rail, differ around the world. Taxes and regulations in various countries can also affect distribution choices. For example, Harley-Davidson has a European distribution center. It ships directly from the United States to Norway, however, to avoid that country's 135 percent luxury tax on each motorcycle. Thus, an organization's AIS must include logistics software that can maximize the efficiency and effectiveness of its shipping function.

Advanced communications systems can provide real-time information on shipping status, and thus provide additional value to customers. For example, if the seller learns that a shipment is going to be late, prompt notification can help that customer revise its plans accordingly.

Billing and Accounts Receivable

The third basic activity in the revenue cycle (circle 3.0 in Figure 11-3) involves billing customers and maintaining accounts receivable. Figure 11-8 shows billing and updating accounts receivable as separate processes and, in practice, these two functions are performed by two separate functions within the accounting department.

Billing

Accurate and timely billing for shipped merchandise is crucial. The billing activity is just an information processing activity that repackages and summarizes information from the sales order entry and shipping activities. It requires information from the

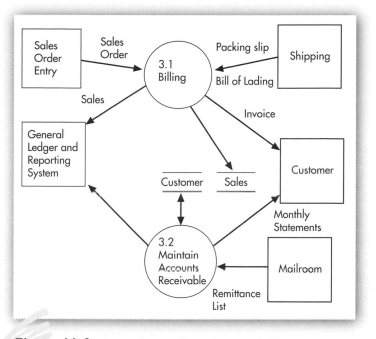

Figure 11-8   Level 1 data flow diagram: billing & accounts receivable

shipping department identifying the items and quantities shipped, and information about prices and any special sales terms from the sales department.

The basic document created in the billing process is the **sales invoice** (see Figure 11-9), which notifies customers of the amount to be paid and where to send payment. Like many companies, AOE still prints paper invoices that it mails to many of its smaller customers. Larger customers, however, receive invoices via EDI.

Information technology provides opportunities to reduce the costs associated with billing. Sending invoices to business via EDI is faster and cheaper than mailing paper documents. For example, Sonoco Products Company estimates that EDI saves it 70 to 80 cents per invoice over processing of paper invoices. Businesses that sell to end consumers can reap similar advantages by convincing their customers to sign up for on-line billing and payment using the Internet. EDI invoices and on-line bill payment also benefit customers by reducing their time and costs (including postage) associated with processing paperwork.

A well-designed AIS can entirely eliminate the need to create and store invoices, at least with customers that have sophisticated systems of their own. To understand this concept, reexamine the information included in a typical sales invoice (see Figure 11-9). The invoice indicates the quantity of each item sold and the price charged for that item; but the price is usually set at the time the order is placed, and the actual quantity sold is known at the time the merchandise is shipped to the customer. Thus, the selling company's AIS already contains all the information needed to calculate the

					Invoice Number 34567

INVOICE

Alpha Omega Electronics
2431 Bradford Lane
St. Louis, MO 63105–2311

Sold To:	Ship To:
Hardware City	Hardware City
35 Appliance Way	6742 Mesa Dr.
Phoenix, AZ 85201	Mesa, AZ 85284

Customer Order # 7291	Our Sales Order # 12345	Date Shipped March 20, 2003	Shipped Via Our Truck	F.O.B. Destination	Terms 1/10, Net 30	Salesperson JKL

Quantity	Item Number	Description	Unit Price	Amount
100	2741	Calculator	17 95	1795 00
50	3315	Pager	49 95	2497 50
			Pay This Amount	4292 50

Thank You!

Figure 11-9   Sample AOE sales invoice

amount of the sale at the time the goods are delivered. Conversely, the buyer knows the price at the time the order is placed, and knows the quantity purchased when the goods are received. Consequently, if both companies have accurate on-line systems, it may be possible to establish an agreement in which the buyer will automatically remit payments within a specified number of days after receiving the merchandise. The seller sends an electronic notification, usually via e-mail, when the goods are shipped and the customer sends an electronic acknowledgment when the goods are received. Ford has established such relationships with many of its main suppliers. Note that the seller can still monitor and determine accounts receivable by tracking shipments to cash remittances: Accounts receivable represents all shipments that have yet to be paid. The attraction of such invoiceless billing is that it saves both the seller and buyer considerable amounts of time and money by eliminating the need to perform a traditional business process (billing) that does not provide any new information.

An integrated AIS also provides the opportunity to merge the billing process with the sales and marketing function, by using data about a customer's past purchase history to send information about related products and services with the monthly statement. Such customized advertising may generate additional sales with little if any incremental costs.

Maintain accounts receivable

The accounts receivable function, which reports to the controller, performs two basic tasks: It uses the information on the sales invoice to debit customer accounts and subsequently credits those accounts when payments are received.

The two basic ways to maintain accounts receivable are the open-invoice and the balance-forward methods. The two methods differ in terms of when customers remit payments, how those payments are applied to update the accounts receivable master file, and the format of the monthly statement sent to customers.

Under the **open-invoice method,** customers typically pay according to each invoice. Usually two copies of the invoice are mailed to the customer, who is requested to return one copy with the payment. This copy is a turnaround document called the **remittance advice.** Customer payments are then applied against specific invoices.

In contrast, under the **balance-forward method,** customers typically pay according to the amount shown on a **monthly statement,** rather than by individual invoices. A monthly statement lists all transactions, including both sales and payments, that occurred during the past month and informs customers of their current account balances (see Figure 11-10). The monthly statement often contains a tear-off portion containing preprinted information, including the customer's name, account number, and balance. Customers are asked to return this stub, which serves as a remittance advice, with payment. Remittances are applied against the total account balance, rather than against specific invoices.

One advantage of the open-invoice method is that it is conducive to offering discounts for prompt payment, as invoices are individually tracked and aged. It also results in a more uniform flow of cash collections throughout the month. A disadvantage of the open-invoice method is the added complexity required to maintain information about the status of each individual invoice for each customer.

Companies with large numbers of customers who make many small purchases each month, such as the credit card companies Visa and MasterCard, or national retail chains such as Sears and J.C. Penney, typically use the balance-forward method. For them, this method is more efficient and reduces costs by avoiding the need to process cash collections for each individual sale. It is also more convenient for the customer to make one monthly remittance.

To obtain a more uniform flow of cash receipts, many of these companies use a process called cycle billing to prepare and mail monthly statements to their customers. Under **cycle billing,** monthly statements are prepared for subsets of customers at different times. For example, the customer master file might be divided into four parts, and each week monthly statements would be prepared for one-fourth of the customers.

MONTHLY STATEMENT Alpha Omega Electronics 2431 Bradford Lane St. Louis, MO 63105–2311							March 2003

Hardware City

35 Appliance Way

Phoenix, AZ 85201

Invoice Number	Date	Current	Past Due 1–30	Past Due 31–60	Past Due 61–90	Past Due Over 90
34567	3/20/2003	4292.50				
34591	3/27/2003	2346.50				
	Totals	6639.00				
		Total Amount Due		6639.00		

Figure 11-10   Sample AOE monthly statement

Cycle billing produces a more uniform flow of cash collections throughout the month and reduces the time that the computer system is dedicated to printing monthly statements. To appreciate these benefits, note that if a credit card company such as Visa or MasterCard prepared monthly statements for all its customers at the same time, its computer system would be tied up for several days.

Image processing technology can improve the efficiency and effectiveness of managing customer accounts. The digital images of customer remittances and accounts can be stored on an optical disk connected to a LAN, where they can be easily retrieved, manipulated, and integrated with other images and data to produce various types of output. Doing so provides employees fast access to all documents relating to a customer and eliminates the time wasted searching through file cabinets for lost paperwork. If a customer needs a duplicate copy of a monthly statement or an invoice to replace a lost original, it can be retrieved, printed, and faxed while talking to the customer on the phone. Image processing also can facilitate resolving customer complaints, because the same image can be viewed simultaneously by more than one person. Thus, a customer account representative and a credit manager could both review an image of a document in question while discussing the problem with the customer on the telephone. Finally, image processing reduces the space and cost associated with

Focus 11-2

Using Image Processing to Improve Cash Collections

Bell Atlantic processes more than 11 million customer remittances each month, sometimes receiving over 0.5 million remittances in a single day. To reduce costs and improve accuracy, Bell Atlantic uses a high-speed image-processing system.

The process begins when Bell Atlantic picks up the mail, which it does several times each day, and scans it electronically. The scanners can detect the magnetic ink on the customer's check, thereby identifying how the checks are positioned in the envelopes. The scanner also determines the number of documents in and the presence of any metal objects (coins or staples) in each envelope. This information is used to sort the envelopes. Those that contain only one check and one return document are opened mechanically and run through a high-speed image-capturing device. The remaining envelopes also are opened mechanically, but their contents are then processed by hand for further sorting. Checks and remittance documents are then run through the image-capturing device.

The system tries to read the handwriting on the check to match it against the customer's balance. The data on checks that cannot be read by the system are keyed in. The checks are then sent through high-speed machines that encode, endorse, and batch them for deposit.

The system cost Bell Atlantic $8 million. The cost savings in reduced clerical work and improved accuracy, however, yielded a payback in only two years.

Source: Scott Humphrey, "Bell Atlantic Reengineers Payment Processing," *Enterprise Reengineering* (October/November 1995): 1–22.

storing paper documents. The savings in this area can be substantial: One optical disk can store up to 20,000 documents, in a fraction of the space. Focus 11-2 describes the use of image processing at Bell Atlantic.

Exceptions: account adjustments and write-offs

Adjustments to a customer's account are sometimes necessary. For example, customer accounts may be credited to reflect either the return of items or allowances granted for damaged goods. To credit a customer's account for returned goods, the credit manager must obtain information from the receiving dock that the goods were actually returned and placed back in inventory. Upon notification from the receiving department that the goods have been returned, the credit manager issues a **credit memo** (see Figure 11-11), which authorizes the crediting of the customer's account. If the damage to the goods is minimal, the customer may agree to keep them for a price reduction. In such cases, the credit manager issues a credit memo to reflect the amount that should be credited to the customer's account. A copy of the credit memo is sent to accounts receivable to authorize an adjustment to the customer's account balance; another copy is sent to the customer.

After repeated attempts to collect payment have failed, it may be necessary to write off a customer's account. In such cases, the credit manager issues a credit memo to authorize the write-off. Unlike the cases involving damaged or returned goods, however, a copy of the credit memo is not sent to the customer.

11121

CREDIT MEMORANDUM

Alpha Omega Electronics
2431 Bradford Lane
St. Louis, MO 63105–2311

Credit To:	Hardware City	Date	April 7, 2003
	35 Appliance Way		
	Phoenix, AZ 85201	Salesperson	FRM

| Apply To Invoice Number | Date | Customer's Order No. |
| 34603 | April 1, 2003 | 7413 |

3	4120	PCS		85.00	255:00

| Reason Credit Issued: | Units damaged during shipment. Returned on April 6, 2003 | |

| Received By: ALZ | Authorized By: PJS |

| **We Credit Your Account For This Amount** | 255:00 |

Figure 11-11   Sample AOE credit memo

Cash Collections

The final step in the revenue cycle is cash collections (circle 4.0 in Figure 11-3). The cashier, who reports to the treasurer (see Figure 11-1), handles customer remittances and deposits them in the bank.

Because cash and customer checks can be stolen so easily, it is important to take appropriate measures to reduce the risk of theft. As discussed more fully in the section on controls, this means that the accounts receivable function, which is responsible for recording customer remittances, should not have physical access to cash or checks. Yet, the accounts receivable function must be able to identify the source of any remittances and the applicable invoices that should be credited. One solution involves mailing the customer two copies of the invoice and requesting that one be returned with the payment. This remittance advice is then routed to accounts receivable and the actual customer payment is sent to the cashier. If the remittance advice also contains a space for the customer to indicate the amount being remitted, an OCR machine can scan in the remittance data, thereby eliminating the potential for mistakes during data entry. An alternative solution is to have mailroom personnel prepare a **remittance list,** which is a document identifying the names and amounts of all customer remittances, and send it to accounts receivable. In place of a remittance list, some companies photocopy all customer remittances and send the copies to accounts receivable while forwarding the actual remittances to the cashier for deposit.

The preceding discussion assumes that customer remittances are sent directly to the company. Another way to safeguard customer remittances is to set up a lockbox arrangement with a bank. A **lockbox** is a postal address to which customers send their remittances. The participating bank picks up the checks from the post office box and deposits them to the company's account. The bank then sends the remittance advices, an electronic list of all remittances, and photocopies of all checks to the company.

Using a lockbox not only prevents theft of customer remittances by employees, but also improves cash-flow management. Having customers send payments to a lockbox eliminates the delay associated with processing customer remittances before depositing them. Cash flow also is improved by selecting several banks around the country to maintain lockboxes, with the locations chosen to minimize the time customer checks are in the mail.

Information technology can provide additional efficiencies in the use of lockboxes. Under an **electronic lockbox** arrangement, the bank electronically sends the company information about the customer account number and the amount remitted as soon as it receives and scans those checks. This method enables the company to begin applying remittances to customer accounts before the photocopies of the checks arrive.

Lockbox arrangements, however, only eliminate the delays associated with internal processing of remittances mailed directly to the company. Electronic funds transfer provides the opportunity to reduce other causes of delay in obtaining access to customer funds. With electronic funds transfer (EFT), customers send their remittances electronically to the company's bank and thus eliminate the delay associated with the time the remittance is in the mail system. Eliminating this check-clearing time also reduces the time lag before the bank makes the deposited funds available to the company. Integrating EFT with EDI, a process referred to as financial electronic data interchange (FEDI), completes the automation of both the billing and cash collections processes. To fully reap the benefits of FEDI, however, requires that both the selling company and its customers use banks that are capable of providing EDI services.

When dealing with customers who are not FEDI capable, or with individual consumers, companies can also speed the collection process by accepting the use of procurement cards (a special type of credit card discussed in Chapter 12) or credit cards. Accepting such payment methods speeds collection, because the card issuer usually transfers the funds within two days of the sale. These benefits must be weighed against the costs of accepting such cards, which typically range from 2 to 4 percent of the gross sales price. Finally, recall that Chapter 3 described one other alternative for receiving customer payment that is available for electronic transactions: acceptance of some form of digital or electronic cash.

This concludes our discussion of basic revenue cycle business activities. The next section describes how the AIS can be designed to efficiently collect and process data about those activities.

INFORMATION PROCESSING PROCEDURES

In response to the Y2K crisis, AOE, like many other organizations, replaced its existing AIS with an integrated ERP system. Figure 11-12 depicts the portion of AOE's new ERP that supports its revenue cycle activities.

The fundamental characteristics of AOE's new revenue cycle system are the sharing of data between activities and the increased integration that results. The on-line sales order processing system handles customer orders, via the Internet, as well as

Figure 11-12   Integrated revenue cycle system for AOE: (a) sales order entry

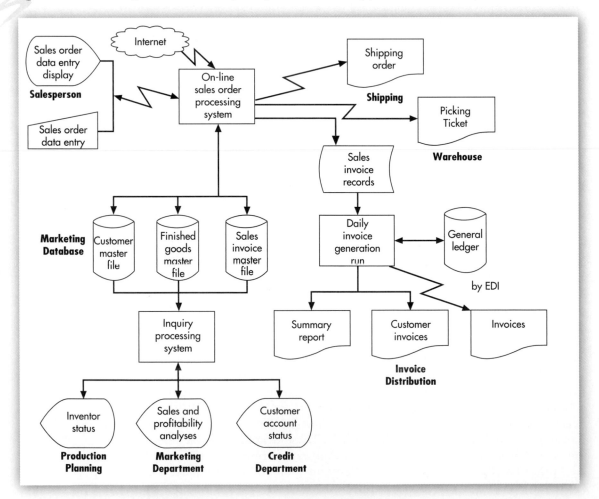

orders via the sales force. Using their laptops, salespeople can enter orders directly in the field, or the sales department can enter customer orders received over the telephone or by mail. Regardless of how the order is initially received, the system quickly verifies customer creditworthiness, checks inventory availability, and notifies the warehouse and shipping departments about the approved sale.

Warehouse and shipping employees enter data about their activities as soon as they are performed, thereby updating information about inventory status in real time. Nightly, the invoice program runs in batch mode, generating paper or electronic invoices for customers who require invoices. At any time, different departments can use the inquiry processing system to ascertain the status of orders and plan their future activities.

Cash receipts processing also is largely automated. AOE's customers either send checks to one of six regional banks with which AOE has established electronic lockboxes, or remit their payments to those banks via EFT. Each day, the bank sends AOE a file containing remittance data, which are then used to update customer accounts and cash.

It is instructive to compare AOE's new processes with the procedures followed in its old (legacy) systems. The appendix to this chapter contains flowcharts and a brief narrative description of AOE's legacy revenue cycle system. Key improvements are as follows:

1. Real-time order entry detects errors, such as missing data, as the order is being entered, and when it is easiest to correct those errors.

2. Credit approval decisions can be made at the time the customer places the order. If special approval is required, the credit manager is notified by e-mail and can immediately make that decision.

Figure 11-12   (b) cash receipts

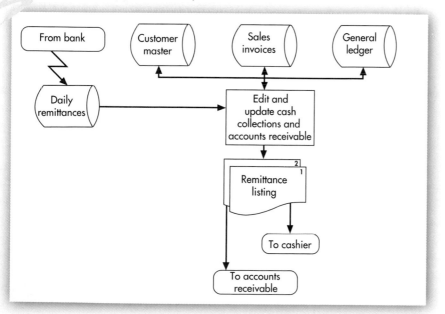

3. Inventory records are more accurate and timely, enabling sales order entry staff to provide customers accurate information about expected delivery dates.

4. The warehouse and shipping departments can better plan activities to minimize the time required to fill customer orders.

5. The system compares data that the shipping department entered with the sales order file, thereby detecting and facilitating correction of any errors prior to shipment.

6. Cash receipts are processed more quickly, improving cash flow.

7. Reports and performance measures are timelier, enhancing management's ability to monitor and improve efficiency and effectiveness.

Realizing these benefits presupposes that adequate controls exist to ensure that the information in the system is available, accurate, secure, and maintainable. The next section discusses applicable control procedures to achieve those objectives.

CONTROL: OBJECTIVES, THREATS, AND PROCEDURES

In the revenue cycle, a well-designed AIS should provide adequate controls to ensure that the following objectives are met:

1. All transactions are properly authorized.
2. All recorded transactions are valid (actually occurred).
3. All valid, authorized transactions are recorded.
4. All transactions are recorded accurately.
5. Assets (cash, inventory, and data) are safeguarded from loss or theft.
6. Business activities are performed efficiently and effectively.

The documents and records described in the previous section play an important role in achieving these objectives. Simple, easy-to-complete documents with clear instructions facilitate the accurate and efficient recording of transaction data. The inclusion of appropriate application controls, such as validity checks and field (format) checks, further increases the accuracy of data entry when using electronic documents. Providing space on paper and electronic documents to record who completed and who reviewed the form provides evidence that the transaction was properly authorized. Prenumbering documents facilitates checking that all transactions have been recorded. Restricting access to blank documents, if paper documents are still used, and to programs that create documents reduces the risk of unauthorized transactions.

Table 11-1 lists the major threats in the revenue cycle and the appropriate control procedures that should be in place to mitigate them. Every company, regardless of its line of business, faces these threats. Therefore, it is important to understand how the AIS can be designed to counter them. This discussion is organized around the four stages of the revenue cycle: sales order entry, shipping, billing and accounts receivable, and cash collections.

Sales Order Entry

The primary objectives of the sales order entry process are to accurately and efficiently process customer orders, ensure that the company gets paid for all credit sales and that all sales are legitimate, and to minimize the loss of revenue arising from poor inventory management. Threats 1 through 4 in Table 11-1 relate to these objectives.

Table 11-1 Threats and Controls in the Revenue Cycle

Process/Activity	Threat	Applicable Control Procedures
Sales Order Entry	1. Incomplete or inaccurate customer orders	Data entry edit checks
	2. Credit sales to customers with poor credit	Credit approval by credit manager, not by sales function; accurate records of customer account balances
	3. Legitimacy of orders	Signatures on paper documents; digital signatures and digital certificates for e-business
	4. Stockouts, carrying costs, and markdowns	Inventory control systems
Shippping	5. Shipping errors: Wrong merchandise Wrong quantities Wrong address	Reconciliation of sales order with picking ticket and packing slip; bar code scanners; Data entry application controls
	6. Theft of inventory	Restrict physical access to inventory; Documentation of all internal transfers of inventory; periodic physical counts of inventory and reconciliation of counts to recorded amounts
Billing and Accounts Receivable	7. Failure to bill customers	Separation of shipping and billing functions; Prenumbering of all shipping documents and periodic reconciliation to invoices; reconciliation of picking tickets and bills of lading with sales orders
	8. Billing errors	Data entry edit controls Price lists
	9. Posting errors in updating accounts receivable	Reconciliation of subsidiary accounts receivable ledger with general ledger; monthly statements to customers
Cash Collections	10. Theft of cash	Segregation of duties; minimization of cash handling; lockbox arrangements; prompt endorsement and deposit of all receipts; Periodic reconciliation of bank statement with records by someone not involved in cash receipts processing
General Control Issues	11. Loss of data	Backup and disaster recovery procedures; access controls (physical and logical)
	12. Poor performance	Preparation and review of performance reports

Threat 1: Incomplete or inaccurate customer orders

A basic threat during sales order entry is that important data about the order will be either missing or inaccurate. Not only does this create inefficiencies due to the need to call back the customer and reenter the order in the system, but it also may negatively affect customer perceptions and, thereby, adversely affect future sales. A variety of data entry edit controls can mitigate this threat. For example, completeness checks can ensure that all required data are entered. Automatic lookup of reference data, such as customer addresses, already stored in the customer master file, prevents errors by eliminating data entry. Reasonableness tests should compare the quantity ordered with item numbers and past sales history. Many of these data entry edit controls, such as completeness checks, are also needed on Web sites to ensure that customers enter all required data.

Threat 2: Credit sales to customers with poor credit

A second threat in sales order entry is the possibility of making sales that later turn out to be uncollectible. Requiring proper authorization for each credit sale diminishes this threat. In general, this is accomplished by setting credit limits for each customer and granting sales staff general authorization to approve additional credit sales to existing customers provided that such sales do not increase the customer's total account balance beyond the approved credit limit. For cases requiring specific authorization, such as new customers or the extension of additional credit to existing customers, someone other than the sales representative should grant approval, especially if the sales staff is paid on commission. The organization chart for AOE (see Figure 11-1) shows this segregation of duties: the credit manager, who sets credit policies and approves the extension of credit to new customers and the raising of credit limits for existing customers, is independent of the marketing function. To enforce this segregation of duties in integrated on-line systems, sales order entry clerks should be granted read-only access to information about individual customer credit limits.

To be effective, however, credit must be approved prior to releasing the goods from inventory. It is also important to maintain accurate and current records of customer account balances and credit limits.

Threat 3: Legitimacy of orders

Another threat concerns the legitimacy of orders. Traditionally, legitimacy of customer orders is established by receipt of a signed purchase order from the customer. As electronic business transactions increase, the use of digital signatures and digital certificates is required to verify the identity of each party.

Threat 4: Stockouts, carrying costs, and markdowns

Yet another threat in the sales order entry process is that sales will be lost due to stockouts. Conversely, excess inventory increases carrying costs and may even require significant markdowns. To address these problems, companies establish accurate inventory control and sales forecasting systems. On-line AISs, as depicted in Figure 11-12, facilitate the use of the perpetual inventory method, thereby ensuring that records about the quantity of inventory available for sale are accurate. Periodic physical counts of inventory also help to verify the accuracy of recorded amounts. Sales forecasts should be regularly reviewed for accuracy and revised frequently. In addition, supplier performance, such as on-time delivery rates, must be monitored.

Shipping

The primary objectives of the shipping function are to fill customer orders efficiently and accurately and to safeguard inventory. Threats 5 and 6 in Table 11-1 relate to these objectives.

Threat 5: Shipping errors

Shipping the wrong items or quantities of merchandise and shipping to the wrong location are serious errors because they can significantly reduce customer satisfaction and thus future sales. They may also result in the loss of assets if customers do not pay for goods erroneously shipped. On-line systems as depicted in Figure 11-12 can reduce the risk of shipping errors if shipping personnel are required to enter the quantities of items being sent before the goods are shipped. This enables detecting, and then correcting, any mistakes before the merchandise leaves the premises by comparing the shipment data with the sales order. The use of bar code scanners to record the picking and shipping of inventory can virtually eliminate data entry errors. At companies where data entry is still performed manually, the use of application controls, such as field checks and completeness tests, can significantly reduce errors. Only after the system has verified that the shipment is correct should the packing slip and bill of lading be printed.

Threat 6: Theft of inventory

Another threat in the shipping stage of the revenue cycle involves the theft of inventory. Theft losses can be extremely large. For example, Exide, Inc., a battery manufacturer, reported a loss of $3.5 million due to employee theft. In addition to a loss of assets, theft also makes inventory records inaccurate, which can lead to problems in filling customer orders.

Several control procedures can reduce the risk of inventory theft. First, inventory should be kept in a secure location to which physical access is restricted. Second, all inventory transfers within the company should be documented. Inventory should be released to shipping employees based only on approved sales orders. In addition, both warehouse and shipping employees should sign the document accompanying the goods (or make the appropriate acknowledgment of the transfer on-line) at the time the goods are transferred from inventory to shipping. This procedure facilitates tracking the cause of any inventory shortages. In addition, such accountability encourages employees to prepare and maintain accurate records. Finally, recorded amounts of inventory should be periodically reconciled with physical counts of inventory on hand, and the employees responsible for inventory custody should be held accountable for any shortages.

Billing and Accounts Receivable

The primary objectives of the billing and accounts receivable functions are to ensure that customers are billed for all sales, that invoices are accurate, and that customer accounts are accurately maintained. Threats 7 through 9 in Table 11-1 relate to these objectives.

Threat 7: Failure to bill customers

Failure to bill customers for items shipped results in the loss of assets and erroneous data about sales, inventory, and accounts receivable. Segregating the shipping and billing functions can diminish this threat. Otherwise, an employee performing both functions could ship merchandise to friends without billing them. Sales orders, picking tickets, packing slips, and sales invoices should be sequentially numbered and then periodically accounted for. Any sales orders or packing slips that cannot be matched to a sales invoice represent shipments that have not been billed, and corrective action should then be taken. When invoices are not generated (e.g., invoiceless systems), it is especially important to ensure that every shipment is recorded.

Threat 8: Billing errors

Billing errors, such as pricing mistakes and billing customers for items not shipped or on back order, represent another potential threat. Overbilling can result in customer dissatisfaction, and underbilling results in the loss of assets. Pricing mistakes can be avoided by having the computer retrieve the appropriate data from the inventory master file. Mistakes involving quantities shipped can be caught by reconciling the quantities listed on the packing slips with those on the sales order. When feasible, the use of bar code scanners can further reduce the probability of data entry errors.

Threat 9: Errors in maintaining customer accounts

Errors in maintaining customer accounts can lead to the loss of future sales and also may indicate possible theft of cash. The following edit checks should be used to ensure accuracy in updating customer accounts:

1. Validity checks on the customer and invoice numbers
2. Closed-loop verification to ensure that the proper account is being credited
3. A field check to ensure that only numeric values are entered for payment amounts

Customer payments are often processed in batches, so batch totals can provide additional means to detect posting errors. For example, after processing customer payments, the sum of all individual customer account balances (the accounts receivable subsidiary file) should equal the total balance of the accounts receivable control account in the general ledger. If the two are not equal, an error in posting has probably occurred and all transactions just entered should be reexamined. To ensure that all remittances were processed, the number of customer accounts updated should be compared with the number of checks received. These reconciliations should be performed by someone other than the individual involved in processing the original transactions because (1) it is easier to catch someone else's mistakes than your own and (2) it provides a means to identify irregularities. Finally, mailing monthly account statements to every customer provides an additional independent review of posting accuracy because customers will complain if their accounts have not been properly credited for payments they remitted.

Cash Collections

The primary objective of the cash collections function is to safeguard customer remittances. Threat 10 in Table 11-1 relates to this objective.

Threat 10: Theft of cash

Special control procedures must be utilized because cash is so easy to steal. Segregation of duties is the most effective control procedure for reducing theft. Employees who have physical access to cash should not have responsibility for recording or authorizing any transactions involving its receipt. Specifically, the following pairs of duties should be segregated:

1. *Handling cash or checks and posting remittances to customer accounts.* A person performing both of these duties could commit the special type of embezzlement called lapping.
2. *Handling cash or checks and authorizing credit memos.* A person performing both of these duties could conceal theft of cash by creating a credit memo equal to the amount stolen.
3. *Issuing credit memos and maintaining customer accounts.* A person performing both of these duties could write off as uncollectible amounts owed by friends.

In general, the handling of money and checks within the organization should be minimized. The optimal methods are a bank lockbox arrangement or the use of EFT or FEDI for customer payments. The costs of these arrangements must be weighed against the benefits of reduced internal processing costs and faster access to customer payments.

If customer payments must be processed internally, prompt documentation of remittances is crucial, because the risk of loss is greatest at the time of first receipt. Thus, a list of all checks received should be prepared immediately after opening the mail. The checks should also be restrictively endorsed at that time. To minimize the risk of misappropriating any cash or checks received, two people should open all incoming mail.

Segregating the recording and custody functions as follows provides additional control: Only the remittance data should be sent to the accounts receivable department, with customer payments being sent to the cashier. Such an arrangement establishes two mutually independent control checks. First, the total credits to accounts receivable recorded by the accounting department should equal the total debit to cash representing the amount deposited by the cashier. Second, the copy of the remittance list that is sent to the internal audit department can be compared with the validated deposit slips and bank statements to verify that all checks the organization received were deposited. Finally, the monthly statements mailed to customers provide another layer of control, because customers would notice the failure to properly credit their accounts for payments remitted.

Retail stores and organizations that receive cash directly from customers should use cash registers that automatically produce a written record of all cash received. In these situations, customers also can play a role in controlling cash collections. For example, many stores use signs to inform customers that their purchase is free if they fail to get a receipt or that receipts marked with a red star entitle them to a discount. Such policies encourage customers to watch that employees actually ring up the cash sale and do so correctly.

All customer remittances should be deposited, intact, in the bank each day. Daily deposits reduce the amount of cash and checks at risk of theft. Depositing all remittances intact, and not using any of them for miscellaneous expenditures, facilitates reconciliation of the bank statement with the records of sales, accounts receivable, and cash collections.

Finally, the employee who reconciles the bank statements should be independent of all other activities involved in handling or recording the receipt of cash. This separation of duties provides an independent check on the cashier and prevents manipulation of the bank statement to conceal the theft of cash.

General Control Issues

Two general objectives pertaining to all revenue cycle activities are that data be available when needed and that all activities be performed efficiently and effectively. Threats 11 and 12 in Table 11-1 are general threats that affect all phases of the revenue cycle.

Threat 11: Loss of data

A significant general threat in the revenue cycle is loss of data about customer accounts. Accurate customer account and inventory records are important not only for external and internal reporting purposes, but also for responding to customer inquiries. Moreover, loss of all accounts receivable data could threaten a company's continued existence. Therefore, those records must be protected from loss or damage.

The master accounts receivable, sales, and cash receipts files must be backed up regularly. Two backup copies of key files, such as the accounts receivable master file, should be made. One should be kept on-site and the other stored off-site. Backup copies of the most recent transaction file also should be made. All disks and tapes should have both external and internal file labels to reduce the possibility of accidentally erasing important files.

Access controls are also important. Leaking customer information to competitors can hurt sales and may even subject the company to legal liability. Unauthorized access also increases the risk of damage to important data files. A system of passwords and user IDs should be used to limit employees' access to and allowable operations on files. For example, only sales staff should be allowed to create sales orders. Moreover, sales staff should have read-only access to customer credit limits and current account balances. Access controls also should exist for individual terminals. For example, the system should be programmed to reject any attempts to enter sales orders from a terminal located at the shipping dock. Finally, logs of all activities, especially any actions involving managerial approval (e.g., extending credit limits), should be recorded and maintained for later review as part of the audit trail.

Threat 12: Poor performance

In addition to ensuring accuracy and safeguarding assets, another objective of internal controls is to encourage efficient and effective performance of duties. Preparing and reviewing reports provides a basis for assessing the efficiency and effectiveness of revenue cycle activities and for diminishing the threat of substandard performance. The potential number of such reports is limited only by management's choice about what activities are important to monitor and control. For example, sales order entry efficiency can be monitored by preparing periodic reports of sales orders processed per individual in a given time period. The efficiency and effectiveness of the sales force can be assessed by **sales analysis reports,** which break down the sales by salesperson, region, or product. Further insights about overall marketing performance can be provided by preparing **profitability analysis reports,** which break down the marginal profit contribution made by each territory, customer, distribution channel, salesperson, product, or other basis.

Reports on the frequency and size of back orders provide insight about the effectiveness of inventory management policies in satisfying customer demands. Similarly, reports that identify slow-moving products help to avoid excessive stockpiling.

The preceding internally focused dimensions of performance provide only one view of success in meeting customer satisfaction goals. Organizations also need to capture and integrate internally generated measures of process efficiency with externally generated data about customer attitudes. Thus, Trevor wants Ann to redesign AOE's AIS to be able to track and store trends in customer satisfaction ratings.

Carefully monitoring accounts receivables also is extremely important because collections significantly affect cash flow. An **accounts receivable aging schedule** lists customer account balances by length of time outstanding and provides information for estimating bad debts. It also provides useful information for evaluating current credit policies and for deciding whether to increase the credit limit for specific customers.

Cash-flow problems are a major reason why many businesses fail. Therefore, a **cash budget,** which provides precise estimates of cash inflows (projected collections from sales) and outflows (outstanding payables), is essential. It can alert an organization to a pending short-term cash shortage, thereby enabling it to plan ahead to secure short-term loans at the best possible rates. Conversely, an organization that knows a surplus of cash is pending can take steps to invest those excess funds to earn the best possible returns. A cash budget could have helped AOE better manage its short-term borrowing needs.

Next, we discuss in more detail how the AIS can be designed to provide these various reports and other information that is useful for effectively managing revenue cycle activities.

REVENUE CYCLE INFORMATION NEEDS AND DATA MODEL

An AIS is designed to collect, process, and store data about business activities to present management with information to support decision making. Operational data are needed to monitor performance and to perform the following recurring tasks:

- ➤ Respond to customer inquiries about account balances and order status
- ➤ Decide whether to extend credit to a particular customer
- ➤ Determine inventory availability
- ➤ Select methods for delivering merchandise

In addition, current and historical information is needed to enable management to make the following strategic decisions:

- ➤ Setting prices for products and services
- ➤ Establishing policies regarding sales returns and warranties
- ➤ Deciding what types of credit terms to offer
- ➤ Determining the need for short-term borrowing
- ➤ Planning new marketing campaigns

Furthermore, the AIS must also supply the information needed to evaluate performance of the following critical processes:

- ➤ Response time to customer inquiries
- ➤ Time required to fill and deliver orders

➤ Percentage of sales that required back orders

➤ Customer satisfaction rates and trends

➤ Analyses of market share and sales trends

➤ Profitability analyses by product, customer, and sales region

➤ Sales volume in both dollars and number of customers

➤ Effectiveness of advertising and promotions

➤ Sales staff performance

➤ Bad debt expenses and credit policies

Notice that both financial and operating information are needed to manage and evaluate revenue cycle activities. For example, evaluating the efficiency and effectiveness of sales order entry requires data not only about sales volumes but also about order processing time. Evaluating the overall effectiveness of all revenue cycle activities also requires information from external sources, such as measures of customer satisfaction. Traditionally, the AIS has provided the internally generated financial measures of performance and managers have turned to other sources for the internal operating and external information they need. This situation is costly, inefficient, and no longer necessary. Database technology makes it possible to redesign the AIS to capture and store both financial and operating data about revenue cycle transactions and to integrate that internally generated data with information from external sources. The effectiveness of the database, however, depends on the quality of the data model underlying it.

Revenue Cycle Data Model

Figure 11-13 shows a simplified REA data model for the revenue cycle of a manufacturing company such as AOE. It provides a means for capturing and storing information about the basic revenue cycle events discussed in this chapter. In addition, two other events important to AOE are included: To evaluate sales force productivity, Trevor wants to collect data about calls on customers; he also wants to separately track the warehouse activities involved in filling customer orders to monitor how that affects AOE's customer service.

Reading the Data Model

Recall that each box in an REA diagram represents a resource, an event, or an agent entity about which information is collected. The labeled diamonds between these entities represent the relationships of interest. If the data model depicted in Figure 11-13 were implemented in a relational database, there would be a table for each entity and for each many-to-many relationship. Table 11-2 lists many of the attributes that would be found in those tables.

Recall also that the cardinalities of those relationships, which are shown in parentheses on the REA diagram, reflect important information about the organization's policies and the nature of its business. Let us consider what the cardinalities depicted in Figure 11-13 reveal about AOE.

Notice that the maximum cardinality associated with the inventory entity is N in each of its relationships with events. This indicates that AOE tracks its inventory by product lines rather than as individual physical units. Thus, the same product line may be discussed in many different sales calls, may be part of many different orders, and

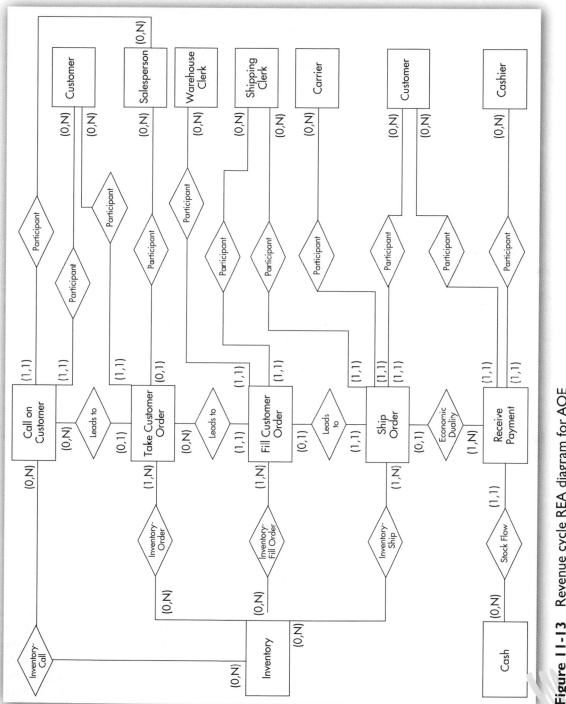

Figure 11-13 Revenue cycle REA diagram for AOE

Table 11-2 Attributes for Relational Tables in Figure 11-13

Table	Attributes (**primary key,** *foreign keys,* other)
Inventory	**Product number,** description, unit cost, unit price, quantity on hand, weight, reorder point, . . .
Cash	**Account number,** *bank ID,* balance, . . .
Call on Customer	**Call number,** date, time, purpose, *customer ID, salesperson number, sales order number,* . . .
Take Customer Order	**Sales order number,** date, *customer ID, salesperson number,* terms, desired delivery date, . . .
Fill Customer Order	**Picking ticket number,** date, time, *warehouse clerk number, shipping clerk number, sales order number,* . . .
Ship Order	**Shipment number,** *invoice number,* date, bill-of-lading number, *picking ticket number, shipping clerk number, carrier number, customer number,* amount due, . . .
Receive Payments	**Remittance number**, date, amount, *customer number, cashier number, invoice number, account number,* . . .
Salesperson	**Employee number,** name, date hired, date of birth, salary, *manager number,* . . .
Warehouse Clerk	**Employee number,** name, date hired, date of birth, salary, *manager number,* . . .
Shipping Clerk	**Employee number,** name, date hired, date of birth, salary, *manager number,* . . .
Carrier	**Carrier number,** name, primary contact, . . .
Customer	**Customer number,** name, bill to address, . . .
Cashier	**Employee number,** name, date hired, date of birth, salary, *manager number,* . . .
Inventory-Call	**Product number, call number**
Inventory-Order	**Product number, sales order number,** quantity, actual sales price, accounting cost
Inventory-Fill Order	**Product number, picking ticket number,** quantity
Inventory-Ship	**Product number, invoice number,** quantity

can be shipped many times. The minimum cardinality associated with the inventory entity is zero, because the inventory table is a master file, which means that its contents pertain to multiple fiscal periods. The event tables, however, store information about transactions for a given fiscal period. At the end of each fiscal year, the contents of the event tables are archived and then cleared. Therefore, at the beginning of each new fiscal year, each row in the inventory table is connected to no rows in the event tables.

Notice that the maximum cardinality for each event entity is also N for its relationship with the inventory entity. When salespeople call on customers, they may discuss many different products. Customers often order multiple product lines, and each fill order and ship order event can involve multiple types of products. The minimum cardinality associated with the call on customer event in the inventory-call relationship is zero, because some sales calls are designed to establish or improve relationships and may not include discussion of specific products. In contrast, the minimum cardinality associated with each of the other events in its relationship with the inventory entity is one, because each order, fill, and shipment must involve at least one product.

The relationship between the events call on customer and take customer order is one-to-many (1:N). The cardinalities associated with these events reflect the following facts: (1) A sales call may not always result in an order, or may result in many orders; (2) orders are linked to the most recent sales call; and (3) some orders may be received without any prior sales calls, resulting instead from other forms of advertising or word of mouth.

The relationship between the take customer order and fill order events is represented as being one-to-many (1:N). AOE sells only to retailers and wholesalers, so each order is generally quite large, often involving hundreds of different products. Therefore, each customer order is picked individually. Sometimes, however, items are out of stock and on back order. In such cases, it takes more than one picking and packing event to completely fill a particular customer order. The minimum cardinalities for each event reflect the fact that orders must be received before they can be filled.

The relationship between the fill order and ship order events is one-to-one (1:1): Once picked, each order is shipped intact to that customer. For economic reasons, AOE sometimes batches several smaller shipments to different customers located in the same city onto one truck. Nevertheless, each shipment is individually tracked for control and performance evaluation purposes. The minimum cardinalities associated with these events reflect the fact that an order must be filled before it can be shipped.

The cardinalities associated with the ship order and receive payment events indicate that AOE allows customers to pay monthly for all shipments they received the prior month, but does not permit customers to make installment payments. The minimum cardinalities associated with each event indicate that AOE sells on credit. It ships products before receiving payment.

The cardinalities associated with the relationship between the receive payment event and the cash resource reflect the fact that each customer payment is deposited into AOE's general checking account but that AOE also maintains other cash accounts (e.g., for payroll and short-term investments).

The relationships between the various events and agents are all N:1. Each event is linked to only one specific customer and internal agent, but each agent can participate in many events during the fiscal year. The minimum cardinality associated with the agents is zero for three reasons. First, AOE maintains information about potential customers. Second, when new employees are hired, they are added to the database prior to performing any activities. Third, the agent tables are master files maintained across fiscal years, whereas the event tables are transaction files that are cleared at the end of each fiscal year. On the event side of each relationship, the minimum cardinality of one reflects the fact that, with one exception, every valid business event must involve both an internal agent and an external agent. The one exception relates to customer orders received through AOE's Web site. In such a case, there is no salesperson involved.

The primary key of the shipping event is the shipment number. The bill of lading is another attribute, but it may be null for deliveries made using AOE's own trucks. Sales invoice number is another attribute of the shipment event. It is not the primary key, however, because AOE is in the process of moving to invoiceless billing with its customers.

Therefore, some shipments do not have an invoice number. Customers with whom invoiceless relationships have been established are instructed to note the shipment number to which their payment applies. Remittance advices sent to customers who still require invoices include the shipment number to facilitate proper credit for payments.

Notice that Figure 11-13 does not include a separate billing event, because it is only an information processing activity, not part of the value chain. Indeed, it is not even a necessary step when companies implement invoiceless sales with customers. The basic economic exchange events in AOE's revenue cycle are ship order and receive payment. The other events are commitments or significant steps in the process about which management needs information for planning, control, and evaluation purposes.

Where are data about accounts receivable stored? Accounts receivable represents sales for which payment has not yet been received. Therefore, accounts receivable can be calculated by taking the difference between the total amount of sales and the amount of cash collections linked to those sales events. To improve query response time, however, the total outstanding balance each customer owes is often stored as an attribute in the customer table.

Finally, notice that information about prices and costs are stored in several places. The inventory table contains information about the standard (list) price and cost of each item because those values are typically constant for the entire fiscal year. The take order—inventory table, however, contains information about not only the quantity ordered but also the actual price and accounting cost assigned to each item. This reflects the fact that AOE may change prices several times during the year. Thus, while the list price is constant, the actual sales price depends on when the sale occurs. Similarly, although the standard cost for each item is constant during the year, the calculated cost (which may be determined using either FIFO, LIFO, weighted-average, or specific identification) will vary throughout the year, especially if a perpetual inventory system is used.

Benefits of the Data Model

Notice how the data model depicted in Figure 11-13 effectively integrates traditional accounting transaction data (e.g., the date and amount of sale) with other operational data (e.g., information about sales calls). It also would be easy to link this internal data with various types of external information. For example, credit rating data about current and potential customers could be downloaded from a commercial database and stored in additional columns in the customer table. Similarly, current customer satisfaction ratings collected from surveys could also be stored in the customer table. If, however, AOE wants to track customer satisfaction over time, a separate customer satisfaction table should be created. Each row in that table would represent a rating by a specific customer at a specific point in time, with information about the survey and possibly including additional comments. Each customer would be linked to (0,N) of these ratings, but each rating would be linked to (1,1) customer records.

One important advantage provided by the REA model depicted in Figure 11-13 is that decision makers can retrieve any desired revenue cycle information with easy-to-use query languages. Thus, implementing the REA data model in a relational database significantly improves the AIS's ability to supply management with the information necessary for effectively managing revenue cycle activities. Focus 11-3 discusses one example of a new type of metric designed specifically to provide a leading indicator of revenue cycle performance.

Focus 11-3

Revenue Margin: A New Metric for Evaluating Revenue Cycle Performance

Companies have long focused on revenue trends as a performance indicator. A better metric for evaluating the quality of growth, however, may be revenue margin. Revenue margin equals gross margin minus all selling costs: payroll, commissions, salesforce-travel-expense reimbursements, customer service and support costs, warranty expenses, marketing and advertising expenses, and distribution and delivery expenses. New database technology makes it easy to calculate this figure.

The value of revenue margin as a metric is that it integrates the effects of changes in sales, pricing, and the costs associated with generating sales on overall company operating profits. Although a financial number, revenue margin reflects such nonfinancial factors as productivity, reputation, and market position strength. Thus, trends in revenue margin provide useful insights for management about the revenue cycle activities' overall performance. Growth in revenue margin indicates that customers are satisfied, productivity is increasing, or both. Conversely, a declining trend indicates potential problems with customer retention, productivity, or pricing pressures due to competition.

Revenue margin is a nontraditional performance metric. It is one example of the kinds of new measures that can be generated more easily because of the increased reporting flexibility that well-designed relational databases provide.

Source: James B. Hangstefer, "Revenue Margin: A Better Way to Measure Company Growth," *Strategic Finance* (July 2000): 41–44.

In addition to giving decision makers quick and easy access to information, a well-designed database can provide strategic benefits to a company's marketing efforts. Companies can "mine" their sales data to target advertising and sales promotions to their customers' needs and desires. Thus, instead of sending mass junk mail promotions to every potential customer in a geographic area, companies can send specific messages to targeted groups of people. The key to effectively conducting such one-to-one marketing is integrating existing transaction data about each customer with lots of other information and storing that information in a manner that is easily accessible. For example, General Motors Corporation uses data collected from its affinity program with MasterCard and its own sales records to determine the type of vehicle information—makes, models, colors, and so on—it should send to specific customers. Similarly, Blockbuster Entertainment Corporation tracks a customer's rental history and mails promotions that suggest titles that may appeal to that customer. Kraft General Foods, Inc. uses information collected from surveys to prepare customized mailings that offer nutrition information and recipes featuring identical Kraft products that a customer has purchased in the past. Siemens Rolm Communications Company tracks customer requests for moving, adding, or changing communications network switches. It uses this information to predict when a customer is approaching capacity limits and would thus be receptive to a sales call recommending the purchase of additional capacity.

The REA data model also facilitates the implementation of collaborative forecasting and replenishment (CFAR) systems with major customers. CFAR integrates actual sales data and information about planned promotions across customers with internally generated data to develop more accurate sales forecasts. The result is improved inventory management and a reduced likelihood of both lost sales due to stockouts and the need for markdowns due to oversupply.

The preceding examples illustrate how companies can use information about their customers to generate increased sales and improve the overall performance of revenue cycle activities. The ability to do so depends on effectively integrating data from both internal and external data sources. Using the REA data model as the basis for redesigning the AIS facilitates such integration. It is also important that adequate control procedures be built into the system to ensure that the data stored therein are accurate and that the confidentiality of customer data is maintained.

Internal Control Considerations

Data accuracy is vital when using a database management system (DBMS). Fortunately, the relational data model provides some built-in controls to ensure data accuracy and consistency. One of the more important of these controls is support for foreign keys and referential integrity. It ensures, for example, that when a new row is added to the take customer order table, the system will verify that the customer number (which appears as a foreign key in that table) actually exists as a primary key in the customer table (that there really is such a customer).

A DBMS also increases the importance of having effective access controls. Most relational DBMSs offer a means to control access by letting different users see only a portion of the database (called a view). For example, sales order entry clerks would see only the portion of Figure 11-13, such as the tables for inventory, customers, and orders, relevant to their job duties. In addition, sales order entry clerks would be permitted to perform only certain operations on those tables. For example, they should not be able to change customer credit limits.

Our discussion of the control threats and exposures listed in Table 11-1 stressed the importance of properly segregating incompatible duties. REA diagrams are useful in evaluating the extent to which incompatible duties are segregated, because they indicate which internal agents participate in each event. The REA model also can indicate if and when events are reviewed and approved by appropriate management. For example, Figure 11-13 should be modified so that the take customer order event is linked not only to the customer and salesperson entities, but also to the credit manager. (We leave the determination of the proper cardinalities for this relationship as homework exercise.)

Moreover, if the REA model is implemented in a DBMS, the computer can be programmed to enforce segregation of duties by rejecting any employee attempts to perform incompatible functions. Conversely, the system can be programmed to list all cases of an employee performing multiple roles, so that the auditors can investigate if adequate compensating controls exist.

SUMMARY AND CASE CONCLUSION

The four basic activities in the revenue cycle are sales order entry, shipping, billing and accounts receivable, and cash collections. The AIS should be designed to maximize the efficiency with which each of these functions is performed. The AIS must also incorporate adequate internal control procedures to mitigate threats such as uncollectible sales, billing errors, and lost or misappropriated inventory and cash. Control procedures also are needed to ensure that the information provided for decision making is both accurate and complete. Finally, to facilitate strategic decision making, the AIS should be designed to accommodate the integration of internally generated data with data from external sources.

At the next executive meeting, Elizabeth summarized the proposals that she, Trevor, and Ann developed to provide the information needed to better manage customer relationships and cash flows. Among the recommendations were the following:

1. Equip the sales force with pen-based laptop computers. Trevor Whitman, vice president of marketing, believes that AOE will still need its sales staff to visit existing customers, to identify which additional products can be profitably carried. Sales staff also will continue to make cold calls on prospective customers to try to convince them to carry AOE's products. As they walk down store aisles, sales representatives can check off the items that need to be restocked and then write in the appropriate quantities. When the order is complete, they can transmit the order back to headquarters. The system can check the customer's credit status and inventory availability and confirm orders within minutes, including an estimated delivery date. After the customer approves the order, the system will immediately update all affected files so that current information about inventory status is available to other sales representatives.

2. Improve billing process efficiency by increasing the number of customers who agree to participate in invoiceless sales relationships and, when possible, using EDI to transmit invoices to those customers who still require them.

3. In an effort to improve customer service, work with major customers to obtain access to their POS data so that AOE can help them better manage their product inventory.

4. Periodically survey customers about their satisfaction with AOE's products and performance.

5. Improve the efficiency of cash collections by encouraging EDI capable customers to move to FEDI so that AOE receives both the funds and remittance data together.

Linda Spurgeon approved these proposals. She then asked Elizabeth and Ann to turn their attention to solving several problems related to AOE's expenditure cycle business activities.

KEY TERMS

- revenue cycle
- sales invoice
- lockbox
- sales order
- open-invoice method
- electronic lockbox
- credit limit
- remittance advice

- back order
- balance-forward method
- picking ticket
- monthly statement
- sales analysis report
- packing slip
- cycle billing
- profitability analysis report

- bill of lading
- credit memo
- accounts receivable aging schedule
- freight bill
- remittance list
- cash budget

CHAPTER QUIZ

1. Which activity is part of the sales order entry process?
   a. setting customer credit limits
   b. preparing a bill of lading
   c. checking customer credit
   d. approving sales returns

2. Which document often accompanies merchandise shipped to a customer?
   a. picking list
   b. packing slip
   c. credit memo
   d. sales order

3. Which method is most likely used when a company offers customers discounts for prompt payment?
   a. open-invoice method
   b. balance-forward method
   c. accounts receivable aging method
   d. cycle billing method

4. Having customers send checks directly to a postal address, rather than to the company, is an example of which of the following?
   a. EFT system
   b. EDI system
   c. image processing
   d. bank lockbox arrangement

5. Which of the following is not likely to be included in a data model of the revenue cycle?
   a. cash collections
   b. sales
   c. orders
   d. purchases

6. What would be most useful for determining which sales region requires additional attention to improve sales?
   a. accounts receivable aging schedule
   b. profitability analysis
   c. sales analysis
   d. cash budget

7. Which document is used to authorize the release of merchandise from the inventory control (warehouse) to shipping?
   a. picking list
   b. packing slip
   c. shipping order
   d. sales invoice

8. For a retail store such as Wal-Mart, the relationship between sales and inventory items is most likely to be represented as being which of the following?
   a. one-to-one
   b. one-to-many
   c. many-to-one
   d. many-to-many

9. For good internal control, who should approve credit memos?
   a. credit manager
   b. sales manager
   c. billing manager
   d. controller
10. For good internal control over customer remittances, the mailroom clerk should separate the checks from the remittance advices and send them to whom?
    a. billing
    b. accounts receivable
    c. cashier
    d. controller

DISCUSSION QUESTIONS

11.1   Customer relationship management systems hold great promise, but their usefulness is determined by the amount of personal data customers are willing to divulge. To what extent do you think concerns about privacy-related issues will affect the use of CRM systems?

11.2   Companies are continually investing in automation tools to support the sales process. Will sales force automation tools ever eliminate the need for sales representatives? Why or why not?

11.3   Many companies are outsourcing their shipping functions to carriers such as UPS and FedEx. The objective of such outsourcing deals is to cut costs. Discuss the advantages and disadvantages of outsourcing functions such as shipping. What control issues are raised by such an arrangement?

11.4   Products that can be digitized, such as music, software, and books, can be delivered over the Internet. What new threats does this create? What control procedures can mitigate those threats?

11.5   Wholesalers have traditionally played an important role in the supply chain. To what extent is such an intermediary role needed on the Internet?

11.6   What accounting- and audit-related issues arise in accepting some form of electronic or digital "cash" from customers in payment for Internet sales?

PROBLEMS

11.1   Use the format of Table 11-1 to compare and contrast how AOE's current integrated revenue cycle system and its old legacy revenue cycle system (as described in the appendix to this chapter) address the various threats and issues related to revenue cycle activities.

11.2   Modify Table 11-1 by indicating if each specific control procedure listed there is preventive (P), detective (D), or corrective (C) in nature.

11.3   What internal control procedure(s) would provide protection against the following threats? If more than one control procedure could be used to solve a problem, rank the alternatives in terms of their effectiveness:
       a. Theft of goods by the shipping dock workers, who claim that the inventory shortages reflect errors in the inventory records

b. Posting the sales amount to the wrong customer account because a customer account number was incorrectly keyed into the system

c. Making a credit sale to a customer who is already 4 months behind in making payments on his account

d. Authorizing a credit memo for a sales return when the goods were never actually returned

e. Writing off a customer's accounts receivable balance as uncollectible to conceal the theft of subsequent collections

f. Billing customers for the quantity ordered when the quantity shipped was actually less due to back ordering of some items

g. Theft of checks by the mailroom clerk, who then endorsed the checks for deposit into the account of a fictitious company

h. Theft of funds by the cashier, who cashed several checks and did not record their receipt

i. Theft of cash by a waiter who destroyed the customer sales ticket for customers who paid cash

11.4 Refer to Figure 11-13 to answer the following questions:

a. If the relationship between shipping and cash collections were one-to-many, what would that reveal about the company's sales policy? What if the relationship was many-to-one? What if it was many-to-many? Think of real company examples that reflect each of these options.

b. What would a one-to-one relationship between inventory and sales imply about the types of products the company sells?

c. Can the relationship between sales and customers ever be one-to-many or many-to-many? Why or why not?

d. What would have to be changed if the company required customers to pay in advance for their orders before the merchandise is shipped?

e. What should be the cardinalities for the relationship between the take customer order event and the credit manager agent? (Hint: Consider the discussion of general versus specific authorization.)

f. Suppose AOE wants to assign customers to specific salespeople. How should this be modeled? What if only preferred customers are assigned to a specific salesperson?

11.5 Your company has just acquired a database management system and wants to develop an REA data model for its revenue cycle activities.

Required

a. Use the following facts, plus the generic description of the revenue cycle included in the chapter, to modify Figure 11-13:

1. The company uses the balance-forward method to bill its customers.

2. The company carries its own credit; customers may pay all or only a portion of their bill each month.

3. There are no back orders.

4. The company wants to track the performance of its customer service representatives in terms of responding to customer inquiries.

5. The company wants to include a sales returns and allowances event. Customers can return unsatisfactory merchandise for credit. In such cases, the company must identify which items are being returned, the quantity being returned, and the reason for the return. There is also a need to record the identity of the employee who approved the return and the total amount of the adjustment to the customer's account. In some cases, a customer may elect to keep the damaged goods and have the account credited for a portion of the purchase price.

6. The company sells both goods and services. Assume that information about services (description, list price) is stored in a resource table called Services. Further, assume that a sale may involve both goods and services, just goods, or just services (e.g., a maintenance check).

b. In addition to modifying the REA diagram, list the attributes that should be stored about the customer service event. Indicate which of these attributes should be the primary key and which, if any, are foreign keys.

c. List the attributes that should be stored about the sales return event.

11.6   Table 11-3 shows some of the relational tables used to implement an REA model of a company's revenue cycle.

Required

a. Identify the primary key of each table.

b. Identify the foreign key(s), if any, of each table.

c. Which tables represent resources? Events? Agents?

Draw an REA diagram of the system. List any assumptions made in assigning cardinalities to relationships.

Table 11-3   Relational Tables for Problem 11-6

Inventory

Part Number	Description	Cost	Price
101	Monitor	$899	$1295
102	CPU	2150	2599
103	CD-ROM drive	95	199
104	Printer	345	499
105	Tape unit	195	259

Inventory-Sales

Part Number	Invoice Number	Quantity
101	25	1
102	25	1
103	25	1
104	26	2

Cash Collections

Remittance Number	Amount	Invoice Number	Customer Number
120	$499	23	1001
121	4851	24	1003
122	4851	27	1001

Sales

Invoice Number	Date	Customer Number	Salesperson Number
23	11/05	1001	12
24	11/05	1003	10
25	11/06	1002	8
26	11/07	1003	12
27	11/07	1001	8
28	11/07	1003	12

Salesperson

Salesperson Number	Name
8	Jones
10	Brown
12	Alawi

Customer

Customer Number	Name	Address
1001	Agrawal	Chicago
1002	Chen	Memphis
1003	Finney	St. Louis

11.7 The Quality Building Supplies Company operates six wholesale outlets that sell roofing materials, electrical and plumbing supplies, lumber, and other building materials to general contractors in a large metropolitan area. The company is studying the feasibility of introducing a guaranteed same-day delivery plan, under which it would guarantee delivery within four hours for orders received from approved customers by noon of that day. For orders received in the afternoon, delivery would be guaranteed by 8 A.M. the next day. The company believes that this system would give it a substantial competitive advantage relative to other regional building wholesalers, because it would enable contractors to maintain smaller inventories yet still be assured of having building supplies when needed.

You have been asked to help design the proposed system. It will be designed to receive customer orders by phone so that contractors can call from the construction site. Customers will be billed monthly for all purchases. You want to streamline the processing of cash collections and minimize the time it takes to deposit those funds in the company's bank account.

Required
a. Specify the factors needed to qualify customers for this new service.
b. Identify the input transactions that this system must process and the output documents (excluding reports) that it should produce.
c. Draw an REA diagram to indicate the information that the new system must capture and maintain.
d. Describe several reports that would be useful to management's implementation of the new credit sales policy. What data need to be collected to produce these reports? What application controls should be in place to ensure that these reports contain complete, accurate, and valid information?
e. Draw a systems flowchart of your proposed system.
f. Describe possible threats to the system and the control procedures required in the new system to address those threats.

11.8 O'Brien Corporation is a midsize, privately owned, industrial instrument manufacturer supplying precision equipment to manufacturers in the Midwest. The corporation is ten years old and operates a centralized AIS. The administrative offices are located in a downtown building and the production, shipping, and receiving departments are housed in a renovated warehouse a few blocks away. The shipping and receiving areas share one end of the warehouse.

The marketing department consists of four sales representatives. Upon obtaining an order over the telephone, a salesperson manually prepares a prenumbered, two-part sales order. One copy of the order is filed by date and the second copy is sent to the shipping department. All sales are on credit, FOB destination. Because of the recent increase in sales, the sales representatives have not had time to check credit histories. As a result, 15 percent of credit sales are either late collections or uncollectible.

The shipping department receives the sales orders and packages the goods from the warehouse, noting any items that are out of stock. The terminal in the shipping department is used to update the perpetual inventory records of each item as it is removed from the shelf. The packages are placed near the loading dock door in alphabetical order by customer name. A shipping clerk signs the sales order, indicating that the order is filled and ready to send.

The sales order is forwarded to the billing department, where a two-part sales invoice is prepared. The sales invoice is prepared upon receipt of the sales order from the shipping department so that the customer is billed only for the items that were sent, not for back orders. Billing sends the customer's copy of the invoice back to shipping, and shipping then inserts it into a special envelope on the package in order to save postage.

The carrier of the customer's choice is then contacted to pick up the goods. In the past, goods were shipped within two working days of receipt of the customer's order; however, shipping dates now average six working days. One reason for this slippage is that two new shipping clerks are still undergoing training. Because these clerks have fallen behind, the two experienced clerks in the receiving department have been assisting them.

The receiving department is located adjacent to the shipping dock, and many different carriers receive merchandise daily. The clerks share a computer terminal with the shipping department. The date, vendor, and number of items received are entered upon receipt to keep the perpetual inventory records current.

Hard copies of the changes in inventory (additions and shipments) are printed monthly. The receiving supervisor checks that the additions are reasonable and forwards the printout to the shipping supervisor, who is responsible for checking the reasonableness of the deductions from inventory (shipments). The inventory printout is stored in the shipping department by date. A complete inventory list is printed only once a year when the entire inventory is counted.

Figure 11-14 presents the document flows employed by O'Brien Corporation.

Required

a. Identify at least five weaknesses in O'Brien Corporation's marketing, shipping, billing, and receiving information system. Describe the exposure resulting from each weakness. Recommend control procedures that should be added to the system to correct the weakness. Format your answer as follows:

Weakness   Threat   Recommended Control Procedure(s)

b. Discuss how O'Brien Corporation could use IT to improve both control and efficiency during sales order processing.

(CMA Examination, adapted)

11.9   Parktown Medical Center, Inc. is a small health care provider owned by a publicly held corporation. It employs seven salaried physicians, ten nurses, three support staff, and three clerical workers. The clerical workers perform such tasks as reception, correspondence, cash receipts, billing, and appointment scheduling. All are adequately bonded.

Most patients pay for services rendered by cash or check on the day of their visit. The clerical staff does not approve credit. The physician who is to perform the respective services approves credit based on an interview. When credit is approved, the physician files a memo with the billing clerk (clerk 2) to set up the receivable from data the physician generates.

The servicing physician prepares a charge slip that is given to clerk 1 for pricing and preparation of the patient's bill. Clerk 1 transmits a copy of the bill to clerk 2 for preparation of the revenue summary and for posting in the accounts receivable subsidiary ledger.

The cash receipts functions are performed by clerk 1, who receives cash and checks directly from patients and gives each patient a prenumbered cash receipt. Clerk 1 opens the mail and immediately stamps all checks "for deposit only" and lists cash and checks for deposit. The cash and checks are deposited daily by the office manager. The list of cash and checks, with the related remittance advices, are forwarded by clerk 1 to clerk 2. Clerk 1 also serves as the office receptionist with general correspondence duties.

Clerk 2 prepares and sends monthly statements to patients with unpaid balances. He also prepares the cash receipts journal and is responsible for the accounts receivable subsidiary ledger. No other clerical employee is permitted access to the accounts receivable subsidiary ledger. Clerk 2 writes off uncollectible accounts only after the physician who performed the

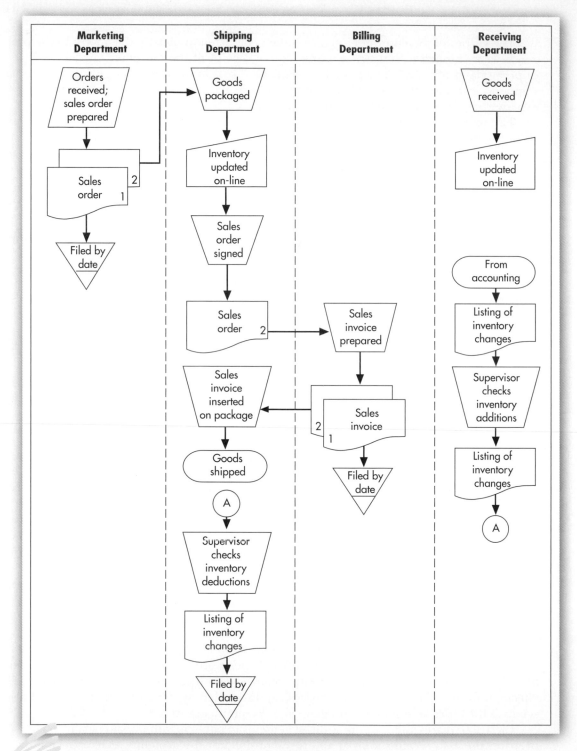

Figure 11-14 Revenue cycle activities for O'Brien Corporation

respective services believes the account will not pay and communicates the write-off to the office manager. The office manager then issues a write-off memo, which clerk 2 processes.

The office manager supervises the clerks, issues write-off memos, schedules appointments for the doctors, makes bank deposits, reconciles bank statements, and performs general correspondence duties.

Additional services are performed monthly by a local accountant who posts summaries prepared by the clerks to the general ledger, prepares income statements, and files the appropriate payroll forms and tax returns. The accountant reports directly to the parent corporation.

Required

Identify at least four control weaknesses at Parktown. Describe the potential threat and exposure associated with each weakness, and recommend how to best correct them.

(CPA Examination, adapted)

11.10 Figure 11-15 depicts the activities performed in the revenue cycle by the Newton Hardware Company.

Required

1. Identify the weaknesses in Newton Hardware's revenue cycle. Explain the resulting threat and suggest methods to correct the weakness. Organize your answer as follows:

   Weakness   Threat   Recommended Improvement

2. Identify ways to use IT to streamline Newton's revenue cycle activities. Describe the control procedures required in the new system.

(CPA Examination, adapted)

11.11 Complete the cell entries in Table 11-4, which lists the various activities performed in the revenue cycle and the journal entries, documents, data, and control issues associated with them.

ANSWERS TO CHAPTER QUIZ

1. c	3. a	5. d	7. a	9. a
2. b	4. d	6. c	8. d	10. c

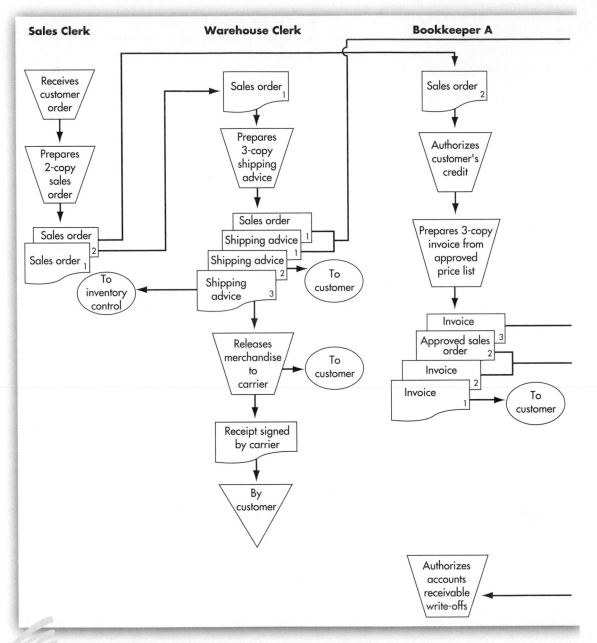

Figure 11-15   Newton Hardware Company: revenue cycle procedures

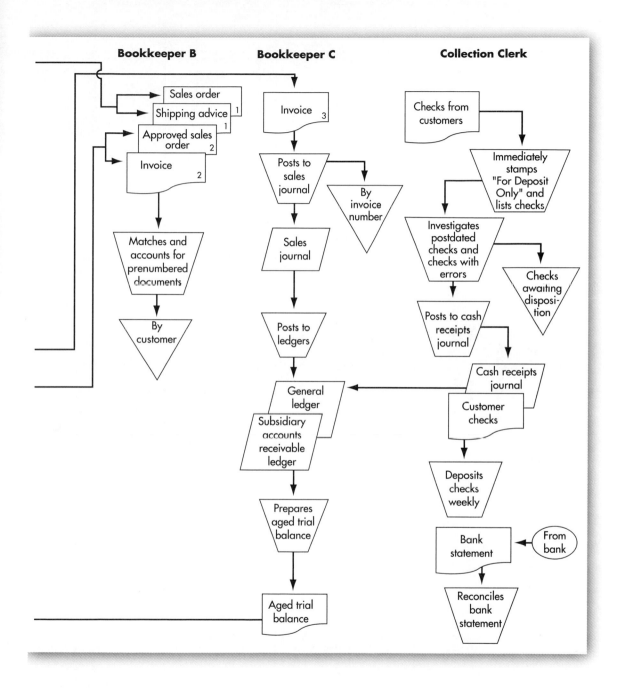

Bookkeeper B **Bookkeeper C** **Collection Clerk**

Sales order

Shipping advice 1

1

Approved sales order 2

Invoice 2

Invoice 3

Checks from customers

Posts to sales journal

By invoice number

Immediately stamps "For Deposit Only" and lists checks

Matches and accounts for prenumbered documents

Sales journal

Investigates postdated checks and checks with errors

Checks awaiting disposition

By customer

Posts to ledgers

Posts to cash receipts journal

Cash receipts journal

General ledger

Customer checks

Subsidiary accounts receivable ledger

Deposits checks weekly

Prepares aged trial balance

Bank statement

From bank

Aged trial balance

Reconciles bank statement

Table 11-4 Overview of Revenue Cycle Business Activities

	Revenue Cycle							
	Contact Customer	Customer Agrees to Sale	Approve Credit	Transfer Goods	Bill Customer	Receive Remittance	Credit Accounts Receivable	Deposit Cash
Accounting transaction				Sale				
Journal entry							Dr. Cash Cr. A/R	
Documents		Purchase order from customer						
Data collected	Name Address Contact person							
Department					Accounting			
Control issues			Only approved customer get credit					
Information required								
Information generated								
Effect of automation								

Source: Adapted from teaching materials developed by Martha Eining, University of Utah.

Case 11-1 AnyCompany, Inc.: An Ongoing Comprehensive Case

Identify a local company (you may use the same company that you identified to complete this case in prior chapters), and answer the following questions:

1. Who are the individuals responsible for sales order preparation, credit checks, safeguarding of physical inventories, shipping, billing, maintaining accounts receivable, and handling cash collections? How are these duties segregated to diminish the threat of errors or irregularities?
2. What documents are used in the system? Are they designed in a manner that makes them easy to complete? Do they collect all the information needed to manage the various revenue cycle business activities? Do the reports generated by the system provide adequate information for decision making?
3. Are data stored in separate files or in a database? How is this information updated? What process is used to update the general ledger? What application controls are in place to ensure accuracy, completeness, and validity of data entry, processing, and output?
4. Document your understanding of the system using flowcharts, data flow diagrams, and REA diagrams. Discuss how current developments in IT could be used to improve the efficiency and effectiveness of existing procedures.

Case 11-2 Elite Publishing Company

Elite Publishing Company has established Business Book Club, Inc. (BBC), a subsidiary that operates as follows: BBC's editors select from among recently published business books those they believe will be most interesting to businesspeople. BBC will purchase these books in large quantities at approximately 40 percent of list price and then sell them to their club members at approximately 75 percent of list price.

Both direct mail and advertisements in selected publications are used to solicit new customers. The advertisements offer an introductory membership bonus whereby new members who purchase one book will receive four free titles. Each month, club members receive a list of new selections and a book order form. For every four books they purchase, members earn one free book.

You have been called upon to design a computerized billing and book inventory system for BBC. The advertising manager wants to know which advertising media are most effective, the credit manager wants to know which accounts are more than 90 days past due, and the editors want to know which books are best-sellers for the club.

Required

1. Draw an REA diagram of the system and prepare a list of attributes that should be stored in the system.
2. Identify the input transactions that this system must process and the output documents and reports that the system should be designed to produce.
3. Describe how IT can be used to maximize efficiency of sales order entry, shipping, billing, and cash collections. Draw a systems flowchart of your proposal.
4. Describe the control procedures that should be included in this system.

AOE's Legacy Revenue Cycle System

AOE's legacy revenue cycle system was characterized by distinct modules to support each of the four basic revenue cycle activities.

SALES ORDER ENTRY

Figure 11A-1 depicts a typical batch-oriented sales order entry process such as the one formerly used at AOE. As they completed calls, sales representatives wrote up orders on preprinted forms. These forms were faxed nightly to the sales order department, where they were assembled in batches of approximately 50 transactions for data entry. Before proceeding with data entry, batch totals (a record count and a hash total of quantities ordered) were manually calculated for each group of 50 transactions. Sales order clerks then entered only the following items for each transaction: customer account number, salesperson number, product numbers and quantities, and requested delivery date. The customer number was used to access the appropriate record in the customer file. The system then retrieved the customer's name and address to complete the sales order. Similarly, the product number was used to access the appropriate record in the inventory file and to retrieve the item description and price.

At this point, a number of edit checks were performed to ensure input accuracy. Transaction records that passed these edit tests represent accurate and valid sales orders. Those that failed one or more tests were listed in an error and exception report for investigation and correction.

As the orders were entered, the system also automatically calculated batch totals. After pro-cessing, these system-generated batch totals were compared with those calculated manually to ensure that all transactions were entered. Any discrepancies were investigated and corrected. The use of small batches facilitated identifying error sources.

The batches of valid sales orders were then merged into one large transaction file to process the orders and update the various master files. The system first calculated the sales amount and compared it with the customer's available credit (credit limit less any outstanding unpaid purchases). Orders that failed this credit check were printed on a credit rejections report. The credit manager evaluated this report and determined whether to increase the customer's credit limit or reject the order. Accepted orders were reentered with the next batch of orders. Customers who were denied credit were notified that their order must be prepaid (these last two steps are not shown in Figure 11A-1).

Next, the system checked availability of inventory to fill accepted orders. If inventory was available, the customer's available credit balance was reduced for the amount of the sale and the quantity available field in the inventory file was reduced for the amount of the order. Otherwise, a back-order record was generated for the needed items. Finally, the sales order, packing slip, and picking tickets were created.

SHIPPING

Figure 11A-2 shows that the picking ticket printed by sales order entry triggered the shipping process. Warehouse workers used the picking ticket to identify which products to remove

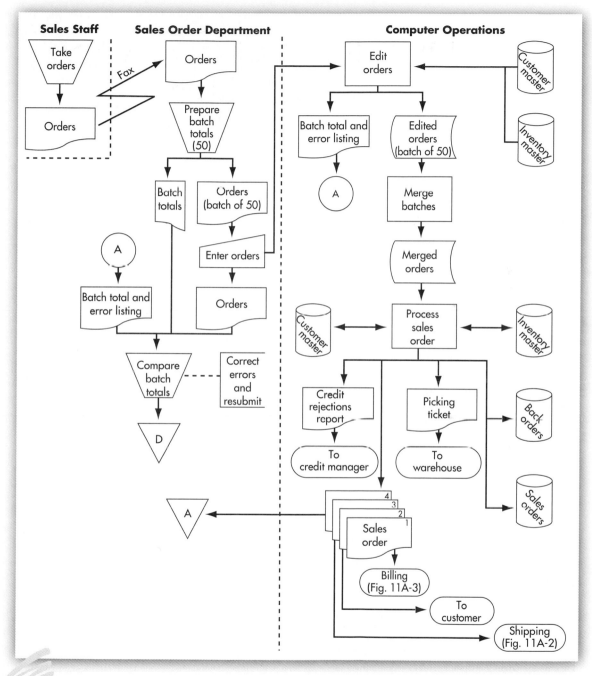

Figure 11A-1 Sales order entry: batch processing

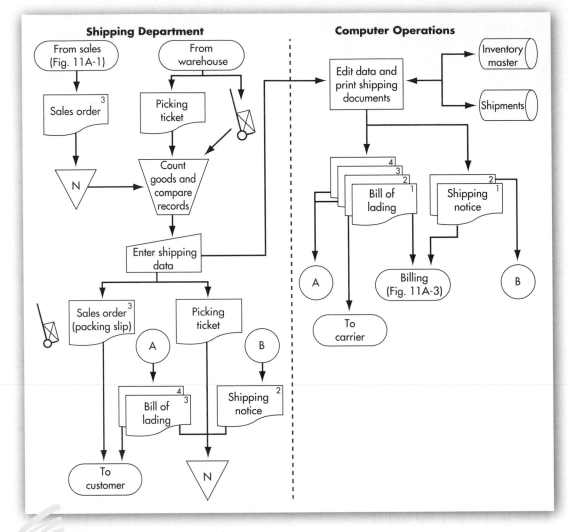

Figure 11A-2   Shipping procedures

from inventory. They marked the quantities picked on the picking ticket, and then brought the inventory and the completed picking ticket to the shipping department.

The shipping department then compared the physical count of inventory with the quantities indicated on the picking ticket and with the quantities indicated on the packing slip (copy 3 of the sales order) that was sent directly to ship-

ping from sales order entry. Discrepancies could arise either because the items were not stored in the location indicated on the picking ticket or because the perpetual inventory records were inaccurate. In such cases, the shipping department initiated the back ordering of the missing items and entered the correct quantities shipped on the packing slip (these steps are not shown in Figure 11A-2).

After the shipping clerk counted the goods delivered from the warehouse, the sales order number, item number(s), and quantities were entered using on-line terminals. A variety of edit checks similar to those described earlier for sales order entry were used to ensure that the shipping data were valid, accurate, and complete. This process updated the quantity-on-hand field in the inventory master file and produced multiple copies of the bill of lading and shipping notices.

BILLING AND ACCOUNTS RECEIVABLE

As shown in Figure 11A-3, AOE prepared invoices only after the shipping department notified billing that the goods had been shipped. When billing received the shipping documents, a clerk matched them with a copy of the sales order that had been sent earlier from the sales order entry department. Throughout the day, the billing clerk generated batches of invoices. The system performed a number of edit checks on the data entered, such as testing the validity of item numbers and comparing the quantities shipped with the quantities indicated on the open sales order.

After these preliminary edit checks, the following operations were performed:

1. New records were created in the sales invoice file, and multiple copies of the sales invoice were printed. Two copies are mailed to the customer, one of which is to be returned with payment.
2. The customer master file was accessed and the customer's account debited for the amount of the sale.
3. The open sales orders were closed to the sales order history file.
4. After all invoices were processed, the system generated a summary journal entry reflecting the total amounts to

be posted to the sales and accounts receivable in the general ledger.

CASH RECEIPTS

Figure 11A-4 depicts a typical batch-oriented approach to processing cash collections, as was formerly used at AOE. The cash collections process began when two mailroom clerks opened the mail. One clerk restrictively endorsed the checks received for deposit to one of the company's bank accounts. The other clerk prepared a remittance list. The checks and one copy of the remittance list were then sent to the cashier, who prepared them for deposit. The second copy of the remittance list was sent to the internal audit department, where it was later used to reconcile the bank statements. The third copy of the remittance list and the remittance advices were sent to accounts receivable for use in updating customer accounts.

An accounts receivable clerk then used an on-line terminal to enter the sum of the remittance list as a batch total, the customer and invoice numbers, and the amount of each payment. The system performed a number of online edit checks to verify the accuracy of data entry. Each customer's account in the customer master file was then credited for the amount remitted, open sales invoices were marked paid and closed to the sales history file, and the total cash received was recorded in the cash receipts file. The system then printed two-part deposit slips and sent them to the cashier. The cashier compared the deposit slips with the checks and remittance list and, after verifying that all customer remittances were accounted for, sent the deposit to the bank. Someone not involved in processing cash collections (in this case, the internal audit department) received the monthly bank statement and prepared the bank reconciliation, thereby providing an independent check on the accuracy and completeness of all deposits. Finally, once a month, the accounts receivable clerk generated and mailed monthly statements to all customers.

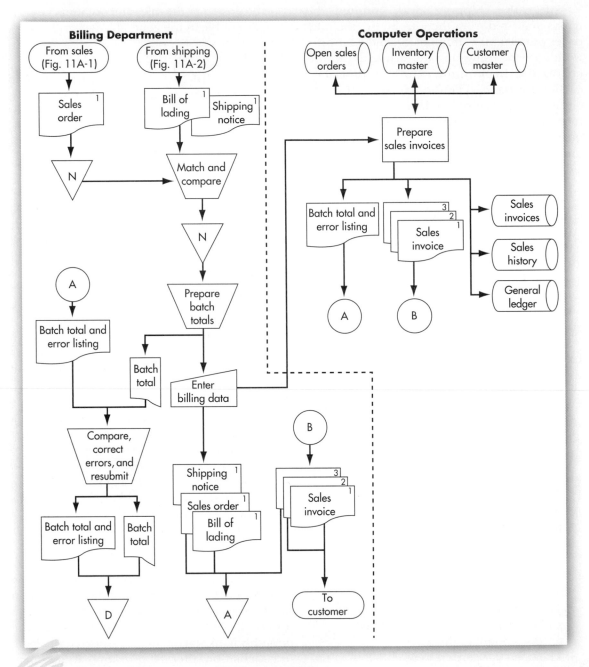

Figure 11A-3   Billing system: batch processing

412

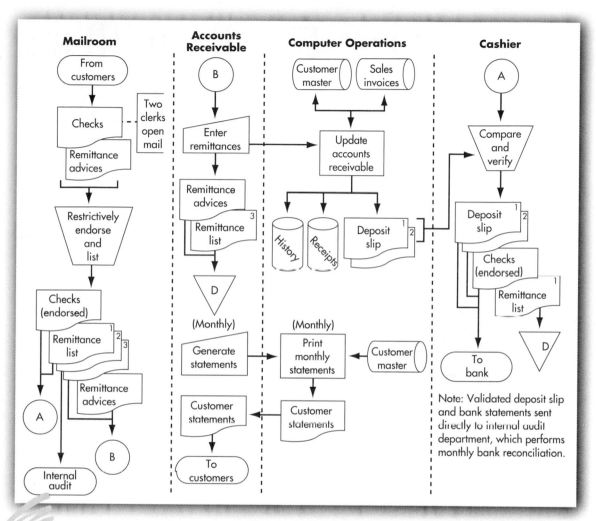

Figure IIA-4 Cash receipts system: batch processing

The Expenditure Cycle: Purchasing and Cash Disbursements

Learning Objectives

After studying this chapter, you should be able to:

■ Describe the basic business activities and related data processing operations performed in the expenditure cycle.

■ Discuss the key decisions to be made in the expenditure cycle and identify the information needed to make those decisions.

■ Document an understanding of the expenditure cycle.

■ Identify major threats in the expenditure cycle and evaluate the adequacy of various control procedures for dealing with those threats.

■ Read and understand a data model (REA diagram) of the expenditure cycle.

Integrative Case: Alpha Omega Electronics

Although AOE's new integrated AIS has enabled it to slash its costs associated with purchasing and accounts payable, Linda Spurgeon, AOE's president, is convinced that additional improvements are needed. She is particularly concerned about issues recently raised by LeRoy Williams, vice president of manufacturing for AOE. LeRoy is upset because several production runs were delayed at the Wichita plant due to components that AOE's inventory records indicated as being in stock but that actually were not on hand. There were also delays at the Dayton plant because suppliers either did not deliver components on time or delivered substandard products.

Linda asked Elizabeth Venko, the controller, and Ann Brandt, AOE's vice president of information systems, for some recommendations on how AOE's AIS could help solve these problems. Specifically, she asked Elizabeth and Ann to address the following issues:

1. What must be done to ensure that AOE's inventory records are current and accurate and to avoid unexpected components shortages like those experienced at the Wichita plant?
2. How could the problems at the Dayton plant be avoided in the future? What can be done to ensure timely delivery of quality components?
3. Is it possible to reduce AOE's investment in materials inventories?
4. How could the information system provide better information to guide planning and production?
5. How could IT be used to further reengineer expenditure cycle activities?

As this case suggests, deficiencies in the information system used to support expenditure cycle activities can create significant financial problems for an organization. The availability of current and accurate information about inventories, suppliers, and the status of outstanding purchase orders is crucial for managing the expenditure cycle effectively. As you read this chapter, think about how changes in AOE's information system could improve the effectiveness and efficiency of its expenditure cycle activities.

INTRODUCTION

The **expenditure cycle** is a recurring set of business activities and related data processing operations associated with the purchase of and payment for goods and services (see Figure 12-1). This chapter focuses on the acquisition of raw materials, finished goods, supplies, and services. Chapters 13 and 14 address two other special types of expenditures: the acquisition of fixed assets and labor services, respectively.

In the expenditure cycle, the primary external exchange of information is with suppliers (vendors). Within the organization, information flows to the expenditure cycle from the revenue and production cycles, inventory control, and various departments about the need to purchase goods and materials. Once the goods and materials arrive, notification of their receipt flows back to those sources from the expenditure cycle. Expense data also flow from the expenditure cycle to the general ledger and reporting function for inclusion in financial statements and various management reports.

The primary objective in the expenditure cycle is to minimize the total cost of acquiring and maintaining inventories, supplies, and the various services the organization needs to function. To accomplish such an objective, management must make the following key decisions:

➤ What is the optimal level of inventory and supplies to carry?
➤ Which suppliers provide the best quality and service at the best prices?
➤ Where should inventories and supplies be held?
➤ How can the organization consolidate purchases across units to obtain optimal prices?
➤ How can IT be used to improve both the efficiency and accuracy of the inbound logistics function?
➤ Is sufficient cash available to take advantage of any discounts suppliers offer?
➤ How can payments to vendors be managed to maximize cash flow?

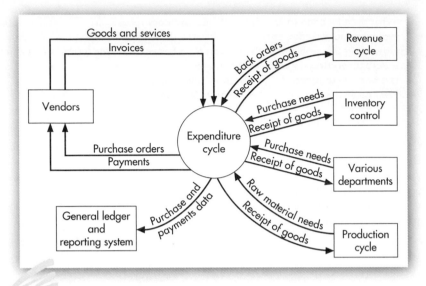

Figure 12-1   Context diagram of the expenditure cycle

In addition, management must be able to monitor and evaluate the efficiency and effectiveness of expenditure cycle processes. That requires easy access to detailed data about the resources employed in the expenditure cycle, the events that affect those resources, and the agents who participate in those events. Moreover, to be useful and relevant for decision making, the data must be accurate, reliable, and timely.

This chapter examines the three basic functions of the AIS in the expenditure cycle: capturing and processing data about business activities, storing and organizing the data to support decision making, and providing controls to ensure the reliability of data and the safeguarding of organizational resources. We begin by describing the basic business activities performed in the expenditure cycle. Then we examine the methods used to collect, store, and process data about those activities. Next, we examine the major control objectives in the expenditure cycle and discuss how to design the AIS to mitigate the threats associated with those activities. We conclude the chapter by presenting an integrated data model that stores and organizes information about expenditure cycle activities to enable management to make key decisions and effectively monitor performance.

EXPENDITURE CYCLE BUSINESS ACTIVITIES

One function of the AIS is to support the effective performance of the organization's business activities by efficiently processing transaction data. Figure 12-2 shows the three basic business activities in the expenditure cycle:

1. Ordering goods, supplies, and services
2. Receiving and storing goods, supplies, and services
3. Paying for goods, supplies, and services

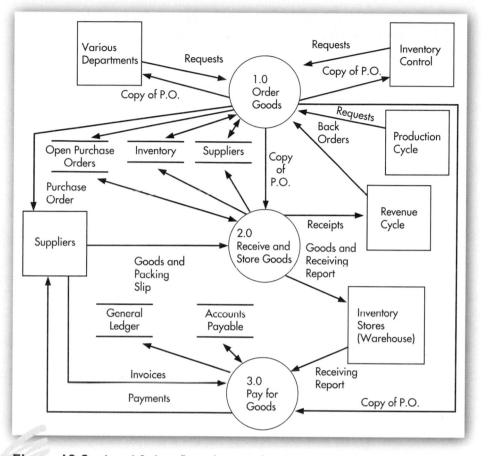

Figure 12-2   Level 0 data flow diagram for the expenditure cycle

Notice that these activities in the expenditure cycle are mirror images of the basic activities performed in the revenue cycle:

➤ The order goods activity generates the purchase order which serves as the customer input to the sales order entry process.

➤ The receive goods activity handles the goods sent by the supplier's shipping function.

➤ The pay for goods activity generates the payments that are processed by the supplier's cash collection activity.

As we will see, these close linkages between the buyer's expenditure cycle activities and the seller's revenue cycle activities have important implications for AIS design. Specifically, by applying new IT developments to reengineer expenditure cycle activities, companies create opportunities for suppliers to reengineer their revenue cycle activities. Conversely, using IT to redesign a company's revenue cycle can create opportunities for customers to modify their own expenditure cycles. In many cases, the changes in one company's operations may *necessitate* changes in the AIS of other companies with which it does business. For example, the major automobile manufacturers may require that suppliers transmit invoices via EDI, or they will not do business with them.

Order Goods

The first major business activity in the expenditure cycle (circle 1.0 in Figure 12-2) is ordering inventory or supplies. The key decisions made in this initial step are identifying what, when, and how much to purchase, as well as identifying from which supplier to purchase. Weaknesses in the inventory control function can create significant problems, as the introductory AOE case demonstrated. Specifically, inaccurate inventory records caused AOE's inventory shortages at the Wichita plant that led to the failure to purchase needed components in a timely manner.

Alternative inventory control methods

The traditional approach to managing inventory is to maintain sufficient stock so that production can continue without interruption even if inventory use is greater than expected or if suppliers are late in making deliveries. This traditional approach is often called the **economic order quantity (EOQ)** approach because it is based on calculating an optimal order size to minimize the sum of ordering, carrying, and stockout costs. *Ordering costs* include all expenses associated with processing purchase transactions. *Carrying costs* are those associated with holding inventory. *Stockout costs* are those that result from inventory shortages, such as lost sales or production delays.

Actual application of the EOQ approach varies depending on the type of item. For high-cost or high-use items, such as the computer chips and displays AOE uses, all three types of costs are included in the formula. For low-cost or low-usage items, such as the screws and springs AOE uses to assemble its products, ordering and carrying costs are usually ignored and the sole objective is to maintain sufficient inventory levels.

The EOQ formula is used to calculate how much to order. The **reorder point** specifies when to order. Companies typically set the reorder point based on delivery time and desired levels of safety stock to handle unexpected fluctuations in demand.

The traditional EOQ approach to inventory control often results in carrying significant amounts of inventory. In recent years many large U.S. manufacturing companies, including Xerox, Ford, Motorola, NCR, Intel, McDonnell Douglas, and Delco Electronics, have adopted alternative methods of inventory control that seek to minimize or even eliminate the amount of inventory on hand.

One alternative approach to managing inventory is called **materials requirements planning (MRP).** MRP seeks to reduce required inventory levels by scheduling production, rather than estimating needs. For example, the production planning department of a company using MRP would prepare a detailed schedule specifying the quantities of each finished product that it wants to manufacture in a specified time period, such as the next three months. Using this schedule and the engineering specifications for each product, one can determine the quantities of raw materials, parts, and supplies needed in production, and the point in time when they will be needed. Thus, MRP systems reduce uncertainties about when raw materials are needed and therefore enable companies to carry less inventory.

A **just-in-time (JIT) inventory system** is another alternative approach to managing inventory. JIT systems attempt to minimize, if not totally eliminate, both carrying and stockout costs. JIT systems are characterized by frequent deliveries of small amounts of materials, parts, and supplies directly to the specific locations that require them when they are needed, rather than by infrequent bulk deliveries to a central receiving and storage facility. Thus, a factory using a JIT system will have multiple receiving docks, each assigned to accept deliveries of items needed at nearby work centers.

A major difference between MRP and JIT systems is production scheduling. MRP systems schedule production to meet estimated sales needs, thereby creating a stock of finished goods inventory. JIT systems schedule production to meet customer demands, thereby virtually eliminating finished goods inventory. Both MRP and JIT systems can reduce costs and improve efficiency. Choosing between them depends, in part, on the types of products a company sells. MRP systems are more effectively used with products that have predictable patterns of demand, such as consumer staples. JIT inventory systems are especially useful for products such as fashion apparel, which have relatively short life cycles and for which demand cannot be accurately predicted. In such cases, it is important to be able to quickly speed up production to meet unanticipated demand as well as to quickly stop production to avoid accumulating large inventories that must be marked down for clearance because the product is no longer in demand.

Purchase requests

The request to purchase goods or supplies is triggered either by the inventory control function or by employees noticing a shortage of materials. The advanced inventory control systems used in large manufacturing companies, such as IBM and Ford, automatically generate purchase requests when the quantity of an item on hand falls below its reorder point. In small companies, however, the employees who use the items note when stock is running low and request that it be reordered. For example, your neighborhood hair stylist is usually responsible for replacing shampoos, hairbrushes, and other supplies. Moreover, even in large companies, office supplies such as copier paper and pencils are often ordered by the employees who use those items when they notice that stock is running low.

Regardless of its source, the need to purchase goods or supplies often results in the creation of a purchase requisition. The **purchase requisition** (Figure 12-3) is a document, or electronic form, that identifies the requisitioner; specifies the delivery location and date needed; identifies the item numbers, descriptions, quantity, and price of each item requested; and may suggest a supplier. The person approving the purchase requisition indicates the department number and account number to which the purchase should be charged.

Generating purchase orders

Purchasing agents (sometimes called buyers) within the purchasing department usually perform the purchasing activity. In manufacturing companies such as AOE, the purchasing function is closely related to the production cycle. Consequently, Ryan McDaniel, the head of the purchasing department at AOE, reports directly to LeRoy Williams, the vice president of manufacturing.

ALPHA OMEGA ELECTRONICS				
PURCHASE REQUISITION				No. 89010
Date Prepared: 07/02/2003	**Prepared by:** Harold Brown *HB*			**Suggested Vendor:** Best Office Supply
Deliver To: Copy Center		**Attention:** Harold Brown		**Date Needed:** 7/15/2003

Item Number	Quantity	Description	Price/Unit
32047	15 boxes	Xerox 4200 paper, 20 wt., 10 ream box	$33.99
80170	5 boxes	Moore 2600 continuous form, 20 lb	$31.99
81756	20 boxes	Dysan 100 HD diskettes, box of 10	$ 6.49
10407	10	IBM 4207 Proprinter ribbon, black	$ 8.99

Approved by: Susan Chen	**Department:** Admin. Services	**Date Approved:** 07/02/2003	**Account No.:** 91887

Figure 12-3   Sample AOE purchase requisition (items in bold are preprinted)

The crucial operating decision in the purchasing activity is selecting suppliers for inventory items. Several factors should be considered in making this decision:

➤ Price
➤ Quality of materials
➤ Dependability in making deliveries

In terms of quality and dependability, supplier reliability is important, especially to JIT systems, because a late delivery or defective parts can bring the entire system to a halt. Consequently, supplier certification is a key component of most JIT systems, and many companies require that their suppliers meet ISO 9000 quality standards. It is important to note that ISO 9000 certification does not guarantee product quality, but only recognizes that the supplier has adequate quality control processes.

Once a supplier has been selected for a product, the supplier's identity should become part of the product inventory master record to avoid repeating the supplier selection process for every subsequent order. (In some cases, however, such as for the purchase of high-cost and low-usage items, management may explicitly want to reevaluate all potential suppliers each time that product is ordered.) A list of potential alternative suppliers for each item should also be maintained, in case the primary supplier is out of stock of a needed item.

To determine the need to switch suppliers, it is important to track and periodically evaluate supplier performance. Properly evaluating suppliers requires more than just data about prices. Companies also incur costs, such as rework and scrap, related to the

Alpha Omega Electronics				No. 2463

Billing Address: 2431 Bradford Lane
St. Louis, MO 63105–2311
(314) 467-2341

Reference the above number on all
invoices and shipping documents

PURCHASE ORDER

To: Best Office Supply
4567 Olive Blvd.
St. Louis, MO 63112–2345

Ship To: AOE, Inc.
1735 Sandy Dr.
Dayton, OH 33421–2243

Vendor Number: 121	Order Date: 07/03/2003	Requisition Number: 89010	Buyer: Fred Mozart	Terms: 1/10, n/30
F.O.B. Destination	Ship Via: Your choice	Delivery Date: 07/15/2003	Remarks:	

Item	Item Number	Quantity	Description	Unit Price
1	32047	15 boxes	Xerox 4200 paper, 20 wt., 10 ream box	$33.99
2	80170	5 boxes	Moore 2600 continuous form, 20 lb.	$31.99
3	81756	20 boxes	Dysan 100 HD Diskettes, box of 10	$6.49
4	10407	10	IBM 4207 Proprinter ribbon, black	$8.99

Approved by: *Susan Beethoven*

Figure 12-4   Sample AOE: purchase order (items in bold are preprinted)

quality of the products purchased. There are also costs associated with supplier delivery performance. The AIS can be designed to capture and track this information. For example, AOE can measure the quality of a supplier's products by tracking how often its items fail to pass inspection in the receiving department. Data on the amount of production that had to be reworked or scrapped because of substandard materials also can be collected. AOE can measure supplier dependability by matching and tracking actual delivery dates versus those promised. Finally, to ensure that purchasing agents consider all these factors, the purchasing function should be evaluated and rewarded by how well it minimizes the total costs, not just the purchase price, of the items acquired.

A **purchase order** (Figure 12-4) is a document or electronic form that formally requests a supplier to sell and deliver specified products at designated prices. It is also a promise to pay and becomes a contract once the supplier accepts it. The purchase order includes the names of the supplier and purchasing agent, the order and requested delivery dates, the delivery location and shipping method, and information about the items ordered. Frequently, several purchase orders are generated to fill one purchase requisition, because different vendors may be the preferred suppliers for the various items requested.

Many companies maintain special purchasing arrangements with important suppliers. One such arrangement is using blanket purchase orders. A **blanket purchase order** is a commitment to purchase specified items at designated prices from a particular supplier for a set time period, often 1 year. Blanket purchase orders reduce the buyer's uncertainty about reliable sources of raw materials and help the supplier plan its capacity and operations more effectively.

Improving efficiency and effectiveness

The major cost driver in the purchasing function is the number of purchase orders processed. Thus, finding ways to reduce the number of orders processed and to streamline the steps involved can yield significant savings. Using EDI or the Internet is one way to improve the purchasing process. Both EDI and the Internet reduce costs by eliminating the clerical work associated with printing and mailing paper documents. The time between recognizing the need to reorder an item and subsequently receiving it also is reduced. Consequently, the risk of running out of stock is diminished, which can significantly increase profitability.

Vendor-managed inventory programs provide another means of reducing purchase and inventory costs. Vendor-managed inventory essentially outsources much of the inventory control and purchasing function. Suppliers are given access to point-of-sales and inventory data and are authorized to automatically replenish inventory when stocks fall to predetermined reorder points.

Reverse auctions provide yet another possible technique to reduce purchasing-related expenses. In reverse auctions, suppliers compete with one another to meet demand at the lowest price. Although early users of reverse auctions reported significant cost savings, the method has limitations. Because the primary focus is on price, reverse auctions are probably best suited to the purchase of commodity items rather than critical components for which quality, vendor reliability, and delivery performance are important.

The Internet has led to the creation of industry-specific trading groups called *trading exchanges*. Most of the successful trading exchanges consist of consortia of the largest firms in an industry. Trading exchanges perform an intermediary function by bringing together large numbers of both buyers and sellers in an electronic marketplace. Usually, the merchandise is a commodity-type item for which the principal differentiation is price. Indeed, because information about supplier delivery performance and financial strength is limited, most companies use trading exchanges primarily to purchase commodities and to fill unanticipated short-term needs. In response, some companies create their own private trading exchanges with their customers and suppliers to share more sensitive data, such as past performance, so that longer-term relationships can be formed.

The number of companies using trading exchanges and the benefits of doing so will increase as standards are established to broaden the intermediary function. Ideally, a company should be able to request a price quote, and the trading exchange would forward it to all potential suppliers. Then the trading exchange would select the supplier that offers the optimal combination of price and service, and automatically generate the purchase order. Developments with Extensible Markup Language (XML) promise to provide a vehicle for establishing and automating the necessary standards.

It is also important to improve the efficiency of the purchasing process for miscellaneous supplies because these purchases usually involve such small dollar amounts that the cost of processing the orders through the same system used to purchase inventory can exceed the cost of the supplies themselves. Moreover, the quantities are often too small to justify using a JIT system. Procurement cards provide a mechanism to improve the efficiency and reduce costs associated with such purchases. A procurement card is a corporate credit card that employees can use at designated suppliers to make specific types of purchases. The company receives one monthly bill summarizing all employee purchases. Spending limits can be set for each card. In addition, the account numbers on the cards can be mapped to specific general ledger accounts, thereby automatically recording miscellaneous purchases in the appropriate accounts. Although the use of procurement cards is steadily increasing, the benefits realized depend on how their use is implemented. Focus 12-1 discusses the results of a recent AICPA survey about the characteristics of effective procurement card use.

Focus 12-1

Effective Use of Procurement Cards

In 2000, the AICPA surveyed over 1,000 companies that used procurement cards and received responses from 188 organizations. The results indicate that procurement cards offer the potential for significant savings. Respondents indicated that invoices for amounts under $2,000 accounted for over 60 percent of all invoices processed by accounts payable but represented less than 20 percent of the total dollar amount of purchases. The average cost to process such transactions with procurement cards was $15, as opposed to $91 under the traditional purchase order approach.

Nevertheless, how procurement cards were used, and the attendant benefits, varied widely. The top 20 percent of companies, in terms of procurement card spending, accounted for over 80 percent of all procurement card spending in the sample. Characteristics that distinguished the companies that used procurement cards most extensively include:

1. Vocal top management support coupled with quantified performance targets
2. Liberal distribution of cards to a large percentage of employees
3. Higher spending limits
4. Fewer record-keeping requirements and fewer spending card audits
5. Ongoing communications about the benefits of using the cards

Sources: Corporate Purchasing Card User Survey: Executive Summary, http://www.aicpa.org/cefm/pcard/execsum.htm; and Richard J. Palmer, "Special Report: Survey Shows How Purchase Cards Can Save Time, Money," *Journal of Accountancy* (May 2000): 18–19.

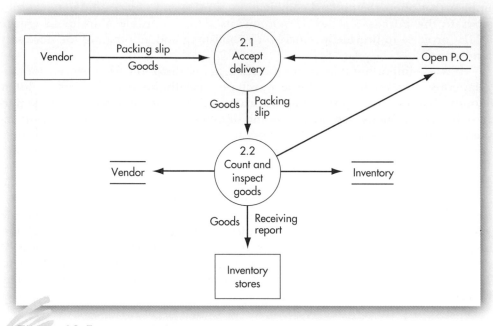

Figure 12-5 Level I DFD of the receiving function

Receive and Store Goods

The second major business activity in the expenditure cycle (circle 2.0 in Figure 12-3) is the receipt and storage of ordered items. The receiving department is responsible for accepting deliveries from suppliers. It usually reports to the warehouse manager, who in turn reports to the vice president of manufacturing. The inventory stores department, which also reports to the warehouse manager, is responsible for storage of the goods. Information about the receipt of ordered merchandise must be communicated to the inventory control function to update the inventory records.

Figure 12-5 shows that the receiving department has two major responsibilities: deciding whether to accept a delivery and verifying the quantity and quality of the goods delivered. The first decision is made based on information provided by the purchasing function: The existence of a valid purchase order indicates that the delivery should be accepted. This decision is important because the acceptance of unordered goods would result in wasted time and space in handling and storing those items until they can be returned. Verifying the quantity of goods delivered is important to ensure that the company pays only for goods actually received and that inventory records are accurately updated.

The **receiving report** is the primary document used in the receiving subsystem of the expenditure cycle; it documents details about each delivery, including the date received, shipper, supplier, and purchase order number (Figure 12-6). For each item received, it shows the item number, description, unit of measure, and quantity. It also

Alpha Omega Electronics		**No. 3113**
RECEIVING REPORT		

Vendor: Best Office Supply	**Date Received:** 07/13/2003
Shipped via: UPS	**Purchase Order Number:** 2463

Item Number	**Quantity**	**Description**
32047	15	Xerox 4200 paper, 20 wt., 10 ream box
80170	5	Moore 2600 continuous form, 20 lb.
81756	20	Dysan 100 HD diskettes, box of 10
10407	10	IBM 4207 Proprinter ribbons, black

Remarks:
Two boxes of Moore 2600 paper received with water damage on outside, but the paper appears to be okay

Received by: *Nathan Hale*	**Inspected by:** *Nathan Hale*	**Delivered to:** *Harold Brown*

Figure 12-6   Sample AOE receiving report (items in bold are preprinted)

contains space to identify the persons who received and inspected the goods as well as for remarks concerning the quality of the items received. A receiving report is typically not used to document the receipt of services, such as advertising and cleaning. Instead, receipt of such services is usually documented by supervisory approval of the supplier's invoice.

When a delivery arrives, a receiving clerk compares the purchase order number referenced on the supplier's packing slip with the open purchase order file to verify that the goods were ordered. The receiving clerk then counts the quantity of goods delivered. Before routing the inventory to the warehouse or factory, the receiving clerk also should examine each delivery for signs of obvious damage.

The three possible exceptions to this process are (1) receiving a quantity of goods different from the amount ordered, (2) receiving damaged goods, or (3) receiving goods of inferior quality that fail inspection. In all three cases, the purchasing department must resolve the situation with the supplier. Usually the supplier will give the buyer permission to correct the invoice for any discrepancies in quantity. In the case of damaged or poor-quality goods, a document called a debit memo is prepared after the supplier agrees to take back the goods or to grant a price reduction. The **debit memo** records the adjustment being requested. One copy of the debit memo is sent to the supplier, who subsequently creates and returns a credit memo in acknowledgment. The accounts payable department is notified and adjusts the account balance owed to that supplier. A copy of the debit memo accompanies the goods to the shipping department to authorize their return to the supplier.

Improving efficiency and effectiveness

Counting and recording inventory deliveries is a labor-intensive task. One way for companies such as AOE to improve the efficiency of this process is to require suppliers to bar code their products. Bar coding enables receiving clerks to scan in the product number, description, and quantity of all items received, thereby virtually eliminating data entry errors. Moreover, although the goods still have to be manually inspected to ensure they meet quality standards, bar code scanners can significantly reduce delivery processing time.

Passive radio frequency identification tags can further streamline the receiving process. These batteryless tags are attached to each crate of goods and emit a signal that a receiving unit embedded in the gates near a company's warehouse unit can read. This eliminates the need for employees to scan the bar codes on items.

Satellite technology provides another way to improve the efficiency of inbound logistics. By equipping trucks with data terminals linked to satellites, companies can track the exact location of all incoming shipments and ensure that adequate staff will be there to unload the trucks. Truck drivers also can be directed to pull up to specific loading docks closest to the place where the goods will be used.

Pay for Goods and Services

The third main activity in the expenditure cycle is approving vendor invoices for payment (circle 3.0 in Figure 12-2). Figure 12-7 shows that this involves two steps. The accounts payable department approves vendor invoices for payment. The cashier, who reports to the treasurer, is responsible for making the payment.

Approve vendor invoices for payment

A legal obligation to pay suppliers arises at the time goods are received. For practical reasons, however, most companies record accounts payable only after receipt and approval of the supplier's invoice. This timing difference is usually not important for daily decision making, but it does require making appropriate adjusting entries to prepare accurate financial statements at the end of a fiscal period.

The objective of accounts payable is to authorize payment only for goods and services that were ordered and actually received. This requires internally generated information from both the purchasing and receiving functions. The existence of a valid purchase order indicates that the goods or services listed on the vendor invoice were actually ordered. Receipt of the goods is noted on the receiving report.

There are two ways to process vendor invoices, referred to as nonvoucher or voucher systems. In a **nonvoucher system,** each approved invoice is posted to individual supplier records in the accounts payable file and is then stored in an open-invoice file. When a check is written to pay for an invoice, the invoice is removed from the open-invoice file, marked paid, and then stored in the paid-invoice file.

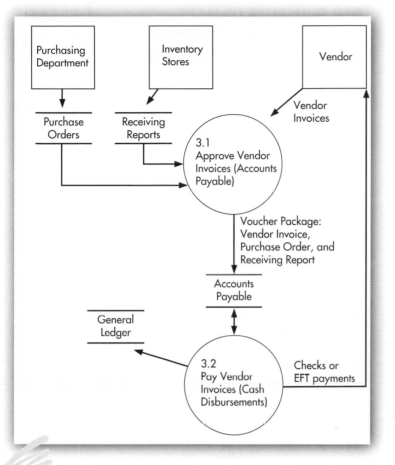

Figure 12-7   Level 1 data flow diagram of the pay for goods function

In a **voucher system,** a document called a disbursement voucher is also prepared. The **disbursement voucher** identifies the supplier, lists the outstanding invoices, and indicates the net amount to be paid after deducting any applicable discounts and allowances (see Figure 12-8). Thus, a disbursement voucher summarizes the information contained in a set of vendor invoices and specifies the general ledger accounts to be debited.

Disbursement vouchers offer three advantages. First, they reduce the number of checks that need to be written, because several invoices may be included on one voucher. Second, because the disbursement voucher is an internally generated document, it can be prenumbered to simplify tracking all payables. Third, because the voucher provides an explicit record that a vendor invoice has been approved for payment, it facilitates separating the time of invoice approval from the time of invoice payment. This makes it easier to schedule both activities to maximize efficiency.

Alpha Omega Electronics DISBURSEMENT VOUCHER				No. 16123	
Date Entered: 07/22/2003			**Debit Distribution**		
Prepared by: *BC*			**Account No.**		**Amount**
Vendor Number: 109			22-140		$868.33
			22-145		629.01
Remit To:			20-699		30.56
Avalon Electronics			20-799		98.45
1401 East Grand					
St. Louis, MO 63106–2211					

Vendor Invoice		**Amount**	**Returns & Allowances**	**Purchase Discount**	**Net Remittance**
Number	**Date**				
5386	07/15/2003	$984.50	$98.45	$17.72	$868.33
5389	07/20/2003	641.85	0.00	12.84	629.01
Voucher Totals:		$1,626.35	$98.45	$30.56	$1,497.34

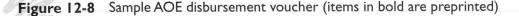

Figure 12-8   Sample AOE disbursement voucher (items in bold are preprinted)

Improving the accounts payable process

The accounts payable process, which matches vendor invoices to purchase orders and receiving reports, is a prime candidate for automation. Processing efficiency can be improved by requiring suppliers to submit invoices electronically, either by EDI or via the Internet, and having the system automatically match those invoices to the appropriate purchase orders and receiving reports. Only those vendor invoices that fail this matching process need be processed manually.

Another option is to eliminate vendor invoices. After all, for most recurring purchases, companies know the prices of goods and services at the time they are ordered. Thus, as soon as receipt of the goods or services is verified, all the information required to pay the supplier is already known. This "invoiceless" approach is called **evaluated receipt settlement (ERS).** ERS replaces the traditional three-way matching process (vendor invoice, receiving report, and purchase order) with a two-way match of the purchase order and receiving report (see Figure 12-9). ERS saves time and money by reducing the number of documents that need to be matched and, hence, the number of potential mismatches. ERS also saves suppliers the time and expense of generating and tracking invoices. This is an example of how improvements in one company's expenditure cycle processes provide benefits to another company's revenue cycle processes.

ERS requires that suppliers quote accurate prices at the time orders are placed and that receiving dock employees accurately count and inspect merchandise received. Typically, ERS systems provide additional process improvements through timely communication: Suppliers electronically notify customers when shipments are coming, and buyers electronically acknowledge receipt of those shipments.

Noninventory purchases provide perhaps the biggest opportunity to improve the efficiency of accounts payable. As noted in Focus 12-1, noninventory purchases typically account for a large proportion of accounts payable transactions, but represent a small proportion of the total dollar value of all purchases. Procurement cards provide one way to eliminate many such small invoices. Issuing corporate credit cards to employees who travel frequently further reduces the number of invoices that need to be processed. It also shifts the burden of reconciling invoices with supporting documents to the employees who incurred the expenses. In addition, electronic forms can be developed for submitting travel expenses. Such forms prevent delays due to math errors, eliminate the need for accounts payable staff to enter the travel expense data, and reduce the time employees must wait to be reimbursed.

Pay approved invoices

The final activity in the expenditure cycle is the payment of approved invoices. The cashier, who reports to the treasurer, performs this activity, often referred to as the cash disbursements function. This segregates the custody function, performed by the cashier, from the authorization and recording functions, performed by the purchasing and accounts payable departments, respectively.

The combination of a vendor invoice and supporting documentation (purchase order and receiving report) forms what is referred to as a **voucher package.** An approved voucher package authorizes disbursement of funds by check or EFT to suppliers.

A key decision in the cash disbursement process is determining whether to take advantage of any discounts offered for prompt payment. A short-term cash flow budget is useful for making this decision. The report lists projected inflows and outflows of cash for a period of time, up to a year in advance. The information in this budget comes from a number of sources. Accounts receivable provides projections of future cash collections. The accounts payable and open purchase order files indicate the amount of current and pending commitments to suppliers, while the human resources function provides information about payroll needs. If the cash flow budget indicates that sufficient cash is available, discounts for prompt payment should be taken because they provide substantial savings. For example, a 1 percent discount for paying within 10 days, instead of 30 days, represents a savings of 18 percent annually.

INFORMATION PROCESSING PROCEDURES

In response to the Y2K crisis, AOE, like many other organizations, replaced its existing AIS with an integrated ERP system. Figure 12-10 depicts the portion of AOE's new ERP system that supports its expenditure cycle activities.

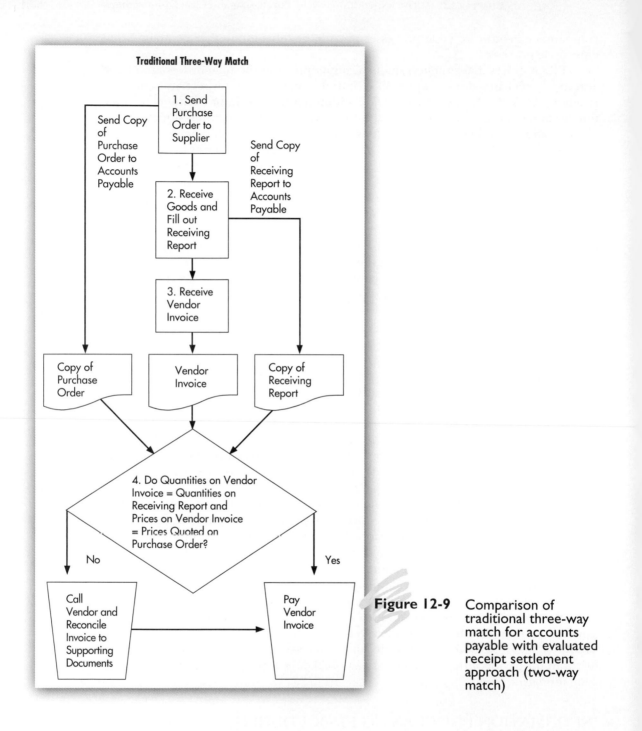

Traditional Three-Way Match

Send Copy of Purchase Order to Accounts Payable

1. Send Purchase Order to Supplier

Send Copy of Receiving Report to Accounts Payable

2. Receive Goods and Fill out Receiving Report

3. Receive Vendor Invoice

Copy of Purchase Order

Vendor Invoice

Copy of Receiving Report

4. Do Quantities on Vendor Invoice = Quantities on Receiving Report and Prices on Vendor Invoice = Prices Quoted on Purchase Order?

No

Yes

Call Vendor and Reconcile Invoice to Supporting Documents

Pay Vendor Invoice

Figure 12-9 Comparison of traditional three-way match for accounts payable with evaluated receipt settlement approach (two-way match)

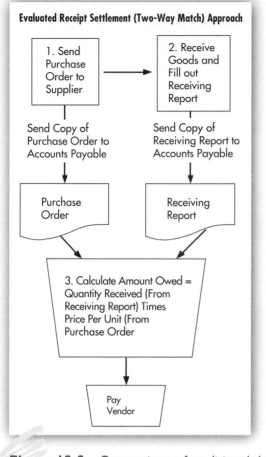

Figure 12-9   Comparison of traditional three-way match for accounts payable with evaluated receipt settlement approach (two-way match) (Continued)

The fundamental characteristics of AOE's new expenditure cycle system are the sharing of data between activities and the increased integration that results. Any department can submit a request to purchase items. Once a request has been approved, the system searches the inventory master file to identify the preferred supplier for that item. The system then creates a purchase order that is sent to the supplier via EDI. (If necessary, paper copies are printed and mailed.) The receiving department has access to the open purchase order file so that it can plan for and verify the validity of deliveries. Accounts payable is notified of orders so that it can plan for pending financial commitments. The department that generated the purchase requisition is also notified that its request has been set in motion.

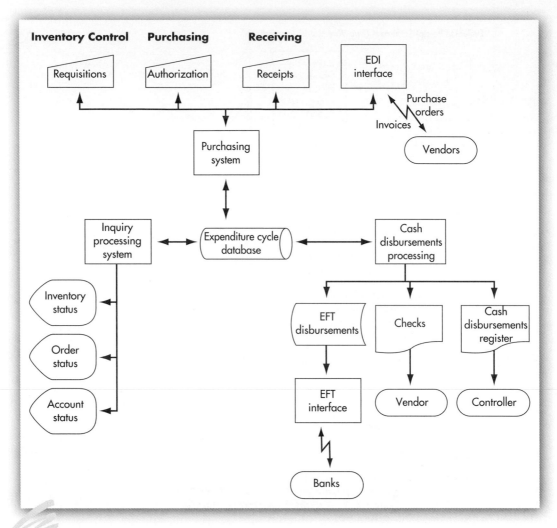

Figure 12-10 Flowchart of AOE's expenditure cycle

Major suppliers send electronic notification of coming deliveries. When a shipment arrives, the receiving dock workers use the inquiry processing system to verify that an order is expected from that supplier. Most suppliers bar code their products to facilitate the counting of the goods. Receiving dock workers also inspect the goods and use an on-line terminal to enter the inventory item numbers, count, and purchase order number. The exact time of the delivery also is recorded to help evaluate vendor performance. The system checks that data against the open purchase order file, and any discrepancies, are immediately displayed on the screen and must be resolved.

Upon transfer of the goods to the warehouse, the inventory stores department verifies the count of the items placed into inventory and enters that data in the system.

For vendors with whom ERS agreements exist, the system automatically schedules a payment according to the agreed upon terms. Other vendors send EDI, and sometimes paper, invoices, which accounts payable clerks enter. Supplier invoices are compared with the information contained in the purchase order and receiving files to ensure accuracy and validity. For purchases of supplies or services that do not usually involve purchase orders and receiving reports, the invoice is sent to the appropriate supervisor for approval. The vendor invoice itself is also checked for mathematical accuracy. The vouchers (or approved invoices in a voucherless system) are then set up for payment by due date.

AOE, like most companies, uses batch processing to pay its suppliers. Each day, the treasurer uses the inquiry processing system to review the vouchers that are due and approves them for payment. AOE makes payments to some of its larger suppliers using FEDI but still prints paper checks for many of its smaller suppliers. When an EFT payment is authorized or a check is printed, the system updates the accounts payable, open-invoice, and general ledger files. For each supplier, the totals of all vouchers are summed and that amount is subtracted from the balance field in that supplier's master file record. The relevant entries in the purchase order and receiving report files are flagged to mark that those transactions have been paid. The invoices that are paid are then deleted from the open-invoice file. A remittance advice is prepared for each supplier, which lists each invoice being paid and the amounts of any discounts or allowances taken. For payments made by EFT, the remittance data accompany the EFT payment as part of the FEDI package. For payments made by check, the remittance advice accompanies the signed check. After all disbursement transactions have been processed, the system generates a summary journal entry, debiting accounts payable and crediting cash, and posts that entry to the general ledger.

After reviewing checks against the voucher package, the cashier signs them. Checks above a specified amount also require the treasurer's signature. After signing them, the cashier then mails the checks and remittance advices to the suppliers. EFT transactions are also performed by the cashier and reviewed by the treasurer.

It is instructive to compare AOE's new processes with the procedures followed in its old (legacy) systems. The appendix to this chapter contains flowcharts and a brief narrative description of AOE's legacy expenditure cycle system. Key improvements to notice are as follows:

1. The quantity of paper documents processed is reduced.
2. More timely and accurate information enables AOE to take advantage of discounts for prompt payment of vendor invoices.
3. Inventory records are more accurate and timely.
4. The warehouse and receiving departments can better plan activities.
5. The system compares data the receiving department entered to the purchase order file, thereby detecting and facilitating correction of any errors on a timely basis.
6. Reports and performance measures are timelier, which enhances management's ability to monitor and improve efficiency and effectiveness.

Realizing these benefits, however, presupposes that adequate controls exist to ensure that the information in the system is available, accurate, secure, and maintainable. The next section discusses applicable control procedures to achieve those objectives.

CONTROL OBJECTIVES, THREATS, AND PROCEDURES

Another function of a well-designed AIS is to provide adequate controls that meet the following objectives:

1. All transactions are properly authorized.
2. All recorded transactions are valid (actually occurred).
3. All valid, authorized transactions are recorded.
4. All transactions are recorded accurately.
5. Assets (cash, inventory, and data) are safeguarded from loss or theft.
6. Business activities are performed efficiently and effectively.

The documents and records described in the previous section play an important role in achieving these objectives. Simple, easy-to-complete documents with clear instructions facilitate the accurate and efficient recording of transaction data. Appropriate application controls, such as validity checks and field (format) checks, further increase the accuracy of data entry when using electronic documents. Providing space on paper and electronic documents to record who completed and who reviewed the form provides evidence that the transaction was properly authorized. Prenumbering all documents facilitates checking that all transactions have been recorded. Restricting access to programs that create documents and to blank documents (if paper documents are still used) reduces the risk of unauthorized transactions.

Table 12-1 lists the major threats and exposures in the expenditure cycle and the applicable control procedures that should be in place to mitigate them. Every company, regardless of its line of business, faces these threats. Therefore, it is important to understand how the AIS can be designed to counter them. Our discussion will be organized around the stages of the expenditure cycle.

Order Goods

The primary objective of the purchasing process is to minimize costs associated with maintaining an adequate supply of all needed materials. The first six threats listed in Table 12-1 pertain to this objective.

Threat 1: Preventing stockouts and/or excess inventory

Stockouts result in lost sales; excess inventory incurs higher than necessary carrying costs. To guard against these threats, companies need to establish an accurate inventory control system. The perpetual inventory method should be used to ensure that information about inventory stocks is always current. Companies should select suppliers that are known to meet their delivery commitments. Supplier performance reports that highlight deviations in product quality, prices, and delivery commitments should be regularly prepared. These reports should be reviewed periodically and new suppliers selected when a supplier's performance falls below acceptable levels.

Bar code technology can improve the accuracy of perpetual inventory records by eliminating the need for human data entry. The effect on accuracy can be dramatic: Studies have found that even expert typists make one mistake for every 300 keystrokes. Bar coding is not a panacea, however. Human error can still occur, especially when bar code scanning is used to record the sale of assorted varieties of a product. For example,

Table 12-1 Threats and Controls in the Expenditure Cycle

Process/Activity	Threat	Applicable Control Procedures
Order goods	1. Preventing stockouts and/or excess inventory	Inventory control systems; perpetual inventory records; bar code technology; periodic counts of inventory
	2. Requesting unnecessary items	Accurate perpetual inventory records; approval of purchase requisitions
	3. Purchasing goods at inflated prices	Solicit competitive bids; use of approved suppliers; approval of purchase orders; budgetary controls
	4. Purchasing goods of inferior quality	Use of approved vendors; approval of purchase orders; monitor vendor performance; budgetary controls
	5. Purchasing from unauthorized suppliers	Approval of purchase orders; restrict access to supplier master file
	6. Kickbacks	Policies; require purchasing employees to disclose financial interests in suppliers; vendor audits
Receive and store goods	7. Receiving unordered goods	Require receiving to verify existence of valid purchase order
	8. Making errors in counting	Use of bar coding technology; document employee performance; incentives for accurate counts
	9. Stealing inventory	Physical access controls; periodic counts of inventory and reconciliation of physical counts to records; document all transfers of inventory
Approve and pay vendor invoices	10. Failing to catch errors in vendor invoices	Double-check invoice accuracy; training of accounts payable staff; use of ERS
	11. Paying for goods not received	Only pay invoices supported by original receiving report; use of ERS; budgetary controls
	12. Failing to take available purchase discounts	Proper filing; cash flow budgets
	13. Paying the same invoice twice	Only pay invoices supported by original voucher package; cancellation of voucher package upon payment; use of ERS; control access to supplier master file
	14. Recording and posting errors in accounts payable	Various data entry and processing edit controls
	15. Misappropriating cash, checks, or EFTs	Restrict access to blank checks, check signing machine, and EFT transfer terminals; segregation of duties of accounts payable and cashier; reconciliation of bank account by someone independent of cash disbursement process; check protection measures including Positive Pay; regular review of EFT transactions
General control	16. Losing data	Backup and disaster recovery plans; physical and logical access controls
	17. Performing poorly	Development and periodic review of appropriate performance reports

if you purchase 24 cans of store-brand soda at a grocery store, the clerk may scan only one can and then manually enter the number purchased. Since the flavors are all priced the same, the amount of the sale is correctly calculated. The perpetual inventory records will be incorrect, however, because the exact count of the flavors sold is not correctly recorded. Consequently, the grocery store may not be able to use POS data to maintain its perpetual inventory records, but must still rely on counting what is actually on the shelves. Nevertheless, because bar coding makes it easier and faster to count inventory, such counts can be more frequent, thereby reducing the risk of running out of stock. For example, employees at many retailers use portable bar code scanners to track inventory status on the floor and to initiate the replenishment process.

Threat 2: Requesting unnecessary items

Companies must also beware of purchasing items that are not currently needed. Accurate perpetual inventory records ensure the validity of purchase requisitions that the inventory control system automatically generates. Supervisors should review and approve purchase requisitions that individual employees initiate.

A related problem is multiple purchases of the same item by different subunits of the organization. As a result, the organization may be carrying a larger inventory than desired, and may fail to take advantage of volume discounts that might be available. This usually occurs because different subunits have different numbering systems for the parts they use. To overcome this problem, the AIS must be designed in a manner that facilitates integrating the databases of various subunits. Then reports linking item descriptions to part numbers can be produced.

Threat 3: Purchasing goods at inflated prices

Companies strive to secure the best prices for raw materials and inventory. Price lists for frequently purchased items should be stored in the computer and consulted when ordering. The prices of many low-cost items can be readily determined from catalogs. Competitive, written bids should be solicited for high-cost and specialized items. Purchase orders should be reviewed to ensure that these policies have been followed.

Budgetary controls are also helpful in controlling expenses. Purchases should be charged to an account that is the responsibility of the person or department approving the requisition. Actual costs should be compared periodically with budget allowances. To facilitate control, these reports should highlight any significant deviations from budgeted amounts for further investigation (the principle of management by exception).

Threat 4: Purchasing goods of inferior quality

In their quest to obtain the lowest possible prices, companies must beware of purchasing inferior-quality products. Substandard products can result in costly production delays. Moreover, the costs of scrap and rework often result in higher total production costs than if higher-quality, more expensive materials had been initially purchased.

Through experience, buyers often learn which suppliers provide the best-quality goods at competitive prices. Such informal knowledge should be incorporated into formal control procedures so that it is not lost when a particular employee leaves the company. Establishing lists of approved suppliers known to provide goods of acceptable quality will achieve this goal. Purchase orders should be reviewed to ensure that only these approved suppliers are being used. In addition, supplier performance data should be collected and periodically reviewed to maintain the accuracy of these approved supplier lists. Finally, purchasing managers should be held responsible for the total cost of purchases, which includes not only the purchase price, but also the quality-related costs of rework and scrap. Doing this requires the AIS to track the latter costs so that they can be allocated back to the purchasing department.

Threat 5: Purchasing from unauthorized suppliers

Purchasing from unauthorized suppliers can result in numerous problems. Items may be of inferior quality or overpriced. The purchase may even cause legal problems, such as violating import quotas. Consequently, all purchase orders should be reviewed to ensure that only approved suppliers are used. It is especially important to restrict access to the approved supplier list, and to periodically review the list for any unauthorized changes. If procurement cards are used for minor purchases, the company should work with the card issuer to limit the types of suppliers that will accept the card.

Threat 6: Kickbacks

Kickbacks are gifts from suppliers to purchasing agents for the purpose of influencing their choice of suppliers. Kickbacks may result in the purchase of goods at inflated prices or of inferior quality. Even if neither of these problems occurs, kickbacks impair the buyer's objectivity. Moreover, employees should not profit from performing their regular business duties.

To prevent kickbacks, companies should prohibit purchasing agents from accepting any gifts from potential or existing suppliers. (Trinkets that are clearly of inconsequential value may be allowed.) In addition, purchasing agents also should be required to sign annual conflict of interest statements, disclosing any financial interests they may have in current or potential suppliers. Because kickbacks are difficult to prevent, detective controls are also necessary. Focus 12-2 discusses one particularly effective detection control: the supplier audit.

EDI-related threats

Using EDI for purchase orders requires additional control procedures. Access to the EDI system should be controlled and limited to authorized personnel through the use of passwords, user IDs, access control matrices, and physical access controls. Procedures to verify and authenticate EDI transactions also are needed. Most EDI systems are programmed to send an acknowledgment for each transaction, which provides a rudimentary accuracy check. Further protection against transmission problems, which can result in the loss of orders, is provided by time-stamping and numbering all EDI transactions. Companies should maintain and periodically review a log of all EDI transactions to ensure that all have been processed and that established policies are being followed. Encryption can ensure the privacy of EDI transactions, which is especially important for competitive bids. Digital signatures should be used to ensure the authenticity of transactions.

Numerous policy-related threats also arise with EDI, each of which must be covered in the trading agreement. Additional complexity occurs when suppliers are

Focus 12-2

Supplier Audits: A Means to Control Purchasing

Ray Mize, a consulting auditor in Kenner, Louisiana, believes that supplier audits may be one of the most effective tools for assessing the effectiveness of expenditure cycle controls. A supplier audit entails visiting a supplier's office to check its records. It is designed to answer a number of questions: Who determines the business requirements for a good or service? How is the good or service consumed, and how is this documented? What is the procurement process, and how is the company assured that the best-quality goods or services were obtained at the best price? Did purchasing agents receive any gifts or favors?

After completing several supplier audits, Mize developed the following list of red flags that identify suppliers likely to represent potential problems:

1. A large percentage of the supplier's gross sales was to one company.

2. The supplier's pricing methods differ from standard industry practice.

3. The supplier does not own the equipment it rents to customers, but is itself renting that equipment from a third party.

4. Entertainment expenses are high in terms of a percentage of the supplier's gross sales.

5. The supplier submits altered or fictitious third-party invoices.

6. The supplier's address on its invoices is fictitious.

Supplier audits can yield substantial returns. Mize reports that the first six supplier audits he performed helped his former employer recover more than $250,000 for such failures as duplicate billings. Audits also uncovered a major violation of the company's conflict of interest policy. Interestingly, Mize notes that virtually all of the suppliers he has audited support the idea of supplier audits, because the process gives them a "good excuse" for not offering purchasing agents gifts or entertainment. This reduces the supplier's costs and results in better procurement terms for the buyer.

Source: B. Ray Mize, Jr., "Vendor Audits," *The CPA Journal* (February 1994): 18–22.

linked to the purchasing company's POS system to automatically manage inventory. Examples of these types of issues include the following:

➤ At what point in the process can the order be canceled?

➤ Which party is responsible for return freight if contract terms are not followed?

➤ Which party is responsible for errors in bar codes and labels?

➤ What happens if errors in the purchasing company's POS system cause additional errors in the amount of goods that suppliers provide?

➤ Can suppliers ship more inventory than ordered if doing so reduces total freight costs by having a full, rather than partial, truckload?

Purchase of services

Thus far, the discussion has centered on the purchase of inventory items. Different procedures are needed to control the purchase of services, such as painting or maintenance work. The major challenge in this area is establishing that the services were actually performed, which may be difficult. For example, visual inspection can indicate if a room has been painted; it does not reveal, however, if the walls were appropriately primed, unless the inspection was done during the painting process, which may not always be feasible.

One way to control the purchase of services is to hold the appropriate supervisor responsible for all such costs incurred by that department. The supervisor is required to acknowledge receipt of the services, and the related expenses are then charged to accounts for which he or she is responsible. Actual versus budgeted expenses should be routinely compared and any discrepancies investigated.

Receive and Store Goods

The primary objectives of the receiving and storage function are to verify the receipt of ordered inventory and to safeguard it against loss or theft. Threats 7 through 9 in Table 12-1 apply to the receipt and storage of inventory.

Threat 7: Receiving unordered goods

Accepting delivery of unordered goods results in costs associated with storing, and later returning, those items. The best control procedure to mitigate this threat is to instruct the receiving department to accept only deliveries for which there is an approved copy of the purchase order. Therefore, the receiving department needs access to the open purchase orders file.

Threat 8: Making errors in counting goods received

Accurate counting of goods received is crucial for maintaining accurate perpetual inventory records. It also ensures that the company pays only for goods actually received. As noted earlier, bar coding technology can improve both the efficiency and accuracy of receiving counts, although it is not foolproof. To encourage the receiving clerk to accurately count what was delivered, many companies design the inquiry processing system so that receiving-dock workers do not see the quantity ordered. (If paper documents are still used, the quantity ordered field is blacked out on the receiving department's copy of the purchase order.) Nevertheless, the receiving clerk still knows the expected quantity of goods because suppliers usually include a packing slip with each order. Consequently, there is a temptation to do just a quick visual comparison of quantities received with those indicated on the packing slip, to quickly route the goods to where they are needed. Therefore, companies must clearly communicate to receiving clerks the importance of carefully and accurately counting all deliveries. An effective means of communication is to require receiving clerks not only to record the quantity received, but also to sign the receiving report (or enter their employee ID numbers in the system). Such procedures indicate an assumption of responsibility, which usually results in more diligent work. Some companies also offer bonuses to receiving clerks for catching discrepancies between the packing slip and actual quantity received before the delivery person leaves. Additional control is provided by requiring the inventory control function, or the appropriate user department, to count the items transferred from receiving and then hold that department responsible for any subsequent shortages.

Threat 9: Stealing inventory

Several control procedures can be used to safeguard inventory against loss. First, inventories should be stored in secure locations with restricted access. Second, all transfers of inventory within the company should be documented. For example, both the receiving department and the inventory stores department should acknowledge the transfer of goods from the receiving dock into inventory. Similarly, both the inventory stores and the production departments should acknowledge the release of inventory into production. This documentation provides the necessary information for establishing responsibility for any shortages, thereby encouraging employees to take special care to record all inventory movements accurately. Finally, it is important to periodically count the inventory on hand and to reconcile those counts with the inventory records.

One annual physical inventory count will generally not be sufficient to maintain accurate inventory records, especially for MRP and JIT systems. Instead, an ABC cost analysis should be used to classify items according to their importance: The most critical items (A items) should be counted most frequently, and the least critical items (C items) can be counted less often. This approach might have alerted management at AOE's Wichita plant in the chapter introductory case about shortages of key components early enough to avoid production delays.

Approve and Pay Vendor Invoices

The objective of approving and paying vendor invoices is to ensure that the company pays only for goods and services that were ordered and received and to safeguard cash. Threats 10 through 15 in Table 12-1 apply to this objective.

Threat 10: Failing to catch errors in vendor invoices

Vendor invoices may contain errors such as discrepancies between quoted and actual prices charged or miscalculations of the total amount due. Consequently, the mathematical accuracy of vendor invoices must be verified and the prices and quantities listed therein compared with those indicated on the purchase order and receiving report. For procurement card purchases, users should be required to keep receipts and verify the accuracy of the monthly statement. Adopting the ERS approach eliminates the potential for errors in vendor invoices, because companies pay by matching counts of what they receive with prices quoted when the goods were ordered.

Even with ERS, freight expenses require special consideration because their complexity creates numerous opportunities for mistakes to occur. The best way to reduce freight-related threats is to provide the purchasing and accounts payable staffs with adequate training on transportation practices and terminology. For example, if the purchase contract says "full freight allowed," then the supplier is responsible for the freight costs. When the purchasing organization is responsible for freight expenses, using a designated carrier for all incoming shipments can reduce costs. The discounts will only be realized, however, if suppliers comply with requests to use that carrier. Therefore, an important detective control is to capture data on all incoming carriers, so that reports identifying suppliers who fail to comply with shipping instructions can be prepared.

Threat 11: Paying for goods not received

The best control to prevent paying for goods not received is to compare the quantities indicated on the vendor invoice with the quantities entered by the inventory control person, who accepts the transfer of those goods from the receiving department. Again, the ERS approach ensures that the company pays only for goods actually received. In regard to services, budgetary controls and careful review of departmental expenses may indicate potential problems that need investigation.

Threat 12: Failing to take available purchase discounts

Failure to take advantage of purchase discounts costs money. Proper filing can significantly reduce the risk of this threat. Approved invoices should be filed by due date, and the system should be designed to track invoice due dates and print a periodic list of all outstanding invoices. A cash flow budget that indicates expected cash inflows and outstanding commitments also can help companies plan to utilize available purchase discounts.

Threat 13: Paying the same invoice twice

The same invoice can be submitted for payment more than once for a variety of reasons. It may be a duplicate invoice that was sent after the company's check was already in the mail, or it may have become separated from the other documents in the voucher package. Although paying invoices a second time is usually detected by the supplier and results in a credit to the company's account, it can affect a company's cash flow needs. In addition, the financial records will be incorrect, at least until the duplicate payment is detected.

Several control procedures can mitigate this threat. First, invoices should be approved for payment only when accompanied by a complete voucher package (purchase order and receiving report). Second, only the original copy of an invoice should be paid. Most duplicate invoices that suppliers send clearly indicate that they are not originals. Payment should never be authorized for a photocopy of an invoice. Third, when the check to pay for an invoice is signed, the invoice and the voucher package should be canceled (marked "paid") in a manner that would prevent their resubmission. Finally, ERS eliminates vendor invoices entirely.

Automating and streamlining accounts payable is not a panacea, however. Automated systems do eliminate most clerical errors associated with processing invoices, and invoiceless accounts payable systems cut costs and improve efficiency. Yet, computers can catch only the types of errors that they have been programmed to identify, whereas vendor invoices involve an infinite number of errors. In addition, unscrupulous suppliers continually devise ways to fool automated accounts payable systems. Therefore, companies must use detective controls to minimize the risk of overpayments to suppliers. Either internal auditors or a consulting firm that specializes in helping companies to detect and recover overpayments to suppliers can do such investigative work.

Finally, in invoiceless accounts payable systems, it is important to control access to the supplier master file and monitor all changes made to it because the supplier master file now contains information about the prices of the various items being purchased. Upon entry of data about the quantity of goods received, the system uses those prices to establish the amount to be paid to suppliers. Thus, unauthorized changes to those prices can result in overpayments to suppliers.

Threat 14: Recording and posting errors in accounts payable

Errors in recording and posting payments to suppliers will result in additional errors in financial and performance reports that, in turn, can contribute to poor decision making. Appropriate data entry and processing controls are necessary to prevent these types of problems. One such control is comparing the difference in supplier account balances before and after processing checks with the total amount of invoices processed. The total of all supplier account balances (or unpaid vouchers, whichever exists) also should be reconciled periodically with the amount of the accounts payable control account in the general ledger.

Threat 15: Misappropriating cash, checks, or EFTs

Because cash is the easiest asset to steal, access to cash and blank checks should be restricted. Checks should be sequentially numbered and periodically accounted for by the cashier. Access to a check-signing machine should be restricted as well.

Fraudulent disbursements, particularly the issuance of checks to fictitious suppliers, are a common type of fraud. Proper segregation of duties can significantly reduce the risk of this threat. The accounts payable function should authorize payment, including the assembling of a voucher package; however, only the treasurer or cashier should sign checks. Checks in excess of a certain amount, such as $5,000 to $10,000, should require two signatures, thereby providing yet another independent review of the expenditure. Finally, access to the approved supplier list should be restricted and any changes to that list should be carefully reviewed and approved. In addition, internal auditors should periodically review the supplier master file to ensure that there are no duplicate entries for suppliers. Many companies that have done this have discovered that, over time, there may be three or four entries for the same supplier, each entered with a slightly different spelling by a different clerk. For example, the same supplier may be listed twice, once as AZBest Ltd. and another time as AZBest Limited.

To ensure that checks are sent to the intended recipients, the cashier should mail the signed checks rather than returning them to accounts payable. The cashier also should cancel all documents in the voucher package to prevent their being resubmitted to support another disbursement. Finally, someone who did not participate in processing either cash collections or disbursements should reconcile all bank accounts. This control provides an independent check on accuracy and prevents someone from misappropriating cash and then concealing the theft by adjusting the bank statement.

Check alteration and forgery are also major problems. Check-protection machines can reduce the risk of this threat by imprinting the amount in distinctive colors, typically a combination of red and blue ink. Using special inks that change colors if altered and printing checks on special papers that contain watermarks can further reduce the probability of alteration. Many banks also provide special services to help protect companies against fraudulent checks. One such service, called Positive Pay, involves sending a daily list of all legitimate checks to the bank, which will then clear only checks appearing on that list. Finally, bank reconciliations are an important detective control for identifying check fraud. If done in a timely manner they facilitate recovery from banks. Indeed, many banks will cover bad check losses only if a company notifies them promptly of any such checks it discovers.

When possible, expenditures should be made by check. Nevertheless, it is often more convenient to pay for minor purchases, such as coffee or pencils, in cash. A petty cash fund, managed by an employee who has no other cash-handling or accounting responsibilities, should be established to handle such expenditures. The petty cash fund should be set up as an imprest fund. An **imprest fund** has two characteristics: It is set at a fixed amount, such as $100, and it requires vouchers for every disbursement. At all times, the sum of cash plus vouchers should equal the preset fund balance. When the fund balance gets low, the vouchers are presented to accounts payable for replenishment. After accounts payable authorizes this transaction, the cashier then writes a check to restore the petty cash fund to its designated level. As with the supporting documents used for regular purchases, the vouchers used to support replenishment of the petty cash fund should be canceled at the time the fund is restored to its preset level.

The operation of an imprest petty cash fund technically violates the principle of segregation of duties, because the same person who has custody of the cash also authorizes disbursements from the fund and maintains a record of the fund balance. The threat of misappropriation is more than offset, however, by the convenience of not having to process small miscellaneous purchases through the normal expenditure cycle. Moreover, the risk of misappropriation can be mitigated by having the internal auditor make periodic unannounced counts of the fund balance and vouchers and by holding the person in charge of the petty cash fund responsible for any shortages discovered during those counts.

Electronic funds transfer (either by itself or as part of FEDI) requires additional control procedures. Because EFT involves the movement of funds, strict access controls are needed. Passwords and user IDs should be used and changed regularly. The user and the location of the originating terminal should be recorded so that the adequacy of access controls can be monitored. All EFT transmissions should be encrypted to prevent alteration. In addition, all EFT transactions should be time-stamped and numbered to facilitate subsequent reconciliation. A control group should be established and given responsibility for monitoring EFT transactions for validity and accuracy and maintaining the adequacy of the controls outlined here. Special programs, called *embedded audit modules,* can be designed into the system to monitor all transactions and identify any that possess specific characteristics. A report of those flagged transactions then can be given to management for review and, if necessary, more detailed investigation.

General Control Issues

Threats 16 and 17 in Table 12-1 are general threats that affect all phases of the expenditure cycle.

Threat 16: Losing data

Data about pending cash disbursement obligations and open orders must be safeguarded from loss or corruption. Both external and internal file labels should be used to reduce the possibility of accidentally erasing important files and to ensure that the most recent version of the master file is being updated. In addition, the purchases, receipts, master accounts payable, and cash disbursements files should be backed up regularly. Two backup copies should be made, one to be stored on-site and the other off-site. These backups should include not only the current and previous versions of the master file, but also the most recent transaction file.

Access controls are also important. A system of passwords and user IDs can limit employee access to various files. For example, only the cashier should be able to alter the field indicating if an invoice has been paid. Access controls also should exist for individual terminals. For example, the system should be programmed to accept approval of invoices only from terminals located in the accounts payable department. When image processing is used, access controls are extremely important to prevent alteration of the source document.

Threat 17: Performing poorly

In addition to ensuring accuracy and safeguarding assets, another objective of internal controls in the expenditure cycle is to encourage efficient and effective performance of business activities. The preparation and review of performance reports is effective in achieving this objective. Several have already been discussed in this chapter, such as reports on supplier performance and lists of outstanding invoices. Reports that help manage inventory are especially valuable. For example, organizations should carefully monitor the percentage of requisitions that are filled from inventory on hand. For critical items, this should be close to 100 percent, but for most items, such a high fill rate is undesirable because it requires carrying too much inventory.

The number of additional performance reports that can be developed is limited only by the controller's ingenuity and by management's decisions about what factors are important to monitor and control. The methods used to store and maintain expenditure cycle data affect the ease with which such reports can be produced, however.

EXPENDITURE CYCLE INFORMATION NEEDS AND DATA MODEL

A third function of the AIS is to provide information useful for decision making. Usefulness in the expenditure cycle means that the AIS must provide the operational information needed to perform the following functions:

- ➤ Determine when and how much additional inventory to order.
- ➤ Select the appropriate suppliers from whom to order.
- ➤ Verify the accuracy of vendor invoices.
- ➤ Decide if purchase discounts should be taken.
- ➤ Monitor cash flow needs to pay outstanding obligations.

In addition, the AIS must provide the following strategic and performance evaluation information:

- ➤ Efficiency and effectiveness of the purchasing department.
- ➤ Analyses of supplier performance such as on-time delivery and quality.
- ➤ Time taken to move goods from the receiving dock into production.
- ➤ Percentage of purchase discounts taken.

Notice that these decisions require both financial and operating data. For example, supplier selection should consider not only price, but also information about supplier performance in meeting delivery dates and quality of goods. Traditionally, the AIS has provided the financial information needed to make expenditure cycle decisions, and other information systems have generated the operating data about expenditure cycle activities. One problem with using separate information systems, however, is that the two sets of resulting data may be inconsistent. For example, many companies are not aware that different subunits may be purchasing the same items, because each unit uses a slightly different name and part number for those items. Consequently, the organization as a whole may be failing to take advantage of potential discounts for volume purchases. Moreover, the existence of multiple, overlapping systems increases costs and reduces efficiency of the systems function. Fortunately, the advent of relational DBMS makes the need to maintain separate information systems for financial and operating data obsolete.

Many expenditure cycle decisions also require externally generated information. For example, data about supplier financial characteristics may be useful in selecting stable suppliers that are likely to meet future commitments. A well-designed data model facilitates the integration of such externally generated information with internally generated financial and operating data about expenditure cycle activities.

Expenditure Cycle Data Model

Figure 12-11 shows an example of an REA data model for the expenditure cycle of a manufacturing company such as AOE. If the data model depicted in this figure were implemented in a relational database, there would be a table for each entity and for each many-to-many relationship.

Table 12-2 lists many of the attributes that would be found in those tables. Most of these attributes and their placement in specific tables should be self-explanatory. The placement of standard and actual costs, however, deserves some explanation.

Standard cost is stored as an attribute of the inventory table because it is the same for all units of a given inventory item for a fiscal year. In contrast, the actual cost of inventory is stored in the order-inventory table. This reflects the fact that purchase prices can vary over time. By storing the cost of each order with the quantity purchased, the system can calculate the actual cost of ending inventory and the cost of goods sold according to any accepted inventory valuation method (LIFO, FIFO, weighted average, or specific identification). If, on the other hand, actual cost were stored as an attribute of the inventory table, it would necessitate using the weighted-average method because all units of a given inventory item would be assigned the same cost. In addition, cost data would be available only in this format; it would be impossible to compute alternative values for inventory because the detailed data about the cost associated with each purchase would not be stored in the database.

Reading the REA Diagram

The cardinalities of the resource-event and event-agent relationships are standard for most organizations and should be self-explanatory. The cardinalities of each event-event relationship, however, may vary for different organizations, depending on their

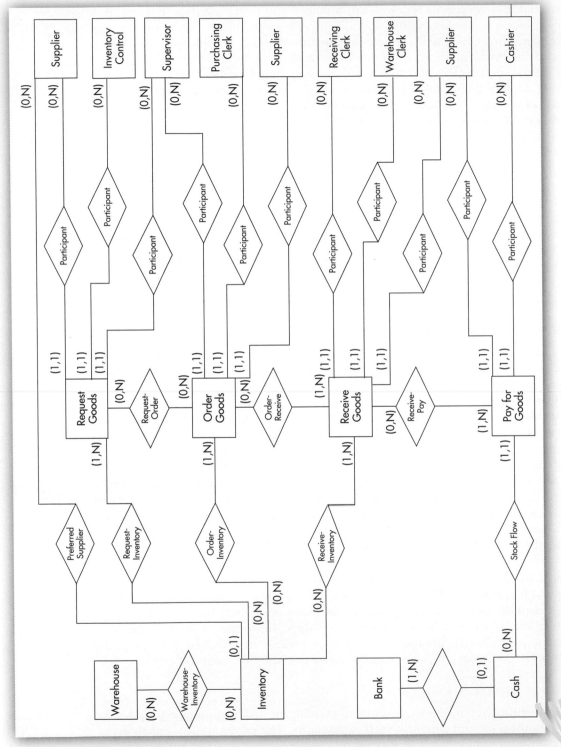

Figure 12-11 Partial REA diagram for expenditure cycle

446

Table 12-2   Partial REA Diagram for Expenditure Cycle

Table Name	Attributes (**primary key, _foreign keys,_ other attributes**)
Warehouse	**Warehouse number,** address, number of employees, . . .
Inventory	**Item number,** description, standard cost, reorder point, quantity on hand, quantity available, _preferred supplier,_ . . .
Bank	**Bank ID,** name, address, . . .
Cash	**Account number,** balance, _bank ID,_ . . .
Request goods	**Requisition number,** date, date needed, _supervisor, inventory control clerk, supplier number,_ . . .
Order goods	**Purchase order number,** date, total amount, _approved by (supervisor), supplier number, clerk number,_ . . .
Receive goods	**Receiving report number,** date, condition of goods, _receiving clerk number, warehouse clerk number,_ vendor invoice number, . . .
Pay for goods	**Check number,** date, amount, _cashier number, supplier number, account number,_ . . .
Cashier[1]	**Employee number,** name, date hired, date of birth, number of dependents, _supervisor,_ . . .
Supplier	**Supplier number,** name, address, performance rating, accounts payable balance, . . .
Warehouse-inventory	**Warehouse number, item number,** quantity, . . .
Request-inventory	**Requisition number, item number,** quantity, . . .
Request-order	**Requisition number, purchase order number,** . . .
Order-inventory	**Purchase order number, item number,** quantity, actual unit cost, . . .
Receive-inventory	**Receiving report number, item number,** quantity, . . .
Order-receive	**Purchase order number, receiving report number,** . . .
Receive-pay	**Receiving report number, check number,** amount applied to invoice, . . .

[1] _Similar tables would exist for all employees, but are omitted to save space._

business practices. Let us examine what the event-event relationship cardinalities in Figure 12-11 reveal about AOE's expenditure cycle business practices.

The relationship between the request goods and order goods events is modeled as many-to-many (M:N). At AOE, each purchase requisition can be for many different items. Since each item may have a different preferred supplier, a single request goods event may be linked to many order goods events. Moreover, for efficiency reasons, each purchase order lists all items to be purchased from a given vendor. Therefore, each order goods event may be linked to many request goods events. The minimum cardinality for each event is zero, because requests precede orders; but sometimes orders are generated automatically by the inventory control program without being specifically requested by any employee.

Figure 12-11 also depicts a many-to-many relationship between the order goods and receive goods events. This reflects the fact that suppliers either make several separate deliveries to fill one purchase order, fill several purchase orders with one delivery, or sometimes make a delivery to fill a single purchase order in full. The minimum cardinalities associated with each event reflect the fact that AOE must place an order first before it receives any inventory.

The relationship between the receive goods and pay for goods events is also depicted as being many-to-many. This reflects the fact that although suppliers bill AOE for each delivery, the company sometimes pays vendor invoices individually, while at other times it writes one check to pay for several invoices. Occasionally AOE makes installment payments for purchases. The minimum cardinalities reflect the typical business practice of buying on credit.

AOE has several warehouses. Consequently, a given inventory item can be stored at more than one warehouse, and each warehouse can store many different inventory items. This is reflected in the many-to-many relationship between the inventory and warehouse entities.

AOE uses one checking account to pay for all its purchases. AOE does, however, have several different bank accounts and sometimes has more than one account at a given bank. Notice that the minimum cardinality for the bank entity is one; AOE maintains information only about banks at which it has accounts. The minimum cardinality associated with the cash entity is zero, however, because AOE also maintains several internal petty cash funds.

Figure 12-11 also includes a relationship between the inventory resource entity and the supplier agent entities. This relationship represents the fact that AOE has developed a list of preferred suppliers for many of the component parts that it purchases.

Why is there no entity for the approve vendor invoices process? The reason is this is just an information processing activity. All the information included on the vendor invoice is already in the system. Purchase prices were set when the order was placed and the quantity received was identified when the goods were delivered. Thus, no additional data are provided when the vendor invoice is received (indeed, as discussed earlier, many companies are moving to invoiceless accounts payable systems). For suppliers who still send invoices, the vendor invoice number is stored as an attribute of the receive goods event.

In Table 12-2, data about the amount owed to specific suppliers are stored as an attribute in the supplier table. This is done only to improve query efficiency. Accounts payable represents those purchases that have not yet been paid for. Therefore, accounts payable could be calculated by computing the difference between total purchases and the cash disbursements linked to those purchase events.

Benefits of the Data Model

Notice that the data model in Figure 12-11 effectively integrates both traditional accounting transaction data (e.g., the date and amount of each purchase) with other operational data (e.g., information about where that item is stored and supplier performance measures, such as delivery date). It also would be easy to link this internally generated data with various types of external information. For example, information about a supplier's financial position and credit rating could be downloaded from a commercial database, appended as an additional column in the supplier table, and used in the supplier selection process. Most importantly, implementing the data model shown in Figure 12-11 in a relational DBMS would enable LeRoy Williams and other decision makers at AOE to directly access and manipulate the information they need by using powerful but easy-to-use query languages.

Internal Control Considerations

Our discussion of the threats listed in Table 12-1 stressed the importance of properly segregating incompatible duties. REA diagrams are useful for this task because they indicate which internal agents participate in each event. In addition, if the REA model is implemented in a DBMS, the computer can be programmed to enforce segregation of duties by preventing the same person from performing incompatible functions. Conversely, the system can be programmed to list all cases of an employee performing multiple roles so that the auditors can investigate if adequate compensating controls exist.

A DBMS also increases the importance of having effective access controls. Most relational DBMSs provide a means to control access by letting users see only a portion of the database (called a *view*). For example, purchasing agents should see only the portion of Figure 12-11 relevant to their job duties, such as the tables for inventory, suppliers, and purchases. Moreover, purchasing agents should be allowed to perform only a restricted set of operations on those tables. For example, to prevent them from making any unauthorized changes to the list of approved suppliers, they should have read-only rights to the supplier table.

Data accuracy is vital when using a DBMS. Fortunately, the relational data model provides some built-in controls to ensure data accuracy and consistency. One of the more important of these controls is support for foreign keys and referential integrity. For example, when a new row is added to the cash disbursements table, the system should automatically verify that the supplier number (which appears as a foreign key in that table) actually exists as a primary key in the supplier table. This control ensures that there really is such a supplier. Finally, the DBMS makes adequate backup and disaster recovery procedures crucial.

SUMMARY AND CASE CONCLUSION

The basic business activities performed in the expenditure cycle include the following:

➤ Ordering goods from suppliers

➤ Receiving goods from suppliers

➤ Approving vendor invoices for payment and paying for goods and services

The efficiency and effectiveness of these activities can significantly affect a company's overall performance. For example, deficiencies in requesting and ordering necessary inventory and supplies can create production bottlenecks and result in lost sales due to stockouts of popular items. Problems in the procedures related to receiving and storing inventory can result in a company's paying for items it never received, accepting delivery and incurring storage costs for unordered items, and experiencing a theft of inventory. Problems in approving vendor invoices for payment can result in overpaying suppliers or failing to take available discounts for prompt payment. Weaknesses in the cash disbursement process can result in the misappropriation of cash.

IT can help improve the efficiency and effectiveness with which expenditure cycle activities are performed. In particular, EDI, bar coding, and EFT can significantly reduce the time and costs associated with ordering, receiving, and paying for goods. In addition, a well-designed data model can allow for the integration of internally generated financial and operating data with externally generated information so that all three types of data can be considered when making important operating and strategic decisions. Finally, proper control procedures, especially segregation of duties, are needed to mitigate various threats such as errors in performing expenditure cycle activities and the theft of inventory or cash.

At the next executive meeting, Ann Brandt and Elizabeth Venko presented their recommendations for improving AOE's expenditure cycle business activities to Linda Spurgeon. Ann indicates LeRoy Williams's plan to conduct more frequent physical counts of key raw materials components will increase the accuracy of the database and reduce the likelihood of future stockouts at the Wichita plant. She also designed a query to produce a daily supplier performance report that will highlight any negative trends before they become the types of problems that disrupted production at the Dayton plant. Ann also indicated that it would be possible to link AOE's inventory and production planning systems with major suppliers to better manage AOE's inventory levels.

Elizabeth Venko stated that she was working to increase the number of suppliers who bar code their shipments. This would not only improve both the efficiency and accuracy of the receiving process, but also the accuracy of AOE's inventory records, thereby providing possible additional reductions in inventory carrying costs. In addition, Elizabeth wants to encourage more suppliers to either send invoices via EDI or agree to ERS, which should improve the efficiency and accuracy of processing invoices and reduce the costs associated with handling and storing paper invoices. Concurrently, Elizabeth plans to increase EFT as much as possible to further streamline the cash disbursements process and reduce the costs associated with processing payments by check.

KEY TERMS

- expenditure cycle
- economic order quantity (EOQ)
- reorder point
- materials requirements planning (MRP)
- just-in-time (JIT) inventory system

- purchase requisition
- purchase order
- blanket purchase order
- receiving report
- debit memo
- nonvoucher system
- voucher system

- disbursement voucher
- evaluated receipts settlement (ERS)
- voucher package
- kickbacks
- imprest fund

CHAPTER QUIZ

1. Which of the following inventory control methods is most likely to be used by a company that purchases inventory in response to customer orders?
   a. JIT   c. MRP
   b. EOQ   d. ABC

2. Which of the following matches is performed in evaluated receipt settlement?
   a. the vendor invoice with the receiving report
   b. the purchase order with the receiving report
   c. the vendor invoice with the purchase order
   d. the vendor invoice, the receiving report, and the purchase order

3. Which of the following documents is not always a part of the voucher package?
   a. purchase order
   b. receiving report
   c. vendor invoice
   d. disbursement voucher

4. Which document is used to establish a contract for the purchase of goods or services from a supplier?
   a. vendor invoice
   b. purchase requisition
   c. purchase order
   d. disbursement voucher

5. Which method would provide the greatest efficiency improvements for the purchase of noninventory items such as miscellaneous office supplies?
   a. bar coding
   b. EDI
   c. procurement cards
   d. Internet trading exchanges

6. Which of the following is not likely to be represented as a separate event in the REA data model of the expenditure cycle?
   a. ordering goods
   b. approving vendor invoices
   c. receiving goods
   d. cash disbursements

7. What is the best control procedure to prevent paying the same invoice twice?
   a. Segregate check-preparation and check-signing functions.
   b. Prepare checks only for invoices that have been matched to receiving reports and purchase orders.
   c. Require two signatures on all checks above a certain limit.
   d. Cancel all supporting documents when the check is signed.

8. For good internal control, who should sign checks?
   a. cashier
   b. accounts payable
   c. purchasing
   d. controller

9. Which of the following procedures is designed to prevent the purchasing agent from receiving kickbacks?
   a. maintaining a list of approved suppliers and requiring all purchases to be made from suppliers on that list
   b. requiring purchasing agents to disclose any financial investments in potential suppliers
   c. requiring approval of all purchase orders
   d. prenumbering and periodically accounting for all purchase orders

10. Which document is used to record adjustments to accounts payable based on the return of unacceptable inventory to the supplier?
    a. receiving report
    b. credit memo
    c. debit memo
    d. purchase order

DISCUSSION QUESTIONS

12.1   In this chapter and in Chapter 11, the controller of AOE played a major role in evaluating and recommending ways to use IT to improve efficiency and effectiveness. Should the company's chief information officer make these decisions instead? Should the controller be involved in making these types of decisions? Why or why not?

12.2   Companies such as IBM and Ingersoll-Rand have moved beyond JIT to JIT-II systems. In JIT-II systems, supplier sales representatives work on-site to monitor inventory levels and have access to current sales data and forecasts. The supplier representatives use this information to reorder goods automatically and meet production needs. Discuss the potential advantages and disadvantages of this arrangement. What special controls, if any, should be developed to monitor JIT-II systems?

12.3   In reverse auctions, suppliers bid to provide goods and services at the lowest price. What are some possible long-term consequences of using reverse auctions to acquire inventory?

12.4   Some people argue that if total quality control principles are followed, there should be little or no shrinkage of inventory and therefore little need for periodic inventory counts. Comment on this argument.

12.5   In what ways can you apply the control procedures discussed in this chapter to paying personal debts (e.g., credit card bills)?

12.6   How might the choice of JIT versus MRP as a technique for managing inventory be affected by the nature of the products being sold?

12.7   In addition to on-time delivery, what other aspects of supplier performance should be monitored?

PROBLEMS

12.1   Which internal control procedure would be most cost-effective in dealing with the following expenditure cycle threats?
   a. A purchasing agent orders materials from a supplier that he partially owns.
   b. Receiving-dock personnel steal inventory and then claim the inventory was sent to the warehouse.
   c. An unordered supply of laser printer paper delivered to the office is accepted and paid for because the "price is right." After jamming all of the laser printers, however, it becomes obvious that the "bargain" paper is of inferior quality.
   d. A vendor's invoice is overcharged for items ordered and delivered.
   e. A company is late in paying a particular invoice. Consequently, a second invoice is sent, which crosses the first invoice's payment in the mail. The second invoice is submitted for processing and also paid.
   f. Inventory records show that an adequate supply of copy paper should be in stock, but none is available on the supply shelf.
   g. The inventory records are incorrectly updated when a receiving dock employee enters the wrong product number at the terminal.
   h. A clerical employee obtains a blank check and writes a large amount payable to a fictitious company.
   i. A fictitious invoice is received and used to pay for goods that were never ordered or delivered.
   j. The petty cash custodian confesses to having "borrowed" $12,000 over the last 5 years.

12.2   The data models for both the revenue and expenditure cycles presented in this chapter and in Chapter 11 contain some common elements such as inventory and cash. Discuss how the two cycles interact with each other. Sketch a combined REA diagram to integrate both cycles.

12.3   Refer to Figure 12-11 to answer the following questions.

a. If the relationship between cash disbursements and receipts was one-to-many, what would that reveal about the company's payment policy?

b. Why is the relationship between inventory and purchases many-to-many? What other possible cardinalities can exist between inventory and purchases? What would they indicate about the company's business practices?

c. Why is the relationship between purchases and receipts many-to-many?

d. If a company regularly bought inventory on an installment payment plan, how would that be reflected in Figure 12-11?

e. Modify Figure 12-11 to include the event of returning defective merchandise. Create any additional tables needed and identify the attributes that would go in those tables. What additional changes, if any, are required to accommodate situations when the supplier adjusts the company's account but does not require actual return of the damaged or nonconforming items?

f. Modify Figure 12-11 to include the purchase of services, such as rent and utilities. Create any additional tables needed and identify the attributes that would go in those tables.

g. Modify Figure 12-11 to reflect situations when suppliers require payment in advance, prior to delivery.

12.4   The following documents are used in the expenditure cycle:

Vendor invoice
Purchase order
Disbursement voucher
Purchase requisition
Packing slip
Receiving report
Check

Required

a. Identify which of these documents are internally generated and which are externally generated.

b. For each internally generated document, how many copies are needed? What is the purpose of each copy? Where does each copy go?

c. Describe the application controls that should be in place if each of these paper documents were replaced by electronic forms.

12.5   Use the format of Table 12-1 to compare and contrast how AOE's current integrated expenditure cycle system and its old legacy expenditure cycle system (as described in the appendix to this chapter) address the various threats and issues related to expenditure cycle activities.

12.6   Modify Table 12-1 by indicating if each specific control procedure listed there is preventive (P), detective (D), or corrective (C) in nature.

12.7   The receiving department at Culp Electronics Company processes inventory deliveries upon arrival by means of on-line data terminals located on the receiving dock. Each inventory receipt entered into the system is processed to update both the inventory master file and the open purchase order file. The system then automatically generates a voucher to authorize a cash disbursement for each receipt.

Required

What items of data should receiving department employees enter?

      Describe several application controls that should be programmed into the system to check the accuracy and validity of the data the receiving department employees enter. Relate your answer specifically to the data items mentioned in part a.

12.8   This problem consists of two parts.

Part I

What is the purpose of each of the following control procedures?

a. Cancellation of the voucher package by the cashier after signing the check
b. Separation of duties of approving invoices for payment and signing checks
c. Prenumbering and periodically accounting for all purchase orders
d. Periodic physical count of inventory
e. Requiring two signatures on checks for large amounts
f. Requiring that a copy of the receiving report be routed through the inventory stores department prior to going to accounts payable
g. Requiring a regular reconciliation of the bank account by someone other than the person responsible for writing checks
h. Maintaining an approved supplier list and checking that all purchase orders are issued only to suppliers on that list

Part II

How can the objectives of the control procedures listed in part I be accomplished in an automated AIS?

12.9   The systems flowchart presented in Figure 12-12 and the following description summarize ConSport Corporation's cash disbursements system:

a. The accounts payable department approves all invoices for payment by matching them with the related purchase requisitions, purchase orders, and receiving reports. The accounts payable clerks focus on matching the supplier names on all documents and skim the remaining information.
b. The supplier file is searched daily for the disbursement vouchers of invoices due to be paid. Both copies of these vouchers are sent to the finance department, along with the other supporting documents. The cashier prepares and signs a check for each supplier and records the check in the check register.
c. The cashier receives the monthly bank statement with canceled checks and prepares the bank reconciliation. If an adjustment is required as a consequence of the bank reconciliation, a two-copy journal voucher is prepared. A copy of the bank reconciliation is sent to the internal audit department.

Required

Identify weaknesses in ConSport's expenditure cycle, explain the resulting problem, and suggest a control procedure that would best prevent or detect and correct each weakness. Use the labels next to each figure to reference your answer.

(CMA examination, adapted)

12.10   In 1995, the Diamond Manufacturing Company purchased over $10 million worth of office equipment under its so-called special ordering system, with individual orders ranging from $5,000 to $30,000. Special orders entail low-volume items that have been included in an authorized user's budget. As part of their annual budgets, department heads request equipment and specify estimated costs. The budget, which limits the types and dollar amounts of office equipment a department head can requisition, is approved at the beginning of the year by the board of directors. A purchase requisition form for all approved equipment pur-

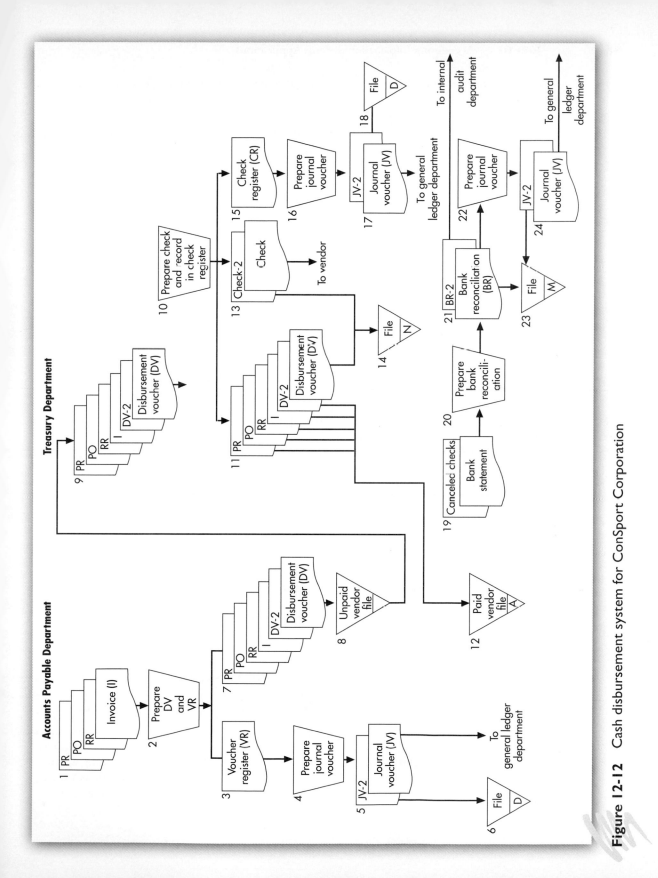

Figure 12-12 Cash disbursement system for ConSport Corporation

chases must be prepared and forwarded to the purchasing department. The special ordering system functions as follows:

Purchasing

Upon receiving a purchase requisition, one of the five purchasing agents (buyers) verifies that the requester is indeed a department head. The buyer next selects the appropriate supplier by searching the various catalogs on file. The buyer then phones the supplier, requests a price quote, and places a verbal order. A prenumbered purchase order is processed, with the original sent to the supplier and copies to the department head, receiving, and accounts payable. One copy is also filed in the open requisition file. When the receiving department verbally informs the buyer that the item has been received, the purchase order is transferred from the open to the filled file. Once a month, the buyer reviews the unfilled file to follow up on open orders.

Receiving

The receiving department gets a copy of each purchase order. When equipment is received, that copy of the purchase order is stamped with the date and, if applicable, any differences between the quantity ordered and the quantity received are noted in red ink. The receiving clerk then forwards the stamped purchase order and equipment to the requisitioning department head and verbally notifies the purchasing department that the goods were received.

Accounts Payable

Upon receipt of a purchase order, the accounts payable clerk files it in the open purchase order file. When a vendor invoice is received, it is matched with the applicable purchase order, and a payable is created by debiting the requisitioning department's equipment account. Unpaid invoices are filed by due date. On the due date, a check is prepared and forwarded to the treasurer for signature. The invoice and purchase order are then filed by purchase order number in the paid invoice file.

Treasurer

Checks received daily from the accounts payable department are sorted into two groups: those over and those under $10,000. Checks for less than $10,000 are machine signed. The cashier maintains the check signature machine's key and signature plate and monitors its use. Both the cashier and the treasurer sign all checks over $10,000.

Required

a. Describe the weaknesses relating to purchases and payments of so-called special orders by the Diamond Manufacturing Company.
b. Recommend control procedures that must be added to overcome weaknesses identified in step a.
c. Describe how the control procedures you recommended in step b should be modified if Diamond reengineered its expenditure cycle activities to make maximum use of current IT (e.g., EDI, EFT, bar code scanning, and electronic forms in place of paper documents).

(CPA examination, adapted)

12.11   Lecimore Company has a centralized purchasing department managed by Tawanda Mason. Tawanda has established policies and procedures to guide the clerical staff and purchasing agents in daily department operations. She is satisfied that these guidelines conform to company objectives and that no major problems exist in the regular operations of the purchasing department.

Lecimore's internal audit department recently performed a routine operational audit of the purchasing department. Tawanda's policies and procedures that were first reviewed are as follows:

➤ All significant purchases are made on a competitive basis. The probability of timely delivery and supplier reliability is taken into account on a subjective basis.
➤ Quality acceptability requirements are provided to all potential suppliers.
➤ The materials manager of the inventory stores department (not the purchasing department) checks supplier adherence to quality specifications. The materials manager inspects the goods upon arrival and ensures that only goods meeting minimum quality standards are transferred to the storeroom.
➤ The materials manager prepares all purchase requests, which are based on the production schedule for the next 4 months.

The internal audit staff then observed the purchasing department's operations and noted the following:

➤ One supplier provides 90 percent of the crucial raw materials Lecimore uses. This supplier has a reliable delivery record and has been the low bidder for several years.
➤ As production plans change, rush orders are made by production directly to the purchasing department. Materials ordered for canceled production runs are stored for future use. The purchasing department absorbs the costs associated with both types of changes because Tawanda believes this is a way of being a "good team player."
➤ As soon as the production department announces changes, purchasing orders the appropriate materials. Tawanda is proud of her staff's quick response time to such orders. Materials on hand are not reviewed before these orders are placed, however.
➤ The materials manager accepts partial and advance shipments and notifies the purchasing department of the receipt of the goods. The purchasing department is responsible for following up on partial shipments; no action is taken to discourage advance shipments.

Required
a. Identify weaknesses and inefficiencies in the purchasing procedures that Tawanda developed for Lecimore.
b. Suggest ways to overcome those weaknesses or inefficiencies.
(CMA Examination, adapted)

12.12 Alden, Inc. has hired you to review its internal controls for the purchase, receipt, storage, and issuance of raw materials. You observed the following:

➤ Raw materials, which consist mainly of high-cost electronic components, are kept in a locked storeroom. Storeroom personnel include a supervisor and four clerks. All are well trained, competent, and adequately bonded. Raw materials are removed from the storeroom only upon written or oral authorization by a production supervisor.
➤ No perpetual inventory records are kept; hence, the storeroom clerks do not keep records for goods received or issued. To compensate, the storeroom clerks perform a physical inventory count each month. The clerks are supervised during this count, and other appropriate procedures are followed.
➤ After the physical count, the storeroom supervisor matches the quantities on hand against a predetermined reorder level. If the count is below the reorder level, the supervisor enters the part number on a materials requisition list that is sent to the accounts payable clerk. The accounts payable clerk prepares a purchase order for each item on the list and mails it to the supplier from whom the part was last purchased.

Table 12-3   Overview of Expenditure Cycle Business Activites

	Request Purchase of Goods	Approve Purchase	Receive Goods	Receive Invoice	Approve Vendor Invoice	Prepare Check	Pay Vendor
				Expenditure Cycle			
Accounting transaction							
Journal entry					Dr. Purchases Cr. A/P		
Documents		Purchase order					
Data collected	• Name • Item #						
Department					Accounting		
Control issues	Order only what is needed						
Information required							
Information generated							
Effect of automation							

Source: Adapted from teaching materials developed by Martha Eining, University of Utah.

> The storeroom clerks receive the ordered materials upon their arrival. The clerks count all items and verify that the counts agree with the quantities on the bill of lading. The bill of lading is then initialed, dated, and filed in the storeroom, to serve as a receiving report.

Required
a. Describe the weaknesses that exist in Alden's expenditure cycle.
b. Suggest control procedures to overcome the weaknesses noted in step a.
c. Discuss how those control procedures would be best implemented in an automated AIS using the latest developments in IT.

(CPA Examination, adapted)

12.13 Table 12-3 lists the various activities performed in the expenditure cycle and the journal entries, documents, data, and control issues associated with them. Complete each of the cell entries in this table.

12.14 Branden Company, a midsize manufacturer of specialized machinery, follows these purchasing procedures:

> Materials purchase requisitions are approved by manufacturing supervisors and then forwarded to the purchasing department.

➤ Purchasing clerks prepare prenumbered purchase orders in triplicate. The original copy is sent to the supplier. The second copy is sent to the receiving department to notify it of an incoming shipment. The third copy is filed in the purchasing department.

➤ When materials are delivered, they are moved directly to the storeroom, with a copy of the receiving report. The receiving department sends another copy of the receiving report and its copy of the purchase order to the purchasing department. The third copy of the receiving report is sent to the accounting department.

➤ Vendor invoices are sent to the purchasing department and directed to the employee who placed that order. This employee checks the invoice for accuracy in terms of discounts, extensions, and footings. The purchasing clerk then compares the invoice with (1) the copy of the purchase order and (2) the copy of the receiving report to verify the quantities ordered and received. The clerk then approves the invoice for payment.

➤ The approved invoice is sent to the accounting department, where it is coded for account distribution, assigned a voucher number, entered in the voucher register, and filed according to payment due date.

Required

Identify weaknesses in Branden's expenditure cycle activities, explain the resulting problems that may occur, and recommend control procedures that should be implemented to correct those weaknesses.

(CPA Examination, adapted)

Case 12-1 AnyCompany, Inc.: An Ongoing Comprehensive Case

Identify a local company (you may use the same company identified to complete this case in previous chapters) and do the following:

1. Identify who is responsible for decisions involving (a) requisitioning, ordering, and receiving inventories; (b) authorizing cash disbursements; and (c) making cash disbursements. Determine if there is adequate segregation of duties regarding these activities.

2. Describe the paper documents and electronic forms the company uses. Evaluate the design of each document or electronic form and assess its appropriateness for its intended use.

3. Draw an REA diagram of the organization's expenditure cycle.

4. Describe how the system updates the master files (or database) after each type of transaction (purchase, receipt, cash disbursement). Draw a systems flowchart of these processes.

5. Identify and evaluate the adequacy of the control procedures used to ensure accuracy and validity of all transaction processing.

6. Examine copies of the reports that the system produces. Identify the major decisions that must be made in the expenditure cycle. Evaluate the adequacy of existing reports in assisting good decision making.

Case 12-2 Blackwell Industries

Blackwell Industries manufactures sporting goods. You have been asked to evaluate the proposed redesign of Blackwell's purchasing system. The new system will use a materials inventory master file, an open purchase order master file, and a supplier history file, all organized and stored in a relational database system. System inputs will include materials inventory receipts and issue transactions, which will be keyed in as they occur from on-line terminals located in the appropriate departments. System outputs will include batches of purchase orders and periodic reports of overdue deliveries, supplier performance, and cash flow commitments. Programs that are separate from the main update program will generate these reports. Managers can also obtain this information by creating on-line queries.

The main update program will begin by reading a transaction record and determining if it is a receipt or issue transaction. Then it will update the appropriate inventory master record. As each issue transaction is processed, the program will also check the quantity on hand in the master inventory record. If it falls below the reorder point, a reorder record will be written to a temporary file on a separate disk. This file will be processed at the end of each day, to prepare purchase orders. For each inventory receipt transaction, the program will update not only the quantity on hand in the inventory master record but also the corresponding open purchase order and supplier history records.

The purchase order preparation program will process the temporary reorder file by first sequencing it by supplier code number. All reorder records for the same supplier will be consolidated into one purchase order. When all reorder records for a supplier have been processed, EDI will generate and transmit a purchase order. The order will also be added to the open purchase order file.

At the end of each day, the open purchase order file will be processed to identify any purchase orders for which delivery is past due, and an overdue deliveries report will be generated. At the end of each month, the supplier history and open purchase order files will be processed to generate supplier performance and cash flow commitments reports.

REQUIRED

1. Prepare a systems flowchart of the main update program.
2. Prepare a systems flowchart of the purchase order preparation program.
3. Draw an REA diagram of the data included in the proposed system.
4. Suggest potential ways that IT could be used to further improve the efficiency of the proposed system.
5. Identify the data that will be input on each transaction record. Suggest appropriate application controls to ensure accurate and reliable input.
6. Identify potential threats relating to the proposed system and suggest appropriate internal control procedures for mitigating them.

ANSWERS TO CHAPTER QUIZ

1. a	**3.** d	**5.** c	**7.** d	**9.** b
2. b	**4.** c	**6.** b	**8.** a	**10.** c

AOE's Legacy Expenditure Cycle System

AOE's legacy revenue cycle system was characterized by distinct modules to support each of the four basic revenue cycle activities.

ORDER GOODS (PURCHASING)

As shown in Figure 12A-1, the receipt of a purchase requisition triggers the process of ordering goods and supplies. Approved purchase requisitions arrive daily from inventory control and various user departments. The purchasing agent uses an on-line terminal to enter the requisition data and create a purchase order. After the item number is entered, the system searches the inventory master file to identify the preferred vendor for that item. The system proceeds to create a purchase order record by retrieving data from the inventory and vendor master files and prompting the purchase agent to enter the remaining data such as quantity needed and desired delivery date. Then the purchase requisition is filed temporarily in numerical order.

The system stores the completed purchase order record in a temporary disk file. At the end of the day, all items to be ordered from the same vendor are consolidated into a single purchase order record. Each of these records is assigned a purchase order number and added to the open purchase order file, and five copies of the purchase order are printed.

The five copies of the purchase order are sent to the purchasing manager for review and approval. After the purchase orders have been signed, the original is sent to the vendor. Copy 2 goes to the receiving department to inform them of anticipated deliveries. Copy 3 goes to accounts payable to notify them of a pending financial commitment. Copy 4 of the purchase order goes to the department that generated the purchase requisition to let it know that its request has been approved. Finally, copy 5 is retained in purchasing, where it is attached to the purchase requisition and filed numerically, by purchase order number, in the open purchase order file.

RECEIVE AND STORE GOODS

Figure 12A-2 shows that the receiving department files the copy of the purchase order sent from the purchasing department alphabetically by vendor. When a delivery arrives, a receiving clerk verifies that the goods were ordered by comparing the purchase order number referenced on the vendor's packing slip with the copy of the purchase order sent earlier by the purchasing department. The receiving clerk then counts and inspects the goods and uses an on-line terminal to enter the inventory item numbers, count, and purchase order number. The system checks that data against the open purchase order file. Any discrepancies are immediately displayed on the screen and must be resolved.

Once the goods are accepted, the system updates the quantity on order and quantity on hand fields in the inventory master file, records the date of receipt in the vendor master file, and notes the quantity received in the open purchase order file. Two copies of a prenumbered receiving report are also printed in the receiving department. One of these accompanies the goods to the inventory stores department, where a clerk signs off to acknowledge

461

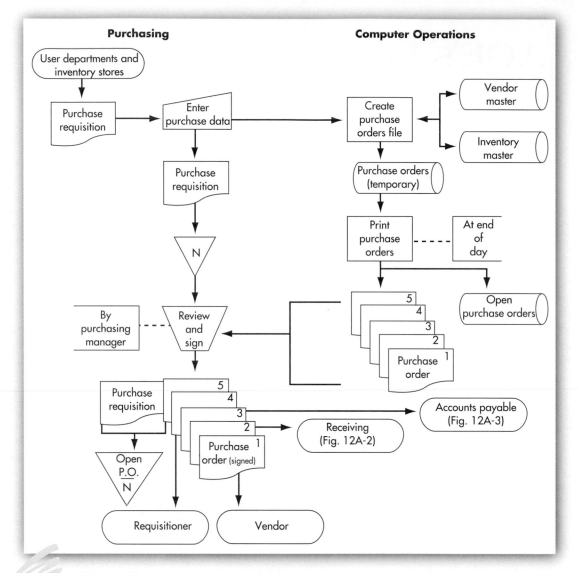

Figure 12A-1   Flowchart of the purchasing system

transfer of the goods into inventory. This signed copy of the receiving report is then sent to accounts payable, where it is used to approve the vendor invoice. The other copy of the receiving report is filed in the receiving department, along with the related purchase order and packing slip.

APPROVE VENDOR INVOICES AND PAY SUPPLIERS

Figure 12A-3 depicts the accounts payable process formerly used at AOE, which is typical of traditional voucher systems. When an invoice is received from a vendor, it is compared with the information contained in copies of the purchase

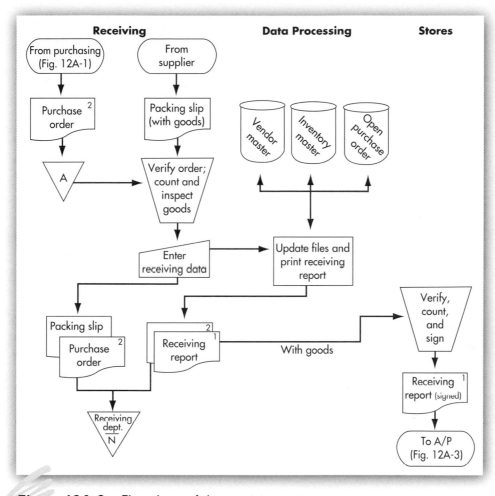

Figure 12A-2 Flowchart of the receiving system

order and receiving report to ensure accuracy and validity. For purchases of supplies or services, which do not usually involve purchase orders and receiving reports, the invoice is sent to the appropriate supervisor for approval. The vendor invoice itself is also checked for mathematical accuracy.

The accounts payable clerk then enters the approved invoice data into the open-invoice file. At this time, the system also updates the open purchase order file to reflect the receipt of the vendor invoice. At the end of each day, the system uses the open-invoice file to update the bal-ances due to each vendor in the vendor master file. Then disbursement vouchers are printed and the accounts payable control account in the general ledger is updated.

The accounts payable clerk compares the disbursement vouchers with the supporting documents (vendor invoice, purchase order, and receiving report) and files them by due date in an unpaid vouchers file. Prior to the due date, the disbursement voucher and supporting documents, or voucher package, are sent to the cashier for payment.

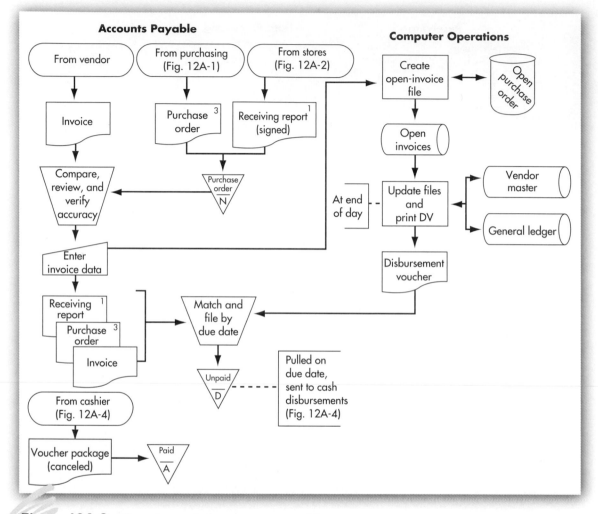

Figure 12A-3 Flowchart of the accounts payable system

Figure 12A-4 depicts the cash disbursements process formerly used by AOE, which reflects a typical batch-oriented accounts payable system. The cashier receives the voucher package, which consists of the vendor invoice, purchase order, receiving report, and disbursements voucher, from the accounts payable department. The cashier reviews each voucher package, computes a batch total of the amounts to be paid, and enters the disbursement data.

The system then uses the disbursement voucher file to update the accounts payable, open-invoice, and general ledger files. For each vendor, the totals of all vouchers are summed and that amount is subtracted from the balance field in that vendor's master file record. The invoices being paid are then deleted from the

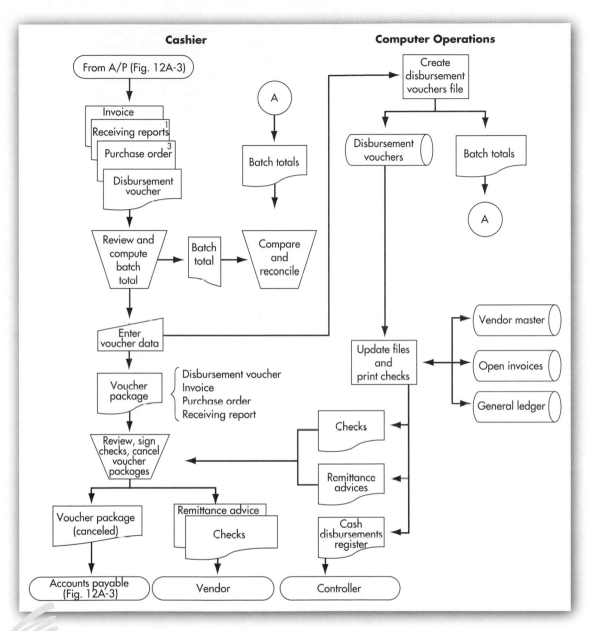

Figure 12A-4 Flowchart of the cash disbursements system

open-invoice file. A remittance advice is prepared for each vendor, listing each invoice being paid and the amounts of any discounts or allowances taken. The checks and remittance advices are then printed. After all disbursement transactions have been processed, the cash disbursements register is printed and sent to the controller. At the same time, the system generates a summary journal entry debiting accounts payable and crediting cash and posts that entry to the general ledger.

The checks and remittance advices are then returned to the cashier for signing. After reviewing the checks against the voucher package, the cashier signs the checks. (Checks above a specified amount also may require the treasurer's signature.) The cashier then mails the checks and remittance advices to the vendors and cancels supporting documents before returning them to accounts payable, where they are filed alphabetically by vendor.

The Production Cycle

Learning Objectives

After studying this chapter, you should be able to:

- Describe the major business activities and related data processing operations performed in the production cycle.
- Explain how a company's cost accounting system can help it achieve its manufacturing goals.
- Identify major threats in the production cycle and evaluate the adequacy of various control procedures for dealing with those threats.
- Discuss the key decisions that must be made in the production cycle and identify the information required to make those decisions.
- Read and understand an REA data model of the production cycle.
- Develop an REA data model for the production cycle.

Integrative Case: Alpha Omega Electronics

LeRoy Williams, vice president for manufacturing at AOE, is concerned about problems associated with the company's change in strategic mission. Two years ago, AOE's top management decided to shift the company from its traditional position as a low-cost producer of consumer electronic products to a product differentiation strategy. Since then, AOE has increased the variety of sizes, styles, and features within each of its product lines.

To support this shift in strategic focus, AOE has invested heavily in factory automation. AOE's cost accounting system has not been changed, however. For example, manufacturing overhead is still allocated based on direct labor hours, even though automation has drastically reduced the amount of direct labor used to manufacture a product. Consequently, investments in new equipment and machinery have resulted in dramatic increases in manufacturing overhead rates. This situation has created the following problems:

1. Production supervisors complain that the accounting system makes no sense, and that they are being penalized for making investments that improve overall efficiency. Indeed, some products now cost more to produce using state-of-the-art equipment than they did before the new equipment was purchased. Yet, the new equipment has increased production capacity while simultaneously reducing defects.
2. The marketing and product design executives have all but dismissed the system's product cost figures as useless for setting prices or determining the potential profitability of new products. Indeed, some competitors have begun to price their products below what AOE's cost accounting system says it costs to produce that item.
3. Although a number of steps have been taken to improve quality, the cost accounting system does not provide adequate measures to evaluate the effect of those steps and to indicate areas that need further improvement. Indeed, LeRoy is frustrated by his inability to quantify the effects of the quality improvements that have occurred.
4. Performance reports continue to focus primarily on financial measures. Line managers in the factory, however, complain that they need more accurate and timely information on physical activities, such as units produced, defect rates, and production time.

LeRoy has expressed these concerns to Linda Spurgeon, AOE's president, who agrees that the problems are serious. Linda then called a meeting with LeRoy; Ann Brandt, AOE's vice president of information systems; and Elizabeth Venko, AOE's controller. At the meeting, Elizabeth and Ann agreed to study how to modify the cost accounting system to more accurately reflect AOE's new production processes. To begin this project, LeRoy agreed to take Elizabeth and Ann on a factory tour so that they could see and understand how the new technology has affected production cycle activities.

As this case suggests, deficiencies in the information system used to support production cycle activities can create significant problems for an organization. The availability of current and accurate information about product costs is crucial for effectively managing the production cycle. As you read this chapter, think about how the introduction of new technology in the production cycle may require corresponding changes in a company's cost accounting system.

INTRODUCTION

The **production cycle** is a recurring set of business activities and related data processing operations associated with the manufacture of products. Figure 13-1 shows how the production cycle is linked to the other subsystems in a company's AIS. The revenue cycle information system (see Chapter 11) provides the information (customer orders and sales forecasts) used to plan production and inventory levels. In return, the production cycle information system sends the revenue cycle information about finished goods that have been produced and are available for sale. Information about raw materials needs is sent to the expenditure cycle information system (see Chapter 12) in the form of purchase requisitions. In exchange, the expenditure cycle system provides information about raw material acquisitions and also about other expenditures included in manufacturing overhead. Information about labor needs is sent to the human resources cycle (see Chapter 14), which in return provides data about labor costs and availability. Finally, information about the cost of goods manufactured is sent to the general ledger and reporting information system (see Chapter 15).

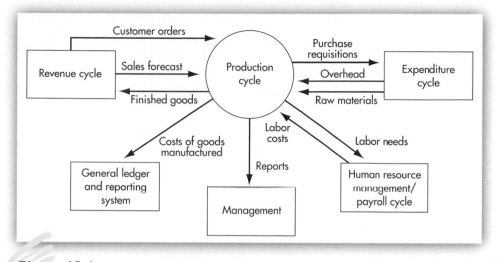

Figure 13-1   Context diagram of the production cycle

A company's AIS plays a vital role in the production cycle. Accurate and timely cost accounting information is essential input to decisions about the following:

➤ Product mix (what to produce)

➤ Product pricing

➤ Resource allocation and planning (e.g., whether to make or buy a product, relative profitability of different products)

➤ Cost management (planning and controlling manufacturing costs, evaluating performance)

These decisions require much more detailed information about costs than the data needed to prepare financial statements in accordance with Generally Accepted Accounting Principles (GAAP). Thus, the design of a company's production cycle AIS must go beyond merely meeting external financial reporting requirements.

This chapter is organized around the three major functions of the AIS in the production cycle. The first section describes production cycle activities and discusses how data about their costs are collected and processed. The second section discusses the major control objectives in the production cycle and explains how the AIS can be designed to achieve them. The final section discusses the key production cycle decisions and presents a data model that shows how the AIS can effectively and efficiently store and organize the information needed to make those decisions.

PRODUCTION CYCLE ACTIVITIES

Figure 13-2 shows the four basic activities in the production cycle: product design, planning and scheduling, production operations, and cost accounting. Figure 13-2 also depicts the principal information flows between each of those activities and the

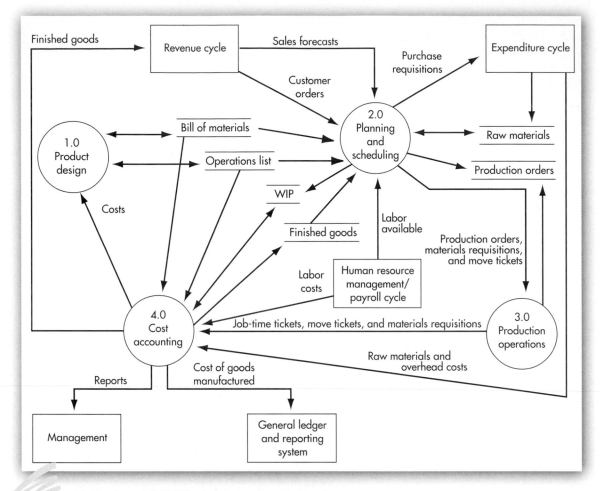

Figure 13-2   Level 0 DFD of the production cycle

other AIS cycles. Although accountants are primarily involved in the fourth step, cost accounting, they also must understand the processes and information needs of the other steps. This knowledge will enable them to work with the information systems function to ensure that the AIS can provide the information needed to manage the four activities of the production cycle.

Product Design

The first step in the production cycle is product design (circle 1.0 in Figure 13-2). The objective of this activity is to design a product that meets customer requirements in terms of quality, durability, and functionality while simultaneously minimizing production costs. Some of these criteria conflict with one another, making the product design task a challenging one.

Documents, forms, and procedures

The product design activity creates two main documents. The first, a **bill of materials,** specifies the part number, description, and quantity of each component used in a finished product. The second is an **operations list,** which specifies the labor and machine requirements needed to manufacture the product. The operations list is sometimes referred to as a routing sheet because it indicates how a product moves through the factory, specifying what is done at each step and how much time that activity should take.

Role of the accountant

Accountants should participate in product design because 65 to 80 percent of product costs are determined at this stage of the production process. Accountants can provide information showing how various design trade-offs affect production costs and thereby profitability. For example, it is possible to significantly reduce the costs of producing a line of related products by increasing the number of common components used in each product. The AIS should be able to provide data about current component usage in various products and the projected costs of using alternative components. Similarly, aspects of product complexity, such as the number of different components and manner of assembly, can significantly affect production time and costs. Therefore, the AIS should be designed to collect and provide information about the machine setup and materials handling costs associated with alternative product designs.

Finally, data about repair and warranty costs associated with existing products can be useful for designing better products. This data should be collected in the revenue cycle. The key is to design the AIS so that the information is available to product designers. Notice that in all of these examples the accountant adds value not by merely measuring costs, but by using cost information proactively to improve long-run profitability.

Planning and Scheduling

The second step in the production cycle is planning and scheduling (circle 2.0 in Figure 13-2). The objective is to develop a production plan efficient enough to meet existing orders and anticipated short-term demand without creating excess finished goods inventories.

Planning methods

Two common methods of production planning are manufacturing resource planning and just-in-time manufacturing. **Manufacturing resource planning (MRP-II)** is an extension of materials resource planning (see Chapter 12) that seeks to balance existing production capacity and raw materials needs to meet forecasted sales demands. MRP-II systems are often referred to as *push manufacturing*, because goods are produced in expectation of customer demand.

Just as MRP-II is an extension of MRP inventory control systems, **just-in-time (JIT) manufacturing systems** extend the principles of just-in-time inventory systems (see Chapter 12) to the entire production process. The goal of JIT manufacturing is to minimize or eliminate inventories of raw materials, work in process, and finished goods. JIT is often referred to as *pull manufacturing*, because goods are produced in response to customer demand. Theoretically, JIT manufacturing systems produce only in response to customer orders. In practice, however, most JIT manufacturing systems develop short-run production plans. For example, Toyota develops monthly production plans so that it can provide a stable schedule to its suppliers. This strategy enables the suppliers to plan their production schedules so that they can deliver their products to Toyota at the exact time they are needed. Thus, both MRP-II and JIT manufacturing systems plan production in advance. They differ, however, in the length of the planning horizon. MRP-II systems may develop production plans for up to 12 months in advance, whereas JIT manufacturing systems use much shorter planning horizons.

Documents, forms, and procedures

The **master production schedule (MPS)** specifies how much of each product is to be produced during the planning period and when that production should occur (see Figure 13-3). Information about customer orders, sales forecasts, and finished goods inventory levels is used to determine production levels. Although the long-range part of the MPS may be modified in response to changes in market conditions, production plans must be frozen a few weeks in advance to provide sufficient time to procure the necessary raw materials, supplies, and labor resources. Moreover, the complexity of scheduling increases dramatically as the number of

Figure 13-3   Sample master production schedule (MPS)

MASTER PRODUCTION SCHEDULE								
Product Number 120				**Description:** VCR				
Lead time:[a]	**Week Number**							
1 week	**1**	**2**	**3**	**4**	**5**	**6**	**7**	**8**
Quantity on hand	500	350[b]	350	300	350	300	450	300
Scheduled production	150[c]	300	250	300	250	400	250	300
Forecasted sales	300	300	300	250	300	250	400	250
Net available	350[d]	350	300	350	300	450	300	350

[a]Time to manufacture product (1 week for VCR).
[b]Ending quantity on hand (net available) from prior week.
[c]Calculated by subtracting quantity on hand from sum of this week's and next week's forecasted sales, plus a 50-unit buffer stock. For example, begin week 1 with 500 units. Projected sales for weeks 1 and 2 total 600 units. Adding 50-unit desired buffer inventory yields 650 units needed by end of week 1. Subtracting beginning inventory of 500 units results in planned production of 150 units during week 1.
[d]Beginning quantity on hand plus scheduled production less forecasted sales.

factories grows. Large manufacturing companies such as Motorola and General Motors must coordinate production at many different plants in different countries. Some of those plants produce basic components such as picture tubes and circuit boards; others assemble the final products. The production information system must coordinate these activities to minimize bottlenecks and the buildup of partially completed inventories.

The MPS is used to develop a detailed timetable that specifies daily production and to determine if raw materials need to be purchased. To do this, it is necessary to "explode" the bill of materials to determine the immediate raw materials requirements for meeting the production goals listed in the MPS (see Table 13-1). These requirements are compared with current inventory levels and, if additional materials are needed, purchase requisitions are generated and sent to the purchasing department to initiate the acquisition process.

Figure 13-2 shows that the planning and scheduling activity produces three other documents: production orders, materials requisitions, and move tickets. A production order authorizes the manufacture of a specified quantity of a particular product. It lists the operations that need to be performed, the quantity to be produced, and the location where the finished product should be delivered. It also collects data about each of those activities (see Figure 13-4).

A **materials requisition** authorizes the removal of the necessary quantity of raw materials from the storeroom to the factory location where they will be used. This document contains the production order number, date of issue, and, based on the bill of materials, the part numbers and quantities of all necessary raw materials (see Figure 13-5). Subsequent transfers of raw materials throughout the factory are documented on **move tickets,** which identify the parts being transferred, the location to which they are transferred, and the time of transfer (see Figure 13-6).

Role of the accountant

The accountant must ensure that the AIS collects and reports costs in a manner consistent with the production planning techniques of the company. This may require making changes to the AIS when new planning techniques are adopted. For example, AOE is thinking about adopting the JIT approach to manufacturing. JIT manufacturing emphasizes working in teams and seeks to maximize the efficiency and synergy of all teams involved in making a particular product. Consequently, Elizabeth Venko realizes that collecting and reporting labor variances at the individual or team level may create dysfunctional incentives to maximize local performance at the expense of plant-wide performance. Therefore, she plans to redesign AOE's AIS so that it collects and reports costs in a manner that highlights the joint contributions of all teams that make a particular product.

Accountants also can help a company choose whether MRP-II or JIT is more appropriate for planning and scheduling its production. If demand for a company's product is predictable and the product has a long life cycle, then an MRP-II approach may be justified. On the other hand, a JIT approach may be more appropriate if a company's products are characterized by short life cycles, unpredictable demand, and frequent markdowns of excess inventory. Thus, the accountant should design the AIS to provide this kind of detailed information about product sales.

Table 13-1   Example of "Exploding" a Bill of Materials

Step 1: Multiply the component requirements for ONE product by the number of products to be produced next period (from the MPS).

Components in Each VCR

Part No.	Description	Quantity	Number of VCRs	Total Requirements
105	Control Unit	1	2,000	2,000
125	Back Panel	1	2,000	2,000
148	Side Panel	4	2,000	8,000
173	Timer	1	2,000	2,000
195	Front Panel	1	2,000	2,000
199	Screw	6	2,000	12,000

Components in Each CD Player

Part No.	Description	Quantity	Number of CD Players	Total Requirements
103	Control Unit	1	3,000	3,000
120	Front Panel	1	3,000	3,000
121	Back Panel	1	3,000	3,000
173	Timer	1	3,000	3,000
190	Side Panel	4	3,000	12,000
199	Screw	4	3,000	12,000

Step 2: Calculate total component requirements by summing products.

Part No.	VCR	CD Player	Total
103	0	3,000	3,000
105	2,000	0	2,000
120	0	3,000	3,000
121	0	3,000	3,000
125	2,000	0	2,000
148	8,000	0	8,000
173	2,000	3,000	5,000
190	0	12,000	12,000
195	2,000	0	2,000
199	12,000	12,000	24,000

Step 3: Repeat steps 1 and 2 for each week during planning horizon.

Part No.	Week 1	Week 2	Week 3	Week 4	Week 5	Week 6
103	3,000	2,000	2,500	3,000	2,500	3,000
105	2,000	2,000	2,500	2,500	2,000	3,000
120	3,000	2,000	2,500	3,000	2,500	3,000
121	3,000	2,000	2,500	3,000	2,500	3,000
125	2,000	2,000	2,500	2,500	2,000	3,000
148	8,000	8,000	10,000	10,000	8,000	12,000
173	5,000	4,000	5,000	5,500	4,500	6,000
190	12,000	12,000	10,000	12,000	10,000	12,000
195	2,000	2,000	2,500	2,500	2,000	3,000
199	24,000	20,000	25,000	27,000	22,000	30,000

					4587
		Alpha Omega Engineering			
		PRODUCTION ORDER			

Order No. 2289	Product No. 4430	Description: Cabinet Side Panel		Production Quantity 1000	
Approved by: *PJS*	Release Date: 02/24/2003	Issue Date: 02/25/2003	Completion Date: 03/09/2003	Deliver to: Assembly Department	

Work Station No.	Product Operation No.	Quantity	Operation Description	Start Date & Time		Finish Date & Time	
MH25	100	1,003	Transfer from stock	02/28	0700	02/28	0800
ML15-12	105	1,003	Cut to shape	02/28	0800	02/28	1000
ML15-9	106	1,002	Corner cut	02/28	1030	02/28	1200
S28-17	124	1,002	Turn & shape	02/28	1300	02/28	1700
F54-5	142	1,001	Finish	03/01	0800	03/01	1100
P89-1	155	1,001	Paint	03/01	1300	03/02	1300
QC94	194	1,001	Inspect	03/02	1400	03/02	1600
MH25	101	1,000	Transfer to assembly	03/02	1600	03/02	1700

Explanation of numbers in Quantity column:

1. *Total of 1,003 sheets of raw material used to produce 1,000 good panels and 3 rejected panels.*
2. *One panel not cut to proper shape, thus only 1,002 units had operations 106 and 124 performed on them.*
3. *One panel not properly turned and shaped; hence only 1,001 panels finished, painted, and received final inspection.*
4. *One panel rejected during final inspection; thus only 1,000 good panels transferred to assembly department.*

Figure 13-4   Sample production order for AOE

Production Operations

The third step in the production cycle is the actual manufacture of products (circle 3.0 in Figure 13-2). The manner in which this activity is accomplished varies greatly across companies, differing according to the type of product being manufactured and the degree of automation used in the production process.

Using various forms of IT in the production process, such as robots and computer-controlled machinery, is referred to as **computer-integrated manufacturing (CIM).** CIM can significantly reduce production costs. For example, Northrop Corporation once had 16,000 sheets of paper containing shop-floor work instructions related to the manufacture of plane fuselages. When on-line terminals were installed at each assembly station, the elimination in paper flow and improved efficiency reduced costs by 30 percent.

Accountants are not required to be experts on every facet of CIM, but they must understand how it affects the AIS. One effect of CIM is a shift from mass production to custom order manufacturing. For example, every Northrop Grumman product is

MATERIALS REQUISITION

No. 2345

Issued To: Assembly	Issue Date: 08/15/2003		Production Order Number: 62913	

Part Number	Description	Quantity	Unit Cost $	Total Cost $
115	Calculator Unit	2,000	2.95	5,900.00
135	Lower Casing	2,000	.45	900.00
198	Screw	16,000	.02	320.00
178	Battery	2,000	.75	1,500.00
136	Upper Casing	2,000	.80	1,600.00
199	Screw	12,000	.02	240.00
Issued by: **AKL**				10,460.00
Received by: *GWS*		Costed by: *ZBD*		

Note: Cost information is entered when the materials requisition is turned in to the cost accounting department.
Other information, except for signatures, is printed by the system when the document is prepared.

Figure 13-5 Sample materials requisition for AOE

Figure 13-6 Sample move ticket for AOE

MOVE TICKET

No. 8753

Production Order Number:	2345	Date Transferred:		08/18/2003
From: Assembly	*KLS*	To: Finishing	*NRC*	
Operation to Perform		Completed	Date	Time
Clean		___X___	08/19/2003	0900
Polish		_____		
Package		_____		
Comments:				

assembled to order. Each product, however, can use any of about 256,000 separate components. Thus, to minimize inventory carrying costs, Northrop's AIS must maintain accurate perpetual inventory records. Its AIS also must have the ability to integrate sales orders with the production system and track the status of all orders. Thus, its AIS must fully integrate information from the revenue, expenditure, and production cycles. ERP systems provide such integration.

Although both the nature of the production process and the extent of CIM vary across companies, every firm requires data about the following four facets of its production operations: raw materials used, labor hours expended, machine operations performed, and other manufacturing overhead costs incurred. In the next section, we discuss the methods used to collect and process this information.

Cost Accounting

The final step in the production cycle is cost accounting (circle 4.0 in Figure 13-2). The three principal objectives of the cost accounting system are (1) to provide information for planning, controlling, and evaluating the performance of production operations; (2) to provide accurate cost data about products for use in pricing and product mix decisions; and (3) to collect and process the information used to calculate the inventory and cost of goods sold values that appear in the company's financial statements.

To successfully accomplish the first objective, as Focus 13-1 explains, the AIS must be designed to collect real-time data about the performance of production activities so that management can make timely decisions. To accomplish the other two objectives, the AIS must collect costs by various categories and then assign those costs to specific products and organizational units. This requires careful coding of cost data during collection, because often the same costs may be allocated in multiple ways, for several different purposes. For example, factory supervisory costs may be assigned to departments for performance evaluation purposes, but to specific products for pricing and product mix decisions.

Types of cost accounting systems

Most companies use either job-order or process costing to assign production costs. **Job-order costing** assigns costs to specific production batches, or jobs, and is used when the product or service being sold consists of discretely identifiable items. For example, construction companies use job-order costing for each house being built. Similarly, public accounting and law firms use job-order costing to account for the costs of individual audits or cases, respectively. AOE currently uses job-order costing.

In contrast, **process costing** assigns costs to each process, or work center, in the production cycle, then calculates the average cost for all units produced. Process costing is used when similar goods or services are produced in mass quantities and discrete units cannot be readily identified. For example, breweries accumulate the costs associated with the various processes (e.g., mashing, primary fermentation, filtering, bottling) in producing a batch of a particular kind of beer, and then compute the average total unit cost for that product. Similarly, mutual funds accumulate the costs associated with handling customer deposits and withdrawals, and then compute the per-unit costs of those transactions.

Focus 13-1

The Importance of Real-Time Production Information

In the late 1990s, many companies successfully integrated the Internet into their revenue and expenditure cycles. Now it is time to do the same for the production cycle. Management requires real-time information about the status of production cycle activities. Access to such information is key to being able to determine immediately if it is possible to fill a new customer order profitably and to make accurate delivery commitments.

Much new production machinery is now Internet compatible. Consequently, manufacturing execution systems (MESs) and paperless shop-floor control (SFC) systems can provide real-time access to data about production cycle activities. Access to such information can provide benefits in the areas of preventive maintenance, product recall, and inventory management.

Internet communication capabilities embedded in new production machinery enable devices to proactively communicate via Internet technology, thereby reducing downtime and improving the flow of goods through the production process. For example, Schneider Electric's Square D–brand circuit breakers alert operators that a breaker is approaching the time when it will fail. But such "smart" devices can do much more than merely signal an alarm. Built-in Internet capabilities mean that the device can automatically send e-mail requests to the manufacturer or maintenance provider to schedule service. Moreover, the service provider can use the Internet communication capabilities to monitor the device remotely, diagnosing the problem and thereby ensuring that the technician arrives with the proper parts to service the machine.

The productivity improvements made possible by such improved maintenance are tremendous. It is estimated that manufacturing plants are shut down due to machinery breakdowns almost 10 percent of the time. For chip manufacturing plants, the estimates are as high as 30 percent downtime.

Real-time detailed data about production activities can also save manufacturers money should there be a need to recall products. The key is to accurately identify which batches of products were affected by the factor underlying the recall. Hudson Foods could have benefited from access to such information. In 1996, it discovered that a batch of hamburger patties shipped from a Nebraska packing plant was contaminated. Because Hudson Food's production cycle information system could not provide timely data about which other shipments might also have included some of the potentially tainted beef, the government forced Hudson Foods to recall 25 million pounds of meat nationwide. Hudson Foods later sold its meat plant, and its remaining operations were eventually taken over by Tyson Foods.

As a result of streamlining revenue and expenditure cycle activities, access to real-time production data reduces inventories. Management requires accurate and timely information about the batches currently in production, particularly about how much raw material is being used and how much is required to complete current production. Without such information, companies often find that even though they have adopted JIT purchasing, inventories are not significantly reduced because they are still being stockpiled at various places in the production process.

Sources: John Teresko, "The Dawn of E-Manufacturing," *IndustryWeek* (October 2, 2000); Michelle Celarier and Roy Harris, "Plucking More Profit from Production: Automated Programs Try to Fill the Gaps ERP Systems Leave on the Shop Floor," *CFO Magazine* (January 1999); Phil Davis, "The Paperless Plant," *Midrange ERP* (April 1999); and Doug Bartholomew, "MES Revisted: Supply-Chain Demands Finally Push Plant-floor Systems to Center Stage," *IndustryWeek* (March 18, 1998).

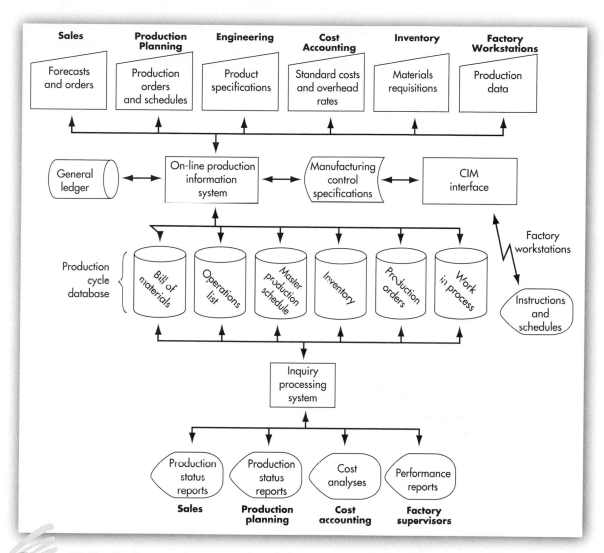

Figure 13-7 On-line production cycle information system

Information processing

Figure 13-7 depicts a typical on-line AIS for the production cycle, as used at AOE. Engineering department specifications for new products result in the creation of new records in both the bill of materials and operations list files. To develop those specifications, engineering accesses both files to examine the design of similar products. It also accesses the general ledger and inventory files for information about the costs of alternative product designs. The sales department enters sales forecasts and customer special order information. The production planning department uses that information and data about current inventory levels to develop the master production schedule.

New records are then added to the production order file to authorize the production of specific goods. At the same time, new records are added to the work-in-process file to accumulate cost data. The list of operations to be performed is displayed at the appropriate workstation. Corresponding instructions also are sent to the CIM interface to guide the operation of computerized machinery and robots. Finally, materials requisitions are sent to the inventory stores department to authorize the release of raw materials to production.

The system shown in Figure 13-7 could be used to implement either a job-order or process costing system. Both systems require accumulating data about four basic kinds of costs: raw materials, direct labor, machinery and equipment, and manufacturing overhead. The choice of job-order or process costing affects only the method used to assign those costs to products, not the methods used for data collection. Let us now examine how these four categories of cost data are collected.

Raw Materials   When production is initiated, the issuance of a materials requisition triggers a debit to work in process for the raw materials sent to production. If additional materials are needed, another debit is made to work in process. Conversely, work in process is credited for any materials not used and returned to inventory. Most raw materials are bar coded so that usage data can be collected by scanning the products when released from, or returned to, inventory. Inventory clerks use on-line terminals to enter usage data for those items that are not bar coded.

Direct Labor   In the past, AOE used a paper document called a **job-time ticket** to collect data about labor activity. This document recorded the amount of time a worker spent on each specific job task. Now, as shown in Figure 13-7, workers enter this data using on-line terminals at each factory workstation. To improve the efficiency of this process, AOE is considering switching to coded identification cards, which workers would run through a badge reader or bar code scanner when they start and finish any task. The time savings associated with using bar coding to automate data collection can be significant. For example, Consolidated Diesel Company, a joint venture between Cummins Engine Company and J.I. Case, found using bar code scanners to capture data about materials usage and labor operations saved about 12 seconds per workstation, resulting in a permanent 15 percent increase in productivity.

Machinery and Equipment   As companies implement CIM to automate the production process, an ever larger proportion of product costs relate to the machinery and equipment used to make that product. Data about machinery and equipment usage are collected at each step in the production process, often in conjunction with data about labor costs. For example, when workers record their activities at a particular workstation, the system can also record information identifying the machinery and equipment used and the duration of such use.

Manufacturing Overhead   Manufacturing costs that are not economically feasible to trace directly to specific jobs or processes are considered **manufacturing overhead.** Examples include the costs of water, power, and other utilities; miscellaneous supplies; rent, insurance, and property taxes for the factory plant; and the salaries of factory supervisors. Most of these costs are collected by the expenditure cycle information system (see Chapter 12), with the exception of supervisory salaries, which are processed by the human resources cycle information system (see Chapter 14).

Accountants can play a key role in controlling overhead costs by carefully assessing how changes in product mix affect total manufacturing overhead. They should go beyond merely collecting such data, however, and identify the underlying factors that drive the changes in total costs. This information then can be used to adjust production plans and factory layout.

Accounting for fixed assets

Thus far, we have focused on accounting for the costs associated with the production of inventory. The AIS also collects and processes information about the property, plant, and equipment used in the production cycle. Indeed, such fixed assets represent a significant portion of total assets for many companies, and so it is important to monitor this investment.

Fixed assets should be bar coded to enable quick and accurate periodic updating of the fixed asset database. At a minimum, every organization should maintain the following information about each of its fixed assets: identifying number, serial number, location, cost, date of acquisition, vendor name and address, expected life, expected salvage value, depreciation method, depreciation charges to date, improvements, and maintenance services performed.

Companies must carefully monitor investments in machinery, plants, and property as well as the disposition of such assets. The next section discusses the necessary controls to monitor such transactions and all other production cycle activities.

CONTROL OBJECTIVES, THREATS, AND PROCEDURES

A second function of a well-designed AIS is to provide adequate controls, to meet the following production cycle objectives:

1. All production and fixed asset acquisitions are properly authorized.
2. Work-in-process inventories and fixed assets are safeguarded.
3. All valid, authorized production cycle transactions are recorded.
4. All production cycle transactions are recorded accurately.
5. Accurate records are maintained and protected from loss.
6. Production cycle activities are performed efficiently and effectively.

The documents and records described in the previous section play an important role in achieving these objectives. Simple, easy-to-complete documents with clear instructions facilitate the accurate and efficient recording of transaction data. Including appropriate application controls, such as validity checks and field (format) checks, further increases the accuracy of data entry when using electronic documents. Providing space on paper and electronic documents to record who completed and who reviewed the form creates evidence that the transaction was properly authorized. Prenumbering all documents facilitates checking that all transactions have been recorded. Restricting access to programs that create documents and, if paper documents are still used, to blank documents, reduces the risk of unauthorized transactions.

Table 13-2 lists the major threats and exposures in the production cycle and the additional control procedures, besides adequate documents and records, which should be in place to mitigate them. As you will see in the following discussion, every company, regardless of its line of business, faces these threats. Therefore, it is important to understand how the AIS can be designed to counter them.

Table 13-2   Threats and Controls in the Production Cycle

Process/Activity	Threat	Applicable Control Procedures
Product design	1. Poor product design	Improved information about the effects of product design on costs Detailed data about warranty and repair costs
Planning and scheduling	2. Overproduction or underproduction	Better production planning systems
	3. Suboptimal investment in fixed assets	Review and approval of fixed asset acquisitions; budgetary controls
Production operations	4. Theft or destruction of inventories and fixed assets	Restrict physical access to inventories and fixed assets Document all movements of inventory through the production process Identification of all fixed assets Periodic physical counts of inventory and fixed assets Proper documentation and review of all transactions involving disposal of fixed assets Adequate insurance
Cost accounting	5. Recording and posting errors resulting in inaccurate cost data	Data entry edit controls; use of bar code scanning where feasible; reconciliation of recorded amounts with periodic physical counts
General threats	6. Loss of data	Backup and disaster recovery planning; restricting access to cost data
	7. Poor performance	Improved and timelier reporting

Product Design

Poor product design drives up costs in several ways. Using too many unique components when producing similar products increases the costs associated with purchasing and maintaining raw materials inventories. It also often results in inefficient production processes because of excessive complexity in changing from the production of one product to another. Poorly designed products are more likely to incur warranty and repair costs.

Product design can be improved with accurate data about the relationship between components and finished goods. For example, automobile manufacturers have realized significant cost savings by increasing the number of common components within and across product lines. Analysis of warranty and repair costs can identify the primary causes of product failure. That information can then be used to redesign products to improve quality.

Planning and Scheduling

Two related threats in the planning and scheduling process are overproduction and underproduction. Overproduction can result in a supply of goods in excess of short-run demands, thereby creating potential cash flow problems because resources are tied up in inventory. Overproduction also increases the risk of carrying inventory that becomes obsolete. Conversely, underproduction can result in lost sales and customer dissatisfaction.

More accurate production planning can prevent over- and underproduction. Improvement requires accurate and current sales forecasts and data about inventory stocks, information that the revenue and expenditure cycle systems can provide. In addition, information about production performance, particularly concerning trends in total time to manufacture each product, should be regularly collected. These data sources should be used periodically to review and adjust the master production schedule.

The risks of over- and underproduction, however, are higher for new innovative products, such as fashion clothing, than for staples and commodities, such as many food items, because it is inherently more difficult to accurately estimate demand for the former. Therefore, companies that produce new and innovative products must invest in flexible supply chains to quickly increase or decrease production in response to realized demand.

Proper approval and authorization of production orders is another control to prevent overproduction of specific items. One means is to restrict access to the production scheduling program using passwords and an access control matrix. It is also important to ensure that the correct production orders are released. Closed-loop verification can accomplish this control: The production planner enters the product number and the system retrieves the description, order quantity, and other relevant data, and requests the user to verify that the correct production order is being released.

Another threat is the unauthorized acquisition of fixed assets, which can result in overinvestment and reduced profitability. The procedures involved in authorizing the purchase of fixed assets vary, depending on the size of the purchase request. A supervisor or manager, who provides details about expected cash flows and other costs and benefits of the proposed expenditure, should first recommend large capital expenditures. All such recommendations should be reviewed by a senior executive or by an executive committee, and the various projects ranked by priority. Smaller capital expenditures (e.g., those costing $10,000 or less) usually can be purchased directly out of departmental budgets, which avoids a formal approval process. Holding managers accountable for their department's return on the fixed assets provides additional incentive to control such expenditures.

Due to the size of fixed asset purchases, companies should invite several competing suppliers to provide bids. A document called a **request for proposal (RFP),** which specifies the desired properties of the asset, is sent to each vendor. The capital investments committee should review the responses and select the best bid.

Once a supplier has been selected, the acquisition of the asset may be handled through the regular expenditure cycle process, as described in Chapter 12. Specifically, a formal purchase order is prepared, receipt of the asset is formally documented using a receiving report, and a disbursement voucher is used to authorize payment to the supplier. The same set of processing controls and edit checks employed for other purchases also should be used for fixed asset acquisitions (for details, refer back to the discussion in Chapter 12).

Production Operations

Theft of inventories and fixed assets is a major threat to manufacturing companies. In addition to the loss of assets, thefts also result in overstated asset balances, which can lead to erroneous analyses of financial performance and, in the case of inventory, underproduction.

To reduce the risk of inventory loss, physical access to inventories should be restricted and all internal movements of inventory should be documented. Thus, materials requisitions should be used to authorize the release of raw materials to production. Both the inventory control clerk and the production employee receiving the raw materials should sign the requisition to acknowledge release of the goods to production. Requests for additional materials in excess of the amounts specified in the bill of materials should be documented and authorized by supervisory personnel. Move tickets should be used to document subsequent movement of inventory through various stages of the production process. The return of any materials not used in production also should be documented.

Proper segregation of duties is important to safeguard inventory. Maintaining physical custody of the raw materials and finished goods inventories is the responsibility of the inventory stores department. Department or factory supervisors have primary responsibility for work-in-process inventories. The authorization function, represented by the preparation of production orders, materials requisitions, and move tickets, is the responsibility of the production planners or, increasingly, of the production information system itself. Bar code scanners and on-line terminals are used to record movement of inventory, thereby maintaining accurate perpetual inventory records. Consequently, proper access controls and compatibility tests are important to ensure that only authorized personnel have access to those records. Finally, an employee without any custodial responsibility should periodically count inventory on hand. Any discrepancies between these physical counts and recorded amounts should be investigated.

Similar controls are needed to safeguard fixed assets. As explained earlier, all fixed assets must be identified and recorded. Managers should be assigned responsibility and accountability for fixed assets under their control. Security measures should be in place to control physical access to fixed assets. Disposal of fixed assessts should be properly authorized and documented. A report of all fixed asset transactions should be printed periodically and sent to the controller, who should verify that each transaction was properly authorized and executed.

Finally, inventories and fixed assets also are subject to loss due to fire or other disasters. Therefore, adequate insurance should be maintained to cover such losses and provide for replacement of those assets.

Cost Accounting

Inaccurate recording and processing of production activity data can diminish the effectiveness of production scheduling and undermine management's ability to monitor and control manufacturing operations. For example, inaccurate cost data can result in inappropriate decisions about which products to make and how to set current selling prices. Errors in inventory records can lead to either over- or underproduction of goods. Inaccuracies in financial statements and managerial reports can distort analyses of past performance and the desirability of future investments or changes in operations.

The best control procedure to ensure that data entry is accurate is to automate data collection using bar code scanners, badge readers, and other devices. When this is not feasible, on-line terminals should be used for data entry. Passwords and user IDs should be used to restrict access to authorized employees. In addition, an access control matrix should be used to limit access to only those portions of the database that a particular employee needs to perform a given job. Check digits and closed-loop verification should be used to ensure that information about the raw materials used, operations performed, and employee number are entered correctly. Validity checks, such as comparing raw materials part numbers to those listed in the bill of materials file, provide further assurance. Finally, to verify the accuracy of database records, periodic physical counts of inventories should be made and compared with recorded quantities.

As with inventory, periodic inspections and counts of all fixed assets should be made, and those figures should be reconciled to recorded amounts. Overstated fixed assets increase expenses through extra depreciation and higher property taxes. Understated fixed assets also can cause problems; for example, inaccurate counts of the number of personal computers in use can cause a company to unknowingly violate software license requirements.

General Threats

As in the other cycles, two general threats in the production cycle are loss of data and poor performance. Loss of production data hinders the monitoring of inventory and fixed assets and makes it difficult to ensure that manufacturing activities are being performed efficiently and effectively. Therefore, inventory and work-in-process records must be protected from both intentional and accidental loss or damage. Regular backing up of all data files is imperative. Additional copies of key master files, such as open production orders and raw materials inventory, should be stored off-site. To reduce the possibility of accidental erasure of important files, all disks and tapes should have both external and internal file labels.

Access controls also are important, because the loss of production trade secrets can destroy a company. For example, a customer of Recon Optical in Barrington, Illinois, obtained access to the company's production database, stole the company's trade secrets, and used that information to compete with Recon. As a result, Recon Optical was forced to lay off 800 of its 1,000 employees. Although companies that are victimized in this manner can sue the perpetrator, any financial compensation may come too late to restore the business.

Unauthorized access also increases the risk of damage to important data files. Using a system of passwords and user IDs can limit access to sensitive files. Moreover, access controls also should apply to terminals. For example, the system should be programmed to reject any attempts to alter inventory records from a terminal located in the engineering department. Finally, logs of all activities, especially any actions involving managerial approval, such as requests for additional raw materials or overtime, should be recorded and maintained for later review as part of the audit trail.

Inefficiencies in production operations result in increased expenses. Quality control problems also increase expenses and may even reduce future sales. Thus, manufacturing activities must be closely monitored and prompt action taken to correct any deviations from standards. The AIS can help control efficiency and quality by preparing appropriate performance reports. In addition to traditional comparisons of actual to budgeted performance, the AIS should produce measures of throughput and quality control.

Throughput: A measure of production effectiveness

Throughput represents the number of good units produced in a given period of time. It consists of three factors, each of which can be separately controlled, as shown in the following formula:[1]

$$\text{Throughput} = (\text{total units produced}/\text{processing time}) \times$$
$$(\text{processing time}/\text{total time}) \times$$
$$(\text{good units}/\text{total units})$$

Productive capacity, the first term in the formula, shows the maximum number of units that can be produced using current technology. Productive capacity can be increased by improving labor or machine efficiency, by rearranging the factory floor layout to expedite the movement of materials, or by simplifying product design specifications.

Productive processing time, the second term in the formula, indicates the percentage of total production time used to manufacture the product. Productive processing time can be improved by improving maintenance to reduce machine downtime or by more efficient scheduling of material and supply deliveries to reduce wait time.

Yield, the third term in the formula, represents the percentage of good (nondefective) units produced. Using better-quality raw materials or improving worker skills can improve yield.

Information about quality control

Information about quality costs can help companies determine the effects of actions taken to improve yield and identify areas for further improvement. Quality control costs can be divided into four areas:

1. *Prevention costs* are associated with changes to production processes designed to reduce the product defect rate.
2. *Inspection costs* are associated with testing to ensure that products meet quality standards.
3. *Internal failure costs* are associated with reworking, or scrapping, products identified as being defective prior to sale.
4. *External failure costs* result when defective products are sold to customers. They include such costs as product liability claims, warranty and repair expenses, loss of customer satisfaction, and damage to the company's reputation.

The ultimate objective of quality control is to minimize the sum of these four types of costs. This objective recognizes the fact that there are trade-offs between cate-

---

[1] This formula was developed by Carole Cheatham in "Measuring and Improving Throughput," *Journal of Accountancy* (March 1990): 89–91.

gories. For example, increasing prevention costs can lower inspection costs as well as internal and external failure costs. The experiences of Lockheed Martin at its Pike County plant in Troy, Alabama, illustrate the potential benefits of increased attention to quality. Factory workers at the plant are organized in teams. Team members continuously monitor a number of quality measures and discuss ways to save time and money. Each new step in the manufacturing process begins by verifying the quality of the previous step. In this way, any quality problems are immediately brought to the attention of the person who made the mistake. Both people then work together to fix the problem, thereby teaching each other how to do their jobs better. Management credits such procedures with cutting the defect rate by 82 percent so that defects now occur only 0.0003 times per million operations. The bottom-line effect of such quality is that the plant has never had a customer reject a single shipped product.

Elizabeth Venko agreed with LeRoy Williams that AOE production managers should receive both throughput and cost-of-quality reports. She also discussed with him the behavioral effects of performance reporting. For example, measuring total production may encourage the buildup of inventories. Similarly, reimbursing departments for scrap and rework may be less effective in promoting quality control efforts than measuring and rewarding departments based on yield. Because of this discussion, LeRoy realizes that he will probably need to closely monitor the effects of any new performance reports and make appropriate modifications to them.

PRODUCTION CYCLE INFORMATION NEEDS AND DATA MODEL

A third function of the AIS is to provide information useful for decision making. In the production cycle, internal and external users need cost information. Internally, management uses information about costs to make decisions about product pricing and product mix, as well as to evaluate performance. Externally, costs must be properly matched with revenues when preparing financial statements. Traditionally, most cost accounting systems have been designed primarily to meet financial reporting requirements and have given only secondary attention to meeting production management's needs. Consequently, in recent years, traditional cost systems have been criticized for not providing adequate information to manage production operations in a modern manufacturing environment. The two major criticisms of traditional cost accounting systems are reflected in the issues raised in the chapter opening case for AOE: Overhead costs are inappropriately allocated to products, and performance measures do not accurately reflect the effects of factory automation.

Criticism 1: Inappropriate Allocation of Overhead Costs

Traditional cost systems use volume-driven bases, such as direct labor or machine hours, to apply overhead to products. Many overhead costs, however, do not vary directly with production volume. Purchasing costs, for example, vary with the number of purchase orders processed. Similarly, receiving costs vary with the number of shipments from suppliers. Setup and materials handling costs vary with the number of different batches that are run, not with the total number of units produced. Thus, allocating these types of overhead costs to products based on output volume overstates the costs of products manufactured in large quantities. It also understates the costs of products manufactured in small batches.

In addition, allocating overhead based on direct labor input can distort costs across products. As investments in factory automation increase, the amount of direct labor used in production decreases. Consequently, the amount of overhead charged per unit of labor increases dramatically. As a result, small differences in the amount of labor used to produce two products can result in significant differences in product costs.

Solution to Criticism 1: Activity-Based Costing

Activity-based costing[2] **(ABC)** can refine and improve cost allocations under both job-order and process cost systems. It attempts to trace costs to the activities that create them, such as grinding or polishing, and only subsequently allocates those costs to products or departments. An underlying objective of activity-based costing is to link costs to corporate strategy. Corporate strategy results in decisions about what goods and services to produce. Activities must be performed to produce these goods and services, which in turn incur costs. Thus, corporate strategy determines costs. Consequently, by measuring the costs of basic activities, such as materials handling or processing purchase orders, ABC provides information to management for evaluating the consequences of strategic decisions.

Activity-based costing versus traditional cost systems

Following are three significant differences between ABC and traditional approaches to product costing:

1. ABC systems attempt to directly trace a larger proportion of overhead costs to products. Advances in IT make this feasible. For example, bar coding facilitates tracking miscellaneous parts used in each product or process stage. When implementing ABC systems, accountants observe production operations and interview factory workers and supervisors to obtain a better understanding of how costs relate to production.

2. ABC systems use a greater number of cost pools to accumulate indirect costs (manufacturing overhead). Whereas most traditional cost systems lump all overhead costs together, ABC systems distinguish three separate categories of overhead:

   - *Batch-related overhead.* Examples include setup costs, inspections, and materials handling. ABC systems accumulate these costs for a batch and then allocate them to the units produced in that batch. Thus, products produced in large quantities have lower batch-related overhead costs per unit than products produced in small quantities.

   - *Product-related overhead.* These costs are related to the diversity of the company's product line. Examples include research and development, expediting, shipping and receiving, environmental regulations, and purchasing. ABC systems try to link these costs to specific products when possible. For example, if a company produces three product lines, one of which generates hazardous waste, an ABC system would charge only that one set of products for all the costs of complying with environmental regulations. Other costs, such as purchasing raw materials, might be allocated across products based on the relative number of purchase orders required to make each product.

   - *Companywide overhead.* This category includes such costs as rent or depreciation. These costs apply to all products. Thus, ABC systems typically allocate them using departmental or plant rates.

---

[2]In this section, we provide an overview of activity-based costing, its effects on the AIS, and its benefits. For additional details on the mechanics of activity-based costing, see any cost accounting textbook.

3. ABC systems attempt to rationalize the allocation of overhead to products by identifying cost drivers. A **cost driver** is anything that has a cause-and-effect relationship on costs. For example, the number of purchase orders processed is one cost driver of purchasing department costs; that is, the total costs of processing purchase orders (e.g., purchasing department salaries, postage) vary directly with the number of purchase orders that are processed. As in this example, cost drivers in ABC systems are often nonfinancial variables. In contrast, traditional costing systems often use financial variables, such as dollar volume of purchases, as the bases for allocating manufacturing overhead.

Benefits of ABC systems

ABC systems cost more to run than traditional cost systems because they require the collection of more production-related data and in greater detail. ABC systems are also more complex, in part because more bases are used to allocate manufacturing overhead. Proponents of ABC systems argue that the increased costs and complexity provide two important benefits: More accurate cost data result in better product mix and pricing decisions, and more detailed cost data improve management's ability to control and manage total costs.

Better Decisions   Traditional cost systems tend to apply too much overhead to some products and too little to others, because too few cost pools are used. This leads to two types of problems, both of which AOE experienced. First, companies may accept sales contracts for some products at prices below their true cost of production. Consequently, although sales increase, profits decline. Second, companies may overprice other products, thereby inviting new competitors to enter the market. Ironically, if more accurate cost data were available, companies would find that they could cut prices to keep competitors out of the market and still make a profit on each sale. ABC systems avoid these problems because overhead is divided into three categories and applied using cost drivers that are causally related to production. Therefore, product cost data are more accurate.

ABC also uses data to improve product design. For example, the costs associated with processing purchase orders can be used to calculate the purchasing-related overhead associated with each component used in a finished product. Engineering can use this information, along with data on relative usage of components across products, to identify unique components that could be replaced by lower cost, more commonly used parts.

Finally, ABC data improve managerial decision making by providing information about the costs associated with specific activities, instead of classifying those costs by financial statement category. Table 13-3 shows an example of how this rearrangement of data can improve managerial analysis by focusing attention on key processes.

Improved Cost Management   Proponents argue that another advantage of ABC is that it clearly measures the results of managerial actions on overall profitability. Whereas traditional cost systems only measure spending to acquire resources, ABC systems measure both the amount spent to acquire resources and the consumption of those resources. This distinction is reflected in the following formula:

$$\text{Cost of activity capability} = \text{Cost of activity used} + \text{Cost of unused capacity}$$

To illustrate, consider the receiving function at a manufacturing firm such as AOE. The total monthly employee cost in the receiving department, including salaries and benefits, represents the cost of providing this function—receiving shipments from suppliers. Assume that the salary expense of the receiving department is $100,000, and

Table 13-3   Comparison of Activity-Based Costing and Traditional Cost Allocation for the Information Systems Department

Traditional Cost Reports, based on General Ledger Account Categories			
	Budget	**Actual**	**Variance**
Salaries	$386,000	$375,000	($11,000)
Computer hardware	845,000	855,000	10,000
Travel	124,000	150,000	26,000
Supplies	25,000	20,000	(5,000)
Total	**$1,380,000**	**$1,400,000**	**$20,000**
Activity-Based Costing Analysis			
	Budget	**Actual**	**Variance**
Systems analysis	$200,000	$210,000	$10,000
Coding	440,000	400,000	(40,000)
Testing	235,000	250,000	15,000
Maintenance	250,000	275,000	25,000
User support	90,000	50,000	(40,000)
Reports	87,000	75,000	(12,000)
Training	78,000	140,000	62,000
Total	**$1,380,000**	**$1,400,000**	**$20,000**

assume that the number of employees is sufficient to handle 500 shipments. The cost per shipment would be $200. Finally, assume that 400 shipments are actually received. The ABC system would report that the cost of the receiving activity used is $80,000 ($200 × 400 shipments) and that the remaining $20,000 in salary expense represents the cost of unused capacity.

In this way, performance reports which ABC systems generate help direct managerial attention to how policy decisions made in one area affect costs in another area. For example, a purchasing department manager may decide to increase the minimum size of orders to obtain larger discounts for bulk purchases. This would reduce the number of incoming shipments that the receiving department must handle, thereby increasing its unused capacity. Similarly, actions taken to improve the efficiency of operations, such as requiring vendors to send products in bar coded containers, increase practical capacity and create additional unused capacity. In either case, ABC performance reports highlight this excess capacity for managerial attention. Management can then try to improve profitability by applying that unused capacity to other revenue-generating activities.

Criticism 2: Inaccurate Performance Measures

In the modern manufacturing environment, the focus must be on total quality management. Consequently, managers need information about how well the production process is functioning, including defect rates, breakdown frequency, percentage of finished goods completed without any rework, and percentage of defects discovered by customers. Although much of this information is collected in the production cycle information system, in traditional cost accounting systems it is not integrated with cost data. Therefore, operational performance measures are not directly linked with their financial consequences.

Indeed, in many companies the cost accounting system has been separate from the production operations information system. The former collects data about the costs of production, storing that information in the work-in-process file. The latter collects data about the physical aspects of manufacturing operations, storing that information in the open production order file. Both types of data are closely related, however, and both are needed for effectively managing the production process. For example, real-time information about production quality enables companies to spot and correct defects immediately, before additional labor and materials are used. Therefore, both cost and operational data should be integrated into one system. Indeed, ABC systems typically require both types of data, using operational data as the drivers to assign costs to products.

Solution to Criticism 2:
Integrated Production Cycle Data Model

Figure 13-8 is a data model for the production cycle of a manufacturing company such as AOE. Data are collected about four main events:

1. Issuance of raw materials
2. Use of labor in production
3. Use of machinery and equipment in production
4. Production of new finished products, represented by the work-in-process event

The REA diagram also includes three abstract entity types—the bill of materials, the job operations list, and the machine operations list—that we will explain shortly.

Reading the E-R diagram

To maximize its usefulness for cost management and decision making, production cycle data must be collected at the lowest possible level of aggregation. Therefore, the event entities depicted in Figure 13-8 do not correspond with the processes depicted in the level 0 DFD for the production cycle presented earlier. Rather, they represent the detailed activities that occur during the production operations stage (circle 3.0 in Figure 13-2).

Let us now examine Figure 13-8 more closely to see what it reveals about the nature of this production cycle. The abstract entity—bill of materials—is used to store information about the raw materials used to make a finished product. It includes data about the standard quantity of each raw material that should be used to make that product. Similarly, the abstract entities—job operations list and machine operations list—specify the labor and machine activities that are to be performed to manufacture each finished product. Both entities also store data about the standard time it should take to perform those operations.

Data about actual raw materials used in production is stored in the raw materials issuance entity. Similarly, information about the actual labor and machine operations performed, including the actual amount of time each activity took, are stored in the job operations and machine operations entities, respectively. Performance can be evaluated by comparing the data in these three event entities with the information

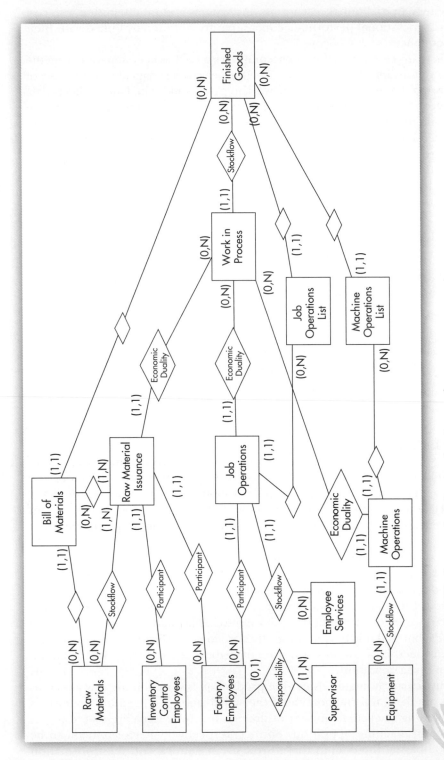

Figure 13-8 Partial REA diagram for the production cycle

Table 13-4   Partial REA Diagram for the Production Cycle

Table	Attributes (**primary key,** *foreign keys,* other attributes)
Raw materials*	**Item number,** description, quantity on hand, standard cost, ...
Employees	**Employee number,** name, date hired, wage rate, *supervisor number,* ...
Supervisor	**Employee number,** name, date hired, number of employees supervising, ...
Equipment	**Equipment ID,** description, cost, depreciation method, accumulated depreciation, salvage value, estimated life, ...
Bill of materials	**Bill of materials number,** *item number, finished goods number,* standard quantity needed, ...
Raw materials issuance	**Raw materials issuance number,** date, time, *factory employee number, inventory control employee number, WIP job number,* ...
Job operations	**Job operation number,** description, *performing employee, WIP job number, job operations list number,* start time, stop time, ...
Job operations list	**Job operations list number,** description, standard time, *finished good number,* ...
Machine operation	**Machine operation number,** description, start time, stop time, *WIP job number, machine operations list number, equipment ID,* ...
Machine operations list	**Machine operations list number,** description, standard time, *finished goods number,* ...
Employee services	**Service category number, pay period number,** total hours worked, total hours allocated, ...
Work in process	**WIP job number,** start date, start time, end date, end time, quantity ordered, quantity produced, date needed, production order number, *finished goods number,* ...
Finished goods*	**Product number,** description, quantity on hand, list price, ...
Raw materials— Raw materials issuances	**Item number, raw materials issuance number,** quantity issued
Bill of materials— Raw materials issuances	**Bill of materials number, raw materials issuance number**

Some companies may want to combine these two inventory tables into one table.

about standards that is stored in the abstract entities (bill of materials, job operations list, and machine operations list).

The work-in-process entity is used to collect and summarize data about the raw materials, labor, and machine operations used to produce a batch of goods. The relationships between work-in-process and those three event entities are all one-to-many, reflecting the fact that each production run may involve a number of raw materials issuances, labor operations, and machine operations. Each of those activities, however, is linked to a specific production run.

Figure 13-8 also depicts a many-to-one relationship between employees and supervisors. This reflects the fact that currently at AOE each employee is assigned to a specific supervisor. Each supervisor, however, is responsible for many employees. Were

AOE to change to a matrix style of organization, where each employee reports to several supervisors, the relationship between factory employees and supervisors would be modeled as being many-to-many.

The employee services entity is a resource—the time that employees are available for work. We discuss this entity in more detail in Chapter 14.

Finally, notice that Figure 13-8 differs from previous REA diagrams in that it shows only one agent associated with the job operations and machine operations events. These internal events differ from the other events discussed throughout this book in that they do not involve an exchange or transfer of resources. Instead, they represent the consumption or use of individual resources such as a specific employee's time or the use of a specific piece of equipment. Therefore, the event is linked to that agent (employee or piece of machinery) for which management wants to collect information for product costing and performance evaluation purposes.

Benefits of the data model

Examination of the table attributes for the data model depicted in Figure 13-8 shows that the data model effectively integrates both financial and nonfinancial measures of production cycle activities. Thus, the REA data model provides managers with access both to traditional financial cost data that can be used to evaluate performance and to operational data that can be used to plan changes in production methods. For example, management can easily track variances related to raw materials usage, labor activities, and machine operations. Analyses of the bill of materials entity can identify which components are used in only a few finished products. This information then can be used to explore possible design modifications that would use more common components. In addition, the data model depicted in Figure 13-8 supports activity-based costing because it captures performance and cost data by each cost driver (job operation, machine operation, and materials issuance).

Figure 13-9 shows another advantage of the REA data model: the ability to easily share data across the revenue, expenditure, production, and human resource management cycles. Thus, when a new customer order is received, the system can quickly check current inventory levels. If additional production is needed to fill the order, the data are immediately routed to the planning and scheduling module, and then labor needs can be determined. This information is shared with the human resource management system to identify any needs for hiring temporary help or scheduling overtime. At the same time, information in the bill of materials is used to identify raw materials needs; data are sent to the inventory control system, which compares it with current inventory levels, and, if necessary, initiates purchase orders for required items. Thus, well-designed data models facilitate the integration of a company's various information systems so that it can optimally respond to new customer orders.

The benefits of such coordination and information sharing can be dramatic. For example, Foxboro, a manufacturer of process controls and systems for oil and chemical refineries, cut its production cycle time from 16 weeks to 6 weeks after it implemented an integrated production cycle database. The new software enabled the design, engineering, purchasing, and manufacturing departments to share a wide range of data, including information about product specifications, the status of pur-

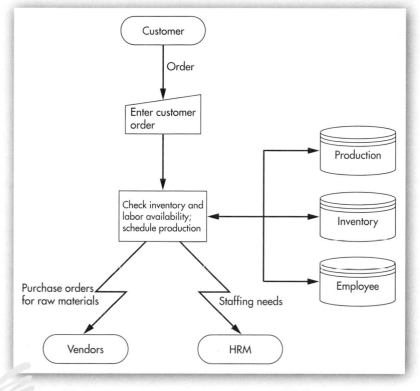

Figure 13-9 Enterprise resource planning (ERP) system for manufacturing

chase orders, and production schedules. With more accurate and timely information, unforeseen delays in production schedules were all but eliminated. It also was easier to adjust the production schedule in response to changes in customer requirements. Moreover, the reduction in cycle time not only improved customer satisfaction, but it also reduced work-in-process inventory levels by 76 percent.

Realizing these benefits, however, depends on the accuracy of the information in the data model, which means that, in a database environment, data entry edit and database update controls are extremely important. Indeed, accuracy, or the lack thereof, can be costly. For example, Elizabeth Venko recalled reading that Red Devil, a manufacturer of tools and supplies for the do-it-yourself home remodeler, routinely overstocked inventory because it did not trust the accuracy of its inventory figures. After implementing a new integrated database system that accurately tracked inventory, Red Devil was able to reduce its inventory by $2 million. Elizabeth wondered if improving the accuracy of AOE's production cycle database could yield similar savings.

SUMMARY AND CASE CONCLUSION

The production cycle consists of four basic activities: product design, production planning and scheduling, production operations, and cost accounting. Companies are continually investing in IT to improve the efficiency of the first three activities. However, for a business to reap the full benefit of these changes, corresponding modifications must be made to the cost accounting portion of the AIS.

Indeed, after completing her tour of the factory, Elizabeth Venko was convinced that some major changes were required in AOE's cost accounting system. For example, although AOE's production operations were highly automated, manufacturing overhead was still being allocated based on direct labor hours. This resulted in distorted product costs due to small differences in the amount of direct labor used to assemble each item. Elizabeth decided that the solution was to do more than merely change the allocation base. Instead, AOE would implement activity-based costing. A number of different pools would be used to accumulate overhead costs, and the appropriate cost drivers would be identified for use in assigning those costs to specific products. Based on her research, including conversations with a controller at another company that had recently implemented an ABC system, Elizabeth believed that these changes would solve AOE's problems with product pricing and mix decisions. In addition, reports prepared by the ABC system would more fairly represent factory supervisor actions.

Elizabeth also decided that two major changes were needed in the reports the AIS produced. First, data about all the costs associated with quality control, not just those involving rework and scrap, should be collected and reported. Second, performance reports should include both nonfinancial and financial measures.

Ann Brandt realized that both of these changes would necessitate a redesign of AOE's production cycle database. Based on her previous experience with redesigning AOE's revenue and expenditure cycle information systems, Ann felt that this could be accomplished best by developing a data model similar to the one depicted in Figure 13-8.

Elizabeth and Ann presented their plans at the next executive meeting. LeRoy Williams was satisfied that the changes would indeed address his complaints about AOE's current production cycle information system. Linda Spurgeon supported the proposal and agreed to fund the necessary changes. Peter Wu, vice president of human resources, was also impressed with Elizabeth and Ann's plans. In fact, he left the meeting resolved to secure their cooperation in helping him to revamp AOE's human resource management/payroll cycle information system.

KEY TERMS

- production cycle
- bill of materials
- operations list
- manufacturing resource planning (MRP-II)
- just-in-time (JIT) manufacturing
- master production schedule (MPS)

- production order
- materials requisition
- move tickets
- computer-integrated manufacturing
- (CIM)
- job-order costing

- request for proposal (RFP)
- process costing
- job-time ticket
- manufacturing overhead
- throughput
- activity-based costing (ABC)
- cost driver

CHAPTER QUIZ

1. Most costs are locked in at which stage in the production cycle?
   a. product design
   b. production planning
   c. production operations
   d. cost accounting

2. Which report or measure provides the most information about production efficiency?
   a. cost-of-quality report
   b. activity-based cost reports
   c. throughput
   d. MPS

3. Where is the list of all components, and their quantities, used to make a finished good found?
   a. operations list
   b. master production schedule
   c. bill of materials
   d. production order

4. Where is information about labor used in production captured?
   a. move ticket
   b. job-time ticket
   c. operations list
   d. bill of materials

5. In an REA data model, information about standard labor hours is stored in which entity?
   a. job operations
   b. job operations type
   c. work in process
   d. employee

6. Activity-based costing can be used to refine which of the following?
   a. job-order costing
   b. process costing
   c. both job-order and process costing
   d. neither job-order nor process costing

7. Which system is most likely to be used by a company that mass produces large batches of standard items in anticipation of customer demand?
   a. job-order costing
   b. standard costing
   c. activity-based costing
   d. process costing

8. The development of an MPS would be most effective in preventing which of the following threats?
   a. recording and posting errors
   b. loss of inventory
   c. production of poor-quality goods
   d. excess production

9. Which control procedure is probably least effective in reducing the threat of inventory loss?
   a. limiting physical access to inventory
   b. documenting all transfers of inventory within the company
   c. regular materials usage reports that highlight variances from standards
   d. periodically counting inventory and investigating any discrepancies between those counts and recorded amounts

10. What is the number of good units produced in a given period of time called?
   a. productive capacity
   b. productive processing time
   c. yield
   d. throughput

DISCUSSION QUESTIONS

13.1   When ABC reports indicate that excess capacity exists, management should either find alternative revenue-enhancing uses for that capacity or eliminate it through downsizing. What factors influence management's decision? What are the likely behavioral side effects of each choice? What implications do those side effects have for the long-run usefulness of ABC systems?

13.2   How might some financial reporting requirements mandated by GAAP, such as absorption accounting, lead to undesirable behaviors by line managers?

13.3   Some companies have eliminated the collection and reporting of detailed analyses on direct labor costs broken down by various activities. Instead, first-line supervisors are responsible for controlling the total costs of direct labor. The justification for this argument is that labor costs represent only a small fraction of the total costs of producing a product and are not worth the time and effort to trace to individual activities. Do you agree or disagree with this argument? Why?

13.4   Typically, McDonald's produces menu items in advance of customer orders based on anticipated demand. In contrast, Burger King produces menu items only in response to customer orders. Which system (MRP-II or JIT) does each company use? What are the relative advantages and disadvantages of each system?

13.5   Describe some of the trade-offs likely to arise when attempting to reduce the quality-control costs associated with prevention, inspection, internal failure, and external failure.

13.6   Products for which demand is predictable and relatively stable are called staples. Products for which demand is unpredictable and which have relatively short life cycles are referred to as innovative products. Identify examples of staples and innovative products and explain whether MRP-II or JIT manufacturing is appropriate for each type of product. What other implications does the type of product have on the value chain activities of inbound logistics, production, and outbound logistics?

13.7   One purported advantage of activity-based costing is it provides more accurate information about costs, thereby improving the product pricing decision. But can cost data really be used in pricing decisions? If the market ultimately determines prices, what is the benefit of more accurate information about costs?

PROBLEMS

13.1   Write a memo discussing the relationships and trade-offs between the concepts of accuracy, precision, and fairness in terms of allocating manufacturing overhead costs.

13.2   What internal control procedure(s) would best prevent or detect the following problems?
   a. A production order was initiated for a product that was already overstocked in the company's warehouse.
   b. A production employee stole items of work-in-process inventory.

   c. The "rush order" tag on a partially completed production job became detached from the materials and lost, resulting in a costly delay.
   d. A production employee prepared a materials requisition and used the document to steal $300 worth of parts from the raw materials storeroom.
   e. A production worker entering job time data on an on-line terminal mistakenly entered 3000 instead of 300 in the "quantity completed" field.
   f. A production worker entering job-time data on an on-line terminal mistakenly posted the completion of operation 562 to production order 7569 instead of production order 7596.
   g. A parts storeroom clerk issued parts in quantities 10 percent lower than those indicated on several materials requisitions and stole the excess quantities.
   h. A parts storeroom clerk stole electronics components and covered up the loss by submitting a form to the accounting department indicating that the missing parts were obsolete and should be written off as worthless.
   i. The quantity-on-hand balance for a key component shows a negative balance.
   j. Materials requisitions are used to authorize the release of the standard quantities of raw materials needed to manufacture a product. At times, production employees use fewer materials to finish the product and steal the remaining parts.
   k. A factory supervisor accesses the operations list file and inflates the standards for work completed in his department. Consequently, future performance reports show favorable budget variances for that department.

13.3 Refer to Figure 13-8 and Table 13-4 to answer the following questions:
   a. The job operations list entity stores information about the standard time it should take to perform a specific job operation. It also indicates whether this operation takes place at the unit, batch, or production run level. The work-in-process entity collects data by production runs. How would you calculate the labor time standards for each production run? How could the data model be modified to make this calculation easier?
   b. The diagram shows that information about the bill of materials is stored as an entity. Why not store that information as a many-to-many relationship between raw materials and finished goods?
   c. The relationship between employees and activities is one-to-many. Is any other type of relationship cardinality possible? If so, for which types of companies?
   d. Figure 13-8 reflects an MRP-II (produce-to-forecast) approach to production. Modify the REA diagram to reflect a JIT (make-to-order) approach to manufacturing.
   e. Modify the REA diagram to include information about equipment repairs and maintenance.
   f. Specify the set of on-line application controls that should be used to control updates to the assembly event table.
   g. Specify the access controls that should be designed into a system based on this data model. Specifically, which employees should be allowed to access each table, and what operations (read, write, update, delete) should they be permitted to perform?

13.4 You have been hired to design a production information system for a new company that will manufacture custom automobile wheels. List all the documents (paper and electronic) that should be included in the system and specify the purposes they serve.

13.5 You have recently been hired as the controller for a small manufacturing firm. One of your first tasks is to develop a report measuring throughput for each of the company's three production departments.
   Required
   Describe the data required and the most efficient and accurate method of collection.

13.6 Table 13-5 represents the first draft of a report on quality-control costs developed by one of your assistants.

Table 13-5   Quality Cost Report for Problem 13-6

	Quality Cost Report June 2003			
Cost Type	June 2003	June 2003	YTD 2003	YTD 2003
Prevention:				
QC Admin.	350	450	1,800	1,700
QC Services	400	550	2,100	2,200
Training	750	900	4,300	4,000
Work Safety	400	200	2,500	1,000
Total Prevent	1,900	2,100	10,700	8,900
Appraisal:				
Inspection	900	1,200	5,000	5,300
Analysis	600	800	4,000	4,900
Supplier	800	400	4,200	2,500
Total Appraise	2,300	2,400	13,200	12,700
Internal Failure:				
Rework	700	1,000	3,000	4,000
Scrap	800	1,100	6,000	6,500
Work. Comp.	500	800	2,800	3,500
Overtime	600	200	3,400	1,000
Overruns	500	900	4,500	5,300
Total Internal	3,100	4,000	19,700	20,300
External Failure:				
Complaints	800	1,200	5,600	6,500
Returns	900	1,300	6,300	9,000
Freight on returns	500	750	3,400	5,400
Total External	2,200	3,250	15,300	20,900

Required
a. Based on the data sources used for this report, what are the most efficient and effective ways to collect the key information needed?
b. Suggest improvements in the design of this report.

13.7 What is the purpose of each of the following control activities?
  a. Documenting the return of any scrapped products to inventory stores
  b. Using an MPS to schedule production
  c. Periodically counting fixed assets and reconciling those counts to the fixed asset subsidiary ledger
  d. Using move tickets to document transfers of work in process between factory departments
  e. Prenumbering and periodic accounting of all materials requisitions
  f. Using passwords to control access to the system that generates production orders
  g. Listing and printing monthly all transactions involving the acquisition or disposal of fixed assets and having the controller review them

13.8 The Joseph Brant Manufacturing Company makes athletic footwear. Processing of production orders is as follows: At the end of each week, the production planning department prepares a list of shoes and quantities to be produced during the next week. Using this list as a source, data entry clerks key in production order release records onto a temporary disk file. Once data entry has been completed, a production order preparation program accesses the operations list (stored on a permanent disk file) and prepares a production order for each shoe to be manufactured. For each new production order, the program (1) prints three copies of a production order document, (2) writes the production order to the open production order master file stored on disk, and (3) prints an operations card identifying each operation required to manufacture that style of shoe.

The operations cards are used as turnaround documents. Each card is sent to the factory department where the operation will be performed. After completing an operation, factory employees mark the elapsed time, quantity completed, and other pertinent data on the card and return it to computer operations. A scanner is then used to read and write the operations data onto a temporary disk file. At the end of each day, this file is processed to update the open production order master file. Once this update has been completed, the program generates departmental production schedules for the next day.

Required
1. Prepare both a data flow diagram and a systems flowchart of all operations described.
2. Describe a comprehensive set of control procedures that should be included in each system. Organize your answer by listing the potential threats and specifying the control procedures that would best address them.

13.9   Assume that Stained Glass Artistry, a new shop that specializes in making stained glass artwork, has hired you to design an integrated database that will provide the owners with the accounting information they need to effectively manage the business. Stained Glass Artistry makes a wide variety of stained glass windows for sale in its store.

A unique job order is assigned to each production run, which includes creating multiple copies of the same basic design. When raw materials are issued to employees, the issuance is documented on a prenumbered raw material issue form. The different kinds of glass needed for the product, and other materials such as copper foil or lead, are issued at one time, so that employees can efficiently produce the design.

Creating a piece of stained glass art involves several different steps, including cutting, foiling, and soldering. The owners want to track how much time each employee spends each day performing each of those various tasks.

The owners have developed raw material and direct labor standards for each design they offer. They want their AIS to track actual costs and standard costs so that they can generate reports that provide price and quantity variance information.

The owners also have provided you with the following list of facts that they want stored in the database.

Attributes in Stained Glass Artistry AIS

(Note: You must create appropriate primary keys for each table; this is the list of other attributes.)

Date hired	Quantity on hand	Color of glass
Style of glass	Quantity to be produced	Actual cost of design
(name or description)	Standard quantity of glass	Quantity issued
Design name	to use in design	Standard cost of design
Standard hours to	Date design produced	Date of birth
make design	Employee name	Standard cost of glass
Wage rate	Time completed task	
Time started task		

Required
1. Draw an integrated REA diagram for Stained Glass Artistry. Include both minimum and maximum cardinalities.
2. Create the set of relational tables required to implement your REA diagram for Stained Glass Artistry in a relational database.

Case 13-1 AnyCompany, Inc.: An Ongoing Comprehensive Case

Visit a local company and obtain permission to study its production information system (you may use the same company identified to complete this case in previous chapters). Write a report that includes the following:

1. DFDs of each of the four major steps in the production cycle (design, planning, operations, and cost accounting).
2. A list of all paper and electronic documents the company uses, with copies if possible, to evaluate each document's design
3. An REA diagram of all the information stored in the system
4. A description of how the system updates the master files (or database) after each type of transaction occurs (materials requisition,

machine operation). Draw a systems flowchart for each step in the production cycle.
5. A list and evaluation of the adequacy of the control procedures used to ensure transaction processing accuracy and validity
6. Your opinion of whether the cost accounting reports produced by the system help managers make good decisions. Suggest changes to improve the use of cost accounting data to help the company attain its strategic objectives.

Case 13-2 The Controller and CIM

Examine issues of *Journal of Accountancy* and *Stategic Finance* for the last two years. Write a brief report on one current development in factory automation and its effects on the AIS. Describe the controller's role in either initiating or responding to the change. In addition, discuss the change's effect on the risk of the various production cycle threats.

ANSWERS TO CHAPTER QUIZ

1. a	**3.** c	**5.** b	**7.** a	**9.** c
2. c	**4.** b	**6.** c	**8.** d	**10.** d

The Human Resources Management and Payroll Cycle

Learning Objectives

After studying this chapter, you should be able to:

■ Describe the major business activities and related data processing operations performed in the human resources management (HRM) /payroll cycle.

■ Identify the major threats in the HRM/payroll cycle and evaluate the adequacy of various internal control procedures for dealing with them.

■ Explain the key decisions to be made in the HRM/payroll cycle and identify the information required to make those decisions.

■ Read and understand a data model (REA diagram) of the HRM/payroll cycle.

■ Create a data model (REA diagram) of the HRM/payroll cycle.

Integrative Case: Alpha Omega Electronics

Peter Wu, the new vice president for human resources at AOE, wants to correct two weaknesses in the company's existing HRM/payroll system. First, payroll processing costs have been rising steadily for years, yet the current system does not provide adequate service. For example, employees are unhappy with the lengthy delays required to obtain information about their benefits and retirement plans. Moreover, Linda Spurgeon wants to provide employees with an expanded flexible benefits plan. Doing so, however, will further increase the demands on the existing system. Thus, Peter must find a way to improve the efficiency and responsiveness of AOE's payroll system.

A second weakness with AOE's current HRM/payroll system is its inability to track employee skill development. Consequently, managers have tended to hire externally to meet new staffing needs, rather than promoting or transferring existing employees. This practice has hurt employee morale. It also impedes evaluating the effectiveness of AEO's investment in training and continuing education. Thus, Peter's other task is to find a way to improve the effectiveness of AEO's HRM system.

Currently AOE, like many companies, has separate HRM and payroll systems. The payroll system, which is under the accounting department's control, produces employee paychecks and maintains the related records as required by government regulations. The payroll system uses batch processing: Hourly employees are paid biweekly; salaried employees and those on commission are paid monthly. The HRM system, which the human resources department runs, maintains files on employee job history, skills, and benefits; these files are updated weekly. Each system maintains its own separate files, sometimes storing the same data, such as pay rates, in different formats. This practice makes it difficult for accounting personnel to prepare reports that combine HRM and payroll data.

Peter met with Elizabeth Venko and Ann Brandt to discuss how to improve the efficiency and effectiveness of AOE's HRM/payroll system. Elizabeth and Ann indicated that it was possible to redesign both activities so that the payroll and HRM systems were integrated. As you read this chapter, think about the relationships between HRM and payroll activities and how an integrated database can make both functions more efficient and effective.

IINTRODUCTION

The **human resources management (HRM)/payroll cycle** is a recurring set of business activities and related data processing operations associated with effectively managing the employee workforce. Following are the more important tasks:

1. Recruiting and hiring new employees
2. Training
3. Job assignment
4. Compensation (payroll)
5. Performance evaluation
6. Discharge of employees, due to voluntary or involuntary termination

In addition, as discussed in Chapter 13, payroll costs also are allocated to products and departments for use in product pricing and mix decisions.

Tasks 1 and 6 are performed once for each employee, whereas tasks 2 through 5 are performed repeatedly for as long as an employee works for the company. In most companies these six activities are split between two separate systems. Task 4, compensating employees, is the payroll system's primary function. The HRM system performs the other five tasks. In many companies, these two systems are organizationally separate: The HRM system is usually the responsibility of the director of human resources, whereas the controller manages the payroll system.

This chapter focuses primarily on the payroll system, because it is one of the largest and most important components of the AIS. The payroll system must be designed to meet government regulations as well as management's information needs. Incomplete or erroneous payroll records not only impair decision making, but also can result in fines and imprisonment! Thus, the design of an efficient and effective payroll system is vital.

It is also important, however, to have a well-designed HRM system. The knowledge and skills of employees are valuable assets and must be carefully managed, developed, and maintained. Companies need effective HRM systems to help assign appropriate employees to different tasks and to facilitate monitoring the continuous development of the organization's intellectual assets.

OVERVIEW

Figure 14-1 presents a context diagram of the payroll system, depicting its relationships with the HRM system and with the other parts of the AIS. This figure shows five major sources of inputs to the payroll system. The HRM department provides information about hirings, terminations, and pay-rate changes due to raises and promotions. Employees initiate changes in their discretionary deductions (e.g., contributions to retirement plans). The various departments provide data about actual hours employees work. Government agencies provide tax rates and instructions for meeting regulatory requirements. Similarly, insurance companies and other organizations provide instructions for calculating and remitting various withholdings.

Checks are the payroll system's principal output. Employees receive individual *paychecks* in compensation for their services. A *payroll check* is sent to the bank to transfer funds from the company's regular accounts to its payroll account. Checks also are issued to government agencies, insurance companies, and other organizations to meet company obligations (e.g., taxes, insurance premiums). In addition, the payroll system produces a variety of reports, which we discuss later, for internal and external use.

Employees are an organization's most valuable asset. Their knowledge and skills affect the quality of the goods and services provided to customers. Indeed, in professional service organizations, such as accounting and law firms, employees' knowledge

Figure 14-1   Context diagram of the payroll portion of the HRM/payroll cycle

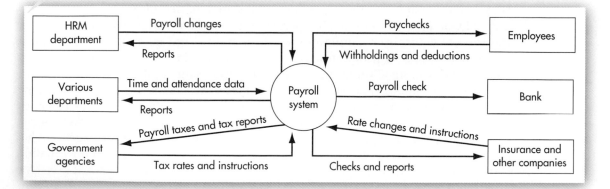

and skills *are* the principal component of the company's product, and labor costs represent the major expense incurred in generating revenues. Even in manufacturing firms, where direct labor costs represent only a fraction of total direct costs, employees are a key cost driver in that the quality of their work affects both overall productivity and product defect rates. Thus, it is not surprising to find that some stock analysts believe that a company's human resources may be worth several times the value of its tangible assets such as inventory, property, and equipment.

Nevertheless, the AIS has not traditionally been used to measure or report on the status of a company's human resources. One reason is the assets reported in financial statements represent resources the organization owns but has not yet consumed. Employees, however, are not "owned" by the company. Consequently, the value of human resources has traditionally been recognized only when they are used, at which time they are either recorded as wages and salary expenses or, in the case of direct labor in manufacturing firms, included as part of the cost of inventory.

This situation is beginning to change. Companies such as Dow Chemical have created new executive positions with such titles as director of intellectual assets. These executives are responsible for measuring and developing the organization's human resources. Other companies, such as Skandia Group, Scandinavia's largest financial services company, have even begun to include human resources information in their annual reports. Skandia divides its intellectual capital assets into two categories: human and structural. Human capital is the knowledge Skandia's employees possess, which can be increased and developed through hiring and training. Structural intellectual capital is knowledge that has been captured and implemented in the form of decision support systems, expert systems, or knowledge databases so that it can be shared throughout the organization. Skandia's director of intellectual capital believes that structural intellectual capital is even more valuable than human intellectual capital, because structural intellectual capital will not quit or work for a competitor and can be used over and over again.

Recognizing the value of employees' knowledge and skills highlights the true costs associated with excessive turnover. Experts estimate that, on average, the costs associated with replacing an employee are 1.5 times that of an employee's annual salary. Thus, organizations that experience below-industry-average turnover rates reap considerable cost savings compared to rivals with higher turnover rates. Of course, some turnover will always occur and may even be desirable. For example, professional consulting organizations have traditionally encouraged some level of turnover because they believe it provides an important source of new ideas. The key is to control and manage turnover rates. It is particularly important to understand and manage the causes of turnover. Employee morale is one of the many factors that affect turnover. As Focus 14-1 indicates, there is increasing evidence that employee morale and attitudes can significantly affect the organization's financial performance.

These examples underscore the need to effectively manage and develop a company's intellectual capital and human resources. To do this, the AIS must be designed to do more than just record time and attendance data and prepare paychecks. Instead, the payroll system should be integrated with the HRM system so that management has easy access not only to data about employee-related costs, but also to information about employees' skills and knowledge.

Focus 14-1

The Effect of Employee Attitudes on the Bottom Line

Sears is one of a growing number of companies that believes it has found a measurable relationship between employee morale and financial performance. For years, Sears collected data on employee satisfaction, actual behaviors with customers, and customer satisfaction. It then hired statisticians from the University of Michigan to analyze that data. The analysis indicated that employee attitudes about their jobs and about the company itself significantly predicted how they interacted with customers. In turn, the quality of such interaction significantly predicted customer retention rates and their propensity to recommend that friends shop at Sears. Those two factors were positively correlated with various financial measures.

As a result of that analysis, Sears began using IT to collect even more detailed data about employee–customer interaction. For example, on a random basis, cash register receipts include a coupon indicating that if the customer calls an 800 number in the next week and answers a series of prerecorded questions by pressing buttons on their touch-tone phone, Sears will send them another coupon good for $5 off on their next purchase. This system makes it possible for Sears to link customer responses to the specific employee with whom a customer interacted.

A Gallup survey of 55,000 workers across a variety of companies found a positive correlation between employee attitudes and profitability. The survey identified four key attitudes: Employees believe they have the opportunity to do what they do best, every day; they believe their opinions count; they think that coworkers are committed to quality; and they understand the connection between their jobs and the company's mission.

Of course, high employee morale and attitudes do not necessarily translate into outstanding financial performance, especially if the latter is measured by stock market returns. For example, Southwest Airlines is consistently rated by *Fortune* magazine as having high employee morale, yet its stock price has not fared as well as companies ranked much lower on employee morale in *Fortune*'s study. Other companies with high employee morale but less-than-stellar stock price performance include Nordstrom, General Mills, and McCormick (the spice maker). Nevertheless, high employee morale does not hurt.

Sources: Stratford Sherman, "Bringing Sears into the New World," *Fortune* (October 13, 1997): 183–184; and Linda Grant, "Happy Workers, High Returns," *Fortune* (January 12, 1998): 81.

The remainder of this chapter is organized in terms of the three basic functions the AIS provides in the HRM/payroll cycle: processing transactional data about employee activities, safeguarding the organization's assets, and providing information for decision making. We begin by describing the basic activities in the payroll cycle. Next, we discuss the control objectives of the HRM/payroll cycle and describe applicable control procedures for mitigating the major potential threats in this cycle. We conclude this chapter with a discussion of key decisions in the HRM/payroll cycle and identify the information needed to make those decisions. We present a data model that satisfies those information needs by effectively integrating payroll data with other HRM information.

PAYROLL CYCLE ACTIVITIES

Figure 14-2 shows the seven basic activities performed in the payroll cycle. Payroll is one AIS application that continues to be processed in batch mode, because (1) paychecks are prepared periodically (weekly, biweekly, or monthly) and (2) most employees are paid at the same time. Figure 14-3 depicts a typical batch-oriented HRM/payroll system like the one AOE uses. We will refer to Figure 14-3 as we discuss the activities depicted in Figure 14-2.

Figure 14-2   Level 0 DFD for the payroll cycle

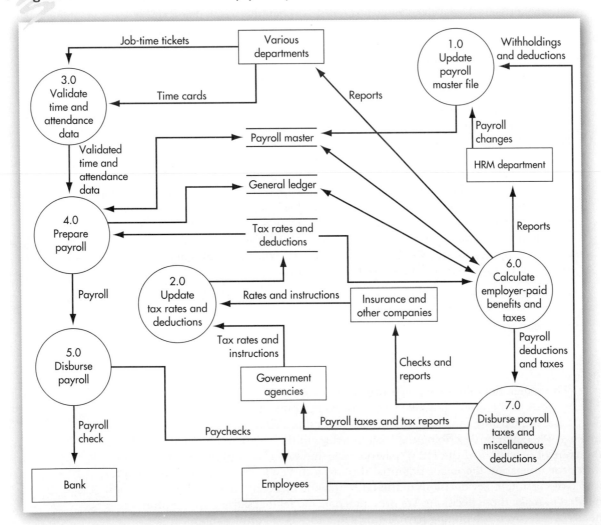

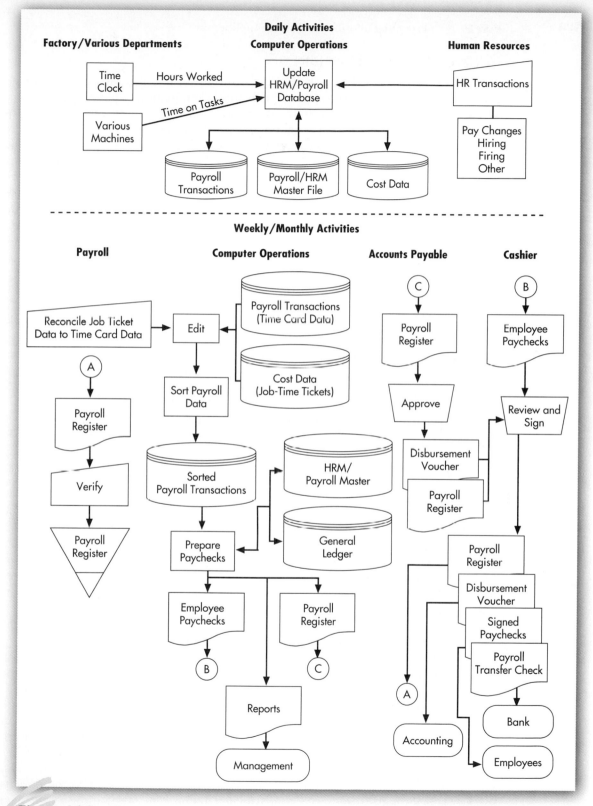

Figure 14-3 HRM/payroll flowchart

Update Payroll Master File

The first activity in the HRM/payroll cycle involves updating the payroll master file to reflect various types of payroll changes: new hires, terminations, changes in pay rates, or changes in discretionary withholdings (circle 1.0 in Figure 14-2). The HRM department provides this information. Although payroll is processed in batch mode, Figure 14-3 shows that the HRM department has on-line access to make these changes to the payroll master file. Appropriate edit checks, such as validity checks on employee number and reasonableness tests for the changes being made, are applied to all payroll change transactions.

It is important that all payroll changes are entered in a timely manner and are properly reflected in the next pay period. Records of employees who quit or are fired should not be deleted immediately, however, because some year-end reports, including W-2 forms, require data about all employees who worked for the organization at any time during the year.

Update Tax Rates and Deductions

The second activity in the HRM/payroll cycle is updating information about tax rates and other withholdings (circle 2.0 in Figure 14-2). The payroll department makes these changes, but the changes occur infrequently. They happen when the payroll department receives updates about changes in tax rates and other payroll deductions from various government units and insurance companies.

Validate Time and Attendance Data

The third step in the payroll cycle is to validate each employee's time and attendance data (circle 3.0 in Figure 14-2). This information comes in various forms, depending on an employee's pay status.

Pay schemes

For employees paid on an hourly basis, many companies use a **time card** to record the employee's arrival and departure times for each work shift. The time card also includes the total hours worked during a pay period. Increasingly, as shown in Figure 14-3, electronic time clocks are replacing paper time cards. As discussed in Chapter 13, manufacturing companies also use job-time tickets to record detailed data about how employees use their time (i.e., which jobs they perform). The data are used to allocate labor costs among various departments, cost centers, and production jobs. Professionals in such service organizations as accounting, law, and consulting firms similarly track the time they spend performing various tasks. These data are used to accurately bill clients.

Employees who earn a fixed salary (e.g., managers and professional staff) seldom record their labor efforts on time cards. Instead, their supervisors informally monitor their presence on the job.

Sales staff often are paid either on a straight commission or on a salary plus commission basis. This requires the staff to carefully record the amount of their sales. In addition, some sales staff are paid bonuses for exceeding targets. Companies in the United States are increasingly extending such incentive bonuses to employees other than sales staff, to motivate greater productivity and better work quality. For example, Nucor Corporation, one of the largest steel producers in the United States, pays its steelworkers an hourly rate set at approximately 60 percent of the industry average, plus a bonus based on the tons of steel they produce and ship. Many companies also offer their nonexecutive employees stock options. Doing so, they claim, motivates employees to actively look for ways to improve service and cut costs so that the value of their compensation package rises.

Using incentives and bonuses requires linking the payroll system and the information systems of sales and other cycles in order to collect the data used to calculate bonuses. Moreover, the bonus/incentive schemes must be properly designed with realistic, attainable goals that can be objectively measured. It is also important that goals be congruent with corporate objectives and that managers monitor goals to ensure that they continue to be appropriate. Indeed, poorly designed incentive pay schemes can result in undesirable behavior. For example, Sears Automotive experienced unintended negative effects from implementing a new incentive plan in the early 1990s that paid its repair staff a commission based on the amount of parts sold and number of hours worked. The intent was to focus employees' attention on how their efforts affected the company's bottom line. The result, however, was a scandal in which it was alleged that Sears employees recommended unnecessary repairs to boost their own pay. The alleged abuses reduced public trust in Sears Automotive and led to lower revenues. Wisely, Sears finally abandoned this incentive system.

Opportunities for using information technology

Figure 14-3 shows how payroll processing can be made more efficient by collecting employee time and attendance data electronically instead of on paper documents. This can reduce the time and potential errors associated with manually recording, verifying, and finally entering employee time and attendance data. For example, badge readers can be used to collect job-time data for production employees. Those data are then automatically fed to the payroll processing system. Similarly, electronic time clocks can transmit time and attendance data directly to the payroll processing program. As discussed in Chapter 13, AOE is planning to implement these techniques to automate collection of time and attendance data for its factory workers.

Similar procedures can be used for professional service staff. For example, AT&T's internal service staff use touch-tone telephones to log in time spent on various tasks, thereby eliminating the use of paper time sheets. The payroll program applies edit checks to verify the accuracy and reasonableness of the data at the time of entry.

Prepare Payroll

The fourth step in the payroll cycle is preparing payroll (circle 4.0 in Figure 14-2). The department in which the employee works provides data about the hours worked and a supervisor usually confirms the data. Pay rate information is obtained from the payroll master file.

Procedures

Figure 14-3 shows the steps in processing payroll. First, the payroll transaction file is sorted by employee number, so that it is in the same sequence as the payroll master file. If the organization is processing payrolls from several divisions, each of these payroll transaction files must also be merged (this step is not shown in Figure 14-3).

The sorted time data file is then used to prepare employee paychecks. For each employee, the payroll master file record and corresponding transaction record are read and gross pay is calculated. For hourly employees, the number of hours worked are multiplied by the wage rate and then any applicable premiums for overtime or bonuses are added. For salaried employees, gross pay is a fraction of the annual salary, where the fraction reflects the length of the pay period. For example, salaried employees paid monthly would receive one-twelfth of their annual salary each pay period.

Next, all payroll deductions are summed and the total is subtracted from gross pay to obtain net pay. Payroll deductions fall into two broad categories: payroll tax withholdings and voluntary deductions. The former includes federal, state, and local income taxes, as well as social security taxes. Voluntary deductions include contributions to a pension plan; premiums for group life, health, and disability insurance; union dues; and contributions to various charities.

Once net pay is obtained, the year-to-date fields for gross pay, deductions, and net pay in each employee's record in the payroll master file are updated. Maintaining accurate cumulative earnings records is important for two reasons. First, because social security tax withholdings and other deductions have cutoffs, the company must know when to cease deductions for individual employees. Second, this information is needed to ensure that the appropriate amounts of taxes and other deductions are remitted to government agencies, insurance companies, and other organizations (such as the United Way). This information also must be included in the various reports filed with those agencies.

Finally, the payroll register and employee paychecks are printed. The **payroll register** is a report that lists each employee's gross pay, payroll deductions, and net pay in a multicolumn format. It is often accompanied by a separate **deduction register,** which lists the miscellaneous voluntary deductions for each employee. Figure 14-4 provides examples of both reports (which need not be printed on paper).

The payroll register also is used to authorize the transfer of funds to the company's payroll bank account. Employee paychecks also typically include an **earnings statement,** which lists the amount of gross pay, deductions, and net pay for the current period, and year-to-date totals for each category.

As each payroll transaction is processed, the system also allocates labor costs to the appropriate general ledger accounts by checking the code on the job-time ticket record. The system maintains a running total of these allocations until all employee payroll records have been processed. These totals, and the column totals in the payroll register, form the basis for the summary journal entry, which is posted to the general ledger after all paychecks have been printed. Table 14-1 describes some of the additional reports produced by the payroll system.

Disburse Payroll

The next step is actual disbursement of paychecks to employees (circle 5.0 in Figure 14-2). Most employees are paid either by check or by direct deposit of the net pay amount into their personal bank account. Unlike cash payments, both methods provide a means to document the amount of wages paid.

Procedures

Figure 14-3 shows that once paychecks have been prepared, the payroll register is sent to the accounts payable department for review and approval. A disbursement voucher

Alpha Omega Electronics			PAYROLL REGISTER					Period Ended 12/03/2003		
						Deductions				
Employee No.	Name	Hours	Pay Rate	Gross Pay	Fed. Tax	FICA	State Tax	Misc.	Net Pay	
37884	Jarvis	40.0	6.25	250.00	35.60	18.75	16.25	27.60	151.80	
37885	Burke	43.6	6.50	295.10	42.40	22.13	19.18	40.15	171.24	
37886	Lincoln	40.0	6.75	270.00	39.20	20.25	17.55	27.90	165.10	
37887	Douglass	44.2	7.00	324.10	46.60	24.31	21.07	29.62	202.50	

Alpha Omega Electronics		DEDUCTION REGISTER					Period Ended 12/03/2003
		Miscellaneous Deductions					
Employee No.	Name	Health Ins.	Life Ins.	Retirement	Union Dues	Savings Bond	Total Misc.
37884	Jarvis	10.40	5.50	7.50	4.20	0.00	27.60
37885	Burke	11.60	5.50	8.85	4.20	10.00	40.15
37886	Lincoln	10.40	5.20	8.10	4.20	0.00	27.90
37887	Douglass	10.20	5.50	9.72	4.20	0.00	29.62

Figure 14-4 Sample payroll deduction registers

is then prepared to authorize the transfer of funds from the company's general checking account to its payroll bank account. Payroll checks should not be drawn on the organization's regular bank account. Instead, for control purposes, a separate payroll bank account should be used. This limits the company's loss exposure to the amount of cash in the separate payroll account.

The disbursement voucher and payroll register are then sent to the cashier. The cashier reviews the payroll register and disbursement voucher and then prepares and signs a check transferring funds to the company's payroll bank account. The cashier also reviews, signs, and distributes the employee paychecks. Thus, the duties of authorizing and recording payroll transactions are segregated from the actual distribution of paychecks. The cashier promptly redeposits any unclaimed paychecks in the company's bank account. To prevent the creation and distribution of fraudulent paychecks, a list of unclaimed paychecks is sent to the internal audit department for further investigation.

The payroll register is then returned to the payroll department, where it is filed by date along with the time cards and job-time tickets. The disbursement voucher is sent to the accounting clerk, who uses it to update the general ledger.

Efficiency opportunity: direct deposit

Direct deposit is one way to improve the efficiency and reduce the costs of payroll processing. Employees who are paid by direct deposit generally receive a copy of the paycheck indicating the amount deposited along with an earnings statement. The payroll

Table 14-1   Examples of Commonly Generated HRM/Payroll Cycle Reports

Report Name	Contents	Purpose
Cumulative earnings register	Cumulative year-to-date gross pay, net pay, and deductions for each employee	Used for employee information and annual payroll reports
Workforce inventory	List of employees by department	Used in preparing labor-related reports for government agencies
Position control report	List of each authorized position, job qualifications, budgeted salary, and position status (filled or vacant)	Used in planning future work-force needs
Skills inventory report	List of employees and current skills	Useful in planning future work-force needs and training programs
Form 941	Employer's quarterly federal tax return (showing all wages subject to tax and amounts withheld for income tax and FICA)	Filed quarterly
Form W-2	Report of wages and withholdings for each employee	Sent to each employee for use in preparing their individual tax returns; due by January 31
Form W-3	Summary of all W-2 forms	Sent to federal government along with a copy of all W-2 forms; due by February 28
Form 1099-Misc.	Report of income paid to independent contractors	Sent to recipients of income for use in filing their income tax returns; due by January 31
Various other reports to government agencies	Data on compliance with various regulatory provisions, state and local tax reports, etc.	To document compliance with applicable regulations

system must generate a series of payroll deposit files, one for each bank through which payroll deposits are made. Each file contains a record for each employee whose account is maintained at a particular bank. Each record includes the employee's name, social security number, bank account number, and net pay amount. These files are sent electronically, using EDI, to each participating bank. The funds are then electronically transferred from the employer's bank account to the employee's account. Direct deposit thus eliminates the need for the cashier to sign individual payroll checks. The cashier does, however, have to authorize the release of funds from the organization's regular checking account.

Direct deposit provides savings to employers by eliminating the cost of purchasing, processing, and distributing paper checks. It also reduces bank fees and postage expenses. These savings are partially offset by the loss of float, which represents the employer's use of the funds between the time the checks are drawn and when they are presented for payment. On balance, however, the savings associated with direct deposit generally exceed its costs. Consequently, most companies now offer their employees the option of direct deposit payment and encourage them to elect this form of payment.

Calculate Employer-Paid Benefits and Taxes

The employer pays some payroll taxes and employee benefits directly (circle 6.0 in Figure 14-2). For example, employers must pay social security taxes, in addition to the amounts withheld from employee paychecks. Circular E, *Employer's Tax Guide*, published by the IRS, provides detailed instructions about an employer's obligations for withholding and remitting payroll taxes and for filing various reports.

Federal and state laws also require employers to contribute a specified percentage of each employee's gross pay, up to a maximum annual limit, to federal and state unemployment compensation insurance funds. In addition, employers often contribute some or all of the amounts to pay for their employees' health, disability, and life insurance premiums. Many companies also offer their employees **flexible benefit plans,** under which each employee receives some minimum coverage in medical insurance and pension contributions, plus additional benefit credits that can be used to acquire extra vacation time or additional health insurance. These plans are sometimes called cafeteria-style benefit plans because they offer a menu of options. Finally, many employers offer and contribute toward a choice of retirement savings plans.

Providing these additional services and benefits places increased demands on a company's HRM/payroll system. For example, the HRM staff of a large company with thousands of employees can spend a considerable amount of time just responding to 401(k) plan inquiries. Moreover, employees want to be able to make changes in their investment decisions on a timely basis. Organizations can satisfy employee demands for such services without increasing costs by providing access to payroll/HRM information on the company's intranet.

Disburse Payroll Taxes and Miscellaneous Deductions

The final activity in the payroll process is paying the payroll tax liabilities and the other voluntary deductions of each employee (circle 7.0 in Figure 14-2). An organization must periodically prepare checks or use electronic funds transfer to pay the various tax liabilities incurred.

Respective government agencies specify the timing of these payments. In addition, the funds voluntarily withheld from each employee's paycheck for various benefits, such as a payroll savings plan, must be disbursed to the appropriate organizations.

Processing Options: Payroll Service Bureaus and Professional Employer Organizations

In an effort to reduce costs, many organizations are outsourcing their payroll and HRM functions to payroll service bureaus and professional employer organizations. A **payroll service bureau** maintains the payroll master file for each of its clients and performs the payroll processing activities described in this section. A **professional employer organization (PEO)** not only processes payroll, but also provides HRM services such as employee benefit design and administration. Because they provide a narrower range of services, payroll service bureaus are generally less expensive than PEOs.

When organizations outsource payroll processing, they send time and attendance data to the payroll service bureau or PEO, and information about personnel changes, at the end of each pay period. The payroll service bureau or PEO then uses that data to prepare employee paychecks, earnings statements, and a payroll register. The payroll processing service also periodically produces employee W-2 forms and other tax-related reports.

Payroll service bureaus and PEOs are especially attractive to small and midsize businesses for the following reasons:

➤ *Reduced costs.* Payroll service bureaus and PEOs benefit from the economies of scale associated with preparing paychecks for a large number of companies. They can charge fees that are typically less than the cost of doing payroll in-house. A payroll service bureau or PEO also saves money by eliminating the need to develop and maintain the expertise needed to comply with the constantly changing tax laws.

➤ *Wider range of benefits.* PEOs pool the costs of administering benefits across all their clients. Consequently, a PEO enables smaller companies to offer the same wide range of benefits that large companies typically provide.

➤ *Freeing up of computer resources.* A payroll service bureau or PEO eliminates one or more AIS applications (payroll and benefits management). The freed-up computing resources can then be used to improve service in other areas, such as sales order entry.

As the basis for competitive advantage increasingly hinges on employees' skills and knowledge, the effective and efficient management of the payroll and HRM functions becomes increasingly important. Thus, as Focus 14-2 shows, HRM consulting represents a potentially lucrative niche for smaller and midsize CPA firms.

CONTROL OBJECTIVES, THREATS, AND PROCEDURES

A second major function of the AIS in the HRM/payroll cycle is to provide adequate internal controls to ensure meeting the following objectives:

1. All payroll transactions are properly authorized.
2. All recorded payroll transactions are valid.
3. All valid, authorized payroll transactions are recorded.
4. All payroll transactions are accurately recorded.
5. Applicable government regulations regarding remittance of taxes and filing of payroll and HRM reports are met.
6. Assets (both cash and data) are safeguarded from loss or theft.
7. HRM/payroll cycle activities are performed efficiently and effectively.

The various documents and records (e.g., time cards, payroll register) described in the previous section play an important role in achieving these objectives. Simple, easy-to-complete documents with clear instructions facilitate the accurate and efficient recording of payroll transactions. Appropriate application controls, such as validity checks and field (format) checks, further increase the accuracy of data entry when using electronic documents. Providing space on both paper and electronic documents

Focus 14-2

HR Services—A Valuable Consulting Niche

HR consulting is a lucrative niche because every company continually faces staffing challenges. Smaller companies already trust their CPAs for financial advice, and so naturally turn to them for help in filling their financial staffing needs. Smaller clients also often cannot afford full-blown internal HR departments. Thus, CPA firms who are interested can supplement the financial services they already provide with HR-related services.

To exploit this new consulting niche, some CPA firms have formed partnerships with HR companies. In such arrangements, the CPA firm focuses on identifying people who possess specific financial skills, while the HR company focuses on complying with employment law regulations.

Other CPA firms have hired HR specialists to run the new consulting service. Some CPAs, such as Ellen Feaver, have become HR experts themselves. Feaver is part of Employee Benefits Resources LLP, located in Helena, Montana. The firm provides a wide range of HR services, such as administering employee benefits and health plans, writing policy manuals, and developing compensation systems. Feaver took courses on employment and management issues and earned the Professional in Human Resources (PHR) designation. She believes that being both a CPA and HR professional gives her a unique competitive advantage.

Source: Phaedra Brotherton, "CPAs Add HR to the Mix," *Journal of Accountancy* (October 2000): 67–76.

to record who completed and who reviewed the form provides evidence that the transaction was properly authorized. Prenumbering all documents facilitates checking that all transactions have been recorded. Restricting access to programs that create documents and, if paper documents are still used, to blank documents, reduces the risk of unauthorized transactions.

Table 14-2 lists the major threats in the HRM/payroll cycle and the applicable control procedures for mitigating those threats. Because every company, regardless of its line of business, faces these threats, it is important to understand how the AIS can be best designed to counter them.

Threat 1: Hiring Unqualified or Larcenous Employees

Hiring unqualified employees can increase production expenses, and hiring a larcenous employee can result in the theft of assets. Both problems are best dealt with by appropriate hiring procedures. Skill qualifications for each open position should be stated explicitly in the position control report. Candidates should be asked to sign a statement on the job application form that confirms the accuracy of the information being submitted and provides their consent to a thorough background check of their credentials and employment history. It is especially important to verify a job applicant's skills and references, including college degrees earned, because research suggests that approximately 30 percent of resumes contain false or embellished information.

Table 14-2   Threats and Controls in the Payroll/HRM Cycle

Process/Activity	Threat	Applicable Control Procedures
Hiring and recruiting	1. Hiring unqualified or larcenous employees	Sound hiring procedures, including verification of job applicant's skills, references and employment history
	2. Violation of employment law	Thorough documentation of hiring procedures; training on current developments in employment law
Payroll processing	3. Unauthorized changes to payroll master file	Segregation of duties: HRM versus payroll and paycheck distribution; access controls; review of all changes
	4. Inaccurate time data	Automation of data collection; various edit checks; reconciliation of time card data with job-time ticket data
	5. Inaccurate processing of payroll	Batch totals and other application controls; payroll clearing account; review of IRS regulations
	6. Theft or fraudulent distribution of paychecks	Direct deposit; paycheck distribution by someone independent of payroll process; investigation of unclaimed paychecks; restricted access to blank paychecks; prenumbering and periodic accounting for all paychecks; use of separate payroll checking account, maintained as an imprest fund; reconciliation of payroll bank account by someone not involved in payroll processing
General	7. Loss or unauthorized disclosure of data	Backup procedures; disaster recovery plans; physical and logical access controls; encryption of data
	8. Poor performance	Development and periodic review of appropriate performance metrics; training programs

It is also important to verify the actual job titles of people listed as references. Finally, when hiring for positions that involve access to financial data and assets, it may be worthwhile to hire a company that performs thorough background checks to verify that the applicant does not have a prior criminal record. Before engaging in a detailed background check, however, it is usually necessary to obtain written permission from the applicant to do so.

Threat 2: Violation of Employment Law

The government imposes stiff penalties on firms that violate provisions of employment law. In addition, organizations can also be subject to civil suits by alleged victims of employment discrimination. In this case, the best control procedure is careful documentation of all actions relating to advertising, recruiting, and hiring new employees, to demonstrate compliance with the applicable government regulations. Continued training to keep current with employment law is also important.

Threat 3: Unauthorized Changes to the Payroll Master File

Unauthorized changes to the payroll master file can result in increased expenses if wages, salaries, commissions, or other base rates used to determine employee compensation are falsified. These problems also result in inaccurate reports on labor costs, which in turn can lead to erroneous decisions.

Proper segregation of duties is the key control procedure for dealing with this threat. As shown in Figure 14-3, only the HRM department should be able to update the payroll master file for hirings, firings, pay raises, and promotions. HRM department employees in turn do not directly participate in payroll processing or paycheck distribution. This segregation of duties prevents someone with access to paychecks from creating fictitious employees or altering pay rates and then intercepting those fraudulent checks. In addition, all changes to the payroll master file should be reviewed and approved by someone other than the person recommending the change. Traditionally, such approval has involved reading and signing a transaction document. For changes processed through on-line terminals, the system must be designed to verify the identity and authority of the persons making and approving the request. A report documenting these changes should also be sent to each department supervisor for review.

Controlling access to the payroll system is also important. Indeed, in a database environment, access controls are vital because many previously separate functions are now performed solely by the system. The system should be programmed to compare user IDs and passwords with an access control matrix that (1) defines what actions each employee is allowed to perform, and (2) confirms what files each employee is allowed to access. Payroll clerks, for example, should not be permitted to change employee pay rates.

Threat 4: Inaccurate Time Data

Inaccuracies in time and attendance records can result in increased labor expenses and erroneous labor expense reports. Moreover, inaccuracies can either hurt employee morale (if paychecks are incorrect or missing) or result in payments for labor services not rendered.

Automation can reduce the risk of *unintentional* inaccuracies in time data. Badge readers and bar code scanners can be used to collect data on employee time and attendance in machine-readable form. If their use is not feasible, on-line terminals should be used. The data entry program should include the following edit checks:

➤ *Field checks* for numeric data in the employee number and hours worked fields
➤ *Limit checks* on the hours worked field
➤ A *validity check* of the employee number

Proper segregation of duties can reduce the risk of *intentional* inaccuracies. As explained earlier, only someone not directly involved in processing payroll should make changes to the payroll master file. Moreover, the appropriate supervisors should approve all such changes.

Time clock data, used for calculating payroll, also should be reconciled to the job-time ticket data, used for costing and managerial purposes, by someone not involved in generating that data. The total time spent on all tasks, as recorded on the job-time tickets, should not exceed the attendance time indicated on an employee's time card. Conversely, all time spent at work should be accounted for on the job-time tickets. To ensure the validity of the data, the employee's supervisor should approve time cards and job-time tickets.

Threat 5: Inaccurate Processing of Payroll

The complexity of payroll processing, especially the various tax law requirements, makes it susceptible to errors. Errors obviously can hurt employee morale, particularly if paychecks are late. In addition to incorrect payroll expense records and reports, processing errors can lead to penalties if the errors result in failure to remit the proper amount of payroll taxes due the government. Similarly, failure to accurately assess garnishments on employees' wages and remit those funds to the appropriate party can also lead to financial penalties.

Three types of control procedures address the threat of payroll errors:

1. *Batch totals.* Even advanced HRM/payroll systems will continue to use batch processing for payroll. Consequently, batch totals should be calculated at the time of data entry and then checked against comparable totals calculated during each stage of processing. Hash totals of employee numbers, for example, are particularly useful. If the original and subsequent hash totals of employee numbers agree, it means that (1) all payroll records have been processed, (2) data input was accurate, and (3) no bogus time cards were entered during processing.

2. *Cross-footing the payroll register.* The total of the net pay column should equal the total of gross pay less total deductions.

3. *A payroll clearing account.* The **payroll clearing account** is a general ledger account that is used in a two-step process to check the accuracy and completeness of recording payroll costs and their subsequent allocation to appropriate cost centers. First, the payroll control account is debited for the amount of gross pay; cash is credited for the amount of net pay, and the various withholdings are credited to separate liability accounts. Second, the cost accounting process distributes labor costs to various expense categories and credits the payroll control account for the sum of these allocations. The amount credited to the payroll control account should equal the amount it was previously debited when net pay and the various withholdings were recorded. This particular internal check is called a zero balance check, because the payroll control account should equal zero once both entries have been posted.

Workers' tax status should be properly classified as either employees or independent contractors, because misclassification can cause companies to owe substantial back taxes, interest, and even penalties. This issue often arises when department managers attempt to circumvent a general hiring freeze by using independent contractors. The HRM department always should review any decisions to hire temporary or outside help. The IRS provides a checklist of questions that can be used to determine if a worker should be classified as an employee or an independent contractor.

Threat 6: Theft or Fraudulent Distribution of Paychecks

Another major threat is the theft of paychecks or the issuance of paychecks to fictitious or terminated employees. This can result in increased expenses and the loss of cash.

Proper segregation of duties relating to the preparation and distribution of paychecks can reduce the risk of this threat.

Payroll check writing controls

The controls related to other cash disbursements, discussed in Chapter 12, also apply to payroll:

➤ Access to blank payroll checks and to the check signature machine should be restricted.

➤ All payroll checks should be sequentially prenumbered and periodically accounted for.

➤ The cashier should sign all payroll checks only when supported by proper documentation (the payroll register and disbursement voucher).

➤ Someone independent of the payroll process should reconcile the payroll bank account.

By limiting the total amount of cash at risk, a separate payroll bank account provides additional protection against forgery or alteration. This account should be operated as an imprest fund; that is, the amount of the check written to replenish the fund should equal the amount of net pay for that period. Thus, when all paychecks have been cashed, the payroll account should have a zero balance. A separate payroll checking account also makes it easier to spot any fraudulent checks when the account is reconciled.

Paycheck distribution controls

Someone who does not authorize or record payroll should distribute paychecks. To see why this segregation of duties is so important, assume that the person responsible for hiring and firing employees also distributes paychecks. This combination of duties could enable that person to conveniently forget to report an employee's termination and subsequently keep that employee's future paychecks. Requiring that the person distributing paychecks positively identify each person picking up a paycheck provides additional control over paycheck distribution. Furthermore, the internal audit department should observe, periodically, the paycheck distribution process.

Special procedures should be used to handle unclaimed paychecks because they indicate the possibility of a problem, such as a nonexistent or terminated employee. Unclaimed paychecks should be returned to the treasurer's office for prompt redeposit. They should also be traced back to time records and matched against the employee master payroll file to verify that they are indeed legitimate.

Threat 7: Loss or Unauthorized Disclosure of Data

The HRM/payroll database is a valuable resource that must be protected from loss or destruction. Protecting the privacy of employee data also is important. For example, morale may suffer if employees learn the salaries of other workers. In addition, unauthorized disclosure of performance evaluation data may subject the organization to lawsuits.

The best control procedure for reducing the risk of unauthorized disclosure of payroll data is using passwords and physical security controls to restrict access to authorized persons. Encryption provides additional control by making HRM/payroll information unintelligible to anyone who succeeds in obtaining unauthorized access to the payroll master file. A payroll service bureau or PEO also mitigates this threat.

Backup and disaster recovery procedures provide the best controls for reducing the risk of payroll data loss. Both internal and external file labels should be used to ensure that the database is not inadvertently erased or processed by the wrong program. Two backup copies of the payroll master file and recent transaction files should be created; one should be stored on-site, the other off-site.

Threat 8: Poor Performance

A general threat in the payroll/HRM process is inefficient and ineffective employee performance. Preparing and reviewing performance reports is an effective means of addressing this threat, especially for employees who telecommute. Careful monitoring of these employees' productivity is necessary to ensure that they are truly working the amount of time for which they are getting paid and that they are not operating a personal business on the side, using company-provided assets. Such monitoring is also necessary to ensure that telecommuting employees do not use company-provided computing resources inappropriately (e.g., visiting pornographic Web sites, sending or forwarding offensive e-mail, or storing and using pirated copies of software).

Training is important to ensure that payroll and HRM staff keep abreast of current developments in employment law and taxes. The HRM function must monitor the training of all employees to help the organization maximize the efficiency and effectiveness of all its business processes. Tracking employee knowledge and skills and capturing that knowledge so that it can be shared throughout the organization also can provide a sustainable competitive advantage. The nature of the data model that stores and maintains payroll and HRM data, however, determines how easy it is to achieve such knowledge management.

KEY DECISIONS, INFORMATION NEEDS, AND DATA MODEL

We discussed how the AIS fulfills the functions of processing payroll transactions and provides controls to safeguard assets. A third function of the AIS in the payroll/HRM cycle is to provide information for managing business activities. The traditional payroll system was designed primarily to meet the needs of external decision makers. Investors, creditors, and various government agencies were generally satisfied with information about a company's periodic salary expenses. Designing the payroll system to satisfy the needs of external users, however, does not ensure the production of all information management needs to use and develop the company's human resources. Instead, the payroll system must be designed to collect and integrate cost data with other types of information to enable management to make the following kinds of decisions:

➤ *Future workforce staffing needs.* How many employees are needed in the next five years to accomplish the organization's strategic plans? Which employees possess the needed skills? Which skills are in short supply? Which skills are in oversupply? How effective are current training programs in maintaining and improving employee skill levels?

➤ *Employee performance.* Which employees should be promoted or receive pay raises? Who should be discharged? Is overall performance improving or declining? Is turnover excessive? Is tardiness or absenteeism a problem?

➤ *Employee morale.* What is the overall level of employee morale and job satisfaction? How can the compensation scheme be used to improve morale, satisfaction, and performance? What additional fringe benefits, if any, should be offered?

➤   *Payroll processing efficiency and effectiveness.* How frequently should employees be paid? Are labor costs being accurately allocated to products and other cost centers? Are all applicable tax reporting requirements being met? How easily can employee requests for information be answered?

Traditionally, the payroll system has provided some of the information needed to answer these questions, such as data about labor costs. The HRM system has normally provided other information, such as data about employee skills. Still other information, such as data about employee morale, has traditionally not been collected by either the payroll or the HRM system. Note that externally generated information, such as data about tax rates and industry averages for turnover and absenteeism, is also needed to make these decisions. This section describes how a well-designed data model facilitates the effective integration of all this information.

Data Model: Payroll and Cost Accounting

Figure 14-5 presents a partial REA data model for payroll processing and cost accounting. If the data model depicted in the figure was implemented in a relational database, then there would be a table for each entity (rectangle) and for each many-to-many relationship. The contents of most of the entities depicted in Figure 14-5, and the cardinalities of the relationships among those entities, should be self-explanatory. Let us briefly discuss several key points.

The basic economic exchange modeled in Figure 14-5 is obtaining the use of an employee's time and skills and in return paying the employee. The get employee services event stores the data traditionally found on time cards and is used to process payroll. Each row in the table captures data about the hours an employee works in a single day. The pay employees table stores data about paychecks issued to employees. Each row in that table represents a paycheck. Employees are paid periodically; therefore, the cardinalities indicate that one paycheck can be linked to many rows (daily time cards) in the get employee services table. Because employees do not normally get paid in installments, each time card is linked to only one paycheck.

The employee service entity represents the resource being acquired: the use of an individual employee's time and skills. This resource cannot be inventoried. Organizations may wish, however, to track and summarize both how much of this resource they acquired and how it was used in a given pay period.

The use employee services event stores data about specific tasks an individual employee performs that were traditionally captured on paper job-time tickets. Indeed, in the production cycle this event is usually called job operations (see Figure 13.8). Each row in this table describes a specific kind of task performed for a specific period. For example, there could be a row for stocking shelves, a row for working the cash register, and a row for unloading deliveries. The objective is to track how much time an employee spends performing different kinds of tasks. As shown in the REA diagrams in previous chapters, however, data are also captured about the performance of each individual event (e.g., each individual sale rung up at a cash register would be recorded as a row in the sales table). Consequently, as shown in the lower portion of Figure 14-5, each row in the use employee services table can be linked to many rows in a specific event table. Each specific event, however, is linked to only one row in the use employee services table.

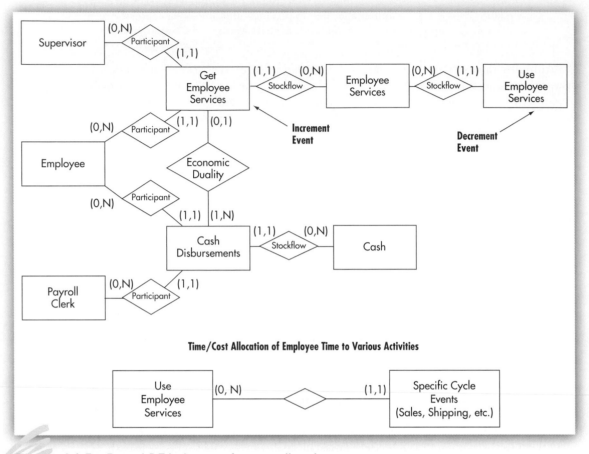

Figure 14-5   Partial REA diagram for payroll and cost accounting

The use employee services table provides additional information not available from the various REA diagrams presented in previous chapters. For example, the revenue cycle REA diagram presented in Figure 11-13 can be queried to answer such questions as "What is the amount of sales a specific salesperson generates?" or "How many sales did each salesperson make?" It does not contain the necessary data, however, to directly answer such questions as "How many hours did a particular salesperson work at the cash register, as opposed to restocking shelves?" The data needed to answer that query is stored in the use employee services table.

Not every organization collects detailed data about their employees' use of time. Typically, manufacturing companies collect such data about employees who participate in the production process for product costing purposes. Similarly, professional services firms collect such data for purposes of billing clients for services rendered. Many retail and service organizations do not collect such detailed data, however. If an organization does not collect detailed data about the time employees spend performing various tasks, then it typically does not implement the use employee services event table or the employee services resource table.

Data Model: Integrating Payroll with HRM Data

Figure 14-6 presents an REA diagram that integrates payroll and HRM data. Notice that the employee entity is linked to almost every other entity in the diagram, reflecting the importance of employees to the organization.

The recruiting event entity stores data about activities performed to notify the public of job openings. The data recorded in this entity are useful for documenting compliance with employment laws and also for evaluating the effectiveness of various methods used to announce job opportunities. The many-to-many relationship between skills and recruiting reflects the fact that each advertisement may seek several specific skills and that, over time, there may be several advertisements for a given skill. The relationship between the recruiting event and job applicants is modeled as being many-to-many because many people typically apply for each job opening, but a given individual may also respond to more than one recruiting event. Also, more than one employee may participate in each recruiting event, and over time a given employee may participate in many such events.

The interview event stores detailed data about each job interview. It is linked to the hire employees event in a many-to-one relationship. This reflects the fact that the hiring event occurs only once, but may result from either one or a number of preceding interviews.

The employees entity stores much of the data typically found in the employee (payroll) master file. The skills entity contains data about the different job skills of interest to the organization. The relationship between skills and employees is modeled as being many-to-many because an employee may possess a number of job skills and, conversely, several employees may possess the same skill.

The training event entity represents the various workshops, training programs, and other opportunities provided for employees to develop and maintain their skills. Thus, this entity stores data that can be used to evaluate the effectiveness and cost of training and development efforts. The relationship between the employees and training entities is many-to-many, because a given employee will, over time, attend numerous training courses and, conversely, a number of employees will attend a specific training class. The relationship between the skills and training entities is one-to-many, because each course is designed to develop a specific skill but several different training courses can develop and enhance a specific skill.

Benefits of the Data Model

If the data model shown in Figure 14-6 were implemented in a relational database, managers could use query languages to easily retrieve the data they need to manage their employees. For example, Peter Wu could write a query to identify which employees at AOE possess a specific skill, such as knowledge of SQL. He could use this type of query to staff special projects or create task forces. The information retrieved by such queries also could be combined with projected future skill needs to plan hiring strategies and to influence the scheduling of future training courses.

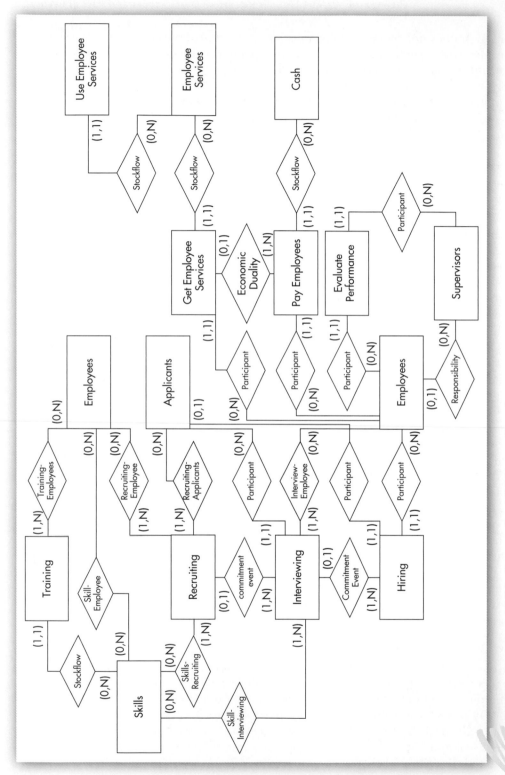

Figure 14-6 Integrated REA diagram for HRM/payroll cycle

Creating a data model for the HRM/payroll cycle like the one depicted in Figure 14-6 also can provide an organization with strategic benefits. First, because it makes information more easily accessible to managers, the data model should result in better decisions concerning how human resources are used and developed. For example, professional services firms have databases of employee expertise. Using these databases, professional staff can quickly identify and solicit the advice of colleagues who have had prior experience in addressing a given problem. This saves staff considerable time in developing solutions to client problems and enables geographically dispersed staff to learn from each other. Well-designed and easily accessible databases are key to such effective sharing and leverage of knowledge. An integrated database such as that depicted in Figure 14-6 also makes it easier for companies to monitor that employees are indeed attending the proper training classes and upgrading their skills.

A second strategic benefit of an integrated HRM/payroll data model is that staff can perform many HRM activities more efficiently, thereby reducing costs. For example, notice that Figure 14-6 includes information about job applicants. On-line resume databases now exist for many professional fields. That information can be downloaded and automatically stored in the job applicant entity, thereby saving considerable time and expense as compared with traditional manual collection and entry of data. Moreover, once in the system, that information can be quickly distributed. For example, Federal Express now scans all resumes and stores them in an image-processing database. This system allows managers who are making hiring decisions to access and print out relevant resumes immediately, rather than waiting for days for the paper documents to be routed to them.

A well-designed HRM database also can be used to reduce recruiting costs. It is not uncommon for several related job openings to arise over a short time. If data about previous applicants are stored in an easily accessible database, much of the clerical work associated with processing applications for subsequent job openings can be avoided.

Control Considerations

The discussion of the threats listed in Table 14-2 stressed the importance of properly segregating incompatible duties. REA diagrams are particularly useful in assessing these controls because they indicate which internal agents participate in each event. In addition, if the REA model is implemented in a DBMS, the computer can be programmed to enforce segregation of duties by preventing one person from performing incompatible functions. Conversely, the system can also be programmed to list all cases of one employee performing multiple roles, so that the auditors can investigate if adequate compensating controls exist.

A DBMS also increases the importance of effective access controls. Most relational DBMSs provide a means to control access by letting users see only a portion of the database (called a view). For example, the view defined for payroll clerks would probably not include access to the data pertaining to the hiring or performance evaluation events. In addition, they would have read-only access to pay rate data in the employee table. This restriction would enable them to obtain the information they need to prepare payroll but would prevent them from making unauthorized changes to that data.

With a DBMS, adequate backup and disaster recovery procedures also become crucial. In addition, data accuracy is vital when using a DBMS. Fortunately, the relational data model provides some built-in controls to ensure data accuracy and consistency. One of the more important of these controls is support for foreign keys and referential integrity. This ensures, for example, that when a new row is added to the pay employee table, the system verifies that the employee number (which appears as a foreign key in that table) actually exists as a primary key in the employee table (i.e., there really is such an employee).

SUMMARY AND CASE CONCLUSION

The HRM/payroll cycle information system consists of two related, but separate, subsystems: HRM and payroll. The HRM system records and processes data about the activities of recruiting, hiring, training, assigning, compensating, evaluating, and discharging employees. The payroll system records and processes data used to pay employees for their services.

The HRM/payroll system must be designed to comply with a myriad of government regulations related to both taxes and employment practices. In addition, adequate controls must exist to prevent (1) overpaying employees due to invalid (overstated) time and attendance data and (2) disbursing paychecks to fictitious employees. These two threats can be best minimized by proper segregation of duties, specifically by having the following functions performed by different individuals:

1. Authorizing and making changes to the payroll master file for such events as hirings, firings, and pay raises
2. Recording and verifying time worked by employees
3. Preparing paychecks
4. Distributing paychecks

Although the HRM and payroll systems have traditionally been separated, many companies, including AOE, are trying to integrate them to manage their human resources more effectively and to provide employees with better benefits and service. Elizabeth Venko and Ann Brandt explained to Peter Wu that this process requires designing the payroll database so that it can be easily linked with the nonpayroll data, such as the employee skills database, maintained in the HRM system. Working together, Elizabeth, Ann, and Peter developed a data model for AOE similar to that shown in Figure 14-6. Peter was impressed with how easily he could retrieve data about employee skills and attendance at training classes from this database. He agreed that this would satisfy the needs of department managers for quick and easy access to such information. Peter also realized that the HRM staff could similarly use this query capability to provide quick response to employee requests for information about their benefits, deductions, or retirement plans. He was even more impressed when Elizabeth and Ann explained that the new system would also allow employees to make direct changes in their retirement savings allocations, medical plan choices, and other benefit options. Freeing the HRM staff from these routine clerical tasks would allow his people to devote more time to strategic activities such as planning for future workforce needs, career counseling, and employee development.

Elizabeth explained that payroll processing itself could continue to be performed in batch mode, because there is no need for on-line processing (employees would continue to be paid only at periodic intervals). Reports, such as the payroll register, however, would be distributed electronically to improve efficiency. Elizabeth also wants to encourage more employees to sign up for direct deposit of their paychecks, thereby reducing the number of checks that need to be printed.

Elizabeth and Ann explained that an access control matrix would be created to maintain adequate segregation of duties in the new system and protect the integrity of the HRM/payroll database. For example, only HRM employees would add new employees, from terminals located in the HRM department.

Linda Spurgeon was pleased with Elizabeth and Ann's work on improving the company's HRM/payroll systems. She indicated that their next task would be to work with Stephanie Cromwell, AOE's chief financial officer, to improve the financial closing process and to help develop reports that would provide better insight into AOE's performance.

KEY TERMS

- human resources management (HRM)/payroll cycle
- time card
- payroll register

- deduction register
- earnings statement
- flexible benefits plan
- payroll service bureau

- professional employer organization (PEO)
- payroll clearing account

CHAPTER QUIZ

1. In an REA diagram of the payroll/HRM cycle, in which entity would information traditionally recorded on time cards be stored?
   a. employee services
   b. get employee services
   c. use employee services
   d. pay employees
2. In an REA diagram of the payroll/HRM cycle, in which entity would information traditionally recorded on job-time tickets be stored?
   a. employee services
   b. get employee services
   c. use employee services
   d. pay employees
3. Which document lists the current amount and year-to-date totals of gross pay, deductions, and net pay for one employee?
   a. payroll register
   b. time card
   c. paycheck
   d. earnings statement
4. On-line processing is most useful for which of these tasks?
   a. preparing payroll checks
   b. reconciling job-time tickets and time cards
   c. paying payroll tax obligations
   d. making changes in employee job status and pay rate

5. Use of a payroll service bureau or a PEO provides all of these benefits *except* which of the following?
   a. integration of payroll and personnel data, such as job skills
   b. lower cost of processing payroll
   c. less need for developing and maintaining payroll tax expertise
   d. fewer staff needed to process payroll
6. Which control procedure would be most effective in detecting the failure to prepare a paycheck for a new employee *before* paychecks are distributed?
   a. validity checks on the employee number on each time card
   b. record counts of time cards submitted and time cards processed
   c. zero balance check
   d. use of a separate payroll bank account
7. Which department should have responsibility for authorizing pay rate changes?
   a. timekeeping
   b. payroll
   c. HRM
   d. accounting
8. To maximize effectiveness of internal controls over payroll, which of the following persons should be responsible for distributing employee paychecks?
   a. departmental secretary
   b. cashier
   c. controller
   d. departmental supervisor
9. Where should unclaimed paychecks be returned?
   a. HRM department
   b. cashier
   c. payroll department
   d. absent employee's supervisor
10. Which of the following entities is most likely to be found in any organization's REA data model?
   a. use employee services
   b. employee services
   c. get employee services
   d. employee time

DISCUSSION QUESTIONS

14.1   This chapter noted many of the benefits that can arise by integrating the HRM and payroll databases. Nevertheless, many companies maintain separate payroll and HRM information systems. Why do you think this is so? (Hint: Think about the differences in employee background and the functions performed by the HRM and payroll departments.)

14.2   Some accountants have advocated that a company's human assets be measured and included directly in the financial statements. For example, the costs of hiring and training an employee would be recorded as an asset that is amortized over the employee's expected term of service. What do you think about this proposal? Should information about human resources appear in a company's published financial statements?

14.3   Some companies such as Skandia Group are attempting to capture employees' knowledge and preserve it. (Skandia refers to this as "transforming human intellectual capital into structural intellectual capital.") One technique is to interview employees and encode their knowledge in an expert system. To what extent should this be done? When an employee develops specialized skills and knowledge on the job, who "owns" that knowledge?

14.4   You are responsible for implementing a new employee performance measurement system that will provide factory supervisors with detailed information about each of their employees on a weekly basis. In conversation with some of these supervisors, you are surprised to learn they do not believe these reports will be useful. They explain that they can already obtain all the information they need to manage their employees simply by observing the shop floor. Comment on that opinion. How could formal reports supplement and enhance what the supervisors learn by direct observation? Why is it difficult to get people to agree to formally document what they think they already know?

14.5   In some aspects, the acquisition and use of employee services is similar to the purchase and use of other resources, such as raw materials and supplies. Discuss the similarities and differences between the way that the purchasing and payroll cycles account for the acquisition of and payment for resources used.

14.6   Direct deposit both reduces the costs of and improves control over payroll distribution. Does this mean that all companies should require their employees to be paid by direct deposit? Why or why not?

14.7   With e-mail and Internet access, employees can "moonlight" while on the job. How should, and can, companies deal with this situation?

14.8   Many large companies find that their existing bureaucratic structure makes innovation difficult. One way some companies have attempted to deal with this problem is to create special teams of employees that are separate from the mainstream, whose sole task is to function like a start-up company and develop new innovative products. Such teams are commonly referred to as "Skunkworks." Discuss the advantages and disadvantages of this approach.

PROBLEMS

14.1   What internal control procedure(s) would be most effective in preventing the following errors or fraudulent acts?
   a. An inadvertent data entry error caused an employee's wage rate to be overstated in the payroll master file.
   b. A fictitious employee payroll record was added to the payroll master file.
   c. During data entry, the hours worked on an employee's time card for one day were accidentally entered as 80 hours, instead of 8 hours.
   d. A computer operator used an on-line terminal to increase her own salary.
   e. A factory supervisor failed to notify the HRM department that an employee had been fired. Consequently, paychecks continued to be issued for that employee. The supervisor pocketed and cashed those paychecks.
   f. A factory employee punched a friend's time card in at 1:00 P.M. and out at 5:00 P.M. while the friend played golf that afternoon.
   g. A programmer obtained the payroll master file and increased his salary.
   h. Some time cards were lost during payroll preparation; consequently, when paychecks were distributed, several employees complained about not being paid.
   i. A large portion of the payroll master file was destroyed when the disk pack containing the file was used as a scratch file for another application.

14.2   Refer to the portion of Figure 14-5 that models payroll processing in order to perform the following two tasks:

a. Modify the expenditure cycle REA diagram (Figure 12-11) to include payroll processing. Assume that management does not want to track how employees use their time.

b. Modify the production cycle REA diagram (Figure 13-8) to include payroll processing.

14.3 Assume that the data model depicted in Figure 14-5 is used to store HRM/payroll data. List the programmed application controls that should be used for adding data to the services provided, performance evaluation, and pay employees tables. Your answer should state which controls should be applied to each data item and the purpose for each control.

14.4 You have been hired to evaluate the payroll system for the Skip-Rope Manufacturing Company. The company processes its payroll in-house. Prepare a list of questions to evaluate Skip-Rope's internal control structure as it pertains to payroll processing for its factory employees. Each question should be phrased so that it can be answered with either a yes or a no; all no answers should indicate potential internal control weaknesses. Include a third column listing the potential problem that could arise if that particular control were not in place.

14.5 The internal audit department of the Newberry Manufacturing Company was assigned to review the payroll department of the Galena, Illinois, plant. The internal audit consisted of (1) tests to verify the numerical accuracy of the payroll department's records, and (2) the determination of the procedures used to process payroll.

The internal audit team found that all numerical items were accurate. The proper hourly rates were used and the wages and deductions were calculated correctly. The payroll register was properly footed, totaled, and posted.

Interviews with plant personnel revealed the following information:

- The payroll clerk receives the time cards from the various department supervisors at the end of each pay period, checks the employee's hourly rate against information provided by the HRM department, and records the regular and overtime hours for each employee.
- The payroll clerk sends the time cards to the plant's computer operations department, where the payroll is processed.
- The computer operations department returns the time cards along with the printed checks and payroll register to the payroll clerk. The payroll clerk then verifies the hourly rate and hours worked for each employee by comparing the detail in the payroll register with the time cards.
- If errors are found, the payroll clerk voids the computer-generated check, prepares another check for the correct amount, and adjusts the payroll register accordingly.
- The payroll clerk obtains the plant's check signature plate from the accounting department and signs the payroll checks.
- An employee of the HRM department picks up and holds the checks until they are delivered to the department supervisors for distribution to employees.

Required

Identify the shortcomings in the payroll procedures at the Newberry Manufacturing Company and suggest steps to correct those weaknesses.

(CMA Examination, adapted)

14.6 Rose Publishing Company devotes the bulk of its work to the development of high school and college textbooks. The printing division has several production departments and employs 400 people. Approximately 95 percent of the staff are paid hourly rates and can earn overtime pay; the remainder earn fixed salaries. All employees are paid weekly.

A manual time card system is used. Each employee punches in and out when entering or leaving the plant. The timekeeping department audits the time cards daily and prepares input sheets for the computerized functions of the payroll system.

Currently, a daily report of the previous day's clock card information, organized by department, is sent to each supervisor in the printing division for verification and approval. Any changes are made directly on the report, signed by the supervisor, and returned to time-keeping. The altered report serves as the input authorization for changes to the system. Because of the volume and frequency of reports, this procedure is the most expensive process in the system.

Timekeeping submits the corrected hourly data to the general and cost accounting departments. General accounting maintains the payroll system that determines weekly pay-roll; prepares weekly checks; summarizes data for monthly, quarterly, and annual reports; and generates W-2 forms. The cost accounting department prepares a weekly and monthly payroll distribution report that shows labor costs for each department.

Competition in college textbook publishing has increased steadily in recent years. Although Rose Publishing has maintained its sales volume, profits have declined. Direct labor cost is believed to be the basic cause of this decline. Insufficient detail on labor utilization is available, however, to enable management to pinpoint the source of the suspected inefficiencies. Consequently the following proposal to redesign the payroll system was developed:

1. The use of an integrated time and labor attendance card (TLAC) system would include direct data entry; cost distribution by project as well as by department; on-line access to time and attendance data for verification, correction, and update; and creation and maintenance of individual employee work history files for long-term analysis.
2. The TLAC system would incorporate uniquely encoded employee badges that electronically record entry to and exit from the plant directly into the system.
3. Labor cost records would be maintained at the employee level, showing the time worked per project in each department. This would allow labor cost to be fully analyzed. Responsibility for correct and timely entry would reside with the departmental supervisors and be verified daily by project managers.
4. On-line terminals would be available in each department for direct data entry. Access to the system would be limited to authorized users through a password and user ID system. Departmental supervisors would be allowed to inspect, correct, verify, and update only time and attendance data for their employees. Project managers would only be able to access information recorded for their projects. Any corrections they want to make would have to be certified outside the system and entered by the affected supervisor.
5. Appropriate data would be maintained at the employee level to allow verification of employee personnel files and individual work history by department and project. Access to employee master file data would be restricted to the HRM department. Work history data would be made available for analysis only at the project or department level and only to supervisors and project managers for whom an employee works.

Required
a. Compared with the existing clock card system, what are the advantages and disadvantages of the recommended system for electronically recording time and attendance data?
b. Identify the items that should be included in the employee master payroll file.
c. The TLAC system allows the employee's departmental supervisor and the HRM department to examine the data contained in an individual employee's payroll master record.
   1. What information should each supervisor be allowed to examine?
   2. What safeguards may be installed to prevent unauthorized access to this data?
d. The recommended system would allow both the departmental supervisors and the project managers to obtain current labor cost distribution data on a limited basis. These restrictions might lead to conflicts between the departmental supervisors and project managers.

1. Why are the specific limitations proposed?
2. How would you recommend resolving any disagreements between the departmental supervisors and project managers about labor cost distributions?

(CMA Examination, adapted)

14.7   The Kowal Manufacturing Company employs about fifty production workers and has the following payroll procedures:
   • The factory supervisor interviews and hires all job applicants. The new employee prepares a W-4 form (Employee's Withholding Exemption Certificate) and gives it to the supervisor. The supervisor writes the hourly rate of pay for the new employee in the corner of the W-4 form and then gives the form to the payroll clerk as notice that a new worker has been hired. The supervisor verbally advises the payroll department of any subsequent pay raises.
   • A supply of blank time cards is kept in a box near the entrance to the factory. All workers take a time card on Monday morning and fill in their names. During the week they record the time they arrive and leave work by punching their time cards in the time clock located near the main entrance to the factory. At the end of the week the workers drop the time cards in a box near the exit. A payroll clerk retrieves the completed time cards from the box on Monday morning. Employees are automatically removed from the payroll master file when they fail to turn in a time card.
   • The payroll checks are manually signed by the chief accountant and then given to the factory supervisor, who distributes them to the employees. The factory supervisor arranges for delivery of the paychecks to any employee who is absent on payday.
   • The payroll bank account is reconciled by the chief accountant, who also prepares the various quarterly and annual tax reports.

Required
List your suggestions for improving the Kowal Manufacturing Company's internal controls over hiring and payroll processing.

(CPA Examination, adapted)

14.8   Arlington Industries manufactures and sells engine parts for large industrial equipment. The company employs over 1,000 workers for three shifts, and most employees work overtime when necessary. Figure 14-7 depicts the procedures followed to process payroll.
Additional information about payroll procedures follows:
   • The HRM department determines the wage rates of all employees. The process begins when a form authorizing the addition of a new employee to the payroll master file is sent to the payroll coordinator for review and approval. Once the information about the new employee is entered in the system, the computer automatically calculates the overtime and shift differential rates for that employee.
   • A local accounting firm provides Arlington with monthly payroll tax updates on tape, which are used to modify the tax rates.
   • Employees record time worked on time cards. Every Monday morning the previous week's time cards are collected from a bin next to the time clock, and new time cards are left for employees to use. The payroll department manager reviews the time cards to ensure that hours are correctly totaled; the system automatically determines if overtime has been worked or a shift differential is required.
   • The payroll department manager performs all other activities depicted in Figure 14-7.
   • The system automatically assigns a sequential number to each payroll check. The checks are stored in a box next to the printer for easy access. After the checks are printed, the payroll department manager uses an automatic check-signing machine to sign the checks. The signature plate is kept locked in a safe. After the checks have been signed, the pay-

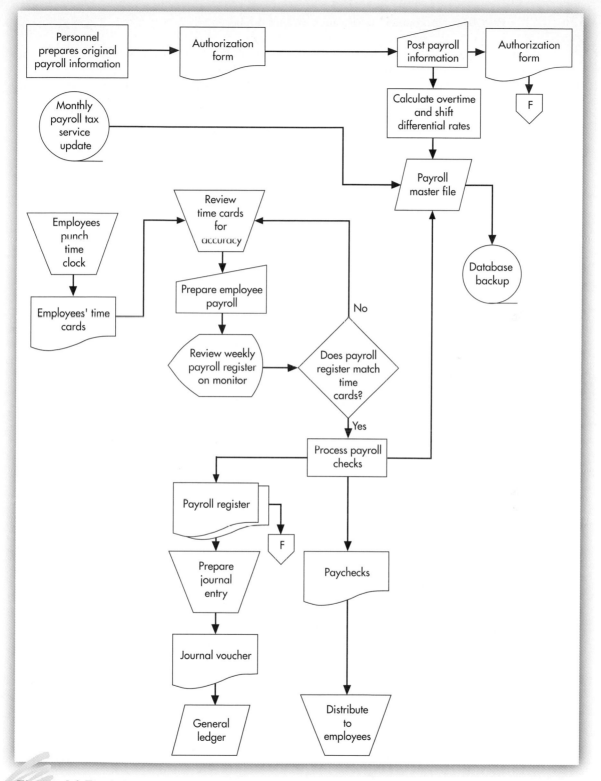

Figure 14-7 Arlington industries flowchart of payroll processing

535

roll manager distributes the paychecks to all first-shift employees. Paychecks for the other two shifts are given to the shift supervisor for distribution.

- The payroll master file is backed up weekly, after payroll processing is finished.

Required

a. Identify and describe five different areas in Arlington's payroll processing system where controls are inadequate.

b. Identify and describe two different areas in Arlington's payroll processing system where controls are satisfactory.

(CMA Examination, adapted)

14.9   The Darwin Department Store pays all of its employees on a salaried basis. Payroll processing is done internally. The payroll master file is maintained on disk. At periodic intervals every month, the HRM department uses on-line terminals to enter batches of payroll file change transactions. After those changes pass the appropriate data entry controls, they are posted to the payroll master file. This run produces a printed report listing all file changes processed.

The payroll run takes place on the last day of each month. Because all employees are paid a fixed salary, there is no transaction input. This run produces printed employee paychecks, earnings registers, a printed summary report, and a payroll register file recorded on disk. The payroll register file is later processed to print a payroll register.

1. What is meant by the term "payroll file change transactions"? Give four examples of these types of transactions.
2. Prepare a flowchart of the processes described.
3. The summary report generated by the payroll run includes accounting journal entries. Describe the contents of these journal entries. What other information is likely to be found on the summary report?
4. Describe a comprehensive set of internal control procedures and policies for this payroll application. Relate each control procedure to a specific objective and explain what threats it is designed to mitigate.
5. Suppose that Darwin decides to pay commissions to its sales staff. What changes would be required in (a) the payroll master file, (b) the payroll run, and (c) the internal control procedures developed in step 4?

14.10 Bernie's Pet Store sells pet food, toys, and supplies. Bernie, the owner, is the only person who places orders with suppliers. He is also the only person who writes checks. Suppliers ship each order individually; if they are out of an item, they back order it and ship it separately as soon as it arrives. Bernie pays each supplier monthly for all purchases made the previous month. Suppliers do not allow him to make installment payments.

Bernie has eight employees, each of whom can check in materials received from suppliers and sell merchandise to customers. Bernie pays his employees weekly.

All sales are made in-store and are paid for immediately by cash, check, or credit card.

When employees are not working the cash register or checking in merchandise, they restock shelves and clean up the premises. Bernie does not want to track each individual restock or clean-up event, but does want to know how much time each employee spends doing those tasks, as well as how much time each employee spends receiving inventory and making sales to customers (since all sales are paid for, in full, at the time of the sale, Bernie wants to just track the time each employee spends at the cash register collecting cash).

Required

Draw an integrated REA diagram for Bernie's Pet Shop. Be sure to include both payroll processing and the ability to track how employees use their time.

14.11 The local community feels that secondary school education is a necessity in our society and that lack of education leads to a number of social problems. As a result, the local school board has decided to take action to reverse the rising dropout rate. The board has voted to provide funds to encourage students to remain in school and earn their high school diplomas. The idea is to treat secondary education like a job and pay students. The board, however, could not agree on the details for implementing this new plan. Consequently, you have been hired to devise a system to compensate students for staying in school and earning their diploma.

As you devise your compensation scheme, be sure it meets the following general control objectives for the payroll cycle:[1]

- All personnel and payroll transactions are properly authorized.
- All employees are assigned to do productive work, and they do it efficiently and effectively.
- All transactions are accurately recorded and processed.
- Accurate records are maintained.
- All disbursements are proper.

Required
Write a proposal that addresses these five questions:
a. How should the students be compensated (e.g., for attendance, grades)?
b. How and by whom will the payments be authorized?
c. How will the payments be processed?
d. How should the payments be made (e.g., in cash or other means)?
e. When will the payments be made?

[1]Adapted from Carol F. Venable, "Development of Diversity Awareness and Critical Thinking," *Proceedings of the Lilly Conference on Excellence in College and University Teaching—West* (Lake Arrowhead, Calif., March 1995); and American Accounting Association Teaching and Curriculum Demonstration Session (Orlando, Fla., August 1995). Reprinted with permission of Dr. Carol Venable.

Case 14-1 AnyCompany, Inc.: An Ongoing Comprehensive Case

Select a local company and study its payroll system (you may use the same company you identified to complete this case in previous chapters). Prepare a report that contains the following:

1. DFD of the payroll system
2. Flowchart of the payroll system (Comment on the company's use, or lack thereof, of IT in payroll processing.)
3. List of the various paper and electronic documents used to process payroll (Evaluate the design of each document and assess its appropriateness for its intended use.)
4. List of the various threats and the control procedures employed to mitigate them (Assess the overall adequacy of internal controls.)
5. List of the reports produced by the system (Evaluate how well those reports meet management's information needs.)
6. REA data model for the company's HRM/payroll processes

Case 14-2 Payroll Service Bureaus and Professional Employer Organizations

Write a brief report describing the advantages and disadvantages of using a payroll service bureau, a professional employer organization, or processing payroll internally. Perform the following research to collect the data for your report:

1. Contact a local payroll service bureau. Find out what services it provides and how much it charges for those services. Ask about the bureau's client base—what size companies does it serve? In what industries does it specialize?
2. Contact a local professional employer organization. Find out what services it provides and how much it charges for those services.

Ask about the company's client base – what size companies does it serve? In what industries does it specialize?
3. Contact two companies that use either a payroll service bureau or a PEO and two that process their own payrolls. Ask them to explain why they do (or do not) process payroll in-house.

ANSWERS TO CHAPTER QUIZ

1. b	**3.** d	**5.** a	**7.** c	**9.** b
2. c	**4.** d	**6.** b	**8.** b	**10.** c

General Ledger and Reporting System

Learning Objectives

After studying this chapter, you should be able to:

- Describe the information processing operations required to update the general ledger and to produce other reports for internal and external users.
- Identify the major threats in general ledger and reporting activities and evaluate the adequacy of various control procedures for dealing with them.
- Read and explain an integrated enterprise-wide REA data model.
- Discuss and design a balanced scorecard for an organization.
- Explain the relationship between on-line transaction processing systems and data warehouses used to support business intelligence.
- Understand the implications of new IT developments, such as XBRL, for internal and external reporting.

Integrative Case: Alpha Omega Electronics

Linda Spurgeon, AOE's president and CEO, is not satisfied with the financial reporting capabilities of AOE's new ERP system. Although the monthly closing process now takes less than two days and provides management with timely information about the firm's financial performance, the new ERP system only provides information about one dimension of AOE's performance. At a recent retreat, AOE's top management developed a multidimensional report, called a *balanced scorecard,* for AOE. The proposed balanced scorecard integrates traditional financial performance measures of key business processes with several other nonfinancial measures. The task now is to ensure that this balanced scorecard can be produced in a timely manner.

In addition, although AOE's new system provides managers with quick and easy access to current-year financial data, trend analysis about performance over the past 5 to 10 years is much more difficult and time consuming. Moreover, Stephanie Cromwell, AOE's chief financial officer, is encountering increased costs associated with providing financial information to interested external parties on a timely basis.

Linda calls a meeting with Elizabeth Venko, AOE's controller, and Ann Brandt, AOE's vice president of information systems, to discuss these concerns. They agree to research how AOE's new information system can be further improved to address these issues.

INTRODUCTION

This chapter discusses the information processing operations involved in updating the general ledger and preparing reports that summarize the results of an organization's activities. As shown in Figure 15-1, the general ledger and reporting system plays a central role in a company's AIS. One of its primary functions is to collect and organize data from the following sources:

Figure 15-1   Context diagram of the general ledger and reporting system

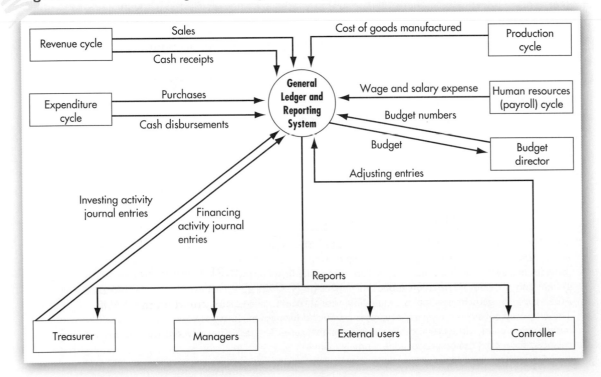

➤ Each of the accounting cycle subsystems described in Chapters 11 through 14 provides information about regular transactions. (Only the principal data flows from each subsystem are depicted, to keep the figure uncluttered.)

➤ The treasurer provides information about financing and investing activities, such as the issuance or retirement of debt and equity instruments and the purchase or sale of investment securities.

➤ The budget department provides budget numbers.

➤ The controller provides adjusting entries.

This information must be organized and stored in a manner that facilitates meeting the varied information needs of internal and external users. Managers need detailed information about the results of operations in their particular area of responsibility. Investors and creditors want periodic financial statements to help them assess the organization's performance. Increasingly, they are demanding more detailed and more frequent reports. Government agencies also have periodic information requirements that must be met.

Consequently, the general ledger and reporting system must be designed to produce regular periodic reports and to support real-time inquiry needs. For example, departmental managers should be able to assess actual versus planned performance at any time so that deviations can be identified early enough to take corrective actions. Likewise, the treasurer must be able to closely monitor cash flows so that deviations from forecasts can be identified in time to adjust short-term borrowing plans.

A logical question to ask at this point, however, concerns the need for a general ledger system. ERP systems can be configured without a general ledger. Moreover, the preceding chapters presented REA data models for the various subsystems of the AIS. Theoretically, implementing these REA data models in each subsystem of the AIS precludes the need for a separate general ledger. Some general ledger accounts, such as inventory and sales, would be represented explicitly as relational tables. Other general ledger accounts, such as accounts receivable and accounts payable, could be derived from data stored in several tables, but also would probably be stored as summary attributes in the customer and vendor tables, respectively.

Nevertheless, we describe a separate general ledger system in this chapter because the organization you work for after graduation will likely still be using a separate general ledger package, usually for reasons of tradition and politics. Note that this practice not only creates redundancy, but also continues the separation of financial from nonfinancial operating data. One unfortunate result is that accountants are often tempted to think that the only important data are those representing the financial aspects of operations. As you learned, such thinking seriously limits the opportunity for accountants to take a proactive value-added role in providing managers with all the information they need to make sound decisions.

What you have learned about relational databases and the REA model is still useful, however. A growing number of general ledger packages are based on the relational data model and support SQL access to financial data; thus, the data modeling skills you have developed in earlier chapters can be productively applied to designing and using the general ledger. It is also likely that as accountants become more comfortable with the concept of producing financial statements directly from a relational database, separate general ledger packages may ultimately disappear.

Therefore, we begin this chapter by describing the basic information processing operations performed to update the general ledger and to prepare reports for both internal management and external users. Next, we discuss major control threats in the general ledger and reporting cycle and the control procedures that can be used to mitigate them. Then we present an integrated enterprise-wide REA data model that can be used to understand how ERP systems interlink the various systems discussed in the preceding four chapters. We conclude the chapter by examining several important new developments in reporting systems.

GENERAL LEDGER AND REPORTING ACTIVITIES

Figure 15-2 is a level 0 DFD depicting the four basic activities performed in the general ledger and reporting system. Figure 15-3 depicts a typical on-line system used to perform those activities.

The first three activities in Figure 15-2 represent the basic steps in the accounting cycle, which culminates in the production of the traditional set of financial statements. The fourth activity indicates that, in addition to financial reports for external

Figure 15-2   Level 0 DFD for the general ledger and reporting system

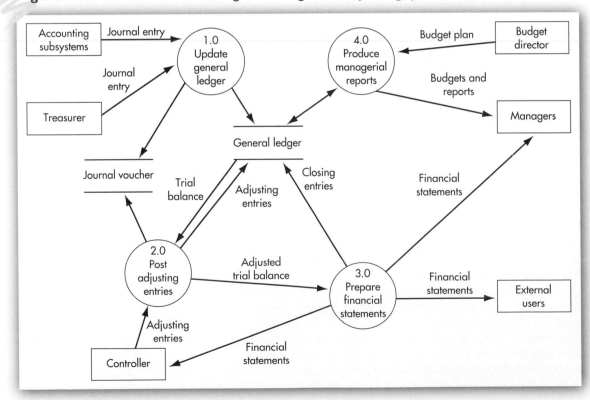

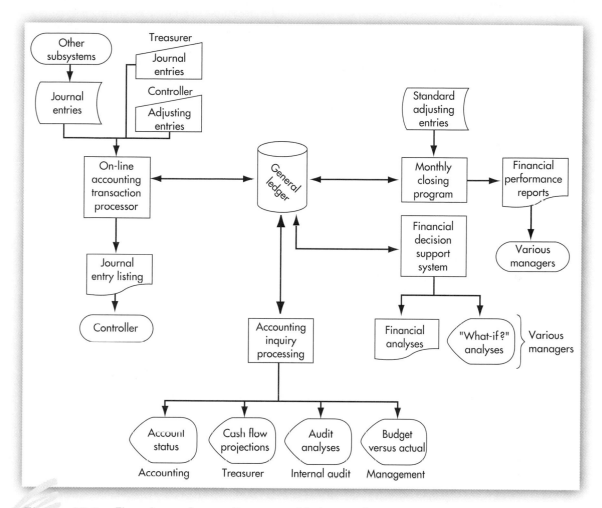

Figure 15-3   Flowchart of an on-line general ledger and reporting system

users, the AIS produces reports for internal management as well. We now examine each of these activities in more detail.

Update General Ledger

As shown in Figure 15-2, the first activity in the general ledger system (circle 1.0) is updating the general ledger. Updating consists of posting journal entries that originate from two sources:

1. *Accounting subsystems.* Each of the accounting subsystems described in Chapters 11 through 14 creates a journal entry to update the general ledger. In theory, the general ledger could be updated for each individual transaction. In practice, however, the various accounting subsystems usually update the general ledger by means of summary journal

entries that represent the results of all transactions that occurred during a given period of time (day, week, or month). For example, the revenue cycle subsystem would generate a summary journal entry debiting accounts receivable and cash and crediting sales for all sales made during the update period. Similarly, the expenditure cycle would generate summary journal entries to record the purchase of supplies and inventories and to record cash disbursements in payment for those purchases.

2. *Treasurer.* The treasurer's office creates individual journal entries to update the general ledger for nonroutine transactions such as the issuance or retirement of debt, the purchase or sale of investment securities, or the acquisition of treasury stock.

Journal entries to update the general ledger may be documented on a form called a **journal voucher.** Figure 15-2 shows that the individual journal entries used to update the general ledger are then stored in the journal voucher file. This file therefore contains the information that would be found in the general journal in a manual AIS. Note, however, that the journal voucher file is a by-product of, not an input to, the posting process. As we will explain later, the journal voucher file forms an important part of the audit trail.

Post Adjusting Entries

The second activity in the general ledger system is posting various adjusting entries (circle 2.0 in Figure 15-2). These adjusting entries originate from the controller's office, after the initial trial balance has been prepared. The **trial balance** is a report that lists the balances for all general ledger accounts. Its name reflects the fact that if all activities have been properly recorded, the total of all debit balances in various accounts should equal the total of all credit balances. Adjusting entries fall into five basic categories:

1. *Accruals* represent entries made at the end of the accounting period to reflect events that have occurred but for which cash has not yet been received or disbursed. Examples include the recording of interest revenue earned and wages payable.

2. *Deferrals* represent entries made at the end of the accounting period to reflect the exchange of cash prior to performance of the related event. Examples include recognizing the portion of advance payments from customers earned during a specific period and expensing the portion of prepaid assets (e.g., rent, interest, and insurance) used this period.

3. *Estimates* represent entries that reflect a portion of expenses that occur over a number of accounting periods. Examples include depreciation and bad debt expenses.

4. *Revaluations* represent entries made to reflect either differences between the actual and recorded value of an asset or a change in accounting principle. Examples include a change in the method used to value inventory, reducing the value of inventory to reflect obsolescence, or adjusting inventory records to reflect the results noted during a physical count of inventory.

5. *Corrections* represent entries made to counteract the effects of errors found in the general ledger.

As shown in Figure 15-2, information about these adjusting entries is stored in the journal voucher file. After all adjusting entries have been made, an adjusted trial balance is prepared. The adjusted trial balance serves as the input to the next step in the general ledger and financial reporting cycle, the preparation of financial statements.

Prepare Financial Statements

The third activity in the general ledger and reporting system is preparing financial statements (circle 3.0 in Figure 15-2). The income statement is prepared first, using data from the revenue and expense account balances in the adjusted trial balance. The balance sheet is prepared next. This activity requires closing entries that zero out all revenue and expense accounts and transferring the net income or loss to retained earnings. In an REA model, this would entail archiving the contents of all event tables. Most organizations perform both monthly and annual closes. The former zeroes out the current month's revenue and expense account balances but leaves the year-to-date totals intact. Thus, an income statement generated immediately after a monthly closing would display all zeroes in the current month column, but would store cumulative numbers in the year-to-date column. The third major financial statement produced is the statement of cash flows. It uses data from the income statement and balance sheet to provide details about the organization's investment and financing activities.

Produce Managerial Reports

The final activity in the general ledger and reporting system (circle 4.0 in Figure 15-2) is producing various managerial reports. Examples of general ledger control reports include (1) lists of journal vouchers by numerical sequence, account number, or date, and (2) lists of general ledger account balances. These reports are used to verify the accuracy of the posting process.

A number of budgets are produced for planning and evaluating performance. The operating budget depicts planned revenues and expenditures for each organizational unit. The capital expenditures budget shows planned cash inflows and outflows for each project. Cash flow budgets compare estimated cash inflows from operations with planned expenditures and are used to determine borrowing needs.

Budgets and performance reports should be developed on the basis of responsibility accounting. **Responsibility accounting** is reporting financial results on the basis of managerial responsibilities within an organization. The result is a set of correlated reports that break down the organization's overall performance by specific subunits, as shown in Figure 15-4. Note that each report shows actual costs and variances from budget for the current month and the year to date, but only for those items that the manager of that subunit controls. Note also the hierarchical nature of the reports: The total cost of each individual subunit is displayed as a single line item on the next-higher-level report.

The contents of the budgetary performance reports should be tailored to the nature of the unit being evaluated. For example, many production, service, and administrative departments are treated as cost centers. Accordingly their performance reports, as shown in Figure 15-4, should highlight actual versus budgeted performance in regard to controllable costs (those that the unit manager can affect directly). In contrast, sales departments are often evaluated as revenue centers. Consequently, their performance reports should compare actual to forecasted sales, broken down by appropriate product and geographic categories. Some departments, such as IT and utilities, charge other units for their services and are evaluated as profit centers. In this case, performance reports should appropriately compare actual revenues, expenses, and profits with their corresponding budgeted amounts. If plants, divisions, and other

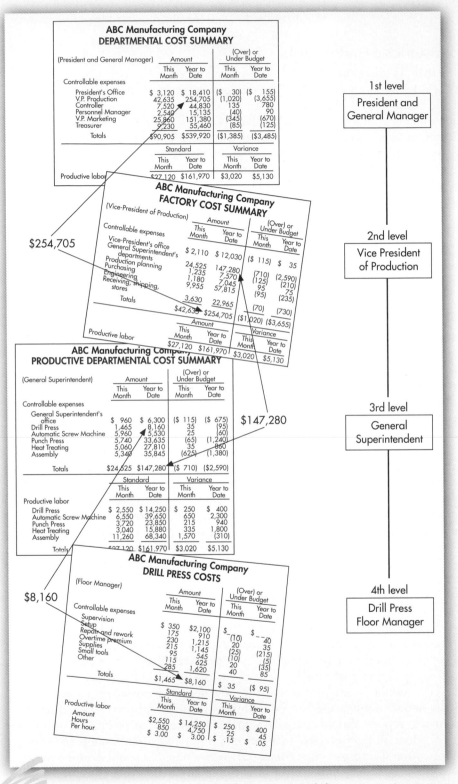

ABC Manufacturing Company
DEPARTMENTAL COST SUMMARY

(President and General Manager)

Controllable expenses	Amount This Month	Amount Year to Date	(Over) or Under Budget This Month	(Over) or Under Budget Year to Date
President's Office	$ 3,120	$ 18,410	($ 30)	($ 155)
V.P. Production	42,635	254,705	(1,020)	(3,655)
Controller	7,520	44,830	135	780
Personnel Manager	2,540	15,135	(40)	90
V.P. Marketing	25,860	151,380	(345)	(670)
Treasurer	9,230	55,460	(85)	(125)
Totals	$90,905	$539,920	($1,385)	($3,485)

	Standard This Month	Standard Year to Date	Variance This Month	Variance Year to Date
Productive labor	$27,120	$161,970	$3,020	$5,130

1st level
President and General Manager

$254,705

ABC Manufacturing Company
FACTORY COST SUMMARY

(Vice-President of Production)

Controllable expenses	Amount This Month	Amount Year to Date	(Over) or Under Budget This Month	(Over) or Under Budget Year to Date
Vice-President's office	$ 2,110	$ 12,030	($ 115)	$ 35
General Superintendent's departments				
Production planning	24,525	147,280	(710)	(2,590)
Purchasing	1,235	7,570	(125)	(210)
Engineering	1,180	7,045	95	75
Receiving, shipping, stores	9,955	57,815	(95)	(235)
	3,630	22,965		
Totals	$42,635	$254,705	($1,020)	($3,655)

	Amount This Month	Amount Year to Date	Variance This Month	Variance Year to Date
Productive labor	$27,120	$161,970	$3,020	$5,130

2nd level
Vice President of Production

$147,280

ABC Manufacturing Company
PRODUCTIVE DEPARTMENTAL COST SUMMARY

(General Superintendent)

Controllable expenses	Amount This Month	Amount Year to Date	(Over) or Under Budget This Month	(Over) or Under Budget Year to Date
General Superintendent's office	$ 960	$ 6,300	($ 115)	($ 675)
Drill Press	1,465	8,160	35	(95)
Automatic Screw Machine	5,960	5,530	25	(60)
Punch Press	5,740	33,635	(65)	(1,240)
Heat Treating	5,060	27,810	35	860
Assembly	5,340	35,845	(625)	(1,380)
Totals	$24,525	$147,280	($ 710)	($2,590)

	Standard This Month	Standard Year to Date	Variance This Month	Variance Year to Date
Productive labor				
Drill Press	$ 2,550	$ 14,250	$ 250	$ 400
Automatic Screw Machine	6,550	39,650	650	2,300
Punch Press	3,720	23,850	215	940
Heat Treating	3,040	15,880	335	1,800
Assembly	11,260	68,340	1,570	(310)
Totals	$27,120	$161,970	$3,020	$5,130

3rd level
General Superintendent

$8,160

ABC Manufacturing Company
DRILL PRESS COSTS

(Floor Manager)

Controllable expenses	Amount This Month	Amount Year to Date	(Over) or Under Budget This Month	(Over) or Under Budget Year to Date
Supervision			$—	$ —
Setup	$ 350	$2,100		
Repair and rework	175	910	(10)	40
Overtime premium	230	1,215	20	35
Supplies	215	1,145	(25)	(215)
Small tools	95	545	(10)	(5)
Other	115	625	20	(35)
	285	1,620	40	85
Totals	$1,465	$8,160	$ 35	($ 95)

	Standard This Month	Standard Year to Date	Variance This Month	Variance Year to Date
Productive labor				
Amount	$2,550	$ 14,250	$ 250	$ 400
Hours	850	4,750	25	45
Per hour	$ 3.00	$ 3.00	$ .15	$ .05

4th level
Drill Press Floor Manager

Figure 15-4 Sample set of reports for a responsibility accounting system

autonomous operating units are treated as investment centers, their performance reports also should provide data for calculating that unit's return on investment.

No matter which basis is used to prepare a unit's budgetary performance report, the method used to calculate the budget standard is crucial. The easiest approach is to establish fixed targets for each unit, store those figures in the database, and compare actual performance with those preset values. One major drawback to this approach is that the budget number is static and does not reflect unforeseen changes in the operating environment. Consequently, individual managers may be penalized or rewarded for factors beyond their control. For example, assume that the budgeted amounts in Figure 15-4 for the general superintendent are based on planned output of 2,000 units. If, however, due to greater than anticipated sales, actual production is 2,200 units, then the negative variances for each expense category may not really indicate inefficiency, but merely reflect the increased level of output.

A solution to such problems is to develop a flexible budget, in which the budgeted amounts vary in relation to some measure of organizational activity. In terms of our previous example, flexible budgeting would entail dividing the budget for each line item in the general superintendent's department into its fixed and variable cost components. In this way, budget standards would be automatically adjusted for any unplanned increases (or decreases) in production. Thus, any differences between these adjusted standards and actual costs can more appropriately be interpreted.

XBRL: An IT Opportunity to Improve Financial Reporting

Communications technology has long been used to reduce both the time and costs of preparing and disseminating financial statements. For example, controllers routinely access public financial reporting databases, such as NAARS and EDGAR, to find examples of how other companies disclose various items. Similarly, tax forms and regulations are available at the IRS Web site. Conversely, many companies can submit required financial and tax filings electronically to the SEC and the IRS, respectively. In addition, many corporate Web sites present the company's financial statements.

Nevertheless, until recently, the electronic dissemination of financial and nonfinancial information was a cumbersome, inefficient process. One problem was that many recipients had different requirements concerning the manner in which information was to be delivered. This meant that organizations had to devote considerable time and expense to formatting the same information in multiple ways. A second related problem was that recipients had to manually reenter much of the information into their own decision analysis tools. For example, recipients had to manually reenter information from financial statements that were presented as HTML documents into EXCEL spreadsheets so that the information could be analyzed.

The underlying cause of both problems lies with the method used to display information on the Internet. HTML code specifies only how a particular data item should be displayed, but provides no information about the content of that data. For example, HTML code can be used to control how information about current sales is displayed (e.g., its location and font characteristics), but does not provide any way to automatically identify that the particular data item represents the value of current year's sales.

This all changed with the development of the extensible business reporting language (XBRL), which is a variant of XML. This general-purpose language is designed to provide a means for communicating the content of data. HTML uses tags to indicate how data are to be formatted. For example, the tag <b> specifies that all subsequent text up to the next </b> tag is to be displayed in bold. XBRL uses similar types of pairs of tags to identify the contents of each data item. For example, an XBRL tag might indicate that the following data item represents accounts receivable.

Today, most people can create Web pages without having to directly write HTML code, because such products as Microsoft Word generate HTML code automatically with the "Save as HTML" option. Most major software vendors are building similar functionality into their products to make XBRL easy to use. Thus, accountants and systems professionals will not need to know how to write XBRL code to take advantage of the benefits it offers.

XBRL provides two major benefits to the creation and electronic dissemination of financial data. First, it enables organizations to publish information only once, using standard XBRL tags. Currently, financial data may be sent to one party as an HTML document, to another as an Adobe Acrobat file, to another as a text file, and to yet another party as a comma-delimited file. This process creates unnecessary costs. In contrast, the same XBRL file could be sent to each of those parties, who could then use the file as they wished. Thus, with XBRL, companies can publish their financial statements one time in a format that anyone can use.

The second benefit of XBRL is that the information the XBRL tags provide is interpretable. This means that recipients will no longer need to manually reenter data they acquired electronically so that decision support tools can analyze them. Instead, if the data contain XBRL tags, they can be fed directly into any analysis tool that understands XBRL. It also means that searching for data on the Internet will be more efficient and accurate. For example, prior to XBRL, searching the Internet for information about contingent liabilities would yield hundreds of sites, most of which have nothing to do with the financial data being sought. With XBRL tagged data, however, the search is limited to information about contingent liabilities reported in financial statements.

XBRL is certainly an important IT development. It is also noteworthy because the accounting profession spearheaded its development (see Focus 15-1). The XBRL development process provides an outstanding illustration of how accountants can actively participate in the ongoing development of IT.

CONTROL OBJECTIVES, THREATS, AND PROCEDURES

The control objectives in the general ledger and reporting system are similar to those in the other AIS cycles discussed in previous chapters:

1. All updates to the general ledger are properly authorized.
2. All recorded general ledger transactions are valid.
3. All valid, authorized general ledger transactions are recorded.
4. All general ledger transactions are accurately recorded.
5. General ledger data are safeguarded from loss or theft.
6. General ledger system activities are performed efficiently and effectively.

Well-designed documents and records play an important role in achieving these objectives. On-line data entry of transactions by the treasurer and the controller, as depicted

Focus 15-1

XBRL—An Accounting-Led IT Development

The origins of XBRL can be traced back to the early 1990s. At that time, a software engineer named Jon Bosak recognized that a critical shortcoming of HTML is its inability to describe the content of the data being presented. Bosak convinced the World Wide Web Consortium (W3C) to sponsor the development of a language with this capability. That project resulted in Bosak and two other software engineers creating a programming language called XML, which stands for extensible markup language. XML is a general-purpose tool that can tag any data with identifying markers.

XML was a step in the right direction. Charles Hoffman, a CPA who worked for a local accounting firm in Tacoma, Washington, however, realized that XML did not go far enough to be a general-purpose language for communicating financial information. What was needed was the ability to not only identify what each piece of data was, but also how it was to be processed and how it related to other data items. Hoffman started work on adding the desired capabilities to XML, but realized that the project required additional support. He sought and obtained the AICPA's help to pursue the development of a prototype set of XML-enhanced financial statements.

As the work progressed, the results were shared with major software companies. They recognized the value of such a common business language and joined in the project. Eventually, many leading software companies, and important user groups, joined in the venture with the AICPA. The result: XBRL. Vendors are currently working on making a wide range of financial and decision support software capable of supporting XBRL. Industry-specific templates are being developed. Similar work is beginning in many other countries. XBRL is on its way to becoming the global computer language for communicating financial data. And it all started with one CPA who was looking for a better way to disseminate financial data on the Internet.

Source: Stanley Zarowin and Wayne E. Harding, "Finally, Business Talks the Same Language," *Journal of Accountancy* (August 2000): 24–30.

in Figure 15-3, facilitates the accurate and efficient recording of general ledger journal entries. In such situations, using appropriate application controls, such as validity checks and field (format) checks, enhances the accuracy of data entry. Recording who completed and reviewed the form provides evidence that the journal entry was properly authorized. Prenumbering all journal entries facilitates checking that all transactions have been recorded. Restricting access to the general ledger program further reduces the risk of unauthorized transactions.

Table 15-1 lists the major threats and exposures in the general ledger and financial reporting system, along with applicable control procedures for mitigating them. Because the general ledger and reporting system involves only information processing activities, there are fewer threats than in the other AIS cycles. Moreover, the threats in the general ledger and reporting system primarily relate to the corruption, loss, or destruction of data. Let us now examine the control procedures that can be used to deal with these threats.

Table 15-1   Threats and Controls in the General Ledger and Reporting Systems

Process/Activity	Threat	Applicable Control Procedures
Updating the general ledger	1. Errors	Input and processing controls; reconciliations and control reports; audit trail
Access to the general ledger	2. Loss of confidential data and/or concealment of theft	Access controls; audit trail
Loss or destruction of the general ledger	3. Loss of data and assets	Backup and disaster recovery procedures

Threat 1: Errors in Updating the General Ledger

Errors made in updating the general ledger can lead to poor decision making based on erroneous information in financial performance reports. The control procedures for dealing with this threat fall into three categories: input edit and processing controls, reconciliations and control reports, and maintenance of an adequate audit trail.

Input edit and processing controls

Figure 15-3 shows two sources of journal entries for updating the general ledger: summary journal entries from the other AIS cycles and direct entries made by the treasurer or controller. The former are themselves the output of a series of processing steps, each of which was subject to a variety of application control procedures designed to ensure accuracy and completeness, as described in the preceding four chapters. Consequently, the primary input edit control for summary journal entries is checking to ensure that they represent activity for the most recent time period.

Journal entries made by the treasurer and controller, however, are original data entry. Consequently, the following types of input edit and processing controls are needed to ensure that they are accurate and complete:

1. A *validity check* to ensure that general ledger accounts exist for each account number referenced in a journal entry
2. *Field (format) checks* to ensure that the amount field in the journal entry contains only numeric data
3. *Zero-balance checks* to verify that total debits equals total credits in a journal entry
4. A *completeness test* to ensure that all pertinent data are entered, especially the source of the journal entry
5. *Closed-loop verification* matching account numbers with account descriptions, to ensure that the correct general ledger account is being accessed
6. Creating a standard adjusting entry file for recurring adjusting entries made each period, such as depreciation expense (Input accuracy is improved without repeatedly keying in these entries. The possibility of forgetting to make a recurring adjusting entry is also reduced, thereby ensuring input completeness.)
7. A *sign check* of the general ledger account balance, once updating is completed, to verify that the balance is of the appropriate nature (debit or credit)

8. Calculating *run-to-run totals* to verify the accuracy of journal voucher batch processing (The computer calculates the new balance of the general ledger account, based on its beginning balance and the total debits and credits applied to that account, then compares that with the actual account balance in the updated general ledger. Any discrepancies indicate a processing error that must be investigated.)

Reconciliations and control report

Reconciliations and control reports can detect if any errors were made during the process of updating the general ledger. One form of reconciliation is the preparation of a trial balance. It indicates if the total debit balances in the general ledger equal the total credit balances; if not, a posting error has occurred. In automated systems, using clearing and suspense accounts generally ensures that the general ledger is always in balance. At the close of a fiscal period, these special accounts should have zero balances; otherwise, an error was made in updating the general ledger.

To illustrate how these types of special accounts are used, assume that one clerk is responsible for recording the release of inventory to customers and another clerk is responsible for recording the billing of customers. The first clerk would make the following journal entry:

Unbilled shipments x x x
    Inventory   x x x

The second clerk would make this entry:

Accounts receivable   y y y
    Unbilled shipments   y y y

Once both entries have been completed, the special clearing account, unbilled shipments, should have a zero balance. If not, an error has been made and must be investigated and corrected.

Another important reconciliation is comparing the general ledger control account balances to the total balance in the corresponding subsidiary ledger. If these two totals do not agree, the difference must be investigated and corrected. It is also important to examine all transactions occurring near the end of an accounting period to verify that they are recorded in the proper time period.

Control reports can help identify the source of any errors that occurred in the general ledger update process. Listing journal vouchers by general account number facilitates identifying the cause of errors affecting a specific general ledger account. Listing the journal vouchers by sequence can indicate the absence of any journal entry postings. Finally, the **general journal listing** shows the details (account number, source reference code, description, and amount debited or credited) of each entry posted to the general ledger. This report indicates if the total debits equal the total credits posted to the general ledger.

The audit trail

The **audit trail** depicts the path of a transaction through the accounting system. Specifically, it provides the information needed to trace all changes made to the general ledger. In particular, an audit trail facilitates the following tasks:

1. Trace any transaction from its original source document (or record in an event table) to the general ledger and to any report or other document using that data.

2. Trace any item appearing in a report back through the general ledger to its original source document (or record in an event table).

3. Trace all changes in general ledger accounts from their beginning balance to their ending balance.

For example, the general journal transaction file indicates the source of all entries made to update the general ledger. The customer master file contains information about the account balances of individual customers, which can be summed and compared with the accounts receivable control account in the general ledger. Users can follow a similar process to reconcile accounts payable, inventory, and equipment balances. In advanced AIS, however, there may no longer be any paper source documents, so it is important to periodically create and archive backup copies of transaction and master files and take steps to ensure that those archived files cannot be altered.

Threat 2: Unauthorized Access to the General Ledger

Unauthorized access to the general ledger can result in confidential data leaks to competitors or corruption of the general ledger. It can also provide a means for concealing the theft of assets. Consequently, it is important to have adequate controls to prevent unauthorized access to the general ledger.

User IDs and passwords should be used to control access to the general ledger and to enforce the proper segregation of duties by limiting the functions that each legitimate user may perform. For example, employees who have custody of assets or the ability to authorize the release of assets should be prevented from updating the general ledger (the recording function). Similarly, management should be given read-only access to the general ledger, as depicted in the bottom of Figure 15-3. The access control matrix should also limit the functions that can be performed at various terminals. Adjusting entries, for example, should be allowed only from terminals in the controller's office.

Controls over the creation of journal voucher records also are important because they authorize changes to general ledger account balances. Thus, the system should check for the existence of a valid authorization code for each journal voucher record before posting that transaction to the general ledger. Otherwise, the integrity of the general ledger may be compromised. Note that this authorization code also forms a part of the audit trail. Indeed, inspection of the audit trail provides a means to detect unauthorized access to the general ledger.

Threat 3: Loss or Destruction of General Ledger

The general ledger is a key component of the organization's accounting information system. Therefore, it is important to provide adequate backup and disaster recovery procedures to protect this asset. Backup controls include the following:

1. Use internal and external file labels to protect the current general ledger against inadvertent destruction.

2. Perform regular backup of the general ledger. At least two backup copies of the general ledger should exist. One copy should be kept on-site where it can be immediately accessed; the other copy should be stored off-site to provide protection against a major disaster such as a fire or an earthquake.

Disaster recovery planning is also crucial. Given the increasing reliance on EDI, EFT, and the Internet to conduct daily business activities, no organization can survive for long if its computers go down. Therefore, organizations need to prepare and periodically practice a plan for dealing with a major disaster that has the potential to shut down their computer systems.

INTEGRATED ENTERPRISE-WIDE DATA MODEL

Figure 15-5 presents an integrated enterprise-wide data model for AOE. Most of this figure represents a merging of the data models as presented in Chapters 11 through 14. Note that this merging primarily involved linking each resource that appeared in those separate data models with the events that increase and decrease that resource. For example, the cash resource is linked to both cash disbursements and cash receipts. Similarly, the raw materials inventory is linked to both purchases and uses in production. Figure 15-5 also models the major events in the financing cycle: the issuance of equity and debt instruments and related periodic payments to investors and creditors.

Note how Figure 15-5 shows the linkages among different subsystems of the AIS. For example, a customer order for finished goods may, if there is insufficient inventory on hand to fill the order, trigger the scheduling of a production run to produce those goods. In turn, this production run may necessitate ordering additional raw materials. ERP systems are designed to automatically trigger these types of related actions across subsystems by linking each subsystem to a common enterprise-wide database. Thus, even though most ERP systems are not specifically based on the REA data model, a model like that depicted in Figure 15-5 can be useful in representing the contents of the ERP database: ERP database.

Most of Figure 15-5 is simply an integration of figures from previous chapters. The lower right corner, however, contains some new entities that represent two important types of financing activities: debt and equity transactions.

The event issue debt is a special kind of cash receipt. It is modeled as a separate event entity because it contains distinctly different attributes from those associated with cash receipts from the sales event, such as the face amount of debt issued, total amount received, date issued, maturity date, and interest rate. Usually, most companies do not deal directly with individual creditors. Instead, they sell their debt instruments through a financial intermediary, which is depicted in Figure 15-5 as the transfer agent. The transfer agent maintains the necessary information about individual creditors, to properly direct both the periodic interest payments and eventual repayment of principal. Therefore, each occurrence of an issue debt event contains data about the aggregate amount received from issuing a set of debt instruments. For example, the issuance of $10,000,000 of 5 percent bonds, which were ultimately purchased by several thousand different individuals for a total of $9,954,000, constitutes one issue debt event.

Debt payments are cash disbursements. Each debt payment event reflects the sending of funds to the transfer agent for the total amount of interest due at that time. Thus, to continue our example, the company would send $125,000 to the transfer agent to make the first quarterly payment on that $10,000,000 of bonds. The transfer agent, in turn, would then send individual checks to each creditor.

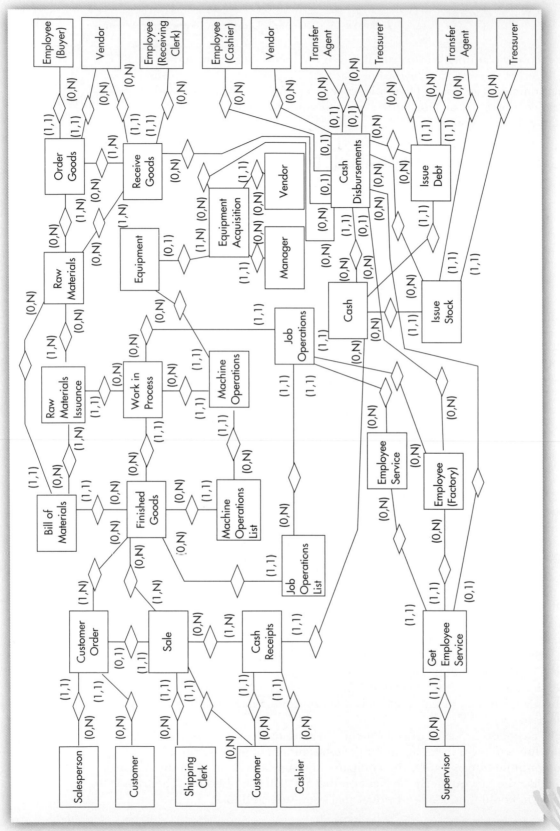

Figure 15-5 Integrated enterprise-wide REA diagram

Equity transactions are modeled in a manner similar to debt transactions. The issue stock event is a special kind of cash receipt associated with the issuance of stock, and the dividend payments are another type of cash disbursement. As with debt, most companies do not deal directly with individual stockholders. Thus, Figure 15-5 shows that both types of equity transactions involve participation by an external transfer agent.

Benefits of an Integrated Data Model

An integrated enterprise-wide data model like that depicted in Figure 15-5 can significantly improve the support provided for managerial decision making. To appreciate this fact, consider how the chart of accounts in a traditional general ledger system limits subsequent analyses of expense data. Expenses are typically recorded and stored in an account that reflects either the nature of the expense, such as travel, or its function, such as campus recruiting visits. With the first alternative, it is easy to prepare reports of total travel expenses, but difficult to identify how much travel expense is associated with campus recruiting. With the second alternative, it is easy to prepare reports that show the costs associated with campus recruiting, but difficult to prepare reports that track total travel costs.

A common response to this problem in file-based general ledger systems is to create more detailed account numbers that identify both the nature and purpose of each expense; thus, there would be separate accounts for campus recruiting travel expenses, sales travel expenses, and so on. The drawback of this approach, however, is that it results in an exponential expansion of the chart of accounts and an increase in the length of each account code. Both of these factors make it more difficult for coding clerks and managers to learn the chart of accounts and apply it correctly. In addition, the ability to further analyze the data remains limited to those categories that were established when the chart of accounts was designed.

In contrast, an integrated enterprise-wide data model avoids these problems and provides greater flexibility for analyzing data. Tables can be created for basic account categories, such as travel expenses. These tables also can include a text attribute for describing the purpose of that expenditure. Managers can then use queries to extract travel expenses by category, such as campus recruiting or trade shows. Moreover, simply changing the condition specified in the query can easily change these categories over time in response to different needs. Thus users are not limited to predetermined expense classification schemes. Yet eliminating a clause that restricts the query's scope also can easily generate reports of total travel expenses for all purposes.

A second benefit of an integrated enterprise-wide data model is it facilitates the integration of financial and nonfinancial information. The importance of this feature is underscored by increasing pressure to expand the scope of the information presented in financial statements. For example, the AICPA Special Committee on Financial Reporting (the Jenkins Committee) recommends that financial reports prepared for external users include nonfinancial information such as measures of customer satisfaction and product cycle times. Similarly, in Chapter 14 we discussed the trend toward including measures of the value of a company's human capital in annual reports. This information also can be easily incorporated in an integrated enterprise-wide data model.

Effective integration of financial and nonfinancial data also results in improved internal reporting. Traditionally, internal reports have focused primarily on financial performance measures. Effective management of an organization, however, requires measuring performance on multiple dimensions because no single measure is sufficient. Instead, top management must have reports that provide a multidimensional perspective on performance. We will discuss this benefit in more detail under the concept of the balanced scorecard.

Internal Control Considerations

As noted earlier, most ERP systems use centralized databases, similar to what is depicted in Figure 15-5, to share data across functions. Such systems typically empower many different individuals to enter data relating to a specific business activity, but this makes it harder to assign responsibility for maintaining data integrity. Moreover, ERP systems often produce process efficiencies by enabling one individual to perform multiple steps in a business process, thereby reducing segregation of duties. Finally, the integrated and all-encompassing nature of ERP systems increases the exposure resulting from a system crash.

These threats can be mitigated, however, through proper design and implementation. The basic principles concerning segregation of duties described in previous chapters can, and should, still be enforced in ERP systems. For example, the employee who enters cash disbursements should not also be able to reconcile the bank account. In addition, employees who have access to master file maintenance should not be able to also perform certain related business processes. For example, the employee who maintains the vendor master file should not also be able to process cash disbursements. An employee able to perform both of those functions could create a fictitious supplier and then disburse funds to that fictitious vendor (i.e., the employee). Similarly, the employee who maintains the customer master file should not also be able to process cash receipts. An employee able to perform both of those functions could commit the type of fraud referred to as lapping. Additionally, employees with programming or system administration responsibilities should not also be able to perform business processes. For example, if an employee with database administration responsibilities also had authority to perform business processes such as cash disbursements, that person could alter the database tables to conceal fraudulent activities. Thus, it is important that internal auditors be involved during the implementation process to prevent these types of segregation of duties weaknesses.

ERP systems also provide tools that facilitate the review and audit of control procedures. One such tool is a detailed trace capability that enables internal auditors to easily follow a transaction through each stage of processing. The database query language typically provided in ERP systems is another potentially useful tool. To illustrate the potential power of these query capabilities, let us examine the process for validating the updates to the sales account in the general ledger. Referring to Figure 15-5, the first step would be writing queries against the data model for the revenue cycle. One such query would sum the amount of all sales during the time period of interest. Other queries would link the sales, shipments, and orders tables to verify the completeness and validity of all recorded sales. Additional queries could be written to trace sales to specific customers and sales staff. In fact, the number of such cross-table links that can be easily generated is limited only by the investigator's imagination. In addition, the system can be configured to create extensive log files that make it possible to identify who authorized a transaction. Thus, ERP systems make it possible to create a richer and more complete audit trail than that typically provided in legacy AISs.

USING INFORMATION FOR DECISION MAKING

As noted throughout this book, a primary function of an AIS is to provide management with the information it needs to make decisions. This section discusses two important topics regarding the use of information for decision making: (1) the balanced scorecard and (2) data warehouses to support business intelligence. Both topics relate to the issues raised in the introductory case concerning the utility of an organization's information systems.

The Balanced Scorecard

A **balanced scorecard**[1] is a report that provides a multidimensional perspective of organizational performance. A balanced scorecard contains measures reflecting four perspectives of the organization: financial, customer, internal operations, and innovation and learning. The financial section contains lagging indicators of the organization's past performance, whereas the other three sections provide leading indicators about likely future performance. For each dimension, the balanced scorecard shows the organization's goals and specific measures that reflect performance in attaining those goals. Together, the four dimensions of the balanced scorecard provide a much more comprehensive overview of organizational performance than that provided by financial measures alone. Indeed, a properly designed balanced scorecard measures key aspects of the organization's strategy and reflects important causal links across the four dimensions. Figure 15-6 shows a sample balanced scorecard for AOE.

AOE's top management, like many companies, agreed on three key financial goals: increased revenue streams through sales of new products, increased profitability as reflected in return on equity, and maintaining adequate cash flow to meet obligations. As shown in Figure 15-6, specific measures and targets were developed to track the attainment of those goals.

Customers are the key to achieving financial goals. Accordingly, the customer perspective of AOE's balanced scorecard contains two key goals: improve customer satisfaction and become the preferred supplier for key customers. In turn, meeting those customer-oriented goals requires efficiently and effectively performing internal business processes. Consequently, the internal perspective portion of AOE's balanced scorecard focuses on those activities most likely to directly affect customer perceptions: service quality, speed of delivery, and product quality. Finally, AOE's top management acknowledged the importance of developing new products and training its workforce to continuously improve service and results. Therefore, measures of those two items are included in the learning and innovation perspective of AOE's balanced scorecard.

Note that the preceding discussion implied a number of hypotheses. For example, increased employee training is expected to improve service quality, as reflected in the percentage of customer orders filled correctly. In turn, improved service quality is expected to result in increased customer satisfaction and in key customers making a greater share of their electronics purchases from AOE. Finally,

---

[1]Robert S. Kaplan and David P. Norton "Transforming the Balanced Scorecard from Performance Measurement to Strategic Management: Part I" *Accounting Horizons* 15:1 (March 2001): 87–104; and Robert S. Kaplan and David P. Norton, "Transforming the Balanced Scorecard from Performance Measurement to Strategic Management: Part II," *Accounting Horizons* 15:2 (June 2001): 147–160.

Dimension Goals	Measure	Target	Current Period	Prior Period
Financial				
New revenue streams	Sales of new products (000s)	104	103	100
Improve productivity	Return on equity (%)	12.5%	12.6%	122.2%
Positive cash flow	Cash from operations (000s)	156	185	143
Customer				
Improve satisfaction	Rating (0–100)	95	93	92
Be a preferred supplier	Percentage of key customers' electronics purchases made from us	20%	20%	18%
Internal operations				
Service quality	Orders filled w/o error (%)	98%	97%	95%
Speed of delivery	Order cycle time (days)	10.4	10.5	11.2
Process efficiency	Defect rate	1.0%	1.1%	1.05%
Innovation and learning				
New products	Number new products	4	4	3
Employee learning	Personnel attending advanced training courses (%)	10%	25%	9%

Figure 15-6   Sample balanced scorecard for AOE

increased customer satisfaction is expected to result in improved profitability and cash flow. Thus, the measures in the learning and innovation, internal, and customer perspective portions of the balanced scorecard can be thought of as leading indicators of financial measures of the organization's strategy. Analyzing trends in the actual measures allows AOE's management to test the validity of those hypotheses. If improvements in one perspective do not generate expected improvements in other areas, top management must reevaluate and probably revise hypotheses about the determinants of organizational success. Indeed, this ability to test and refine strategy is one of the major benefits the balanced scorecard provides.

Accountants and systems professionals should participate in the development of a balanced scorecard. Top management should specify the goals to be pursued in each dimension. Accountants and information systems professionals can help management choose the most appropriate measures for tracking achievement of those goals. In addition, they can provide input concerning the feasibility of collecting the data that would be required to implement various proposed measures.

Using Data Warehouses for Business Intelligence

Timely access to information is important. In today's fast-paced global economy, management must constantly monitor and reevaluate the organization's financial and operating performance in light of its strategic goals. Firms must be able to alter their plans quickly in response to changes in their environment. Consequently, many organizations are adopting on-line general ledger systems similar to that depicted in Figure 15-3. When such systems include well-structured databases similar to the one depicted in Figure 15-5, management has ready access to the information needed to make timely operating and tactical decisions.

Such systems are not sufficient, however, to support management's strategic decision-making needs, because databases structured like the one shown in Figure 15-5 are designed to support the organization's transaction processing needs. Accordingly, they typically contain data for only the current fiscal year, plus perhaps one additional month to enable comparisons of the current month's activities to those of the same month a year ago. Thus, the event tables, which contain the data traditionally contained in journals in a manual AIS, are, like journals, closed out and archived at the end of each fiscal year. Strategic decision making, however, requires access to large amounts of historical data. For example, when evaluating marketing strategies, management may need access to data about sales broken down by products, by salesperson, and by customer for the past five years.

To provide the information needed for strategic decision making, organizations are building separate databases called data warehouses. A **data warehouse** contains both detailed and summarized data for a number of years and is used for analysis, rather than transaction processing. Because they contain information for multiple years, data warehouses are enormous. Indeed, it is not unusual for them to contain tens, or even hundreds, of terabytes of data. Consequently, data warehouses are usually separate systems from the AIS used to support the organization's daily business activities so that performance of those activities is not adversely affected by the computer processing resources consumed in analyzing the data contained in the data warehouse. In addition, organizations often build separate data warehouses for various functions. For example, an organization may build one data warehouse for the finance function, another for the human resources function, and so forth. Such smaller warehouses are often referred to as **data marts.**

Data warehouses and data marts do not replace an organization's transaction processing databases. Instead, they complement those databases by providing support for strategic decision making. It is important to remember that data warehouses and data marts are not used for transaction processing. Consequently, they are not usually updated in real time, but instead are periodically updated to reflect the results of all transactions that have occurred since the last update.

Data warehouses differ from the databases used to support transaction processing not only in size, but also in how they are structured. Whereas transaction-processing databases are designed so as to minimize redundancy and thereby maximize the efficiency of updating them to reflect the results of current transactions, data warehouses are often designed to be purposely redundant to maximize query efficiency. Thus, instead of being based on the REA data model, data warehouses are usually designed to be dimensional in nature. The most common dimensional architecture is referred to as the star schema, which is so named because the data are arranged in a manner resembling a star (see Figure 15-7).

At the center of the star is a fact table that is linked to several relevant dimensions. In the figure, the fact table contains information about purchases of raw materials, in terms of both units and dollar values. Relevant dimensions may include the location where the material is stored, the item, the purchasing agent and department, the

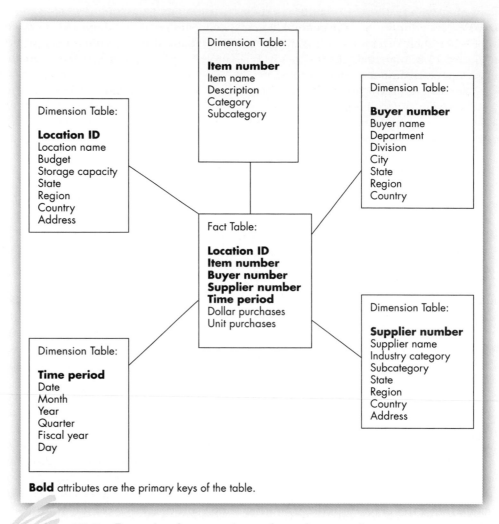

Figure 15-7   Example of a star schema for a data warehouse

supplier, and the time period. A data warehouse consists of numerous such stars, one for each important set of fact data. Further information about the star schema is beyond the scope of this text, but can be found in any textbook used for courses on data warehousing.

The process of accessing the data contained in a data warehouse and using it for strategic decision making is often referred to as **business intelligence.** There are two main techniques used in business intelligence: online analytical processing (OLAP) and data mining. **On-line analytical processing (OLAP)** is using queries in which the user guides the investigation of hypothesized relationships in the data. For example, a manager may begin with a query that breaks down purchases by supplier for the last three years. This may be followed by additional queries that "drill down" to lower levels (similar to the hierarchy of reports depicted in Figure 15-4) by, for example, grouping purchases by different items and by fiscal periods. **Data mining** is using sophisticated statistical analysis, including artificial intelligence techniques such as neural networks, to "discover" unhypothesized relationships in the data. For example, credit card companies use data mining to identify patterns of usage indicative of fraud. Similarly, data mining techniques can be used to identify previously unknown relationships in sales data that can then be used as the basis for future promotions.

Data warehousing can provide significant benefits to an organization. Proper controls are needed, however, to reap those benefits. Focus 15-2 summarizes the major issues to address.

Focus 15-2

Data Warehousing Control Issues

Like any systems project, controls are needed to ensure that data warehouses and data marts are secure and that the information they contain is reliable. The following seven steps outline a thorough process for addressing potential security and integrity concerns with data warehousing:

1. *Data identification.* Designing the appropriate controls for a data warehouse or data mart requires knowledge about what is stored therein. A complete inventory of all data items stored in the warehouse must be taken and the results organized and documented in an easily retrievable manner.

2. *Data classification.* Once the contents of a data warehouse have been identified, management must classify the data in terms of security risk. Experts recommend using three classes: data that can be made publicly available, confidential data to which access should be restricted, and top-secret data that are highly sensitive and mission critical. Beware that by making such classifications without following through with differential security procedures only makes an intruder's job easier.

3. *Data valuation.* Designing the optimal level of controls over data includes weighing the costs of controls versus the benefits. Thus, it is important to attach a value to each class of data identified in step 2, against which the costs of proposed controls can be compared.

4. *Vulnerability identification.* This step entails risk assessment. Of particular relevance are the four SysTrust criteria for systems reliability: availability, integrity, security, and maintainability.

5. *Control identification.* Potential controls must be identified to deal with each threat previously identified. Access controls are certainly important. Encryption may be necessary to protect data classified as being top secret. Controls also are needed to ensure that data integrity is maintained when the contents of the data warehouse or data mart are updated.

6. *Selection of cost-effective controls.* After threats and potential controls have been identified, a cost-benefit analysis can suggest the optimal methods for controlling vulnerabilities.

7. *Evaluation.* Once the data warehouse or data mart is in use, the effectiveness of existing control procedures in addressing the various threats must be periodically reassessed. Risk assessment also should be reperformed periodically, especially in light of any significant changes in technology.

Source: Slemo Warigon, "Data Warehouse Control & Security," *Internal Auditor* (February 1998): 54–60.

SUMMARY AND CASE CONCLUSION

The general ledger and financial reporting system integrates and summarizes the results of the various accounting subsystems for the revenue, expenditure, production, and human resources cycles. The general ledger is the central master file in the AIS. Consequently, it is important to implement control procedures to ensure its accuracy and security. Important controls include edit checks of the journal voucher records posted to the general ledger, access controls, an adequate audit trail, and appropriate backup and disaster recovery procedures.

The outputs produced by the general ledger system fall into two primary categories: financial statements and managerial reports. The former are prepared periodically in accordance with GAAP and are distributed to both internal and external users. The latter are prepared for internal use only and therefore often include comparisons between actual and budgeted performance. The usefulness of these reports, whether presented in the form of tables or graphs, is affected by how well they are designed.

In addition to printed reports, the general ledger system should also support inquiry processing by decision makers. This requires adequate controls to limit access to, and permissible operations on, the data in the general ledger. Designing the general ledger in accordance with the relational data model facilitates inquiry processing by making the data more easily accessible to desktop tools found on most personal computers.

Organizations must provide information to a wide variety of users including government agencies, industry analysts, financial institutions, and individual decision makers. XBRL provides a mechanism for improving the efficiency of generating such information, as well as for using information obtained from external sources. Elizabeth Venko and Ann Brandt propose that AOE take advantage of the new capabilities XBRL provides to improve the efficiency and reduce the costs associated with providing financial information to external users.

Elizabeth and Ann informed Linda Spurgeon and Stephanie Cromwell that AOE's new integrated transaction processing database, similar to that depicted in Figure 15-5, facilitates collecting, storing, and retrieving the data needed to create a balanced scorecard. Ann points out, however, that a separate data warehouse that contains not only current, but also detailed historical data, will have to be built to satisfy AOE's business intelligence needs.

This chapter concludes our examination of the various cycles in an AIS. You have learned that accounting information systems have three main objectives: (1) to process transactions for accountability purposes, (2) to maintain adequate controls to ensure the integrity of the organization's data and the safeguarding of its assets, and (3) to provide information to support decision making. One other theme that appears throughout this book is the need for accountants to move beyond the traditional role of scorekeeper and to actively seek to add value to their organization. It is especially important that accountants participate in decisions concerning the adoption of new technology. The next three chapters discuss the activities involved in designing, acquiring, and implementing new information systems.

Accountants should participate in decisions about adopting new technology and implementing new information systems, because they have the training to properly evaluate the relative costs and benefits, as well as the economic risks, underlying such investments. Effectively participating in decisions concerning technology, however, requires accountants to not only keep abreast of current accounting developments, but also to stay informed about advances in IT. Thus, as an accountant, you must make a commitment to lifelong learning. We wish you well in this endeavor.

KEY TERMS

- journal voucher
- balanced scorecard
- trial balance
- data warehouses
- responsibility accounting
- data marts
- business intelligence
- general journal listing
- audit trail
- on-line analytical processing (OLAP)
- data mining

CHAPTER QUIZ

1. From where do adjusting entries usually come?
   a. treasurer
   b. controller
   c. various accounting cycle subsystems, such as sales order entry
   d. unit managers
2. Preparing performance reports that contain data only about items that a specific organizational unit controls is an example of which of the following?
   a. flexible budget system
   b. responsibility accounting system
   c. closing the books
   d. management by exception
3. What is the technique used to perform exploratory business intelligence called?
   a. data warehousing
   b. OLAP
   c. data mining
   d. querying
4. Which of the following shows the implied linkages among the portions of the balanced score-card?
   a. Financial → Internal → Learning and innovation → Customer
   b. Learning and innovation → Internal → Customer → Financial
   c. Customer → Financial → Internal → Learning and innovation
   d. Internal → Customer → Learning and innovation → Financial
5. Writing a query to identify trends in sales of a product by salesperson and by customer over the past five years is an example of which of the following?
   a. data mining
   b. responsibility accounting
   c. transaction processing
   d. OLAP
6. Measures of cycle time would most likely appear in which part of the balanced scorecard?
   a. innovation and learning
   b. customer
   c. internal operations
   d. financial
7. Which of the following would be a good measure of innovation and learning?
   a. percentage of on-time deliveries
   b. percentage of sales from products less than two years old
   c. market-share percentage
   d. customer satisfaction ratings

8. Traditionally, when is the general ledger updated?
   a. when each transaction occurred
   b. at year end
   c. monthly
   d. on demand
9. What is the new common business reporting computer language developed, in part, by the accounting profession called?
   a. XML
   b. XBRL
   c. SQL
   d. HTML
10. In performance reports, setting the comparison standards on the basis of the actual level of activity that occurred is an example of which of the following?
    a. responsibility accounting
    b. long-range planning
    c. variance analysis
    d. flexible budgeting

DISCUSSION QUESTIONS

15.1 The data model shown in Figure 15.5 should accommodate the unified storage of financial and nonfinancial operating data. How can you effectively combine both types of information in one report? For example, how can you compare and relate a 15 percent reduction in scrap and rework costs with an 8 percent increase in customer satisfaction and a 10 percent increase in sales?

15.2 What effect does the classification of an organizational unit as a cost, revenue, profit, or investment center have on the types of managerial reports produced for that unit?

15.3 It has been proposed that companies should provide users with a computer-readable copy, either on disk or through the Internet, of the organization's general ledger instead of its financial statements. This would permit users to analyze data in whatever manner they desire. Assuming that this approach is technologically feasible, should it be done? Why or why not?

15.4 Digital assets are not used up when they are consumed. Moreover, the variable costs associated with distributing those assets may be close to zero. What implications do these properties have for accounting for digital assets? (Hint: Think about depreciation and cost of goods sold.)

15.5 Many companies are participating in studies to develop benchmarks for evaluating the efficiency of their accounting departments. These studies typically report such statistics as the total costs of the accounting department as a percentage of revenues, documents processed per accounting clerk each month, and monthly closing times. Both best and average figures are usually reported for these categories. Discuss the usefulness and limitations of using such measures to evaluate the accounting department of a specific company.

15.6 Some companies are abandoning the practice of budgeting, because they claim that the costs outweigh the benefits. They argue that instead of comparing actual performance to budgeted standards, closely monitoring trends in actual performance over time would be more effective. Deviations from historical trends would signal the need to take corrective actions. Discuss the advantages and disadvantages of this practice.

15.7   The balanced scorecard measures organizational performance along four dimensions. Is it possible that measures on the customer, internal operations, and innovation and learning dimensions could be improving without any positive change in the financial dimension? If so, what are the implications of such a pattern?

PROBLEMS

15.1   Which control procedure would be most effective in addressing the following problems?
   a. When entering a nonroutine journal entry, the accounting clerk inadvertently transposes two digits in the debit amount.
   b. When entering a nonroutine journal entry, the accounting clerk inadvertently transposes two digits in the account code.
   c. Last Tuesday, an accounting clerk forgot to mark the source journal voucher as being entered after keying in the data for the issuance of debt. Consequently, another accounting clerk entered that same data on Wednesday.
   d. The credit manager makes an entry authorizing the write-off of a friend's account.
   e. The general ledger master file is stored on disk. For some reason, the disk is no longer readable. It takes the accounting department a week to reenter the past month's transactions from source documents in order to create a new general ledger master file.
   f. An accounting clerk, unsure as to which department to charge for a loss on the disposition of some fixed assets, debited a suspense account to make the entry balance. Consequently, performance evaluation reports did not correctly show the results of this transaction.
   g. The budget director accessed the payroll file and discovered the salaries of every other financial executive.
   h. The treasurer inadvertently omitted the credit portion of the journal entry submitted to account for the repurchase of treasury stock.
   i. During data entry, the controller transposed two digits in the debit portion of the adjusting entry for bad debt expense.
   j. The treasurer forgot to submit a journal entry to record the accrual of interest on a short-term CD.
   k. A nonexistent customer account number is entered during the posting of cash receipts. Consequently, the accounts receivable subsidiary ledger is out of balance with the general ledger control account.

15.2   Give two specific examples of nonroutine transactions that may occur in processing cash receipts and updating accounts receivable. Also specify the control procedures that should be in place to ensure the accuracy, completeness, and validity of those transactions.

15.3   An important control procedure involves the periodic reconciliation of general ledger accounts with their subsidiary ledgers. Explain how this control procedure works in the context of accounts payable. Your answer should specify how to verify the accuracy, completeness, and validity of all entries involving purchases, purchase returns, purchase discounts, and cash disbursements.

15.4   Figure 15-1 is a context diagram for the general ledger and reporting cycle that shows the principal data flows to and from the general ledger.
   Required
   a. List the source documents or journals underlying each data flow into the general ledger.
   b. Identify at least two additional data flows resulting from the revenue and expenditure cycle systems, and specify the source documents or journals that would support those flows.

15.5   Refer to the example of responsibility coding depicted in Figure 15-4.

Required

a. Design a coding scheme that will support the production of this set of reports. Make and state any assumptions you believe are necessary.

b. Write a brief (half-page) explanation of how your coding scheme works.

c. Suggest improvements in the set of reports depicted in Figure 15-4.

15.6   As manager of a local pizza parlor, you want to develop a balanced scorecard so you can more effectively monitor the restaurant's performance.

Required:

a. Propose at least two goals for each dimension and explain why those goals are important to the overall success of the pizza parlor.

b. Suggest specific measures for each goal developed in step a.

c. Explain how to gather the data needed for each measure developed in step b.

15.7   Write a brief report describing the current status of XBRL. Your report should address the following issues.

a. Extent of usage of XBRL by industry

b. Extent of current support for XBRL by various software vendors

c. Extent of internationalization of XBRL standards

d. Actual costs and benefits of using XBRL

15.8   Obtain the annual report of a company assigned by your professor. Read the management discussion and analysis section and develop a balanced scorecard that reflects that company's vision, mission, and strategy.

Case 15-1   AnyCompany, Inc.: An Ongoing Comprehensive Case

Select a local company and obtain permission to study its general ledger and financial reporting system. Write a report that addresses the following issues:

1. Analyze the structure of its general ledger. How does it reflect the nature of the company's line of business? Is the system file-based or is it organized as a database?

2. How often is the general ledger updated? Why?

3. Is an operating budget used for performance evaluation purposes? If so, what is the basis for setting the budget?

4. What control procedures are in place to safeguard the general ledger's integrity?

5. How often do various unit managers receive reports on their unit's financial performance? Do any of those reports combine financial with nonfinancial data? If so, how?

6. Evaluate the tabular reports produced by the system. Are they easy to understand? Are they appropriate for their intended use?

7. To what extent does the company use XBRL for financial reporting?

8. Does the company prepare a balanced scorecard? If so, evaluate it. If not, develop one that reflects the organization's goals, mission, and strategy.

Case 15-2 Evaluating a General Ledger Package

Accounting magazines such as *Journal of Accountancy* and *Strategic Finance* periodically publish reviews of accounting software. Obtain a copy of a recent software review article and read its comments about a general ledger package to which you have access. Using the software, write a report that indicates whether, and why, you agree or disagree with the review's opinions about the following features of the general ledger package:

1. Ease of installation.
2. Flexibility in the initial setup of the chart of accounts and during subsequent modifications.
3. Frequency of updates from subsystems (sales, cash receipts, etc.).
4. Control procedures available to restrict access.
5. Control procedures to ensure accuracy of input and processing.
6. Report flexibility (how easy it is to design reports, etc.).
7. Adequacy of the audit trail (e.g., what reference data are automatically provided versus how much of the audit trail has to be manually constructed).

ANSWERS TO CHAPTER QUIZ

1. b	**3.** c	**5.** d	**7.** b	**9.** b
2. b	**4.** b	**6.** c	**8.** c	**10.** d

C h a p t e r   1 6

Introduction to Systems Development and Systems Analysis

Learning Objectives

After studying this chapter, you should be able to:

■ Explain the five phases of the systems development life cycle.

■ Discuss the people involved in systems development and the roles they play.

■ Explain the importance of systems development planning and describe planning techniques.

■ Discuss the various types of feasibility analysis and calculate economic feasibility.

■ Explain why systems change triggers behavioral reactions, what form this resistance to change takes, and how to avoid or minimize the resulting problems.

■ Discuss the key issues and steps in systems analysis.

Integrative Case: Shoppers Mart

Several months ago, Ann Christy, a successful accountant, was promoted to controller of Shoppers Mart (SM), a small but rapidly growing regional chain of discount stores. Since her promotion she has been assessing how the accounting function could better serve Shoppers Mart. She has held meetings with the president and CEO and with other key managers at headquarters. She has also spent several weeks visiting various SM stores and talking one on one with store managers and employees. Her findings are as follows:

1. Store managers cannot obtain information other than what is contained on SM's periodic, preformatted reports. As soon as they request information from several functional areas, the system bogs down.

2. The sales and purchasing department cannot get timely information about what products are or are not selling well. As a result, stores are often out of popular items and overstocked with products that customers are not buying.

3. Top management is concerned that SM is losing market share to larger rivals with better prices and selection. The current system cannot provide management with the information it needs to analyze and solve this problem.

After analyzing the situation, Ann is convinced that Shoppers Mart needs a new information system that is flexible, efficient, and responsive to user needs. Ann knows that a new system will never be successful unless it has top management's complete support. Before she asks for approval and funding for the new system, Ann schedules a meeting with the head of systems development. She has the following questions:

1. What process must the company go through to obtain and implement a new system?

2. What types of planning are necessary to ensure the system's success? Who will be involved and how? Do any special committees need to be formed? What resources need to be planned for? How should all of the planning be documented?

3. How will employees react to a new system? What problems might this changeover cause, and how can they be minimized?

4. How should the new system be justified and sold to top management? How can expected costs and benefits be quantified to determine if the new system will indeed be cost-effective?

INTRODUCTION

Because we live in a highly competitive and ever-changing world, organizations continually face the need for new, faster, and more reliable ways of obtaining information. To meet this need, an information system must continually undergo changes, ranging from minor adjustments to major overhauls. Occasionally, the needed changes are so drastic that the old system is scrapped and replaced by an entirely new one. Change is so constant and frequent that at any given time most organizations are involved in some system improvement or change. Companies usually change their systems for one of the following reasons:

➤ *Changes in user or business needs.* Increased competition, business growth or consolidation, mergers and divestitures, new regulations, or changes in regional and global relationships can alter an organization's structure and purpose. To remain responsive to company needs, the system must change as well.

➤ *Technological changes.* As technology advances and becomes less costly, an organization can make use of the new capabilities or existing ones that were previously too expensive.

➤ *Improved business processes.* Many companies have inefficient business processes that require updating. For example, the ordering system at Nashua, an office supply manufacturer, caused customer frustration and dissatisfaction. When a customer called, a clerk would take information and promise to call back. Before doing so, the clerk had to access two separate systems: a mainframe system to verify customer information and perform a credit check, and a PC-based system to calculate pricing. If the customer was still interested, the clerk accessed another centralized system to determine inventory availability. When the system was redesigned, it took three minutes to process a telephone order instead of two days.

➤ *Competitive advantage.* Increased quality, quantity, and speed of information can result in an improved product or service and may help lower costs. For example, Wal-Mart invests heavily in technology to provide information about customers and their purchases to increase sales. Bell Atlantic increased revenues by investing $2.1 billion in a new system. This is a shift in management focus, since previously 90 percent of new systems were designed to automate labor and reduce expenses.

➤ *Productivity gains.* Computers automate clerical and repetitive tasks and significantly decrease the performance time of other tasks. Expert systems place specialized knowledge at the disposal of many others. Carolina Power and Light was able to eliminate 27 percent of its information systems staff when it installed a new system that significantly outperformed the old one.

➤ *Growth.* Companies outgrow their systems and must either upgrade or replace them entirely.

➤ *Downsizing.* Companies often move from centralized mainframes to networked PCs or to Internet-based systems to take advantage of their price/performance ratios. This places decision making and its corresponding information as far down the organization chart as possible. For example, Consolidated Edison of New York downsized from a mainframe-based system to a client/server system and eliminated 100 clerical positions. The new system does much more than the old one, including handling workflow management, user contact, database queries, automatic cash processing, and voice/data integration.

This chapter discusses five topics. The first is the systems development life cycle, the process that organizations follow to obtain and implement a new AIS. The second is the planning activities that are necessary during the development life cycle. The third is the feasibility analysis that is prepared to demonstrate that a new AIS is feasible. The fourth is the behavioral aspects of change that companies must deal with to successfully implement a new system. The last topic is a discussion of systems analysis, the first step in the development life cycle.

SYSTEMS DEVELOPMENT

Whether systems changes are major or minor, most companies go through a systems development life cycle. The steps in that cycle and the people involved in systems development are discussed in this section.

The Systems Development Life Cycle

Ann Christy asked the manager of systems development to explain the process Shoppers Mart would use to design and implement a new system. This five-step process, known as the **systems development life cycle (SDLC),** is shown in Figure 16-1 and briefly explained in the next section.

Systems analysis

As organizations grow and change, management and employees recognize the need for more or better information and request a new or improved information system. The first step in systems development is systems analysis. During **systems analysis,** the information needed to purchase or develop a new system is gathered. Requests for systems development are prioritized to maximize the use of limited development

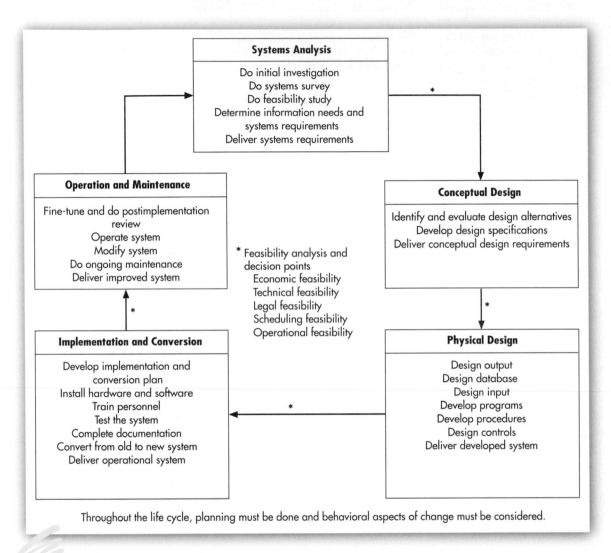

Figure 16-1   The systems development life cycle

resources. If a project passes the initial screening, the current system is surveyed to define the nature and scope of the project and to identify its strengths and weaknesses. Then an in-depth study of the proposed system is conducted to determine its feasibility.

If the proposed system is feasible, the information needs of system users and managers are identified and documented. This is the most important part of systems analysis, as these needs are used to develop and document systems requirements. Systems requirements are used to select or develop a new system. To summarize the work done during systems analysis, a report is prepared and submitted to the information systems steering committee.

Conceptual design

During **conceptual design,** the company decides how to meet user needs. The first task is to identify and evaluate appropriate design alternatives. There are many different ways to obtain a new system, including buying software, developing it in-house, or outsourcing the system to someone else. Detailed specifications outlining what the system is to accomplish and how it is to be controlled must be developed. This phase is complete when conceptual design requirements are communicated to the information systems steering committee.

Physical design

During **physical design,** the company translates the broad, user-oriented requirements of the conceptual design into detailed specifications that are used to code and test the computer programs. Input and output documents are designed, computer programs are written, files and databases are created, procedures are developed, and controls are built into the new system. This phase is complete when physical system design results are communicated to the information systems steering committee.

Implementation and conversion

The **implementation and conversion** phase is the capstone phase during which all the elements and activities of the system come together. Because of this phase's complexity and importance, an implementation and conversion plan is developed and followed. As part of implementation, any new hardware or software is installed and tested. New employees may need to be hired and trained, or existing employees relocated. New processing procedures must be tested and perhaps modified. Standards and controls for the new system must be established and system documentation completed. The organization must convert to the new system and dismantle the old one. After the system is up and running, any fine-tuning adjustments needed are made and a postimplementation review is conducted to detect and correct any design deficiencies. The final step in this phase is to deliver the operational system to the organization, at which time the development of the new system is complete. A final report is prepared and sent to the information systems steering committee.

Operations and maintenance

The new—and now operational—system is used as needed in the organization. During its life, the system is periodically reviewed. Modifications are made as problems arise or as new needs become evident, and the organization uses the improved system. This process is referred to as the **operations and maintenance phase.** Eventually a major modification or system replacement is necessary and the SDLC begins again.

In addition to these five phases, three activities (planning, managing the behavioral reactions to change, and assessing the ongoing feasibility of the project) are performed throughout the life cycle. These three activities, as well as systems analysis, are discussed in this chapter. The different approaches to obtaining an AIS are discussed in Chapter 17. The last four SDLC phases are explained in Chapter 18.

The Players

Many people must cooperate to successfully develop and implement an AIS. This section discusses the roles of those involved.

Management

One of the most effective ways to generate systems development support is a clear signal from top management that user involvement is important. With respect to systems development, top management's most important roles are providing support and encouragement for development projects and aligning information systems with corporate strategies. Other key roles include establishing system goals and objectives, reviewing information system department performance and leadership, establishing project selection and organizational structure policies, and participating in important system decisions. The principal roles of user management are to determine information requirements for departmental projects, to assist systems analysts with project cost and benefit estimations, to assign key staff members to development projects, and to allocate appropriate funds to support systems development and operation.

Accountants

Accountants may play three roles during systems design. First, as AIS users they must determine their information needs and system requirements and communicate them to system developers. Second, as members of a project development team or information systems steering committee, they help manage systems development. Third, accountants should take an active role in designing system controls and periodically monitoring and testing the system to verify that the controls are implemented and functioning properly. All systems should contain sufficient controls to ensure the accurate and complete processing of data. The system also should be easy to audit. If addressed at the start of development, auditability and control concerns can be maximized. Trying to achieve them after a system has been designed is inefficient, time consuming, and costly. Control and audit issues are discussed in depth in Chapters 7 through 10.

Information systems steering committee

Because AIS development spans functional and divisional boundaries, organizations usually establish an executive-level **steering committee** to plan and oversee the information systems function. The committee often consists of high-level management people, such as the controller and systems and user department management. The steering committee sets policies that govern the AIS and ensures top-management participation, guidance, and control. The steering committee also facilitates the coordination and integration of information systems activities to increase goal congruence and reduce goal conflict.

Project development team

Each development project has a team of systems specialists, managers, accountants and auditors, and users that guides its development. They plan each project, monitor it to ensure timely and cost-effective completion, make sure proper consideration is given to the human element, and communicate project status to top management and the steering committee. Team members should communicate frequently with users and hold regular meetings to consider ideas and discuss progress so there are no surprises upon project completion. A team approach usually produces more effective results and facilitates user acceptance of the implemented system.

Systems analysts and programmers

Systems analysts study existing systems, design new ones, and prepare specifications that are used by computer programmers. Analysts interact with systems technology and employees throughout the organization to successfully bridge the gap between the user and technology. Analysts are responsible for ensuring that the system meets user needs.

Computer programmers write computer programs using the specifications developed by the analysts. They also modify and maintain existing computer programs.

External players

Many people outside an organization play a role in systems development, including customers, vendors, auditors, and governmental entities. For example, Wal-Mart has told its vendors that if they want to do business with the company, then the vendors must implement and use electronic data interchange (EDI).

PLANNING SYSTEMS DEVELOPMENT

As shown in Figure 16-1, several activities must be performed at various times throughout the SDLC. One such activity is planning. The organization must have a long-range plan, each systems development project requires a plan, and each phase of each development plan must also be planned. This section discusses these plans and a number of techniques used to develop them.

Imagine that you built a two-bedroom house. Several years later you add a bedroom, then another bedroom and a bathroom. Over the years you add a family room, recreation room, deck, and two-car garage. In addition, you expand the kitchen and the dining area. Without prior thought to what you would eventually want in a home, your house will end up as a poorly organized patchwork of rooms surrounding the original structure. In addition, the cost of the house can end up greatly exceeding its value. This scenario also applies to an AIS that is not properly planned. The result is a costly and poorly integrated system that is difficult to operate and maintain.

Systems development planning is an important step for the following key reasons:

➤ *Consistency.* Planning enables the system's goals and objectives to correspond to the organization's overall strategic plan.

➤ *Efficiency.* Systems are more efficient, subsystems are coordinated, and there is a sound basis for selecting new applications for development.

➤ *Cutting edge.* The company remains abreast of the ever-present changes in IT.

➤ *Lower costs.* Duplication, wasted efforts, and cost and time overruns are avoided. The system is less costly and easier to maintain.

➤ *Adaptability.* Management is better prepared for future resource needs, and employees are better prepared for the changes that will occur.

When development efforts are poorly planned, a company must often return to a prior phase and correct errors and design flaws, as shown in Figure 16-2. Such a process is costly and results in delays, frustration, and low morale. Two types of systems

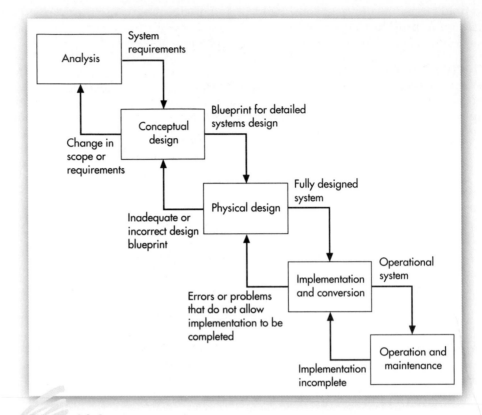

Figure16-2   Reasons for returning to a prior SDLC phase

development plans are needed: individual project plans prepared by project teams and a master plan developed by the information systems steering committee.

1. *Project development plan.* The basic building block of information systems planning is the **project development plan.** Each project development plan contains a cost/benefit analysis; developmental and operational requirements, including human resource, hardware, software, and financial resource requirements; and a schedule of the activities required to develop and operate the new application.

2. *The master plan.* A **master plan** is a long-range planning document that specifies what the system will consist of, how it will be developed, who will develop it, how needed resources will be acquired, and where the AIS is headed. The master plan also should provide the status of projects in process, prioritize planned projects, describe the criteria used for prioritization, and provide timetables for development. The projects with the highest priority should be the first to be developed. The importance of this decision dictates that it be made by top management and not by computer specialists. A planning horizon of approximately five years is reasonable for any master plan. The plan should be updated at least once each year. MCI, which uses a five-year plan, updates parts of its

Table 16-1   Components of the Systems Master Plan at Shoppers Mart

Organizational goals and objectives	Status of systems being developed
Company mission statement and goals	Proposed systems priorities
Information systems strategic plan and goals	Approved systems development
Organizational constraints	Proposals under consideration
Organizational approach to AIS	Development timetables and schedules
Organizational and AIS priorities	Forecast of future developments
Inventory and assessments	Forecasts of information needs
Current systems	Technological forecasts
Approved systems	Environmental/regulatory forecasts
Current hardware	Audit and control requirements
Current software	External user needs
Current AIS staff	
Assessment of current strengths and weaknesses	

plan as often as biweekly. The table of contents of the master plan used at Shoppers Mart is shown in Table 16-1.

Systems planning at MCI has been an important factor in its success, as explained in Focus 16-1.

Planning Techniques

Two techniques for scheduling and monitoring systems development activities are PERT and the Gantt chart. The **program evaluation and review technique (PERT)** requires that all activities and the precedent and subsequent relationships among them be identified. The activities and relationships are used to draw a PERT diagram, which consists of a network of arrows and nodes representing, respectively, project activities that require an expenditure of time and resources and the completion and initiation of activities. Completion time estimates are made and the **critical path**—the path requiring the greatest amount of time—is determined. If any activity on the critical path is delayed, then the whole project is delayed. If possible, resources are shifted to critical path activities to reduce project completion time.

A **Gantt chart** (Figure 16-3) is a bar chart with project activities listed on the left-hand side and units of time (days or weeks) across the top. For each activity a bar is drawn from the scheduled starting date to the ending date, thereby defining expected project completion time. As activities are completed, they are recorded on the Gantt chart by filling in the bar; thus, at any time it is possible to determine quickly which activities are on schedule and which are behind. The capacity to show, in graphical form, the entire schedule for a large, complex project, including progress to date and current status, is the primary advantage of the Gantt chart. The charts do not show, however, the relationships among various project activities.

Focus 16-1

Planning Helps MCI Cope with Popular New Service

WHEN MCI's Friends & Family service was introduced, order entry transaction volume soared 70 percent in three months. Fortunately, MCI was able to keep response times for the order entry system within acceptable bounds. One reason MCI was prepared was due to planning. Computer capacity planning and performance management are vital activities at MCI, where double-digit annual growth is the norm and computing does not just support the business—it is the business. Five-year plans are updated annually, annual plans are revised quarterly, and quarterly plans may change biweekly. MCI's capacity planning staff has such a good track record that top management will accept, with little question, a recommendation to spend millions on a system.

The planning process takes input from three sources. Sales projections go into a computer model developed by MCI, as do service-level objectives such as response time. Out of the model flows capacity requirements for each of MCI's five data centers, indicating the need for hardware resources such as off-line and on-line storage, main memory, and processor power. Capacity planners also factor in advance notice of new software coming from MCI's applications developers and forecasts of new technology from industry research firms and vendors.

Once applications are in production, MCI uses a variety of automated tools to spot abnormal patterns, looming bottlenecks, and other trouble spots. When they are found, the consulting group works with users and software developers to fine-tune applications or to ease workloads.

FEASIBILITY ANALYSIS

As shown in Figure 16-1, a **feasibility study** (also called a "business case") is prepared during systems analysis and updated as necessary during the remaining steps in the SDLC. The extent of these studies varies, depending on the size and nature of the system. For example, the study for a large-scale system is generally quite extensive, whereas one for a desktop system might be conducted informally. The feasibility team should include management, accountants skilled in controls and auditing, systems personnel, and users.

At major decision points (see Figure 16-1), the steering committee uses the study to decide whether to terminate a project, proceed unconditionally, or proceed if specific problems are resolved. Although a project can be terminated at any time, the early go-no-go decisions are particularly important as each subsequent SDLC step requires more time and monetary commitments. As the project proceeds, the study is updated and the project's viability is reassessed. The further along a development project is, the less likely it is to be canceled if a proper feasibility study has been prepared and updated.

Although uncommon, systems have been scrapped after implementation because they did not work or failed to meet an organization's needs. For example, Bank of America hired a software firm to replace a 20-year-old batch system used to manage billions of dollars in institutional trust accounts. After two years of development, the new system was implemented despite warnings that it was not adequately tested. Ten months

PROJECT PLANNING CHART

Project Number _____ 01 - 650 _____
Project Name _____ Labor Cost Anaylsis Module _____
Project Leader _____ J. Flaherty _____

Page __1__ of __1__
Prepared by __S. Doe__
Date __12 / 8 / 03__

ACTIVITY		WEEK STARTING																						
No.	**Name**	11/17	11/24	12/1	12/8	12/15	12/22	12/29	1/5	1/12	1/19	1/26	2/2	2/9	2/16	2/23	3/2	3/9	3/16	3/23	3/30				
1-1	Organize implementation team																								
1-2	Prepare system support procedures																								
1-3	Develop conversion plan																								
1-4	Develop testing plan																								
2-1	Prepare program specifications																								
2-2	Revise system documentation																								
2-3	Perform programming tasks																								
3-1	System test																								
4-1	Install system support procedures																								
5-1	Acceptance test																								
6-1	Conversion																								

Figure 16-3 Sample Gantt chart

later the system was scrapped, the bank's top systems and trust executives had resigned, and the company had taken a $60 million write-off to cover expenses related to the system. During the ten months the system was in place, the company lost 100 institutional accounts with $4 billion in assets. Focus 16-2 describes a project at Blue Cross/Blue Shield that was scrapped after six years of work and a $120 million investment.

Five important aspects to be considered during a feasibility study are as follows:

1. **Technical feasibility.** Can the planned system be developed and implemented using existing technology?
2. **Operational feasibility.** Does the organization have access to people who can design, implement, and operate the proposed system? Can people use the system and will they use it?
3. **Legal feasibility.** Does the system comply with all applicable federal and state laws and statutes, administrative agency regulations, and the company's contractual obligations?
4. **Scheduling feasibility.** Can the system be developed and implemented in the time allotted? If not, it will have to be modified, postponed, or replaced by an alternative selection.
5. **Economic feasibility.** Will system benefits justify the time, money, and other resources required to implement it?

Economic feasibility, the most important and frequently analyzed of the five aspects, is now discussed in greater depth. The feasibility analysis that Ann performed for Shoppers Mart is shown in Table 16-8.

Focus 16-2

Blue Cross/Blue Shield Abandons Runaway

BLUE CROSS/BLUE SHIELD of Massachusetts hoped that its new information system would usher in a new era. After six years and $120 million, however, the System 21 project was behind schedule and significantly over budget. The project was canceled, and Blue Cross turned its computer operation over to Electronic Data Systems (EDS) Corporation, an outside contractor.

Although information system failures of this magnitude are unusual, they happen more often than one would expect. According to a KPMG survey, 35 percent of all major information system projects become a runaway—a project that is millions of dollars over budget and months or years behind schedule. Other surveys show that almost every Fortune 200 company has had at least one runaway.

One major reason for the development problems was Blue Cross's failure to properly supervise the project. Blue Cross hired an independent contractor to develop the software, but neglected to appoint someone to coordinate and manage the project in-house. Top management did not establish a firm set of priorities regarding essential features and the sequence of application development.

When the developers presented the claims processing software to Blue Cross, the developers thought it was a finished product. The managers and users at Blue Cross had other ideas. They were not happy with the software and requested numerous changes. As a result, the whole project was delayed. This led to ever-increasing cost overruns. By the time System 21 was launched, Blue Cross had fallen far behind its competitors in its ability to process an ever-swelling load of paperwork. In fact, during a six year period it lost one million subscribers and came close to bankruptcy. It also had a poorly integrated system—nine different claims processing systems running on hardware dating back to the early 1970s.

The lesson that Blue Cross learned with System 21 was a painful one. The system it spent six years building was abandoned, and it turned its hardware over to EDS. Fortunately, although the system died, the patient survived.

Calculating economic feasibility costs and benefits

Determining economic feasibility requires a careful investigation of the costs and benefits of a proposed system. Because accountants are familiar with cost concepts, they provide a significant contribution to this evaluation. The basic framework for feasibility analysis is the **capital budgeting model** in which cost savings and other benefits, as well as initial outlay costs, operating costs, and other cash outflows, are translated into dollar estimates. The estimated benefits are compared with the estimated costs to determine if the system is cost beneficial. When possible, benefits and costs that are not easily quantifiable should be estimated and included in the feasibility analysis. If they cannot be accurately estimated, they should be listed and the likelihood of their occurring and the expected impact on the organization evaluated.

Some of the tangible and intangible benefits a company might obtain from a new system are cost savings; improved customer service, productivity, decision making, and data processing; better management control; and increased job satisfaction and employee morale.

Equipment costs are an initial outlay cost if the system is purchased and an operating cost if rented or leased. Equipment costs vary from $1,000 for PC systems to millions of dollars for enormous mainframes. Equipment costs are usually less than the cost of acquiring software and maintaining, supporting, and operating the system. Software acquisition costs include the purchase price of software as well as the time and effort required to design, program, test, and document software. The human resource costs associated with hiring, training, and relocating staff can be substantial. Site preparation costs may also be incurred for large computer systems. In addition, there are costs involved in installing the new system and converting files to the appropriate format and storage media.

The primary operating cost is maintaining the system. Studies show that between 65 and 75 percent of an organization's systems efforts are spent in maintaining current information systems. In addition, there may be significant annual cash outflows for equipment replacement and expansion and software updates. Human resource costs include the salaries of systems analysts, programmers, operators, data entry operators, and management. Costs are also incurred for supplies, overhead, and financial charges. Initial outlay and operating costs are summarized in Table 16-2.

Capital budgeting

During systems design, several alternative approaches to meeting system requirements are developed. Various feasibility measures are then used to narrow the list of alternatives. Capital budgeting techniques are used to evaluate the economic merits of the alternatives. Three common capital budgeting techniques are as follows:

1. **Payback period.** This figure represents the number of years required for the net savings to equal the initial cost of the investment. The project with the shortest payback period is usually selected.
2. **Net present value (NPV).** With the NPV method, all estimated future cash flows are discounted back to the present, using a discount rate that reflects the time value of money. The initial outlay costs are deducted from the discounted cash flows to obtain the NPV. A positive NPV indicates the alternative is economically feasible. When comparing projects, the one with the highest positive NPV is usually accepted.
3. **Internal rate of return (IRR).** The IRR is the effective interest rate that results in an NPV of zero. A project's IRR is compared with a minimum acceptable rate to determine acceptance or rejection. When comparing projects, the proposal with the highest IRR is usually selected.

Payback, NPV, and IRR are illustrated in Ann's feasibility analysis for Shoppers Mart, shown in Table 16-8.

BEHAVIORAL ASPECTS OF CHANGE

Individuals participating in systems development are agents of change who are continually confronted by people's reactions and resistance to change. The **behavioral aspects of change** are crucial, because the best system will fail without the support of the people it serves. Niccolo Machiavelli discussed resistance to change some 400 years ago:[1]

---

[1]Niccolo Machiavelli, *The Prince,* translated by Luigi Rice, revised by E. R. P. Vincent (New York: New American Library, 1952).

Table 16-2   Initial Outlay and Operating Costs

Hardware	Maintenance/backup
Central processing unit	Hardware/software maintenance
Peripherals	Backup and recovery operations
Communications hardware	Power supply protection
Special input/output devices	Documentation
Upgrade and expansion costs	Systems documentation
Software	Training program documentation
Application, system, general-purpose, utility,	Operating standards and procedures
and communications software	Site preparation
Updated versions of software	Air-conditioning, humidity, and dust controls
Application software design, programming,	Physical security (access)
modification, and testing	Fire and water protection
Staff	Cabling, wiring, and outlets
Supervisors	Furnishing and fixtures
Analysts and programmers	Installation
Computer operators	Freight and delivery charges
Input (data conversion) personnel	Setup and connection fees
Recruitment and staff training	Conversion
Consultants	Systems testing
Supplies and overhead	File and data conversions
Preprinted forms	Parallel operations
Data storage devices	Financial
Supplies (paper, ribbons, toner)	Finance charge
Utilities and power	Legal fees
	Insurance

It must be considered that there is nothing more difficult to carry out, nor more doubtful of success, nor more dangerous to handle, than to initiate a new order of things. For the reformer has enemies in all those who could profit by the old order, and only lukewarm defenders in all those who could profit by the new order. This lukewarmness arises partly from fear of their adversaries, who have the laws in their favor, and partly from the incredulity of mankind, who do not truly believe in anything new until they have had an actual experience of it.

Organizations must be sensitive to and consider the feelings and reactions of persons affected by change. They also should be aware of the type of behavioral problems that can result from changes, as discussed in this section.

Why Behavioral Problems Occur

An individual's view of change as good or bad will usually depend on how he or she is personally affected by it. For example, management views change positively if it increases profits or performance or reduces costs. An employee, on the other hand, will view the same change as bad if his or her job is terminated or adversely affected.

To minimize adverse behavioral reactions, one must first understand why resistance takes place. Some of the more important factors include the following:

➤ *Personal characteristics and background.* Generally speaking, the younger and more highly educated people are, the more likely they are to accept change. Likewise, the more comfortable people are with technology, the less likely they are to oppose changes in an AIS.

➤ *Manner in which change is introduced.* Resistance is often a reaction to the methods of instituting change rather than to change itself. For example, the rationale used to sell the system to top management may not be appropriate for lower-level employees. The elimination of menial tasks and the ability to advance and grow are often more important to users than are increasing profits and reducing costs.

➤ *Experience with prior changes.* Employees who had a bad experience with prior changes are more reluctant to cooperate when future changes occur.

➤ *Top-management support.* Employees who sense a lack of top-management support for change wonder why they themselves should endorse it.

➤ *Communication.* Employees are unlikely to support a change unless the reasons behind it are explained.

➤ *Biases and natural resistance to change.* People with emotional attachments to their duties or coworkers may not want to change if those elements are affected.

➤ *Disruptive nature of the change process.* Requests for information and interviews are distracting and place additional burdens on people. These disturbances can create negative feelings toward the change that prompted them to occur.

➤ *Fear.* Many people fear the unknown and the uncertainty accompanying change. They also fear losing their jobs, losing respect or status, failure, technology, and automation.

How People Resist AIS Changes

Behavioral problems may begin as soon as people find out that a system change is being made. Initial resistance is often subtle, manifested by tardiness, subpar performance, or failure to provide developers with information. Major behavioral problems often occur after the new system has been implemented and the change has become a reality. Major resistance often takes one of three forms: aggression, projection, or avoidance.

Aggression

Aggression is behavior that is usually intended to destroy, cripple, or weaken the system's effectiveness. It may take the form of increased error rates, disruptions, or deliberate sabotage. One organization introduced an on-line AIS, only to discover soon thereafter that the data input devices were inoperable; some had honey poured into them, others had been mysteriously run over by forklifts, and still others had paper clips inserted in them. Employees had also entered erroneous data into the system. More subtle forms of aggression can also undermine the system's intended use. In another organization, disgruntled workers used the new system to gang up on an unpopular foreman. Instead of clocking in and out as they moved from one station to another, they punched in at the foreman's department for the entire day and proceeded to work in different areas. This adversely affected the foreman's performance evaluation, as he was charged for hours that did not belong to his operation.

Projection

Projection involves blaming the new system for any and every unpleasant occurrence. For example, missing and incorrect data, which were present but undetected in a manual system, are blamed on a new automated system until the actual cause is determined. In essence, the system becomes the scapegoat for all real and imagined problems and errors. If these criticisms are not controlled or answered, the integrity of the system can be damaged or destroyed.

Avoidance

Dealing with problems through **avoidance** is a common human trait. For example, a person who cannot decide between two job offers may delay a decision until one company withdraws its offer and the decision is made for him. Likewise, one way for employees to deal with a new AIS is to avoid using it in the hope that the problem (the system) can be ignored or that it will eventually go away.

Preventing Behavioral Problems

The human element is often thought to be the most significant problem a company encounters in designing, developing, and implementing a system. Although there is no one best way to overcome behavioral problems, people's reactions can be improved by observing the following guidelines:

- ➤ *Meet user's needs.* It is essential that the form, content, and volume of system output be designed to satisfy user needs.

- ➤ *Keep communication lines open.* Managers and users should be fully informed of system changes as soon as possible. They should be told what changes are being made and why, and they should be shown how the new system will benefit them. The objective is to help employees identify with the company's efforts to improve the system. This helps ensure that employees feel they are key players in the company's future goals and plans. Open communication also helps prevent damaging and inaccurate rumors and misunderstandings. Employees should be told who they can contact if they have questions or concerns.

- ➤ *Maintain a safe and open atmosphere.* It is vital that everyone affected by systems development has an attitude of trust and cooperation. If employees become hostile, it will be difficult to change their attitude or to implement the system successfully.

- ➤ *Obtain management support.* When possible, a powerful champion, who can provide resources for the system and motivate others to assist and cooperate with systems development, should be appointed.

- ➤ *Allay fears.* The organization should provide assurances (to the extent possible) that no major job losses or responsibility shifts will occur. These goals can be achieved through relocation, attrition, and early retirement. If employees are terminated, severance pay and outplacement services should be provided.

- ➤ *Solicit user participation.* Those who will use or be affected by the system should participate in its development by providing data, making suggestions, and helping make decisions. Participation is ego enhancing, challenging, and intrinsically satisfying. Users who participate in development are more knowledgeable, better trained, and more committed to using the system.

- ➤ *Provide honest feedback.* To avoid misunderstandings, users should be told which suggestions are being used and how, which suggestions are not being used and why, and which ones will be incorporated at a later date.

➤ *Make sure users understand the system.* Effective use or support cannot be obtained if users are confused about or do not understand the system. Generally, those who have a working knowledge of computers often underestimate user training needs.

➤ *Humanize the system.* System acceptance is unlikely if individuals believe the computer is controlling them or has usurped their positions.

➤ *Describe new challenges and opportunities.* System developers should emphasize important and challenging tasks that can be performed with the new system. It also should be emphasized that the system may provide greater job satisfaction and increased opportunities for advancement.

➤ *Reexamine performance evaluation.* User's performance standards and criteria should be reevaluated to ensure that they are satisfactory in view of changes brought on by the new system.

➤ *Test the system's integrity.* The system should be properly tested prior to implementation to minimize initial bad impressions.

➤ *Avoid emotionalism.* When logic vies with emotion, it rarely stands a chance. Emotional issues related to change should be allowed to cool, handled in a nonconfrontational manner, or sidestepped.

➤ *Present the system in the proper context.* Users are vitally interested in how system changes affect them personally. Relevant explanations should be presented that address their concerns, rather than the concerns of managers or developers.

➤ *Control the user's expectations.* A system is sold too well if users have unrealistic expectations of its capabilities and performance. Be realistic when describing the merits of the system.

➤ *Keep the system simple.* Avoid complex systems that cause radical changes. Make the change seem as simple as possible by conforming to existing organizational procedures.

Observing these guidelines is both time-consuming and expensive. As a result, workers tend to skip the more difficult steps to speed up systems development and installation. However, the problems caused by not following these guidelines are usually more expensive and time-consuming to fix than preventing behavioral problems in the first place.

SYSTEMS ANALYSIS

When a new or improved system is needed, a written **request for systems development** is prepared. The request describes the current system's problems, the reasons for the change, and the proposed system's goals and objectives as well as its anticipated benefits and costs. The project development team conducts the analysis. The five steps in the analysis phase and their objectives are shown in Figure 16-4 and discussed in this section.

Initial Investigation

An **initial investigation** is conducted to screen projects. The person conducting an initial investigation must gain a clear picture of the problem or need, determine the project's viability and expected costs and payoffs, evaluate the project's scope and the nature of the new AIS, and recommend whether the development project should be initiated as proposed, modified, or abandoned.

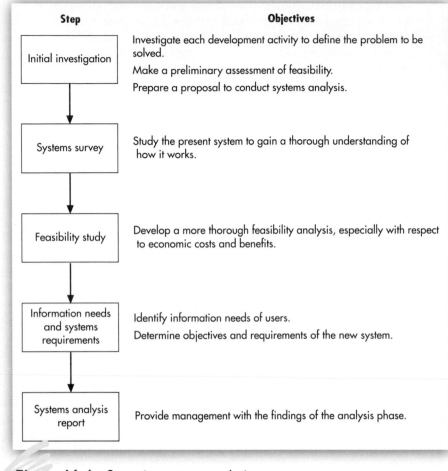

Figure 16-4   Steps in systems analysis

During the initial investigation the exact nature of the problem(s) under review must be determined. In some instances what is thought to be the cause of the problem is not the real source. For example, a governmental accountant once asked a consultant to develop an AIS to produce the information he needed on fund expenditures and available funds. Further investigation showed that the agency's system already provided the information. The accountant simply did not understand the reports he was receiving.

The project's scope (what it should and should not seek to accomplish) also must be determined. A new AIS is useful when problems are a result of lack of information, inaccessibility of data, and inefficient data processing. However, a new AIS is not the answer to organizational problems, such as the controller managing too many employees. Likewise, if a manager lacks organization skills or if a failure to enforce existing procedures causes control problems, a new AIS is not the answer.

Table 16-3   Table of Contents for Reports Prepared During Systems Analysis at Shoppers Mart

Shoppers Mart Proposal to Conduct Systems Analysis	Shoppers Mart Systems Survey Report	Shoppers Mart Systems Analysis Report
Table of Contents	**Table of Contents**	**Table of Contents**
I. Executive Summary	I. Executive Summary	I. Executive Summary
II. System Problems and Opportunities	II. System Goals and Objectives	II. System Goals and Objectives
III. Goals and Objectives of Proposed System	III. System Problems and Opportunities	III. System Problems and Opportunities
IV. Project Scope	IV. Current Systems Operations	IV. Project Scope
V. Anticipated Costs and Benefits	A. Policies, Procedures, and Practices Affecting System	V. Relationship of Project to Overall Strategic Information Systems Plan
VI. Participants in Development Project	B. Systems Design and Operation (Intended and Actual)	VI. Current Systems Operations
VII. Proposed Systems Development Tasks and Work Plan	C. Systems Users and Their Responsibilities	VII. User Requirements
VIII. Recommendations	D. Systems Outputs, Inputs, and Data Storage	VIII. Feasibility Analysis
	E. Systems Controls	IX. Systems Constraints
	F. Systems Strengths, Weaknesses, and Constraints	X. Recommendations for New System
	G. Costs to Operate System	XI. Proposed Project Participants and Work Plan
	V. User Requirements Identified During Survey	XII. Summary
		XIII. Approvals
		XIV. Appendix of Documents, Tables, Charts, Glossary of Terms

If a project is approved, a **proposal to conduct systems analysis** is prepared. It is assigned a priority and added to the master plan, and the development team begins the survey of the existing AIS. As the investigation progresses, the proposal will be modified as more information becomes available. The table of contents for the Shoppers Mart proposal, shown in Table 16-3, is representative of the information in a proposal to conduct systems analysis.

Systems Survey

During the **systems survey** an extensive study of the current AIS is undertaken. This survey may take weeks or months, depending on the complexity and scope of the system. The objectives of a systems survey are as follows:

➤ Gain a thorough understanding of company operations, policies, and procedures; data and information flow; AIS strengths and weaknesses; and available hardware, software, and personnel.

➤ *Make preliminary assessments of current and future processing needs, and determine the extent and nature of the changes needed.*

➤ *Develop working relationships with users and build support for the AIS.*

➤ *Collect data that identify user needs, conduct a feasibility analysis, and make recommendations to management.*

Data about the current AIS can be gathered internally from employees as well as from documentation such as organization charts and procedures manuals. External sources include consultants, customers and suppliers, industry associations, and government agencies. The advantages and disadvantages of four common methods of gathering data are summarized here and in Table 16-4.

An *interview* helps gather answers to "why" questions: Why is there a problem? Why does the AIS work this way? Why is this information important? Care must be taken, however, to ensure that an interviewee's personal biases, self-interests, or desire to say what he or she thinks the interviewer wants to hear do not produce inaccurate information.

Ann Christy's interviews at Shoppers Mart were successful because of her approach and preparation. For each interview, she made an appointment, explained the purpose beforehand, indicated the amount of time needed, and arrived on time. Before each session she studied the interviewee's responsibilities and listed the points she wanted to cover. She put each interviewee at ease by being friendly, courteous, and tactful. Her questions dealt with the person's responsibilities, how the person interacted with the AIS, how the system might be improved, and the person's information needs. She let the interviewee do most of the talking and paid special attention to nonverbal communication, because subtle overtones and body language can be as significant as direct responses to questions. She took notes and augmented them with detailed impressions shortly after the interview. She asked permission to tape especially important interviews.

Questionnaires are used when the amount of information to be gathered is small and well defined, is obtained from many people or from those who are physically removed, or is intended to verify data from other sources. Questionnaires take relatively little time to administer, but developing a quality questionnaire can be challenging and require significant time and effort.

Observation is used to verify information gathered using other approaches and to determine how a system actually works, rather than how it should work. It can be difficult to interpret observations properly, because observed people may change their normal behavior or make mistakes. Observation effectiveness is maximized by identifying what is to be observed, estimating how long it will take, obtaining permission, and explaining what will be done and why. The observer should not make value judgments, and notes and impressions should be formally documented as soon as possible. For example, a systems analyst could observe a customer representative interacting with customers to better understand what customer representatives do and what information they need.

Systems documentation describes how the AIS is intended to work. Throughout the systems survey, the project team should be alert to differences between intended and actual systems operation. These differences provide important insights into problems and weaknesses. If documentation is unavailable or incomplete, it may be worthwhile to develop it.

Table 16-4   Advantages and Disadvantages of Data Gathering Methods

	Advantages	Disadvantages

Interviews	Can answer "why" questions
	Interviewer can probe
	  and follow up
	Questions can be clarified
	Builds positive relationships
	  with interviewee
	Builds acceptance and support
	  for new system
		Time-consuming
		Expensive
		Personal biases or self-
		  interest may produce
		  inaccurate information

Questionnaires	Can be anonymous
	Not time-consuming
	Inexpensive
	Allows more time to think
	  about responses
		Does not allow in-depth
		  questions or answers
		Cannot probe or follow up
		  on responses
		Questions cannot be
		  clarified
		Impersonal; does not build
		  relationships
		Difficult to develop
		Often ignored or
		  completed superficially

Observation	Can verify how system *actually*
	  works, rather than how it
	  should work
	Results in greater understanding
	  of system
		Time-consuming
		Expensive
		Difficult to interpret
		  properly
		Observed people may alter
		  behavior

Systems documentation	Describes how system
	  should work
	Written form facilitates
	  review, analysis
		Time consuming
		May not be available
		  or easy to find

Document findings and model the existing system

The information gathered during the analysis phase must be documented so it can be used throughout the systems development project. Documentation consists of questionnaire copies, interview notes, memos, and document copies. Another way of documenting a system is to model it. **Physical models** illustrate *how* a system functions by describing the flow of documents, the computer processes performed and the people performing them, the equipment used, and any other physical elements of the system. **Logical models** illustrate *what* is being done, regardless of how that

Table 16-5   Systems Analysis and Design Tools and Techniques

CASE (Chapter 17)	Forms design checklist (Chapter 18)
Data dictionary (Chapter 4)	Gantt charts (Chapter 16)
Data flow diagrams (Chapter 6)	PERT charts (Chapter 16)
Data modeling (Chapter 5)	Prototyping (Chapter 17)
Document flowcharts (Chapter 6)	Record layouts (Chapter 4)
E-R diagrams (Chapter 5)	System flowcharts (Chapter 6)

flow is actually accomplished. The logical model focuses on the essential activities and the flow of information, not on the physical processes of transforming and storing data. Table 16-5 lists the analysis and design tools and techniques accountants and system developers use to create an AIS and identifies the chapter where each is discussed in this text.

Analyze the existing system

Once data gathering is complete, the survey team evaluates the AIS's strengths and weaknesses to develop ideas for how to design and structure the new AIS. When appropriate, strengths should be retained and weaknesses corrected. For example, if output is being duplicated, consolidating reports might produce cost savings. Sometimes, however, revolutionary rather than evolutionary change is needed and an entirely new system is developed. This process, called *reengineering*, is discussed in Chapter 17.

Prepare systems survey report

The systems survey culminates with a **systems survey report.** Table 16-3 shows the table of contents for the Shoppers Mart systems survey report. The report is supported by documentation such as memos, interview and observation notes, questionnaire data, file and record layouts and descriptions, input and output descriptions, copies of documents, flowcharts, and data flow diagrams.

Feasibility Study

At this point in systems analysis, a more thorough feasibility analysis is conducted to determine the project's viability. Especially important is economic feasibility, as discussed earlier in the chapter. The feasibility analysis is updated regularly as the project proceeds and costs and benefits become clearer.

Information Needs and Systems Requirements

Once a project is deemed to be feasible, the company identifies the information needs of AIS users and documents systems requirements. See Table 16-6 for examples of systems requirements.

Table 16-6   Posible Contents of System Requirements

Processes	A description of all processes in the new system, including what is to be done and by whom
Data elements	A description of the data elements needed, including their name, size, format, source, and significance
Data structure	A preliminary data structure, showing how the data elements will be organized into logical records
Outputs	A copy of system outputs and a description of their purpose, frequency, and distribution
Inputs	A copy of system inputs and a description of their contents, source, and who is responsible for them
Documentation	A description of how the new system and each subsystem will operate
Constraints	A description of constraints such as deadlines, schedules, security requirements, staffing limitations, and statutory or regulatory requirements
Controls	Controls to ensure the accuracy and reliability of inputs, outputs, and processing
Reorganizations	Organizational reorganization needed to meet the user's information needs, such as increasing staff levels, adding new job functions, restructuring, or terminating existing positions or jobs

Determining information needs can be a challenging process due to the sheer quantity and variety of information that must be specified, even for a relatively simple AIS. In addition, it may be difficult for employees to articulate their information needs or they may identify them incorrectly. Figure 16-5 is a humorous view of the types of communication problems associated with this process.

To illustrate the importance of accurately determining systems requirements, consider the example of Corning Corporation. When the company began investigating the quality of the ophthalmic pressings it manufactures and sells to the makers of prescription lenses, it found that 35 percent of its drafting documents contained errors. Corning also found that the drafting errors became increasingly expensive to correct at each subsequent stage of the manufacturing process. It cost $250 if the errors were discovered before the toolmakers cut the tools, $20,000 if discovered before the assembly line began production, and up to $100,000 after the tools were sent to the customer. As a result of the study, several corrective actions were implemented that reduced the error rates from 35 percent to 0.2 percent. The same type of cost relationship exists in information systems development. The cost to correct an error increases as development proceeds through the SDLC phases.

Systems objectives and constraints

Many organizations take a **systems approach** to determining information needs and system requirements; problems and alternatives are viewed from the standpoint of the entire organization, rather than from any single department or interest group.

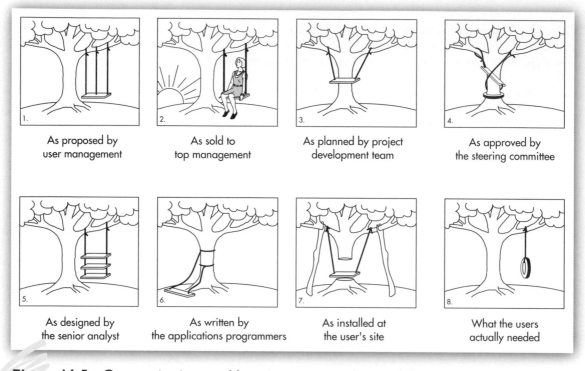

Figure 16-5   Communications problems in systems analysis and design

It is important to determine system objectives so that analysts and users can focus on those elements most vital to the AIS's success (see Table 16-7); however, it is difficult for a system to satisfy every objective. For example, designing adequate internal controls must be viewed as a trade-off between the objectives of economy and reliability. Similarly, cutting clerical costs must balance the objectives of capacity, flexibility, and customer service.

Organizational constraints usually make it impossible to develop all parts of a new AIS simultaneously. Therefore, the system is divided into smaller subsystems, or modules, that are analyzed, developed, and installed independently. When changes are made to the system, only the affected module needs to be changed. Great care should be taken to ensure that the modules are properly integrated into a workable system.

A system's success often depends on the project team's ability to cope with the constraints under which the organization is operating. Common constraints include governmental agency requirements, management policies and guidelines, lack of sufficiently qualified staff, the capabilities and attitudes of system users, available technology, and limited financial resources. To maximize system performance, the effects of these constraints on system design must be minimized.

Table 16-7   AIS Objectives

Usefulness	Information produced by the system should help management and users in decision making.
Economy	The benefits of the system should exceed the cost.
Reliability	The system should process data accurately and completely.
Availability	Users should be able to access the system at their convenience.
Timeliness	Crucial information should be produced first and then less important items as time permits.
Customer service	Courteous and efficient customer service should be provided.
Capacity	System capacity should be sufficient to handle periods of peak operation and future growth.
Ease of use	The system should be user-friendly.
Flexibility	The system should accommodate reasonable operating or system requirements changes.
Tractability	The system should be easily understood by users and designers and facilitate problem solving and future systems development.
Auditability	Auditability should be built into the system from the beginning of systems development.
Security	Only authorized users should be granted access or allowed to change system data.

Strategies for determining requirements

One or more of the following four strategies are used to determine AIS requirements:

1. *Ask users what they need.* Though this is the simplest and fastest strategy, many people do not realize or understand their true needs. Although they may know how to do their jobs, they may not be able to break them down into the individual information elements they use. It is sometimes better to ask users questions pertaining to what decisions they make and what processes they are involved in and then help them design systems to address their answers. Users must think beyond their current information needs so that new systems do not simply replicate the current information in new and improved formats.

2. *Analyze existing systems.* Both internal and external systems should be analyzed. A partial solution may already exist, thus eliminating the problem of reinventing the wheel.

3. *Examine existing system use.* This strategy differs from the previous one by taking into account that certain modules may not be used as intended, may be augmented by manual tasks, or may be avoided altogether. This approach helps determine if a system can be modified or must be replaced.

4. *Create a prototype.* When it is difficult to identify a usable set of requirements, a developer can quickly rough out a system for users to critique. Once users see something on the screen, they can begin to identify what they like and dislike and request changes. This iterative process of looking at what is developed and then improving it continues until users agree on their needs. Prototyping is discussed in Chapter 17.

Documentation and approval of user requirements

Detailed requirements for the new AIS that explain exactly what the system must produce should be created and documented. How to produce the required features is determined during the design phase of the SDLC. The requirements list should be supported by sample input and output forms as well as charts to make it easier for readers to conceptualize the system. A nontechnical summary that captures important user requirements and development efforts to date is often prepared for management.

When user requirements have been determined and documented, the project team meets with the users, explains the requirements, and obtains their agreement and approval. When an agreement is reached, user management should sign the appropriate system requirements documents to indicate approval.

Systems Analysis Report

Systems analysis is concluded by preparing a **systems analysis report,** to summarize and document the analysis activities and serve as a repository of data from which systems designers can draw. The report shows the new system's goal and objectives, the scope of the project and the new system, how the new system fits into the company's master plan, the user's processing requirements and information needs, the feasibility analysis, and recommendations for the new system. The Shoppers Mart report, shown in Table 16-3, shows in more detail the information typically contained in the report.

A go–no-go decision is generally made three times during systems analysis: (1) during the initial investigation, to determine whether to conduct a systems survey; (2) at the end of the feasibility study, to determine whether to proceed to the information requirements phase; and (3) at the completion of the analysis phase, to decide whether to proceed to the next phase.

After systems analysis is completed, projects developed using the SDLC approach move to the conceptual design phase and then to physical design, implementation and conversion, and operation and maintenance. These topics are discussed in the next two chapters.

SUMMARY AND CASE CONCLUSION

An extensive analysis of Shoppers Mart's current system and core business processes was conducted. After the analysis, Ann Christy, in consultation with the information systems steering committee, decided she wanted the corporate office to gather daily sales data from each store. Analyzing the prior day's sales will help Shoppers Mart adapt quickly to customer needs. Providing sales data to suppliers will help avoid stockouts and overstocking.

Coordinating buying at the corporate office will help Shoppers Mart to minimize inventory levels and negotiate lower wholesale prices. Stores will send orders electronically the day they are prepared. Based on store orders, the previous day's sales figures, and warehouse inventory, Shoppers Mart will send purchase orders to suppliers. Suppliers will process orders and ship goods to regional warehouses or directly to the stores the day orders are received. Each store will have the flexibility to respond to local sales trends and conditions by placing local orders. Accounts payable will be centralized so the firm can make payments electronically.

Ann reviewed the system with the legal department and the AIS staff and was assured that it complied with all legal considerations and was technologically feasible. Top management and the information systems steering committee will decide how to allocate time and resources for this massive project and will communicate all staff assignments to systems management and personnel.

Ann's team conducted an economic feasibility study and determined that the project makes excellent use of funds. As shown in Table 16-8, the team estimated that initial outlay costs for the system are $5 million (new hardware and initial systems design $2 million each; software $400,000; and training, site preparation, and conversion $200,000 each).

The team estimated what it would cost to operate the system for its estimated six-year life, as well as what the system would save the company. The following recurring costs were identified: hardware expansion, additional software and software updates, systems maintenance, added personnel to operate the system, communication charges, and overhead. The system will also save Shoppers Mart money by eliminating clerical jobs, generating working capital savings, increasing sales and profits, and decreasing warehouse costs. The costs and savings for years 1 through 6, which are expected to rise from year to year, are shown in Table 16-8.

Ann calculated the annual savings minus the recurring additional costs and then calculated the after-tax cash savings for each year. The $5 million system can be depreciated over the 6-year period (see Table 16-8 for the rates). For example, the depreciation in year 1 of $1 million reduces net income by that amount. Because the company does not have to pay taxes on the $1 million at its tax rate of 34 percent, it ends up saving an additional $340,000 in year 1. Finally, Ann calculated the net savings for each year.

Shoppers Mart has a 10 percent cost of capital. Ann used this rate to calculate the NPV of the investment, which is over $3 million. The internal rate of return is a lofty 25 percent. Ann realized how advantageous it would be for the company to borrow the money (at 10 percent interest rates) to produce a 25 percent return on that borrowed money. In addition, payback occurs in the fourth year.

Ann presented the system to top management and described its objectives. Challenges to her estimates were plugged into the spreadsheet model so that management could see the effect of the changed assumptions. Even the stiffest challenges to Ann's numbers showed a positive return. As a result of the meeting, top management was supportive of the new system. They requested some changes and told Ann to proceed.

Ann soon found management's enthusiastic support crucial to the system's success. Several employees with vested interests in the current system believed it was adequate and were critical of her ideas. Some employees remembered the problems Shoppers Mart had when the current system was implemented a few years ago. Ann concluded that those who resisted the new system were afraid of the change and its effect on them personally. To counter the negative behavioral reactions, Ann took great pains to explain to all employees how the new system would benefit them individually and the company as a whole. With management's approval, she assured employees they would not lose their jobs and that all affected employees would be retrained. She involved the two most vocal opponents to the system change in planning activities, and soon they became two of its biggest advocates.

Ann set up a steering committee and was granted approval to put the managers of all affected departments on the committee. A master plan for developing the system was formulated, and the system was broken down into manageable projects. The projects were prioritized, and project teams were formed to begin work on the highest priority projects. Documentation standards were developed and approved.

Table 16-8 Economic Feasibility Study for Shoppers Mart's New Information System

	Initial Outlay	Year 1	Year 2	Year 3	Year 4	Year 5	Year 6
Initial outlay costs							
Hardware	$2,000,000						
Software	400,000						
Training	200,000						
Site preparation	200,000						
Initial systems design	2,000,000						
Conversion	200,000						
Total initial outlays	$5,000,000						
Recurring costs							
Hardware expansion			$260,000	$300,000	$340,000	$380,000	$400,000
Software			150,000	200,000	225,000	250,000	250,000
Systems maintenance		$60,000	120,000	130,000	140,000	150,000	160,000
Personnel costs		500,000	800,000	900,000	1,000,000	1,100,000	1,300,000
Communication charges		100,000	160,000	180,000	200,000	220,000	250,000
Overhead		300,000	420,000	490,000	560,000	600,000	640,000
Total costs		$960,000	$1,910,000	$2,200,000	$2,465,000	$2,700,000	$3,000,000
Savings							
Clerical cost savings		$600,000	$1,200,000	$1,400,000	$1,600,000	$1,800,000	$2,000,000
Working capital savings		900,000	1,200,000	1,500,000	1,500,000	1,500,000	1,500,000
Profits from sales increases			500,000	900,000	1,200,000	1,500,000	1,800,000
Warehousing efficiencies			400,000	800,000	1,200,000	1,600,000	2,000,000
Total savings		$1,500,000	$3,300,000	$4,600,000	$5,500,000	$6,400,000	$7,300,000
Savings minus recurring costs		$540,000	$1,390,000	$2,400,000	$3,035,000	$3,700,000	$4,300,000
Less income taxes (34% rate)		(183,600)	(472,600)	(816,000)	(1,031,900)	(1,258,000)	(1,462,000)
Cash savings (net of tax)		$356,400	$917,400	$1,584,000	$2,003,100	$2,442,000	$2,838,000
Savings on taxes due to depreciation deduction		340,000	544,000	326,400	195,500	195,500	98,600
Net savings	($5,000,000)	$696,400	$1,461,400	$1,910,400	$2,198,600	$2,637,500	$2,936,600

Payback occurs in the fourth year when the savings net of taxes of $6,266,800 exceed the costs of $5,000,000.

Net present value (interest rate of 10%):

(5,000,000)		(5,000,000)
696,400 × 0.9091 =		633,097
1,461,400 × 0.8265 =		1,207,847
1,910,400 × 0.7513 =		1,435,284
2,198,600 × 0.6830 =		1,501,644
2,637,500 × 0.6209 =		1,637,624
2,936,600 × 0.5645 =		1,657,711
Net present value		3,073,206
Internal rate of return is		25.04%

Depreciation on initial investment of $5,000,000:
Tax Rate 34%

Year	Rate (%)	Depreciation	Tax Savings
1	20.00	1,000,000	340,000
2	32.00	1,600,000	544,000
3	19.20	960,000	326,400
4	11.50	575,000	195,500
5	11.50	575,000	195,500
6	5.80	290,000	98,600

KEY TERMS

- systems development life cycle (SDLC)
- systems analysis
- conceptual design
- physical design
- implementation and conversion
- operations and maintenance
- steering committee
- systems analysts
- computer programmers
- project development plan
- master plan
- program evaluation and review technique (PERT)

- critical path
- Gantt chart
- feasibility study
- technical feasibility
- operational feasibility
- legal feasibility
- scheduling feasibility
- economic feasibility
- capital budgeting model
- payback period
- net present value (NPV)
- internal rate of return (IRR)
- behavioral aspects of change
- aggression

- projection
- avoidance
- request for systems development
- initial investigation
- proposal to conduct systems analysis
- systems survey
- physical models
- logical models
- systems survey report
- systems approach
- systems analysis report

CHAPTER QUIZ

1. Which of the following is *not* one of the reasons why companies make changes to their AISs?
   a. gain a competitive advantage
   b. increase productivity
   c. keep up with company growth
   d. downsize
   e. All of the above are reasons why companies change an AIS.
2. The planning technique that identifies implementation activities and their relationships, constructs a network of arrows and nodes, and then determines the critical path through the network is referred to as which of the following:
   a. Gantt chart
   b. PERT diagram
   c. physical model
   d. data flow diagram
3. The purchasing department is designing a new AIS. Who is best able to determine departmental information requirements?
   a. steering committee
   b. controller
   c. top management
   d. purchasing department
4. Which of the following is the correct order of the steps in systems analysis?
   a. initial investigation, determination of information needs and system requirements, feasibility study, system survey
   b. determination of information needs and system requirements, system survey, feasibility study, initial investigation
   c. system survey, initial investigation, determination of information needs and system requirements, feasibility study
   d. initial investigation, system survey, feasibility study, determination of information needs and system requirements

5. Which of the following is the long-range planning document that specifies what the system will consist of, how it will be developed, who will develop it, how needed resources will be acquired, and its overall vision?
   a. steering committee agenda
   b. master plan
   c. systems development life cycle
   d. project development plan

6. Resistance is often a reaction to the methods of instituting change rather than to change itself.
   a. True
   b. False

7. Increased error rates, disruptions, and sabotage are examples of which of the following?
   a. aggression
   b. avoidance
   c. projection
   d. payback

8. What is the most significant problem a company encounters in designing, developing, and implementing a system?
   a. the human element
   b. technology
   c. legal challenges
   d. planning for the new system

9. Determining whether the organization has access to people who can design, implement, and operate the proposed system is referred to as which of the following?
   a. technical feasibility
   b. operational feasibility
   c. legal feasibility
   d. scheduling feasibility
   e. economic feasibility

10. Which of the following is *not* one of the tangible or intangible benefits a company might obtain from a new system?
    a. cost savings
    b. improved customer service and productivity
    c. improved decision making
    d. improved data processing
    e. All are benefits of a new system.

DISCUSSION QUESTIONS

16.1   The approach to long-range AIS planning described in this chapter is important for large organizations with extensive investments in computer facilities. Should small organizations with far fewer information systems employees attempt to implement planning programs? Why or why not? Be prepared to defend your position to the class.

16.2   Assume you are a consultant advising a firm on the design and implementation of a new system. Management has decided to let several employees go after the system is implemented. Some have many years of company service. How would you advise management to communicate this decision to the affected employees? To the entire staff?

16.3   While reviewing a list of benefits from a computer vendor's proposal, you note an item that reads "improvements in management decision making—$50,000 per year." How would you interpret this item? What influence should it have on the economic feasibility and the computer acquisition decision?

16.4   This chapter suggests that an organization should make special efforts to ease fears among its employees about potential job or seniority loss. One advantage of mechanizing a system, however, is a reduction of clerical costs, which often results in job losses. Are these two concepts inconsistent? What policies should be consistent with both concepts?

16.5   The president of Monteer Signature Homes is perplexed by requests for computers from three different areas of the firm. The EDP manager wants $4.5 million to upgrade the mainframe computer. The vice president of engineering wants $450,000 to buy a client/server system. The vice president of finance wants $200,000 to purchase laptop computers. Rapid growth is putting a strain on computer resources and keeping profits down. Payroll, accounting, inventory, and engineering functions are computerized whereas other tasks are manual. The firm is organized by business functions, with vice presidents for manufacturing, marketing, engineering, finance, and human resources. The president wonders if a steering committee is needed. Discuss the objectives, responsibilities, and composition of an information systems steering committee. Justify your recommendations concerning its membership and the selection of a chairperson.

(CIA Examination, adapted)

16.6   Describe some examples of systems analysis decisions that involve a trade-off between each of the following pairs of objectives:
a. economy and usefulness
b. economy and reliability
c. economy and customer service
d. simplicity and usefulness
e. simplicity and reliability
f. economy and capacity
g. economy and flexibility

16.7   For years, Jerry Jingle's dairy production facilities led the state in total sales volume. However, recent declines left Jerry wondering what his company was doing wrong. When he asked several customers to rate his products, they seemed satisfied but did note several areas of concern. First on the list was the dairy company's record of late deliveries and incomplete orders. Further discussion with some of the company's production employees (not the cows) revealed several problems, including bottlenecks in milk pasteurization and homogenization due to a lack of coordination in job scheduling, mix-ups in customers' orders, and improperly labeled products. How would you suggest Jerry address the company's problems? What types of data gathering techniques would be helpful at this early stage?

16.8   The following problem situations could arise in any manufacturing firm. What questions should you ask to understand the problem?
• Customer complaints about product quality have increased.
• Accounting sees an increase in the number and dollar value of bad debt write-offs.
• Operating margins have declined the past four years due to higher-than-expected production costs from idle time, overtime, and reworking of products.

16.9   For each of the following items, discuss which data gathering method(s) are most appropriate and why:
a. Surveying the adequacy of internal controls in the purchase requisition procedure
b. Identifying the controller's information needs

c. Determining how cash disbursement procedures are actually performed
d. Surveying the opinions of employees concerning the move to a total quality management program
e. Investigating an increase in uncollectible accounts

PROBLEMS

16.1   Yuping Chai has seen the future, and so far she wants no part of it. The offices at Sierra Manufacturing Company, where Chai is vice president, have just been automated. Sitting at her desk in Sacramento, Chai can push buttons on a computer terminal's keyboard and staff memos will appear on the screen. She can respond with her own memos, which will instantly be sent to colleagues, either for immediate viewing or for storage and later retrieval. By pressing a few other buttons, she can view company financial data stored in the corporate computer. Chai can do all that and more, but instead she has unplugged the terminal. "I think most managers, including me, are talkers," she states. "I would much rather talk than push buttons." Chai's resistance exemplifies the reaction of some professionals and executives who are being forced to make major psychological and behavioral adjustments as they begin to move into a paperless world.

Required
a. What do you believe is the real cause of Chai's resistance to the computer system?
b. As a colleague of Chai, how could you help her realize the benefits of computerization and overcome her computer phobia?

16.2   Mary Smith is the bookkeeper for Dave's Distributing Company, a distributor of soft drinks and juices. Because the company is rather small, Mary performs all the daily accounting tasks herself. Dave, the president and owner of the company, supervises the warehouse/delivery and front office staff, but he also spends much of his time jogging and skiing.

For several years profits were good and sales grew faster than industry averages. Although the accounting system was working well, bottlers were pressuring Dave to computerize. With a little guidance from a CPA friend and with no mention to Mary, Dave bought a new personal computer and some accounting software. Only one day was required to set up the hardware, install the software, and convert the files. The morning the vendor installed the computer, Mary's job performance changed dramatically. Although the software company provided two full days of training, she had trouble learning the new system. As a result, Dave decided she should run both the manual and computer systems for a month to verify the new system's accuracy.

Mary continually complained that she lacked the time and expertise to run both systems by herself. She also complained that she did not understand how to run the new computer system. To keep accounts up to date, Dave spent two to three hours a day running the new system himself. Dave found that much of the time spent running the system was devoted to identifying discrepancies between the computer and manual results. When the error was located, it was almost always in the manual system. This significantly increased Dave's confidence in the new system.

At the end of the month Dave was ready to scrap the manual system, but Mary said she was not ready. Dave went back to skiing and jogging, and Mary went on with the manual system. When the computer system fell behind, Dave again spent time catching it up. He also worked with Mary to make sure she understood how to operate the computer system.

Months later Dave was still keeping the computer system up to date and training Mary. He was at the height of frustration. "I'm sure Mary *knows* how to run the system, but she doesn't seem to *want* to. I can do all the accounting work on the computer in two or three hours a day, but she can't even do it in her normal eight-hour workday. What should I do?"

Required

a. What events may have contributed to the new system's failure?

b. In retrospect, how should Dave have handled the computerization of the accounting system?

c. At what point in the decision-making process should Mary have been informed? Should she have had some say in whether the computer was purchased? If so, what should have been the nature of her input? If Mary had not agreed with Dave's decision to acquire the computer, what should Dave have done?

d. A hard decision must be made regarding Mary. Significant efforts have been made to train her, but they have been unsuccessful. What would you recommend at this point? Should she be fired? Threatened with the loss of her job? Moved somewhere else in the business? Given additional training?

16.3   Wright Company employs a computer-based data processing system to maintain company records. The present system was developed in stages over the past five years and has been fully operational for the past two years. During the design process, department heads were asked to specify the types of information and reports they would need. Company management also asked for several reports. By the time the development stage began, there were several staff changes and the new department heads requested additional reports. The information systems department complied with these changes, and reports were discontinued only upon the request of a department head. Few reports were actually discontinued, and a large number of reports are generated each period.

Company management is concerned about the quantity of information the system produces. Internal auditing was asked to evaluate the system's effectiveness and determined that more information was being generated than could be used effectively. They noted the following reactions to this information overload.

- Many department heads did not act on certain reports during periods of peak activity. They let them accumulate in the hope of catching up later.
- Some department heads had so many reports they did not act at all, or misused the information.
- Frequently, no action was taken until another manager needed a decision made. Department heads did not develop a priority system for acting on the information.
- Department heads often developed information from alternative, independent sources. This was easier than searching the reports for the needed data.

Required

a. Indicate if each of the observed reactions is a functional or dysfunctional behavioral response. Explain your answer in each case.

b. Recommend procedures to eliminate any dysfunctional behavior and prevent its recurrence.

(CMA Examination, adapted)

16.4   The controller of Tim's Travel (TT), a rapidly growing travel corporation, is deciding between upgrading the company's existing computer system or replacing it with a new MANTIS XIT-470. The present system is four years old. Upgrading will cost $97,500 and will extend its useful life for another seven years. The book value is $19,500, although it would sell for $24,000. Upgrading will eliminate one employee at a salary of $19,400; the MANTIS will eliminate two employees. Annual operating costs are estimated at $15,950 per year. Upgrading is expected to increase profits 3.5 percent above last year's level of $553,000.

The BetaTech Company has quoted a price of $224,800 for the new MANTIS, which has a useful life of seven years. Annual operating costs are estimated to be $14,260. The average processing speed of the MANTIS is 12 percent faster than that of other systems in its price range, which would increase TT's profits by 4.5 percent.

Tim's present tax rate is 35 percent and money is worth 11 percent. Also assume that after seven years the salvage value, net of tax, would be $12,000 for the MANTIS and $7,500 for the present system. For tax purposes, computers are depreciated over five full years (six calendar years; a half year the first and last years) and the depreciation percentages are as follows:

Year	Percent (%)
1	20.00
2	32.00
3	19.20
4	11.52
5	11.52
6	5.76

Required

Using a spreadsheet package, prepare an economic feasibility analysis to determine if TT should rehabilitate the old system or purchase the MANTIS. As part of the analysis, compute the after-tax cash flows for years 1 through 7 and the payback, NPV, and IRR of each alternative.

16.5   Rossco Incorporated is considering purchasing a new Z-660 computer to maximize office efficiency. The proposal estimates that initial systems design would cost $54,000; hardware, $74,000; and new software, $35,000. One-time initial training costs are expected to be $11,000, an additional $20,000 will be required to install the system, and $12,000 will be required to convert the files. A net reduction of three employees, whose average salaries are $40,000 per year, is expected if the new machine is acquired. A just completed special study found that computerization could decrease average yearly inventory by $150,000. Annual operating costs, other than employee wages, are expected to be $30,000 per year higher than those for the current manual system.

The expected life of the machine is four years, with an estimated salvage value of zero. The effective tax rate is 40 percent. For purposes of the feasibility study, assume that all costs associated with the computer purchase will be depreciated equally over the four-year life using the straight-line method. Assume that Rossco can invest money made available from the reduction in inventory at 11 percent annually. Also, assume that all cash flows, except for the initial investment and start-up costs, are at the end of the year. Assume 365 days in a year.

Required

Use a spreadsheet to perform a feasibility analysis to determine if Rossco should purchase the computer. Compute the following as part of the analysis:

a. Initial investment

b. After-tax cash flows for years 1 through 4

    c. Payback period
    d. Net present value
    e. Internal rate of return

16.6   XYZ Conglomerate Company has completed a feasibility study to upgrade its computer system. Management received the information in Table 16-9, which shows the benefits of the new system.
Required
As a board member, which of the benefits would you accept as relevant to the cost justification of the system? Defend your answer.
(SMAC Examination, adapted)

16.7   The Alkin Chemical Company manufactures and sells chemicals for agricultural and industrial use. The company has grown significantly over the past five years. However, the company's AIS is the original one developed and installed by the former president's son while he was in college. Much of the information generated by the system is irrelevant, and more appropriate and timely information is needed.

    The controller is concerned that actual monthly cost data for most production processes are compared with actual costs of the same processes for the previous year. However, the production supervisors contend that the system is adequate because it accounts for discrepancies. The current year's costs seldom vary from the previous year's costs when adjusted for inflation; thus, the supervisors feel that costs are under control.

    The vice president of manufacturing has found that preparing even the simplest of cost analyses requires that she spend days compiling information generated by the current system. She believes the system should be flexible enough for managers to develop quickly their own recurring reports.

    As a result of these concerns, the new president has appointed a committee to review the system. It will determine management's information needs for cost control and decision purposes and ensure that the company's and employees' behavioral needs are met. The vice president of finance and administration chairs the committee.

    Shortly after announcing the formation of this committee, the vice president of finance overheard a cost accountant say, "I've been doing it this way since the company began and now this committee plans to make my job redundant." Several employees in the general accounting department also assumed that their positions would be eliminated or changed significantly. Several days later, the vice president of finance and administration overheard one production manager state that he believed the system was in need of revision because the most meaningful information he was receiving came from a junior salesperson.

Required
a. Identify the behavioral implications of using an AIS that does not appear to meet management's needs.
b. Identify and explain the problems employees have with the AIS.
c. Identify policies or practices the company could follow during systems implementation that would reduce costs without laying off employees.
(SMAC Examination, adapted)

16.8   Recent years have brought an explosive growth in electronic communication: Computers, photocopiers, fax machines, word processors, electronic mail, teleconferencing, and sophisticated management information systems have changed the way information is received, processed, and transmitted. With the decreasing costs of computer equipment and the

Table 16-9 Benefits to Be Derived from the New System

1. Production
   a. Marketing forecasting is presently in dollars per product line. Calculation of units by product line takes an estimated 2 man-days, a total of $80. This saving would be repeated each time the market forecast was updated, presumably monthly. The program to calculate the forecast in units would be more accurate than the present method of applying factors to dollar value. $ 960
   b. More effective inventory control would permit an overall reduction in inventory. The ability to quickly establish total requirements would help to overcome parts stockout situations. For this calculation we estimate a 10 percent inventory reduction. The cost of capital at XYZ Conglomerate Company approximates 20 percent, and the benefit then approximates 20 percent of $100,000. $20,000
   c. Evaluation of changes to plans will be possible in detail. This is not so under our manual system. Parts explosions are time consuming and can only be done monthly. The impact here would be increased production flexibility and the reduction of sales losses due to finished goods stockouts. We estimate that this can be valued as the equivalent of hiring two clerks. $15,000 $35,960
2. Engineering
   a. Use of the computer in filing and updating bills of material would save 40 percent of the industrial engineer's time. $ 4,000
   b. The improved updating of files, which includes the bills of material and product structure files, which affect many areas, should save a minimum 25 percent of one clerk (if we took all areas, this would probably be closer to 50 percent). $ 1,500
   c. Estimated clerical savings in labor calculations, rates, and bonus detail is 2 days per week, or 40 percent of one person. $ 2,000 $ 7,500
3. Sales
   a. Improved reporting will enable sales staff and sales management to react more quickly to prevailing conditions. The implied benefit would be sales increases, especially during promotions, and a better sales/expense ratio. We are assuming an improvement in sales of only $1,000 per person, for a total of $5,000. $ 5,000
4. Marketing
   Revised reports and an improved forecasting system will help establish sales trends and will help the production department in flexibility and inventory control.
5. Accounting
   a. Standard costing of all bills of material, and in fact, the side effect of being able to cost new products quickly, can be expressed as the equivalent of saving 30–40 percent of the plant accountant's time. $ 3,000
   b. A revised incentive earnings and payroll system installed on the computer should reduce the payroll department clerical labor from 3 days to 1 day— possible benefit of 40 percent of one clerk. $ 2,400 $ 5,400

Total $53,860

increasing power of automation, the full impact of computerization has yet to be felt. Although the development of computer applications is directed at being user-friendly or user oriented, the integration of computers into the organization has had both positive and negative effects on employees.

Required

a. Describe the benefits that companies and their employees can receive from electronic communication.

b. Discuss the organizational impact of introducing new electronic communication systems.

c. Explain (1) why an employee might resist the introduction of electronic communication systems, and (2) the steps an organization can take to alleviate this resistance.

(CMA Examination, adapted)

16.9   PWR Instruments manufactures precision nozzles for fire hoses. The president, Ronald Paige, an engineer, started the corporation, which has been successful and has experienced steady growth. Reporting to Ronald are six vice presidents representing the company's major functions—marketing, production, research and development, information services, finance, and human resources. The information services department was just established during the past fiscal year, when PWR began developing a new computer-based information system. The new database system employs a server connected to several terminals and personal computers in each of the six departments. The personal computers can both download data from and upload data to the main computer. For example, financial analysts can access the data stored on the main computer through the personal computers and use the latter as smart terminals on a stand-alone basis. PWR is still in the process of designing and developing new applications for its computer system.

Ronald has recently received the management letter prepared by the company's external audit firm, and has called a meeting with his vice presidents to review the recommendations. One major item that Ronald wants to discuss is the recommendation that PWR form an information systems steering committee.

Required

a. Explain why the external auditor would recommend that PWR establish an information systems steering committee, and discuss its specific responsibilities. What advantages can such a steering committee offer PWR?

b. Identify the PWR managers who would be most likely to serve on the committee.

(CMA Examination, adapted)

16.10   Almost 500 years ago, Machiavelli wrote in *The Prince,* "It must be considered that there is nothing more difficult to carry out, nor more doubtful of success, nor more dangerous to handle, than to initiate a new order of things." This statement is as applicable today as it was in 1520.

Implementing organizational change is one of the most demanding assignments that any executive faces. It has been suggested that every change requires three steps: unfreezing the current situation, implementing the change, and finally refreezing the effected change. This view, however, lacks the specific details needed by an operating manager who must initiate the change.

Required

a. Identify and describe the specific steps a manager must take to implement an organizational change.

 b. Suppose an organization does make a change that affects employees directly or affects how they conduct their operations.

  1. Explain why employees generally resist change.

  2. Outline and describe the ways a manager can reduce the resistance to change.

(CMA Examination, adapted)

16.11 Don Richardson, vice president of marketing for the JEM Corporation, has just emerged from another strategic planning session aimed at developing a new line of business. The company's management team has been discussing these plans for several months, since major organizational changes will be required to implement the strategic plan. Rumors about the plans have been circulating the office for months, and several employees who are anxious about the expected changes have already confronted Don. His only response has been to tell them that an official announcement of this new business plan is expected shortly.

  When he returns to his office, Don is met by an ad hoc committee composed of his department managers. The sales manager, Susan Williams, has been the most vocal of the group and, as expected, is acting as spokesperson. "Mr. Richardson, it is imperative that we speak to you right away. The employees are becoming very apprehensive about the proposed changes, and lately their job performance has slacked off."

  "That's right," adds George Sussman, accounting manager. "My subordinates are asking me all sorts of questions concerning this new line of business, and I don't have any answers for them. They're not buying the 'official announcement' line any longer. I suspect that some of them are already looking for jobs in the event that department 'changes' phase out their positions."

Required

 a. Describe the general steps in the decision-making process that a company should follow before choosing to implement a major organizational change.

 b. Explain why employees generally resist organizational change.

 c. Discuss ways JEM Corporation can alleviate employee resistance to change.

(CMA Examination, adapted)

16.12 Remnants, Inc. is a large company that manufactures and markets designer clothing throughout the United States. From its St. Louis headquarters, Remnants has developed a regional system for marketing and servicing its products. Each region functions as a profit center because of the authority given to regional managers within their territories.

  Each regional organization consists of an accounting and a budget department, a human resources and training department, and several area offices to market and service the products. Each area office consists of sales, service, and administrative departments, the managers of which ultimately report to one area manager.

  The New York area office departed from the standard organizational structure by establishing a branch office to market and service the firm's products in the Boston area. A branch manager who reports directly to the area manager heads the local office.

  In recent years the Boston branch manager has encouraged the area manager to consider a new information system to handle the local branch's growing information needs. The New York area manager and the eastern regional manager have concluded that they should establish a project team with employees from the regional office, the area office, and the branch office to (1) assess the information needs at the Boston branch office and (2) develop system recommendations, if necessary. The following employees have been appointed to the project team, with Keith Nash acting as chairperson.

Eastern Region Office

Kurt Johnson, Budget Supervisor
Sally Brown, Training Director

New York Office

Keith Nash, Administrative Director

Boston Branch

Heidi Meyer, Branch Manager and Sales Manager
Bobby Roos, Assistant Branch Manager and Service Manager
Joe Gonzalez, Salesperson
Juana Martinez, Serviceperson

Required

a. A project team, similar to the one organized at Remnants, Inc., is organized to contribute its skills to accomplish a given objective. Characteristics of group members can influence the functioning and effectiveness of a project team. Identify some of these characteristics.
b. Due to the team's composition, what sources of conflict can you see arising among its members? Do you think the group will succeed in its objective to develop an information system for the Boston branch office? Why or why not?
c. What contribution would a person who holds a position as budget supervisor make in a project team such as this one?

16.13 Managers face a continual crisis in the systems development process: Information systems departments develop systems that businesses cannot use. At the heart of the problem is a proverbial "great divide" that separates the world of business from the world of information systems. Few departments seem able or ready to cross this gap.

A major reason for the resulting information systems development crisis is that many large systems currently handling corporate information needs are seriously out of date. As a result, companies are looking for ways to improve existing systems or to build new ones.

Another reason for the crisis is the widespread use of PC-based systems that has spawned a high level of user expectation that IS departments are not meeting. As computer education increases, users are seeking more powerful applications that are not available on many older systems.

The costs of the great divide can be devastating for unprepared companies. An East Coast chemical company spent more than $1 million on a budgeting and control system that was never used. The systems department created an administrative budgeting system; the company's expertise was technical excellence, not budgets. As a result, the new system completely missed the mark when it came to meeting business needs.

Another example of poor systems development comes from a Midwestern bank. It used an expensive computer-aided software engineering (CASE) tool to develop a system that users ignored because there had been no design planning. A senior analyst for Franklin Savings Association said, "They built the system right, but, unfortunately, they didn't build the right system."

So what is the solution? The first step in effective systems design is a thorough business analysis, not a systems analysis. A business analysis includes a thorough review of how a business operates and how the functions of the business relate. Only with this understanding can systems professionals and business managers communicate effectively when developing an integrated system.

In addition, businesses are seeking managers who have a systems background, because they provide a liaison between the systems department and the finance and accounting departments, helping business managers to clearly communicate their needs.

What is still missing is more involvement between systems staff and end users. Systems designers must take more time to interact with end users. In addition, business managers must provide their employees with the training time required to make the system work right.

Required

a. What is the great divide in the systems development process? What are the reasons for this gap?
b. What are the suggested solutions to the information crisis? How will the systems approach to development help?
c. Discuss the role that a systems designer, a business manager, and an end user can take to narrow the great divide.
d. Who plays the most vital role in the effective development of the system?

16.14 Joanne Grey, a senior consultant, and David Young, a junior consultant, were assigned by their firm to conduct a systems analysis for a client. The objective of the study was to consider the feasibility of integrating and automating certain clerical functions. Joanne had previously worked on jobs for this client, but David had been hired only recently.

During the first morning on the job, Joanne directed David to interview a departmental supervisor and learn as much as he could about the department's operations. David went to the supervisor's office, introduced himself, and made the following statement: "Your company has hired my firm to study the way your department works and to make recommendations as to how its efficiency could be improved and its cost lowered. I would like to interview you to determine what goes on in your department."

David questioned the supervisor for about 30 minutes, but found him to be uncooperative. David then gave Joanne an oral report on how the interview had gone and what he had learned about the department.

Required

Describe several flaws in the approach taken to obtain information about the operation of the department under study. How should this task have been performed?

16.15 Business organizations often are required to modify or replace a portion or all of their financial information system to keep pace with their growth and take advantage of improved IT. The process involved in modifying or replacing an AIS requires a substantial commitment of time and resources. When an organization undertakes a change in its AIS, a systems analysis takes place.

Required

a. Explain the purpose and reasons for surveying an organization's existing system during a systems study.
b. Identify and explain the general activities and techniques that are commonly used during the systems analysis.
c. Systems analysis is often carried out by a project team composed of a systems analyst, a management accountant, and other persons in the company who would be knowledge-

able and helpful in the systems study. What would be the management accountant's role in systems analysis?

(CMA Examination, adapted)

16.16 The following list presents specific project activities and their scheduled starting and completion times:

Activity	Starting Date	Ending Date
A	Jan. 5	Feb. 9
B	Jan. 5	Jan. 19
C	Jan. 26	Feb. 23
D	Mar. 2	Mar. 23
E	Mar. 2	Mar. 16
F	Feb. 2	Mar. 16
G	Mar. 30	Apr. 20
H	Mar. 23	Apr. 27

Required

a. Using a format similar to that illustrated in Figure 16-3, prepare a Gantt chart for this project. Assume that each activity starts on a Monday and ends on a Friday.

b. Assume today is February 16 and activities A and B have been completed, C is half completed, F is a quarter completed, and the other activities have not yet commenced. Record this information on your Gantt chart. Is the project behind schedule, on schedule, or ahead of schedule? Explain.

c. Discuss the relative merits of the Gantt chart and PERT as tools for project planning and control.

Case 16-1   AnyCompany, Inc.:
An Ongoing Comprehensive Case

Identify a local company (you may use the same company that you identified to complete Case 1.1) and perform the following steps:

1. Schedule a visit with a member of the AIS staff. With help, identify the most significant revision in the company's AIS (for some, this may mean the initial design and implementation). Discuss the following issues.

   a. What groups were organized to oversee systems design/revision and implementation? How was the implementation strategy developed?

   b. What problems did the company run into when it was developing/revising its system? How did the company handle these problems?

   c. Which staff members were affected by the change in the AIS? In general terms, how did employees react to the changes? What did the project development team do to minimize potential negative effects of the system change?

d. If the company were starting the project over again, what would it do differently? Why?

2. Review the documentation that covers system design/revision and implementation. Take a few moments to review any project development plans and the master plan, if available.

3. If appropriate, ask to review the feasibility analysis surrounding the implementation of the AIS.

4. From your interview and your observations, write a brief report summarizing your findings. Consider the following issues:

a. How well did the company organize the design/revision and implementation of the AIS?

b. What suggestions do you have for improving the company's development and implementation procedures?

Case 16-2 Audio Visual Corporation

Audio Visual Corporation (AVC) manufactures and sells visual display equipment. The company's headquarters are outside Boston. The majority of sales are made through seven geographical sales offices located in Los Angeles, Seattle, Minneapolis, Cleveland, Dallas, Boston, and Atlanta. Each sales office has a warehouse located nearby that carries an inventory of new equipment and replacement parts. The remainder of the sales are made through manufacturers' representatives.

AVC's manufacturing operations are conducted in a single plant, which is highly departmentalized. In addition to the assembly department are several departments responsible for various components used in the visual display equipment. The plant also has maintenance, engineering, scheduling, and cost accounting departments.

Early in 1996, management decided that its AIS needed upgrading. As a result, the company installed a mainframe at corporate headquarters and local area networks at each of the seven sales offices.

The integration of the new computer and the LANs into the AVC AIS was carried out by the information systems staff. The systems manager and the four systems analysts who had the major responsibility for the integration were hired by the company in the spring of 1997. The department's other employees—programmers, machine operators, and keypunch operators—have been with the company for several years.

During its early years, AVC had a centralized decision-making organization. Top management formulated all plans and directed all operations. As the company expanded, some of the decision making was decentralized, although the information processing was still highly centralized. Departments had to coordinate their plans with the corporate office, but they had more freedom in developing their sales programs. However, information problems developed, and the information systems department was assigned the task of improving the company's information processing system once the new equipment was installed.

The systems analysts reviewed the current AIS prior to the acquisition of the new computer and identified its weaknesses. They then designed new applications to overcome these problems. During the 18 months since the acquisition of the new equipment, the following applications have been redesigned or developed and are now operational: payroll, production scheduling, financial statement preparation, customer billing, raw material use in production, and finished goods inventory by warehouse. The operating departments of AVC affected by the systems changes were rarely consulted or contacted until the system was operational and the new reports were distributed to the operating departments.

AVC's president is very pleased with the information systems department's work. During a recent conversation with an individual who was interested in AVC's new system, the president stated, "The systems people are doing a good job and I have full confidence in their work. I touch base with them frequently, and they have encountered no difficulties in doing their work. We paid a lot of money for the new equipment and the systems people certainly cost enough, but the combination of the new equipment and new information systems staff should solve all of our problems."

Recently, two additional conversations regarding the computer and the AIS have taken place. One was between Jerry Adams, plant manager, and Bill Taylor, the information systems manager; the other was between Jerry Adams and Terry Williams, the new human resources manager.

BILL TAYLOR–JERRY ADAMS CONVERSATION

JERRY: Bill, you're trying to run my plant for me. I'm supposed to be the manager, yet you keep interfering. I wish you would mind your own business.

BILL: You've got a job to do, but so does my department. As we analyzed the information needed for production scheduling and by top management, we saw where improvements could be made in the workflow. Now that the system is operational, you can't reroute work and change procedures, because that would destroy the value of the information we're processing. And while I'm on that subject, it's getting to the point where we can't trust the information we're getting from production. The documents we receive from production contain a lot of errors.

JERRY: I'm responsible for the efficient operation of production. Quite frankly, I think I'm the best judge of production efficiency. The system you installed has reduced my workforce and increased the workload of the remaining employees, but I don't see that this has improved anything. In fact, it might explain the high error rate in the documents.

BILL: This new computer cost a lot of money, and I'm trying to ensure that the company gets its money's worth.

JERRY ADAMS–TERRY WILLIAMS CONVERSATION

JERRY: My best production assistant, the one I'm grooming to be a supervisor when the next opening occurs, came to me today and said he was thinking of quitting. When I asked him why, he said he didn't enjoy the work anymore. He's not the only one who is unhappy. The supervisors and department heads no longer have a voice in establishing production schedules. This new computer system has taken away the contribution we used to make to company planning and direction. We seem to be going back to the days when top management made all the decisions. I have more production problems now than I used to. I think it boils down to a lack of interest on the part of my management team. I know the problem is within my area, but I thought you might be able to help me.

TERRY: I have no recommendations for you now, but I've had similar complaints from purchasing and shipping. I think we should explore your concerns during tomorrow's plant management meeting.

QUESTIONS

Evaluate the preceding information, and answer the following questions:

1. Apparently the development of and transition to the new computer-based system has created problems among AVC's staff.

Identify and briefly discuss the apparent causes of these problems.
2. How could the company have avoided these problems in the first place? How could they prevent them from happening in the future?

(CMA Examination, adapted)

ANSWERS TO CHAPTER QUIZ

1. e	**3.** d	**5.** b	**7.** a	**9.** b
2. b	**4.** d	**6.** a	**8.** a	**10.** e

AIS Development Strategies

Learning Objectives

After studying this chapter, you should be able to:

- Describe how organizations purchase application software, vendor services, and hardware.
- Explain how information system departments develop custom software.
- Explain how end-users develop, use, and control computer-based information systems.
- Explain why organizations outsource their information systems, and evaluate the benefits and risks of this strategy.
- Explain the principles and challenges of business process reengineering.
- Describe how prototypes are used to develop an AIS, and discuss the advantages and disadvantages of doing so.
- Explain what computer-aided software engineering is and how it is used in systems development.

Integrative Case: Shoppers Mart

Ann Christy was elated that the new system Shoppers Mart so badly needed was approved and that she and her team had accurately assessed the company's needs. Ann realized she needed to determine if it would be better to purchase a software system from an outside vendor, develop the system in-house, or hire a company that specialized in systems like the one she envisioned to develop and operate the new system. More specifically, she needed answers to the following questions:

1. Could Ann buy the software she needed? If so, how should she approach the process of buying hardware and software and selecting a vendor?
2. How do companies go about developing software in-house? Is this the best approach for Shoppers Mart?

3. How extensively should the system make use of end-user-developed software?
4. Should Shoppers Mart make the needed improvements to its existing system, or should it consider reengineering its business processes and then develop a system to support the new processes?
5. Was outsourcing the information system a viable alternative to obtaining a new system? Did the benefits of outsourcing outweigh its risks?
6. If the company decided to develop the system in-house, should it speed up the development process by using advanced techniques such as prototyping or computer-assisted software engineering?

Ann decided to investigate the various design alternatives to determine what course of action was best for Shoppers Mart.

INTRODUCTION

Traditionally, accountants have experienced the following difficulties in developing an AIS:

➤ Demands for development resources are so numerous that AIS projects can be backlogged for several years.

➤ A newly designed AIS does not always meet user needs. The problem may not be discovered until the system is in use, often after a lengthy development process. It is hard for users to visualize how the AIS will look or how it will operate by reviewing design documentation. In addition, when systems developers do not understand the company's business needs or user needs, it is hard for them to make meaningful suggestions for improvement.

➤ The development process can take so long that the system no longer meets company needs. For example, Fannie Mae spent eight years and $100 million developing the largest loan accounting system in the world. Unfortunately, when the system was finally completed, it no longer met most of Fannie Mae's business needs.

➤ Users are unable to specify their needs adequately. Often they do not know exactly what they need, and when they do, they sometimes cannot communicate these ideas to systems developers.

➤ Changes to the AIS are often difficult to make after requirements have been frozen into specifications. If users are allowed to keep changing the requirements, the AIS may take forever to finish and costs increase each time the AIS is reworked.

In today's fast-changing world, many companies find themselves in the position of Shoppers Mart. They must meet user information needs quickly and efficiently. In this chapter you will learn three ways to obtain a new information system: purchasing prewritten software, developing software in-house, and hiring an outside company (outsourcing) to develop and operate the system. You will also learn three ways to hasten or improve the development process: business process reengineering, prototyping, and computer-aided software engineering (CASE) tools.

PURCHASE SOFTWARE

In the early days of computers it was rare that a company was able to buy software that could meet its needs. As the software industry has matured, however, more companies have begun to purchase software. Because of software's easy availability and lower cost, an estimated 80 percent of companies currently installing computers are either using or considering canned software packages.

Written by software development companies, **canned software** is sold on the open market to a broad range of users with similar requirements. Some companies combine software and hardware and sell them as a package. These are called **turnkey systems,** because the vendor installs the entire system and the user needs only to "turn the key." Many turnkey systems are written by vendors who specialize in a particular industry. For example, specific systems are geared toward doctors and dentists, automobile repair and service companies, full-service restaurants, fast-food outlets, video rental businesses, and other retail stores.

The Internet has given companies a new way to acquire software. **Application service providers (ASPs)** host Web-based software on their computers and deliver the software to their clients over the Internet. In this case, companies do not have to buy, install, and maintain canned software. Instead, they "rent" the software they need from an ASP. The advantages of doing this include a reduction of software costs and administrative overhead, automated software upgrades, scalability as the business grows, global access to information, access to skilled IT personnel, and the ability to focus on core financial competencies rather than IT requirements.

Soon it is likely that application systems will be developed in-house only by very large organizations or companies with unique requirements. However, even today, many large organizations purchase software from outside suppliers. For example, Pacific Gas & Electric Company signed a $750,000 contract that calls for the license and installation of Dun & Bradstreet's General Ledger software to replace its in-house-developed general ledger system. A recent Deloitte & Touche survey found that most chief information officers expect to replace their current systems with commercially available packages rather than use custom-developed systems.

A major problem with canned software is that it often does not meet all of a company's information or data processing needs. This disadvantage can often be overcome by modifying canned software. Generally, the best way to accomplish this is to have the software vendor, rather than the in-house programming staff, make the modifications. Modifications that are unauthorized by the vendor may not be supported and may make the program unreliable and unstable. Some companies have used this approach quite successfully. For example, about 90 percent of Dow Chemical's software consists of canned packages that have been modified to match its business processes, whereas the rest is custom software written in-house.

Purchasing Software and the SDLC

Companies that buy rather than develop AIS software still follow the SDLC process, as follows:

➤ *Systems analysis.* Companies must conduct an initial investigation, system survey, and feasibility survey. They must also determine AIS requirements.

➤ *Conceptual systems design.* An important part of conceptual design is determining if software that meets AIS requirements is already available. If so, a make-or-buy decision must be made.

➤ *Physical design.* If software is purchased, some of the physical design phase, such as designing and coding the program, can be omitted. However, it may be necessary to modify the purchased software to better meet company needs. Even when software is purchased, companies often design output, input, files, and control procedures.

➤ *Implementation and conversion.* Companies must plan implementation and conversion activities, select and train personnel, install and test the hardware and software, document procedures, and convert from the old to the new AIS. They do not, however, develop and test software modules or document the computer program itself.

➤ *Operation and maintenance.* The AIS is operated like any other software, and the vendor usually maintains the software.

Selecting a Vendor

Deciding to make or purchase software can be made independently of the decision to acquire hardware, service, maintenance, and other AIS resources. Likewise, these resources can be purchased independently of the software, although the hardware and vendor decisions may depend on the software decision.

Vendors can be found by looking in the phone book, obtaining referrals, scanning computer or trade magazines, attending conferences, or using search organizations. Some vendors flourish for a while and then go out of business. Additionally, many companies offer computer services but have little experience or capital. When vendors go out of business, they often leave the companies that use their products high and dry. As a result, it is important to be selective when choosing a vendor.

Acquiring Hardware and Software

Once AIS requirements have been defined, an organization is ready to purchase software and hardware. Companies requiring only a PC, a word processor, and a spreadsheet can usually complete their own research and make a selection. Companies that are buying large or complex systems, however, send vendors a **request for proposal (RFP),** which is an invitation to propose a system by a specified date. Each proposal is evaluated, with the best systems investigated in depth to verify that company requirements can be met. A formal approach to acquiring system resources, such as an RFP, is important for the following reasons:

1. *Saves time.* The same information is provided to all vendors, eliminating repetitive interviews and questions.
2. *Simplifies the decision-making process.* All responses are in the same format and based on the same information.
3. *Reduces errors.* The chances of overlooking important factors are reduced.
4. *Avoids potential for disagreement.* Both parties possess the same expectations and pertinent information is captured in writing.

When an RFP is solicited based on exact hardware and software specifications, the total costs are usually lower and less time is required for vendor preparation and company evaluation. However, this does not permit the vendor to recommend alternative technology. In contrast, a generalized RFP contains a problem definition and requests a system that meets specific performance objectives and requirements. This allows the requesting company to leave the technical issues to the vendor. Disadvantages of this approach include a greater difficulty in evaluating proposals and the potential for more costly bids.

Generally speaking, the more information a company provides to a vendor, the better the company's chances of receiving a system that meets its requirements. Vendors need detailed specifications for the new AIS, including the required applications, inputs and outputs, files and databases, frequency and methods of file updating and inquiry, and unique characteristics or requirements. It is also essential to distinguish between mandatory and desirable requirements.

Evaluating Proposals and Selecting a System

Proposals that are missing important information, fail to meet minimum requirements, or are ambiguous should be eliminated. Proposals that pass this preliminary screening should be carefully compared with the proposed AIS requirements to determine (1) if they meet all mandatory requirements and (2) how many of the desirable requirements they meet. The top vendors can be invited to demonstrate their system using company-supplied data. This measures the system's performance and validates the vendor's claims. Table 17-1 presents criteria that can be used to evaluate hardware, software, and vendors.

One way to compare system performance is to use a **benchmark problem**—a data processing task with input, processing, and output jobs typical of those the new AIS will be required to perform. Processing times are calculated and compared, and the AIS with the lowest time is judged the most efficient.

Another approach is **point scoring,** which is illustrated in Table 17-2. For each system evaluation criterion, a weight is assigned based on its relative importance. Vendors are assigned a score for each criterion based on how well its proposal measures up to the standard. The total of the weighted scores provides a basis for comparing and contrasting the various systems. Based on the point-scoring approach in this example, vendor 3 offers the best system. Its system scored 190 points more than vendor 2, the second-place candidate.

Requirements costing estimates the cost of purchasing or developing features that are not present in a particular AIS. The total cost for each AIS is computed by adding the acquisition cost and the purchasing or developing costs. The resulting totals represent the costs of systems with all required features and provide an equitable basis for comparison.

Neither point scoring nor requirements costing is totally objective. In points scoring, the weights and the points used are assigned subjectively and dollar estimates of costs and benefits are not included. Requirements costing overlooks intangible factors such as reliability and vendor support. In any event, the final choice among vendor proposals is not likely to be clear-cut, because it must rely to some extent on subjective factors and cost considerations.

Once the best AIS has been identified, the software should be thoroughly test-driven, other users contacted to see how satisfied they are, vendor personnel evaluated, and proposal details confirmed. The company wants to verify that the AIS that appears to be the best on paper actually is the best in practice. The lessons that

Table 17-1   Hardware, Software, and Vendor Evaluation Criteria

Hardware evaluation	Is the cost of the hardware reasonable, based on its capabilities and features?
	Can the hardware run the desired software?
	Are the CPU's processing speed and capabilities adequate for the intended use?
	Are the secondary storage capabilities adequate?
	Are the input and output speeds and capabilities adequate?
	Does the system have adequate communication capabilities?
	Is the system expandable?
	Is the hardware based on the most recent technology, or on technology that is old or soon to be out of date?
	Is the hardware available now? If not, when?
	Is the system under consideration compatible with existing hardware, software, and peripherals?
	How do evaluations of the system's performance compare with those of its competitors?
	What is the availability and cost of support and maintenance?
	What guarantees and warranties come with the system?
	Are financing arrangements available (if applicable)?
Software evaluation	Does the package meet all mandatory specifications?
	How well does the package meet desirable specifications?
	Will program modifications be required to meet company needs?
	Does the software contain adequate controls?
	Is the performance (speed, accuracy, reliability) adequate?
	How many other companies use the software?
	Are other users satisfied with the package?
	Is the package well documented?
	Is the software compatible with existing corporate software?
	Is the software user-friendly?
	Can the software be demonstrated and test driven?
	Does the software have an adequate warranty?
	Is the software flexible and easily maintained?
	Is on-line inquiry of files and records possible?
	Will the vendor keep the package up-to-date?
Vendor evaluation	How long has the vendor been in business?
	How large is the vendor?
	Is the vendor financially stable and secure?
	How much experience does the vendor have with the hardware and software?
	How well does the vendor stand behind its products? How good is its guarantee?
	Does the vendor regularly update its products?
	Does the vendor provide financing?
	Will the vendor put promises in a contract?
	Will the vendor supply a list of customers as references?
	Does the vendor have a reputation for reliability and dependability?
	Does the vendor provide hardware and software support and maintenance?
	Does the vendor provide implementation and installation support?
	Does the vendor have high-quality, responsive, and experienced personnel?
	Does the vendor provide training?
	How responsive and timely is vendor support?

Table 17-2   Point Scoring Evaluation of Vendor Proposals

Criterion	Weight	Vendor 1		Vendor 2		Vendor 3	
		Score	Weighted Score	Score	Weighted Score	Score	Weighted Score
Hardware compatibility	60	6	360	7	420	8	480
Hardware speed	30	6	180	10	300	5	150
Memory expansion	60	5	300	7	420	8	480
Hardware current	30	9	270	9	270	6	180
Software compatibility	90	7	630	7	630	9	810
On-line inquiry capabilities	40	9	360	10	400	8	320
Controls	50	7	350	6	300	9	450
Positive references	40	10	400	8	320	6	240
Documentation	30	9	270	8	240	7	210
Easily maintained; updated regularly	50	7	350	8	400	9	450
LAN and WAN capabilities	50	8	400	7	350	8	400
Vendor support	70	6	420	9	630	10	700
Totals			4,290		4,680		4,870

Geophysical Systems Corporation learned from its vendor selection process highlight the importance of a thorough vendor evaluation (see Focus 17-1).

Despite the availability of good software packages, many organizations meet their information needs by writing their own software. The next section discusses in-house software development. The subsequent section then discusses software that users develop themselves.

DEVELOPMENT BY AN IN-HOUSE INFORMATION SYSTEMS DEPARTMENT

Despite the availability of good canned software packages, many organizations develop their own software because their requirements are unique or their size and complexity necessitate a custom package.

Developing **custom software** is difficult and error prone, and it consumes a great deal of time and resources. After end-users define their requirements, analysts work with them to determine the format of paper and screen outputs. The analysts then identify the data required for each input and the data to be retained in the files. Analysts also develop detailed program specifications to be interpreted and coded by a programmer. Because of the many and varied development tasks, the process requires a significant amount of discipline and management supervision. Accountants often

Focus 17-1

A Software Purchase that Went Awry

GEOPHYSICAL SYSTEMS Corporation (GSC), which specializes in developing drilling equipment, developed a device that uses sonar to analyze the production potential of oil and gas discoveries. GSC needed a software program to analyze the data generated by the company's sonar device. GSC hired Seismograph Service Corporation and paid it $20 million to write the computer system. To its dismay, GSC found that the Seismograph system could not accurately process the massive volume of data and perform the complex computations needed. When this failing became apparent, GSC's clients canceled their contracts. As a result, the company went from yearly sales of $40 million and profits of $6 million to filing for bankruptcy two years later.

GSC sued Seismograph, claiming that the supplier's system failed to perform as promised. In addition, it claimed that Seismograph knew the system would not be able to perform as desired before it began the development project. The jury agreed, awarding GSC over $48 million as compensation for lost profits and the cost of the computer system. Seismograph appealed on the basis that its system did work and that GSC's sales decline resulted from a slump in oil prices.

GSC's experience is not uncommon; many systems development projects do not produce the intended results.

help develop custom software, either as project supervisors, users, or development team members.

Custom software is usually developed and written in-house. Chapter 18 discusses in more depth the process used to develop software. Alternatively, organizations may engage an outside company, such as Accenture or EDS, to develop a package or assemble one from their inventory of program modules. These modules are adapted, combined, and organized to form a customized product that meets a company's specific requirements. When contracting with an outside organization, a company should maintain control over the development process. The following guidelines are recommended:

➤ *Carefully select a developer.* The outside developer should have experience in the company's industry, a good understanding of business in general, and an in-depth understanding of how the company conducts its business.

➤ *Sign a contract.* The contract should place responsibility for meeting the company's requirements on the developer and allow the company to discontinue the project if certain key conditions are not met.

➤ *Plan and monitor each step.* All aspects of the project should be designed in detail, and there should be frequent checkpoints for monitoring the project.

➤ *Maintain effective communication.* The relationship between the company and the developer should be rigorously defined: Frequent communication is necessary.

➤ *Control all costs.* Costs should be tightly controlled and cash outflows minimized until the project has been completed and accepted.

Arthur D. Little and other information systems consultants tell clients to develop custom software only if it provides a significant competitive advantage. For example, there is usually no measurable benefit to having a custom-written payroll or accounts receivable system. On the other hand, there may be significant benefits to sophisticated, just-in-time inventory management or product manufacturing software. If a software application will not provide a competitive advantage, Little advises its clients to buy software from an outside supplier.

There is no single right answer to the build-or-buy decision. Different companies come to different conclusions. For example, Gillette once developed its own software, but recently decided to move from proprietary systems to off-the-shelf software when possible. Its rationale is that it gains a greater competitive advantage from deciding *how* software should be used than from determining *what* software should be used and then creating it. If canned software does not meet all of Gillette's needs, it is modified using high-level development tools. Pepsi, on the other hand, has moved in the opposite direction. It once bought most of its mainframe software but, after moving to a client/server architecture, it could not find software sophisticated enough to meet its needs. Although Pepsi still buys software when it can find it, it has had to create most of its newly installed software.

This section has discussed why many organizations have information systems staff develop their software. Organizations also are finding it productive to allow users to develop systems to meet their own information needs. The next section discusses this approach.

End-User–Developed Software

End-user computing (EUC) is the hands-on development, use, and control of computer-based information systems by users. In other words, EUC is people using IT to meet their information needs rather than relying on systems professionals. For example, a savings and loan in California wanted a system to track loan reserve requirements. Its information systems department said the system would take 18 months to develop. Rather than wait, the loan department used a PC and a database program to develop a functional program in a single day. Enhancing the program took several more days. Not only did the loan department cut the development time from 18 months to a few days, it ended up with the exact information it needed because users developed the system themselves.

After the automobile was introduced, a famous sociologist predicted that the automobile market would not exceed 2 million cars because only that many people would be willing to serve as chauffeurs. Instead, tens of millions of cars are sold annually to people who drive themselves. It was once predicted that the telephone system would collapse because the geometric growth in calls would require everyone to be telephone operators. Instead, equipment was developed that automated many of the functions previously performed by operators.

Since the introduction of the computer, the demand for information systems has grown astronomically. If a company wanted to eliminate its information backlogs, almost everyone would have to become a programmer. Does this sound similar to the automobile and the telephone examples? The solution involves end-users who meet their own information needs. As with telephones, technology is being developed to automate much of the process for us. Just as most people learn to drive automobiles, increased computer literacy and easier-to-use programming languages will allow almost everyone to operate powerful computers.

With the advent of inexpensive PCs and a wide variety of powerful and inexpensive software, users began developing their own systems to create and store data, access and download company data, and share data and computer resources in networks. As end-users began to meet their initial needs, two things happened. First, users realized computers could be used to meet more and more information needs. Second, increased access to data created many new uses and needs for information. The result has been a tremendous growth in end-user computing, a growth that is expected to continue accelerating through this century.

The growth in end-user computing has significantly altered the information system staff's role. They continue to develop and maintain the transaction processing systems and company-wide databases on which end-users draw to meet their information needs. In addition, staff provide users with technical advice and operational support and make as much information available to end-users as possible. Although this has resulted in more work for the systems staff, it has been counterbalanced by a decreased demand for their traditional services.

If the end-user computing trend continues, it will represent 75 to 95 percent of all information processing by the end of this decade. Because you will be an end-user or have a significant involvement with end-user computing no matter where you work, it is essential to have an understanding of end-user computing concepts.

Appropriate End-User Development and Use

End-user development (EUD) occurs when information users, such as managers, accountants, and internal auditors, develop their own applications using computer specialists as advisors. End-user development is inappropriate for complex systems, such as those that process a large number of transactions or update database records. Therefore, it is not used for processing payroll, accounts receivables and payables, general ledger, or inventory. Following are examples of appropriate end-user developments:

➤ Retrieving information from company databases to produce simple reports or to answer one-time queries

➤ Performing "what if," sensitivity, or statistical analyses

➤ Developing applications using prewritten software such as a spreadsheet or a database system

➤ Preparing schedules and lists, such as depreciation schedules, accounts receivable aging, and loan amortizations

Benefits of End-User Computing

One reason end-user computing has increased so significantly is that it offers the following advantages.

User creation, control, and implementation

Accountants and other end-users, rather than the information systems department, control the development process. They decide what information needs are important and if a system should be developed. The sense of ownership that comes with end-user development helps users develop better systems.

Systems that meet user needs

When end-users develop their own systems, the systems are more likely to meet the users' needs. Users also can discover flaws that the systems people would not catch. The user-analyst-programmer communication problems inherent in traditional program development are avoided.

Timeliness

Much of the lengthy delay inherent in the traditional systems development process is avoided, such as expensive and time-consuming cost-benefit analysis, detailed requirements definitions, and the inevitable delays and red tape inherent in the approval process.

Freeing up systems resources

The more information needs users can meet, the more time the information systems department must spend on other information and maintenance activities. This reduces both the visible and the invisible backlog of systems development projects.

Versatility and ease of use

Most end-user computing software is easy to understand and use. Users can change the information they produce or modify their application anytime their requirements change. With a laptop computer, work can be completed at home, on a plane, or almost anywhere.

As the foregoing paragraphs explain, end-user computing has significant advantages. Equally important are the disadvantages, which are discussed next. The benefits and risks associated with end-user computing are summarized in Table 17-3.

Table 17-3   Benefits and Risks of End-User Computing

Benefits	Risks
Users control development process and decide what systems are created and implemented.	End-user systems are more likely to contain errors or be flawed in some way.
The systems that are developed are more likely to meet user needs.	Systems are implemented that have not been adequately tested.
Systems are developed when needed.	Systems are more likely to be inefficient or use more resources than necessary.
Systems resources are freed up for other tasks.	Systems are often poorly controlled and documented.
Systems are usually easy to use and modify.	Systems are more likely to be incompatible with other systems in the organization.
	Greater likelihood of producing duplicate systems or wasting organization resources.
	Often results in greater overall system costs.

Risks of End-User Computing

There are some significant drawbacks to end-user computing and to eliminating analyst/ programmer involvement in the development process.

Logic and development errors

Because end-users have little experience in systems development, they are more likely to make errors and less likely to recognize when errors have occurred. The user-developer may solve the wrong problem, poorly define system requirements, apply an inappropriate analytical method, use the wrong software, or use incomplete or out-dated information. Often the error is caused by faulty logic or by incorrectly using formulas or software commands.

For example, employees at an oil and gas company developed a complex spread-sheet to analyze a proposed acquisition. Based on the results, company management scheduled a meeting to propose the acquisition to the board of directors. Before the company made the presentation, consultants from the company's CPA firm tested the model to see if they agreed with its results and gave their approval. Shortly before his speech, one of the presenters performed his own tests so he would understand how the model worked and could answer any tough questions the board threw at him. He discovered a few formulas he thought distorted the projections of what the company could attain by selling properties of the acquired company, the restatement of oil and gas reserves, and the consolidated balance sheet of the two combined entities. He called in the group that developed the spreadsheet and several partners of the CPA firm. When the formulas were corrected they showed that the acquisition would have led to significant losses. The presentation to the board was canceled, the person who developed the spreadsheet was fired, and the CPA firm no longer does any audit or consulting work for the company.

Inadequately tested applications

Users are not as likely to rigorously test their applications, either because they do not recognize the need to do so or because of the difficulty or time involved. One result is an application with the types of errors mentioned previously.

Inefficient systems

Most end-users are not programmers and have not been trained in systems develop-ment. Although the systems they develop may get the job done, they are not always efficient. For example, a bank clerk spent three weeks developing a program that examined each cell in a spreadsheet and changed its value to zero if it was a negative amount. When the 60-page program began returning a "too many nested ifs" error message, the clerk called in a computer consultant. Within five minutes the consultant developed a finished application using a built-in spreadsheet function.

Poorly controlled and documented systems

Many end-users do not implement controls to protect their system. User-created sys-tems are often poorly documented because the user considers the task boring or unimportant. Users fail to realize that without documentation, others cannot under-stand how their system works.

System incompatibilities

Some companies add end-user equipment without considering the technological implications. As a result, they have a diversity of hardware and software that is difficult to support or to network. For example, Aetna Life & Casualty spent more than $1 billion a year on IT in an attempt to gain a competitive advantage. The result was 50,000 PCs from a few dozen manufacturers, 2,000 minicomputers and servers, 108 word processing systems, 19 incompatible e-mail systems, and 36 different communications networks. Aetna Life & Casualty finally realized it needed to shift its emphasis from trying to own the latest technology to the effective use of technology. Aetna standardized its systems and now uses only a few different types of PCs, Microsoft software products, two electronic mail systems, and one network. The result is compatibility across all systems and significantly less cost.

Duplication of systems and data and wasted resources

If end-users are unaware that other users have similar information needs, duplicate systems occur. Inexperienced users also may take on more than they are able to accomplish, which ends up wasting time and resources.

Increased costs

A single PC purchase is inexpensive, but buying PCs for hundreds or thousands of workers is costly. Updating the hardware and software every few years is also expensive. End-user computing also has a high opportunity cost if it diverts users' attention from their primary job. In addition, it increases time and data demands on the company mainframe and on information systems people use for support and assistance.

A proper balance between maximizing the benefits and minimizing the risks of end-user systems can be achieved by providing systems analysts as advisers and requiring user-created systems to be reviewed and documented prior to use. In addition, users can be trained in the systems analysis process so they can identify and adequately meet their needs and review the work of other users.

Managing and Controlling End-User Computing

Organizations use several different approaches to manage and control end-user computing. Giving the systems department control over end-user computing discourages end-user computing's growth, denies the organization of most of its benefits, and is not in the company's best long-term interests. However, if there are no controls over end-users, such as what end-user computing tools are purchased or how they are used, then chaos can easily result. It also can be difficult to support the system. It is best to provide enough guidance and standards to adequately control the system yet allow users the flexibility they need.

For instance, a **help desk** can encourage, support, coordinate, and control end-user activities. The 60 help desk analysts and technicians at Schering-Plough handle more than 9,000 calls a month. The front-line analysts use expert system software to quickly find the answers to their questions and then provide callers with scripted answers. The second-line technicians handle the more complicated queries. Other companies use multimedia software with animation or videos to help first-line staffers walk callers through a complicated process. Duties of the help desk include the following:

➤ Providing hot-line assistance to help resolve problems

➤ Serving as a clearinghouse for information, coordination, and assistance

➤ Training end-users how to use specific hardware and software, and providing corresponding technical maintenance and support

➤ Evaluating new end-user hardware and software products

➤ Assisting with application development

➤ Developing and implementing standards for (1) hardware and software purchase to ensure compatibility; (2) documentation and application testing; and (3) controlling security issues such as fraud, software piracy, and viruses

➤ Controlling corporate data so (1) authorized end-users can access and share it; (2) it is not duplicated; and (3) access to confidential data is restricted

OUTSOURCE THE SYSTEM

We have discussed two approaches to obtaining software: buying it and developing it in-house. A third way to acquire software is to outsource the information system.

Outsourcing is hiring an outside company to handle all or part of an organization's data processing activities. In a mainframe outsourcing agreement, the outsourcers buy their client's computers and hire all or most of the client's employees. They then operate and manage the entire system on the client's site, or they migrate the system to the outsourcer's computers. Many mainframe outsourcing contracts are in effect for 10 years or more and cost from hundreds of thousands to millions of dollars a year. For example, several years prior to its bankruptcy filing Enron signed a $750 million agreement with EDS to outsource its entire information system. EDS bought Enron's computers, software, and transmission network. It also hired all 550 of Enron's information systems staff at comparable wages and benefits. Enron paid EDS a fixed annual fee, plus additional fees based on processing volume. During the 10-year life of the contract, Enron expected to save $200 million, which was almost 25 percent of its computing costs.

In a client/server or a PC outsourcing agreement, an organization outsources a particular service, a segment of its business, a particular function, or PC support. Most Fortune 2000 companies outsource anywhere from 10 percent to 80 percent of their PC support functions. For example, Taco Bell outsourced its PC help desk services. Royal Dutch Shell, the international oil company, has 80,000 PCs worldwide and has outsourced most of its installation, maintenance, training, help desk, and technical support.

The Growth in Outsourcing Applications

Outsourcing was initially used for standardized applications such as payroll, accounting, and purchasing or by companies that were struggling to survive and wanted a quick infusion of cash from selling their hardware. However, in 1989, Eastman Kodak surprised the business world by hiring three different companies to operate its computer systems. Kodak outsourced its data processing operations and sold its mainframes to IBM. It outsourced its telecommunications functions to DEC and its PC operations to Businessland (and later Entek Information Services). When the performance of DEC and Entek began to slip, Kodak opened those services to new bids. Kodak continues to perform its own information systems strategic planning and development, but the responsibility of system implementation and operation belongs to the outsourcers. The results have been dramatic. Capital expenditures for computers fell 90 percent while operating expenses decreased between 10 and 20 percent. Kodak expects the annual information systems savings to reach approximately $130 million over the 10-year period of the agreement.

Several years ago Xerox signed what was then the largest outsourcing deal in history: a $3.2 billion, 10-year contract with EDS to outsource its computing, telecommunications, and software management in 19 countries. The company moved to outsourcing to cut costs, to speed up the move from a mainframe architecture to client/server computing, and to free management to focus on strategic management issues rather than on day-to-day concerns. However, Xerox retained control over its systems functions, such as strategic planning and new application development, to support its reengineering efforts.

The success of Kodak and Xerox motivated other organizations to outsource their information systems. For example, 15 of the top 25 Fortune 500 companies outsource some or all of their information systems. Companies now spend over $100 billion a year to outsource their IT functions.

The Benefits of Outsourcing

This section discusses the benefits of outsourcing; the disadvantages are discussed in the next section. The advantages and disadvantages of outsourcing are summarized in Table 17-4.

A business solution

Outsourcing is a plausible business solution, rather than just an information systems solution. Outsourcing is a viable strategic and economic approach because it allows companies to concentrate on their core competencies. Kodak believes in focusing its

Table 17-4   Advantages and Disadvantages of Outsourcing

Advantages	Disadvantages
It is a business as well as an information system solution.	Outsourcing contracts are not very flexible due to their length.
It allows a company to better use its assets and scarce resources.	Companies may lose control of their system and data. This may result in abuse, such as confidential data shared with competitors.
It provides access to greater expertise and more advanced technology.	Over time, a company may lose sight of its information needs and how the system can provide it with competitive advantages.
It can lower a company's overall information systems costs.	It is expensive and difficult to reverse the outsourcing decision and replace the hardware, software, and people.
It can result in faster and more efficient systems development.	Many outsourcing goals and benefits are never realized.
It helps eliminate the peaks and valleys of system usage.	The service some outsourcers provide is poor.
It facilitates downsizing.	

efforts on what it does best—selling film and cameras—and leaving data processing to more qualified computer companies. Kodak treats outsourcers as partners and works closely with them to meet its strategic and operational data processing objectives.

Asset utilization

Organizations with millions of dollars tied up in IT can improve their cash position and reduce annual expenses by selling those assets to an outsourcer. With technology changing so rapidly, the AIS function can drain a company's cash reserves as it tries to keep up with the latest advancements. For example, Health Dimensions, a hospital management company, outsourced the data processing functions of its four hospitals so it could use its limited monetary resources for revenue-generating purchases.

Access to greater expertise and more advanced technology

Many companies cannot afford to retain a staff to manage and develop the increasingly complex networks required in today's businesses. Continental Bank and Del Monte Foods turned to outsourcing because the cost and time involved in staying at the cutting edge of technology were rising significantly. Washington Water Power Company began outsourcing when the prospect of upgrading and replacing its obsolete computer system seemed too daunting a task.

Lower costs

Outsourcing can decrease information systems costs by 15 to 30 percent. Outsourcers can pass along some of the savings achieved from standardizing users' applications, buying hardware at bulk prices, splitting development and maintenance costs between projects, and operating at higher volumes. Continental Bank will save $100 million (20 percent of IT costs) during the life of its 10-year contract. However, companies such as Occidental Petroleum and USX have rejected outsourcing as costing more than internal AIS development and operation.

Improved development time

Experienced industry specialists often can develop and implement a system faster and more efficiently than in-house staff. Outsourcers also can help a company cut through much of the internal politics surrounding systems development.

Elimination of peaks and valleys usage

Many companies have seasonal businesses that require heavy computer power during part of the year but very little the remainder of the year. For example, from January to March, W. Atlee Burpee & Company processes mail order and wholesale requests for its seeds and gardening products. During this period its IBM mainframe operated at 80 percent capacity, functioning at 20 percent the rest of the time. Systems personnel were underused most of the time. Burpee turned to outsourcing and now pays Computer Science Corporation according to how much the system is used. In doing so, Burpee cut its processing costs in half.

Facilitation of downsizing

Companies that downsize are often left with an unnecessarily large AIS function. General Dynamics downsized dramatically in the early 1990s due to reduced spending in the defense industry. It sold its data centers to Computer Sciences Corporation (CSC) for $200 million and transferred 2,600 employees to CSC. It signed a $3 billion,

10-year outsourcing contract even though its information systems function was rated number one in the aerospace industry.

Risks of Outsourcing

Companies that outsource often experience one or more of the following drawbacks.

Inflexibility

Many outsourcing contracts are signed for 10 years. If during this time problems arise, if the company is dissatisfied, or if the company goes through extensive structural changes, the contract is difficult or costly to break. In such cases companies may find themselves in a technological straitjacket. Before they merged, Integra Financial Corp. and Equimark Corp. held contracts with different outsourcers. After the merger, one of the contracts had to be eliminated, at a cost of $4.5 million.

Loss of control

A company that outsources a significant portion of its AIS runs the risk of losing control of its system and data. In addition, when an external party processes its business data, the company is exposed to possible abuse such as sharing confidential data. For that reason, Ford's outsourcing agreement with Computer Sciences Corporation excludes CSC from taking on other automobile manufacturers as clients.

Reduced competitive advantage

Over the long run, a company can lose a fundamental understanding of its own information systems needs and how the system can provide it with competitive advantages. A system that does not evolve and improve cannot add value and help achieve corporate objectives. In addition, outsourcers cannot be expected to be as motivated as their clients in trying to meet a particular industry's competitive challenges. However, up to 80 percent of a company's business processes can be considered standard (payroll cash disbursements, accounts receivable). This disadvantage can be mitigated significantly by outsourcing these standard functions and customizing the 20 percent of business processes that provide competitive advantage.

Locked-in system

Once a company outsources its system and sells its data processing centers, it is expensive and difficult to reverse the process. If the company is unable to buy back the data processing facilities, it will have to buy new equipment and hire a new data processing staff, often at prohibitive costs. Blue Cross of California decided that the performance of its outsourcer, EDS, was so poor that it would end the agreement; however, when Blue Cross started to initiate the change it realized that it knew virtually nothing about its system and could not afford to discharge EDS. In contrast, LSI Logic, a chip manufacturer, terminated its agreement with IBM and brought its system back in-house at significant dollar and personnel costs when it installed an ERP system.

Unfulfilled goals

Critics point out that many outsourcing goals and benefits are never realized. At least one study has shown that some alleged benefits, such as increased efficiency, are a myth. USF&G Corporation canceled its $100 million contract with Cigna Information Services after 18 months, because Cigna could not implement the changes needed to make the system work properly.

Poor service

Some companies complain of receiving poor service from their outsourcing company. Common complaints are that responsiveness to changing business conditions is slow or nonexistent and migration to new technologies is poorly planned.

A problem with some systems is that they are simply automated ways of doing business the same way it was done before computers. Business process reengineering, a radical approach to introducing massive changes into information systems and improving the development process, is discussed in the next section.

BUSINESS PROCESS REENGINEERING

Despite the trillion-plus dollars spent on IT in the past decade, productivity has not increased significantly. One reason is that many business processes are relics from pre-computer days when work was based on economies of scale and specialization of labor. Work was organized as a sequence of narrowly defined tasks, flowing between specialists who did little thinking or reasoning. Workers simply had to carry out their assigned tasks as efficiently as possible. When computers came along, businesses used them to speed up their manual and paper flow processes and procedures.

In recent years the work environment has changed drastically. Many current systems are not designed to handle the flood of new information available today. Nor can they take advantage of the steady stream of new technology that makes it possible to do things differently. With powerful databases and almost unlimited storage, we have access to more and better information than ever before. An approach is needed that, instead of paving cow-paths, blazes new trails.

Many management gurus now advocate radical change, or what they refer to as **business process reengineering (BPR).** BPR is the thorough analysis and complete redesign of business processes and information systems to achieve dramatic performance improvements. It is a revolutionary process that challenges traditional organization structures, rules, assumptions, work flows, job descriptions, management procedures, controls, and organizational values and cultures.

BPR reduces a company to its essential business processes and focuses on *why* they are done rather than on the details of *how* they are done. It then completely reshapes organizational work practices and information flows to take advantage of technological advancements. This is done to simplify the system, to make it more effective, and to improve a company's quality and service.

CSC Index, a consulting firm, measured the cost and time savings and the reduction in defects before and after helping 15 clients complete reengineering efforts. CSC found that fundamentally changing business processes produced an average improvement of 48 percent in cost, 80 percent in time, and 60 percent in defects. After Citibank reengineered a credit analysis system, employees spent 43 percent of their time (instead of 9 percent) recruiting new business instead of completing paperwork on closed deals. Within two years, profits increased by over 750 percent. By reengineering its customer

Table 17-5   Seven Principles of Business Processing Reengineering

1. Organize around outcomes, not tasks.
2. Have output users perform the process.
3. Have those who produce information process it.
4. Centralize and disperse data.
5. Integrate parallel activities.
6. Empower workers, use built-in controls, and flatten the organizational chart.
7. Capture data once, at its source.

service operations, Datacard Corporation increased its sales sevenfold. A process that took a full day and five phone calls was replaced with one that took an hour.

The Principles of Reengineering

What are the secrets to reengineering? How can a company minimize the costs and maximize the benefits? Michael Hammer, a leading proponent of reengineering, set forth seven principles that help organizations successfully reengineer business processes.[1] These principles are summarized in Table 17-5.

Organize around outcomes, not tasks

In a reengineered system, the traditional approach of assigning different parts of a business process to many people is not appropriate. This approach, with its numerous handoffs, results in delays and errors. Instead, when possible, one person is given responsibility for the entire process. Each person's job is designed around an objective or an outcome, such as a finished component or a completed process, rather than one of many tasks necessary to produce the finished component or complete the process.

At Mutual Benefit Life (MBL), an insurance company, approving an insurance application previously included 30 steps performed by 19 people in five departments. Because paperwork had to be transferred among so many people, an approval took anywhere from 5 to 25 days. When MBL reengineered its business processes, it eliminated existing job descriptions and departmental boundaries. It created the position of case manager and gave each manager the authority to perform all application approval tasks. A number of information systems, including an expert system, support case managers who can call on specialists for help with any particularly difficult application. Because one person is in charge of the entire process, there is no handing off of files. This has resulted in fewer errors, decreased costs, and a dramatically improved turnaround time. Case managers now handle more than twice the volume of new applications, allowing the company to eliminate 100 field positions. A new application can now be processed in as little as four hours, with an average turnaround of only two to five days.

---

[1] Much of this section is adapted from Michael Hammer, "Reengineering Work: Don't Automate, Obliterate," *Harvard Business Review* (July–August 1990): 104–112.

Require those who use the output to perform the process

Owners and managers often organize their companies into separate departments, each specializing in a separate task. Because each department passes its completed product off to someone else, departments are customers of one another. This strategy may work well for specialized projects, but it can hurt a company's performance when it comes to less significant tasks. For example, consider the problem when accounting wants to order nonstrategic or inexpensive goods such as office supplies. It must requisition the supplies from purchasing, which is responsible for selecting suppliers and ordering goods. This system is slow, cumbersome, and can actually cost the company more, in time and money, than the supplies are worth.

One large manufacturer had this exact problem before reengineering its business processes. The manufacturer took advantage of IT and set up a computerized database of approved vendors (maintained by purchasing), developed an expert system for purchasing nonstrategic items, and linked all departments in a network. The new process enables users, with the help of the expert system and the database, to order their own supplies. The purchasing process is now much faster, simpler, and less costly because the department that orders the supplies is the one that actually uses them.

Require those who produce information to process it

Most organizations process their acquisition/payment information the way Ford Motors once did. Previously, Ford's purchasing department prepared a multicopy purchase order, sending one copy to the vendor, another to accounts payable, and keeping one for itself. When goods were received, the receiving department prepared a multicopy receiving report and sent one copy to accounts payable and kept the other. The vendor prepared a multicopy invoice and sent one copy to accounts payable. Accounts payable processed all three documents and matched 14 different data items on the three documents before a payment could be processed. Accounts payable spent most of its time trying to reconcile all of the mismatches. Payments were delayed, vendors were unhappy, and the process was time-consuming and frustrating. It took more than 500 employees to process Ford's accounts payable.

In Ford's reengineered system, the people who produce the information also process it. Purchasing agents create and process their purchase orders by entering them into an on-line database. Vendors ship goods but do not send an invoice. When the goods arrive, the receiving clerk enters three items of data into the system: part number, unit of measure, and supplier code. The computer compares the receiving information with the outstanding purchase order data. If they do not match, the goods are returned. If they do match, the goods are accepted and the computer prepares the vendor's check, which is sent by accounts payable. The reengineered system saves a significant amount of money, much of it achieved through a 75 percent reduction of accounts payable staff.

Centralize and disperse data

To achieve economies of scale and to eliminate bureaucracy and redundant resources, companies centralize operations. To be more responsive to their customers and to provide better service, they decentralize operations. With current technology, companies no longer have to choose between these two approaches. Corporate-wide databases can centralize data, and telecommunications technology can then disburse it to the necessary locations. In effect, companies can have the advantages of both approaches.

Hewlett-Packard (HP) had a decentralized purchasing system that successfully served the needs of its 50 manufacturing units. However, HP could not take advantage of its extensive buying power to negotiate quantity discounts. HP reengineered its system and introduced a corporate-wide purchasing department that developed and maintained a shared database of approved vendors. Each plant continued to meet its unique needs by making its own purchases from the approved vendors. The corporate office tracked the purchases of all 50 plants, negotiated quantity discounts and other vendor concessions, and resolved disputes with vendors. The result was a significantly lower cost of goods purchased, a 50 percent reduction in lead times, a 75 percent reduction in failure rates, and a 150 percent improvement in on-time deliveries.

Integrate parallel activities

Certain processes, such as product development, are performed in parallel and then integrated at the end. For example, Chrysler had one department that worked exclusively on designing engines, another on transmissions, another on frames, and so on. Unfortunately, the departments often did not communicate as well as they should have. At the integration and testing phase they often found that the components did not fit together properly. As a result, they had to be redesigned at considerable expense.

Chrysler reengineered its product development process to place at least one person from each department area on a team. Each team was put in charge of a particular automobile. As a result, Chrysler was able to decrease its product development time significantly and reduce costly redesigns.

Empower workers, use built-in controls, and flatten the organizational chart

Most organizations have a layer of employees who do the work and several layers who record, manage, audit, or control the efforts of the former group. The logic behind this organization is that the workers are not able either to make correct decisions, to monitor and control the process themselves, or both. In a reengineered system, the people who do the work are empowered with this type of decision-making responsibility. This results in a faster response time to problems and increases the quality of the task performed. Information technology, such as expert systems, can help workers make correct decisions and avoid mistakes. This same principle also states that controls should be built into the process itself. For example, the system could be programmed with preventive controls so that it would proceed only when all relevant data have been entered and edited by the system for validity, correctness, and reasonableness. Controls could also be placed in the system to detect and correct any errors that might make their way into the system.

When Mutual Benefit Life empowered its case managers with decision-making ability, it was able to eliminate several layers of managers. Those who were retained changed their focus from supervision and control to support and facilitation.

Capture data once, at its source

Historically, each functional area has designed and built its own AIS. As a result, information was entered into several different applications. For example, a vendor number was entered in the accounts payable system as well as the purchasing system. Each functional area had to collect the same piece of information (usually on different forms), enter it into its system, and store it. This is both inefficient and expensive. In addition, there were discrepancies between the individual systems as a result of data capture and data entry errors. EDI and source data automation devices such as bar coding now allow data in a reengineered system to be captured electronically at the source. The data can be entered once in an on-line database and made available to all who need them. This approach reduces errors, eliminates data processing delays, and reduces clerical and other costs.

A few years ago management at Sun Microsystems decided to solve the problem of its information systems not being able to easily communicate with each other. In addition, certain data needed to be entered as many as 10 times into incompatible systems. The system was reengineered and now data entered into any system worldwide are entered only once and made available to all who need them.

Underlying each of these seven principles is the efficient and effective use of the latest information systems technology. Future advances will allow even more powerful reengineering efforts. Radio- and satellite-based communications technology, coupled with powerful handheld computers, will have a significant impact on the way companies do business. With image processing, multiple users can use a document simultaneously. *Active documents* that automatically know where to go will also have an impact. For example, suppose you are buying a mail order computer. After the sales clerk creates the *active order*, it will automatically be sent to shipping, inventory control, sales and marketing, the credit card company, and your customer record. With an active document, the decision about where the information on the document is to go need only be made once. From then on, all orders will automatically be sent to the appropriate location.

Challenges Faced by Reengineering Efforts

Business process reengineering can be a challenging venture. Not only must a company be rethought and completely reorganized, but people must abandon the old ways of doing things and learn new jobs and new ways of operating. As a result, many reengineering efforts fail or do not accomplish all they set out to do. To successfully complete the reengineering process, a company must face and overcome the following obstacles:

➤ *Tradition.* The inefficient business processes that are being reengineered oftentimes are decades old. Traditional ways of doing things do not often die easily, especially practices associated with the organization's culture. Successful reengineering requires changes in employee culture and beliefs.

➤ *Resistance.* Change, especially radical change, is always met with a great deal of resistance. Throughout the process, managers must continually reassure, persuade, and provide support to those affected so that the necessary changes will work.

➤ *Time requirements.* Reengineering is a lengthy process, almost always taking 2+ years to complete.

➤ *Cost.* It is costly to thoroughly examine and question a company's business processes to find a faster and more efficient way of operating.

➤ *Lack of management support.* Reengineering is still in its infancy and, since few companies have completed full-blown reengineering projects, many top managers have not yet been converted to its benefits. Many are afraid of the "big hype, few results" syndrome. Without top management support, reengineering has little chance of succeeding. Information systems management lacks the power and influence to push a reengineering project successfully.

➤ *Risk.* Information systems management is aware that pushing a reengineering project can be a risky career move. If it is a success, they will be looked on with great favor in the organization. If not, they may very well be looking for new jobs.

➤ *Skepticism.* Some members of the information systems community are skeptical about reengineering. They view it as traditional systems development, but in a new wrapper with a fancy name. One big obstacle to reengineering is outlasting the non-believers and the cynics who say it cannot be done.

➤ *Retraining.* Many reengineering efforts dramatically change the way work is done; thus, employees have to be retrained, which is time-consuming and expensive.

➤ *Controls.* An important element of an information system is the controls that ensure system reliability and integrity. People involved in reengineering efforts must be careful not to reengineer important controls out of the system. For example, a key element of internal control is a separation of duties and, if that control is reengineered out of the new system, compensating controls have to be built into the system to take its place.

Sometimes systems under development do not need to be reengineered, but the development team would like to hasten the development process significantly. Prototyping, as discussed next, is a good way to do just that.

PROTOTYPING

Prototyping is an approach to systems design in which a simplified working model of a system is developed. This **prototype,** or first draft, is quickly and inexpensively built and provided to users for testing. Experimenting with the prototype allows users to determine what they do and do not like about the system. Based on their reactions and feedback, the developers modify the system and again present it to the users. This iterative process of trial usage and modification continues until the users are satisfied that the system adequately meets their needs.

The basic premise of prototyping is that it is easier for people to express what they like or dislike about a prototype than to imagine what they want in a system. In other words, if users can try out an actual application, they can provide feedback as to what they do and do not like about it. Even a simple system that is not fully functional demonstrates features far better than diagrams, drawings, verbal explanations, or volumes of documentation.

UNUM Life Insurance used prototyping to show how a new system using image processing would work. UNUM wanted to use new technologies to link its system with all external and internal systems and their users. However, top management had a hard time getting middle managers to envision how they wanted to use image processing and to understand the issues involved in the change. After viewing a prototype, the managers caught on to the possibilities and issues associated with image processing. Up to that point, these managers thought image processing only meant replacing file cabinets. Only after viewing the prototype did they realize its business potential.

Developers who use prototyping still go through the systems development life cycle discussed in Chapter 16, but prototyping allows them to condense and speed up

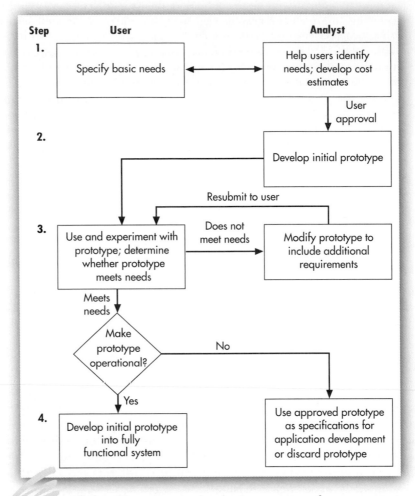

Figure 17-1 The steps to developing a system from a prototype

parts of the analysis and the design phases. For example, prototyping does a good job of capturing user needs and helps developers and users make many of the conceptual and physical design decisions. As a result, current practice leans heavily toward prototyping, so that projects can be completed as quickly as possible before planned systems become obsolete.

Steps in Developing a Prototype

As shown in Figure 17-1, four steps are involved in developing a prototype. The first step is to identify basic system requirements by meeting with users to agree on the size and scope of the system and to decide what the system should include and exclude. The developer and users also determine decision-making and transaction processing outputs, as well as the inputs and data needed to produce these outputs. The emphasis is on *what* output should be produced rather than *how* it should be produced. The developer must ensure that users' expectations are realistic and that their basic information requirements can be met. The designer uses the information requirements to develop cost, time, and feasibility estimates for alternative AIS solutions. Because only general requirements are identified, determining requirements for the prototype is less formal and time consuming than in the traditional SDLC approach. Users develop detailed system requirements as they interact with the prototype.

The second step is to develop an initial prototype that meets the agreed-on requirements. The emphasis is on speed and low cost rather than efficiency of operation. The goal is to implement the prototype within a short time period, perhaps days or weeks. Because of these time limitations, some aspects of the system are sacrificed in the interests of simplicity, flexibility, and ease of use. Therefore, nonessential functions, system controls, exception handling, validation of input data, processing speed, and efficiency considerations are ignored at this point. It is critical, however, that users see and use tentative versions of data entry display screens, menus, input prompts, and source documents. They must also respond to prompts, query the system, judge response times, and issue commands.

Certain tools help designers develop prototypes. These tools can help designers create files, screens, reports, and program code much faster and with much less effort than conventional programming languages. The tools include fourth-generation languages (4GLs), CASE tools, databases, high-level query languages, generalized report writers, and various application software packages.

When the prototype is finished, the developer returns to the users and demonstrates the system. The users are instructed to experiment with the system and comment on what they do and do not like about its content and performance.

The third step is an iterative process in which users identify changes, developers make changes, and the system is again turned over to the users for evaluation and experimental use. This iterative process continues until the users are satisfied with the system. A typical prototype will go through four to six iterations.

The fourth step is to use the system approved by the users. As shown in Figure 17-1, an approved prototype is typically used in one of two ways. Half of all prototypes are turned into fully functional systems referred to as **operational prototypes.** To make the prototype operational, the developer must incorporate needed controls, improve operational efficiency, provide backup and recovery, and integrate the prototype with the systems with which it interfaces. Changes may be necessary to allow the program to accept real input, access real data files, process data, make the necessary computations and calculations, and produce real output.

In many instances it is not practical to modify the prototype to make it a fully functional system. These **nonoperational,** or **throwaway, prototypes** can be used in several ways. The prototype may be discarded; and the system requirements identified during the prototyping process can be used to develop a new system. The system development life cycle is followed to develop the system, with the prototype as the model for development. The prototype also can be used as the initial prototype for an expanded system designed to meet the needs of many different users. Finally, if the users and the developer decide that the system under consideration is unsalvageable, the prototype can be discarded completely. In this instance, the company has saved itself years of development work and a lot of money by avoiding the much more costly traditional SDLC process.

When to Use Prototyping

In most cases prototyping supports rather than replaces the SDLC. Prototyping is appropriate when there is a high level of uncertainty about the AIS, it is unclear what questions to ask, the final AIS cannot be clearly visualized because the decision process is still unclear, speed is an issue, or there is a high likelihood of failure. Systems that are especially good candidates for prototyping are decision support systems, executive information systems, expert systems, and information retrieval systems. Prototyping is also appropriate for systems that involve experimentation and trial-and-error development or when the requirements evolve as the system is used. Prototyping is not usually appropriate for large or complex systems that serve major organizational components or cross a number of organizational boundaries. Nor are they commonly used for developing standard AIS components such as accounts receivable and payable or inventory management. A summary of the conditions that make prototyping an appropriate design methodology is presented in Table 17-6.

Advantages of Prototyping

The advantages of prototyping are discussed in the following subsections. The advantages and disadvantages are summarized in Table 17-7.

Better definition of user needs

Because of intensive end-user involvement, prototyping usually results in a good definition of user needs. Many users find that systems developed using prototypes do

Table 17-6   Conditions that Favor the Use of Prototyping

Users lack a full understanding of their needs, or their needs change rapidly.
System requirements are hard to define.
System inputs and outputs are not known.
The task to be performed is unstructured or semistructured.
Designers are uncertain about what technology to use.
The system to be developed is crucial and needed quickly.
The risk associated with developing the wrong system is high.
The users' reactions to the new system are important development considerations.
Many design strategies must be tested.
The development staff is experienced with 4GL and other prototyping tools.
The design staff has little experience developing the system or application under consideration.
The system will be used infrequently (and therefore processing efficiency is not a major concern).

Table 17-7   Advantages and Disadvantages of Prototyping

Advantages	Disadvantages
Usually produces a better definition of user needs than other approaches.	Requires a significant amount of user time.
Greater user involvement and satisfaction and less risk that the system will not be used.	Shortcuts used in developing a prototype may result in inefficient systems.
Systems can be developed much more quickly.	May not lead to a comprehensive and thorough requirements analysis.
Errors are more likely to be detected and eliminated.	Developers may shortchange the testing and documentation process.
Users can see and use the system and have more opportunities to make changes.	May result in a number of negative behavioral reactions.
Less costly than other approaches.	Unending iterations and revisions may be proposed because changes are so easy to make.

not need modification for quite some time because they were done right the first time. When significant changes are needed, it is usually because business requirements have changed.

Higher user involvement and satisfaction

When user requirements are met, the results are greater user satisfaction and less risk that the AIS will not be used. Early user involvement helps to build a climate of acceptance rather than skepticism and criticism about the new AIS.

Faster development time

It only takes a few days or weeks to get a prototype system up and running, which allows users to immediately evaluate significant changes in the way business is transacted. In contrast, it may take a year or more under the traditional approach before the new system can be evaluated. After that time the system may no longer be useful, and enough time has passed for user resistance to build. John Hancock Mutual Life Insurance developed the prototype of an executive information system in only 1 month, as described in Focus 17-2.

Fewer errors

Because the user experiments with and uses each version of the prototype, errors are detected and eliminated early in the development process. In addition, it is much easier to identify and terminate an infeasible AIS before a great deal of time and expense are incurred.

More opportunity for changes

Under the traditional SDLC approach, the design team is responsible for identifying AIS requirements the first time around. These requirements are then frozen so that

Focus 17-2

Prototyping: The Third Dimension

AN ARCHITECT develops two-dimensional blueprints that show how a custom home will look, but that is not the same as walking through a model of the proposed home. A look at the third dimension, walking through the home, lets you actually see the rooms and get a feel for the layout. Creating customized software provides a similar challenge. Users must try to visualize the look and feel of their software from written specifications. Prototypes help users who have ideas or plans but do not know how to turn them into reality, as well as users who have a problem but do not know how to begin solving it. A prototype lets them walk through the proposed system and experiment with its look and feel before committing to the expense of application development.

John Hancock Mutual Life Insurance Company was dissatisfied with the traditional development process: determining user specifications (getting information from high-level executives was especially difficult), writing them up, developing the system, and presenting it to the end-users. The typical reaction from a user was, "I may have said that this is what I wanted, but it isn't."

To counter these problems, Hancock used a prototyping approach to develop an executive information system (EIS). The EIS was needed because the company was dissatisfied with its inability to obtain data quickly and easily from the existing system.

A team was formed that included systems development consultants from IBM, user representatives, systems analysts, and programmers. The prototyping process was highly interactive, and the continual involvement of the end-users eliminated a great deal of misunderstanding. The programmers on the team started programming almost immediately. They prepared sample screens for the first interview session with users. The development staff sat down with users and showed them how the system would work. Users were then given a chance to try the screens. Almost immediately, users could determine if what they said they wanted was really what they needed.

The result was a prototype for an EIS that took only one month to build. The prototype allows top management at Hancock to access and query current and historical financial data and measurements. Top managers who had been skeptical when the project began were impressed by how much the team was able to accomplish in a single month.

the team can complete the AIS. With prototyping, users can continue to suggest changes until the system is exactly what they want.

Less costly

Some prototype systems can be developed for 10 to 20 percent of the cost of traditional systems. For example, one utility company claimed a 13-to-1 improvement in development time over traditional methods using COBOL when prototyping was used to develop 10 major applications.

Disadvantages of Prototyping

Prototyping has the following disadvantages:

Significant user time

Prototyping can be successful only if users are willing to devote a significant amount of time to working with the AIS and providing the developer with feedback and suggestions. Prototyping may require a greater involvement and commitment than busy users are willing to give.

Less efficient use of system resources

The shortcuts that make rapid prototyping iterations possible do not always allow for efficient use of computer resources. As a result, poor performance and reliability and high maintenance and support costs may be incurred. As systems become less expensive and faster, however, the exposure from this limitation is reduced.

Incomplete systems development

In large or complex systems with many users, prototyping may not lead to a comprehensive and thorough requirements analysis.

Inadequately tested and documented systems

Because prototypes are used heavily before acceptance, developers are often tempted to shortchange the testing and documentation process.

Negative behavioral reactions

If a prototype is a throwaway, users may react negatively to learning the system and then not being able to use it. They may also become dissatisfied if all their demands for improvements are not met or if they have to go through too many iterations.

Never-ending development

If prototyping is not managed properly, it may never be completed. Unending iterations and revisions may be proposed because changes are simple to make.

Another tool for improving the development process is a set of software tools referred to as CASE. They are discussed in the next section.

COMPUTER-AIDED SOFTWARE ENGINEERING

Software developers have been compared with the shoemaker's children who had to go barefoot: They develop software for others, yet fail to create software to simplify their own work. The development of powerful **computer-aided software** (or **systems**) **engineering (CASE)** tools, an integrated package of computer-based tools that automate important aspects of the software development process, has changed all that. CASE tools are used to plan, analyze, design, program, and maintain an information system. They also are used to enhance the efforts of managers, users, and programmers in understanding information needs.

Many companies are currently using CASE tools. For example, Florida Power's $86 million customer information system was created using a CASE tool sold by Accenture. The system has been so successful that Accenture packaged it for other utility companies. America West Airlines has more than half of its 90 programmers developing applications using a PC-based CASE tool. Its employees use the tool to model data and business processes, and then the tool uses this information to design and construct a system.

CASE tools do not replace skilled designers. Instead they provide a host of well-integrated tools that give developers effective support for all SDLC phases. CASE software typically has tools for strategic planning, project and system management, database design, screen and report layout, and automatic code generation.

Advantages and Disadvantages of CASE Technology

CASE tools provide the following important advantages:

➤ *Improved productivity.* Sony reported that CASE tools increased productivity by over 600 percent. CASE can generate bug-free code from system specifications as well as automate repetitive tasks. Using an integrated CASE tool, a programmer at Baptist Medical System developed a system in one week that was estimated to take four months.

➤ *Improved program quality.* CASE tools simplify the enforcement of structured development standards, thus improving the quality of development and reducing the threat of serious design errors. CASE tools also can check the internal accuracy of the design and detect inconsistencies.

➤ *Cost savings.* Savings of 80 to 90 percent are possible. At DuPont, an application estimated to require 27 months at a cost of $270,000 was finished in 4 months for $30,000. Over 90 percent of the code was generated directly from design specifications.

➤ *Improved control procedures.* CASE tools encourage the development of system controls, security measures, and system auditability and error handling procedures early in the design process.

➤ *Simplified documentation.* CASE tools automatically document the system as the development process progresses.

Some of the more serious problems with CASE technology include the following:

➤ *Incompatibility.* Some CASE tools do not interact effectively with other systems.

➤ *Cost.* CASE technology is expensive, with some packages in excess of $300,000. As a result, many small companies cannot afford integrated CASE tools.

➤ *Unmet expectations.* According to a Deloitte & Touche survey, only 37 percent of the chief information officers using CASE believe they achieved the expected benefits.

SUMMARY AND CASE CONCLUSION

A company can use many different strategies to obtain a new AIS. First, as the quality and quantity of vendor-written software increase, more and more companies are purchasing canned software. Second, they can use their information systems departments to develop their software or allow end-users to develop their own software. When vendor-written software does not meet all of a company's needs, some companies buy the software and then modify it themselves or, preferably, ask the vendor to make the needed modifications. Third, companies can hire an outsourcing company to handle data processing activities.

There are many ways to speed up or improve the development process. One way to improve the development process is business process reengineering, which is the thorough analysis and complete redesign of business processes and information systems to achieve dramatic performance improvements. It is a revolutionary process that challenges traditional organization structures, rules, assumptions, work flows, job descriptions, management procedures, controls, and organizational values and cultures associated with poor performance.

A second way to improve and speed up the development process is to design a prototype, a simplified working model of a system. A prototype is quickly and inexpensively built and given to users to test drive so they can decide what they like and dislike about the system. Their reactions and feedback are used to modify the system, which is again given to the users to test. This iterative process of trial usage and modification continues until the users are satisfied that the system adequately meets their needs.

A third way to improve the development process is to use computer-aided software engineering tools to automate important aspects of the software development process. CASE tools are used to plan, analyze, design, program, and maintain an information system. They are also used to enhance the efforts of managers, users, and programmers in understanding information needs. CASE software typically has tools for strategic planning, project and system management, database design, screen and report layout, and automatic code generation.

Ann considered the different strategies discussed in this chapter and eliminated several of them. She decided against outsourcing the AIS because she did not feel that option would provide Shoppers Mart with the type of system that management wanted. She also believed her team could do a better and faster job developing the system than an outsourcer. Ann did not think that prototyping would be effective, because Shoppers Mart needed a large and complex system that would serve the needs of many users in many functional areas. Ann discussed the new system with top management and the systems staff and decided that the company's business processes did not need to be radically overhauled; that is, the system does not need to be reengineered.

Ann narrowed her options down to purchasing a system or designing one in-house. If Shoppers Mart decides to develop its own software, Ann will investigate the various CASE packages on the market to see if they will add value to the development process.

No matter which approach she chooses, Ann wants to facilitate as much end-user development as is practical and useful. Ann will make the final decision during the conceptual design phase (Chapter 18). To gather the information she needs to decide whether to purchase software, Ann prepares and sends an RFP to vendors. The RFP asks the vendors to propose software and hardware to meet the company's needs as identified during systems analysis.

KEY TERMS

- canned software
- turnkey systems
- application service provider (ASP)
- request for proposal (RFP)
- benchmark problem
- point scoring
- requirements costing

- custom software
- end-user computing (EUC)
- end-user development (EUD)
- help desk
- outsourcing
- business process reengineering (BPR)
- prototyping

- prototype
- operational prototypes
- nonoperational (throwaway) prototypes
- computer-aided software (or systems) engineering (CASE)

CHAPTER QUIZ

1. Which of the following is not one of the difficulties accountants have experienced using the traditional systems development life cycle?
   a. AIS development projects are backlogged for years.
   b. Changes are not possible after requirements have been frozen.
   c. The AIS that is developed does not meet their needs.
   d. All of the above are difficulties with the SDLC.
2. Companies that buy rather than develop an AIS must still go through the systems development life cycle.
   a. True
   b. False
3. Which of the following statements is false?
   a. As a general rule, companies should buy rather than develop software if they can find a package that meets their needs.
   b. As an AIS increases in size and complexity, there is a greater likelihood that canned software can be found that meets user needs.
   c. A company should not attempt to develop its own custom software unless experienced, in-house programming personnel are available and the job can be completed less expensively on the inside.
   d. As a general rule, a company should develop custom software only when it will provide a significant competitive advantage.
4. When buying large and complex systems, vendors are invited to submit systems for consideration. What is such a solicitation called?
   a. request for quotation
   b. request for system
   c. request for proposal
   d. good faith estimate
5. To compare system performance, a company can create a data processing task with input, processing, and output jobs. This task is performed on the system under consideration and the processing times are compared. The AIS with the lowest time is the most efficient. What is this process called?
   a. benchmarking
   b. requirements costing
   c. point scoring
   d. performance testing
6. Which of the following statements is true?
   a. Because the AIS is so crucial, companies never outsource the entire AIS.
   b. Most mainframe outsourcing contracts are for two to three years and cost thousands of dollars a year.
   c. In elaborate agreements, outsourcers often buy the client's computers and hire all or most of its information systems employees.
   d. Only companies struggling to survive and wanting a quick infusion of cash from selling their hardware use outsourcing.
7. Which of the following is not a benefit of outsourcing?
   a. It offers a great deal of flexibility because it is relatively easy to change outsourcers.
   b. It can provide access to the expertise and special services provided by outsourcers.
   c. It allows companies to move to a more sophisticated level of computing at a reasonable cost.
   d. It is a cost-effective way to handle the peaks and valleys found in seasonal businesses.

8. Which of the following is a true statement with respect to prototyping?
   a. In the early stages of prototyping, system controls and exception handling may be sacrificed in the interests of simplicity, flexibility, and ease of use.
   b. A prototype is a scaled-down, first-draft model that is quickly and inexpensively built and given to users to evaluate.
   c. The first step in prototyping is to identify system requirements.
   d. All of the above statements are true.
9. Which of the following is not an advantage of prototyping?
   a. better definition of user needs
   b. adequately tested and documented systems
   c. higher user involvement and satisfaction
   d. faster development time
10. When is it most appropriate to use prototyping?
    a. when there is a little uncertainty about the AIS
    b. when it is clear what user needs are
    c. when the final AIS cannot be clearly visualized because the decision process is still unclear
    d. when there is a low likelihood of failure

DISCUSSION QUESTIONS

17.1 What is the accountant's role in the computer acquisition process? Should the accountant play an active role, or should all the work be left to computer experts? In what aspects of computer acquisition might an accountant provide a useful contribution?

17.2 A city in the Midwest, with a population of 45,000, purchased a computer and began developing application programs with in-house programmers. Four years later, only one major application had been developed and it was neither complete nor functioning properly. Moreover, none of the application software running on the system met the users' minimum requirements. Both the hardware and the software frequently failed. A similarly configured system, fully programmed with canned software, would have saved the city nearly $500,000. Moreover, the city's annual data processing costs exceeded the annual costs of a new turnkey system with packaged software.

   Why do you think the city was unable to produce quality, workable systems? Would the city have been better off purchasing canned software? Do you think the city would have been able to find software to adequately meet its needs? Why or why not?

17.3 Custom, canned, and modified canned software all have advantages and disadvantages. In this age of increasing computerization, which do you feel will become predominant? Will any of the methods be phased out? Does your response vary depending on the type and size of user organizations?

17.4 You are a systems consultant for Cooper, Price, and Arthur, CPAs. During your country club's annual golf tournament, your partner is Frank Fender, owner of an automobile dealership. He describes a proposal he received from Turnkey Systems and asks for your opinion. The system will handle inventories, receivables, payroll, accounts payable, and general ledger accounting. Turnkey personnel would install the $70,000 system and train Fender's employees. Identify the major themes you would touch on in responding to Fender. Identify the advantages and disadvantages of using a turnkey system to operate the organization's accounting system.

17.5 Sara Jones is the owner of a rapidly growing department store and faces stiff competition. The store is using an out-of-date AIS, resulting in poor customer service, late and error-prone billing, and inefficient control and monitoring of inventory. If the store is to continue growing, its AIS must be upgraded. However, the company is not exactly sure what it wants the AIS to accomplish. Sara has heard about prototyping, but she does not know what it is and whether it would help her. What would you tell Sara if she asked you to define and explain prototyping? Include an explanation of the advantages and disadvantages of prototyping and the circumstances in which it would be most appropriate.

17.6 Clint Grace is the owner of a chain of regional department stores and has been in the business for more than 30 years. He has definite ideas about how department stores should be run. He is financially conservative and is reluctant to make expenditures that do not have a clear financial payoff.

In recent years the stores' profitability has declined sharply and customer dissatisfaction is at an all-time high. Store managers never know exactly how much inventory is on hand and when purchases are needed until a shelf is empty. Clint asks you to study the reason for the profitability decline and to recommend a solution. During your research you find that the current AIS is inefficient and unreliable and that the company's processes and procedures are out of date.

You believe the solution is to reengineer the business processes at the department stores and in the central office. What are some challenges you might face in reengineering Clint's stores? Knowing what you do about Clint's personality, how will you present your recommendation?

PROBLEMS

17.1 Don Otno is confused. He has been researching software options but cannot decide among three alternatives. He has come to you for help.

Don started his search at Computers Made Easy (CME), a computer store in his office complex. He almost wished he had looked no further. Steve Young, the manager of CME, appeared to be knowledgeable and listened attentively as Don explained his problems, needs, and concerns. Steve stated that he had a series of software packages that would, with a few exceptions, come close to meeting Don's needs. He could fix Don up with both hardware and software, and Don could start implementing the package almost immediately. The system's price was unexpectedly reasonable.

Impressed but wanting to shop around, Don visited Custom Designed Software (CDS). After three hours, he left convinced that CDS could produce a program that was exactly what he needed. Cost and time estimates had not been established, but CDS assured him that the cost would be reasonable and that the programs would only take a few months to complete.

Seeking a third opinion, Don visited Modified Software Unlimited (MSU). The MSU representative said customized packages were very good but expensive, whereas canned software was inexpensive but rarely met more than a few needs. The best of both worlds could be achieved by having MSU modify the package that came closest to meeting Don's needs.

On the way back to his office, Don stopped by CME and asked Steve about customized and modified software. Steve expressed enough concerns about both that Don came full circle, and he began thinking canned software was best. Late that night Don realized that he was not able to make an objective decision. He was swayed by whichever vendor he was talking with at the time. The next morning he called you for help.

Required

a. At Don's request you agree to conduct a study and submit a report showing the advantages and disadvantages of each vendor's approach. Outline the report's contents, identifying the advantages and disadvantages of each approach.

b. Recommend the course of action that you feel would be best for Don, and support your decision.

17.2 One unhappy federal agency spent almost $1 million on a development contract for an integrated human resources/payroll system that produced no usable software. The original contract was for $445,158 and 15 months. The agency terminated the contract after 28 months and $970,000. The agency had not fully developed user requirements or system specifications for the proposed software when it issued the RFP. There were a number of problems:

- The contractor did not understand the desired software systems.
- User requirements were never adequately defined and frozen. Changes delayed completion schedules and caused disagreements about whether new requirements were included in the original scope of work.
- The contract did not specify systems requirements or performance criteria and the terminology was vague. The contract was amended 13 times to add or delete requirements and to reimburse the contractor for the extra costs resulting from agency-caused delays. The amendments increased the cost of the contract to $1,037,448.
- The contractor complained of inexcusable agency delays, such as taking too much time to review items submitted for approval. The agency blamed the delays on the poor quality of the documentation under review.
- The agency did not require each separate development phase to be approved before work continued. When the agency rejected the general system design, the contractor had to scrap work already completed.

   The agency eventually became convinced that the contractor could not deliver the software at an acceptable time and cost; the agency then canceled the contract and tried to withhold payment for poor performance. A negotiated settlement price of $970,000 was agreed on. None of the software was ever used by the agency.

Required

a. Who is to blame for the agency's problems? How could the agency have done a better job of managing the systems development project? What could the contractor have done differently?

b. Can we generalize from this case that organizations and governmental agencies should not try to have custom software written for them? Explain your answer.

17.3 Wong Engineering Corporation (WEC) operates in 25 states and three countries. WEC faced a crucial decision: choosing a network operating system and software that would maximize functionality, manageability, and acceptance of the system by end-users. WEC developed and followed a four-step approach:

Step 1: Develop the evaluation criteria. WEC organized a committee to develop proper evaluation criteria. Committee members interviewed users and developed the following criteria:

Menu or graphical user interface

Ease of use

Scope of vendor support

Ease of LAN management and administration

Cost, speed, and performance
Wide-area communications abilities
Ability to access other computing platforms
Security
Fault tolerance and recovery abilities
Ability to connect workstations to the network
Global naming services
Printing capabilities
Upgrade and enhancement options
Stability of the vendor

WEC organized the criteria into the following four categories and prioritized them.

1. *Business criteria* refer to overall business, economic, and competitive issues.
2. *Operational criteria* refer to tactical issues and operating characteristics.
3. *Organizational criteria* refer to people issues such as the LAN's impact on the information systems structure.
4. *Technical criteria* refer to hardware, software, and communications issues.

The evaluation committee used a weighting scale of 1 to 5, with 5 as the highest, to select the top three evaluation criteria for each category. Criteria vital to short-term and long-term business goals were given a 5. "Wish list" criteria were weighted a 3. Inapplicable criteria were given a 1.

Step 2: Define the operating environment. A number of data gathering techniques were used to collect information from which an information systems model was developed. The model revealed the need to share accounting, sales, marketing, and engineering data at three organizational levels: the district, division, and home office. In addition, district offices needed access to centralized financial information to handle payroll. WEC decided it needed a distributed network that allows users throughout the organization access to company data.

Step 3: Identify the operating alternatives. Using the criteria developed in step 1, WEC evaluated each package identified. Each committee member established personal matrices for each product, and then members compared notes during a roundtable discussion.

Step 4: Test and prototype products. The highest-scoring products were tested further using prototypes. Finally, WEC selected the product that fit the organization's needs most completely.

Required

a. Discuss the evaluation committee's role in the selection process. How should members of the committee be selected? What advantages and problems result from using a committee to make the selection?
b. What data gathering techniques could WEC use to assess user needs? To select a vendor?
c. What is the benefit of analyzing the operating environment before selecting the software? What data gathering techniques should a company employ in understanding the operating environment?
d. In selecting a system using the point scoring method, how should the committee resolve scoring disputes? List at least two methods.
e. Assume the point scoring approach narrowed the process to three candidates. Should a purchase decision be made on the point scoring process alone? What other procedure(s) should the committee employ in making the final selection?

17.4 Mark Mitton is the accountant acting as liaison to the information systems department for a mid-size retail firm in Salem, Oregon. Mark has been investigating several computer systems and has narrowed the selection to the best three systems. Mark developed a shopping list of features the

Table 17-8   An Alternative Evaluation Matrix

Selection Criteria	Weight	System 1	System 2	System 3
Software				
Fulfillment of business needs	100	6	8	9
Acceptance in marketplace	30	6	7	6
Quality of documentation	50	7	9	8
Quality of warranty	50	4	8	7
Ease of use	80	7	6	5
Control features	50	9	7	9
Flexibility	20	4	5	9
Security features	30	4	4	8
Modularity	30	8	5	4
Integration with other software	30	8	9	6
Quality of support utilities	50	9	8	5
Vendor				
Reputation and reliability	10	3	9	6
Experience with similar systems	20	5	5	6
Installation assistance	70	9	4	6
Training assistance	35	4	8	6
Timeliness of maintenance	35	5	4	4
Hardware				
Internal memory size (RAM)	70	5	6	8
Hard-drive capacity	40	9	9	5
Graphics capabilities	50	7	7	8
Processing speed	30	8	8	5
Overall performance	40	9	4	4
Expandability	50	7	2	5
Support for LAN technology	30	3	4	7

system needs. He carefully reviewed each system, talked to other users, and interviewed appropriate systems representatives. Using a point-scoring system, Mark assigned weights to each factor to coincide with his evaluation. Mark developed Table 17-8 to help him select the best system.

Required

a. Use a spreadsheet program to develop a point scoring matrix and determine which of the three systems Mark should select.

b. Mark's coworker, Susan Shelton, did not agree with Mark's weightings. Susan suggested the following changes.

Flexibility	60
Reputation and reliability	50
Quality of support utilities	10
Graphics capability	10

On the basis of the changes, which vendor should Mark recommend?

c. Mark's manager suggested the following changes to Susan's weightings:

Reputation and reliability	90
Installation assistance	40
Experience with similar systems	40
Training assistance	65
Internal memory size	10

Will the manager's changes affect the decision about which system to buy?

d. What can you conclude about point scoring from the changes made by Susan and Mark's manager? Develop your own weighting scale to evaluate the selection of the three software packages. What other selection criteria would you use? Be prepared to discuss your results with the class.

e. What are the weaknesses of the point scoring method?

17.5 Nielsen Marketing Research USA (NMR), with operations in 29 countries, is the recognized world leader in the production and dissemination of marketing information. Nielsen was a pioneer in the development of the decision support information business and has been the primary supplier for more than 70 years. NMR's most recognizable product is the Nielsen television ratings.

Nielsen is one of the largest users of computer capacity in the United States. Its information system has consistently ranked above average in efficiency for its industry. However, NMR commissioned IBM to evaluate outsourcing its information processing. NMR wants to know if outsourcing will allow it to concentrate on giving its customers value-added services and insights and if it can increase its flexibility, promote rapid growth, and provide it with more real-time information.

Required

What are the benefits and risks of outsourcing for NMR? Do you think the benefits of outsourcing outweigh the risks? Explain your answer.

17.6 The Pedaler, one of the largest bicycle manufacturers in the world, has grown significantly in the 20 years since it was formed. Eighteen years ago the company began using a computer to handle its data processing needs. Since then, it has spent several million dollars on hardware and software.

For the past several years the information systems department has effectively handled company needs. During the slow season, systems employees have light schedules, work on special projects, and spend one to two weeks at training seminars. During the peak season, employees average five hours of overtime per week. Recently, the Pedaler has grown so fast that the information system is struggling to keep up. Realizing the benefit such a system provides, management is thinking of expanding the department at a cost of $1 million over the next three years. Due to its rapid expansion, the Pedaler would have to borrow the money for this project. Investing in a new system, however, may slow the company's growth or, worse, add significantly to debt.

At the last board of directors meeting, outsourcing was suggested as a possible solution. Brian Cycle, the president, has asked you, an independent consultant specializing in AIS strategies, for advice.

Required

Write a one-page memo explaining outsourcing and summarizing the benefits and drawbacks of outsourcing the Pedaler's information systems functions. Address issues about how outsourcing fits the Pedaler's situation, if it can save the Pedaler money, and if it can effectively meet the needs of a growing company.

17.7 Meredith Corporation publishes books and magazines, owns and operates television stations, and provides a real estate marketing and franchising service. Meredith is dissatisfied with its ability to retrieve correct and timely inventory information from its AIS. Each division either developed its own inventory system or already had one in place when Meredith acquired the AIS. As a result, Meredith has 11 different inventory systems, which are unable to communicate with each other. Management wants to tie the systems together and have one consistent inventory pool from which to extract the information needed for making good business decisions. Meredith has decided to use prototyping to develop the system.

Required
a. When interviewing Meredith's personnel, what three key questions would you ask to determine systems requirements? What type of information are you attempting to elicit from each question?
b. What do you think are Meredith's basic information needs?
c. Explain how the prototyping process would work for Meredith. What would the system developer do during the iterative process step? Why would you want the fewest iterations possible?
d. What tools will you use to design your prototype? Why would you use them instead of conventional programming languages?
e. Would you want this prototype to be operational or nonoperational? Why? If it were an operational prototype, what would have to happen? If it were a nonoperational prototype, how would the prototype be used?
f. Suppose the company decides the prototyped system is not practical, abandons the system, and takes some other approach to solving its inventory problem. Docs that mean prototyping is not a valid systems development approach? Explain your answer.

17.8 The following list outlines the activities a company may perform in the process of reengineering its business. Match each activity with one of the seven principles of reengineering.

Reengineering Activities
a. One person processes an employment application from beginning to end.
b. The department manager using the yearly budget is also the one who prepared it.
c. The purchasing manager has the authority to handle every aspect of purchase making.
d. Each plant issues its own purchase orders, and a new corporate department coordinates purchasing across all the plants.
e. All customer service representatives share a corporate-wide database that contains customer sales data.
f. A sales clerk enters a customer's order into a computer terminal. The order is then automatically sent over the network to shipping, inventory control, and the credit manager. In addition, the database is updated immediately.

Seven Principles of Reengineering
1. Organize the business and information system around outcomes, not individual tasks.
2. Have output users perform the process.
3. Have those who produce information process it.
4. Use IT to achieve the benefits of both centralization and decentralization of data.
5. Integrate parallel processes instead of performing them separately and trying to integrate them at the end of the process.

6. Flatten the organizational chart by giving workers the power to make decisions and use built-in controls.
7. Capture data only once, at its source, using source data automation.

17.9 The management of Quickfix would like to decrease costs and increase customer service by reengineering its computer repair procedures. Currently, when a defective or broken computer needs servicing, the customer calls one of five regional customer service centers. A customer service representative manually logs in the relevant customer information and then searches through a list to find the closest qualified technician. That technician is then contacted by phone to see if the repair fits into his or her schedule. If not, the representative finds the next closest technician. When a technician who can perform the service is located, the customer and repair information is provided over the phone. The technician then calls the customer and makes arrangements to pick up the broken computer and replace it with a loaner. Making these arrangements takes one to two days and sometimes more if technicians are not available or do not promptly return calls.

The broken computer is sent to a repair depot. Typically, the entire repair process takes another four to seven days. Overall, it can take up to three weeks for an item to be repaired. When a customer calls to see if the computer is ready, the customer service representative must then call the technician, find out the status of the item, and call the customer back. Throughout the entire repair process, usually five phone calls take place between the customer, the customer service representative, and the technician.

There are three main problems with this process: (1) It is time-consuming; (2) it is inconvenient for a customer to have a computer removed, a new one installed, and then the old one reinstalled; and (3) customer service representatives do not have immediate access to information about items currently being repaired.

Required
a. Identify the basic activities that occur when an item is repaired and around which the reengineered process should be developed.
b. Describe how the current repair process can be reengineered to achieve the goal of more timely repair and increased customer service.
c. What will be the specific benefits of reengineering the repair process?

17.10 Selling goods to a manufacturer that employs a just-in-time (JIT) inventory system requires immediate and reliable information from a company's AIS—just ask Sony Corporation of America. The need for faster information is partially a result of Sony's shift in business strategies. Over the past decade Sony has increased market penetration by supplying electronic parts to computer manufacturers. However, the AIS, originally built for the consumer market, was simply not prepared to handle this shift in information needs.

The problems with the system are readily apparent. One of Sony's biggest obstacles is that it does not get the information it needs, when it needs it, from its factories. As a result, it cannot provide good delivery information to its customers, which in turn causes a big problem: If Sony is not responsive to its customers' needs, it will probably lose them.

To speed system development, Sony's information systems organization is employing a computer-aided software engineering (CASE) tool from Texas Instruments. The tool lets systems designers use local workstations linked to a mainframe and uses artificial intelligence features to develop program code.

To use the CASE tool, the designer enters statements that describe the data the company will use and the relationships among the data files that will store this information. The CASE tool checks the data relationships to ensure that they are consistent. After any inconsistencies have been corrected, the CASE tool produces code that describes the relationships. The information is then stored in a global encyclopedia of corporate information. This process continues until a model of how the company operates is developed. The CASE tool allows this model to be updated and altered as relationships change.

Sony is finding several advantages to using CASE technology. For instance, it requires that developers possess a certain business expertise, which makes designers more effective in translating business problems into systems solutions. The CASE system has also provided a significant productivity boost. Recent smaller development projects at Sony have seen sixfold increases in programming productivity. CASE tools also require significant planning long before any source code is written. Such planning minimizes wasted programming time and the possibility of a runaway system.

Required
a. What are the benefits of CASE technology? How does CASE technology improve the systems development process?
b. Discuss why CASE technology might not be used in systems development.

17.11   Conduct a search (using written materials, the Internet, electronic databases, etc.) for successful and failed implementations of information systems. Per your professor's instructions, prepare an oral or written summary of a successful and a failed information system implementation. Include in your summary the approach used to acquire or develop the system (purchase software, develop it, modify it, outsource it).

Case 17-1   AnyCompany, Inc.: An Ongoing Comprehensive Case

Visit a local company and obtain permission to study its systems development approach. Once you have lined up a company, do the following:

1. With a member of the information systems staff, discuss the following issues.
   a. What procedures does the company follow in determining its hardware and software needs? How does the company select software, hardware, and vendors?
   b. Does the company outsource any of its data processing activities? If so, what benefits is it now deriving, and to what risks is it exposed? Does the company think the decision was a good one? If it does not outsource, has it considered the option? If so, why was it rejected?
   c. Has the company used prototyping? If so, what benefits did it derive? What were the disadvantages? Does the company continue to use prototypes, or has it discontinued their use? If it has not used prototypes, was the approach considered? If so, why was it rejected?
2. Summarize your findings in a written report and be prepared to share them with the class.

Case 17-2 Professional Salon Concepts

Steve Cowan is the owner of Professional Salon Concepts (PSC), a distribution company for hair salon products, in Joliet, Illinois. Steve started working for his father, a distributor of barber and beauty salon products, at age 16, and a decade later decided to start his own business. He rented a small warehouse, hired four people, and began selling products carrying the name of famous hairstylist Paul Mitchell. Unfortunately, hairstylists ignored the products and did not buy them. Steve eventually had to let his people go and moved his products to an inexpensive basement location.

The tables turned for Steve when he conducted a free two-hour seminar at a local hair salon demonstrating how hairstylists could successfully use his products. He left with a $1,000 order and the realization that he had found his niche. He decided to sell only to salons that allowed him to run a seminar in which he could demonstrate his products.

PSC has done very well using Steve's strategy. Sales reached $7 million as PSC grew to 45 employees and 3,000 salon customers. Warehouse operations ran smoothly due to Paul Mitchell's specialized product line, which was 75 percent of PSC's business. PSC carried 1,000 products, compared with 10,000 for the average salon distributor. This more focused product line enabled PSC to achieve a 24-hour turnaround on orders, in contrast to more than two days for the competition. To achieve this quick turnaround, Steve sometimes worked late packing orders so he could drive them to the UPS hub a few towns away by the 2:00 A.M. deadline.

Steve bought PSC's first computer, and installed a $3,000 accounting package, which served his accounting needs very well. In fact, Steve thought everything was going great until Terri Klimko, a consultant from PSC's second-largest supplier, stopped by. Terri asked Steve the following questions designed to reveal how well he knew his business:

- Do you know exactly to whom you ship each month?
- Do you know how much each customer bought, by supplier?
- Can you rank your customer sales?
- Can you break your sales down by product?
- Do you know how the profit per client breaks down into product lines?
- Do you know how revenues per salesperson vary over the days of the week?

Steve's answer was an uncomfortable "no" to each question. Terri told him that people who cannot answer these questions are losing money. That upset Steve and he terminated the session, politely dismissing Terri. Although Steve was unimpressed with Terri's advice, he was impressed with her. They started dating and were soon married. Shortly after the marriage, she joined the company.

Steve realized that Terri's skills could be used either to help PSC's business grow or to help PSC internally. Believing it was more important to expand the business, he asked Terri to help make the salons more profitable. With PSC's help, she developed a template to break down and analyze every aspect of their business. The template helped salon owners determine such statistics as how much each hairstylist brings in per client, how many clients receive extra services, and how many clients, and which ones, buy hair products. The Cowans soon became more like partners to their customers than trainers and educators. If a salon had employee problems, the Cowans would help settle the issues. If a salon fell behind in a grand opening, the Cowans lent a hand. The only catch was the salons had to buy PSC's products. The better the customer, the more time the Cowans gave.

PSC began selling turnkey systems and support services at cost to help salons answer questions like those Terri posed to Steve. Unfortunately, PSC's computer could not answer those same questions. Steve asked Mike Fenske, a consultant, for help, and sent to Mike as much raw data as could be extracted from his PC-based accounting system. Mike entered it into a database and wrote programs to produce the information Steve wanted. The system worked, but it was very slow—so slow that accounts payable and purchasing information was handled manually. The system also failed to answer all of Terri's questions, and her list was getting longer. To make matters worse, only a few months of detailed information were available at any time. To partially alleviate some of these problems, Steve hired Mike, his brother-in-law, as the company's controller.

After reading a special industry report, Steve realized that his company was well positioned in every aspect except investment in technology. Steve and Mike knew it was time to purchase a new system. They considered outside consultants but felt they would take too much time trying to understand PSC's special needs. In addition, Mike believed consultants knew little about the detailed workings of the software they recommend. They decided to evaluate and select the software themselves and rely on the vendor for installation help.

Steve and Mike spent months researching software and attending demonstrations before settling on a generic AIS software program. They paid the $20,000 price tag and the vendor began installing the system and training PSC personnel. Three days prior to conversion, Steve met a distributor from North Dakota at a social gathering. The distributor described how his system not only provided the detailed accounting and customer reporting features, but also met his distributorship's inventory management and order fulfillment needs. Steve was so impressed that he excused himself and called Mike, telling him to halt the conversion. They immediately went to North Dakota to check out the system, then flew to Minneapolis to visit DSM, the software developer.

DSM did a great job of demonstrating the software and provided Steve and Mike with several great references. The only hitch was DSM's inability to demonstrate two features that were particularly important to Steve. The first was the ability to adjust orders automatically to reflect outstanding customer credits and back orders. The second was the ability to determine the least expensive way to pack and ship each order. DSM's salespeople assured Steve and Mike that those features would be up and running on the package by the time it was delivered to PSC.

Before committing to the system, Steve and Mike sat down to determine if it was economically feasible. They estimated $234,000 in yearly savings in the following manner:

$144,000 Most of PSC's orders consisted of several boxes, 95 percent of which were sent COD. PSC's old system had no way of writing orders for shipments of more than one box. In other words, an order shipped in five boxes had required five sales invoices and five separate COD tickets. The new system would allow PSC to generate one sales order and ship one box COD. The other four would be shipped by regular delivery, which was much less costly than COD delivery. Eliminating the need to ship every box COD would save the company $144,000 a year.

$50,000 PSC paid an outside accounting firm $40,000 a year to prepare its financial statements. The new software would prepare most of those statements automatically.

$40,000 Because the old system did not have credit-managing capabilities, it was hard to detect past due accounts. Steve believed earlier detection of past due accounts would result in faster collections, fewer lost customers, and fewer write-offs.

Unknown The major reason for acquiring the system was to improve customer service by making more detailed customer information available.

Steve and Mike estimated annual maintenance costs of $10,000 and an annual return on investment of $224,000. Because the system would pay for itself in less than a year, Steve bought it and wrote off his $20,000 investment in the other system.

At the end of 1993, DSM technicians arrived at PSC to install the software. To Steve's dismay, the promised features were not part of the package and there was no immediate plan to add them. Although Steve and Mike were upset, they realized they had to shoulder some of the blame for not insisting on seeing the two features before signing the deal. A subsequent search found a program that automatically determined the cheapest way to pack and ship an order. DSM agreed to pay half of the $10,000 cost to integrate it into the program. DSM also offered to create the module to reflect customer credits and back orders for another $20,000, but Steve declined. These problems pushed the conversion date back several months.

PSC spent the first three months of 1994 preparing to implement the new system. Training PSC employees to use the new system was particularly important. For example, adding a customer to the database required only one screen with the old system, while the new software required six screens. Employees were taught to shout "Fire!" if they came upon a problem they could not handle. Mike, or one of the DSM programmers, would come to their assistance and explain the error and the proper method of correction. During implementation, the new system was tested for glitches by processing real data. Looking back, Mike admits three months were not nearly enough for the training and testing. They should have used twice as much time to identify and eliminate glitches.

PSC dismantled the old system and converted to the new one on April 20, 1994. Before long, telephone operators grew confused and forgot how to move from one part of the system to another. They began bumping up against unfamiliar error messages and getting themselves into situations they had not been trained to handle. Soon everyone was yelling "Fire!" at the same time. In less than 1 hour, so many people were waiting for help that the programmers stopped explaining the correct procedures and simply ran from operator to operator correcting problems. Mistakes were repeated numerous times, and the situation intensified. Some employees, feeling embarrassed and ashamed at their inability to work the new system, broke down and cried openly.

Steve was running the warehouse area and was not having much fun either. On a normal day, PSC has 200 to 300 boxes ready for 3:30 P.M. shipment. On conversion day, a lone box sat ready to go. Facing the first default on his 24-hour turnaround promise since he started PSC, Steve, and Terri, Mike, and a few others, stayed long after midnight packing boxes and loading them on trucks. They just barely made it to the nearest UPS hub on time.

The next day, order entry and shipping ran much smoother. However, when Steve sat down to retrieve the data he needed to monitor sales, he could not figure out how to get the information from the system. Needless to say, he was not feeling too kindly toward his $200,000 system or the company that sold it to him.

It took Steve several weeks to figure out how to get the data he needed to monitor sales. When he did, he was horrified that sales had dropped nearly 15 percent. They had focused so hard on getting the system up and running that they had taken their eyes off the customers. To make matters worse, Steve could not get information on sales by customer, salesperson, or product, and he could not figure out why or where sales were falling.

However, things quickly improved after "Hell Week." Orders are now entered just as quickly as before, and printed copies are not needed for filing purposes. Warehouse operations are improved, thanks to the integrated add-in program. The new system provides pickers with the most efficient path to follow when picking orders. It also tells them which items to pack in which boxes based on destination and weight. The system selects a carrier and prints out labels for the boxes. Order turnaround time was shaved to 20 minutes from five hours.

Months after the system was installed, it still does not do everything Steve needs it to do, including some things the old system did. Nor does it answer all of Terri's questions. Steve is confident, however, that the system will eventually provide PSC with a distinct competitive advantage. He is negotiating with DSM to write the credit and back order module.

With all that has happened, Steve believes that the step up to the new system was necessary, even the right move, for his growing company. With the exceptions of taking the DSM salesperson's word and not taking enough time to practice with the system, Steve feels PSC did as good a job as it could have in selecting, installing, and implementing a new system.

Write a memo to address the following questions. Be prepared to defend your position to the class.

1. Do you agree with Steve's assessment that PSC did a good job selecting, installing, and implementing the new system considering the exceptions he noted? If so, why?

Or do you feel PSC could have done a better job? If so, what did it do wrong and what should it have done differently?

2. How could PSC have avoided the problem of the missing features?

3. How could PSC have avoided some of the conversion and reporting problems it faced?

4. Based on what you read about economic feasibility in Chapter 16, evaluate Steve's analysis. Do you agree with his numbers and his conclusions? Explain your answer.

5. How could PSC's customers use the new multibox shipping approach to defraud PSC?

6. On a scale of 1 to 5, with 1 being the best, how would you rate the service that PSC received from DSM? Could it have been improved? If so, how?

Source: Adapted from David H. Freeman, "Computer Upgrade: To Hell and Back," *INC. Technology* (June 15, 1994): 46–53.

ANSWERS TO CHAPTER QUIZ

1. d	3. b	5. a	7. a	9. b
2. a	4. c	6. c	8. d	10. c

Chapter 18

Systems Design, Implementation, and Operation

Learning Objectives

After studying this chapter, you should be able to:

- Discuss the conceptual systems design process and the activities in this phase.
- Discuss the physical systems design process and the activities in this phase.
- Discuss the systems implementation and conversion process and the activities in this phase.
- Discuss the systems operation and maintenance process and the activities in this phase.

Integrative Case: Shoppers Mart

Ann Christy, the controller at Shoppers Mart, presented the results of her systems analysis to top management and received permission to develop a new AIS (Chapter 16 conclusion). The following week she planned the rest of the project. Ann is concerned because many development projects bog down during the design and implementation phases. She certainly does not want to have a runaway project on her hands—one that she cannot control. She believes that her staff has adequately determined the requirements for the new system and wants to be sure that the rest of the development process is completed correctly. She decides to schedule another meeting with the head of systems development to discuss the following questions:

1. She must determine what type of system will best meet Shoppers Mart's needs and then make a proposal to management. Should her team develop what they consider to be the best approach to meeting Shoppers Mart's needs? Should they develop several approaches?
2. What can be done to ensure that system output will meet user needs? When and how should input, such as accounting transactions, be captured and who should capture it? Where should AIS data be stored and how should the data be organized and accessed?
3. How should Shoppers Mart convert from its current to its new AIS? How much time and effort will be needed to maintain the new AIS? In what capacity should Ann's accounting staff participate?

658

INTRODUCTION

Developing quality, error-free software is a difficult and time-consuming task, but most companies that seek to implement a new system want it immediately. As developers feel the pressure to perform system miracles, they begin skipping the basic steps of systems analysis and design and start writing code. Omitting systems analysis steps only leads to disaster, as developers create well-structured systems that fail to meet user needs or solve any of their business problems. An American Management Systems study revealed that 75 percent of all large systems either are not used, are not used as intended, or generate meaningless reports.

In a recent survey, KPMG found that 35 percent of all major information systems projects were classified as runaways—hopelessly incomplete and over budget. Skipping or skimping on systems analysis and design steps is a major factor in runaway occurrence, although not the only cause. Runaways can consume a great deal of time and money and in the end produce no usable results, as illustrated by the following examples:

➤ Pacific Gas & Electric (PG&E) pulled the plug on a client/server information system for all of its residential and commercial customers. People in and out of the utility labeled the system, five years in development, a financial disaster with no end product. To fix the problem, PG&E used several consulting firms, including three of the Big Five CPA firms.

➤ California's Department of Motor Vehicles decided to overhaul its system, which was originally developed in 1965. The system was so difficult to maintain that it took the equivalent of 18 programmers working for an entire year to add a social security number file to the drivers' license and vehicle registration file. After seven years, $44 million, and not a single usable application, the state canceled the project.

Many of these problems can be attributed to ineffective or incomplete systems analysis and design efforts. Effective systems analysis and design can ensure that developers correctly define the business problem and design the appropriate solution. As discussed in Chapter 16, systems analysis is a crucial phase in the systems design life cycle (SDLC). It begins with problem recognition, feasibility analysis, and a study and documentation of the existing system. The goal is to define the new system's requirements so it will take the organization where it needs to go. This chapter discusses the other four steps (see Figure 16-1) in the systems development life cycle: conceptual systems design, physical systems design, systems implementation and conversion, and operation and maintenance. Chapter 17 discusses how some of the steps in the SDLC can be shortened or made more effective.

Accountants must understand the development process, as they are involved in it in several ways—as users helping to specify their needs, as members of the development team, and as auditors after the system is complete. Accountants should help keep the project on track by evaluating and measuring benefits, monitoring costs, and ensuring that the project stays on schedule.

CONCEPTUAL SYSTEMS DESIGN

In the **conceptual systems design** phase, the developer creates a general framework for implementing user requirements and solving problems identified in the analysis phase. As shown in Figure 18-1, there are three main steps in conceptual design: evaluate design alternatives, prepare design specifications, and prepare the conceptual systems design report. The following sections explain these in more detail.

Evaluate Design Alternatives

There are many ways to design an AIS, so accountants and others involved in systems design must continually make design decisions. For example: Should the company mail hard copy purchase orders or use EDI? Should the company have a large centralized mainframe and database, or distribute computer power to the stores using minicomputers, PCs, distributed databases, LANs, and WANs? Should data entry be

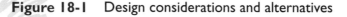

Figure 18-1 Design considerations and alternatives

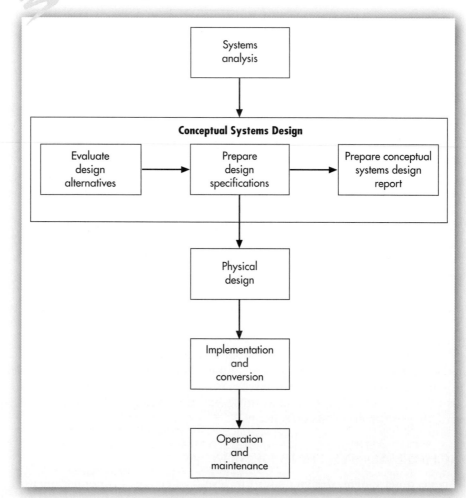

through keyboard, optical character recognition, point-of-sale devices, or in some combination of these?

In addition, there are many different ways that a company can approach the systems development process. It could purchase software from a vendor, ask that the in-house information systems staff develop the software, request that the people who are going to use the system design it, or hire an outside company to develop and manage the information system. The company could modify, enhance, or replace existing software or completely reengineer all of its business processes and develop software to support these new processes. These alternatives, which must be considered in conceptual systems design, are discussed in more detail in Chapter 17.

The design team should identify a variety of design alternatives and evaluate each with respect to the following standards: (1) how well it meets organizational and system objectives, (2) how well it meets user needs, (3) whether it is economically feasible, and (4) its advantages and disadvantages. The steering committee evaluates the alternatives and selects the one that best meets the organization's needs. Table 18-1 presents examples of conceptual and physical design considerations and their corresponding design alternatives.

Table 18-1   Design Considerations and Alternatives

Design Consideration	Design Alternatives
Communications channel configuration	Point-to-point, multidrop, or line sharing
Communications channels	Telephone lines, coaxial cable, fiber optics, microwave, or satellite
Communications network	Centralized, decentralized, distributed, or local area
Data storage medium	Tape, disk, diskette, hard drive, CD, or paper
Data storage structure	Files or database
File organization and access	Random, sequential, or indexed-sequential access
Input medium	Keying, OCR, MICR, POS, EDI, or voice
Input format	Source document, turnaround document, source data automation, or screen
Operations	In-house or outsourcing
Output frequency	Instantaneous, hourly, daily, weekly, or monthly
Output medium	Paper, screen, voice, diskette, CD, or microfilm
Output scheduling	Predetermined times or on demand
Output format	Narrative, table, graph electronic file or communication
Printed output	Preprinted forms, turnaround document, or system-generated forms
Processing mode	Manual, batch, or real time
Processor	Personal computer, minicomputer, or mainframe
Software acquisition	Canned, custom, or modified
Transaction processing	Batch or on-line
Update frequency	Instantaneous, hourly, daily, weekly, or monthly

Prepare Design Specifications

Once a design alternative has been selected, the project team develops the **conceptual design specifications** for the following elements:

1. *Output.* Because the system is designed to meet users' information needs, output specifications must be prepared first. For example, to evaluate store sales using a sales analysis report, Shoppers Mart must decide (a) how often to produce the report (daily or weekly), (b) what the report should contain (store number, sales volume, etc.), (c) what the report will look like, and (d) if users require a hard copy or screen (or both) output.

2. *Data storage.* Development decisions for Shoppers Mart include which data elements must be stored to produce the sales report, whether the data should be stored in sequential or random order, what type of file or database to use, and which field size is appropriate for the data items.

3. *Input.* Design considerations for Shoppers Mart include which sales data to enter, sale location and amount, and where, when, and how to collect data. Inputs are considered only after the desired output is identified.

4. *Processing procedures and operations.* Design considerations for Shoppers Mart include how to process the input and stored data in order to produce the sales report, and also the sequence in which the processes must be performed.

Prepare the Conceptual Systems Design Report

At the end of the conceptual design phase, the project development team prepares and submits a **conceptual systems design report.** The purpose of this report is to (1) guide physical systems design activities, (2) communicate how management and user information needs will be met, and (3) help the steering committee assess system feasibility. The main component is a description of one or more recommended system designs. This description contains the contents of each output, database, and input; processing flows and the relationships among the programs, files, inputs, and outputs; hardware, software, and resource requirements; and audit, control, and security processes and procedures. Any assumptions or unresolved problems that may affect the final systems design should be discussed. The table of contents of the Shoppers Mart report is shown in Table 18-7, in this chapter's summary.

PHYSICAL SYSTEMS DESIGN

During the **physical systems design** phase, the company determines how the conceptual AIS design is to be implemented. Physical design translates the broad, user-oriented AIS requirements of conceptual design into detailed specifications that are used to code and test the computer programs. As shown in Figure 18-2, the steps that occur during this phase include designing output, creating files and databases, designing input, writing computer programs, developing procedures, and building controls into the new AIS. The following subsections describe these activities in detail.

Output Design

The objective of output design is to determine the nature, format, content, and timing of printed reports, documents, and screen displays. Tailoring the output to user needs

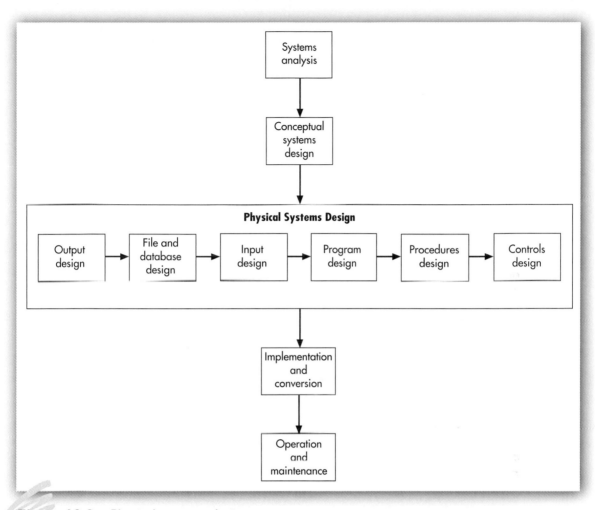

Figure 18-2   Physical systems design

requires cooperation between users and designers. Some important output design considerations are summarized in Table 18-2.

Output usually fit into one of the following four categories:

1. **Scheduled reports** have a prespecified content and format and are prepared on a regular basis. Examples include monthly performance reports, weekly sales analyses, and annual financial statements.

2. **Special-purpose analysis reports** have no prespecified content or format and are not prepared on a regular schedule. They are prepared in response to a management request to evaluate an issue, such as which of three new products would provide the highest profits.

Table 18-2   Output Design Considerations

Consideration	Concern
Use	Who will use the output, why and when do they need it, and what decisions will they need to make based on it?
Medium	Should output be paper, screen, voice response, diskette, microfilm, or some combination of these?
Format	The format that clearly conveys the most information should be selected (table, narrative, graphic); for example, large volumes of data can be condensed easily into graphs that are easy to read and interpret.
Preprinted	Should paper output be on a preprinted form, such as a check or purchase order? Should turnaround documents be used?
Location	Where should AIS output be sent?
Access	Who should have access to hard copy and computer screen output?
Detail	Lengthy output should be preceded by an executive summary and a table of contents. Headings and legends organize data and highlight important items. Detailed information is placed in an appendix.
Timeliness	How often should AIS output be produced?

3. **Triggered exception reports** have a prespecified content and format but are prepared only in response to abnormal conditions. Excessive absenteeism, cost overruns, inventory shortages, and situations requiring immediate corrective action trigger such reports.

4. **Demand reports** have a prespecified content and format but are prepared only on request. Both triggered exception reports and demand reports can be used effectively to facilitate the management process.

The AIS developers prepare an output sample, and users evaluate it to ensure that it is complete, relevant, and useful. Unacceptable output is modified and reviewed as many times as necessary to make it acceptable. To avoid the expense and time delays resulting from changes made later in the SDLC, many organizations require users to sign a document stating that the form and content are acceptable.

File and Database Design

It is important that the various divisions or departments of a company store data in compatible formats. This helps companies avoid the problem that AT&T faced: 23 business units and a jumble of incompatible systems. It was difficult for some of the units to share e-mail with other units. Perhaps more importantly, the business units did not maintain customer records in formats that allowed them to be easily shared. AT&T undertook a five-year project to create a "single view" of each customer so that customer data can be shared across all business units.

In Chapter 4 you learned about files and databases and how to design them. Some of the more important file and database design considerations are summarized in Table 18-3.

Table 18-3   File and Database Design Considerations

Consideration	Concern
Medium	Should data be stored on hard drive, disk, diskette, CD, tape, or paper?
Organization and access	Should sequential, indexed-sequential, or random-access methods be used?
Processing mode	Should manual, batch, or real-time processing be used?
Maintenance	What procedures are needed to maintain data effectively?
Size	How many records will be stored in the database and how large are they? How fast is the number of records expected to grow?
Activity level	What percentage of the records will be added or deleted each year? What percentage will need to be updated?

Input Design

When evaluating input design, the design team must identify the different types of data input and optimal input methods. There are two principal types of data input: forms and computer screens. These two types of input are discussed in the next two subsections. Considerations in input design are shown in Table 18-4.

Table 18-4   Input Design Considerations

Consideration	Concern
Medium	Should AIS data be entered using a keyboard; an OCR, MICR, or POS terminal; EDI; or voice input?
Source	Where do data originate (a computer, customer, remote location, etc.), and how does that affect data entry?
Format	What format (source or turnaround document, screen, source data automation) efficiently captures the data with the least effort and cost?
Type	What is the nature of AIS data?
Volume	How much data are to be entered?
Personnel	What are the data entry operators' abilities, functions, and expertise? Is additional training necessary?
Frequency	How often does AIS data need to be entered?
Cost	How can costs be minimized without adversely affecting efficiency and accuracy?
Error detection and correction	What errors are possible, and how can they be detected and corrected?

Table 18-5   Principles of Good Forms Design

General Considerations
- Are preprinted data used to the maximum extent possible?
- Are the weight and grade of the paper appropriate for the planned use?
- Are bold type, double-thick lines, and shading used appropriately to highlight different parts of the form?
- Is the form a standard size?
- Is the size of the form consistent with requirements for filing, binding, or mailing?
- If the form will be mailed to external parties, is the address positioned so that the form can be used in a window envelope?
- Are copies of the form printed in different colors to facilitate proper distribution?
- Are there clear instructions on how to complete the form?

Introductory Section of Form
- Does the name of the form appear at the top, in bold type?
- Is the form prenumbered consecutively?
- If the form will be distributed to external parties, are the company's name and address preprinted on the form?

Main Body of Form
- Is logically related information (e.g., customer name, address) grouped together?
- Is there sufficient room to record each data item?
- Is the ordering of data items consistent with the sequence in which those items are most likely to be acquired?
- Are standardized explanations preprinted so that codes or check-offs can be used instead of requiring written user entries?

Conclusion Section of Form
- Is space provided to record the final disposition of the form?
- Is space provided for a signature(s) to indicate final approval of the transaction?
- Is space provided to record the date of final disposition or approval?
- Is space provided for a dollar or other numeric total?
- Is the distribution of each copy of the form clearly indicated?

Forms design

Some information systems still capture input data on paper and later transfer those data to a computer medium. Although more and more systems are moving away from the use of paper documents and toward source data automation techniques, forms design is still an important topic. A number of important forms design principles are summarized in Table 18-5. This checklist is a useful tool for evaluating existing forms and designing new ones.

Designing computer screens

When data must be keyed into a system, it is more efficient to enter them directly on a computer screen than on paper for subsequent entry. As a result, it is important to understand how to design computer screens for input as well as for output. Computer screens are most effective when the following principles are used:

➤ Organize the screen so that data can be entered quickly, accurately, and completely. Minimize data input by retrieving as much information as possible from the system. For example, entering a customer number could automatically cause the system to retrieve the customer's name, address, and other key information.

➤ Enter data in the same order as displayed on paper forms used to capture the data.

➤ Complete the screen from left to right and top to bottom. Group logically related data together.

➤ Design the screen so that users either can jump from one data entry location to another using a single key or go directly to screen locations.

➤ Make it easy to correct mistakes. Clear and explicit error messages that are consistent across all screens are essential. There should be a help feature to provide on-line assistance.

➤ Restrict the amount of data on a screen to avoid clutter. Limit the number of menu options on a single screen.

Program Design

Program development is one of the most time-consuming activities in the entire SDLC. Programs should be subdivided into small, well-defined modules to reduce complexity and enhance reliability and modifiability, a process called **structured programming.** Modules should interact with a control module rather than with each other. To facilitate testing and modification, each module should have only one entry and exit point.

To improve the quality of their software, organizations should develop programming standards (rules for writing programs). This contributes to consistency among programs, making them easier to read and maintain. Organizations should also conduct a structured program walk-through to find incorrect logic, errors, omissions, or other problems.

Although accountants need not be computer programmers, they should understand how software is created. Program preparation time may range from a few days to a few years, depending on program complexity.

Following are eight steps for developing software. Step 1 is performed as a part of the systems analysis phase of the systems development life cycle. Step 2 is done during conceptual systems design and may carry over to the beginning of physical design. Most of the effort in steps 3 and 4 is done during systems design and is completed during systems implementation. Steps 5 and 6 are begun in systems design, but most of the work is done during systems implementation. Step 7 is completed during systems implementation and conversion. Step 8 is part of the operation and maintenance phase.

1. *Determine user needs.* Systems analysts consult with users and draw up an agreement about software requirements.

2. *Develop a plan.* A development plan is produced and documented.

3. *Write program instructions (code).* The overall program approach and major processing tasks are identified before each program step is planned in greater detail. Designing a program from the top down to more detailed levels is referred to as **hierarchical program design.** This is where the computer code (or program instructions) is written.

4. *Test the program.* **Debugging** is the process of discovering and eliminating program errors. After a program is coded, a visual and mental review, referred to as **desk checking,** is conducted to discover keying or programming errors. During program compilation, syntax errors are uncovered. A program is tested for logic errors using test data that

simulate as many real processing situations or input data combinations as possible. Test data should include all valid transactions and all possible error conditions. Large programs are often tested in three stages: individual program modules, the linkages between modules and a control module, and interfaces between the program being tested and other application programs. Focus 18-1 discusses the difficulty of testing software and the consequences of releasing software with undetected errors. Many software developers state that 20 to 30 percent of software development costs should be allocated to testing, debugging, and rewriting software.

Focus 18-1

Software Bugs Take Their Toll

AN $18.5 MILLION rocket explodes seconds after liftoff. Telephone networks mysteriously crash in three cities, leaving 10 million customers without service. A nuclear plant releases hundreds of gallons of radioactive water near Lake Huron. These three events have one disturbing fact in common: They were caused by tiny errors (bugs) buried in computer programs. The term "bug" was coined during World War II when a researcher, puzzled by a computer shutdown, removed a moth stuck between two electric relays. Some examples of these electronics pests follow:

- Without warning, Washington, D.C., Los Angeles, and Pittsburgh residents lost local phone service at almost the same time each morning. The culprit was three missing digits in several million lines of programming that control the phone companies' call-switching computers.

- During the Persian Gulf War, a software error prevented a Patriot missile from destroying an incoming Iraqi Scud missile that killed 28 people.

- The American Airlines reservations system shut down for almost 12 hours, crippling 14,000 travel agencies nationwide and forcing American's agents to write tickets by hand.

- A bug in a linear accelerator—a device that uses X-rays to treat cancer victims—caused the accelerator to deliver a radiation overdose, killing one patient and leaving two others deeply burned and partly paralyzed.

- Ashton-Tate, a powerhouse in PC software, never recovered after it shipped bug-filled software.

Where do these bugs originate? To create software, a programmer writes millions of lines of code. One incorrect letter or punctuation mark in a line of code—even a missing period—can cause a computer to issue an incorrect command or no command at all. For instance, a flaw in DSC's call-switching computers sent hundreds of erroneous messages to other DSC computers, asking for assistance in rerouting calls when no help was necessary. The flood of messages shut down the computers and gave callers busy signals for hours.

Bugs exist in most software and are almost impossible to eliminate. A program containing bugs can work adequately for quite some time until suddenly, with no warning, the bug triggers something and the computer suddenly goes haywire.

Programmers go to great pains to detect and eliminate bugs before software is shipped; but no one has the time or money to find every bug, or to simulate the exact situations the computer program will encounter in the real world. It would take 3,000 years to completely test a program with several hundred instructions if one performed 1,000 tests a second. Instead, software is tested with assumptions about how it will be used. Only a certain amount of information—for instance, the number of paychecks to be sent out each Friday—is used to test the program. No one can predict that a few enterprising customers will add more information than the software can handle.

A former Lotus Development product manager estimated that Lotus often found 5,000 bugs in each product. The company would fix serious flaws before shipping the product and ignore minor or cosmetic flaws and those that were highly unlikely to ever cause a problem. If software developers took the time to find every one of these flaws, they would miss getting their product out to market on a timely basis and thus lose market share to competitors able to get their products out on time.

Software developers also cannot predict if computer users will work faster than the software itself.

The linear accelerators that killed and maimed cancer patients were controlled by an operator who typed extremely fast. She accidentally selected the X-ray mode and then switched to the electron beam. The software was not quick enough to recognize the change and the machine beamed radiation at full power to a tiny spot on the patients' bodies. The bug was so subtle it took programmers a year to detect and eliminate it.

The sheer volume of software code needed in a complex program makes finding bugs difficult. There are over 2.5 million lines of code in systems that check for cracks in the engine wheel of a space shuttle and 12 million in a phone company's call-switching computer. Finding a flaw in this code is as difficult as looking for one misspelled name in the New York City phone book.

Source: Adapted from John Schneidawind, "Getting the Bugs Out," *USA Today* (August 29, 1991): 1–2.

5. *Document the program.* Documentation explains how programs work and is used to help correct and resolve errors. Flowcharts, data flow diagrams, record layouts, E-R diagrams, REA data models, narrative descriptions of the system, and related items should be retained as part of program documentation and organized into a meaningful documentation manual.

6. *Train program users.* Program documentation is often used to train users.

7. *Install the system.* All system components, including the programs, are combined and the company begins to use the system.

8. *Use and modify the system.* Factors that require existing programs to be revised, referred to as **program maintenance,** include requests for new or revised reports; changes in input, file content, or values such as tax rates; error detection; and conversion to new hardware.

Procedures Design

Everyone who interacts with the newly designed AIS should follow procedures that answer the who, what, when, where, why, and how questions related to all AIS activities. Procedures should cover input preparation, transaction processing, error detection and correction, controls, reconciliation of balances, database access, output preparation and distribution, and computer operator instructions. Procedures may take the form of system manuals, user instruction classes, training materials, or on-line help screens. Development teams, users, or teams representing both groups may write procedures.

Controls Design

The often-heard adage in the computer industry, "garbage in, garbage out," emphasizes that improperly controlled input, processing, and database functions produce information of little value. Controls must be built into an AIS to ensure its effectiveness, efficiency, and accuracy. They should minimize errors and detect and correct them

Table 18-6 Controls Design Considerations

Consideration	Concern
Validity	Are all system interactions valid? For example, how can the AIS ensure that cash disbursements are made only to legitimate vendors?
Authorization	Are input, processing, storage, and output activities authorized by the appropriate managers? For example, how can the AIS ensure that payroll additions have been authorized?
Accuracy	Is input verified to ensure accuracy? What controls are in place to ensure that data passed between processing activities are not lost?
Security	Is the system protected against (a) unauthorized physical and logical access to prevent the improper use, alteration, destruction, or disclosure of information and software and (b) the theft of system resources?
Numerical control	Are documents prenumbered to prevent errors or intentional misuse and to detect when documents are missing or stolen?
Availability	Is the system available for operation and use at times set forth in service-level statements or agreements? Can users enter, update, and retrieve data during the agreed upon times?
Maintainability	Can the system be modified as required without affecting system availability, security, and integrity? Are only authorized, tested, and documented changes made to the system and related data? Are resources available to manage, schedule, document, and communicate the changes to management and authorized users?
Integrity	Is data processing complete, accurate, timely, and authorized? Is data processing free from unauthorized or inadvertent system manipulation?
Audit trail	Can transaction data be traced from source documents to final output (and vice versa)? For example, if a customer calls with a question, can transaction details be easily accessed?

when they do occur. Accountants play a vital role in this area. Some of the more important control concerns that must be addressed are summarized in Table 18-6. Controls are discussed in greater detail in Chapters 7 through 9.

Physical Systems Design Report

At the end of the physical design phase, the team prepares a **physical systems design report.** (Table 18-8 later in the chapter shows a table of contents for the report prepared at Shoppers Mart.) This report becomes the basis for management's decision whether or not to proceed to the implementation phase.

SYSTEMS IMPLEMENTATION

Systems implementation is the process of installing hardware and software and getting the AIS up and running. This process generally consists of developing a plan, developing and testing software, preparing the site, installing and testing hardware, selecting and

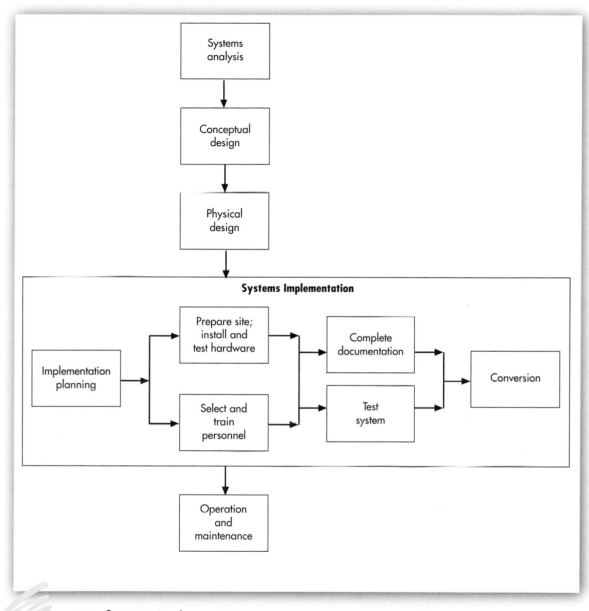

Figure 18-3   Systems implementation

training personnel, developing documentation, and testing the system. These activities are illustrated in Figure 18-3 and are discussed in this section. Systems conversion is discussed later in the chapter.

The state of Virginia has been especially successful in designing and implementing its AIS. In fact, it serves as a model for other governmental agencies. Focus 18-2 describes the improvements the state has made to its AIS.

Focus 18-2

Stars Saves Virginia $80 Million

HUNDREDS of thousands of Virginia taxpayers now receive tax refunds within a week of filing instead of the usual two to three months. They owe the quick turnaround to Jane Bailey, director of AIS at the Department of Taxation. Jane managed the development of the State Tax Accounting and Reporting System (STARS), a multisystem project that took nine years to complete. STARS has been so successful that the IRS, 27 states, and a Canadian province have sent teams to Richmond to see if a little magic might rub off on their own systems development and implementation efforts.

The state's central IT group strongly recommended that the department engage outside contractors for the job, saying Jane's six-person staff was far too small and unsophisticated to overhaul the vast and motley collection of manual and batch systems formerly in place. Jane insisted, however, on going with an inside job. She was able to convince management by letting them know that once the system was developed, she would maintain it and she would be able to respond quickly to tax law changes.

Jane's staff eventually swelled to 45 people. She insisted that these employees be first-rate individuals. If she could not hire the experts and specialists she needed, she retained them as consultants and then used them to train her existing staff. In addition, she recruited five management analysts to redesign business processes, write user documentation, and train users. Ten people from her staff are management analysts who work full-time on user procedures and issues. Seeing user involvement as crucial, Jane succeeded in getting six managers from user areas assigned full time to the project.

Over the years, the scope of STARS expanded to encompass more functions and more users, and its budget climbed from its original $3 million to $11 million. A major new piece of software was installed every three to six months. Users had to adapt, often getting 15 new screens at a time. The megaproject eventually involved putting together 1,500 programs, 40 IBM databases, and 350 on-line screens in 25 applications for 1,800 users.

The state, which asked for a Chevrolet, got a Cadillac; and the payoff has been impressive. STARS users estimate that it saved the state $80 million over five years, most of it from added collections from would-be tax cheats.

Implementation Planning

An **implementation plan** consists of implementation tasks, expected completion dates, cost estimates, and the person or persons responsible for each task. The plan specifies when the project should be complete and when the AIS is operational. The implementation team should identify risk factors that decrease the likelihood of successful implementation, and the plan should contain a strategy for coping with each of the identified risk factors.

Plan for organizational changes

AIS changes may require adjustments to a company's existing organizational structure. New departments may be created and existing ones eliminated or reduced in size. The structure and status of the data processing department itself may change. For example, Blue Cross and Blue Shield of Wisconsin contracted for a new $200 million system. The system—initiated by technical staff who did not understand the company's business or vision—did not work properly. It sent hundreds of checks to a nonexistent town, made $60 million in overpayments, and resulted in the loss of 35,000 clients. One reason the system failed was that its implementation should have included an organizational restructuring.

Site Preparation

A PC, or other small computer, requires little site preparation. A large system may require extensive changes, such as additional electrical outlets, data communications facilities, raised floors, humidity controls, special lighting, and air conditioning. Security measures, such as fire protection and an emergency power supply, also may be necessary. Space is needed for equipment, storage, and offices. Site preparation is a lengthy process and should begin well in advance of the installation date.

Select and Train Personnel

Employees can be hired from outside the company or transferred internally. Hiring from within the company is the less costly, more effective alternative, because employees already understand the firm's business and operations. Transferring employees who are displaced as a result of the new system could boost employee loyalty and morale.

Studies of large companies show that over 90 percent of employees have computers, but more than a third feel they lack the skills necessary to use them adequately. Because effective training is time-consuming and expensive, companies take shortcuts. In addition, those who understand the system are so busy trying to maintain and upgrade it that they lack the time to provide training. When users are not adequately trained, the company will not achieve the expected benefits and return on its investment. The hidden cost of inadequate training is that users turn for help to coworkers who have mastered the system, resulting in less productive coworkers and increased company costs.

Effective AIS training must consist of more than just the hardware and software skills needed to use the new AIS. Employees must be oriented to new policies and operations, and training should be planned and scheduled so it occurs just before systems testing and conversion. Many types of training programs are available to companies: technical training from vendors, self-study manuals, computer-assisted instruction, videotape presentations, role-playing, case studies, and experimenting with the AIS under the guidance of experienced users.

Boots the Chemists, a London-based international pharmacy chain with more than 1,000 stores, developed a novel approach to training. Store employees, nervous about a forthcoming computer system, were invited to a party at a store where a new POS system had been installed. They were asked to try to harm the system by pushing the wrong buttons or fouling up a transaction. Employees quickly found they could not harm the system and that it was easy to use.

Complete Documentation

Three types of documentation must be prepared for new systems:

1. *Development documentation* describes the new AIS. It includes a system description; copies of output, input, and file and database layouts; program flowcharts; test results; and user acceptance forms.
2. *Operations documentation* includes operating schedules; files and databases accessed; and equipment, security, and file retention requirements.
3. *User documentation* teaches users to operate the AIS. It includes a procedures manual and training materials.

Test the System

Inadequate system testing was one reason for the Blue Cross and Blue Shield system failure, described earlier. The developers underestimated the complexity of the system and promised an overly optimistic delivery time of 18 months. One shortcut they took to meet that deadline was to deliver an untested system.

Documents and reports, user input, operating and control procedures, processing procedures, and computer programs should all be given a trial run in realistic circumstances. In addition, capacity limits and backup and recovery procedures should be tested. Following are three common forms of testing:

1. **Walk-throughs** are step-by-step reviews of procedures or program logic. The development team and system users attend walk-throughs early in system design. The focus is on the input, files, outputs, and data flows of the organization. Subsequent walk-throughs, attended by programmers, address logical and structural aspects of program code.
2. **Processing of test transactions** determines if a program operates as designed. Valid and erroneous data are processed to determine if transactions are handled properly and errors are detected and dealt with appropriately. To evaluate test results, the correct system response for each test transaction must be specified in advance.
3. **Acceptance tests** use copies of real transaction and file records rather than hypothetical ones. Users develop the acceptance criteria and make the final decision whether to accept the AIS.

Chemical Bank suffered the consequences of not adequately testing an upgrade to its ATM system. Shortly after its installation, New York customers who withdrew cash from one of the bank's 900 ATMs found their accounts were debited twice. Before the problem could be corrected, 150,000 withdrawals with a total value of $8 million were posted twice to customer accounts. Thousands of small accounts were overdrawn or emptied, which annoyed and angered customers. Chemical Bank lost a great deal of credibility with its customers as a result of the glitch.

Even software purchased from an outside vendor must be tested thoroughly before being installed. Kane Carpets learned this lesson after it installed an AIS custom-tailored to the floor covering industry. No sooner was the software up and running than Kane began experiencing serious problems. For example, its inventory control system told its salespersons that orders could not be filled when the product was in fact available, and vice versa. As a result, Kane lost many of its customers.

SYSTEMS CONVERSION

Conversion is the process of changing from the old AIS to the new. Many elements must be converted: hardware, software, data files, and procedures. The process is complete when the new AIS has become a routine, ongoing part of the system.

Conversion Approaches

Four conversion approaches are used to change from an old to a new system:

> ➤ **Direct conversion** immediately terminates the old AIS when the new one is introduced. For example, Shoppers Mart could discontinue its old system on Saturday night and use its new AIS on Monday morning. Direct conversion is appropriate when the old AIS has no value or the new one is so different that comparisons between the two are meaningless. The approach is inexpensive, but it provides no backup AIS. Unless a system has been carefully developed and tested, therefore, direct conversion carries a high risk of failure. Focus 18-3 discusses the problems at Sunbeam Corp., in part caused by attempting a direct conversion with no backup system.

> ➤ **Parallel conversion** operates the old and new systems simultaneously for a period of time. For example, Shoppers Mart could process transactions with both systems, compare the output, reconcile the differences, and correct problems with the new AIS. After the new system proves itself, Shoppers Mart could discontinue the old system. Parallel processing protects companies from errors, but it is costly and stressful for employees to process all transactions twice. However, because companies often experience problems during conversion, parallel processing has gained widespread popularity.

> ➤ **Phase-in conversion** gradually replaces elements of the old AIS with the new one. For example, Shoppers Mart could implement its inventory system, then disbursements, followed by sales collection, and so forth, until the whole system is functional. These gradual changes mean that data processing resources can be acquired over time. The disadvantages are the cost of creating the temporary interfaces between the old and the new AIS and the time required to make the gradual changeover.

> ➤ **Pilot conversion** implements a system in just one part of the organization, such as a branch location. For example, Shoppers Mart could install its new POS system at one of its stores using a direct, parallel, or phase-in approach. When problems with the system are resolved, the new system could be implemented at the remaining locations. This approach localizes conversion problems and allows training in a live environment. The disadvantages are the long conversion time and the need for interfaces between the old and the new systems, which coexist until all locations have been converted. Owens-Corning Fiberglass implemented its accounts payable, travel and expense, and payroll systems by getting the system up and running in one plant and then moving it to all the others one by one.

Data Conversion

Data conversion can be time-consuming, tedious, and expensive. The difficulty and magnitude of the task can be easily underestimated. Data files may need to be modified in three ways. First, files may be moved to a different storage medium—for

Focus 18-3

Sunbeam Corp. and the Price of Direct Conversion

Sunbeam Corp., a consumer products company, hired new CEO AL Dunlap to turn the company around. While turning Scott Paper Company around, Al made such drastic cost cuts that he was nicknamed Chainsaw Al.

At Sunbeam, Al also made drastic cost-cutting moves, many of which went too far and ended up hurting the company much more than they helped. His restructuring plan called for eliminating 87 percent of the company's products and half of its 6,000 employees. Included in the cost-cutting plan were the information systems staff, as the systems function was to be outsourced. Al terminated computer personnel who were making $35,000 a year only to discover they could earn $125,000 a year elsewhere! He then had to replace them with contract workers who had to be paid significantly more than $35,000. Ironically, some of the contract workers turned out to be terminated employees.

During the turnaround effort, the company decided to modernize its information system. To minimize costs, Sunbeam used a direct conversion approach. Unfortunately, the new system did not work, and since there was no backup system, the entire system was down for months. The result was total chaos. Orders were lost and some customers did not receive their shipments.

Others customers received their orders two or three times, while others received the wrong order.

Customers were very upset and began calling at all hours about their orders. Unfortunately, Sunbeam had no way to respond to them, as employees could not track orders or shipments. With no system, customers who did not receive their orders could not be billed automatically. As a result, Sunbeam had to manually bill its customers. Imagine the headache this was for large customers such as Wal-Mart.

Due to poor management and the lack of an AIS for such a long period of time, the price of Sunbeam's stock plummeted, and in the summer of 1998 Al Dunlap was fired. Shareholder lawsuits were filed and governmental entities, including the SEC, began investigating the company. The SEC is now claiming that Al perpetrated an accounting fraud at Sunbeam. The SEC contends that at least $62 million of the $189 million in income that Sunbeam reported in 1997 did not comply with accounting rules. Arthur Andersen, Sunbeam's auditors, paid out $110 million in damages to settle a shareholder class-action suit filed against the accounting firm. In February 2001, Sunbeam filed for Chapter 11 bankruptcy protection.

Source: John A. Byrne, "Chainsaw," *Business Week* (October 18, 1999): 128–149.

example, from tapes to disks. Second, data content may be changed; for example, fields and records may be added or deleted. Third, file or database format may be changed.

The first step in the data conversion process is to decide which data files need to be converted. Then they must be checked for completeness and any data inaccuracies and inconsistencies should be removed. Actual data conversion is next. Validating the new files, to ensure data were not lost during conversion, follows. If the file conversion is lengthy, the new files must be updated with the transactions that occurred during data conversion. Once the files and databases have been con-

Table 18-7 Factors to Investigate During Postimplementation Review

Factors	Questions
Goals and objectives	Does the system help the organization meet its goals, objectives, and overall mission?
Satisfaction	Are the users satisfied with the system? What would they like changed or improved?
Benefits	How have users benefited from the system? Were the expected benefits achieved?
Costs	Are actual costs in line with expected costs?
Reliability	Is the system reliable? Has the system failed and, if so, what caused its failure?
Accuracy	Does the system produce accurate and complete data?
Timeliness	Does the system produce information on a timely basis?
Compatibility	Are the hardware, software, data, and procedures compatible with existing systems?
Controls and security	Is the system safeguarded against unintentional errors, fraud, and unauthorized intrusion?
Errors	Do error-handling procedures exist, and are they adequate?
Training	Are systems personnel and users adequately trained to support and use the system?
Communications	Is the communications system adequate?
Organizational changes	Are any organizational changes brought about by the system beneficial or harmful? If harmful, how can they be resolved?
Documentation	Is system documentation complete and accurate?

verted and tested for accuracy, the new system is functional. The system should be monitored for a time to make sure it runs smoothly and accurately. The final activity is to document the conversion activities.

OPERATION AND MAINTENANCE

The final step in the SDLC is to operate and maintain the new system. A **postimplementation review** should be conducted on a newly installed AIS to ensure it meets its planned objectives. Some important factors to consider and questions to answer during the postimplementation review are listed in Table 18-7. Any problems uncovered during the review should be brought to management's attention and the necessary adjustments made. When the review has been completed, a **postimplementation review report** is prepared. The table of contents in Table 18-8 illustrates what this report should contain. User acceptance of the postimplementation review report is the final activity in the systems development process. Control of the AIS is passed to the data processing department. Work on the new system is not finished, however.

Table 18-8 Table of Contents for Shoppers Mart Documentation Reports

Shoppers Mart Conceptual Systems Design Report	Shoppers Mart PhysicalSystems Design Report	Shoppers Mart Postimplementation Review Report
Table of Contents	**Table of Contents**	**Table of Contents**
I. Executive Summary of Conceptual Systems Design	I. Executive Summary of Physical Systems Design	I. Executive Summary of Postimplementation Review
II. Overview of Project Purpose and Summary of Findings to Date	II. Overview of Project Purpose and Summary of Findings to Date	II. Overview of Development Project
III. Recommended Conceptual Design(s) of Proposed System	III. Major Physical Design Recommendations	III. Evaluation of the Development
A. Overview of Recommended Design(s)	A. Output Design	A. Degree to Which System Objectives Were Met
B. Objectives to Be Achieved by Design(s)	B. Input Design	B. Analysis of Actual Versus Expected Costs and Benefits
C. Impact of Design(s) on Information System and Organization	C. Database Design	C. User Reactions and Satisfaction
D. Expected Costs and Benefits of Design(s)	D. Software (Processing) Design	IV. Evaluation of Project Development Team
E. Audit, Control, and Security Processes and Procedures	E. Hardware Design	V. Recommendations
F. Hardware, Software, and Other Resource Requirements	F. Controls Design	A. Recommendations for Improving the New System
G. Processing Flows: Relationships of Programs, Databases, Inputs, and Outputs	G. Procedures Design	B. Recommendations for Improving the System Development Process
H. Description of System Components (Programs, Databases, Inputs, and Outputs)	IV. Assumptions and Unresolved Problems	VI. Summary
IV. Assumptions and Unresolved Problems	V. Summary	
V. Summary	VI. Appendixes, Glossary	
VI. Appendixes, Glossary		

Studies show that, over the life of a system, only 30 percent of the work takes place during development. The remaining 70 percent is spent maintaining the system. Most maintenance costs relate to software modifications and updates.

The experience of the Hartford Insurance Group illustrates the cost of maintenance. Approximately 70 percent of its personnel resources are devoted to maintaining existing systems. Hartford must maintain an inventory of 34,000 program modules containing 24 million lines of code. The job is even more difficult because recent changes in insurance regulations and business strategies have reduced the structure of the code and increased its complexity.

SUMMARY AND CASE CONCLUSION

Ann Christy tackled the sales processing portion of the AIS first. She gave the project development team her systems analysis report and accompanying data. During conceptual systems design, the team visited stores with similar operations and identified ways to meet AIS requirements. Alternative approaches were discussed with users, management, and the steering committee and were narrowed down to Ann's original approach. Ann considered buying software but did not find any that did what she and the company wanted to accomplish. The team developed conceptual design specifications for the output, input, processing, and data storage elements.

The company decided to use screen-based output as much as possible and to capture data electronically using POS devices. Data that cannot be captured electronically will be entered using PCs. Each store will have a LAN that connects all its PCs and POS devices to a local database. The POS cash registers will be used to capture and feed sales data electronically to this database. Each store will be linked electronically to the central office using a wide area network. All sales data, store orders, and other summary-level information will be uploaded to the corporate database daily. The corporate database will download the information needed to manage the store. The central office will use EDI to order goods and pay suppliers. The table of contents for the conceptual systems design report is shown in Table 18-8.

During physical design, the development team designed each report identified during conceptual design in screen or hard copy format. The reports were shown to users and reworked until everyone involved was satisfied. The team then designed all files, databases, and input screens. Next came the detailed design of the software programs needed to collect and process data and produce the output. The team also developed new procedures for handling data and operating the AIS. The accountants and the internal audit staff were especially helpful during the design of the controls needed to protect the system against errors and fraud. The physical systems design report table of contents is shown in Table 18-8.

Ann and her staff started implementation planning early. A location for the new mainframe was identified, and site preparation began during the design phase. First the hardware and then the software was installed and tested, followed by testing of the entire AIS. The new AIS was staffed almost exclusively with existing employees trained as the system was tested. System documentation was completed before data from the old AIS was converted to the new one.

Ann and her staff used a variety of conversion approaches. Because corporate-wide mainframe data were vitally important, Ann used a parallel conversion strategy. The new and old systems were operated together for a month, and the results were compared. When the bugs in the new AIS were ironed out, the old AIS was discontinued. A pilot approach was used for the store's AIS. The AIS was installed at several stores and all problems were resolved before implementing the system at the remaining Shoppers Marts. Conversion was not easy and required a fair amount of overtime and duplicate processing. After a few months, Ann and her staff conducted a postimplementation review and made some adjustments to enhance the already high user acceptance of and satisfaction with the new AIS. The table of contents for the postimplementation report is shown in Table 18-8.

Ann made a final presentation to top management after the AIS was installed and operating. She was widely congratulated and even heard the president mention to an executive vice president that she "was worth keeping an eye on" for even more responsibility in the firm.

KEY TERMS

- conceptual systems design
- conceptual design specifications
- conceptual systems design report
- physical systems design
- scheduled reports
- special-purpose analysis reports
- triggered exception reports
- demand reports

- structured programming
- hierarchical program design
- debugging
- desk checking
- program maintenance
- physical systems design report
- systems implementation
- implementation plan
- walk-throughs
- processing of test transactions

- acceptance tests
- conversion
- direct conversion
- parallel conversion
- phase-in conversion
- pilot conversion
- postimplementation review
- postimplementation review report

CHAPTER QUIZ

1. The developers of your new system have proposed two different AIS designs and have asked you to evaluate them. This evaluation process is most likely to be a part of which SDLC step?
   a. systems analysis
   b. conceptual design
   c. physical design
   d. implementation and conversion
   e. operation and maintenance
2. What is the purpose of the conceptual systems design report?
   a. to guide physical systems design activities
   b. to communicate how management and user information needs are met
   c. to help the steering committee assess system feasibility
   d. a and b
   e. a, b, and c
3. Which of the following is the correct order of the steps in physical systems design?
   a. input, file and database, output, controls, procedures, program
   b. file and database, output, input, procedures, program, controls
   c. output, input, file and database, procedures, program, controls
   d. output, file and database, input, program, procedures, controls
4. A monthly payroll register showing all hourly employees, the number of hours they worked, their deductions, and their net pay is most likely which of the following?
   a. scheduled report
   b. special-purpose analysis
   c. triggered exception report
   d. demand report

5. Which of the following is not a consideration in input design?
    a. Which errors are possible and how can they be detected and corrected?
    b. How can data be entered (keyboards, OCR, or POS terminal)?
    c. Which format efficiently captures the input data with the least effort and cost?
    d. How often should the system produce reports and forms?
6. Which of the following procedures is most likely to help improve program development?
    a. physical model
    b. IT strategic plan
    c. walk-through
    d. record layout
7. Which of the following statements is true?
    a. An American Management Systems study revealed that 95 percent of all large systems either are not used, are not used as intended, or generate meaningless reports.
    b. KPMG found that 65 percent of all major information systems projects were classified as runaways—hopelessly incomplete and over budget.
    c. Many software developers state that 35 to 40 percent of software development costs should be allocated to testing, debugging, and rewriting software.
    d. Over the life of a system, only 30 percent of information systems work takes place during development; the remaining 70 percent is spent maintaining the system.
8. Which of the following describes the systems testing approach that uses real transaction and file records rather than hypothetical ones?
    a. walk-through
    b. processing of test transactions
    c. acceptance test
    d. parallel conversion test
9. The process of discontinuing an old system as soon as a new one is introduced is called
    a. direct conversion
    b. parallel conversion
    c. phase-in conversion
    d. pilot conversion
10. Which of the following describes designing a program from the top down to more detailed levels?
    a. hierarchical program design
    b. top-down program design
    c. parallel program design
    d. unstructured program design

DISCUSSION QUESTIONS

18.1   Prism Glass Company is converting from a manual data processing system to a computerized one. To expedite the implementation of the system, the CEO has asked your consulting team to postpone establishing standards and controls until after the system is fully operational. How should you respond to the president's request?

18.2   When a company converts from one system to another, many areas within the organization are affected. Explain how conversion to a new system will affect the following groups, both individually and collectively.
    a. Personnel
    b. Data storage
    c. Operations
    d. Policies and procedures
    e. Physical facilities

18.3   The following notice was posted in the employee cafeteria on Monday morning:

To: All Accounting and Clerical Employees

From: I.M. Krewel, President

Subject: Termination of Employee Positions

Effective this Friday, all accounting and clerical employees not otherwise contacted will be terminated. Our new computer system eliminates the need for most of these jobs. We're grateful for the loyal service you've rendered as employees and wish you success. You may wish to pick up your final checks on Friday before you go.

Discuss the president's approach to human resource management. What are the possible repercussions of this episode? Assuming that job termination is the best alternative available, how would you approach the situation?

18.4   In which phase of the systems development cycle would each of the following positions be most actively involved? Justify your answers.

a. Managerial accountant

b. Programmer

c. Systems analyst

d. Financial vice president

e. Information systems manager

f. Auditor

18.5   During which of the five SDLC stages is each task, labeled a through m, performed? More than one answer may apply for each activity.

1. Systems analysis
2. Conceptual (general) system design
3. Physical (detailed) systems design
4. Implementation and conversion
5. Operation and maintenance

a. Write operating procedures manuals.
b. Develop program and process controls.
c. Identify alternative systems designs.
d. Develop a logical model of the system.
e. Identify external and administrative controls.
f. Test the system.
g. Train personnel.
h. Evaluate the existing system.
i. Analyze the achievement of systems benefits.
j. Modify and alter programs.
k. Analyze total quality management (TQM) performance measures.
l. Conduct a feasibility analysis.
m. Align AIS development plans with business objectives.

PROBLEMS

18.1   The Glass Jewelry Company manufactures costume jewelry. You have just been hired as the management accountant in charge of the accounting and control functions. During your introductory meeting with the president, he outlined your first project: the design and implementation of a new AIS. He stated that the new system must be fully implemented within six months. Total company sales for the past year were $10 million. Sales are expected to double within the next 18 months.

Required

a. Outline the procedures you would follow to complete the assigned project. Your response should include a description of the following:

 1. Various sources of information
 2. Methods of documenting information collected
 3. Methods of verifying the information collected

b. One of the subsystems that you plan to design is the accounts payable system. This system will contain a number of programs, two of which include Enter Invoices and Print Payable Checks. For each of these programs, describe its purpose and outline the application control considerations.

(SMAC Examination, adapted)

18.2 Chaotic order processing at Wang Laboratories had long been accepted by its customers as the cost of doing business with the computer giant. The tremendous growth of Wang throughout the 1970s left the company with a serious revenue tracking problem: Customers would often wait months for Wang to fill orders and process invoices. Repeated attempts by Wang's understaffed AIS department to solve these problems always met with failure.

Finally, Wang Laboratories hired a small consulting organization in 1980 to solve its revenue tracking problems and expedite prompt receipt of payments. The 18-month project turned into a doubly long nightmare. After three years and $10 million, the consultants were dismissed from the unfinished project.

The reasons for the project failure were clear. First, the project was too large and far too complex for the appointed consulting team. According to one consultant, the systems development process was so dynamic that the failure to complete the project quickly was self-defeating, as modifications took over the original design.

Second, management had no clear vision of the new AIS and lacked a strong support staff. As a result, a number of incompatible tracking systems sprang up throughout the company's distributed computer system.

Third, the consulting firm had little experience with the desired technology: a complex database that represented the heart of the new system.

Finally, the project had too many applications. Interdependencies among subprograms and subroutines left consultants with few completed programs. Every program was linked to several subprograms, which in turn were linked to several other programs. Programmers would begin an initial program only to find that several subroutines were necessary. They eventually found themselves lost in a morass of subroutines with no completed program.

Wang's ultimate solution to the crisis came from the internal AIS department. However, the revenue tracking system that the internal staff developed suffered quality problems for years.

Required

The president of Wang Laboratories has asked you, as a member of the AIS staff, to write a memo explaining the failure of the systems development project.

a. Outline the specific reasons for the development failure. What role did the consultants play in the project's failure?
b. Identify the organizational issues that management must address in the future.
c. Recommend any future steps the company could take to guarantee the quality of consulting services.

18.3 Tiny Toddlers Company, a large multinational manufacturer of children's toys and furniture, is planning the design and implementation of a distributed data processing system to assist its sales force. The company has 10 sales offices in Canada and 20 in the United States. The company's sales departments have been set up in a regional structure: Each sales office maintains its own customers and is responsible for granting credit and collecting receivables.

The proposed system will not only permit inquiries, but will also allow entry of daily sales and maintenance of the customer master file. Reports used by each sales office to maintain the customer master file and to enter the daily sales orders are shown in Figures 18-4 and 18-5.

Required

Evaluate the reports shown in Figures 18-4 and 18-5 using the following format.

Report Weakness   Explanation   Recommendation(s)

(SMAC Examination, adapted)

18.4   Mickie Louderman is the new assistant controller of Pickens Publishers, a growing company with sales of $35 million. She was formerly the controller of a smaller company in a similar industry, where she was in charge of accounting and data processing and had considerable influence over the entire computer center operation. Prior to Mickie's arrival at Pickens, the

Figure 18-4   Customer maintenance form for Tiny Toddlers

CUSTOMER MAINTENANCE FORM	
New Customer?	☐
	Yes _____
	☑
	No 24671
Name	The Little Ones Furniture Store
New Address	5 St. Antoine Street N. Quebec City
Old Address	305 St. Antoine Street S. Quebec City
Salesperson #	02
Requested Credit Limit	50,000
Sales Office	Eastern Canada
Pricing Code	25
Estimated Sales	300,000
Credit Limit	10,000
Currency	U.S.A. ☐, Canada ☐
Bank	Canadian Credit Bank 50 St. Antoine Street Quebec City
Bank Line	_____
Rating	Satisfactory
_____ Sales Manager	
_____ Credit Manager	

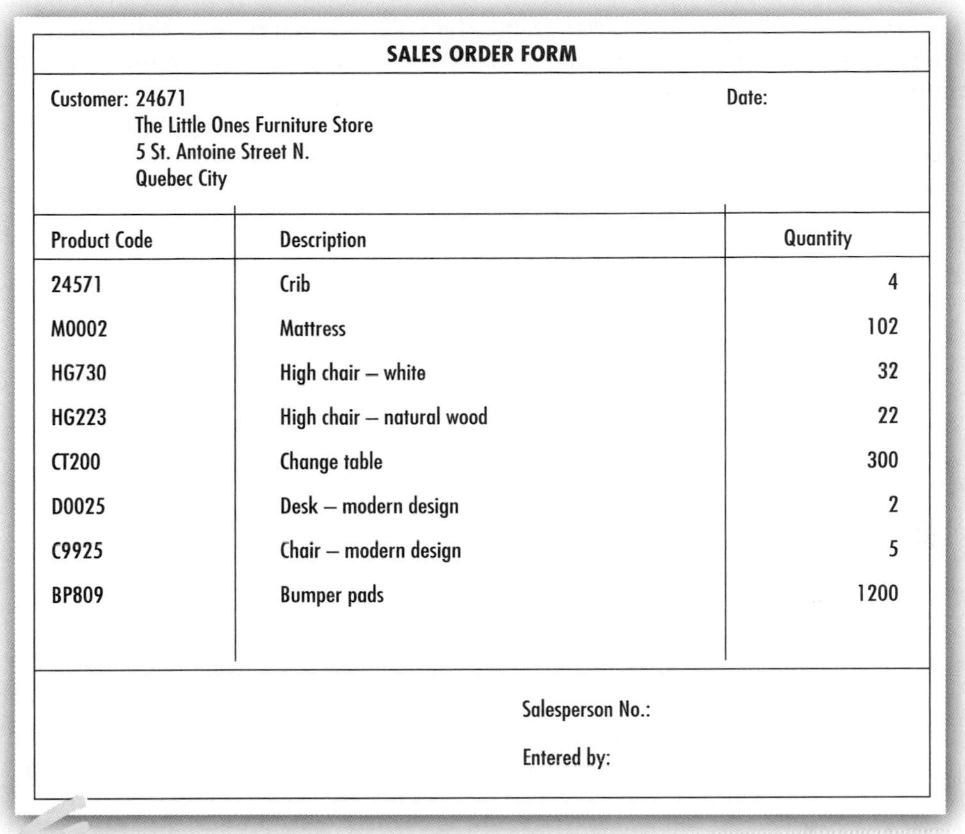

SALES ORDER FORM

Customer: 24671   Date:
      The Little Ones Furniture Store
      5 St. Antoine Street N.
      Quebec City

Product Code	Description	Quantity
24571	Crib	4
M0002	Mattress	102
HG730	High chair – white	32
HG223	High chair – natural wood	22
CT200	Change table	300
D0025	Desk – modern design	2
C9925	Chair – modern design	5
BP809	Bumper pads	1200

Salesperson No.:

Entered by:

Figure 18-5   Sale order form for Tiny Toddlers

company revamped its entire computer operations center, placing increased emphasis on decentralized data access, personal computers with mainframe access, and on-line systems.

John Richards, the controller of Pickens, has been with the company for 28 years and is near retirement. He has given Mickie managerial authority over both the implementation of the new system and the integration of the company's accounting-related functions. Her promotion to controller will depend on the success of the new AIS.

Mickie began to develop the new system by using the same design characteristics and reporting format as she had used at her former company. She sent details of the new AIS to the departments that interfaced with accounting, including inventory control, purchasing, human resources, production control, and marketing. If they did not respond with suggestions by a prescribed date, she would continue the development process. Mickie and John determined a new schedule for many of the reports, changing the frequency from weekly to monthly. After a meeting with the director of computer operations, Mickie selected a programmer to help her with the details of the new reporting formats.

Most of the control features of the old system were maintained to decrease the initial installation time, while a few new ones were added for unusual situations; however, the procedures for maintaining the controls were substantially changed. Mickie appointed herself the decisive authority for all control changes and program testing that related to the AIS, including the screening of control features related to batch totals for payroll, inventory control, accounts receivable, cash deposits, and accounts payable.

As each module was completed, Mickie told the corresponding department to implement the change immediately, to take advantage of the labor savings. However, incomplete instructions accompanied these changes, and specific implementation responsibility was not assigned to departmental personnel. Mickie believes that operations people should learn as they go, reporting errors as they occur.

Accounts payable and inventory control were the initial areas of the AIS to be implemented, and several problems arose in both. Mickie was disturbed that the semimonthly runs of payroll, which were weekly under the old system, had abundant errors and, consequently, required numerous manual paychecks. Frequently, the control totals of a payroll run would take hours to reconcile with the computer printout. To expedite matters, Mickie authorized the payroll clerk to prepare journal entries for payroll processing.

The new inventory control system failed to improve the carrying level of many stock items, causing several critical raw material stockouts that resulted in expensive rush orders. The new system's primary control procedure was the availability of ordering and use information. The information was available to both inventory control and purchasing personnel so that both departments could issue purchase orders on a timely basis. Because the inventory levels were updated daily, Mickie discontinued the previous weekly report.

Because of these problems, system documentation is behind schedule and proper backup procedures have not been implemented in many areas. Mickie has requested budget approval to hire two systems analysts, an accountant and an administrative assistant, to help her implement the new system. John is disturbed by her request, because her predecessor had only one part-time assistant.

Required
a. List the steps Mickie should have taken during the design of the AIS to ensure that end-user needs were satisfied.
b. Identify and describe three areas where Mickie has violated the basic principles of internal control during the implementation of the new AIS.
c. Refer to Mickie's approach to implementing the new AIS.
   1. Identify and describe its weaknesses.
   2. What recommendations do you have that would improve the situation and allow development to continue on the remaining areas of the AIS?

(CMA Examination, adapted)

18.5 Columbia Corporation is a midsize, diversified manufacturing company. Ryon Pulsipher has been promoted recently to manager of the company's property accounting division. Ryon has had difficulty responding to requests from other departments for information about the company's fixed assets. Five of the requests and problems Ryon has been involved with follow:
1. The controller has requested schedules of individual fixed assets to support the balance in the general ledger. Although Ryon has furnished the necessary information, it has always been late. The manner in which the records are organized makes it difficult to obtain information easily.
2. The maintenance manager wishes to verify the existence of a punch press that he thinks was repaired twice. He has asked Ryon to confirm the asset number and location of the press.
3. The insurance department wants data on the cost and book values of assets to include in its review of current insurance coverage.

4. The tax department has requested data that can be used to determine when Columbia should switch depreciation methods for tax purposes.
5. The company's internal auditors have spent a significant amount of time in the property accounting division in a recent attempt to confirm the annual depreciation expense.

The property account records that are at Ryon's disposal consist of a set of manual books. These records show the date the asset was acquired, the account number to which the asset applies, the dollar amount capitalized, and the estimated useful life of the asset for depreciation purposes.

After many frustrations, Ryon realized that his records are inadequate and that he cannot supply data easily when requested. He has decided to discuss his problems with the controller, Gig Griffith.

RYON: Gig, something has to give. My people are working overtime and can't keep up. You worked in property accounting before you became controller. You know that I can't tell the tax, insurance, and maintenance people everything they need to know from my records. Also, the internal auditing team is living in my area and that slows down the work pace. The requests of these people are reasonable, and we should be able to answer their questions and provide the needed data. I think we need an automated property accounting system. I would like to talk with the AIS people to see if they can help me.

GIG: Ryon, I think you have a great idea. Just be sure you are personally involved in the design of any system so that you get all the information you need. Keep me posted on the project's progress.

Required

a. Identify and justify four major objectives Columbia Corporation's automated property accounting system should possess to respond to departmental requests for information.
b. Identify the data that should be included in the computer record for each asset included in the property account.

(CMA Examination, adapted)

18.6 A savings and loan association has decided to develop a new AIS. The internal auditors have suggested planning the systems development process in accordance with the SDLC concept. The following nine items have been identified as major systems development activities that will have to be completed.

1. System test
2. User specifications
3. Conversion
4. System planning study
5. Technical specifications
6. Postimplementation planning
7. Implementation planning
8. User procedures and training
9. Programming

Required

a. Arrange the nine items in the sequence in which they should logically occur.
b. One major subactivity that will occur during system implementation is the conversion of data files from the old system to the new one. Indicate three types of documentation for a file conversion work plan that would be of particular interest to an auditor.

(CMA Examination, adapted)

Case 18-1 AnyCompany, Inc.: An Ongoing Comprehensive Case

Visit a local company and obtain permission to study its systems development approach. Once you have lined up a company, do the following:

1. With a member of the information systems staff, discuss the procedures the company follows in designing and implementing AIS changes.
    a. When a decision is made to change an existing system, how does the company approach conceptual systems design? Who determines which design alternatives are selected? What is the output from conceptual systems design?
    b. How does the company handle the physical design procedures involved in the development of the system? If available, view any documentation or flowcharts used in the development of a prior system.
    c. What implementation strategy does the company employ? What conversion procedures does the company find most

effective in making the transition from an old system to a new one?
2. Obtain the documentation manual for one of the company's software programs. Evaluate the effectiveness of the documentation and identify its strengths and weaknesses. What suggestions do you have for improvement?
3. Summarize the results of your findings in a memo report.
    a. How effective are the company's conceptual and physical design procedures?
    b. How effective are the company's implementation, conversion, operation, and maintenance procedures?
    c. What recommendations do you have for improving the company's AIS development procedures?

Case 18-2 Citizen's Gas Company

Citizen's Gas Company is a midsize gas distribution company that provides natural gas service to approximately 200,000 customers. The

customer base is divided into three revenue classes. Data by customer class is as follows:

Class	Customers	Sales in Cubic Feet	Revenues
Residential	160,000	80 billion	$160 million
Commercial	38,000	15 billion	$ 25 million
Industrial	2,000	50 billion	$ 65 million
		145 billion	$250 million

Residential customer gas use is primarily for residential heating and is thus highly correlated with the weather. Commercial and industrial customers, on the other hand, may use gas for

heating purposes, but consumption does not necessarily depend on the weather.

The largest 25 of the company's 2,000 industrial customers account for $30 million of the industrial revenues. Each of these 25 customers uses gas for both heating and industrial purposes and has a consumption pattern governed almost entirely by business factors.

The company obtains its gas supply from 10 major pipeline companies. The pipeline companies provide gas in amounts specified in contracts that extend over periods ranging from 5 to 15 years. For some contracts, the supply is in equal monthly increments, whereas for others the supply varies in accordance with the heating season. Supply over and above the contract amounts is not available, and some contracts contain take-or-pay clauses—that is, the company must pay for the volumes specified in the contract, regardless of the amount of gas it uses.

To assist in matching customer demand with supply, the company maintains a gas storage field. Gas can be pumped into the storage field when supply exceeds customer demand; likewise, gas can be obtained when demand exceeds supply. There are no restrictions on the use of the gas storage field except that the field must be filled to capacity at the beginning of each gas year (September 1). Consequently, when the contractual supply for the remainder of the gas year is less than that required to satisfy projected demand and replenish the storage field, the company must curtail service to the industrial customers (except for quantities that are used for heating). The curtailments must be carefully controlled so that an oversupply does not occur at year-end. Similarly, care must be taken to ensure that curtailments are adequate during the year to protect against the need to curtail commercial or residential customers, to replenish the storage field at year-end.

In recent years the company's planning efforts have not provided a firm basis for the establishment of long-term contracts. The current year has been no different. Planning efforts have not been adequate to control the supply during the current gas year. Customer demand has been projected only as a function of the total number of customers. Commercial and industrial customers' demand for gas has been curtailed. This has resulted in lost sales and caused an excess of supply at the end of the gas year.

In an attempt to correct the problems at Citizen's Gas, the president has hired a new director of corporate planning. The director has been presented with a conceptual design for a system to assist him in the analysis of the supply and demand of natural gas. The system should provide a monthly gas plan for each year for the next five years, with particular emphasis on the first year. The plan should provide a set of reports that assists in the decision-making process and that contains all necessary supporting schedules. The system must provide for the use of actual data during the course of the first year to project demand for the rest of the year and the year in total. The president has indicated to the director that he will base his decisions on the effect alternative plans have on operating income.

1. Discuss the criteria that must be considered in specifying the basic structure and features of Citizen's Gas Company's new system to assist in planning its natural gas needs.
2. Identify the major data items that should be incorporated into Citizen's Gas Company's new system to provide adequate planning capability. For each item identified, explain why the data item is important, and describe the level of detail that would be necessary for the data to be useful.

(CMA Examination, adapted)

ANSWERS TO CHAPTER QUIZ

1. b	**3.** d	**5.** d	**7.** d	**9.** a
2. e	**4.** a	**6.** c	**8.** c	**10.** a

Glossary

acceptance tests   Tests of new systems using specially developed transactions and acceptance criteria. The test results are evaluated to determine if the system is acceptable.

access control matrix   An internally maintained list that the computer uses to verify that the person attempting to access system resources is authorized to do so. The matrix usually consists of a list of user codes, a list of all files and programs maintained on the system, and a list of the accesses each user is authorized to make.

accounting cycle   The activities corresponding to an organization's major accounting transactions. There are five major accounting cycles: acquisition and cash disbursements, payroll and personnel, sales and collection, capital acquisition and repayment, and inventory and warehousing.

accounting information system (AIS)   The human and capital resources within an organization that are responsible for (1) the preparation of financial information and (2) the information obtained from collecting and processing company transactions. The AIS is a subset of the management information system.

accounts receivable aging schedule   A report listing customer account balances by length of time outstanding; it provides useful information for evaluating current credit policies and for deciding whether to increase the credit limit for specific customers. It also provides information for estimating bad debts.

activity-based costing (ABC)   A cost system that attempts to trace costs to the activities, such as grinding or polishing, that create them, and only subsequently allocates those costs to products or departments.

ad hoc queries   Nonrepetitive requests for reports or answers to specific questions about the contents of the system's data files.

adjusted trial balance   A trial balance prepared after all adjusting entries have been made. The income statement can be produced from the adjusted trial balance.

administrative controls   The plan of organization and all methods and procedures that are concerned with operational efficiency and adherence to managerial policies.

administrative documentation   A description of the overall standards and procedures for the data processing facility, including policies relating to justification and authorization of new systems or systems changes, standards for systems analysis, design, and programming; and procedures for file handling and file library activities.

agents   In the REA data model, the people and organizations that participate in events.

aggression   A way of resisting change that is intended to destroy, cripple, or lessen the effectiveness of a system.   Aggression may take the form of increased error rates, disruptions, or deliberate sabotage.

application   The problem or data processing task to which a computer's processing power is applied.

application controls   Controls that relate to the data input, files, programs, and output of a specific computer application, rather than the computer system in general. Contrast with *general controls*.

application programmer   A person who formulates a logical model, or user view, of the data to be processed and then writes an application program using a programming language.

application service provider (ASP)   A company that provides access to and use of application programs via the Internet. The ASP owns and hosts the software; the contracting organization accesses the software remotely via the Internet.

application software   The programs that perform the data or information-processing tasks required by the user. Common types of application software in accounting include accounts receivable and payable, inventory control, and payroll.

artificial intelligence (AI)   A field of study in which researchers are attempting to develop computers that have the ability to reason, think, and learn like a human being.

691

asynchronous transmission Data transmission in which each character is transmitted separately. A start bit is required before the character and a stop bit after it because the interval of time between transmission of characters can vary. Contrast with *synchronous transmission*.

ATM card A bank card that many businesses accept in lieu of credit and debit cards.

attributes Characteristics of interest in a file or database; the different individual properties of an entity. Examples of attributes are employee number, pay rate, name, and address.

audit committee The committee responsible for overseeing a corporation's internal control structure, financial reporting process, and compliance with related laws and regulations. It is comprised of outside members of the board of directors.

audit hooks Concurrent audit techniques that embed audit routines into application software to flag certain kinds of transactions that might be indicative of fraud.

audit log A log kept on magnetic tape or disk of all computer system transactions that have audit significance.

audit trail A traceable path of a transaction through a data processing system from source documents to final output.

auditing A systematic process of (1) objectively obtaining and evaluating evidence regarding assertions about economic actions and events to ascertain the degree of correspondence between those assertions and established criteria; and (2) communicating the results to interested parties.

authenticity Being able to determine, with almost absolute certainty, who sent a message.

authorization The empowerment of an employee to perform certain functions within an organization, such as to purchase or sell on behalf of the company. Authorization can be either general or specific. *General* authorization is when regular employees are authorized to handle routine transactions without special approval. *Specific* authorization is when an employee must get special approval before handling a transaction.

automated flowcharting program A program that interprets the source code of a program and generates a flowchart of the logic used by the program.

avoidance A way of resisting change by not using the new system.

back order A document authorizing the purchase or production of items for which sufficient quantity is not available to meet customer orders.

back-end (or **lower**) **CASE** These CASE tools support the later SDLC phases. Programmers generate structured program code from database specifications and from screen and report layouts.

backup file Duplicate copy of a current file.

balance-forward method Method of maintaining accounts receivable in which customers typically pay according to the amount shown on a monthly statement, rather than by individual invoices. Remittances are applied against the total account balance, rather than against specific invoices.

balanced scorecard A management report that measures four dimensions of performance: financial, internal operations, innovation and learning, and customer perspectives of the organization.

bandwidths The differences between the highest and the lowest frequencies of a communications channel. Usually expressed in cycles per second (hertz).

bar codes Special identification labels found on most merchandise. A code includes vertical lines of differing widths that represent binary information that is read by an optical scanner.

batch processing Accumulating transaction records into groups or batches for processing at some regular interval such as daily or weekly. The records are usually sorted into some sequence (such as numerically or alphabetically) before processing.

batch totals Sums of the instances of numerical items, calculated for a batch of documents. These totals are calculated prior to processing the batch and are compared with machine-generated totals at each subsequent processing step to verify that the data were processed correctly.

behavioral aspects of change Systems development causes changes in organizations that may result in people changing their behavior. Organizations must be sensitive to and consider the feelings and reactions of persons affected by such changes.

benchmark problem A data processing task that is executed by different computer systems. The results are used to measure systems performance and to make comparative evaluations among systems.

bill of lading   A legal contract that defines responsibility for the goods while they are in transit. It identifies the carrier, source, destination, any special shipping instructions, and indicates which party (customer or vendor) must pay the carrier.

bill of materials   A document that specifies the part number, description, and quantity of each component used in a product.

biometric identification   Using unique physical characteristics such as fingerprints, voice patterns, retina prints, signature dynamics, and the way people type certain groups of characters to identify people.

bits   Binary digits that are the smallest storage location in a computer. A bit may be either "on" or "off," or "magnetized" or "nonmagnetized." A combination of bits (usually eight) is used to represent a single character of data.

bits per second (BPS)   A unit of measurement describing the number of bits of data transmitted electronically in 1 second.

blanket purchase order or **blanket order**   A commitment to purchase specified items at designated prices from a particular supplier for a set time period, often one year.

broadband lines   Communications channels that are capable of handling high-speed data transmissions, usually in the range of 20,000 to 500,000 bps. Their primary use is for high-speed data transmission between computer systems.

budget   The formal expression of goals in financial terms. Budgets are financial planning tools. Contrast with *performance report*.

bus network   Type of network organization in which all devices are attached to a main channel called a "bus." Each network device can access the other devices by sending a message to its address. Each device reads the address of all messages sent on the bus and responds to the messages sent to it.

business cycle   A group of related business processes. The five major business cycles are marketing, purchasing and inventory control, production, personnel, and finance.

business intelligence   The process of accessing the data contained in a data warehouse and using it for strategic decision making. There are two main techniques used in business intelligence:

online analytical processing (OLAP) and data mining.

business process reengineering (BPR)   The thorough analysis and complete redesign of business processes and information systems to achieve dramatic performance improvements.

byte   A group of adjacent bits that is treated as a single unit by the computer. The most common size for a byte is 8 bits. An 8-bit byte can be used to represent an alphabetic, numeric, or special character, or two numeric characters can be "packed" into a single 8-bit byte.

callback system   A routing verification procedure. After the user dials in and is authenticated, the computer disconnects and calls the user back as an additional security precaution.

canned software   Programs written by computer manufacturers or software development companies for sale on the open market to a broad range of users with similar needs.

capacity check   An input validation routine that ensures that data will fit into its assigned field.

capital budgeting model   An estimate of funds to be appropriated for the acquisition of major capital assets and for investment in long-term projects. The estimated benefits are compared with the costs to determine if the system is cost beneficial.

cardinality   A property of a database relationship, indicating the number of occurrences of one entity that may be associated with a single occurrence of the other entity. Three types of cardinalities are one-to-one, one-to-many, and many-to-many.

carrying costs   The costs associated with holding inventory.

cash budget   A budget that shows projected cash inflows and outflows. A cash budget can provide advance warning of cash flow problems in time to permit corrective action to be taken.

cathode ray tube (CRT)   A type of monitor used in some personal computers and computer terminals.

CD-ROM   A storage device that uses laser optics for reading data rather than magnetic storage devices. Although CD-ROM discs are "read only," the discs are useful for storing large volumes of data (roughly 600 megabytes per disc).

central processing unit (CPU)   The hardware that contains the circuits that control the interpretation and execution of instructions and that serves as the principal data processing device. Its major components are the arithmetic-logic unit, the memory, and the control unit.

centralized data processing system All the data processing equipment, personnel, and controls located in the same geographical area.

centralized network A large, centralized computer system that handles a company's data processing needs. Such a system requires complex software and is designed to provide a company with an "economy of scale" advantage in data processing operations.

centralized system Data processing is done at a centralized processing center. User terminals are linked to the centralized host computer so that users can send data to the host computer for processing and access data as needed.

certificate authority An independent organization that issues digital certificates.

character Letters, numeric digits, or other symbols used for representing data to be processed by a computer.

chart of accounts A listing of all balance sheet and income statement account number codes for a particular company.

check digit A redundant digit in a data field that provides information about the other digits in the data field. It is used to check for errors or loss of characters in the data fields as a result of data transfer operations. If data are lost or erroneously changed, the fact that the check digit does not match the other data in the field will signal that an error has occurred.

check digit verification The edit check in which a check digit is recalculated to verify that an error has not been made. This calculation can be made only on a data item that has a check digit.

checkpoint Any one of a series of points during a long processing run at which an exact copy of all the data values and status indicators of a program are captured. Should a system failure occur, the system could be backed up to the most recent checkpoint and processing could begin again at the checkpoint rather than at the beginning of the program.

client/server system An arrangement of a LAN where information requested by a user is first processed as much as possible by the server and then transmitted to the user. Contrast with *fileserver*.

closed-loop verification An input validation method in which data that have just been entered into the system are sent back to the sending device so that the user can verify that the correct data have been entered.

coding (1) Assigning numbers, letters, or other symbols according to a systematic plan so that a user can determine the classifications to which a particular item belongs. (2) Writing program instructions that direct a computer to perform a specific data processing task.

cold site A location that provides everything necessary to quickly install computer equipment in the event of a disaster-stricken organization.

collusion Cooperation between two or more people in an effort to thwart internal controls.

commitments Promises to engage in future economic exchanges.

Committee of Sponsoring Organizations (COSO) A private sector group consisting of the American Accounting Association, the AICPA, the Institute of Internal Auditors, the Institute of Management Accountants, and the Financial Executives Institute.

communications channel The line, or link, between the sender and the receiver in a data communications network.

communications network An information system consisting of one or more computers, a number of other hardware devices, and communication channels linked into a network.

communications software A program that controls the transmission of data electronically over communications lines.

compatibility check (or **compatibility test**) A procedure for checking a password to determine if its user is authorized to initiate the type of transaction or inquiry he or she is attempting to initiate.

compensating controls Control procedures that will compensate for the deficiency in other controls.

completeness test An on-line data entry control in which the computer checks if all data required for a particular transaction have been entered by the user.

computer audit software (CAS) See *generalized audit software*.

computer console A hardware device that computer operators use to interact with large computer systems.

computer crime Any illegal act for which knowledge of a computer is essential for the crime's perpetration, investigation, or prosecution.

computer fraud See *computer crime.*

computer-integrated manufacturing (CIM) A manufacturing approach in which much of the manufacturing process is performed and monitored by computerized equipment, in part through the use of robotics and real-time data collection on manufacturing activities.

computer program See *program.*

computer programmers Persons who develop, code, and test computer programs.

computer programming The process of writing software programs to accomplish a specific task or set of tasks.

computer security The policies, procedures, tools, and other means of safeguarding information systems from unauthorized access or alteration and from intentional or unintentional damage or theft.

computer security officer An employee independent of the information system function who monitors the system and disseminates information about improper system uses and their consequences.

computer system The input/output devices, data storage devices, CPU, and other peripheral devices that are connected together. The software necessary to operate the computer is also considered a part of the system.

computer virus A segment of executable code that attaches itself to an application program or some other executable system component. When the hidden program is triggered, it makes unauthorized alterations to the way a system operates.

computer-aided software (or systems) engineering (CASE) Software used by analysts to document and manage a systems development effort.

computer-based information system Information system in which a computer is used as the data processor; the equipment, programs, data, and procedures for performing a set of related tasks on a computer.

concatenated key The combination of two fields in a database table that together become a unique identifier or key field.

conceptual design specifications Once a conceptual design alternative has been selected, systems requirements are specified for systems output, data storage, input, and processing procedures and operations.

conceptual systems design A phase of the systems development life cycle in which the systems designer proposes a systems design without considering the physical restrictions of particular hardware and software.

conceptual systems design report A document specifying the details of the conceptual systems design that is used by physical systems designers to identify the hardware, software, and procedures necessary to deliver the system.

conceptual-level schema The organization-wide schema of the entire database. It lists all data elements in the database and the relationships between them. Contrast with *external-level schema* and *internal-level schema.*

concurrent audit techniques A software routine that continuously monitors an information system as it processes live data in order to collect, evaluate, and report to the auditor information about the system's reliability.

concurrent update controls Controls that lock out one user to protect individual records from potential errors that could occur if two users attempted to update the same record simultaneously.

configuration For a network, the entire interrelated set of hardware. For a microcomputer, the configuration references the complete internal and external components of the computer including peripherals.

context diagram The highest level of a data flow diagram. It provides a summary-level view of a system. It shows the data processing system, the input and output of the system, and the external entities that are the sources and destinations of the system's input and output.

continuous and intermittent simulation (CIS) A concurrent audit technique that embeds an audit module into a database management system, rather than the application software.

control account The general ledger account that summarizes the total amounts recorded in the subsidiary ledger. Thus, the accounts payable control account in the general ledger represents the total amount owed to all vendors. The balances in the subsidiary accounts payable ledger indicate the amount owed to each specific vendor.

control environment   The organization's environment as related to controls. It consists of many factors, including management's philosophy, the audit committee, and the organizational structure.

control risk   The risk that a significant control problem will fail to be prevented or detected by the internal control system.

control totals   Batch totals used to ensure that all data are processed correctly. Examples are the number of transactions processed and the dollar amount of all updates.

conversion   The process of changing from one form or format to another. See also *data conversion, media conversion, software conversion, system conversion,* and *hardware conversion.*

corrective controls   Procedures established to remedy problems that are discovered through detective controls.

cost driver   Anything that has a cause-and-effect relationship on costs. For example, the number of purchase orders processed is one cost driver of purchasing department costs.

cracking   See *hacking.*

credit limit   The maximum allowable account balance for each customer, based on past credit history and ability to pay.

credit memo   A document authorizing the billing department to credit the customer's account. Usually issued for sales returns, allowances granted for damaged goods kept by the customer, or to write off uncollectible accounts. Approved by the credit manager.

critical path   The path requiring the greatest amount of time to complete a project. If any of the activities on the critical path is delayed, the whole project is delayed. If possible, resources are shifted to critical path activities to reduce project completion time.

cross-footing balance test   A procedure in which worksheet data are totaled both across and down and then the total of the horizontal totals is compared to the total of the vertical totals to ensure the worksheet balances.

cryptography   See *data encryption.*

custom software   Computer software that is developed and written in-house to meet the unique needs of a particular company.

cycle billing   A procedure for producing monthly statements for subsets of customers at different times. For example, the customer master file might be divided into four parts, and each week monthly statements would be prepared for one-fourth of the customers.

data   Characters that are accepted as input to an information system for further storing and processing. After processing, the data become information.

data administrator (DA)   The person responsible for developing general policies and procedures governing all organizational data, not just what is stored in the database. The DA is ultimately responsible for understanding the information needs of the organization to decide what should be included in the database.

data communications   The transmission of data from a point of origin to a point of destination.

data communications network   Communication system that bridges geographical distances, giving users immediate access to a company's computerized data. It also allows multiple companies or computer services to be linked for the purpose of sharing information.

data definition language (DDL)   A database management system language that ties the logical and physical views of the data together. It is used to create the database, to describe the schema and subschemas, to describe the records and fields in the database, and to specify any security limitations or constraints imposed on the database.

data destination   A component of data flow diagrams which represent an entity outside of the system that receives data produced by the system.

data dictionary   An ordered collection of data elements that is essentially a centralized source of data about data. Each data element used in the organization is a record in the data dictionary that contains data about that data element.

data diddling   Changing data before they enter, as they enter, or after they have already been entered into the system. The change can be made to delete data, to change data, or to add data to the system.

data encryption (or **cryptology**)   The translation of data into a secret code for storage or data transmission purposes. Encryption is particularly important when confidential data are being transmitted from remote terminals, because data transmission lines can be electronically monitored without the user's knowledge.

data flow   A component of a data flow diagram that represents a piece of data flowing into or out of a process.

data flow diagram (DFD)   A diagram that concentrates on identifying the types of data and their flow through various types of processing. The physical nature of the data (e.g., physical document, electronic) is ignored; the diagram simply identifies the content of the data, the source, and the destination.

data independence   A data organization approach in which the data and the application programs that use the data are independent. This means that one may be changed without affecting the other.

data leakage   The unauthorized copying of company data, often without leaving any indication that it was copied.

data maintenance   The periodic processing of transactions to update stored data. The four types of data maintenance are additions, deletions, updates, and changes.

data manipulation language (DML)   A database management system language that is used to update, replace, store, retrieve, insert, delete, sort, and otherwise manipulate the records and data items in the database.

data mart   A smaller data warehouse that is built by an organization for various functions such as finance and human resources.

data mining   A method for accessing information stored in a data warehouse by using statistical analysis or artificial intelligence techniques to "discover" relationships in the data.

data model   An abstract representation of the contents of a database.

data modeling   The process of defining a database so that it faithfully represents all key components of an organization's environment. The objective is to explicitly capture and store data about every business activity that the organization wishes to plan, control, or evaluate.

data processing center   The room that houses a company's computer system (the hardware, software, and people who operate the system).

data processing cycle   The operations performed on data in computer-based systems to generate meaningful and relevant information. The data processing cycle has four stages: data input, data processing, data storage, and information output.

data processing schedule   A schedule of data processing tasks designed to maximize the use of scarce computer resources.

data query language (DQL)   A high-level, English-like command language that is used to interrogate a database. Most DQLs contain a fairly powerful set of commands that are easy to use, yet provide a great deal of flexibility.

data redundancy   The storage of the same item of data in two or more files within an organization.

data source   A component of a data flow diagram that represents a source of data outside the system being modeled.

data store   A component of a data flow diagram that represents the storage of data within a system.

data transmission controls   Methods of monitoring the network to detect weak points, maintain backup components, and ensure that the system can still communicate if one of the communications paths should fail.

data value   The actual value stored in a field. It describes a particular attribute of an entity.

data warehouses   Very large databases.

database   A set of interrelated, centrally controlled data files that are stored with as little data redundancy as possible. A database consolidates many records previously stored in separate files into a common pool of data records and serves a variety of users and data processing applications.

database administrator   The person responsible for coordinating, controlling, and managing the data in the database.

database management system (DBMS)   The specialized computer program that manages and controls the data and interfaces between the data and the application programs.

database query language   Easy-to-use programming language that lets the user ask questions about the data stored in a database.

database system   The combination of the database, the database management system, and the application programs that access the database through the database management system.

debit memo   A document used to record an adjustment to the balance due a vendor, reflecting a reduction in the amount owed.

debugging   The process of checking for errors in a computer program and correcting the errors that are discovered.

decentralized system An information processing system that has an independent CPU and a data processing manager at each location.

decision support system (DSS) An interactive computer system designed to help with the decision-making process by providing access to a computer-based database or decision-making model.

decision table A tabular representation of program logic that indicates the possible combinations of logic conditions and the courses of action taken by the computer program for each condition.

deduction register A report listing the miscellaneous voluntary deductions for each employee.

default value A control that helps preserve the integrity of data processing and stored data by leaving a field blank if a standard value is to be used.

delete anomaly A problem that can arise in a poorly designed relational database when attributes that are not characteristics of the primary key of a relation are stored in that table. Deleting a row from that table may result in the loss of all information about those attributes that are not characteristics of the primary key. For example, if customer addresses are only stored in the sales invoice table, then deleting the row representing the only sale to a particular customer results in the loss of all information about that customer.

demand reports Reports that have a prespecified content and format but are prepared only in response to a request from a manager or other employee.

denial-of-service attack An attack that bombards the receiving server with so much information that it shuts down.

desk checking A visual and mental review of a newly coded program to discover keying or program errors.

detection risk The risk that the auditors and their audit procedures will not detect a material misstatement.

detective controls Controls designed to discover control problems soon after they arise.

digest The message used to create a digital signature, which is usually a digital summary of a plaintext business document.

digital certificate Identifies the owner of a particular private key and the corresponding public

key and the time period during which the certificate is valid.

digital fingerprint A hash number that identifies and validates a digital certificate.

digital signature A piece of data signed on a document by a computer. A digital signature cannot be forged and is useful in tracing authorization.

direct access An access method that allows the computer to access a particular record without reading any other records. Because each storage location on a direct access storage device has a unique address, the computer can find the record needed as long as it has the record's address.

direct access storage device (DASD) A storage device (such as a disk drive) that can directly access individual storage locations to store or retrieve data.

direct conversion An approach to converting from one system to another in which the old system is discontinued, after which the new system is started (also known as "burning the bridges" or "crash conversion").

disaster recovery plan Plan that prepares a company to recover its data processing capacity as smoothly and quickly as possible in response to any emergency that could disable the computer system.

disbursement voucher A document that identifies the vendor, lists the outstanding invoices, and indicates the net amount to be paid after deducting any applicable discounts and allowances.

diskette A round piece of flexible magnetic film enclosed within a protective cover. It is a popular storage medium for microcomputers.

distributed data processing (DDP) A system in which computers are set up at remote locations and then linked to a centralized mainframe computer.

document flowchart A diagram illustrating the flow of documents through the different departments and functions of an organization.

documentation Written material consisting of instructions to operators, descriptions of procedures, and other descriptive material. Documentation may be classified into three basic categories: administrative, systems, and operating.

documents Records of transaction or other company data such as checks, invoices, receiving reports, and purchase requisitions.

download   To transmit data or software maintained on a large host (mainframe) computer to a personal computer for use by an individual working at the personal computer.

downsizing   Shifting data processing and problem solving from mainframes to smaller computer systems. Downsizing saves money and allows the end user to be more involved in the processing of the data.

dumpster diving   See *scavenging*.

earnings statement   A report listing the amount of gross pay, deductions, and net pay for the current period; year-to-date totals for each category are also listed.

eavesdropping   When a computer user observes transmissions intended for someone else. One way unauthorized individuals can intercept signals is by setting up a wiretap.

e-business   All uses of advances in information technology, particularly networking and communications technology, to improve the ways in which an organization performs all of its business processes.

echo check   A hardware control that verifies transmitted data by having the receiving device send the message back to the sending device so that the message received can be compared with the message sent.

e-commerce   The electronic execution of business transactions such as buying and selling.

economic espionage   The theft of information and intellectual property.

economic exchanges   An event in which one agent gives a resource to another agent.

economic feasibility   The dimension of feasibility concerned with whether the benefits of a proposed system will exceed the costs.

economic order quantity (EOQ)   The optimal order size so as to minimize the sum of ordering, carrying, and stockout costs. Ordering costs include all expenses associated with processing purchase transactions. Carrying costs are the costs associated with holding inventory. Stockout costs represent costs, such as lost sales or production delays, which result from inventory shortages.

edit checks   Accuracy checks performed by an edit program.

edit programs   Computer programs that verify the validity and accuracy of input data.

electronic commerce   The use of advances in networking and communications technology to improve the ways in which a company interacts with its suppliers and customers.

electronic data interchange (EDI)   The use of computerized communication to exchange business data electronically in order to process transactions.

electronic data processing (EDP)   Processing data utilizing a computer system. Little or no human intervention is necessary while data are being processed.

electronic envelope   A method for protecting e-mail messages by using public or private key techniques to encrypt and decrypt the messages.

electronic funds transfer (EFT)   The transfer of funds between two or more organizations or individuals using computers and other automated technology.

electronic lockbox   A lockbox arrangement in which the bank electronically sends the company information about the customer account number and the amount remitted as soon as it receives and scans those checks. This enables the company to begin applying remittances to customer accounts before the photocopies of the checks arrive.

electronic vaulting   Electronically transmitting backup copies of data to a physically different location. Electronic vaulting permits on-line access to backup data when necessary.

e-mail bomb   A type of denial-of-service attack in which the receiver's e-mail server is bombarded with hundreds of e-mail messages per second.

e-mail forgery   Altering e-mail to make it appear that it came from a different source.

e-mail threats   Unwarranted threats sent to victims by e-mail. The threats usually require some follow-up action, often at great expense to the victim.

embedded audit modules   Special portions of application programs that track items of interest to auditors, such as any unauthorized attempts to access the data files.

embezzlement   The fraudulent appropriation of business property by an employee to whom it has been entrusted. It is often accompanied by falsification of records.

employee fraud   Type of internal fraud in which an employee or group of employees uses company resources for personal gain.

employee goofing   Surfing the Internet for personal entertainment on company time.

end-user computing (EUC) The creation, control, and implementation by end users of their own information system.

end-user development (EUD) When information users develop applications on their own, rather than going through the information systems department.

end-user system (EUS) Information system developed by the users themselves, rather than professionals in the information systems department, to meet their own operational and managerial information needs. An EUS draws upon the information in existing corporate databases to meet users' information needs.

enterprise resource planning (ERP) system A system that integrates all aspects of an organization's activities into one accounting information system.

entity The item about which information is stored in a record. Examples include an employee, an inventory item, and a customer account.

entity integrity rule A design constraint in a relational database, requiring that the primary key have a non-null value. This ensures that a specific object exists in the world and can be identified by reference to its primary key value.

entity-relationship (E-R) diagram A graphical depiction of a database's contents. It shows the various entities being modeled and the important relationships among them. An entity is any class of objects about which data are collected. Thus, the resources, events, and agents that comprise the REA data model are all entities. An E-R diagram represents entities as rectangles; lines and diamonds represent relationships between entities.

error log The record of data input and data processing errors.

error message A message from the computer indicating that it has encountered a mistake or malfunction.

error report A report summarizing errors by record type, error type, and cause.

evaluated receipt settlement (ERS) An "invoice-less" approach to the accounts payable process. ERS replaces the traditional three-way matching process (vendor invoice, receiving report, and purchase order) with a two-way match of the purchase order and receiving report. ERS saves time and money by reducing the number of potential mismatches. ERS also saves suppliers the time and expense of generating and tracking invoices.

events In the REA data model, the various business activities about which management wants to collect information.

executive information system (EIS) Information system designed to provide executives with the needed information to make strategic plans, to control and operate the company, to monitor business conditions in general, and to identify business problems and opportunities.

expected loss A measure of loss based on the potential loss associated with a control problem and the risk, or probability, that the problem will occur.

expenditure cycle A recurring set of business activities and related data processing operations associated with the purchase of and payment for goods and services.

expert system (ES) A computerized information system that allows nonexperts to make decisions about a particular problem that are comparable with those of experts in the area.

exposure A measure of risk derived by multiplying the potential magnitude of an error, in dollars, by the error's estimated frequency (probability) of occurrence.

external label A label on the outside of a magnetic storage medium (e.g., tape or disk) that identifies the data contained on the storage medium.

external-level schema An individual user's or application program's view of a subset of the organization's database. Each of these individual user views is also referred to as a subschema. Contrast with *conceptual-level schema* and *internal-level schema*.

extranet The term used for the linked intranets of two or more companies.

fault tolerance The capability of a system to continue performing its functions in the presence of a hardware failure.

feasibility study An investigation to determine if the development of a new application or system is practical. This is one of the first steps in the systems evaluation and selection process.

feedback Informational output of a process that returns as input to the process, initiating the actions necessary for process control.

field The part of a data record that contains the data value for a particular attribute. All records of a particular type usually have their fields in the same order. For example, the first field in all accounts receivable records may be reserved for the customer account number.

field check   An edit check in which the characters in a field are examined to ensure they are of the correct field type (e.g., numeric data in numeric fields).

file   A set of logically related records, such as the payroll records of all employees.

file access   The way the computer finds or retrieves each record it has stored.

file maintenance   The periodic processing of transaction files against a master file. This maintenance, which is the most common task in virtually all data processing systems, includes record additions, deletions, updates, and changes. After file maintenance, the master file will contain all current information.

file organization   The way data are stored on the physical storage media. File organization may be either sequential or direct (random, nonsequential, or relative).

File-server   An arrangement of a LAN where an entire file is sent to the user and then processed by the user, not the server. Contrast with *client-server system.*

financial audit   A review of the reliability and integrity of financial and operating information and the means used to identify, measure, classify, and report such information.

financial electronic data interchange (FEDI)   The combination of EFT and EDI that enables both remittance data and funds transfer instructions to be included in one electronic package.

financial total   The total of a dollar field, such as total sales, in a set of records. It is usually generated manually from source documents prior to input and compared with machine-generated totals at each subsequent processing step. Any discrepancy may indicate a loss of records or errors in data transcription or processing.

financial value-added network (FVAN)   An independent organization that offers specialized hardware and software to link various EDI networks with the banking system for EFT.

financing cycle   A recurring set of business activities and related data processing operations associated with obtaining the necessary funds to run the operations, repay creditors, and distribute profits to investors.

firewall   A combination of security algorithms and router communications protocols that prevent outsiders from tapping into corporate databases and e-mail systems.

flexible benefits plan   A plan under which each employee receives some minimum coverage in medical insurance and pension contributions, plus additional benefit "credits" that can be used to acquire extra vacation time or additional health insurance. These plans are sometimes called cafeteria-style benefit plans because they offer a menu of options.

flowchart   A diagrammatical representation of the flow of information and the sequence of operations in a process or system.

flowcharting symbols   A set of objects that are used in flowcharts to show how and where data move. Each symbol has a special meaning that is easily conveyed by its shape.

flowcharting template   A piece of hard, flexible plastic on which the shapes of flowcharting symbols have been diecut.

Foreign Corrupt Practices Act (1977)   Among other things, requires all publicly owned corporations subject to the Securities Exchange Act of 1934 to keep reasonably detailed records and maintain an internal accounting control system.

foreign key   An attribute appearing in one table that is itself the primary key of another table.

forensic accountants   Accountants who specialize in fraud auditing and investigation. Upon qualification, forensic accountants may receive a Certified Fraud Examiner (CFE) certificate.

fraud   Any and all means a person uses to gain an unfair advantage over another person.

fraudulent financial reporting   Intentional or reckless conduct, whether by act or omission, that results in materially misleading financial statements.

freight bill   A document that indicates the amount the customer should pay to the carrier for delivered goods. May be either a separate document or a copy of the bill of lading.

front-end (or upper) CASE   These CASE tools support the early stages of the SDLC, such as analysis and design.

Gantt chart   A bar graph used for project planning and control. Project activities are shown on the left, and units of time are shown across the top. The time period over which each activity is expected to be performed is represented with a horizontal bar on the graph.

general authorization When regular employees are authorized to handle routine transactions without special approval.

general controls Controls that relate to all or many computerized accounting activities, such as those relating to the plan of organization of data processing activities and the separation of incompatible functions. Contrast with *application controls*.

general journal The general journal is used to record infrequent or nonroutine transactions, such as loan payments and end-of-period adjusting and closing entries.

general journal listing A report showing the details (account number, source reference code, description, and amount debited or credited) of each entry posted to the general ledger.

general ledger Contains summary-level data for every asset, liability, equity, revenue, and expense account of the organization.

general ledger and reporting system The information-processing operations involved in updating the general ledger and preparing reports that summarize the results of the organization's activities.

generalized audit software (GAS) A software package that performs audit tests on the data files of a company.

goal conflict Occurs when a decision or action of one subgoal or subsystem is inconsistent with another subgoal or subsystem.

goal congruence Occurs when employees can achieve their assigned subgoals while contributing to the achievement of their organization's overall goal.

grandfather-father-son concept A method for maintaining backup copies of files on magnetic tape or disk. The three most current copies of the data are retained, with the son being the most recent.

graphical user interface (GUI) Operating environment where the user selects commands, starts programs, or lists files by pointing to pictorial representations (icons) with a mouse. A Macintosh computer, Microsoft's Windows, and IBM's OS/2 are all GUI environments.

group decision support software (GDSS) Software that encourages and allows everyone in a group to participate in decision making. A GDSS brings a group of people together to share information, exchange ideas, explore differing points of views, examine proposed solutions, arrive at a consensus, or vote on a course of action.

groupware Software that combines the power of computer networks with the immediacy and personal touch of the face-to-face brainstorming session. Groupware lets users hold computer conferences, decide when to hold a meeting, make a calendar for a department, collectively brainstorm on creative endeavors, manage projects, and design products.

hacking Unauthorized access and use of computer systems, usually by means of a personal computer and telecommunications networks.

hard disk A magnetic storage disk made of rigid material and enclosed in a sealed disk unit to reduce the chances of the magnetic medium being damaged by foreign particles. A hard disk has a much faster access time and greater storage capacity than a floppy disk.

hardware Physical equipment or machinery used in a computer system.

hash total A total generated from values for a field that would not usually be totaled, such as customer account numbers. It is usually generated manually from source documents prior to input and compared with machine-generated totals at each subsequent processing step. Any discrepancy may indicate a loss of records or errors in data transcription or processing.

header label Type of internal label that appears at the beginning of each file and contains the file name, expiration date, and other file identification information.

help desk An in-house group of analysts and technicians who answers employees' questions with the purpose of encouraging, supporting, coordinating, and controlling end-user activity.

hierarchical network A variation of the star network. The configuration looks like a hierarchical organization chart.

hierarchical organization structure An organizational structure created by subdividing organizational goals and tasks into a graded series of lower-level goals and tasks.

hierarchical program design The process of designing a program from the top level down to the detailed level.

home page A "storefront" or site on the Internet that is set up by individuals and firms to provide useful and interesting information about the individual or firm.

hot site Completely operational data processing facility configured to meet the user's requirement that can be made available to a disaster-stricken organization on short notice.

human resources (payroll) cycle The recurring set of business activities and related data processing operations associated with effectively managing the employee workforce.

impersonation See *masquerading*.

implementation The process of installing a computer. It includes selecting and installing the equipment, training personnel, establishing operating policies, and getting the software onto the system and functioning properly.

implementation and conversion The capstone phase in the SDLC where the elements and activities of the system come together. Implementation includes installing and testing new hardware and software, hiring and training employees, and testing new processing procedures. Standards and controls must be established and documented. The final step, conversion, consists of dismantling the old system and converting it into the new one.

implementation plan A written plan that outlines how the new system will be implemented. The plan includes a timetable for completion, who is responsible for each activity, cost estimates, and task milestones.

imprest fund A cash account with two characteristics: (1) It is set at a fixed amount, such as $100, and (2) vouchers are required for every disbursement. At all times, the sum of cash plus vouchers should equal the preset fund balance.

index file A master file of record identifiers and corresponding storage locations.

index sequential access method (ISAM) A file organization and access approach in which records are stored in sequential order by their primary key on a direct access storage device. An index file is created, which allows the file to be accessed and updated randomly.

information Data that have been processed and organized into output that is meaningful to the person who receives it. Information can be mandatory, essential, or discretionary.

information overload The state in which additional information cannot be used efficiently and has no marginal value.

information processing The process of turning data into information. This process has four stages: data input, data processing, data storage, and information output.

information system An organized way of collecting, processing, managing, and reporting information so that an organization can achieve its objectives and goals. Formal information systems have an explicit responsibility to produce information. In contrast, an informal information system is one that arises out of a need that is not satisfied by a formal channel. It operates without a formal assignment of responsibility.

information systems audit Reviews the general and application controls of an AIS to assess its compliance with internal control policies and procedures and its effectiveness in safeguarding assets.

inherent risk The susceptibility of a set of accounts or transactions to significant control problems in the absence of internal control.

initial investigation A preliminary investigation to determine if a proposed new system is both needed and possible.

input Data entered into the computer system either from an external storage device or from the keyboard of the computer.

input controls Ensure that only accurate, valid, and authorized data is entered into the system.

input controls matrix A matrix that shows the control procedures applied to each field of an input record.

input device Hardware used to enter data into the computer system.

input validation routines Computer programs or routines designed to check the validity or accuracy of input data.

input/output bound Describes a system that can process data faster than it can receive input and send output. Consequently the processor has to wait on the I/O devices.

inquiry processing Processing user information queries by searching master files for the desired information and then organizing the information into an appropriate response.

insert anomaly A problem that can arise in a poorly designed relational database when attributes that are not characteristics of the primary key of a relation are stored in that table. The problem is that new information about those attributes cannot be entered in the database without violating the integrity rules. For example, assume that information about vendors is only stored as part of the purchases table. Data about potential new vendors, or about alternate suppliers, could not be added until a purchase from them was made. Otherwise, the purchase order number column, the primary key of the purchases table, would have a null value, violating the entity integrity rule.

integrated CASE   A software package that combines upper and lower CASE tools, linked by the data repository.

Integrated Circuits   Small silicon chips that contain the circuitry used by the computer.

Integrated Services Digital Network (ISDN)   An extensive digital network with built-in intelligence to permit all types of data (voice, data, images, facsimile, video, etc.) to be sent over the same line.

integrated test facility   A testing technique in which a dummy company or division is introduced into the company's computer system. Test transactions may then be conducted on these fictitious master records without affecting the real master records. These test transactions may be processed along with the real transactions, and the employees of the computer facility need not be aware that testing is being done.

Integration   The combining of subsystems.

Integrity   Protecting data from unauthorized tampering.

Interface   The common boundary between two pieces of hardware or between two computer systems. It is the point at which the two systems communicate with each other.

Interface Devices   Devices used by computer systems to communicate with each other. Examples include modems, hubs, and network interface cards.

internal control flowchart   A type of flowchart that shows the internal control structure of a company. Often used by auditors in the planning stage of an audit.

internal control structure   The plan of organization and all the coordinate methods and measures adopted within a business to safeguard its assets, check the accuracy and reliability of its accounting data, promote operational efficiency, and encourage adherence to prescribed managerial policies.

internal controls   Controls within a business organization that ensure information is processed correctly.

internal labels   Labels written in machine-readable form on a magnetic storage medium (e.g., tape or disk) that identify the data contained on the storage medium. Internal labels include volume, header, and trailer labels.

internal rate of return (IRR)   The effective interest rate that equates the present value of the total costs to the present value of the total savings.

internal-level schema   A low-level view of the entire database describing how the data are actually stored and accessed. It includes information about pointers, indexes, record lengths, and so forth. Contrast with *external-level schemas* and *conceptual-level schemas.*

Internet   An international network of independently owned computers that operate as a giant, seamless computing network. No one owns it and no single organization controls its use. Data are not centrally stored but are stored on computers called Web servers.

Internet misinformation   False or misleading information spread using the Internet.

Internet service providers (ISPs)   Companies that provide connections to the Internet for individuals and other companies. Major ISPs include MCI, GTE, and Sprint.

Internet terrorism   Crackers using the Internet to disrupt electronic commerce and destroy company and individual communications.

intranet   An internal network that can connect to the main Internet and be navigated with simple browser software. It is usually closed off from the general public.

inventory control   The function of determining what, when, and how much inventory to purchase.

inverted file   A file containing inverted lists for selected attributes.

inverted list   A method for organizing records in a database. An inverted list has an index containing pointers to each record.

job-order costing   A cost system that assigns costs to specific production batches or jobs; it is used when the product or service being sold can be distinctly identified.

job-time ticket   A document used to collect data about labor activity, recording the amount of time a worker spent on each specific job task.

journal voucher Form that is used to summarize a group of transactions. For example, a group of documents would be gathered and their total entered on the journal voucher.

just-in-time (JIT) inventory system A system that minimizes or virtually eliminates manufacturing inventories by scheduling inventory deliveries at the precise times and locations needed. Instead of making infrequent bulk deliveries to a central receiving and storage facility, suppliers deliver materials in small lots at frequent intervals to the specific locations that require them.

just-in-time (JIT) manufacturing Manufacturing systems with short planning horizons whose goal is to minimize or eliminate inventories of raw materials, work in process, and finished goods. JIT is often referred to as pull manufacturing because goods are produced in response to customer demand. Theoretically, JIT manufacturing systems produce only in response to customer orders. In practice, however, most JIT manufacturing systems develop short-run production plans.

key A unique identification code assigned to each data record within a system.

key verification Method used to check the accuracy of data entry by having two people enter the same data using a key-operated device. The computer then compares the two sets of keystrokes to determine if the data were entered correctly.

key-to-disk encoder Several keying stations are linked to a minicomputer that has an attached disk memory. Data may be entered simultaneously from each of the key stations and pooled on the disk file.

key-to-tape encoder A device for keying in data and recording the data on magnetic tape.

kickbacks Gifts given by vendors to purchasing agents for the purpose of influencing their choice of suppliers.

kiting Fraud scheme in which the perpetrator conceals a theft of cash by creating cash through the transfer of money between banks.

LAN See *local area network*.

LAN interface The hardware device that interfaces between the local area network (LAN) cable and the hardware devices (computers, printers, etc.) connected to the LAN.

lapping Concealing a cash shortage by means of a series of delays in posting collections to accounts.

legal feasibility The dimension of feasibility that determines if there will be any conflicts between the system under consideration and the organization's ability to discharge its legal obligations.

limit check An edit check to ensure that a numerical amount in a record does not exceed some predetermined limit.

line count Total number of lines entered during a data processing session.

linked list A method for organizing records in a database. Each record includes a pointer field containing the address of the next record on the list.

local area network (LAN) A network that links microcomputers, disk drives, word processors, printers, and other equipment located within a limited geographical area, such as one building.

lockbox A postal address to which customers send their remittances. This post office box is maintained by the participating bank, which picks up the checks several times each day and deposits them to the company's account. The bank then sends the remittance advices, an electronic list of all remittances, and photocopies of all checks to the company.

logic errors Errors that occur when the instructions given to the computer do not accomplish the desired objective. Contrast with *syntax errors*.

logic time bomb A program that lies idle until some specified circumstance or a particular time triggers it. Once triggered, the bomb sabotages the system by destroying programs or data.

logical access The ability to use computer equipment to access company data.

logical models Descriptions of a system that focus on the essential activities and flow of information in the system, irrespective of how the flow is actually accomplished.

logical view The manner in which users conceptually organize, view, and understand the relationships among data items. Contrast with *physical view*.

logistics management The planning and control of the physical flow of materials through an organization, through purchasing, inventory management, and production management.

macro   (1) A series of keystrokes or commands that can be given a name, stored, and activated each time the keystrokes must be repeated; (2) programming command.

magnetic disks   Magnetic storage media consisting of one or more flat round disks with a magnetic surface on which data can be written.

magnetic ink character recognition (MICR)   The recognition of characters printed by a machine that uses special magnetic ink.

magnetic tape   A secondary storage medium that is about 1/2 inch in width and that has a magnetic surface on which data can be stored. The most popular types are seven-track and nine-track tapes.

main memory   The internal memory directly controlled by the CPU, which usually consists of the ROM and RAM of the computer.

mainframe computers   (1) Same as CPU. (2) Large digital computers, typically with a separate stand-alone CPU. They are larger than minicomputers.

management audit   A review of how well management is utilizing company resources and how well company operations and programs follow established objectives and are being carried out as planned.

management by exception   A method for interpreting variances displayed on performance reports. If the performance report shows actual performance to be at or near budgeted figures, a manager can assume that the item is under control and that no action needs to be taken. On the other hand, significant deviations from budgeted amounts, in *either* direction, signal the need to investigate the cause of the discrepancy and take appropriate action to correct the problem.

management control   Activities by management designed to motivate, encourage, and assist officers and employees to achieve corporate goals and objectives as effectively and efficiently as possible and to observe corporate policies.

management information system   The set of human and capital resources in an organization that are dedicated to collecting and processing data so that all levels of management have the information they need to plan and control the activities of the organization.

manual information system   Information system in which most of the data processing load is completed by people without the use of computers.

manufacturing overhead   All manufacturing costs that are not economically feasible to trace directly to specific jobs, or processes.

manufacturing resource planning (MRP-II)   A comprehensive, computerized planning and control system for manufacturing operations. It is an enhancement of materials requirements planning that incorporates capacity planning for factory work centers and scheduling of production operations.

many-to-many (M:N) relationship   A relationship between two entities where the maximum cardinality for both entities in the relationship is many (N).

mapping programs   Programs activated during regular processing that provide information as to which portions of the application program were not executed.

masquerading   When a perpetrator gains access to a system by pretending to be an authorized user. This approach requires that the perpetrator know the legitimate user's identification numbers and passwords.

master file   A permanent file of records that reflects the current status of relevant business items such as inventory and accounts receivable. The master file is updated with the latest transactions from the current transaction file.

master plan   A document specifying the overall information system plan of an organization.

master production schedule (MPS)   Specifies how much of each product is to be produced during the planning period, and when that production should occur.

materiality   The concept that an auditor should focus on detecting and reporting only those errors, deficiencies, and omissions that could possibly have a significant impact on decisions.

materials requirements planning (MRP)   An approach to inventory management that seeks to reduce required inventory levels by *scheduling* production to meet sales forecast demands, rather than *estimating* needs.

materials requisition   Authorizes the removal of the necessary quantity of raw materials from the storeroom to the factory location in which production operations are to begin.

maximum cardinality   The second symbol in a cardinality pair next to an entity in the REA data model. It represents the maximum number of occurrences on the other side of the relationship that can be linked to each occurrence on the entity's side.

message   (1) The data transmitted over a data communication system. (2) The instructions that are given to an object in object-oriented languages.

minimum cardinality   The first symbol in the cardinality pair next to an entity in the REA data model. It represents the minimum number of occurrences on the other side of the relationship that need to be linked to each occurrence on the entity's side.

misappropriation of assets   See *employee fraud.*

modem   Modulator/demodulator, a communications device that converts the computer's digital signals into analog signals that can be sent over phone lines. The modem can be internal (mounted on a board within the computer) or external (a freestanding unit).

modified canned software   Canned software that has been modified to meet the particular needs of the user.

modular conversion   An approach for converting from an old system to a new system in which parts of the old system are gradually replaced by the new until the old system has been entirely replaced by the new.

monitor   (1) A video display unit or CRT. (2) Software that controls how a system operates.

monthly statement   A document summarizing all transactions that occurred during the past month and informing customers of their current account balance.

move tickets   Documents that identify the internal transfer of parts, the location to which they are transferred, and the time of the transfer.

multiattribute search file organization   A file organization scheme that allows data records to be accessed by means of secondary keys. Examples include linked lists and inverted lists.

multimedia   Computer-based applications that combine text, 3-D graphics, full-screen video, sound, and animation.

mutual authentication scheme   A routing verification procedure that requires both computers to exchange their passwords before communication takes place.

narrative description   Written, step-by-step explanation of the system components and how the components interact.

narrowband lines   Phone lines designed to accept data transmissions of up to 300 bps. This type of line is not suitable for transmitting audible or voicelike signals.

net present value (NPV)   A value determined by discounting all estimated future cash flows back to the present, using a discount rate that reflects the time value of money to the organization.

network   (1) A group of interconnected computers and terminals; a series of locations tied together by communications channels. (2) A data structure involving relationships among multiple record types.

network administrator   One who installs, manages, and supports a LAN. The network administrator also controls access to the system and maintains the shared software and data.

network interface card (NIC)   The device needed to connect a computer or peripheral to a data communications network.

neural networks   Computing systems that imitate the brain's learning process by using a network of interconnected processors that perform multiple operations simultaneously and interact dynamically. Neural networks recognize and understand voice, face, and word patterns much more successfully than do regular computers and humans.

nonoperational (or **throwaway**) **prototypes**   Prototypes that are discarded, but the system requirements identified from the prototypes are used to develop a new system.

nonvoucher system   A method for processing accounts payable in which each approved invoice is posted to individual vendor records in the accounts payable file and is then stored in an open invoice file. Contrast with *voucher system.*

normalization   The process of following the guidelines for properly designing a relational database that is free from delete, insert, and update anomalies.

off-line devices   Devices that are not connected to or controlled by the main CPU. Off-line devices are used to prepare data for entry into the computer system (e.g., key-to-tape encoder, keypunch/verification equipment). Contrast with *on-line devices.*

one-to-many (1:N) relationship   A relationship between two entities where the maximum cardinality of one entity in the relationship is one

(1) and the maximum cardinality for the other entity in that relationship is many (N).

one-to-one (1:1) relationship   A relationship between two entities where the maximum cardinality for each entity in the relationship is one (1).

on-line analytical processing (OLAP)   Tools that provide access to information stored in a data warehouse by using queries to investigate hypothesized relationships.

on-line batch processing   Processing in which the computer captures the data electronically and stores it so that it can be processed later.

on-line devices   Hardware devices that are connected directly to the CPU by cable or telephone line (e.g., CRT terminal, disk drive).

on-line processing   Processing individual transactions as they occur and from their point of origin rather than accumulating them to be processed in batches. Online processing requires the use of online data entry terminals and direct access file storage media so that each master record can be accessed directly.

on-line, real-time processing   The computer system processes data immediately after capture and provides updated information to the user on a timely basis. On-line, real-time processing usually entails one of two forms of processing: on-line updating and inquiry processing.

open-invoice method   Method for maintaining accounts receivable in which customers typically pay according to each invoice. Usually two copies of the invoice are mailed to the customer, who is requested to return one copy with the payment.

operating budget   A report that projects an organization's revenues and expenses for a given time period, usually a month or a year. Typically, operating budgets are structured along the lines of financial statements.

operating documentation   All information required by a computer operator to run a program, including the equipment configuration used, variable data to be entered on the computer console, and descriptions of conditions leading to program halts and related corrective actions.

operating system   A software program that controls the overall operation of a computer system. Its functions include controlling the execution of computer programs, scheduling, debugging, assigning storage areas, managing data, and controlling input and output.

operational audit   See *management audit.*

operational control   Decisions that are concerned with the efficient and effective performance of specific tasks in an organization.

operational document   A document that is generated as an output of transaction processing activities. Examples include purchase orders, customer statements, and employee paychecks. Contrast with *source document.*

operational feasibility   The dimension of feasibility concerned with whether a proposed system will be used by the people in an organization. It also is concerned with how useful the system will be within the operating environment of the organization.

operational prototypes   Prototypes that are further developed into fully functional systems.

operations and maintenance   The last phase of the system development life cycle where follow-up studies are conducted to detect and correct design deficiencies. Minor modifications will be made as problems arise in the new system.

operations list   A document that specifies the labor and machine requirements needed to manufacture the product. Also referred to as a routing sheet because it indicates how a product moves through the factory, specifying what is done at each step and how much time each operation should take.

opportunity   The condition or situation that allows a person to commit and conceal a dishonest act.

Optical Character Recognition (OCR)   The use of light-sensitive hardware devices to convert characters readable by humans into computer input. Since OCR readers can read only certain items, a special machine-readable font must be used.

optical disk   A mass storage medium that is capable of storing billions of bits. Lasers are used to write to and read from an optical disk.

output   The information produced by a system. Output is typically produced for the use of a particular individual or group of users.

output controls   Controls that regulate system output.

outsourcing   Hiring an outside company to handle all or part of the data processing activities.

packing slip   A document identifying the contents of the shipment.

parallel conversion   A systems conversion approach in which the new and old systems are run simultaneously until the organization is assured that the new system is functioning correctly.

parallel simulation An approach auditors use to detect unauthorized program changes and data processing accuracy. The auditor writes his or her own version of a program and then reprocesses data. The output of the auditor's program and the client's program are compared to verify that they are the same.

parity bit An extra bit added to a byte, character, or word. The parity bit is magnetized as needed to ensure that there is always an odd (or even) number of magnetized bits. The computer uses the odd (or even) parity scheme to check the accuracy of each item of data.

parity checking As a computer reads or receives a set of characters, it sums the number of 1-bits in each character to verify that it is an even number. If not, the corresponding character must contain an error.

password A series of letters, numbers, or both that must be entered to access and use system resources. Password use helps prevent unauthorized tampering with hardware, software, and the organization's data.

password cracking Using illicit means to steal a file containing passwords and then using them.

payback period The number of years required for the net savings to equal the initial cost of the investment.

payroll clearing account A general ledger account used to check the accuracy and completeness of recording payroll costs and their subsequent allocation to appropriate cost centers.

payroll register A listing of payroll data for each employee for the current payroll period.

payroll service bureau An organization that maintains the payroll master file for each of its clients and performs their payroll processing activities for a fee.

performance evaluations A project development control that requires evaluating each module or task as it is completed.

performance objectives The overall goals that an entity wishes to achieve.

performance report Lists the budgeted and actual amounts of revenues and expenses and also shows the variances, or differences, between these two amounts. Used for financial control. Contrast with *budget*.

peripherals The hardware devices (such as those used for input, output, processing, and data communications) that are connected to the CPU.

personal digital assistant (PDA) A handheld computer that has had a significant impact on personal productivity.

personal identification number (PIN) A confidential code that allows an individual to gain access to a system and the data or resources stored in that system.

phase-in conversion See *modular conversion*.

phreaker A hacker who attacks phone systems.

physical access Ability to physically use computer equipment.

physical design (1) A phase of the system development life cycle where the broad, user-oriented requirements of the conceptual design are implemented by creating a detailed set of specifications that are used to code and test the computer programs. (2) The fourth stage of the database design process. It consists of taking the conceptual design and converting it into physical storage structures.

physical model The description of physical aspects of a database (e.g., field and file sizes, storage and access methods, and security procedures).

physical possession identification A method of identifying people by an item they physically possess, such as an ID card.

physical systems design The phase of the systems development life cycle in which the designer specifies the hardware, software, and procedures for delivering the conceptual systems design.

physical systems design report A report prepared at the end of the physical design phase that describes the system. Management uses this report to decide whether or not to proceed to the implementation phase.

physical view The way data are physically arranged and stored on disks, tapes, and other storage media. EDP personnel use this view to make efficient use of storage and processing resources. Contrast with *logical view*.

picking ticket A document authorizing the release of merchandise to the shipping department. The picking ticket is often printed so that the item numbers and quantities are listed in the sequence in which they can be most efficiently retrieved from the warehouse.

piggybacking When a perpetrator latches on to a legitimate user who is logging in to a system. The legitimate user unknowingly carries the perpetrator with him as he is allowed into the system.

pilot conversion The implementation of a system in just one part of the organization, such as a branch location. This approach localizes conversion problems and allows training in a live environment. Disadvantages are the long conversion times and the need to interface the old system with the new system.

point scoring An objective procedure in which weighted selection criteria are used to evaluate the overall merits of vendor proposals.

point-of-sale (POS) recorders Electronic devices that function as both a terminal and a cash register. They are used commonly in retail stores to record sales information at the time of the sale and to perform other data processing functions.

policies The rules that provide a formal direction for achieving performance objectives and that enable performance.

policy and procedures manual A management tool for assigning authority and responsibility. It details management's policy for handling specific transactions.

postimplementation review Review made after a new system has been operating for a brief period. The purpose is to ensure that the new system is meeting its planned objectives, to identify the adequacy of system standards, and to review system controls.

postimplementation review report A report that analyzes a newly delivered system to determine if the system achieved its intended purpose and was completed within budget.

preformatting An on-line data entry control in which the computer displays a form on the screen and the user fills in the blanks on the form as needed.

pressure A person's motivation for committing a fraud.

preventive controls A control system that places restrictions on and requires documentation of employee activities so as to reduce the occurrence of errors and deviations. Because preventive controls operate from within the process being controlled, they are perhaps the type of control most consistent with the original meaning of the term *internal control*.

preventive maintenance A program of regularly examining the hardware components of a computer and replacing any that are found to be weak.

primary activities Activities in the value chain that are performed to create, market, and deliver products and services to customers and provide post-delivery service and support. Primary activities include production, shipping and receiving, and marketing.

primary key A unique identification code assigned to each record within a system. The primary key is the key used most frequently to distinguish, order, and reference records.

private key system An encryption system in which both the sender and the receiver have access to the key but do not allow others access to the same key.

process A set of actions, automated or manual, that transform data into other data or information.

process costing A cost system that assigns costs to each process, or work center, in the production cycle, and then calculates the average cost for all units produced. Process costing is used when masses of similar goods or services are sold.

processing controls Controls that ensure that all transactions are processed accurately and completely and that all files and records are properly updated.

processing of test transactions Running hypothetical transactions through a new system to test for processing errors.

production cycle The recurring set of business activities and related data processing operations associated with the manufacture of products.

production order A document authorizing the manufacture of a specified quantity of a particular product. It lists the operations to be performed, the quantity to be produced, and the location to which the finished product is to be delivered.

professional employer organization (PEO) An organization that processes payroll and also provides HRM services such as employee benefit design and administration.

profitability analysis report Reports used to assess overall marketing performance by breaking down the marginal profit contribution made by each territory, customer, distribution channel, salesperson, product, or other basis. Contrast with *sales analysis report*.

program A set of instructions that can be executed by a computer.

program evaluation and review technique (PERT) A commonly used technique for planning, coordinating, controlling, and scheduling complex projects such as systems implementation.

program flowchart A diagrammatical representation of the logic and sequence of processes used in a computer program.

program maintenance The revision of a computer program to meet new program instructions, satisfy system demands such as the need for a new report, correct an error, or make changes in file content.

program tracing A technique used to obtain detailed knowledge of the logic of an application program, as well as to test the program's compliance with its control specifications.

project development plan A proposal to develop a particular computer system application. It contains an analysis of the requirements and expectations of the proposed application.

project development team A group of people consisting of specialists, management, and users that develop a project's plan and direct the steps of the systems development life cycle. The team monitors costs, progress, employees, and gives status reports to top management and to the steering committee.

project milestones Significant points in a development effort at which a formal review of progress is made.

projection A way of resisting change by blaming anything and everything on the new system. The system becomes the scapegoat for all real and imagined problems and errors.

prompting An on-line data entry control that uses the computer to control the data entry process. The system displays a request to the user for each required item of input data and then waits for an acceptable response before requesting the next required item.

proposal to conduct systems analysis A document calling for the analysis of either an existing or a proposed system. This document is prepared by a user or department and requests the information systems function to analyze the feasibility of developing a system to perform a specific function.

protocol The set of rules governing the exchange of data between two systems or components of a system.

prototype A simplified working model of an information system used in prototyping.

prototyping An approach to systems design in which a simplified working model, or prototype, of an information system is developed. The users experiment with the prototype to determine what they like and do not like about the system. The developers make modifications until the users are satisfied with the system.

public key infrastructure (PKI) An approach to encryption that uses two keys: a public key that is publicly available and a private key that is kept secret and known only by the owner of that pair of keys. With PKI, either key (the public or private) can be used to encode a message, but only the other key in that public-private pair can be used to decode that message.

public key system An encryption system that uses two separate keys: a public key that is available to everyone and a private key known only to the user.

purchase order A document that formally requests a vendor to sell and deliver specified products at designated prices. It is also a promise to pay and becomes a contract once the vendor accepts it.

purchase requisition A document that identifies the requisitioner, specifies the delivery location and date needed, identifies the item numbers, descriptions, quantity, and price of each item requested, and may suggest a vendor.

query A request for specific information from a computer. Queries are often used with a database management system to extract data from the database.

query languages Languages used to process data files and to obtain quick responses to questions about those files.

query-by-example (QBE) languages Graphical query languages for retrieving information from a relational database.

random access memory (RAM) A temporary storage location for computer instructions and data. RAM may have data both written to it and read from it.

random surveillance Way of detecting fraud by having auditors periodically audit the system and test system controls. Informing employees that the auditors will conduct random surveillance is a deterrent to computer crime.

range check An edit check designed to verify that a data item falls within a certain predetermined range of acceptable values.

rationalization The excuse that fraud perpetrators use to justify their illegal behavior.

REA data model   A data model developed explicitly for use in designing AIS databases. The name REA is an acronym signifying that the data model contains information about three fundamental types of objects: resources, events, and agents. Resources represent identifiable objects that have economic value to the organization. Events represent all of an organization's business activities. Agents represent the people or organizations about which data are collected.

read-only memory (ROM)   Internal CPU memory that can be read but usually may not be changed.

real-time notification   A variation of the embedded audit module in which the auditor is notified of each transaction as it occurs by means of a message printed on the auditor's terminal.

real-time system   A system that is able to respond to an inquiry or provide data fast enough to make the information meaningful to the user. Real-time systems are usually designed for very fast response.

reasonable assurance   The concept that an auditor cannot seek complete assurance that an item is correct, since to do so would be prohibitively expensive. Instead, the auditor accepts a reasonable degree of risk that the audit conclusion is incorrect.

reasonableness test   An edit check of the logical correctness of relationships among the values of data items on an input record and the corresponding file record. For example, a journal entry that debits inventory and credits wages payable is not reasonable.

receiving report   A document that records details about each delivery, including the date received, shipper, vendor, and purchase order number.

record   A set of logically related data items that describe specific attributes of an entity, such as all payroll data relating to a single employee.

record count   A total of the number of input documents to a process or the number of records processed in a run.

record layout   A document that illustrates the arrangement of items of data in input, output, and file records.

recovery procedures   A set of procedures that is followed if the computer quits in the middle of processing a batch of data. The procedures allow the user to recover from hardware or software failures.

redundant data check   An edit check that requires the inclusion of two identifiers in each input record (e.g., the customer's account number and the first five letters of the customer's name). If these input values do not match those on the record, the record will not be updated.

reengineering   The thorough analysis and complete redesign of all business processes and information systems to achieve dramatic performance improvements. Reengineering seeks to reduce a company to its essential business processes.

referential integrity rule   A constraint in relational database design requiring that any non-null value of a foreign key must correspond to a primary key in the referenced table. For example, if vendor number is a foreign key in the inventory table, to indicate the preferred source of that item, then any vendor number appearing in that table must appear as a primary key value in the vendor table. This constraint ensures consistency in the database. Note, however, that the foreign key can be null, if there is no existing relationship between the two tables. For example, a null value for vendor number in any row in the inventory table would indicate that there is no preferred vendor for that inventory item.

relational data model   A database model in which all data elements are logically viewed as being stored in the form of two-dimensional tables called "relations." These tables are, in effect, flat files where each row represents a unique entity or record. Each column represents a field where the record's attributes are stored. The tables serve as the building blocks from which data relationships can be created.

relations   The tables used to store data in a relational database.

remittance advice   An enclosure included with a customer's payment that indicates the invoices, statements, or other items paid.

remittance list   A document listing all checks received in the mail.

remote batch processing   Accumulating transaction records in batches at some remote location and then transmitting them electronically to a central location for processing.

reorder point   The level to which the inventory balance of an item must fall before an order to replenish stock is initiated.

report System output organized in a meaningful fashion. Used by employees to control operational activities, by managers to make decisions, and by investors and creditors to gather information about a company's business activities. Prepared for both internal and external use.

report writers Software that lets a user specify the data elements to be printed. The report writer searches the database, extracts the desired items, and prints them out in the user-specified format.

reprocessing An approach auditors use to detect unauthorized program changes. The auditor verifies the integrity of an application program and then saves it for future use. At subsequent intervals, and on a surprise basis, the auditor uses the previously verified version of the program to reprocess data that have been processed by the version used by the company. The output of the two runs is compared and discrepancies are investigated.

request for proposal (RFP) A request by an organization or department for vendors to bid on hardware, software, or services specified by the organization or department.

request for systems development A written request for a new or improved system. The request describes the current system's problems, why the change is needed, and the proposed system's goals and objectives as well as its anticipated benefits and costs.

requirements costing A system evaluation method in which a list is made of all required features of the desired system. If a proposed system does not have a desired feature, the cost of developing or purchasing that feature is added to the basic cost of the system. This method allows different systems to be evaluated based on the costs of providing the required features.

requirements definition The second step in the database design process. It entails defining the scope of a proposed database system, determining general hardware and software requirements, and identifying user information needs.

resources Those things that have economic value to an organization, such as cash, inventory, supplies, factories, and land.

response time The amount of time that elapses between making a query and receiving a response.

responsibility accounting A system of reporting financial results on the basis of managerial responsibilities within an organization.

revenue cycle The recurring set of business activities and related information-processing operations associated with providing goods and services to customers and collecting cash in payment for those sales.

ring network A configuration in which the data communications channels form a loop or circular pattern when the local processors are linked together. Contrast with *star network*.

risk The likelihood that a threat or hazard will actually come to pass.

rollback A process whereby a log of all pre-update values is prepared for each record that is updated within a particular interval. If there is a system failure, the records can be restored to the pre-update values and the processing started over.

round-down technique A fraud technique used in financial institutions that pay interest. The programmer instructs the computer to round down all interest calculations to two decimal places. The fraction of a cent that was rounded down on each calculation is put into the programmer's own account.

routing sheet See *operations list*.

routing verification procedures Controls to ensure that messages are not routed to the wrong system address. Examples are header labels, mutual authentication schemes, and dial-back.

sabotage An intentional act where the intent is to destroy a system or some of its components.

salami technique A fraud technique in which tiny slices of money are stolen from many different accounts.

sales analysis report Reports used to assess the efficiency and effectiveness of the sales by breaking down sales by salesperson, region, or product. Contrast with *profitability analysis report*.

sales invoice A document notifying customers of the amount to be paid and where to send payment.

sales order The document created during sales order entry, listing the item numbers, quantities, prices, and terms of the sale.

scanning routines Software routines that search a program for the occurrence of a particular variable name or other combinations of characters.

scavenging The unauthorized access to confidential information by searching corporate records. Scavenging methods range from searching trash cans for printouts or carbon copies of confidential information to scanning the contents of computer memory.

scheduled reports   Reports that are generated by a system at specified time intervals.

scheduling feasibility   The dimension of feasibility that determines if the system being developed can be implemented in the time allotted.

schema   A description of the types of data elements that are in the database, the relationships among the data elements, and the structure or overall logical model used to organize and describe the data.

secondary key   A field that can be used to identify records in a file. Unlike the primary key, it does not provide a unique identification.

secondary storage   Storage media, such as magnetic disks or magnetic tape, on which data that are not currently needed by the computer can be stored. Also called *auxiliary storage*.

security measures and controls   Controls that are built into an information system to ensure that data are accurate and free from errors. Security measures also protect data from unauthorized access.

segregation of duties   The separation of assigned duties and responsibilities in such a way that no single employee can both perpetrate and conceal errors or irregularities.

semiconductor   A tiny silicon chip upon which a number of miniature circuits have been inscribed.

semistructured decisions   Decisions that require subjective assessment and judgment to supplement formal data analysis.

sequence check   An edit check that determines if a batch of input data is in the proper numerical or alphabetical sequence.

sequential access   An access method that requires data items to be accessed in the same order in which they were written.

sequential file   A way of storing numeric or alphabetical records according to a key (e.g., customer numbers from 00001 to 99999). To access a sequential file record, the system starts at the beginning of the file and reads each record until the desired record is located.

sequential file processing   Processing a master file sequentially from beginning to end. The master and transaction files are processed in the same predetermined order, such as alphabetically.

server   High-capacity computer that contains the network software to handle communications, storage, and resource-sharing needs of other computers in the network. The server also contains the application software and data common to all users.

sign check   An edit check that verifies that the data in a field have the appropriate arithmetic sign.

single key encryption systems   Encryption systems that use the same key to encrypt and decrypt a message.

smart cards   Plastic cards that contain a microprocessor, memory chips, and software; can store up to three pages of text. Used in Europe as a credit or ATM card.

snapshot technique   An audit technique that records the content of both a transaction record and a related master file record before and after each processing step.

social engineering   Fraudulently gaining information to access a system by fooling an employee.

software   A computer program that gives instructions to the CPU; also used to refer to programming languages and computer systems documentation.

software agents   Computer programs that learn how to do often-performed, tedious, time-consuming, or complex tasks.

software piracy   The unauthorized copying of software.

source code (or **source program)**   A computer program written in a source language such as BASIC, COBOL, or assembly language. The source program is translated into the object (machine language) program by a translation program such as a compiler or assembler.

source data automation (SDA)   The collection of transaction data in machine-readable form at the time and place of origin. Examples of SDA devices are optical scanners and automated teller machines.

source documents   Contain the initial record of a transaction that takes place. Examples of source documents, which are usually recorded on preprinted forms, include sales invoices, purchase orders, and employee time cards. Contrast with *operational document*.

spamming   E-mailing the same message to everyone on one or more Usenet newsgroups or LISTSERV lists.

special-purpose analysis reports Reports that have no prespecified content or format and are not prepared according to any regular schedule; rather, they are generally prepared in response to a management request to investigate a specific problem or opportunity.

specialized journals Specialized journals are used to simplify the process of recording large numbers of repetitive transactions; commonly used for the following types of transactions: credit sales, cash receipts, purchases on account, and cash disbursements.

specific authorization When an employee must get special approval before handling a transaction.

standards The required procedures implemented to meet the policies.

star network A configuration in which there is a centralized real-time computer system to which all other computer systems are linked. Contrast with *ring network.*

steering committee An executive-level committee to plan and oversee the information systems function. The committee typically consists of management from the systems department, the controller, and other management affected by the information systems function.

stockout costs The costs, such as lost sales or production delays, that result from inventory shortages.

storage Placement of data in internal memory or on a medium such as magnetic disk or magnetic tape, from which they can later be retrieved.

strategic plan An organization's multiple-year plan that serves as a technological road map and lays out the projects the company must complete to achieve its long-range goals.

strategic planning Decisions that establish the organization's objectives and policies for accomplishing those objectives.

stratified sampling A sampling approach in which a population is divided into two or more groups to which different selection criteria can be applied.

structured decisions Decisions that are repetitive, routine, and understood well enough that they can be delegated to the lower-level employees of an organization.

structured programming A modular approach to programming in which each module performs a specific function, stands alone, and is coordinated by a control module. Also referred to as "GOTO-less" programming because modular design makes GOTO statements unnecessary.

structured query language (SQL) The standard text-based query language provided by most, but not all, relational DBMSs. Powerful queries can be built using three basic keywords: SELECT, FROM, and WHERE.

structured relationships Relationships in the REA data model in which every event entity is linked to a resource entity and two agent entities.

structured walkthrough A formal review process in program design in which one or more programmers walk through the logic and code of another programmer to detect weaknesses and errors in program design.

subschema (1) A subset of the schema that includes only those data items used in a particular application program or by a particular user. (2) The way the user defines the data and the data relationships.

subsidiary ledgers Used to record the detailed data for any general ledger account that has many individual subaccounts. Subsidiary ledgers are commonly used for accounts receivable, inventory, fixed assets, and accounts payable.

subsystems Smaller systems that are a part of the entire information system. Each subsystem performs a specific function that is important to and that supports the system of which it is a part.

superzapping The use of a special system program to bypass regular system controls to perform unauthorized acts. A superzap utility was originally written to handle emergencies, such as restoring a system that had crashed.

supply chain An extended system that includes an organization's value chain as well as its suppliers, distributors, and customers.

support activities Activities in the value chain that enable the primary activities to be performed efficiently and effectively. Examples include administration, purchasing, and human resources.

synchronous transmission Data transmission in which start and stop bits are required only at the beginning and end of a block of characters. Contrast with *asynchronous transmission.*

syntax errors Errors that result from using the programming language improperly or from incorrectly typing the source program.

system (1) An entity consisting of two or more components or subsystems that interact to achieve a goal. (2) The equipment and programs that comprise a complete computer installation. (3) The programs and related procedures that perform a single task on a computer.

system control audit review file (SCARF) A concurrent audit technique that embeds audit modules into application software to continuously monitor all transaction activity and collect data on transactions having special audit significance.

system flowchart A diagrammatical representation that shows the flow of data through a series of operations in an automated data processing system. It shows how data are captured and put into the system, the processes that operate on the data, and system outputs.

system performance measurements Measurements used to properly evaluate and assess a system. Common measurements include throughput (output per unit of time), utilization (percentage of time the system is being productively used), and response time (how long it takes the system to respond).

system review A step in internal control evaluation in which it is determined if the necessary control procedures have been prescribed.

systems analysis (1) A rigorous and systematic approach to decision making, characterized by a comprehensive definition of available alternatives and an exhaustive analysis of the merits of each alternative as a basis for choosing the best alternative. (2) Examination of the user information requirements within an organization to establish objectives and specifications for the design of an information system.

systems analysis report Comprehensive report prepared at the end of the systems analysis and design phase that summarizes and documents the findings of analysis activities.

systems analysts The people who are responsible for developing the company's information system. The analyst's job generally involves designing computer applications and preparing specifications for computer programming.

systems approach Way of handling systems change by recognizing that every system must have an objective, a set of components, and a set of interrelationships among the components. The systems approach proceeds step by step, with a thorough exploration of all implications and alternatives at each step.

systems concept A systems analysis principle that states that alternative courses of action within a system must be evaluated from the standpoint of the system as a whole rather than from the standpoint of any single subsystem or set of subsystems.

systems design The process of preparing detailed specifications for the development of a new information system.

systems development life cycle (SDLC) Five procedures and steps that a company goes through when it decides to design and implement a new system. The five steps are systems analysis, conceptual design, physical design, implementation and conversion, and operation and maintenance.

systems documentation A complete description of all aspects of each systems application, including narrative material, charts, and program listings.

systems implementation The task of delivering a completed system to an organization for use in day-to-day operations.

systems software Software that interfaces between the hardware and the application program. Systems software can be classified as operating systems, database management systems, utility programs, language translators, and communications software.

systems survey The systematic gathering of facts relating to the existing information system. A systems analyst generally carries out this task.

systems survey report The culmination of the systems survey. It contains documentation such as memos, interview and observation notes, questionnaire data, file and record layouts and descriptions, input and output descriptions, and copies of documents, flowcharts, and data flow diagrams.

SysTrust An information systems assurance service introduced by the AICPA and the Canadian Institute of Chartered Accountants (CICA) that independently tests and verifies a system's reliability. SysTrust uses four principles to determine if a system is reliable: availability, security, maintainability, and integrity.

tagging An audit procedure in which certain records are marked with a special code before processing. During processing, all data relating to the marked records are captured and saved so that the auditors can verify them later.

tape drive The device that controls the movement of the magnetic tape and that reads and writes on the tape.

tape file protection ring A circular plastic ring that determines when a tape file can be written on. When the ring is inserted on a reel of magnetic tape, data can be written on the tape. If the ring is removed, the data on the tape cannot be overwritten with new information.

technical feasibility The dimension of feasibility concerned with whether a proposed system can be developed given the available technology.

terminal An input/output device for entering or receiving data directly from the computer. Also referred to as cathode ray tube (CRT) or visual display terminal (VDT).

test data Data that have been specially developed to test the accuracy and completeness of a computer program. The results from the test data are compared with hand-calculated results to verify that the program operates properly.

test data generator program A program that takes the specifications describing the logic characteristics of the program to be tested and automatically generates a set of test data that can be used to check the logic of the program.

test of control A test whose objective is to determine if control procedures are being followed correctly.

threats Potential losses to an organization arising from hazards such as embezzlement, employee carelessness or theft, or poor management decisions.

throughput (1) The total amount of useful work performed by a computer system during a given period of time. (2) A measure of production efficiency representing the number of "good" units produced in a given period of time.

time card A document that records the employee's arrival and departure times for each work shift. The time card records the total hours worked by an employee during a pay period.

token ring A LAN configuration that forms a closed loop. A token is passed around the ring to indicate that a device is free to send or receive a message.

trailer label Type of internal label that appears at the end of each file and serves as an indicator that the end of the file has been reached.

transaction cycles A group of related business activities (e.g., the set of business activities consisting of sales order entry, shipping, billing, and cash receipts constitutes the revenue cycle). The five major transaction cycles are revenue, expenditure, production, human resource management/payroll, and general ledger and reporting.

transaction file A relatively temporary data file containing transaction data that are typically used to update a master file.

transaction log A detailed record of every transaction entered in a system through data entry.

transaction processing A process that begins with capturing transaction data and ends with an informational output.

transcription error An error occurring during data conversion from a manual to an automated environment in which one digit of a number is written incorrectly during the conversion (e.g., a "4" in the tens position transcribed as a "9," which would cause an error of 50 in the value of the number).

Transmission Control Protocol/Internet Protocol (TCP/IP) The protocol enabling communications on the Internet. It creates what is called a packet-switching network. When a message is ready to be sent over the Internet, the TCP breaks it up into small packets. Each packet is then given a header, which contains the destination address, and the packets are then sent individually over the Internet. The IP uses the information in the packet header to guide the packets so that they arrive at the proper destination. Once there, the TCP reassembles the packets into the original message.

transposition error An error that results when the numbers in two adjacent columns are inadvertently exchanged (for example, 64 is written as 46).

trap door A set of computer instructions that allows a user to bypass the system's normal controls.

trial balance A report listing the balances of all general ledger accounts. It is so named because one of its purposes is to allow the accountant to verify that the total debit balances in various accounts equal the total credit balances in other accounts.

triggered exception reports Preformatted reports generated only when certain conditions exist (e.g., the amount of raw materials on hand falls below the safety stock amount). They bring the information about the existing conditions to the attention of a decision maker.

Trojan horse A set of unauthorized computer instructions in an authorized and otherwise properly functioning program. It performs some illegal act at a preappointed time or under a predetermined set of conditions.

tunneling   An Internet security approach in which data are sent between firewalls in small encrypted segments called "packets."

tuple   (pronounced to rhyme with the word *couple*). A row in a relation. A tuple contains data about a specific occurrence of the type of entity represented by that database table. For example, each row in the inventory table contains all the pertinent data about a particular inventory item.

turnaround document   A document, readable by humans, that is prepared by the computer as output, sent outside the system, and then returned as input into the computer. An example is a utility bill.

turnkey system   A system that is delivered to customers is ready (theoretically) to be turned on. A turnkey system supplier buys hardware, writes application software that is tailored both to that equipment and to the specific needs of its customers, and then markets the entire system.

uninterruptible power system (UPS)   An alternative power supply device that protects against the loss of power and fluctuations in the power level.

Universal Product Code (UPC)   A machine-readable code that is read by optical scanners. The code consists of a series of bar codes and is printed on most products sold in grocery stores.

UNIX   A flexible and widely used operating system for 16-bit machines.

unstructured decisions   Nonrecurring and non-routine decisions that require considerable judgment and intuition.

update anomaly   A problem that can arise in a poorly designed relational database. If attributes that are not characteristics of the primary key of a relation are stored in that table, then that data item is stored in many different rows. For example, if customer addresses are stored in the sales invoice table, then the address for a given customer is stored many times (once for each sale). Consequently, if the value of that data item is not changed in every row in which it is stored, inconsistencies in the database will result.

updating   Changing stored data to reflect more recent events (e.g., changing the accounts receivable balance because of a recent sale or collection).

user ID   A knowledge identifier such as an employee number or account number that users enter to identify themselves when signing on to a system.

user identification (ID) and authentication system   A system that requires users to identify themselves by entering a unique user ID when they sign on to the system.

Users   All people who interact with the system. Users are those who record data, manage the system, and control the system's security. Those who use information from the system are end users.

utility programs   A set of prewritten programs that perform a variety of file and data-handling tasks (e.g., sorting or merging files) and other housekeeping chores.

utilization   The percentage of time a system is being productively used.

validity check   An edit test in which an identification number or transaction code is compared with a table of valid identification numbers or codes maintained in computer memory.

value chain   The linking together of all the primary and support activities in a business. Value is added as a product passes through the chain.

value system   The combination of several value chains into one system. A value system includes the value chains of a company, its suppliers, its distributors, and its customers.

value-added network (VAN)   Public network that adds value to the data communications process by handling the difficult task of interfacing with the multiple types of hardware and software used by different companies.

virtual private network (VPN)   A network that controls access to an extranet by encryption and authentication technology.

voice input   A data input unit that recognizes human voices and converts spoken messages into machine-readable input.

volume label   A type of internal label that identifies the contents of each separate data recording medium, such as a tape, diskette, or disk pack.

voucher   A document that summarizes the data relating to a disbursement and represents final authorization of payment.

voucher package   The set of documents used to authorize payment to a vendor. It consists of a purchase order, receiving report, and vendor invoice.

voucher system   A method for processing accounts payable in which a disbursement voucher is prepared, instead of posting invoices directly to vendor records in the accounts payable subsidiary ledger. The disbursement voucher identifies the vendor, lists the outstanding invoices, and indicates the net amount to be paid after deducting any applicable discounts and allowances. Contrast with *nonvoucher system.*

walk-throughs   Meetings, attended by those associated with a project, in which a detailed review of systems procedures and/or program logic is carried out in a step-by-step manner.

war dialing   Searching for an idle modem by programming a computer to dial thousands of phone lines. Finding an idle modem often enables a cracker to gain access to the network to which it is connected.

Web servers   Large computers on the Internet that are scattered worldwide and contain every imaginable type of data. Each Web server can have tens of thousands of networks and users attached to it.

white-collar criminals   Typically businesspeople who commit fraud. White-collar criminals usually resort to trickery or cunning and their crimes usually involve a violation of trust or confidence.

wide area information servers (WAIS)   Tools for searching the Internet's huge information libraries.

wide area network (WAN)   A telecommunications network that covers a large geographic area anywhere in size from a few cities to the whole globe. A WAN uses telephone lines, cables, microwaves, or satellites to connect a wide variety of hardware devices in many different locations.

wiretap   To listen (eavesdrop) in on an unprotected communications line.

worm   Similar to a virus except that it is a program rather than a code segment hidden in a host program. A worm also copies itself and actively transmits itself directly to other systems.

WORM   "Write once, read many." For example, an optical disk can be written on once, but later read many times.

zero-balance check   An internal check that requires the balance of the payroll control account to be zero after all entries to it have been made.

Index